Good Guide to Dog Friendly Pubs, Hotels and B&Bs 2017

6th Edition

Edited by Cath Phillips

Walks consultant Tim Locke
Additional research Fiona Stapley,
Patrick Stapley and Fiona Wright

EBURY
PRESS

3 5 7 9 10 8 6 4

Published in 2017 by Ebury Press, an imprint of Ebury Publishing
20 Vauxhall Bridge Road,
London SW1V 2SA

Ebury Press is part of the Penguin Random House
group of companies whose addresses can be
found at global.penguinrandomhouse.com

Penguin
Random House
UK

First published by Ebury Press in 2017

www.penguin.co.uk

A CIP catalogue record for this book is available from
the British Library

ISBN 9781785034442

Printed and bound in Great Britain by Clays Ltd, Elcograf S.p.A.

Typeset by Integra

The Penguin Random House Group is committed to a sustainable
future for our businesses, our readers and our planet. This book
is made from Forest Stewardship Council® certified paper.

Contents

Around 8.5 million households in Britain own a dog. They are an integral part of a family and when their owners go away, the dog often goes too. As editor of the *Good Pub Guide*, I travel regularly around the UK and, increasingly, I take my labrador with me since the majority of good pubs welcome dogs in the bar. The warmth of this welcome often extends to a bowl of water, biscuits and other treats such as pig's ears and a sausage or two, or even special doggy menus. If you take a dog into a pub, you should have it on a lead and it's wise to check before-hand if there is a resident dog (we always mention this if we know).

If you're looking for somewhere to spend the night, many pubs with bedrooms now welcome dogs to sleep over too. On some occasions, of course, a pub may not be appropriate, and (as its name suggests) this *Dog Friendly Guide to Pubs, Hotels and B&Bs* offers a fine mix of other places, ranging from the simple to the luxurious. As a bonus, many are also situated in lovely walking country.

Establishments can change their policy on welcoming dogs if a canine guest (or its owner) has behaved badly, so if you come to make a reservation and find things have changed, do please let us know. Mean-while, we hope this Guide helps to make travelling with your dog a happy and rewarding experience.

Fiona Stapley
Editor, *Good Pub Guide*

Introduction

Welcome to the 6th edition of the *Dog Friendly Guide!* Again, we have chosen places that offer a real welcome to dogs and their owners. These are all establishments that we would happily include in a 'non-dog' guidebook – indeed, many of them are distinguished entries in our sister publication, the *Good Pub Guide*. But apart from pubs, they span a tremendous range of styles, from simple B&Bs or farmhouses through venerable inns to luxurious hotels. We have put particular effort into tracking down places with plenty of good walks nearby.

Information in this Guide was correct when it was researched during 2016. Unfortunately, over the years, we have found that establishments can change their policy on welcoming dogs. One bad experience with a dog (or their owner) can be enough to cause a place to completely rescind their canine welcome. It's therefore possible that by the time you come to make a reservation, a handful of entries in the Guide will no longer welcome dogs.

Do please help by telling us about places you have visited with your dog. You can email us (feedback@goodguides.com), write to Dog Friendly Guide, FREEPOST RTJR-ZCYZ-RJZT, Perrymans Lane, Etchingham, East Sussex TN19 7DN (no stamp needed if you post in the UK), or use the pre-printed forms at the back of the book.

Ten tips for top dog holidays

Making sure your dog enjoys a break as much as you do boils down mainly to common sense and a little forethought. And do think of other people – a little consideration for staff and other visitors goes a long way.

1. Always phone the establishment to discuss with the owners or manager what their rules are regarding dogs before you book a room. If you turn up with two large rottweilers without pre-booking, you might not get the warm reception you were hoping for. Many places set aside bedrooms that are particularly suitable for dogs, such as ground-floor rooms or rooms with

access to the outside. And there is often a charge for dogs –
confirm this when booking.

2. Check your pet insurance to see that it covers personal liability –
knocking over furniture or tripping up people, for example.

3. Check which areas your dog is allowed into, as some places
will only allow them in bedrooms and not in public areas.

4. Many establishments do not allow dogs to be left alone in
bedrooms as they could become anxious (howling or barking and
annoying other guests) or bored (chewing furniture, climbing on to
beds and so forth). You may therefore have to put your dog in the
car, or in a cage in the room, while you're in the restaurant.

5. Make sure to take your dog's own bedding, a towel for drying
muddy paws and any favourite toys. Some places do provide
dog beds, bowls and food, but it's often best to stick to regular
mealtimes and the food your pet is used to.

6. Hairy dogs need a really thorough brushing beforehand, to
minimise errant hairs.

7. Obviously, you wouldn't want to take a really unsociable dog away
with you. Many proprietors have dogs and other animals of their
own (and children, of course), and will not want a visiting pet that
is difficult with them – or with other guests.

8. Do keep your dog under control all the time – we find that it's
more relaxing to keep even the best-behaved dogs on leads. This
is particularly relevant if you're staying on farms or estates where
there is livestock.

9. When you leave, make sure that there is no evidence that your
dog has been there – either inside or out.

10. If you're hoping to explore the area, most proprietors will be able
to point you in the direction of good nearby walks, and some
attractions have special kennels where you can leave your dog;
it's worth checking this beforehand.

In the countryside with your dog

Many dogs appreciate the countryside as much as their owners do.
Whether your dog likes hills, open heaths or coastal landscapes, there's
plenty of choice across Britain. However, access is by no means unlim-
ited, and the law requires you to keep your dog under control and put
it on a lead when crossing fields that contain livestock. A farmer has
the right to shoot dogs that are worrying his farm animals: though this
is not a common occurrence, it does happen from time to time. If your
dog is on a lead and you're both chased by a farm animal, it's generally
safer to let the dog off the lead than to risk injury to yourself.

It's considerate to carry plastic bags to clean up your dog's mess, and
to make sure your dog keeps well away from birds' nests (bear in mind
that some birds lay their eggs on the ground) and other wildlife.

Places you can generally walk your dog in England and Wales are:

- **Public roads**, though of course they're not always ideal.
- Most **beaches**. Some popular beaches ban dogs in the summer – and even more than anywhere else, it's always considerate to clean up after your dog on beaches.
- Paths and tracks on **National Trust land** (apart from National Trust gardens and house estates, where you need a ticket to get in, though some of these welcome dogs on leads) that are dedicated as public land and have free access. These include areas of coast, woodlands and open land.
- **Canal towpaths** unless there's a sign to the contrary.
- Paths and tracks in areas of forest owned by the **Forestry Commission**, though note that these may be temporarily closed during felling operations.
- Areas designated as **country parks**. Many of these are owned by local authorities, and you're allowed to wander where you like within them.
- Anywhere along a **public footpath, public bridleway** or **public byway** (the three together are also known generically as **public rights of way**). Bridleways are also open to horse riders and cyclists, and byways are open to all traffic, so unless these have a paved surface they can be very muddy in wet weather. Public rights of way are normally signposted from roads, and may have **waymark arrows** (red for byways, blue for bridleways and yellow for footpaths). '**Permissive paths**' or '**licensed paths**' cross private land and are not public rights of way; the landowner has the right to close them at any time.
- Under the Countryside and Rights of Way Act you have a '**right to roam**' on **access land** in uncultivated countryside in England and Wales.

Scotland has different laws about access to the countryside. There are some legal rights of way, but not many, and they aren't indicated as such on Ordnance Survey (OS) maps. Access tends to be established on an informal basis: there's a general tolerance towards walkers, who can effectively go anywhere on moorland and mountains outside the grouse-shooting and deer-stalking seasons (12 August-10 December and mainly 1 July-20 October, respectively). Dogs may not be welcome on moorland because of nesting game birds; look out for notices, or check locally at tourist information centres.

What the right to roam means
Right to roam grants access on foot to many areas of moors, mountains, downland, heaths and registered commons that have been designated

as **access land**. Here you have the right to walk wherever you like without sticking to paths, although in practice the lie of the land may determine your route in places. Note that not all uncultivated land is access land, and it doesn't include farmland, woods, coast or parkland; even in areas of open-looking hills such as the South Downs, the right to roam is quite limited.

Since access areas were established in 2004, many new stiles and gates have been built to allow entry, though you do sometimes have to leave the same way you came in. Access land is marked at key points with brown and white circular pictograms depicting a walker wandering through lumpy terrain, and marked on Ordnance Survey Explorer 1:25,000 maps.

Do note the restrictions on access: you must keep dogs on a short lead (no longer than two metres) if near livestock, and at all times from 1 March to 31 July; dogs may also, at any time, be banned temporarily or permanently from particular areas where, for example, birds may be nesting. You are not allowed to cycle, ride a horse, light fires, camp or feed livestock; if you do, you lose your right to roam for 72 hours. There may also be local restrictions on night-time access.

Maps and other useful information
OS maps In England and Wales, the first point of reference is the local Ordnance Survey map. Both the purple-covered Landranger series (at a scale of 1:50,000, or about one and a quarter inches to the mile) and the orange-covered Explorer series (at a scale of 1:25,000, or about two and a half inches to the mile) show rights of way (crosses for byways, long dashes for bridleways and short dashes for footpaths, sometimes overprinted with diamonds to denote long-distance routes; in red on Landranger maps and in green on Explorer maps; restricted byways – shown by alternating dashes and dots on Landrangers and by knobbly dashes on Explorers – are open to all except mechanically propelled vehicles). Access land is marked with a yellow tint and a dark orange border on Explorer maps only; they also indicate with an 'i' in an orange circle the primary access points, which have an information board; but other gates and stiles are not shown. Other areas of land that are always open (National Trust, National Trust for Scotland and Forestry Commission) are shown on Explorer and Landranger maps with purple boundaries.

Dog stiles and gates Bridleways and byways use gates rather than stiles, which makes things much easier for dog-walking, as dogs can find stiles baffling. Some councils and landowners are increasingly installing easily climbed stiles, or gates rather than stiles, or excellent stiles with dog gates built into them – and there's now a legal requirement for councils to take into account the needs of the less mobile when stiles or gates are installed. In the meantime, finding out if a particular path has dog-friendly crossing points isn't straightforward, and it's best to ask locally. Some local tourist information centres stock leaflets showing stile-free walks suitable for dogs.

Dogs on trains are carried free of charge (up to two dogs per passenger), and must be kept on a lead or in a basket. For journey planning, see www.nationalrail.co.uk for trains, and www.traveline.info for buses.

Guided walks are run by all sorts of organisations. The largest of these is the Ramblers (formerly the Ramblers' Association), which has local clubs across the country. Leaders may or may not allow dogs, so it's always worth checking first. For details of group walks and other events, as well as a wealth of information about where to walk, access rights and walking gear, see www.ramblers.org.uk. You can try a Ramblers walk for free, but will be expected to join if you go on several. You could also meet up with local walkers through www.meetup.com, which has dozens of walking groups for a range of levels of fitness and experience, arranged by locality. There's also the splendid Great North Dog Walk (www.cooksondogwalk.co.uk), held each June in north-east England. A major fund-raising event, it has made it into the Guinness World Records as the largest dog walk ever held, with the number of dogs now taking part well in excess of 20,000.

Finally, although it's not really connected to dog-walking, if you're into cycling and want to take your dog along with you, there are **dog cycle trailers** that hitch on to the back of your bike, allowing your dog to enjoy the ride. A search on www.google.co.uk for dog + "cycle trailers" comes up with plenty of results.

How the Guide works

Each county chapter is divided into two sections – **Dog Friendly Pubs**, followed by **Dog Friendly Hotels, Inns and B&Bs**.

The maps at the back of the book will help you locate pubs that allow dogs in the bar – they are indicated with a ●. Places where dogs are allowed in the bedrooms are indicated with a ▣.

Dog Friendly Pubs (where dogs are allowed in at least one bar)

We give opening hours and note any days that places are closed altogether, whether they have a restaurant, and if they offer bar food. Typical food service times in pubs are 12-2pm and 7-9pm Monday to Saturday; the kitchen often closes a bit earlier on Sundays. We give specific hours for each place and also note days when no food is served, but suggest you check first before planning an expedition that depends on having a meal.

Some of these pubs also offer accommodation (we've said if this is the case and given the price of a standard double room), but note that they don't allow dogs into those bedrooms. If they did, the pub would appear in the Hotels section.

Dog Friendly Hotels, Inns and B&Bs (where dogs are welcome in some or all of the bedrooms)

Some establishments are extremely dog-focused, welcoming dogs in every bedroom and all public areas (although restaurants are usually out of bounds). Others have a certain number of bedrooms set aside for dogs (often ground-floor ones with direct access to the garden or car park) and allow them in some, but not all, public areas – usually the bar and often a lounge or conservatory too. Others accept only small dogs or only on the condition that they are never left alone in bedrooms. We've tried to be as specific as possible with such details (though you should always check when booking).

Many pubs and hotels have water bowls and a jar of treats in the bar, but some places make a special effort in the bedrooms too, providing a dog bed or blanket, a bowl or two, sometimes even a map outlining local walks. We've said if this is the case.

Increasingly, venues charge for dogs staying overnight (usually to compensate for the extra cleaning required), though many still don't. If we give a price, this is per dog per night: £10 seems to be standard. If the charge is for the duration of your stay, not per night, we say so. If no price is given, then there is no charge.

All this information is listed at the end of each entry.

The bedroom price is given at the front of each entry, along with the total number of rooms. This price is for two people sharing a standard double room with its own bathroom for one night, midweek, in high season. It includes breakfast, VAT and any automatic service charge that we know about. We say if dinner is included, which it may be at more remote places. The price is for a dog-friendly room, so this may be more expensive than a standard bedroom if the venue only allows dogs into certain rooms.

Remember that the price is a guide, not a guarantee. Rates can vary greatly throughout the year; many places offer cheaper rates if you book well in advance, or online, and winter prices are often lower than summer ones. It's always worth checking for special deals. If we know that the back rooms are the quietest, or the front ones have the best views, or the ones in the new extension are more spacious, then we say so.

We always mention a restaurant if we know there is one and we commend food if we have information supporting a positive recommendation. Many B&Bs will suggest nearby pubs for dinner if they do not offer an evening meal.

We also say if the venue is closed for more than a week at any point in the year; some places close for a couple of weeks (or even months) in winter, especially in remoter or colder areas. But we don't mention closures day by day: if a restaurant-with-rooms, say, is always shut on a Sunday and Monday, you'll discover that yourself when booking.

Let's go for a walk

Many of the places listed in this Guide are in particularly lovely countryside and some of them have great walks right on their doorsteps.
This selection gives just a handful of pubs that are perfectly sited
for a walk, a drink and a meal with your canine friend. We've only
provided an outline to the walk itself, so you will need an OS map
(1:25,000 scale Explorer sheets are the best) to help you plan and
follow your exact route, though in some instances where the walks
follow obvious physical features such as coastline or canals you
might not need a map, and in London the *A-Z* or Google maps will
do the trick.

BEDFORDSHIRE

Prince of Wales, Ampthill (page 3)

There's free access to Ampthill Park – a surprisingly wild expanse
just north-west of Ampthill, with woodland and grassland, and once
a hunting ground of Henry VIII. Car parks are on the south side, off
the B530, and the park is crossed by the Greensand Ridge Walk. You
can extend the stroll by walking north from the church to the ruins of
Houghton House.

BERKSHIRE

Crown & Garter, Inkpen (page 6)

A few minutes' walk north-east along Great Common Road from
the pub leads to Inkpen Common nature reserve, a patch of ancient
heathland, with three types of heather and a variety of birdlife;
kissing gates rather than stiles make it easy for most dogs. In total
contrast, a mile south down the lane gets you to car parks at the
top of the downs on either side of Walbury Hill, a really bracing
place in the wind, and with huge views north. The easy chalk

track along the top of the escarpment west leads past the macabre landmark of Combe Gibbet.

BUCKINGHAMSHIRE

White Horse, Hedgerley (page 19)

Around Hedgerley are some splendid broad-leafed woodlands, laced with paths and with plenty of potential for walks. They're at their most spectacular when carpets of bluebells appear in spring or when the leaves turn in autumn (autumn colours are especially famed at Burnham Beeches to the south-west). Almost next to the White Horse is the entrance to Church Wood RSPB reserve (they request that you keep your dog on a lead, especially during the April to June nesting season), known for its woodland birds, including great spotted woodpeckers, nuthatches and tree creepers.

CHESHIRE

Pheasant, Burwardsley (page 43)

The well waymarked Sandstone Trail runs close to the Pheasant, through a stretch of woodland and sandstone crags of the Peckforton Hills. The going underfoot (or underpaw) can be rough and slippery in places and you'll need to keep your dog under control if venturing further south to the top of Raw Head, at 746 feet (227 metres) the highpoint of the range. Here a sandstone cliff has been weathered into honeycomb patterns, and just below the summit is a cave quarried out of the hillside and known as the Queen's Parlour. North from Burwardsley the Trail takes in a very attractive section through forest beneath the sham-medieval Peckforton Castle.

CORNWALL

Bush, Morwenstow (page 58)

The well trodden route past Morwenstow church and to the clifftops is the obvious walk here. The eccentric 19th-century vicar Rev Hawker built the church and rectory, and buried many salvaged shipwreck victims in the churchyard: the rectory's chimney pots mimic the towers of churches in places he'd formerly lived. Ten minutes' walking brings you to the cliffs, and just before the coast path reaches Higher Sharpnose you'll find the driftwood shack, now maintained by the National Trust, where Hawker would contemplate and smoke opium.

CUMBRIA

Sun, Coniston (page 73)

Highly contrasting but equally rewarding walking options are found at Coniston. You'll find easy strolling along Coniston Water, reached in a few minutes from the village via Lake Road, then, where the road bends left, fork right at the signpost for the lake. The route passes the ancient-looking Coniston Hall and soon offers glorious views across the water; you can continue for up to 3 miles (5km) on a delightful lakeside path that goes in and out of woodland. Alternative expeditions for energetic dogs involve walking up to the Coppermines Valley above the west side of the village, with spectacular remnants of long-defunct mines punctuating the slopes below Coniston Old Man. The lane up from Coniston begins steeply, then rises past the Miners Bridge and waterfall.

Britannia, Elterwater (page 74)

You walk straight out of this pub into some of the choicest walking country in England, with easily managed gates. Easy options follow the Cumbria Way along the river – eastwards en route to Skelwith Force waterfall you sneak a view of the strangely elusive Elterwater, not otherwise easy to see up close. Westwards, the Great Langdale Beck enters Langdale proper: the walking is through flat fields but the views of the Langdale Pikes are hugely rewarding. Tougher dogs might enjoy the walk up to Stickle Tarn, marvellously placed beneath the Langdale Pikes summits, or an extended 9-mile (14.5km) tour of the dale taking in the lower reaches of Lingmoor Fell and scenically sited Blea Tarn, which has its own car park.

Old Dungeon Ghyll, Langdale (page 76)

Some wonderful low-level walking from here follows a bridleway section of the Cumbria Way, with easily managed gates. West of Old Dungeon Ghyll is an easily managed track along the valley of Mickleden Beck, with formidable peaks rising ahead and on either side: you can walk for about 2 miles (3km) before the terrain steepens appreciably.

Langstrath, Stonethwaite (page 69)

You can enjoy very satisfying views of Borrowdale on an easy, level, 2-mile (3km) circular walk from Stonethwaite – over Stonethwaite Bridge, then left along Stonethwaite Beck to the next hamlet, Rosthwaite, where you cross over and take the lane on the far

side of the B5289, then left on the path by the River Derwent, over
the next bridge and back on the lane to Stonethwaite.

DERBYSHIRE

Monsal Head Hotel, Monsal Head (page 87)

The view from here lures you down to the Monsal Trail, which
goes over the old railway viaduct you can see below, and along a
railway trackbed. It's easy going for dogs, and if you'd rather not
take in the steep path from the hotel to the Trail, you can start from
a car park and picnic site on the A6 at the valley floor level. Either
direction is beautiful: westwards extends a mile (1.6km) until you're
diverted away from a tunnel entrance and past the old textile mill at
Cressbrook and into Millers Dale.

DEVON

Masons Arms, Branscombe (page 100)

The path network helps keep you and your dog off the narrow
lanes, and the walkers' routes are well marked, if sometimes steep.
From the Masons Arms you can follow the lane or field path to
Branscombe Mouth, where to the east beyond the caravan park is
the strange netherworld of collapsed chalk cliffs known as Hooken
Undercliff – one of the most startling coastal features in all Devon.
Or you could head west from Branscombe Mouth on to the coast
path, through woods in places, later striking inland to drop down
past Branscombe church, where there's a choice of road or path to
get you back to the starting point.

Rock, Haytor Vale (page 103)

One of the best viewpoints in Dartmoor is nearby: drive up to the car
park at Haytor Rocks, and use the groups of rocks, the abandoned
quarries and the old tram tracks to guide you round the moor.

Rugglestone, Widecombe (page 97)

Good, breezy moorland strolls in the vicinity include eastwards up
to Rugglestone Rock and the Logan Stone, and from Widecombe
village to the wide ridge of Hameldown – the latter reached by
following the lane towards Natsworthy then branching up a steadily
rising track, alongside a wall on the right. It can be boggy on the
moor in places, but that is more than compensated for by the
wonderful feeling of space.

DORSET

George, Chideock (page 111)

The busy A35 is something of a deterrent to starting a walk, but once you're away from it (best to drive the short lane to Seatown), the walk up from Seatown to Golden Cap has one of the great Dorset views, from the county's highest coastal point. You need to be careful with the cliff drops, but there's generally plenty of space for dogs at the top.

Square & Compass, Worth Matravers (page 116)

Several routes lead out to the cliffs from here: the easiest, and least interesting, is along the road west to Renscombe Farm, then left on the lane down to the atmospherically unadorned ancient chapel on the clifftop at St Aldhelm's Head (1.5 miles/2.4km total); it's more fun, but much more challenging, to keep west on a path from Renscombe Farm to join the switchback coast path above Chapman's Pool. This is wonderful in either direction, but it's not recommended for vertigo sufferers, and there are stiles on the way. Eastwards you can edge round the coast and return to Worth Matravers along the valley floor of Winspit Bottom.

GLOUCESTERSHIRE

Eight Bells, Chipping Campden (page 129)

The Cotswold Way starts and finishes by the market hall at Chipping Campden, from where you can follow this well signposted National Trail north-west, turning right by St Catharine's Church and following Back Lane and rising out of town. After a brief section along Kincomb Lane, the Way continues as a track leading on to the top of the escarpment of Dover's Hill, for tremendous views over the western Midlands. You can return by the same route or devise a more elaborate circuit around Dover's Hill. Another nearby excellent strolling ground along the Cotswold Way is Broadway Hill, with its folly tower looking far across the Vale of Evesham to the Malverns.

HAMPSHIRE

Royal Oak, Fritham (page 147)

You can wander at will through much of the New Forest, but be aware that ponies and deer may be at large, the presence of which might either frighten your dog or encourage it to give chase. Finding a path isn't difficult; more of a problem is losing your way, as there's a huge network of paths. From the end of the public road near the Royal

Oak you can step straight into the wilds, which here vary pleasantly between planted forest and open heathland.

Wykeham Arms, Winchester (page 159)

The water meadows adjoining the city make for idyllic strolling: you can join them by turning on to College Walk near Wolvesey Castle, following the signs for the Hospital of St Cross (an ancient almshouses institution), which takes about 20 minutes. A satisfying add-on for dogs that like a bit of a climb is the modest summit of St Catherine's Hill, from the entrance to the hospital. At the top are Iron Age ramparts and a mysterious 'mizmaze' cut into the turf, supposedly for knights to do penance by crawling round it; the view extends right across Winchester.

HEREFORDSHIRE

Saracens Head, Symonds Yat (page 162)

Crossing the river is half the fun here: from the Saracens Head, a rope-hoisted ferry will get you and your dog across for a small fee. On the other side, turn left along the riverside track to the 'chicken wire' bridge a mile or so downstream, then double back on the obvious riverside route along the other side. For such an easy walk, this is extraordinarily scenic and has plenty to look at, both on and away from the river; abseilers and canoeists are often in evidence. To make it more of a challenge, you could wander up to the Symonds Yat viewpoint, high above the pub, with its classic view of the river's great meander.

ISLE OF WIGHT

Sentry Mead, Totland (page 175)

The coastal path is only a short stroll away, at the end of Madeira Road. Turn left along the esplanade and once past the houses you head beneath rugged cliffs and rise to the heathery expanses of Headon Warren, an area of National Trust land with remains of a 19th-c gun battery and a Bronze Age barrow. From there you dip down to Alum Bay, where a chairlift can take you to the shore to view the multicoloured sand cliffs. You can extend this walk along the wonderfully open, grassy, whaleback downland that stretches from the western tip of the island above the Needles chalk pinnacles, past the monument to Alfred Lord Tennyson on Tennyson Down, to Freshwater Bay. And if you and your dog are feeling super-energetic, join up the sections of the walk by taking part of the path along the reedy River Yar.

KENT

Red Lion, Stodmarsh (page 184)

The Red Lion is perfectly positioned for one of the great wildlife walks of Kent, along the Stour and through Stodmarsh National Nature Reserve – though you will need to keep your dog on a short lead because of the abundance of wildlife. This hugely important wetlands site (binoculars strongly recommended), with its watermeadows and reedy lagoons, is a major bird sanctuary and harbours rarities such as bitterns and marsh harriers. From the Red Lion, walk away from the village on the track past a car park near the entrance to the Reedbed Hide and explore the path across the marshes past the Marsh Hide to the Grove Ferry Road, where you can return along the river to complete a fascinating 5 miles (8km).

LINCOLNSHIRE

Chequers, Woolsthorpe (page 210)

An uncomplicated and extremely pleasant walk for dogs of all abilities along the Grantham Canal can easily be joined from Woolsthorpe (although you may prefer to drive the unexceptional road section as far as the canal). With the pub sign on your right, follow Main Street and continue at the next junction along Sedgebrook Road, forking right at the sign for the Dirty Duck pub beyond the end of the village on a road crossing the canal. You can make a circular walk of 8.5 miles (13.5km) by following the towpath east to bridge 66, then doubling back on a field path soon skirting Denton Reservoir and carrying on through the ironstone village of Denton. At the south end of the village, a field path runs parallel to the A607 south-west until you meet the signposted Viking Way long-distance path which leads back to Woolsthorpe.

NORFOLK

Blakeney Hotel, Blakeney (page 215)

All of the Norfolk Coast Path here is gloriously straightforward dog-walking terrain – easy to find, easy underfoot and plenty to enjoy looking at. From Blakeney, and many other places along the coast, the route follows the top of a grassy dyke around the marshes. Eastwards it loops around past the remains of Blakeney Chapel to Cley-next-the-Sea (the frequent Coasthopper bus service is a useful means of travelling between Cley, Blakeney and other points on the coast; they will take dogs for no charge provided they're not a risk to other passengers; for details call 01553 776980 or visit www.stagecoachbus.com).

Westwards, the coast path heads along the landward side of the marshes to Morston, from where there's a seasonal boat service to the long coastal spit of Blakeney Point.

Orange Tree, Thornham (page 220)

A favourite spot for bird-watchers, Thornham's quiet saltmarsh inlets can be followed out towards the coast via Ship Lane and Staithe Lane, where you're close to the Titchwell RSPB reserve. Then you're into a different terrain of expansive dunes as you carry on westwards past Gore Point to Holme-next-the-Sea. Either return the same way or go on to the A149 to pick up the Coasthopper bus back.

NORTHUMBRIA

Jolly Fisherman, Craster (page 228)

The low-lying coast is consistently beautiful hereabouts, and for much of the way there are good paths along or just above the shore, in many places along sandy beaches backed by dunes. From Craster, the stand-out walk is northwards 1.5 miles (2.5km) to the spectacular ruins of 14th-century Dunstanburgh Castle; you can carry on past a golf course to Dunstan Steads Farm for a less eventful but easy and level return route along farm tracks.

SHROPSHIRE

Royal Oak, Cardington (page 251)

The village sits on the brink of some of the loveliest hill walks in this part of the world. Your dog can experience it without climbing at all by walking along the lane west from Cardington past Wilstone Farm; Caer Caradoc soon comes into view. If you want to tackle it, you'll face a steep walk up but you'll be rewarded with colossal views from its satisfyingly compact summit; easier options include the gentle moorland tracks over Hope Bowdler Hill to the south.

SOMERSET

Crown, Churchill (page 262)

The Crown is well positioned for one of the very best walks in the Mendips, around Dolebury Warren and towards Burrington Combe. From the pub, head along the Batch southwards, then fork left to cross the A38, where you'll find a lane leading past a small car park: from there it's an easily managed valley-floor track with gates. It's worth continuing for a mile (1.6km) to a junction of tracks where you can return by turning left up over Dolebury Warren – an open hill with lots of space for dogs – with far-reaching views from the Iron Age hill fort at the western end. You can extend the walk further east to take in the moorland above the limestone gorge of Burrington Combe; the road along the floor of the gorge is unfenced and pleasant to walk along.

SUFFOLK

Crown (page 285), Harbour Inn (page 286) and Swan (page 292), all Southwold

Plenty of space on the beach and some lovely areas of common provide plenty of possibilities for dog-walkers. Southwold has a long beach and a spacious common: dogs are allowed on the Denes (the southern stretch of the beach) but barred from certain areas near the pier during the holiday season. From there, you can continue round to the mouth of the canalised River Blyth, where a summer ferry sometimes operates to Walberswick (giving scope for carrying on along the Dunwich river and towards Walberswick National Nature Reserve); follow the river upstream to the bridge, then go right up to Southwold Common and back into the town to complete a very uncomplicated 2.5 miles (4km).

SURREY

Percy Arms, Chilworth (page 296)

The sandy woodland tracks leading over St Martha's Hill make for some super dog-walking options, along the North Downs Way. There's a path on the left side of the primary school that heads to the Tillingbourne, a lovely stream in woodland – if you follow it eastwards, you pass remains of defunct gunpowder mills; further on is Albury Pond and the main ascent to the hilltop. You can avoid a lot of the effort by starting from the car park half a mile east of the summit. At the very top sits the mostly Victorian St Martha's Church, far from any road, looking out over the Weald towards the South Downs.

Mill at Elstead, Elstead (page 297)

A mile or so south of Elstead is Thursley Common, one of the best Surrey heaths for walking, with sandy paths and tracks running between large expanses of heather and patches of woodland. Several ponds make attractive points to head for. A useful starting point is the Moat car park and picnic site just off the road to Thursley, or you can follow a path south-east from Elstead from Thursley Road near the junction with the B3001.

SUSSEX

Fox Goes Free, Charlton (page 303)

Just north of the village and with very much of the look of the South
Downs as they were before modern agriculture, Levin Down is a nature
reserve crossed by public paths, and is a habitat for numerous butterflies
and chalkland wildflowers. Southwards a quiet lane and a track lead up
towards Goodwood Racecourse, at the west end of which is parking
space giving on to the Trundle; masts mark the top of an impressive Iron
Age hill fort (open access and plenty of space) with massive ramparts
and a huge view extending to the Isle of Wight and Beachy Head.

Tiger, East Dean (page 306)

With the free car park adjoining the village green, this makes the
perfect starting point for the finest coastal walk in the South-East,
taking in the grassy rollercoaster clifftops of the Seven Sisters in one
direction and using the quiet tracks through Friston Forest in the other.
The cliff edges are sheer and very crumbly, so you may need to keep
your dog well supervised, but there's free access so you can wander
some way inland. There are plenty of options for shortening it: the
easiest walks include starting at Birling Gap and strolling up to Belle
Tout lighthouse, or parking at Crowlink (off the main road at Friston,
just above East Dean) and walking down over the grass and on to the
clifftops. The information centre is at Seven Sisters Country Park.

WILTSHIRE

Castle (page 331) and Woolley Grange (page 341), both Bradford-on-Avon

Suitable for dogs of all levels of fitness and energy, Barton Farm
Country Park lies on the town's southern peripheries. The 36-acre
(14.5-hectare) park is an old farm estate with a tithe barn, and lies
between the River Avon and the Kennet & Avon Canal. Here you'll
encounter plenty of grassy open space, and you can carry on along
the verdant towpath of the canal as far as your dog desires.

WORCESTERSHIRE

Nags Head, Malvern (page 349)

From the top of the long Malverns ridge there are terrific views across
the Midlands and into the Welsh borders, and an almost bewildering
number of paths to get you up to the top. It's all very dog-friendly

and somewhat more easily managed and municipal than you might expect for a range of hills that looks formidably alpine from the hazy distance, with benches sited every few paces on amiable grassy terrain. Worcestershire Beacon, the highest point, is close to the town centre of Malvern and is easily reached by walking past St Ann's Well, the original source of Malvern water.

YORKSHIRE

Lion, Blakey Ridge (page 353)

Either side of the road from here are splendid level walks through the moor, on former railway tracks that once served the ironstone quarries. On the east side, the track loops around lazily, giving effortless views over Farndale.

Bridge Inn, Grinton (page 363)

Swaledale is connoisseurs' walking territory, though the number of stiles can make it tricky for dog-walking, and the field crossing is often quite intricate. On the far side of the Swale from Grinton, a riverside path makes a pleasant half-mile amble, and on the open moors on all sides are opportunities for striding out. A particularly satisfying circular route could be made from Reeth, up the north side of Arkle Beck in its deep-set valley, then taking any of several paths leading up to the valley rim of Fremington Edge for an enjoyably blustery contrast.

LONDON

Holly Bush, North London (page 377)

Hampstead Heath could stake a claim as London's premier dog-walking terrain, a 790-acre (320-hectare) countrified expanse that's large enough to lose yourself in and hilly enough to sustain interest wherever you wander. There's free access to all of it, and your dog can dip into ponds, explore woodlands and glades and run around through grasslands. You might like to head past Hampstead Ponds and up Parliament Hill, one of the highest points in London at 322 feet (98 metres), with an outstanding view over the capital. From there you could carry on to Kenwood House's grounds for refreshment at the café and a stroll round the gardens; entrance is free. There's a wide choice of access points from Hampstead itself, with large car parks at East Heath Road, Jack Straw's Castle, Parliament Hill Lido and Kenwood House, and plenty of buses passing by.

SCOTLAND

Border Hotel, Kirk Yetholm (page 398)

As Kirk Yetholm is at the very end of the long-distance Pennine Way, you might like to follow it in reverse for a distance and greet walkers who have nearly made it all the way. The first stretch is along a surfaced, but virtually traffic-free, farm road. After the last building the route climbs appreciably up on to the high moors of the Cheviots, reaching a saddle between the Curr and Black Hag – a total distance from Kirk Yetholm of about 4 miles (6.5km).

Burts Hotel, Melrose (page 398)

Two objectives to join together here: one is the River Tweed, just north of Melrose, with a riverside path making the most of the Borders views. The other are the Eildon Hills, a mile or so south of Melrose, and reached by a field path. They rise just enough to feel like proper summits, and one of them – Eildon Hill North – is ringed by Iron Age ramparts, but it's only about 900 feet (275 metres) of ascent. The view from the top takes in the Cheviots, the Moorfoots and the Lammermuir Hills. You can join the hills with the river by walking along the Tweed east to Newstead, climbing the Eildons from there, then dropping to Melrose (4.5 miles/7km).

WALES

Pen-y-Gwryd, Llanberis (page 418)

There's really nothing here along the level, but energetic dogs may like the walk up from here following the miners' track northwards to the saddle between Glyder Fach and Y Foel Goch. If you choose not to continue up to either of these summits you can just enjoy the superlative view of Tryfan ahead.

Harp, Old Radnor (page 420)

The view from the open ground in front of the pub may well inspire you to venture on to Radnor Forest, the upland mass a few miles away. One of the most useful access points is New Radnor, from where you can climb up through forestry plantations and skirt the prominent peak known as the Whimble or take a path through the churchyard, round the contour and across the entrance to Harley Dingle (used for munitions testing, but a highly scenic route skirts it). A couple of miles west of New Radnor, along the A44, is a car park for the 15-minute walk along a forest road to the entrance to a chasm on the left, at the end of which is Water-Break-Its-Neck, a marvellously tucked-away waterfall that sprays appreciably after prolonged rain and often has a show of icicles in deep winter. There are lots of sheep on the open hills, so you'll need to keep your dog on a lead for much of the way.

Stackpole Inn, Stackpole (page 412)

Just to the south of the pub, Bosherston Lakes have free access, with gorgeous walks along the water's edge, and the eastern arm is suitable for wheelchair users. A rich wildlife haunt, it's home to numerous species of breeding birds, dragonflies and damselflies, and in June and July the lilies are at their showiest. At the southern end, you can venture on to Broad Haven, a wonderfully unspoilt sandy beach. The coast path from here eastwards is mostly level, and encompasses St Govan's Head, near which St Govan's Chapel is an extraordinary medieval structure ensconced beneath the cliffs.

Bedfordshire

DOG FRIENDLY PUBS

BEDFORD
Park

TL0550

(01234) 273929 – www.theparkbedford.co.uk
Corner of Kimbolton Road (B660) and Park Avenue, out past Bedford Hospital; MK40 2PA

Civilised and individual oasis – a great asset for the town

There's always a wide mix of customers here popping in and out all day and the atmosphere is chatty and bustling. Appealing décor has thoughtful touches, and you can choose where to sit according to your mood: a more or less conventional bar with heavy beams, panelled dado and leaded lights in big windows, a light and airy conservatory sitting room with easy chairs well spread on a carpet, and an extensive series of softly lit rambling dining areas, carpeted or flagstoned. Charles Wells Bombardier Burning Gold and Eagle and Courage Directors on handpump, inventive bar nibbles and an excellent choice of wines by the glass; background music. The sheltered brick-paved terrace has good timber furniture, some under canopies, and attractive shrub plantings.

Little Gems Country Dining Pubs ~ Manager Steve Cook ~ Real ale ~ Open 8am-11.30pm; 9am-11.30pm Sat; 9am-11pm Sun ~ Bar food 12-3, 6-10; 12-10 Sat; 12-8 Sun ~ Restaurant ~ Children in one bar and restaurant ~ Dogs allowed in bar ~ Wi-fi

FLITTON
White Hart

TL0535

(01525) 862022 – www.whitehartflitton.co.uk
Village signed off A507; MK45 5EJ

Simply furnished and friendly village pub with bar and dining area, real ales, interesting food and seats in the garden

The rewarding food is one of the big draws to this friendly village pub, but they do keep B&T Golden Fox and Shefford Bitter on handpump and 20 wines – as well as champagne and prosecco – by the glass. The minimally decorated front bar has dark leather tub chairs around low tables, contemporary leather and chrome seats at pedestal tables, and Farrow & Ball painted walls; TV. Steps lead down to a good-sized, simply furnished back dining area with red plush seats and banquettes on dark wooden floorboards. The nice garden has neat shrub borders, and teak seats and tables on a terrace shaded by cedars and weeping willows. A 13th-c church is next door.

Free house ~ Licensees Phil and Clare Hale ~ Real ale ~ Open 12-2.30, 6-midnight; 12-3,
6-1am Sat; 12-5 Sun; closed Sun evening, Mon ~ Bar food 12-2, 6.30-9 (9.30 Fri, Sat); 12-2.30
Sun ~ Restaurant ~ Children welcome ~ Dogs allowed in bar ~ Wi-fi

OAKLEY   TL0053

Bedford Arms

(01234) 822280 – www.bedfordarmsoakley.co.uk
High Street; MK43 7RH

**Nice old village inn with real ales, wines by the glass, fish and other
popular food in two dining rooms and seats in the garden**

Each of the interconnected rooms in this updated 16th-c pub has different
contemporary décor. The pubbiest part has straightforward wooden
furniture on bare boards, flower prints on the walls, daily papers, a decorative
woodburning stove with a flat-screen TV above it, and Charles Wells
Bombardier Burning Gold and Eagle and Courage Directors on handpump
and 30 wines by the glass; darts. The four cosy, individually decorated rooms
leading off the main bar are the nicest places for a drink and chat. One has a
large circular pine table (just right for a private party), another has farmhouse
chairs and a cushioned pew beside a small fireplace, the third has ladderback
chairs and shiny tables on ancient floor tiles and the last is very much Victorian
in style. The stone-floored dining rooms have tartan-covered seating or wicker
chairs, while the light, airy conservatory overlooks the pretty garden where
there are seats for warm weather. The daily fresh fish dishes are quite special.

Wells & Youngs ~ Tenants Tim and Yvonne Walker ~ Real ale ~ Open 12-11 (10.30 Sun) ~
Bar food 12-2.30, 6.15-9.30; 12-4 Sun ~ Restaurant ~ Children welcome ~ Dogs allowed in
bar ~ Wi-fi

RAVENSDEN   TL0754

Horse & Jockey

(01234) 772319 – www.horseandjockey.info
Village signed off B660 N of Bedford; pub at Church End, off village road; MK44 2RR

Contemporary comfort, with enjoyable food and good range of drinks

Both drinkers and diners receive a genuine welcome in this friendly place. It's
carefully run by enthusiastic licensees and the pleasantly modern interior
has a quiet colour scheme of olive greys and dark red, careful lighting, leather
easy chairs in the bar, a wall of meticulously arranged old local photographs
and maybe copies of *Country Life* and daily papers; background music and
board games. Adnams Ghost Ship and Southwold and Black Sheep Holy Grail
on handpump and 20 wines by the glass served by charming staff. The bright
dining room has nice chunky tables and high-backed seats, well lit prints and
a contemporary etched glass screen; it overlooks a sheltered terrace with
smart, up-to-date tables and chairs under cocktail parasols on decking and
a few picnic-sets on the grass beside. The handsome medieval church with
churchyard is further off.

Free house ~ Licensees Darron and Sarah Smith ~ Real ale ~ Open 12-3, 6-11 (midnight
Sat); 12-8 Sun ~ Bar food 12-2, 7-9; 12-6 Sun ~ Restaurant ~ Children welcome ~ Dogs
allowed in bar ~ Wi-fi

WOOTTON   TL0046

Legstraps

(01234) 854112 – www.thelegstraps.co.uk
Keeley Lane; MK43 9HR

Bustling village pub with a nice range of food from open kitchen, local ales and wines by the glass

There's a good mix in this village pub between drinkers and diners and the kind, efficient staff welcome everyone. The low-ceilinged bar has an elegant feel with contemporary and comfortable upholstered chairs around all size of tables, big flagstones, a woodburning stove in a brick fireplace with a leather sofa and box wall seats to either side, and leather-topped stools against the pale planked counter. They keep Fullers London Pride and Sharps Doom Bar on handpump, good wines by the glass and quite a few gins. The dining rooms have bold paintwork, similar furnishings to the bar, polished bare boards and flower prints on one end wall with paper butterflies on another.

Free house ~ Licensee Ian Craig ~ Real ale ~ Open 12-3, 5.30-11; 12-midnight Fri, Sat; 12-7 Sun; closed Mon ~ Bar food 12-2, 6-9 (9.30 Fri, Sat); 12-4 Sun ~ Restaurant ~ Children welcome ~ Dogs allowed in bar ~ Wi-fi

DOG FRIENDLY HOTELS, INNS AND B&Bs

AMPTHILL   TL0338

Prince of Wales

(01525) 840504 – www.princeofwales-ampthill.com
24 Bedford Street, Ampthill, Bedfordshire MK45 2NB

£70; 5 rooms. This attractive red-brick place is more an open-plan bar/brasserie than a straightforward pub, with comfortable, stylish furnishings and modern prints on mainly cream walls, a log fire in a brick fireplace, big burgundy leather armchairs and sofas, flagstone floors and church candles; the partly ply-panelled dining room has dark leather dining chairs around sturdy tables, and notably good food (Thursday is steak night); real ales, plenty of wines by the glass, good coffee and excellent service; picnic-sets on a nicely planted two-level lawn and on a terrace by the car park. Dogs allowed in all bedrooms and bar.

FLITWICK   TL0234

Hallmark Hotel Flitwick Manor

(01525) 712242 – www.hallmarkhotels.co.uk/hotels/flitwick
Church Road, Flitwick, Bedfordshire MK45 1AE

£134; 18 thoughtfully decorated rooms with antiques and period pieces. Georgian country house surrounded by acres of rolling gardens and wooded parkland; log fire in entrance hall, comfortable, tranquil lounge and library, and smart restaurant with imaginative food using home-grown and local produce; tennis and croquet. Dogs allowed in downstairs bedrooms; welcome pack; £20.

HOUGHTON CONQUEST

TL0441

Knife & Cleaver

(01234) 930789 – www.theknifeandcleaver.com
The Grove, Houghton Conquest, Bedfordshire MK45 3LA

£99; 9 attractively decorated chalet rooms around courtyard. Comfortably civilised and extended village inn, real ales and good choice of wines by the glass, a blazing winter fire, enjoyable food from bar and separate smart dining room, tables on a terrace alongside the neatly kept, attractive garden; friendly helpful staff; nearby walks; seven scottie dogs and one parrot. Dogs allowed in two bedrooms (with private gardens) but not bar; £5.

Berkshire

MAP 2

DOG FRIENDLY PUBS

BRAY   SU9079

Crown

(01628) 621936 – www.thecrownatbray.co.uk
*1.75 miles from M4 junction 9; A308 towards Windsor, then left at Bray signpost
on to B3028; High Street; SL6 2AH*

**Ancient low-beamed pub with knocked-through rooms, enjoyable food,
real ales and plenty of outside seating**

The main emphasis here is on dining (not surprising given that the owner is
Heston Blumenthal), but there's also a little bar area with high stools around
an equally high table, simple tables and chairs beside an open fire and regulars
who drop in for a chat and a drink: Courage Best and Directors and a couple
of changing guest beers on handpump and around 18 wines by the glass. The
snug rooms have some panelling, heavy old beams – some so low you may have
to mind your head – plenty of timbers at elbow height where walls have been
knocked through, a second log fire and neatly upholstered dining chairs and
cushioned settles; board games. The covered and heated courtyard has modern
slatted chairs and tables and there are plenty of picnic-sets in the large, enclosed
back garden.

Scottish Courage ~ Lease David Hyde ~ Real ale ~ Open 11.30-11; 11.30-10.30 Sun ~ Bar
food 12-2.30 (3 Sat), 6-9.30 (10 Fri, Sat); 12-8 Sun ~ Children welcome ~ Dogs allowed in
bar ~ Wi-fi

BRAY   SU9079

Hinds Head

(01628) 626151 – www.hindsheadbray.com
High Street; car park opposite (exit rather tricky); SL6 2AB

**First class food in top gastropub, traditional surroundings, fine wines
and real ales**

The thoroughly traditional L-shaped bar in this handsome old place has dark
beams and panelling, polished oak parquet, blazing log fires, red-cushioned
built-in wall seats and studded leather carving chairs around small round
tables, and latticed windows. High chairs line the counter where they keep
beers from local breweries such as Oakham Green Devil IPA, Rebellion IPA
and Roasted Nuts and Windsor & Eton Canberra on handpump, 14 wines by the
glass from an extensive list, 18 malt whiskies and a dozen specialist gins and

whiskies with interesting ways of serving them. This is Heston Blumenthal's second pub in the village.

Free house ~ Licensee Nabiel El-Nakib ~ Real ale ~ Open 11.30 (12 Mon)-11; 12-6.30 Sun ~ Bar food 12-2.30, 6.15-9.15 (9.30 Fri, Sat); 12-3.30 Sun ~ Restaurant ~ Children welcome ~ Dogs allowed in bar ~ Wi-fi

HARE HATCH   SU8077
Horse & Groom

(0118) 940 3136 – www.brunningandprice.co.uk/horseandgroom
A4 Bath Road W of Maidenhead; RG10 9SB

Spreading pub with attractively furnished, timbered rooms, enjoyable food and seats outside

Well trained, courteous staff in this handsome old coaching inn warmly welcome all customers and offer a splendid range of drinks including a good changing range of 15 wines by the glass, Brakspears Bitter and Oxford Gold, Ringwood Fortyniner and Wychwood Hobgoblin on handpump, Weston's farm cider, 20 gins and 40 malt whiskies. There are plenty of signs of great age in the interconnected rooms – and much of interest too: beams and timbering, a pleasing variety of well spread individual tables and chairs on mahogany-stained boards, oriental rugs and some carpet to soften the acoustics, and open fires in attractive tiled fireplaces. Also, a profusion of mainly old or antique prints and mirrors, book-lined shelves, house plants and daily papers. A sheltered back garden has picnic-sets and the front terrace has teak tables and chairs under parasols.

Brunning & Price ~ Manager Josh Nicholson ~ Real ale ~ Open 11.30-11 ~ Bar food 12-10 (9 Sun) ~ Well behaved children welcome ~ Dogs allowed in bar ~ Wi-fi

INKPEN   SU3764
Crown & Garter

(01488) 668325 – www.crownandgarter.co.uk
Inkpen Common: Inkpen signposted with Kintbury off A4; in Kintbury turn left into Inkpen Road, then keep on into Inkpen Common; RG17 9QR

Carefully run country pub with modern touches blending with original features, enjoyable food and seats outside; bedrooms

For somewhere that feels so remote, this is a substantial and rather fine old brick inn. There's a spreading bar area with wooden stools against the counter where they serve West Berkshire Good Old Boy and Ramsbury Gold on handpump and ten wines by the glass. Leading off here is a snug area with a leather armchair and sofa by an open fire in a raised brick fireplace. Throughout, an assortment of upholstered dining chairs are grouped around simple tables on pale floorboards, with armchairs here and there, cushioned wall seating, mirrors and modern artwork on contemporary paintwork and wallpaper that depicts bookcases (in the smart restaurant) and old suitcases. The front terrace has seats and tables under parasols. There's a separate bakery and coffee shop (which becomes a private dining space in the evening). Disabled access.

Free house ~ Licensee Romilla Arber ~ Real ale ~ Open 8.30am-11pm; 8.30-6 Sun ~ Bar food 12-2 (2.30 Sun), 6.30-9 ~ Restaurant ~ Children welcome ~ Dogs allowed in bar ~ Wi-fi ~ Bedrooms: £130

NEWBURY   SU4767
Newbury
(01635) 49000 – www.thenewburypub.co.uk
Bartholomew Street; RG14 5HB

Lively pub with thoughtful choice of drinks, good food and plenty of bar and dining space

Once found, you're sure to go back to this cheerful, stylish town pub. The bar has an assortment of wooden dining chairs around sturdy farmhouse and other solid tables on bare boards, comfortable leather sofas, big paintings on pale painted walls and church candles. They keep a fantastic choice of drinks: a beer named for them (from Greene King), Timothy Taylors Landlord, Upham Punter and Tipster and a guest beer on handpump, a farm cider, 20 malt whiskies, around 23 wines by the glass, an extensive cocktail list and a fine range of coffees and teas (including tea grown in Cornwall). There is also an upstairs cocktail bar that leads out on to a roof terrace with an electric folding canopy roof. Light and airy, the dining rooms have wall benches and church chairs around more rustic tables on more bare boards, local artwork and shelves full of cookery books. The downstairs courtyard holds a smoker, which is put to great use.

Free house ~ Licensee Peter Lumber ~ Real ale ~ Open 12-11 (midnight Fri, 2am Sat, 10 Sun) ~ Bar food 12-3 (4 Sat), 6-10; 12-4 Sun ~ Restaurant ~ Children welcome ~ Dogs allowed in bar ~ Wi-fi

PEASEMORE   SU4577
Fox
(01635) 248480 – www.foxatpeasemore.co.uk
4 miles from M4 junction 13, via Chieveley: keep on through Chieveley to Peasemore, turning left into Hillgreen Lane at small sign to Fox Inn; village also signposted from B4494 Newbury–Wantage; RG20 7JN

Friendly downland pub on top form under its expert licensees

After a walk around the lovely surrounding countryside, this bustling, cheerful pub is just the place to head for – and you can be sure of a genuine welcome from the first class licensees. The long bare-boards bar has strategically placed high-backed settles (comfort guaranteed by plenty of colourful cushions), a warm woodburning stove in a stripped-brick chimney-breast and, for real sybarites, two luxuriously carpeted end areas, one with velour tub armchairs. Friendly, efficient, black-clad staff serve Ridgeside Black Night, West Berkshire Good Old Boy and a changing guest on handpump, 15 wines by the glass and summer farm cider; background music. This is downland horse-training country, and picnic-table sets at the front look out to the rolling fields beyond the quiet country lane – on a clear day as far as the Hampshire border hills 20 miles south; there are more on a smallish sheltered back terrace.

Free house ~ Licensees Philip and Lauren Davison ~ Real ale ~ Open 12-2.30, 6-11; 12-11 Sat; 12-6 Sun; closed Mon, Tues ~ Bar food 12-2, 6-9; 12-3, 5.30-9 Sat; 12-4 Sun ~ Restaurant ~ Children welcome ~ Dogs allowed in bar ~ Wi-fi

RUSCOMBE

SU7976

Royal Oak

(0118) 934 5190 – www.burattas.co.uk
Ruscombe Lane (B3024 just E of Twyford); RG10 9JN

Wide choice of popular food at welcoming pub with interesting furnishings and paintings, and local beer and wine

Known locally as Buratta's, this deservedly busy place is run by charming, hands-on licensees. The bars are open-plan and carpeted and cleverly laid out so that each area is fairly snug, but it still maintains an overall feel of a lot of people enjoying themselves. A good variety of furniture runs from dark oak tables to big chunky pine ones with mixed seating to match; the two sofas facing each other are popular. Contrasting with the old exposed ceiling joists, mostly unframed modern paintings and prints decorate the walls, which are painted in cream, white and soft green. Binghams (the brewery is just across the road) Space Hoppy IPA and Twyford Tipple and Fullers London Pride on handpump, 15 wines by the glass (they stock wines from the Stanlake Park vineyard in the village), several malt whiskies and attentive service. Picnic-sets are ranged around a venerable central hawthorn in the garden behind (where there are ducks and chickens); summer barbecues. The pub is on the Henley Arts Trail. Do visit the landlady's antiques and collectables shop, which is open during pub hours.

Enterprise ~ Lease Jenny and Stefano Buratta ~ Real ale ~ Open 12-3, 6-11; 12-4 Sun; closed Sun and Mon evenings ~ Bar food 12-2.30, 6-9.30; 12-3 Sun ~ Restaurant ~ Children welcome ~ Dogs welcome ~ Wi-fi

SHEFFORD WOODLANDS

SU3673

Pheasant

(01488) 648284 – www.thepheasant-inn.co.uk
Under 0.5 miles from M4 Junction 14 – A338 towards Wantage, first left on B4000; RG17 7AA

Bustling bars, a separate dining room, highly thought-of food and beer and seats outside; bedrooms

Good, enjoyable food and a warm welcome consistently attract happy customers here. The various interconnecting bar rooms have a mix of elegant wooden dining chairs and settles around all sorts of tables, big mirrors here and there, plenty of horse-related prints, photos and paintings (including a huge mural) – the owners are keen racegoers – and a warm fire in a little brick fireplace. One snug little room, with log-end wallpaper, has armchairs, a cushioned chesterfield and a flat-screen TV. A beer named for the pub (from Marstons), Marstons Pedigree, Ramsbury Gold and Ringwood Best on handpump and quite a few good wines by the glass. There's also a separate dining room; background music. Seats in the garden have attractive views.

Upham ~ Tenant Jack Greenall ~ Real ale ~ Open 11-11; 12-10.30 Sun ~ Bar food 12-3, 6-9.30; 12-5, 6-9 Sun ~ Children welcome ~ Dogs allowed in bar ~ Wi-fi ~ Bedrooms: £110

SONNING
Bull

SU7575

(0118) 969 3901 – www.bullinnsonning.co.uk
Off B478, by church; village signed off A4 E of Reading; RG4 6UP

Pretty timbered inn in attractive spot, plenty of character in old-fashioned bars, friendly staff and good food; bedrooms

As this is a fine black and white timbered 16th-c inn near the River Thames, there are always plenty of customers; it probably looks its best in early summer when the wisteria is flowering and the courtyard is full of bright flower tubs. Inside, the two old-fashioned bar rooms have low ceilings and heavy beams, cosy alcoves, leather armchairs and sofas, cushioned antique settles and low wooden chairs on bare boards, and open fireplaces. Fullers HSB, Honey Dew, London Pride, Oliver's Island and a couple of guests on handpump served by helpful staff, 16 good wines by the glass, cocktails and a farm cider. The dining room has a mix of wooden chairs and tables, rugs on parquet flooring and shelves of books; TV. If you bear left through the ivy-clad churchyard opposite, then turn left along the bank of the river, you come to a very pretty lock. The Thames Valley Park is close by.

Fullers ~ Manager Christine Mason ~ Real ale ~ Open 10am-11pm (midnight Sat); 12-10.30 Sun ~ Bar food 10-9.30 ~ Restaurant ~ Children welcome ~ Dogs allowed in bar ~ Wi-fi ~ Tribute acts monthly ~ Bedrooms: £105

SWALLOWFIELD
George & Dragon

SU7364

(0118) 988 4432 – www.georgeanddragonswallowfield.co.uk
Church Road, towards Farley Hill; RG7 1TJ

Busy country pub with enjoyable bar food, real ales, friendly service and seats outside

The long-serving licensees here care for both their pub and their customers – and it shows. It's a comfortable, easy-going place and the various interconnected rooms have plenty of character: beams (some quite low) and standing timbers, a happy mix of nice old dining chairs and settles around individual wooden tables, rugs on flagstones, lit candles, a big log fire and country prints on red or bare brick walls; background music. Ringwood Best, Sharps Doom Bar and Upham Punter on handpump, quite a few wines by the glass and several gins and whiskies. There are picnic-sets on gravel or paving in the garden and the website has details of walks that start and end at the pub.

Free house ~ Licensee Paul Dailey ~ Real ale ~ Open 12-11 (10 Sun) ~ Bar food 12-2.30, 7-9.30; 12-3, 7-9 Sun ~ Restaurant ~ Children welcome lunchtime only ~ Dogs allowed in bar ~ Wi-fi

UPPER BASILDON
Red Lion

SU5976

(01491) 671234 – www.theredlionupperbasildon.co.uk
Off A329 NW of Pangbourne; Aldworth Road; RG8 8NG

Laid-back country pub with friendly family atmosphere, popular food and a good choice of drinks

Handy after a walk for either a drink or a meal, this is a popular pub with plenty of customers. There's pale blue-grey paintwork throughout (even on the beams), and the bars have chapel chairs, a few pews and miscellaneous stripped tables on bare floorboards, and a green leather chesterfield and armchair; maybe hops on timbering and little plants on each table. Courage Directors, Sharps Doom Bar, Upham Punter and West Berkshire Good Old Boy on handpump, a dozen wines from an extensive list and a farm cider. Beyond a double-sided woodburning stove, a pitched-ceiling area has much the same furniture on cord carpet, though a big cut-glass chandelier and large mirror give it a slightly more formal dining feel. Maybe daily papers including the *Racing Post*, occasional background music and regular (usually jazz-related) live music. There are sturdy picnic-sets in the sizeable enclosed garden and summer barbecues and hog roasts.

Enterprise ~ Lease Alison Green ~ Real ale ~ Open 11-3, 5-11; 11-11 Sat; 11-10.30 Sun ~ Bar food 12-2.30, 6-9 (9.30 Fri, Sat); 12-3.30, 6-7.30 Sun ~ Restaurant ~ Children welcome ~ Dogs allowed in bar ~ Wi-fi

WHITE WALTHAM   SU8477
Beehive

(01628) 822877 – www.thebeehivewhitewaltham.co.uk
Waltham Road (B3024 W of Maidenhead); SL6 3SH

Attractive village pub with welcoming staff and enjoyable food and drinks choice; seats in garden with table service

After refurbishments, the garden has been extended and updating of some facilities inside the pub has made quite a difference. The atmosphere remains bustling and friendly, helped along by the hospitable landlord and his friendly staff. To the right of the entrance are several comfortably spacious areas with leather chairs around sturdy tables, while to the left is a neat bar brightened up by cheerful scatter cushions on comfortable built-in wall seats and captain's chairs. Rebellion IPA, Sharps Doom Bar and Hook Norton Old Hooky on handpump, 20 wines by the glass from a good list and farm cider; background music. An airy dining room has glass doors opening on to the front terrace where teak seats and picnic-sets take in the rather fine view. The bigger back garden has plenty of seats and tables, and the village cricket field is opposite. Disabled access and facilities.

Enterprise ~ Lease Dominic Chapman ~ Real ale ~ Open 12-2.30, 5-11; 12-11 Sat; 12-8 Sun ~ Bar food 12-2.30, 6-9.30 (10 Fri, Sat); 12-4 Sun ~ Restaurant ~ Children welcome ~ Dogs allowed in bar ~ Wi-fi

WOOLHAMPTON   SU5766
Rowbarge

(0118) 971 2213 – www.brunningandprice.co.uk/rowbarge
Station Road; RG7 5SH

Canalside pub with plenty of interest in rambling rooms, six real ales, good bistro-style food and lots of outside seating

In warm weather you can make the most of the setting here, with wooden chairs and tables on a decked terrace and picnic-sets among trees by the Kennet & Avon Canal. Six rambling rooms with beams and timbering are connected by open doorways and knocked-through walls. The décor is gently themed to represent the nearby canal with hundreds of prints and photographs (some of rowing and boats) and oars on the walls, as well as old glass and stone bottles in nooks and crannies, big house plants and fresh flowers, plenty of candles and several open fires; the many large mirrors create an impression of even more space. Throughout there are antique dining chairs around various nice old tables, settles, built-in cushioned wall seating, armchairs, a group of high stools around a huge wooden barrel table, and rugs on polished boards, stone tiles or carpeting. Friendly, helpful staff serve Phoenix Brunning & Price Original plus guests such as Butts Blackguard Porter, Grand Union Best, Itchen Valley Hampshire Rose, Ramsbury Red Velvet and Tring Side Pocket for a Toad on handpump, 20 wines by the glass, 30 gins and 65 malt whiskies; background music and board games.

Brunning & Price ~ Manager Stephen Butt ~ Real ale ~ Open 11-11 (10.30 Sun) ~ Bar food 12-10 (9.30 Sun) ~ Restaurant ~ Children welcome ~ Dogs allowed in bar ~ Wi-fi

DOG FRIENDLY HOTELS, INNS AND B&Bs

CHIEVELEY   SU4574
Crab & Boar
(01635) 247550 – www.crabandboar.com
Wantage Road, Chieveley, Newbury, Berkshire RG20 8UE

£95; 14 comfortable bedrooms, including five with private courtyards and hot tubs. Stylish inn with friendly yet gently civilised atmosphere in interconnected bars and dining rooms; the L-shaped bar is light and airy at one end, cosier at the other, with leather armchairs and sofas in front of a woodburning stove in a large fireplace, while the dining rooms are decorated with old fishing reels, a large boar's head, photos and prints and a mix of attractive chairs and tables on bare floorboards or carpet; real ales and good wines by the glass served by courteous staff, and notably good modern food; garden with elegant metal or teak tables and chairs on gravel and grass, plus a fountain and an outside bar. Dogs allowed in several bedrooms, bar and part of the restaurant (but not on furniture); bowl.

EAST GARSTON   SU3676
Queens Arms
(01488) 648757 – www.queensarmshotel.co.uk
Newbury Road, East Garston, Hungerford, Berkshire RG17 7ET

£120; 12 attractive rooms. Smart but chatty dining pub right in the heart of racehorse-training country with a roomy, opened-up bar, antique prints (many featuring jockeys), daily papers (the most prominent being the *Racing Post*), traditional pubby seats and tables on a wooden floor, local beers and a fair choice of whiskies; a lighter dining area has horse and country prints, a pleasing mix of furniture, enjoyable classic food served by friendly staff and tasty breakfasts; garden and patio, plenty of downland walks nearby. Dogs allowed in all bedrooms and bar.

ETON
Christopher Hotel

SU9677

(01753) 852359 – www.thechristopher.co.uk
110 High Street, Eton, Windsor, Berkshire SL4 6AN

£158; 34 well equipped rooms – those in the main house have the most character. Early 18th-c former coaching inn just across the river from Windsor Castle; the relaxed, informal half-panelled bar has sofas and armchairs on stripped floorboards and offers some sort of food all day including morning coffee and afternoon teas, and the smart restaurant serves enjoyable bistro-style meals; a small outside terrace has seats and tables and there's a field behind for dogs to exercise in; resident spaniels George and Harry. Dogs allowed in courtyard bedrooms; £10.

HUNGERFORD
Bear Hotel

SU3368

(01488) 682512 – www.thebearhotelhungerford.co.uk
41 Charnham Street, Hungerford, Berkshire RG17 0EL

£75–£165; 39 modern, well equipped rooms, some with views over the river. Civilised and carefully restored 13th-c hotel with open fires, a bright bar with wooden chairs and tables on floorboards, real ales and good wines by the glass; separate beamed restaurant with similar furniture; seats in the courtyard and riverside terrace (often used for private events); walks by canal or on nearby common. Dogs allowed in four bedrooms and bar; £10 per stay.

KINTBURY
Dundas Arms

SU3866

(01488) 658263 – www.dundasarms.co.uk
53 Station Road, Kintbury, Berkshire RG17 9UT

£145; 8 comfortable bedrooms, including five in old stable block with private riverside terraces. Handsome, carefully updated inn between the River Kennet and the Kennet & Avon Canal, surrounded by ducks and banks of spring daffodils; relaxed informal bar (the counter decorated with highly polished old penny pieces) with sporting prints above a high oak dado, neat little cushioned arts-and-crafts chairs around stripped or polished tables on floorboards, and cheerful helpful staff serving real ales, farm cider and 14 wines by the glass; also smart two-level restaurant and a cosy, tartan-carpeted sitting room with wing chairs and a good winter log fire flanked by glass-fronted bookcases; large, pretty back garden has water on each side and well spaced tables on grass, and pleasant nearby walks. Dogs allowed in river terrace bedrooms and elsewhere except restaurant; bed, bowl and treats; £25.

MAIDENS GREEN
Winning Post

SU9072

(01344) 882242 – www.winningpostwinkfield.co.uk
Winkfield Street, Maidens Green, Windsor, Berkshire SL4 4SW

£130; 10 quiet bedrooms with garden views. Gently civilised but easy-going 18th-c inn, handy for Ascot and Henley, with welcoming staff and chatty locals (several with dogs – ours got a treat); beamed open-plan rooms connected by timbering with leather and wood tub chairs, a long cushioned settle, big flagstones and contemporary paintwork on planked walls; real ales and highly regarded food (including breakfast for non-residents); dining areas include one long room with huge horse photos, tartan banquettes, a woodburning stove, hanging lanterns and bowler hat lights, while the Winning Enclosure room has horse-racing wall photos and a large raised fireplace; partly covered terrace with seating and a rather smart smokers' hut. Dogs allowed in some bedrooms and bar.

PANGBOURNE   SU6376
Elephant

(01189) 842244 – www.elephanthotel.co.uk
Church Road, Pangbourne, Berkshire RG8 7AR

£105; 22 interestingly decorated rooms. Victorian hotel decorated in colonial style with indian furniture on oriental rugs and bare boards, lots of elephant ornaments, a comfortable lounge with sofas and armchairs in front of an open fire, a bustling friendly bar with pubby furniture, prints on the walls and local beers, and an elegant restaurant; food is very good and ranges from simple to inventive, and service is helpful and cheerful; there's also a garden with tables. Dogs allowed in some bedrooms and elsewhere except restaurant; bed, bowl, treats and food menu; £20.

STREATLEY   SU5980
Swan at Streatley

(01491) 878800 – www.swanatstreatley.com
High Street, Streatley, Reading, Berkshire RG8 9HR

£110; 41 recently refurbished, appealing rooms, many overlooking the water. Well run, friendly Thames-side hotel with comfortable, relaxed lounges and bars, consistently good food in attractive restaurant, café in restored boathouse, a popular spa with sauna, steam room, treatments and gym, and flower-filled gardens where dogs may walk – other walks nearby; you can hire self-drive electric boats (not in winter) – great fun. Dogs allowed in some bedrooms and most public areas (not dining room); £20.

YATTENDON   SU5574
Royal Oak

(01635) 201325 – www.royaloakyattendon.co.uk
The Square, Yattendon, Newbury, Berkshire RG18 0UF

£95; 10 attractive light rooms. Handsome old inn by the village square and close to Newbury Racecourse (so it does get busy on race days); plenty of civilised character in spacious, charming rooms; beams and panelling, appealing chairs and tables on quarry tiles or wooden floorboards, interesting prints on brick, cream or red walls, four log fires, lovely flowers, real ales (brewed in the village) and carefully chosen wines; the food is modern and imaginative and the breakfasts delicious; attractive garden with seats. Dogs allowed in all bedrooms and anywhere in the pub.

Buckinghamshire

MAPS 2, 3 & 4

DOG FRIENDLY PUBS

ADSTOCK   SP7330

Old Thatched Inn

(01296) 712584 – www.theoldthatchedinn.co.uk
Main Street, off A413; MK18 2JN

Pretty thatched dining pub with keen landlord, friendly staff, five real ales and good food

An enthusiastic landlord runs this attractive thatched dining pub surrounded by rolling farmland. The small front bar area has low beams, sofas on flagstones, high bar chairs and an open fire and they keep Fullers London Pride, Sharps Doom Bar, Thwaites Wainwright, Timothy Taylors Boltmaker and Tring Side Pocket for a Toad on handpump, 14 wines by the glass, a dozen malt whiskies and four ciders; courteous service. A dining area leads off with more beams and a mix of pale wooden dining chairs around miscellaneous tables on a stripped wooden floor; background music. There's also a modern conservatory restaurant at the back with well spaced tables on bare boards. The sheltered terrace has tables and chairs under a gazebo. This is an attractive village.

Free house ~ Licensee Andrew Judge ~ Real ale ~ Open 12-11 (midnight Sat, 10.30 Sun) ~ Bar food 12-2.30, 6-9.30 (5-9 Sat); 12-8 Sun ~ Restaurant ~ Well behaved children welcome ~ Dogs allowed in bar ~ Wi-fi

BOVINGDON GREEN   SU8386

Royal Oak

(01628) 488611 – www.royaloakmarlow.co.uk
0.75 miles N of Marlow, on back road to Frieth signposted off West Street (A4155) in centre; SL7 2JF

Civilised dining pub with nice little bar, a fine choice of wines by the glass, real ales and imaginative food

It's the modern british food that most customers are here to enjoy, but they do keep Rebellion IPA on handpump, alongside changing guests such as Timothy Taylors Landlord and Woodfordes Wherry, 24 wines by the glass (plus pudding wines), several gins and farm cider. The low-beamed cosy snug, closest to the car park, has three small tables and a woodburning stove in an exposed brick fireplace (with a big pile of logs beside it). Several other attractively decorated areas open off the central bar with half-panelled walls variously painted in pale blue, green or cream (though the dining room ones are red). Throughout, there's a mix of church chairs, stripped wooden tables and chunky wall seats, with rugs on the partly wooden, partly flagstoned floors, co-ordinated cushions and curtains, and a very bright, airy feel. Thoughtful extra touches enhance the tone: a bowl of olives on the bar, carefully laid-out newspapers and fresh flowers or candles on the tables. Board games and background music. A sunny terrace with good solid tables leads to an appealing garden with pétanque, ping pong, badminton and swing ball; there's also a smaller side garden and a kitchen herb garden.

Salisbury Pubs ~ Manager James Molier ~ Real ale ~ Open 11-11; 12-10.30 Sun ~ Bar food 12-2.30, 6.30-9.30; 12.3, 6-10 Fri, Sat; 12-9 Sun ~ Restaurant ~ Children welcome ~ Dogs welcome ~ Wi-fi

BRILL
SP6514
Pheasant
(01844) 239370 – www.thepheasant.co.uk
Windmill Street; off B4011 Bicester–Long Crendon; HP18 9TG

Long-reaching views, a bustling bar with local ales, attentive staff and tasty food; bedrooms

There are plenty of seats and tables on the decked area and in the garden here, offering marvellous views over the windmill opposite (one of the oldest post windmills still in working order) and into the distance across five counties. Inside, it's more or less open-plan, with a raftered bar area, leather tub seats in front of a woodburner, and Chiltern Beechwood, Vale Brill Gold and a guest from Skinners on handpump and a dozen wines by the glass served by charming, attentive staff. Dining areas have high-backed leather or dark wooden chairs, attractively framed prints and books on shelves; background music. Good walks from the door. Roald Dahl used to drink here, and some of the tales the locals told him were worked into his short stories.

Free house ~ Licensee Marilyn Glover ~ Real ale ~ Open 12-11 (midnight Fri, Sat) ~ Bar food 12-9; 12-2.30, 6-9 winter; 12-9 winter Sat; 12-5 winter Sun ~ Children welcome ~ Dogs allowed in bar ~ Wi-fi ~ Bedrooms: £95

BRILL
SP6513
Pointer
(01844) 238339 – www.thepointerbrill.co.uk
Church Street; HP18 9RT

Carefully restored pub in a pretty village with rewarding food, local ales and interesting furnishings

Next to the church and by the village green, this handsome place is very stylishly furnished: low beams, windsor chairs, elegant armchairs and sofas with brocaded cushions, open fires or woodburners in brick fireplaces and animal-hide stools by the counter. A beer named for the pub (from the XT Brewing Company), Vale Best Bitter and Brill Gold (brewed in the village) and Rebellion Zebedee on handpump, a dozen fair-priced wines by the glass, a gin and a whisky menu and friendly, attentive staff. The airy and attractive restaurant has antique Ercol chairs around pale oak tables, cushioned window seats, rafters in a high vaulted ceiling and an open kitchen. French windows open on to the sizeable garden. Do visit their deli next door where you can buy their own produce and freshly baked bread (open Wednesday, Thursday and Friday afternoons and Saturday morning). Tolkien is said to have based the village of Bree in *The Lord of the Rings* on this pretty village.

Free house ~ Licensees David and Fiona Howden ~ Real ale ~ Open 12-11 (midnight Sat); 12-10 Sun; closed Mon ~ Bar food 12-2.30, 6.30-9 (10 Fri, Sat); 12.30-5 Sun ~ Restaurant ~ Children welcome ~ Dogs allowed in bar ~ Wi-fi

BUTLERS CROSS   SP8407

Russell Arms

(01296) 624411 – www.therussellarms.co.uk
Off A4010 S of Aylesbury, at Nash Lee roundabout; or off A413 in Wendover, passing station; Chalkshire Road; HP17 0TS

Attractive old place with good food and local ales, friendly landlord and staff, and seats in sunny garden

Recently refurbished, this is an 18th-c beamed pub (and former coaching inn and servants' quarters for nearby Chequers, the prime minister's country retreat). The simply furnished bar has stools and chairs around polished tables on new pale floorboards, higher stools against the counter and well kept Chiltern Beechwood, St Austell Tribute and Tring Side Pocket for a Toad on handpump, 24 wines by the glass and artisan gins served by welcoming staff; background music and board games. The two dining areas have an open fire with logs piled high to either side of it and a woodburner in an inglenook, an eclectic collection of wheelback, mate's and elegant high-backed and cushioned chairs around scrubbed tables on bare boards, some panelling, tartan curtains and fresh flowers. One wall has a blown-up photo of Chequers with smaller photos of past prime ministers. French windows lead to a suntrap terrace with teak furniture and there are steps up to the garden with picnic-sets. The pub is handy for Chilterns walks.

Free house ~ Licensee James Penlington ~ Real ale ~ Open 10am-11pm; 12-10.30 Sun; closed Mon ~ Bar food 12-2.30, 6.30-9; 12-4 Sun ~ Restaurant ~ Children welcome ~ Dogs allowed in bar ~ Wi-fi

DENHAM   TQ0487

Swan

(01895) 832085 – www.swaninndenham.co.uk
Village signed from M25 junction 16; UB9 5BH

Double-fronted dining pub in quiet village with interesting furnishings, log fires, fine choice of drinks and large garden

In a quiet and lovely village, this is a handsome Georgian pub that cleverly manages to appeal to both diners and drinkers. The stylishly furnished bars have a nice mix of antique and old-fashioned chairs and solid tables, rich heavily draped curtains, log fires, newspapers and fresh flowers. Friendly staff serve Rebellion IPA and a guest such as Caledonian Flying Scotsman on handpump, over 20 wines by the glass (plus pudding wines) and a good choice of vodkas and liqueurs; background music. In warm weather, the extensive back garden is a big draw (it's also floodlit at night) and there are seats and tables on a sheltered terrace, with more on a spacious lawn. It can get busy at weekends, when parking may be tricky. The wisteria is lovely in May.

Little Gems Country Dining Pubs ~ Manager Mark Littlewood ~ Real ale ~ Open 11.30-11.30; 12-11 Sun ~ Bar food 12-2.30, 6-9 (9.30 Fri); 12-9.30 Sat; 12-8 Sun ~ Restaurant ~ Children welcome ~ Dogs allowed in bar ~ Wi-fi

FINGEST SU7791

Chequers

(01491) 638335 – www.chequersfingest.com
Off B482 Marlow–Stokenchurch; RG9 6QD

Friendly, spotlessly kept old pub with big garden, real ales and interesting food

This is good walking country with quiet pastures sloping up to beechwoods, and you can make your way on foot from here to other pubs in this chapter. The unaffected public bar has real country charm, and other neatly kept old-fashioned rooms are warm, cosy and traditional, with large open fires, horsebrasses, pewter tankards and pub team photographs on the walls. Brakspears Bitter and Ringwood Boondoggle on handpump alongside quite a few wines by the glass, several malt whiskies and farm cider; board games and a house cat and dog. French doors from the smart back dining extension open to a terrace (plenty of picnic-sets), which leads to the big, beautifully tended garden with fine views over the Hambleden Valley. This 15th-c, white-shuttered brick and flint pub is in a charming spot opposite a unique twin-roofed Norman church tower – probably the nave of the original church.

Brakspears ~ Tenants Jaxon and Emma Keedwell ~ Real ale ~ Open 12-3, 5.30-11; 12-11.15 Sat; 12-10.30 Sun; closed Mon ~ Bar food 12-2 (3 Sat, 4 Sun), 7-9 (9.30 Fri, Sat) ~ Restaurant ~ Children welcome ~ Dogs allowed in bar ~ Wi-fi

FORTY GREEN SU9291

Royal Standard of England

(01494) 673382 – www.rsoe.co.uk
3.5 miles from M40 junction 2, via A40 to Beaconsfield, then follow sign to Forty Green, off B474 0.75 miles N of New Beaconsfield; keep going through village; HP9 1XT

Full of history and character, with fascinating antiques in rambling rooms and good choice of drinks and food

Until after the Battle of Worcester in 1651 (when Charles I hid in the high rafters of what is now its food bar), this ancient pub used to be called the Ship. It's been trading for nearly 900 years and the leaflet documenting the pub's history is really interesting. The rambling rooms have some fine old features to look out for: huge black ship's timbers, lovely worn floors, carved oak panelling, roaring winter fires with handsomely decorated iron firebacks and cluttered mantelpieces – there's also a massive settle apparently built to fit the curved transom of an Elizabethan ship. Nooks and crannies are filled with a collection of antiques, including rifles, powder-flasks and bugles, ancient pewter and pottery tankards, lots of tarnished brass and copper, needlework samplers and richly coloured stained glass. Chiltern Ale and Elgoods Windsor Knot plus four changing guests on handpump, a carefully annotated list of bottled beers and malt whiskies, farm ciders, perry, somerset brandy and around a dozen wines by the glass. You can sit outside in a neatly hedged front rose garden or under the shade of a tree; look out for the red gargoyle on the wall facing the car park. The inn is used for filming television programmes such as *Midsomer Murders*.

Free house ~ Licensee Matthew O'Keeffe ~ Real ale ~ Open 11am-11.30pm; 12-10.30 Sun ~ Bar food 12-10 ~ Children welcome ~ Dogs welcome ~ Wi-fi

FULMER

SU9985

Black Horse

(01753) 663183 – www.theblackhorsefulmer.com
Village signposted off A40 in Gerrards Cross, W of junction with A413; Windmill Road; SL3 6HD

Appealingly reworked dining pub, friendly and relaxed, with enjoyable up-to-date food, exemplary service and pleasant garden; bedrooms

There's always a good mix of customers popping in and out of this extended 17th-c pub as it's helpfully open all day. It's a charming and thoughtfully run country pub with a lot of character: there's a proper bar in the middle and two cosy areas to the left with low black beams, rugs on bare boards, settles and other solid pub furniture and several open log fires. Greene King IPA and London Glory and a monthly guest ale on handpump, 21 wines by the glass and 20 malt whiskies; staff are friendly and efficient even when pushed. Background music, TV. The main area on the right is set for dining and leads to the good-sized suntrap back terrace where there's a summer barbecue bar. This is a charming conservation village and the pub is next to the church.

Greene King ~ Lease Matt Birchall ~ Real ale ~ Open 11am-midnight; 12-10.30 Sun ~ Bar food 8.30am-9.30pm (10 Fri, Sat); 12-7 Sun ~ Restaurant ~ Children welcome ~ Dogs allowed in bar ~ Wi-fi ~ Quiz Mon 8pm Sept-Apr ~ Bedrooms: £130

GREAT MISSENDEN

SP9000

Nags Head

(01494) 862200 – www.nagsheadbucks.com
Old London Road, E – beyond Abbey; HP16 0DG

Well run and pretty inn with beamed bars, an open fire, a good range of drinks and modern cooking; bedrooms

Built in the 15th c as three small cottages, this is now a quietly civilised dining pub. There's a low-beamed area on the left, a loftier part on the right, a mix of small pews, dining chairs and tables on carpet, Quentin Blake prints on cream walls and a log fire in a handsome fireplace. Rebellion IPA and a couple of guests such as Malt IPA and Vale Red Kite on handpump from the unusual bar counter (the windows behind face the road), 26 wines by the glass from an extensive list and half a dozen vintage Armagnacs. There's an outside dining area beneath a pergola and seats on the extensive back lawn. Roald Dahl used this as his local and the Roald Dahl Museum & Story Centre is just a stroll away.

Free house ~ Licensee Adam Michaels ~ Real ale ~ Open 11-11 (midnight Sat); 11-10.30 Sun ~ Bar food 12-2.30, 6.30-9.30; 12-7 Sun ~ Restaurant ~ Children welcome ~ Dogs allowed in bar ~ Wi-fi ~ Bedrooms: £95

HAMBLEDEN

SU7886

Stag & Huntsman

(01491) 571227 – www.thestagandhuntsman.co.uk
Off A4155 Henley–Marlow; RG9 6RP

Friendly inn with nice bar, plenty of dining space and good food, welcoming staff and country garden; bedrooms

You'll be sure to find cheerful, chatty regulars in this handsome pub that's set on the far edge of one of the prettiest Chilterns villages. Visitors are made welcome too, and the little bar has a thriving atmosphere, stools against the counter, built-in cushioned wall seating, simple tables and chairs and bare floorboards. Rebellion IPA, Sharps Doom Bar and a couple of guest beers on handpump and several wines by the glass, served by warmly friendly staff. There's also a sizeable open-plan room with armchairs beside a woodburning stove in a brick fireplace, and a sofa and stools around a polished chest on more boards; this leads into the dining room with all sorts of wooden or high-backed red leather dining chairs around a variety of wooden tables, and hunting prints and other pictures on floral wallpaper. Darts and background music. There are seats in the country garden.

Free house ~ Licensee Claire Hollis ~ Real ale ~ Open 11-11 ~ Bar food 12-2.30, 6-9.30; 12-3, 6-9 Sun ~ Restaurant ~ Children welcome ~ Dogs allowed in bar ~ Wi-fi ~ Bedrooms: £100

HEDGERLEY

SU9687

White Horse

(01753) 643225

2.4 miles from M40 junction 2; at exit roundabout take Slough turn-off following alongside M40; after 1.5 miles turn right at T junction into Village Lane; SL2 3UY

Old-fashioned drinkers' pub with lots of beers, home-made lunchtime food and a cheery mix of customers

A fine range of real ales in this charming, convivial country gem might include Rebellion IPA and up to seven daily changing guests, sourced from all over the country and tapped straight from casks kept in a room behind the tiny hatch counter. Their Easter, May, Spring and August bank holiday beer festivals (they can get through about 130 beers during the May event) are highlights of the local calendar. This marvellous range of drinks extends to craft ales in cans or bottles, three farm ciders, eight wines by the glass, 15 malt whiskies and winter mulled wine. The cottagey main bar has plenty of unspoilt character with beams, brasses and exposed brickwork, low wooden tables, standing timbers, jugs, ballcocks and other bric-a-brac, a log fire, and a good few leaflets and notices about village events. A little flagstoned public bar on the left has darts, shove-ha'penny and board games. A canopied extension leads out to the garden where there are tables, occasional barbecues and lots of hanging baskets; a few tables in front of the building overlook the quiet road. Good walks nearby, and the pub is handy for the Church Wood RSPB reserve and popular with walkers and cyclists; it's often crowded at weekends.

Free house ~ Licensees Doris Hobbs and Kevin Brooker ~ Real ale ~ Open 11-2.30, 5-11; 11-11 Sat; 12-10.30 Sun ~ Bar food 12-2 (2.30 weekends) ~ Children allowed in canopied extension area ~ Dogs allowed in bar ~ Wi-fi

LONG CRENDON

SP6908

Eight Bells

(01844) 208244 ~ www.8bellspub.com

High Street, off B4011 N of Thame; car park entrance off Chearsley Road, not 'Village roads only'; HP18 9AL

Good beers and sensibly priced seasonal food in nicely traditional village pub with charming garden

Luckily, nothing changes here – which is just how people like it. The little bare-boards bar on the left has Ringwood Best, XT Four, Thwaites Wainwright and a changing guest ale on handpump or tapped from the cask, 16 wines by the glass and three farm ciders; service is cheerful. A bigger low-ceilinged room on the right has a log fire, daily papers and a pleasantly haphazard mix of tables and simple seats on ancient red and black tiles; one snug little hidey-hole with just three tables is devoted to the local morris men – frequent visitors. Board games, TV and background music. The small back garden is a joy in summer when there are well spaced picnic-sets among a colourful variety of shrubs and flowers; aunt sally. The interesting old village is known to many from TV's *Midsomer Murders*.

Free house ~ Licensee Paul Mitchell ~ Real ale ~ Open 12-11; 12-10 Sun ~ Bar food 12-9; 12-4 Sun ~ Restaurant ~ Children welcome ~ Dogs welcome ~ Wi-fi ~ Live music last Sun of month

MILTON KEYNES   SP8939
Swan
(01908) 665240 – www.theswan-mkvillage.co.uk
Broughton Road, Milton Keynes village; MK10 9AH

Well thought-out rooms with open fires in inglenooks, enjoyable food and drink and seats outside

Original features mix well with contemporary furnishings in this pretty thatched pub and the beamed main bar area has plush armchairs to each side of an inglenook fireplace, several high tables and chairs dotted about, a cushioned wall banquette with scatter cushions, and wooden dining chairs and chunky tables on flagstones. Youngs Bitter and Wells Bombardier plus guests like Black Sheep Holy Grail and Courage Directors on handpump, 30 wines by the glass, good coffees and courteous service. Leading off to the left is a cosy room with a gas stove, more cushioned banquettes and similar tables and chairs on parquet flooring, bookcase-effect wallpaper and photos of the pub. The spreading, partly beamed restaurant, with views of the open kitchen, has all manner of wooden and pretty fabric-covered dining chairs, cushioned settles and wall seats and a few curved banquettes (creating snug, private areas) on floorboards, and a woodburning stove. Doors open on to an outside dining area overlooking the garden, where there are seats and picnic-sets on grass.

Little Gems Country Dining Pubs ~ Manager Grant Owen ~ Real ale ~ Open 11-11 (midnight Fri, Sat); 12-10.30 Sun ~ Bar food 12-3, 6-9.30; 12-10 Fri, Sat; 12-8 Sun ~ Restaurant ~ Children welcome but must be well behaved ~ Dogs allowed in bar ~ Wi-fi

PENN   SU9093
Old Queens Head
(01494) 813371 – www.oldqueensheadpenn.co.uk
Hammersley Lane/Church Road, off B474 between Penn and Tylers Green; HP10 8EY

Stylishly updated pub with highly enjoyable food, a good choice of drinks and walks nearby

The open-plan rooms in this smart pub have lots of different areas to sit in, all with different aspects, and are decorated in a stylish mix of contemporary and chintz. There are well spaced tables, a modicum of old prints and comfortably varied seating on flagstones or broad dark boards. Stairs lead up to an attractive (and popular) two-level dining room, partly carpeted, with stripped rafters. The active bar side has Greene King Old Speckled Hen and Ruddles County and a guest like Belhaven IPA on handpump, over 20 wines by the glass (plus pudding wines), a dozen gins and a good choice of liqueurs; the turntable-top bar stools let you swivel to face the log fire in the big nearby fireplace. Daily papers and background music. The sunny terrace overlooks St Margaret's church and there are picnic-sets on the sheltered L-shaped lawn. Walkers and their dogs head here after visiting the ancient beechwoods of Common or Penn Woods; dogs might be offered a biscuit.

Little Gems Country Dining Pubs ~ Manager Tina Brown ~ Real ale ~ Open 11.30-11.30 ~ Bar food 12-2.30, 6.30-9.30; 9.30-3, 6.30-10 Fri, Sat (snacks all afternoon); 12-9 Sun ~ Restaurant ~ Children welcome ~ Dogs allowed in bar ~ Wi-fi

PRESTWOOD SP8799

Polecat

(01494) 862253 – www.thepolecatinn.co.uk
170 Wycombe Road (A4128 N of High Wycombe); HP16 0HJ

Enjoyable food, real ales and a chatty atmosphere in several smallish civilised rooms; attractive sizeable garden

Civilised but easy-going, this is an enjoyable pub with plenty of customers. Several smallish rooms opening off the low-ceilinged bar have an assortment of tables and chairs, various stuffed birds, stuffed white polecats in one big cabinet, small country pictures, rugs on bare boards or red tiles, and a couple of leather wing chairs by a good open fire. Malt Golden Ale and Prestwoods Best, Rebellion IPA and Zebedee and a guest beer on handpump, 30 wines by the glass, quite a few gins and home-made cordials. The garden is most attractive with lots of spring bulbs, colourful summer hanging baskets and tubs and plenty of herbaceous plants; there are picnic-sets under parasols on neat grass out in front beneath a big fairy-lit pear tree, more on a large well kept lawn at the back and a large children's play area.

Free house ~ Licensee Philip Whitehouse ~ Real ale ~ Open 11.30-11; 12-6 Sun; 11.30-3, 6.30-11 winter ~ Bar food 12-9; 12-3 Sun ~ Restaurant ~ Children welcome ~ Dogs allowed in bar ~ Wi-fi

STOKE MANDEVILLE SP8310

Bell

(01296) 612434 – www.bellstokemandeville.co.uk
Lower Road; HP22 5XA

Friendly landlord and staff, a fine choice of drinks, interesting food and seats outside

Run with enthusiasm by a friendly landlord, this extended red-brick Victorian pub is popular for both food and drinks. The interconnected bar and dining areas have an easy-going atmosphere, flagstones or polished pine floorboards and prints, drawings and maps of local interest and hunting prints on the walls above a dark blue dado; background music and board games. High stools line the counter where they keep Wells Bombardier, Youngs Bitter and a guest ale on handpump and 20 wines (including sweet wines) by the glass; there are some equally high stools and tables opposite. Throughout are high-backed cushioned wooden and farmhouse chairs, wall settles with scatter cushions, and rustic benches around a medley of tables, some painted beams and a woodburning stove; a snug alcove has just one table surrounded by cushioned wall seats. The little side terrace has picnic-sets and there are more on grass beside a weeping birch.

Distinct Pub Company ~ Lease James Penlington ~ Real ale ~ Open 10am-11pm (10.30pm Sun) ~ Bar food 12-9.30 (8.30 Sun) ~ Restaurant ~ Children welcome ~ Dogs allowed in bar ~ Wi-fi

THE LEE
SP8904

Old Swan

(01494) 837239 – www.theoldswanpub.co.uk
Swan Bottom, back road 0.75 miles N of The Lee; HP16 9NU

Country pub with character bars and dining areas, friendly service, real ales, highly thought-of food and seats in big garden

As there are good surrounding walks and cycling routes, you'll find plenty of cheerful customers in this friendly 16th-c pub. The attractively furnished linked rooms have heavy beams, flagstones and old quarry tiles, high-backed antique settles and window seats with scatter cushions, little plush stools and straightforward dining chairs around wooden tables and a log fire in an inglenook cooking range. High bar stools line the counter where they keep Chiltern Ale, Sharps Doom Bar and a guest such as Rebellion Waterloo on handpump and several wines by the glass. The big, spreading back garden has picnic-sets and contemporary seating around rustic tables; children's play area.

Free house ~ Licensees Phil and Jane Joel ~ Real ale ~ Open 12-3, 6-9; 12-11 Fri, Sat; 12-7 Sun; closed Mon lunchtime ~ Bar food 12-2.30, 7-9; 12-2.30, 6.30-9 Fri, Sat; 12-3 Sun; not Sun evening, Mon ~ Restaurant ~ Children welcome ~ Dogs allowed in bar ~ Wi-fi

DOG FRIENDLY HOTELS, INNS AND B&Bs

AYLESBURY
SP7912

Hartwell House

(01296) 747444 – www.hartwell-house.com
Oxford Road, Aylesbury, Buckinghamshire HP17 8NR

£390; 30 extremely comfortable rooms and suites in main house over three floors, and 6 rooms and 10 suites in restored 18th-c stables (Hartwell Court) with private garden and statues. Elegant Grade I listed building with Jacobean and Georgian façades, wonderful decorative plasterwork and panelling, fine paintings and antiques, a marvellous gothic central staircase, splendid morning room, a library, fine wines and excellent food in three dining rooms and exceptional service; 90 acres of parkland with ruined church, lake and statues; spa with indoor swimming pool, sauna, gym, beauty rooms and a café-bar; tennis, croquet and fishing; dog-walking in grounds and on nearby footpaths. Dogs allowed in Hartwell Court suites only; bed, water bowl and snacks.

MARLOW
SU8586

Macdonald Compleat Angler

(01628) 484444/405401 – www.macdonald-hotels.co.uk/compleatangler
Bisham Road, Marlow, Buckinghamshire SL7 1RG

£253; 64 pretty, stylish rooms named after fishing flies and overlooking garden or river. Famous Thames-side hotel with oak-panelled, 400-year-old bar, comfortable lounge, smart indian restaurant and conservatory-style modern british restaurant with riverside terrace, imaginative food using the best produce, and courteous, helpful service; coarse fishing and private launches and boats for hire. Dogs allowed in some bedrooms and in bar/lounge; £10.

Cambridgeshire

MAP 5

DOG FRIENDLY PUBS

BRANDON CREEK
TL6091
Ship
(01353) 676228 – www.theshipbrandoncreek.co.uk
A10 Ely–Downham Market; PE38 0PP

Fine riverside spot with plenty of outside seating, cosy snug and busy bar, four ales, good wines by the glass and well liked food

With up to five real ales and a thoughtful menu, this 17th-c waterside pub does get packed at peak times. It's a friendly place and the carefully modernised bar at the centre of the building has massive stone masonry in the sunken former forge area, a big log fire at one end and a woodburning stove at the other, interesting old fenland photographs and prints, and paintings by local artists. Adnams Southwold, plus a couple of guests such as Cottage Try Me and Two Rivers Hares Hopping on handpump,14 wines by the glass and farm cider; board games and background music. There's a cosy snug on the left with another open fire and a restaurant overlooking both the Great Ouse and the Little Ouse rivers; seats on the terrace and in the riverside garden make the most of the position. They have moorings for visiting boats.

Free house ~ Licensee Mark Thomas ~ Real ale ~ Open 12-11 ~ Bar food 12-3, 6-9; 12-9 Sat; 12-8 Sun ~ Restaurant ~ Children welcome ~ Dogs allowed in bar ~ Wi-fi ~ Live music Fri evening

CAMBRIDGE
TL4459
Punter
(01223) 3633221 – www.thepuntercambridge.com
Pound Hill, on corner of A1303 ring road; CB3 0AE

Good enterprising food in relaxed and interestingly furnished surroundings

As a former coaching inn, the rambling and informal linked rooms here have quite a bit of character. There are paintings, antique prints and a pleasing choice of seating on old dark floorboards – pews, elderly dining chairs and Lloyd Loom easy chairs. One prized corner is down a few steps, behind a wooden railing. The scrubbed tables feature candles in bottles or assorted candlesticks, and staff are quick and friendly. Adnams Ghost Ship, an ale named for the pub from Oakham, Sharps Doom Bar and a guest ale from the local Turpins Brewery on handpump and decent wines by the glass;

board games and background jazz music. The flagstoned and mainly covered former coachyard has tables and picnic-table sets; beyond is a raftered barn bar, similar in style, with more pictures on papered walls, a large rug on dark flagstones and a big-screen TV.

Punch ~ Lease Sarah Lee ~ Real ale ~ Open 12-midnight (11.30 Sun) ~ Bar food 12-3, 5-9; 12-10 Fri, Sat; 12-9 Sun ~ Children welcome ~ Dogs welcome ~ Wi-fi

DUXFORD   TL4746

John Barleycorn

(01223) 832699 – www.johnbarleycorn.co.uk
Handy for M11 junction 10; right at first roundabout, then left at main village junction; CB22 4PP

Pretty pub with friendly staff, attractive beamed interior, enjoyable food and seats outside; bedrooms

This comfortable early 17th-century inn looks very much like a perfect English country pub with its low thatched roof and shuttered windows. It has a lot of character and the standing timbers and brick pillars create alcoves and different drinking and dining areas: hops on heavy beams and nice old floor tiles, log fires, all manner of seating from rustic blue-painted cushioned settles through white-painted and plain wooden dining chairs to some rather fine antique farmhouse chairs and quite a mix of wooden tables. There's also a lot to look at, including china plates, copper pans, old clocks, a butterchurn, a large stuffed fish and plenty of pictures on blue or pale yellow walls. Greene King Abbot and IPA and guests such as Harviestoun Bitter & Twisted and Joules Slumbering Monk on handpump and ten wines by the glass; background music. There are blue-painted picnic-sets beside pretty hanging baskets on the front terrace and more picnic-sets among flowering tubs and shrubs in the back garden. The pub was used by the young airmen of Douglas Bader's Duxford Wing during World War II. The Air Museum is close by.

Greene King ~ Tenant Nicholas Kersey ~ Real ale ~ Open 11-11 (10.30 Sun) ~ Bar food 11-3, 5-9.30; 12-3, 5-8.30 Sun ~ Children welcome ~ Dogs allowed in bar ~ Wi-fi ~ Bedrooms: £79.50

ELTON   TL0894

Crown

(01832) 280232 – www.thecrowninn.org
Off B671 S of Wansford (A1/A47), and village signposted off A605 Peterborough–Oundle; Duck Street; PE8 6RQ

Pretty pub with interesting food, several real ales, well chosen wines and a friendly atmosphere; stylish bedrooms

This is a lovely golden-stone and thatched pub. The softly lit beamed bar has leather and antique dining chairs around a nice mix of chunky tables on bare boards, an open fire in a stone fireplace and good pictures and pubby ornaments on pastel walls. The beamed main dining area has fresh flowers and candles and similar tables and chairs on stripped wooden flooring, and there's a dining extension too. High bar chairs against the counter are popular with locals, and they keep a house beer (from Kings Cliffe Brewery), Greene King IPA and Oakham JHB on handpump, well chosen wines by the glass and farm cider; board games, background music and TV. There are tables outside on the front terrace, and Elton Mill and Lock are nearby. This is a charming village. To find the pub, follow the brown sign towards Nassington.

Free house ~ Licensee Marcus Lamb ~ Real ale ~ Open 12-11 ~ Bar food 12-2 (4 bank holidays), 6.30-9 ~ Restaurant ~ Children welcome ~ Dogs allowed in bar ~ Wi-fi ~ Bedrooms: £125

FEN DRAYTON

TL3468

Three Tuns

(01954) 230242 – www.the3tuns.co.uk

Eastbound on A14, take first exit after Fenstanton, signed Fen Drayton and follow to pub; westbound on A14, exit at junction 27 and follow signs to village on Cambridge Road; High Street; CB24 5SJ

Lovely old pub with traditional furnishings in bar and dining room, real ales, tasty food and seats in garden

There's a happy mix of people drinking and dining at this pretty thatched village pub and log fires in each room help create a warm and relaxed atmosphere, all helped along by the friendly licensees. The three rooms are more or less open-plan with heavy-set moulded Tudor beams and timbers, a mix of burgundy cushioned stools, nice old dining chairs and settles in the friendly bar and wooden dining chairs and tables on red-patterned carpet in the dining room; framed prints of the pub too. Greene King IPA and Old Speckled Hen and a couple of guests such as Timothy Taylors Landlord and Titanic Best Bitter on handpump and a dozen wines by the glass. A well tended lawn at the back has seats and tables, a covered dining area and a play area for children.

Greene King ~ Tenants Mr and Mrs Baretto ~ Real ale ~ Open 12-3, 6-11; 12-11 summer Fri, Sat; 12-4 Sun ~ Bar food 12-2, 6-9 (9.30 Fri, Sat); 12-2 Sun ~ Restaurant ~ Children welcome ~ Dogs allowed in bar ~ Wi-fi

GRANTCHESTER

TL4455

Rupert Brooke

(01223) 841875 – www.therupertbrooke.com

Broadway; junction Coton Road with Cambridge–Trumpington Road; CB3 9NQ

Plenty of space for drinking and dining in airy, refurbished dining pub with modern food and local ales

Smartly refurbished, this is a stylish place at the end of the high street with an emphasis on dining – though they do keep Woodfordes Wherry and a guest from Milton on handpump and several wines by the glass, served by courteous staff. The contemporary wood-clad extension has huge windows, elegant wooden or leather dining chairs around polished tables on floorboards and leads back to a bar area where there are sofas in a cosy nook by the stairs. The two-level restaurant looks into the open kitchen and has mushroom-coloured button-back wall banquettes, pendant lights and photographs of Rupert Brooke as a child. Stairs lead upstairs to a club room with direct access out to a roof terrace.

Free house ~ Licensee David Harrison ~ Real ale ~ Open 12-11; 12-7 Sun ~ Bar food 12-3, 6.30-9; 12-5 Sun ~ Restaurant ~ Children welcome ~ Dogs allowed in bar ~ Wi-fi

HEMINGFORD ABBOTS
TL2870

Axe & Compass

(01480) 463605 – www.axeandcompass.co.uk
High Street; village signposted off A14 W of Cambridge; PE28 9AH

Thatched pub with several linked rooms, a good range of drinks and food served by friendly staff and seats outside

This is a charming village and the partly 15th-c pub is very much its hub. The interconnected rooms have plenty of space and a cheerful mix of customers; the simple, beamed public bar has mate's chairs and stools around wooden tables on lovely ancient floor tiles, and an open two-way fireplace (not in use) into the snug next door where there's a woodburning stove. The main room has more beams and standing timbers, tweed tartan-patterned chairs and armchairs and cushioned wall seating around nice old tables on wood floors, local photographs and stools against the counter where they serve Adnams Lighthouse, Sharps Doom Bar and Woodfordes Reedlighter on handpump, 12 wines by the glass and local cider; there's a second woodburner in a small brick fireplace. Background music and board games. The long dining room has more photos on green walls and high-backed dark leather dining and other chairs around pale wooden tables. The garden, between the pretty thatched pub and the tall-spired church, has a fenced-off area with play equipment, contemporary seats and tables on the terrace and picnic-sets on grass; walks along the river. Disabled facilities.

Enterprise ~ Lease Emma Tester ~ Real ale ~ Open 12-11 (10 Mon winter) ~ Bar food 12-2.30 6-9; 12-9 Sat; 12-4 Sun; maybe longer hours on summer weekends ~ Restaurant ~ Well behaved children welcome ~ Dogs allowed in bar ~ Wi-fi ~ Live music first Fri of month; quiz Tues

HEMINGFORD GREY
TL2970

Cock

(01480) 463609 – www.cambscuisine.com/the-cock-hemingford
Village signposted off A14 eastbound, and (via A1096 St Ives road) westbound; High Street; PE28 9BJ

Imaginative food in pretty pub with extensive wine list, four interesting beers, a bustling atmosphere and a smart restaurant

A great favourite, run with much care and attention to detail. The bar rooms have white-painted or dark beams and lots of contemporary pale yellow and cream paintwork, fresh flowers and church candles, artworks here and there, and throughout a really attractive mix of old wooden dining chairs, settles and tables. They've sensibly kept the traditional public bar (on the left) for drinkers only: it has an open woodburning stove on a raised hearth, bar stools, wall seats and a carver, and steps that lead down to more seating. Brewsters Hophead and Great Oakley Wagtail with guests such as Elgoods Cambridge Bitter and Nene Valley Dark Horse on handpump, 19 wines by the glass mainly from the Languedoc-Roussillon region, and Cromwell cider (made in the village); they hold a beer festival every August Bank Holiday weekend. In marked contrast, the stylishly rustic restaurant on the right – you must book to be sure of a table – is set for dining, with flowers on each table, pale wooden floorboards and another woodburning stove. There are seats and tables among stone troughs and flowers on the terrace and in the neat garden, and pretty hanging baskets. This is a delightful village on the River Ouse.

Free house ~ Licensees Oliver Thain and Richard Bradley ~ Real ale ~ Open 11.30-3, 6 (5 Fri)-11; 11.30-11 Sat; 12-10.30 Sun ~ Bar food 12-2.30, 6.30-9; 12-2.30, 6-9.30 Fri, Sat; 12-2.45, 6.30-8.30 Sun ~ Restaurant ~ No children after 6pm ~ Dogs allowed in bar ~ Wi-fi

HORNINGSEA
TL4962

Crown & Punchbowl

(01223) 860643 – www.cambscuisine.com/the-crown-and-punchbowl
Just NE of Cambridge; CB25 9JG

Impressive food and thoughtful drinks choice in carefully refurbished old inn; seats outside; bedrooms

Given the track record of the other pubs in this little group, we know this will be a winner. It's a 17th-c former coaching inn that's been transformed and extended without losing original features or character. The beamed bar has a woodburning stove in a brick fireplace, leather banquettes and rustic old chairs, stripped boards, terracotta walls and an attractively carved counter where they serve freshly carved ham and home-made pickles. Behind the bar they keep Brewsters Hophead, Milton Pegasus and a changing guest tapped from the cask and 20 wines by the glass (with a focus on the Languedoc-Roussillon region), home-made punches (alcoholic and non-alcoholic), lavender lemonade and local cider. The timbered dining room has leather cushioned chairs around wooden tables on pale boards, wall panelling and candlelight. Another conservatory-style room has large windows and ceramic light fittings (a nod to the village's history as a centre for Roman pottery). There are rustic seats out the front. This is sister pub to the Cock at Hemingford Grey and Tickell Arms in Whittlesford.

Free house ~ Licensees Oliver Thain and Richard Bradley ~ Real ale ~ Open 12-3, 6 (5 Fri)-11; 12-11 Sat; 12-10.30 Sun ~ Bar food 12-2.30, 6.30-9 (9.30 Fri, Sat); 12-3, 6.30-8.30 Sun ~ Restaurant ~ Children welcome ~ Dogs allowed in bar ~ Wi-fi ~ Bedrooms: £140

KEYSTON
TL0475

Pheasant

(01832) 710241 – www.thepheasant-keyston.co.uk
Just off A14 SE of Thrapston; brown sign to pub down village loop road, off B663; PE28 0RE

Smart but friendly country dining pub with appealing décor and attractive garden

This neatly kept, thatched white building has come a long way since it was the village smithy – it's now a civilised dining pub with attentive, neat staff and first class food. The main bar has pitched rafters high above, with lower dark beams in side areas, and the central serving area has padded stools along the leather-quilted counter and dark flagstones, with hop bines above the handpumps for Adnams Southwold, Brewsters Hop A Doodle Doo and Digfield Chiffchaff, and a tempting array of 14 wines by the glass. Nearby are armchairs, a chesterfield, quite a throne of a seat carved in 17th-c style, other comfortable seats around low tables, and a log fire in a lofty fireplace. The rest of the pub is mostly red-carpeted with dining chairs around a variety of polished tables, large sporting prints, some hunting-scene wallpaper and lighted candles and tea-lights. The attractively planted and well kept garden behind has tables on lawn and terrace, and there are picnic-sets in front. This is a quiet farming hamlet.

Free house ~ Licensee Simon Cadge ~ Real ale ~ Open 12-3, 6-11; 12-11 Sat; 12-5 Sun; closed Sun evening, Mon ~ Bar food 12-2 (2.30 Fri, Sat), 6.30-9.30; 12-3.30 Sun ~ Restaurant ~ Children welcome ~ Dogs allowed in bar ~ Wi-fi

KIMBOLTON   TL0967

New Sun

(01480) 860052 – www.newsuninn.co.uk
High Street; PE28 0HA

Interesting bars and rooms, tapas menu plus other good food, and a pleasant back garden

This pleasant old pub fits in well with the village's delightfully harmonious high street and is usefully open all day. The cosiest room is perhaps the low-beamed front lounge with standing timbers and exposed brickwork, a couple of comfortable armchairs and a sofa beside a log fire, and books on shelves. This leads into a narrower locals' bar with Charles Wells Bombardier and Eagle and a weekly changing guest on handpump, 17 wines by the glass (including champagne and pudding wines) and a dozen gins; background music, board games, piano and quiz machine. The traditionally furnished dining room opens off here. An airy conservatory with high-backed leather dining chairs has doors leading to the terrace where there are smart seats and tables under giant umbrellas. Note that some of the nearby parking spaces have a 30-minute limit.

Wells & Youngs ~ Lease Stephen and Elaine Rogers ~ Real ale ~ Open 11.30-11; 12-10.30 Sun ~ Bar food 12-2.15 (2.30 Sun), 7-9.30; not Sun or Mon evenings ~ Restaurant ~ Well behaved children welcome away from bar ~ Dogs allowed in bar ~ Wi-fi

PETERBOROUGH   TL1899

Brewery Tap

(01733) 358500 – www.thebrewery-tap.com
Opposite Queensgate car park; PE1 2AA

Fantastic range of real ales including their own brews, popular thai food and a lively, friendly atmosphere

The own-brewed Oakham Ales (housed in a striking modern conversion of an old labour exchange) and thai food may seem an unusual combination – but it obviously works. The open-plan contemporary interior has an expanse of light wood and stone floors and blue-painted iron pillars holding up a steel-corded mezzanine level. It's stylishly lit by a giant suspended steel ring with bulbs running around the rim and steel-meshed wall lights. A band of chequered floor tiles traces the path of the long sculpted pale wood bar counter, which is boldly backed by an impressive display of bottles in a ceiling-high wall of wooden cubes. There's also a comfortable downstairs area, a big-screen TV for sporting events, background music and regular live bands and comedy nights. A two-storey glass wall divides the bar from the brewery, giving fascinating views of the two-barrel brew plan from which they produce their own Oakham Bishops Farewell, Black Hole Porter, Citra, Inferno, JHB and seasonal ales; also, up to eight guests, quite a few whiskies and several wines by the glass. It gets very busy in the evening.

Own brew ~ Licensee Jessica Loock ~ Real ale ~ Open 12-11 (1am Fri, 2am Sat); 12-10.30 Sun ~ Bar food 12-2.30, 5.30-10.30; 12-10.30 Fri, Sat; 12-3.30, 5.30-9.30 Sun ~ Restaurant ~ Children welcome during food service times only ~ Dogs allowed in bar ~ Wi-fi ~ Live music nights Fri-Sun

REACH   TL5666

Dyke's End

(01638) 743816 – www.dykesend.co.uk
From B1102 follow signpost to Swaffham Prior and Upware; village signposted; CB25 0JD

Candlelit rooms in former farmhouse, with enjoyable food and own-brewed beer

This looks every inch the classic English pub, situated next to the church in a charming village-green setting, and it remains proud of its old-fashioned values such as no background music, games machines, food sachets or paper napkins. The simply decorated ochre-walled bar has stripped heavy pine tables and pale kitchen chairs on dark boards. In a panelled section on the left are a few rather smarter dining tables with candles, and on the right there's a step down to a red-carpeted part with the small red-walled servery and sensibly placed darts at the back; board games. Adnams Southwold, Timothy Taylors Landlord and a couple of changing guest beers on handpump alongside a decent wine list, and Old Rosie cider. There are picnic-sets under parasols on the front grass.

Free house ~ Licensee George Gibson ~ Real ale ~ Open 12-2.30, 6-11; 12-11 Sat; 12-10.30 Sun; closed Mon ~ Bar food 12-1.45; 6.45-8.45; not Sun evening, Mon ~ Restaurant ~ Children allowed but must be well behaved ~ Dogs welcome ~ Wi-fi

WHITTLESFORD   TL4648

Tickell Arms

(01223) 833025 – www.cambscuisine.com/the-tickell-whittlesford
2.4 miles from M11 junction 10: A505 towards Newmarket, then second turn left signposted Whittlesford; keep on into North Road; CB22 4NZ

Light and refreshing dining pub with good enterprising food and pretty garden

Although the main emphasis is on the dining area (through an ornate glazed partition), there is a proper L-shaped bar here with floor tiles and – under bowler-hatted lampshades over the counter – Brewsters Hophead, Elgoods Cambridge Bitter, Milton Pegasus and Nethergate Old Growler on handpump, 20 fairly priced wines by the glass including champagne, and farm cider. Also, three porcelain handpumps from the era of the legendarily autocratic regime of the Wagner-loving former owner Kim Tickell; these are now orphaned and decorate a high 'counter' that's suspended between a pair of ornate cast-iron pillars and lined with bentwood bar stools. Staff are neatly dressed and friendly. Tables in the dining room vary from sturdy to massive, with leather-cushioned bentwood and other dining chairs and one dark pew, and fresh minimalist décor in palest buff. This opens into an even lighter limestone-floored conservatory area, partly divided by a very high-backed ribbed-leather banquette. The side terrace has comfortable tables, and in the secluded garden beyond there are pergolas and a pond. This is sister pub to the Cock in Hemingford Grey and the Crown & Punchbowl at Horningsea.

Free house ~ Licensees Oliver Thain, Richard Bradley and Max Freeman ~ Real ale ~ Open 12-2.30, 6-11; 12-11 Sat; 12-10.30 Sun ~ Bar food 12-2.30, 6.30-9 (9.30 Fri); 12-3, 6-9.30 Sat; 12-3, 6-8 Sun ~ Restaurant ~ Children must be over 10 in pub and over 5 in evening restaurant ~ Dogs allowed in bar ~ Wi-fi

DOG FRIENDLY HOTELS, INNS AND B&Bs

BALSHAM   TL5850

Black Bull

(01223) 893844 – www.blackbull-balsham.co.uk
27 High Street, Balsham, Cambridge, Cambridgeshire CB21 4DJ

£120; 5 comfortable rooms in single-storey extension. Thatched 17th-c inn
with a friendly landlord serving an interesting range of real ales, plenty of
wines by the glass from a good list, 15 malt whiskies and interesting juices;
dividers and standing timbers break up the beamed bar and there's also an
open fire, leather sofas and leatherette-seated dining chairs; well regarded
food available in the restaurant – housed in a listed barn with a high-raftered
oak-panelled roof; seats in a small back garden and on a front terrace beside
a long old-fashioned verandah; sister pub to the Red Lion at Hinxton. Dogs
allowed in bedrooms and bar; £10.

ELY   TL5480

Lamb

(01353) 663574 – www.thelamb-ely.com
2 Lynn Road, Ely, Cambridgeshire CB7 4EJ

£90; 37 comfortable rooms. Pleasant, neatly kept 15th-c coaching inn near the
cathedral, an attractive bar with high-backed chairs around a mix of tables and
scatter cushions along a leather-seated wall bench, wooden flooring, real ales and
wines by the glass, and enjoyable british food served by friendly staff in the smart
restaurant; limited car parking; walks nearby. Dogs allowed in bedrooms and bar;
bowl; £10 per stay.

HINXTON   TL4945

Red Lion

(01799) 530601 – www.redlionhinxton.co.uk
32 High Street, Hinxton, Cambridge, Cambridgeshire CB10 1QY

£125; 8 well equipped rooms in separate building. Pink-washed 16th-c inn
(handily placed for the Imperial War Museum at Duxford and for the M11) with
a low-beamed bar with oak chairs and tables on bare boards, leather chesterfield
sofas, an open fire, an old wall clock and a relaxed, friendly atmosphere; several
real ales, 22 wines by the glass, 15 malt whiskies and first class service; good
food is served in an informal dining area and a smart restaurant (with oak rafters
and traditional dry peg construction) decorated with pictures and clocks; the
lovely landscaped garden has teak tables and chairs, picnic-sets, a dovecote and
views of the village church; sister pub is the Black Bull in nearby Balsham. Dogs
allowed in bedrooms and bar; £10.

HUNTINGDON   TL2471
Old Bridge
(01480) 424300 – www.huntsbridge.com
1 High Street, Huntingdon, Cambridgeshire PE29 3TQ

£188; 24 very comfortable rooms, some overlooking the river. Ivy-clad Georgian hotel by the Great Ouse river with seats on waterside terrace and a landing stage for visiting boats; a traditional pubby bar with a wide mix of chatty customers, comfortable sofas and low wooden tables on polished floorboards, a log fire, an exceptional wine list (and wine shop), local beers and first class service; enticing food is served in the Terrace room and the more formal panelled restaurant, and breakfasts are delicious. Dogs allowed in some bedrooms, bar and lounge; bowl.

UFFORD   TF0904
White Hart
(01780) 740250 – www.whitehartufford.co.uk
Main Street, Ufford, Stamford, Cambridgeshire PE9 3BH

£90; 10 comfortable rooms, including two in a converted cart shed. 17th-c stone inn (formerly a farmhouse) with a comfortable and friendly atmosphere and plenty of drinking and dining space; farm tools, chamber pots, scatter cushions on leather benches, old chairs and tables, a woodburning stove, exposed stone walls – and also an elegant beamed restaurant and an airy Orangery serving flavoursome food; real ales, 21 wines by the glass and 11 gins; three acres of gardens include a sunken dining area with plenty of seating, steps up to various quiet corners, and lovely flowers and shrubs. Dogs allowed in cart-shed bedrooms and bar; £15.

WANSFORD   TL0799
Haycock Hotel
(01780) 782223 – www.macdonaldhotels.co.uk/haycock
London Road, Wansford, Peterborough, Cambridgeshire PE8 6JA

£150; 48 individually decorated rooms. Recently refurbished 16th-c golden-stone coaching inn with relaxed, comfortable lounges, a pubby bar with real ales and wines by the glass, and a smart, stylish restaurant serving contemporary british food using top quality local produce; friendly, efficient staff; seats in the flower-filled garden. Dogs can walk in the grounds – plenty of nearby country walks too. Dogs allowed in garden bedrooms; £15.

Cheshire

MAP 7

DOG FRIENDLY PUBS

ALDFORD   SJ4259

Grosvenor Arms

(01244) 620228 – www.brunningandprice.co.uk/grosvenorarms
B5130 Chester–Wrexham; CH3 6HJ

Spacious place with impressive range of drinks, wide-ranging imaginative menu, good service, suntrap terrace and garden

Part of the Grosvenor Estate and by the village green, this is a large brick and half-timbered pub with a good mix of customers of all ages. The various rooms have plenty of interest and individuality and a buoyantly chatty atmosphere – and staff are well trained and attentive. Spacious cream-painted areas are sectioned by big knocked-through arches with a variety of floor finishes (wood, quarry tiles, flagstones, black and white tiles), and the richly coloured turkish rugs look well against these natural materials. Good solid pieces of traditional furniture, plenty of pictures and attractive lighting keep it all intimate. A handsomely boarded panelled room has tall bookshelves lining one wall; good selection of board games. Phoenix Brunning & Price Original, Weetwood Eastgate and guests such as New Plassey Midnight Mild, Sharps Doom Bar and Thwaites Lancaster Bomber are served from a fine-looking bar counter and they offer 20 wines by the glass, over 80 whiskies, 30 gins and distinctive soft drinks such as peach and elderflower cordial and Willington Fruit Farm pressed apple juice. Lovely on summer evenings, the airy terracotta-floored conservatory has lots of gigantic low-hanging flowering baskets and chunky pale wood garden furniture. It opens out to a large elegant suntrap terrace and a neat lawn with picnic-sets.

Brunning & Price ~ Manager Tracey Owen ~ Real ale ~ Open 11-11; 12-10.30 Sun ~ Bar food 12-9 (10 Fri, Sat) ~ Children welcome ~ Dogs allowed in bar ~ Wi-fi

ALLOSTOCK   SJ7271

Three Greyhounds

(01565) 723455 – www.thethreegreyhoundsinn.co.uk
4.7 miles from M6 junction 18: A54 E then forking left on B5803 into Holmes Chapel, left at roundabout on to A50 for 2 miles, then left on to B5082 towards Northwich; Holmes Chapel Road; WA16 9JY

Relaxing, civilised and welcoming, with enjoyable food and drink all day

The rooms are interconnected by open doorways and décor throughout is restful: thick rugs on quarry tiles or bare boards, candles and soft lighting, dark grey walls (or interesting woven wooden ones made from old brandy barrels)

hung with modern black-on-white prints. There's an appealing variety of wooden dining chairs, cushioned wall seats, little stools and plenty of plump purple scatter cushions around all sorts of tables – do note the one made from giant bellows. A smashing choice of drinks includes 12 interesting wines by the glass, 50 brandies, a farm cider and Caledonian Byley Bomber and Weetwood Three Greyhounds (named for the pub) plus quickly changing guests such as Caledonian Deuchars IPA, Dunham Massey Little Bollington Bitter and Tatton Red Red Rye on handpump; unobtrusive background music. Above the old farm barns is a restored private dining and party room called the Old Dog House. The big side lawn has picnic-table sets under parasols, with more tables on a decked side verandah with a Perspex roof. Shakerley Mere nature reserve is just across the road. The pub is owned by Tim Bird and Mary McLaughlin, who also run the Cholmondeley Arms in Cholmondeley and the Bulls Head and Church Inn in Mobberley.

Free house ~ Licensee James Griffiths ~ Real ale ~ Open 12-11 (midnight Sat); 12-10.30 Sun ~ Bar food 12-9.15 (9.30 Sat, 8.45 Sun) ~ Children welcome until 7pm ~ Dogs allowed in bar ~ Wi-fi ~ Live music every second Fri

ASTON
SJ6146

Bhurtpore

(01270) 780917 – www.bhurtpore.co.uk
Off A530 SW of Nantwich; in village follow Wrenbury signpost; CW5 8DQ

Fantastic range of drinks (especially real ales) in warm-hearted pub with some unusual artefacts; big garden

Enthusiastic customers come here on a regular basis to try the ever-changing range of around 11 real ales sourced from all over the country. Examples include Abbeydale A Chocwork Orange, Acorn Drop Kick, Burton Bridge Spring Ale, Cheshire Brewhouse TRYPA, Copper Dragon Golden Pippin, Hobsons Shropshire Stout, Ossett Citra, Rat Bohemian Ratsody, Salopian Lemon Dream, Three Tuns Clerics Cure and a changing guest from Derby. They also stock dozens of unusual bottled beers and fruit beers, a great many bottled ciders and perries and farm cider, over 100 different whiskies, 43 gins, 20 vodkas, carefully selected soft drinks and 14 wines from a good list; summer beer festival. The pub name commemorates the siege of Bhurtpore (a town in India) during which local landowner Sir Stapleton Cotton (later Viscount Combermere) was commander-in-chief. The connection with India also explains some of the quirky artefacts in the carpeted lounge bar – look out for the sunglasses-wearing turbanned figure behind the counter; also good local period photographs and some attractive furniture in the comfortable public bar; board games, pool, TV and games machine. Weekends tend to be pretty busy.

Free house ~ Licensee Simon George ~ Real ale ~ Open 12-11.30 (midnight Fri, Sat); 12-11 Sun ~ Bar food 12-2, 5.30-9.30 (8.30 Mon); 12-9.30 Fri, Sat; 12-8.30 Sun ~ Restaurant ~ Children welcome ~ Dogs allowed in bar ~ Wi-fi

BARTHOMLEY
SJ7752

White Lion

(01270) 882242 – www.whitelionbarthomley.co.uk
M6 junction 16, B5078 N towards Alsager, then Barthomley signed on left; CW2 5PG

Timeless 17th-c thatched village tavern with classic period interior, up to half a dozen real ales and good value lunchtime food

This charming black and white tavern is very much part of the local community and popular with a good mix of people – it's also one of the most attractive buildings in a pretty village. The bar has a blazing open fire, heavy oak beams dating from Stuart times, attractively moulded black panelling, Cheshire prints on the walls, latticed windows and uneven wobbly old tables. Up some steps, a second room has another welcoming open fire, more oak panelling, a high-backed winged settle and a paraffin lamp hinged to the wall; shove-ha'penny; local societies make good use of a third room. Banks's Bitter, Jennings Cocker Hoop and Sneck Lifter, Marstons Burton Bitter and Pedigree and Sunbeam Best Bitter on handpump served by genuinely friendly staff. The gents' are across an open courtyard. In summer, seats on cobbles outside offer nice village views and the early 15th-c red sandstone church of St Bertoline (where you can learn about the Barthomley massacre).

Marstons ~ Tenant Peter Butler ~ Real ale ~ Open 11.30-11 (10.30 Sun) ~ Bar food 12-2 Mon, Tues; 12-3 Weds-Sun ~ Children welcome away from bar counter ~ Dogs allowed in bar ~ Wi-fi

BOSTOCK GREEN   SJ6769

Hayhurst Arms

(01606) 541810 – www.brunningandprice.co.uk/hayhurstarms
London Road, Bostock Green; CW10 9JP

Interesting pub with a marvellous choice of drinks, a wide choice of rewarding food, friendly staff and seats outside

Cleverly renovated to incorporate the former stables and coach house, this is a handsome pub with lots to look at inside. The long main bar is divided into different dining areas by elegant support pillars, and it's light and airy throughout: big windows, house plants, bookshelves, standard lamps, metal chandeliers and prints, old photographs and paintings arranged frame-to-frame above wooden dados. The varied dark wooden dining chairs are grouped around tables of all sizes on rugs, quarry tiles, wide floorboards and carpet, and three open fireplaces have big mirrors above, with hefty leather armchairs to the sides. A couple of cosier rooms lead off; background music and board games. Phoenix Brunning & Price Original and Weetwood Eastgate Ale, with guests such as Cwrw Ial Limestone Cowboy, Mobberley Maori and Sandstone Desert Dragon, Mild and Onyx on handpump, 25 wines by the glass, 70 malt whiskies and 25 gins; staff are efficient and courteous. The outside terrace has good quality tables and chairs under parasols, and the village green opposite has swings and a play tractor.

Brunning & Price ~ Manager Christopher Beswick ~ Real ale ~ Open 11-11 (10.30 Sun) ~ Bar food 12-10 (9.30 Sun) ~ Children welcome ~ Dogs allowed in bar ~ Wi-fi

BUNBURY   SJ5658

Dysart Arms

(01829) 260183 – www.brunningandprice.co.uk/dysart
Bowes Gate Road; village signposted off A51 NW of Nantwich; and from A49 S of Tarporley – coming in this way on northernmost village access road, bear left in village centre; CW6 9PH

Civilised chatty dining pub with thoughtfully laid-out rooms, enjoyable food and a lovely garden with pretty views

Although the interior has been opened up here, the neatly kept rooms still retain a cottagey feel as they ramble around the pleasantly lit central bar. Cream walls keep it light, clean and airy, with deep venetian-red ceilings adding cosiness. Each room (some with good winter fires) is nicely furnished with an appealing variety of well spaced sturdy wooden tables and chairs, a couple of tall filled bookcases and just the right amount of carefully chosen bric-a-brac, properly lit pictures and plants. Flooring ranges from red and black tiles to stripped boards and some carpet. Phoenix Brunning & Price Original and Weetwood Best Bitter with guests such as Copper Dragon Best Bitter and Ossett Elizabeth Rose on handpump alongside a good selection of 17 wines by the glass and around 20 malts; background music and board games. There are sturdy wooden tables on the terrace and picnic-sets on the lawn in the neatly kept and slightly elevated garden, and the views of the splendid church at the end of this pretty village and the distant Peckforton Hills beyond are lovely.

Brunning & Price ~ Manager Kate John ~ Real ale ~ Open 11.30-11; 12-10.30 Sun ~ Bar food 12-9.30 (9 Sun) ~ Children welcome ~ Dogs allowed in bar ~ Wi-fi

BURLEYDAM   SJ6042
Combermere Arms
(01948) 871223 – www.brunningandprice.co.uk/combermere
A525 Whitchurch–Audlem; SY13 4AT

Roomy and attractive beamed pub successfully mixing a good drinking side with imaginative all-day food

There are plenty of nooks and crannies in this partly 16th-c pub that's been cleverly extended without losing its character. The many rambling yet intimate-feeling rooms are attractive and understated and filled with all sorts of antique cushioned dining chairs around dark wood tables, rugs on wood (some old, some new oak) and stone floors, prints hung frame-to-frame on cream walls, bookshelves, deep red ceilings, panelling and open fires. Phoenix Brunning & Price Original and Weetwood Cheshire Cat Blonde Ale and guests such as Acorn Barnsley Bitter, Copper Dragon Golden Pippin, Sharps Doom Bar and Timothy Taylors Boltmaker on handpump, 100 malt whiskies, 20 wines by the glass from an extensive list and three farm ciders; board games and background music. Outside there are good solid wood tables and picnic-sets in a pretty, well tended garden.

Brunning & Price ~ Manager Lisa Hares ~ Real ale ~ Open 11-11 ~ Bar food 12-10 (9 Sun) ~ Children welcome ~ Dogs allowed in bar ~ Wi-fi

CHESTER   SJ4066
Albion
(01244) 340345 – www.albioninnchester.co.uk
Albion Street; CH1 1RQ

Strongly traditional pub with comfortable Edwardian décor and captivating World War I memorabilia; pubby food and good drinks

For over 40 years, the charming licensees here have amassed an absorbing collection of World War I memorabilia; in fact, this is an officially listed site of four war memorials to soldiers from the Cheshire Regiment. It's a genuinely friendly, old-fashioned pub and the peaceful rooms are filled with big engravings of men leaving for war and similarly moving prints of wounded veterans, as well as flags, advertisements and so on. There are also leatherette and hoop-backed chairs around cast-iron-framed tables, lamps, an open fire in the Edwardian fireplace and dark floral William Morris wallpaper (designed on the first day of World War I). You might even be lucky enough to hear the vintage 1928 Steck pianola being played; there's an attractive side dining room too. Big Rock Harvest Pale Ale, Moorhouses Pride of Pendle and Weetwood Cheshire Cat Blonde Ale on handpump, new world wines, fresh orange juice, organic bottled cider and fruit juice, over 25 malt whiskies and a good selection of rums and gins. An attractive way to reach the place is along the city wall, coming down at Newgate/Wolfsgate and walking along Park Street. No children. Please note: if the pub is quiet they may close early, so it's best to ring ahead and check.

Punch ~ Lease Mike and Christina Mercer ~ Real ale ~ No credit cards ~ Open 12-3, 5 (6 Sat)-11; 12-2.30 Sun ~ Bar food 12-2, 5-8 (8.30 Sat) ~ Restaurant ~ Dogs allowed in bar ~ Bedrooms: £90

CHESTER   SJ4066

Architect

(01244) 353070 – www.brunningandprice.co.uk/architect
Nicholas Street (A5268); CH1 2NX

Busy pub by the racecourse with interesting furnishings and décor, attentive staff, a good choice of drinks and super food

This lively establishment is almost two separate places connected by a glass passage. The pubbiest part, with a more bustling feel, is the garden room where they serve Phoenix Brunning & Price Original and Weetwood Eastgate alongside guests such as Barngates Pale, Cheshire Brewhouse Cheshire Set, Peerless Pale, Salopian Hop Twister and Titanic Plum Porter on handpump, 18 wines by the glass, 74 whiskies and farm cider. Throughout there are elegant antique dining chairs around a mix of nice old tables on rugs or bare floorboards, hundreds of interesting paintings and prints on green, cream or yellow walls, house plants and flowers on windowsills and mantelpieces, and lots of bookcases. Also, open fires, armchairs in front of a woodburning stove or tucked into cosy nooks, candelabra and big mirrors, and a friendly, easy-going atmosphere; background music and board games. Big windows and french doors look over the terrace, where there are plenty of good quality wooden seats and tables under parasols. There are views over Roodee Racecourse (binoculars are provided).

Brunning & Price ~ Manager Natalie Shaw ~ Real ale ~ Open 10.30am-11pm; 10.30-10.30 Sun ~ Bar food 12-10 (9.30 Sun) ~ Children welcome ~ Dogs allowed in bar ~ Wi-fi

CHESTER   SJ4166

Old Harkers Arms

(01244) 344525 – www.brunningandprice.co.uk/harkers
Russell Street, down steps off City Road where it crosses canal; CH3 5AL

Well run canalside building with a lively atmosphere, fantastic range of drinks and extremely good food

You can watch boats on the Shropshire Union Canal next to this cleverly converted warehouse from the tall windows that run the length of the main bar. The striking industrial interior with its high ceilings is divided into user-friendly spaces by brick pillars. Walls are covered with old prints hung frame-to-frame, there's a wall of bookshelves above a leather banquette at one end, the mixed dark wood furniture is set out in intimate groups on stripped-wood floors and attractive lamps lend some cosiness; board games. Cheerful staff serve Phoenix Brunning & Price Original and Weetwood Cheshire Cat Blonde Ale with guests such as Acorn Blonde, Titanic Plum Porter and Woodfordes Norfolk Nog on handpump, 120 malt whiskies, 20 wines from a well described list and six farm ciders.

Brunning & Price ~ Manager Paul Jeffery ~ Real ale ~ Open 10.30am-11pm; 12-10.30 Sun ~ Bar food 12-9.30 ~ Children welcome but no babies, toddlers or pushchairs ~ Dogs allowed in bar ~ Wi-fi

COTEBROOK   SJ5765

Fox & Barrel

(01829) 760529 – www.foxandbarrel.co.uk
A49 NE of Tarporley; CW6 9DZ

Attractive building with stylishly airy décor, an enterprising menu and good wines

Food here is excellent and, of course, many customers are here to dine, but they do have high chairs against the bar counter and cushioned benches and settles where drinkers feel quite at home. Friendly staff serve Caledonian Deuchars IPA, Weetwood Eastgate and a couple of guests such as Black Sheep Golden Sheep and Wincle Lord Lucan on handpump; they also have 16 wines by the glass from a good list. A big log fire dominates the bar while a larger uncluttered beamed dining area has attractive rugs and an eclectic mix of period tables on polished floorboards, with extensive wall panelling hung with framed old prints. The front terrace has plenty of smart tables and chairs under parasols; at the back, there are picnic-sets on grass and some nice old fruit trees. There's a big new car park at the front.

Free house ~ Licensee Gary Kidd ~ Real ale ~ Open 12-11 (10.30 Sun) ~ Bar food 12-9.30 (9 Sun) ~ Children welcome ~ Dogs allowed in bar ~ Wi-fi

DELAMERE   SJ5667

Fishpool

(01606) 883277 – www.thefishpoolinn.co.uk
Junction A54/B5152 Chester Road/Fishpool Road, a mile W of A49; CW8 2HP

Something for everyone in extensive interestingly laid-out pub, with a good range of food and drinks served all day

Cleverly and stylishly laid out, this place has plenty of snug, cosy areas leading off a big, cheerful open section with unusual and varied furnishings and décor. A lofty central area, partly skylit – and full of contented diners – has a row of booths facing the long bar counter, and numerous other tables with banquettes or overstuffed small armchairs on pale floorboards laid with rugs; then comes a conservatory overlooking picnic-sets on a flagstone terrace, and a lawn beyond. Off on two sides are many rooms with much lower ceilings, some with heavy dark beams, some with bright polychrome tile or intricate parquet flooring: William Morris wallpaper here, dusky paintwork or neat bookshelves there, sofas, armchairs, a fire in an old-fashioned open range, lots of old prints and some intriguing objects including carved or painted animal skulls; background music. Weetwood Best, Cheshire Cat and Eastgate plus guests such as Wincle Nimrod and Wibbly Wallaby on handpump, 13 wines by the glass, ten malt whiskies and farm cider; unobtrusive background music; upstairs lavatories. Sister pubs are the Pheasant in Burwardsley and the Bears Paw in Warmingham.

Free house ~ Licensee Andrew Nelson ~ Real ale ~ Open 11-11 ~ Bar food 12-9.30 (10 Fri, Sat); 12-9 Sun ~ Restaurant ~ Children welcome ~ Dogs allowed in bar ~ Wi-fi

KETTLESHULME   SJ9879

Swan

(01663) 732943
B5470 Macclesfield–Chapel-en-le-Frith, a mile W of Whaley Bridge; SK23 7QU

Charming 16th-c pub with enjoyable food, good beer and an attractive garden

The interior of this pretty white cottage is snug and cosy, with latticed windows, very low dark beams hung with big copper jugs and kettles, timbered walls, antique coaching and other prints and maps, ancient oak settles on a turkish carpet and log fires; the dining room has an open kitchen. Marstons Bitter on handpump with a couple of guest beers from breweries such as Phoenix and Whim, and 12 wines by the glass served by courteous, friendly staff. The front terrace has teak tables, another two-level terrace has further tables and steamer benches under parasols, and there's a sizeable streamside garden. The pub is handy for walks in the relatively unfrequented north-west part of the Peak District National Park.

Free house ~ Licensee Robert Cloughley ~ Real ale ~ Open 12-11 (midnight Sat); 12-10.30 Sun; closed Mon lunchtime ~ Bar food 12-9; 12-4 Sun; no food Mon ~ Restaurant ~ Children welcome ~ Dogs allowed in bar ~ Wi-fi

MACCLESFIELD

SJ9271

Sutton Hall

(01260) 253211 – www.brunningandprice.co.uk/suttonhall
Leaving Macclesfield southwards on A523, turn left into Byrons Lane signposted Langley, Wincle, then just before canal viaduct fork right into Bullocks Lane; OS Sheet 118 map reference 925715; SK11 0HE

Historic building set in attractive grounds, with a fine range of drinks and well trained, courteous staff

Nearly 500 years ago, this was a manor house. It's now a busy pub and some of the remaining original features have been carefully restored to blend cleverly with up-to-date touches; the hall at the heart of the building is especially noteworthy – in particular the entrance space. There's a charming series of rooms (a bar, a library with books on shelves and a raised open fire and dining areas) divided by tall oak timbers: antique oak panelling, warmly coloured rugs on broad flagstones, bare boards and tiles, lots of pictures placed frame-to-frame, and two more fires. Background music and board games. The atmosphere is nicely relaxed and a good range of drinks includes Phoenix Brunning & Price Original plus Beartown Bearly Literate, Conwy Riptide, Weetwood Eastgate and Wincle Lord Lucan on handpump, 18 wines by the glass from an extensive list, 65 malt whiskies and 30 gins; service is attentive and friendly. The pretty gardens have spaciously laid-out tables (some on their own little terraces), sloping lawns and fine mature trees.

Brunning & Price ~ Manager Syd Foster ~ Real ale ~ Open 11-11 (10.30 Sun) ~ Bar food 12-10 (9.30 Sun) ~ Restaurant ~ Children welcome ~ Dogs allowed in bar ~ Wi-fi

MOBBERLEY

SJ7879

Bulls Head

(01565) 873395 – www.thebullsheadpub.co.uk
Mill Lane; WA16 7HX

Terrific all-rounder with interesting food and drink and plenty of pubby character

They hold live music twice a month in this particularly well run, friendly pub plus quiz evenings and themed food events – it's worth checking their website regularly. There's always a good mix of both locals and visitors and the whole place has been kept nice and pubby with just a touch of modernity. A fine range of drinks includes Wincle White Bull (named for the pub) and Weetwood Bulls Head Bitter, Cheshire Cat Blonde Ale and Mobberley Wobbly Ale on handpump (useful tasting notes too), 15 wines by the glass, around 80 whiskies and local gins. Several rooms are furnished quite traditionally, with an unpretentious mix of wooden tables, cushioned wall seats and chairs on fine old quarry tiles, black and pale grey walls contrasting well with warming red lampshades, and pink bare-brick walls and pale stripped-timber detailing; also, lots of mirrors, hops, candles, open fires, background music and board games. Dogs get a warm welcome (they're allowed in the snug) with friendly staff dispensing doggie biscuits from a huge jar, and they keep popular walk leaflets; seats outside in the big garden. The pub is owned by Tim Bird and Mary McLaughlin, who also own the Church Inn (also in Mobberley), the Three Greyhounds in Allostock and Cholmondeley Arms at Cholmondeley.

Free house ~ Licensee Barry Lawlor ~ Real ale ~ Open 12-10.30 (11 Weds-Sat); 12-10.30 Sun ~ Bar food 12-9.15 (9.45 Fri, Sat); 12-8.45 Sun ~ Children welcome but no under-10s after 7pm ~ Dogs allowed in bar ~ Wi-fi ~ Live music twice a month

MOBBERLEY

SJ7980

Church Inn

(01565) 873178 – www.churchinnmobberley.co.uk
Brown sign to pub off B5085 on Wilmslow side of village; Church Lane; WA16 7RD

Nicely traditional, friendly country pub with bags of character; good food and drink

The small, snug interconnected rooms in this pretty brick building have all manner of nice old tables and chairs on wide floorboards, low ceilings, plenty of candlelight and friendly young staff; it's best to book in advance to be sure of a table. The décor in soothing greys and dark green, with some oak-leaf wallpaper, is perked up by a collection of stuffed grouse and their relatives, and a huge variety of pictures; background music. Beartown Best Bitter, Mallorys Mobberley Best (George Mallory, lost near Everest's summit in 1924, is remembered in the church with a stained-glass window) and Tatton Church Ale-Alujah and Gold on handpump, and unusual and rewarding wines, with 16 by the glass; wine tastings can be booked in the upstairs private dining room. They give out a detailed leaflet describing a good four-mile circular walk from the pub, passing sister pub the Bulls Head en route. Dogs are welcomed in the bar with not just a tub of snacks on the counter, but maybe even the offer of a meaty 'beer'. The sunny garden snakes down to an old bowling green with lovely pastoral views and a side courtyard has sturdy tables and benches. The village church is opposite. The pub shares owners with the Three Greyhounds in Allostock, Cholmondeley Arms at Cholmondeley and Bulls Head in this village.

Free house ~ Licensee Simon Umpleby ~ Real ale ~ Open 12-11 (10.30 Sun) ~ Bar food 12-9.15 ~ Children welcome but no under-10s after 6pm ~ Dogs allowed in bar ~ Wi-fi

MOTTRAM ST ANDREW

SJ8878

Bulls Head

(01625) 828111 – www.brunningandprice.co.uk/bullshead
A538 Prestbury–Wilmslow; Wilmslow Road/Priest Lane; E side of village; SK10 4QH

Superb country dining pub, a thoughtful range of drinks and interesting food, plenty of character and well trained staff

Consistently well run, this is a highly enjoyable pub. There is a bustling bar but perhaps the main emphasis is on the dining areas at the far end. Four levels stack up alongside or above one another, each with a distinctive décor and style, from the informality of a sunken area with rugs on a tiled floor, through a comfortable library/dining room, to another with an upstairs conservatory feel and the last, with higher windows and more of a special-occasion atmosphere. The rest of the pub has an appealing and abundant mix of old prints and pictures, comfortable seating in great variety, a coal fire in one room, a blazing woodburning stove in a two-way fireplace dividing two other rooms and an antique black kitchen range in yet another. Phoenix Brunning & Price Original and Wincle Sir Philip with guests such as Moorhouses White Witch, Pennine Real Blonde and Timothy Taylors Landlord on handpump, around 20 wines by the glass, 50 malt whiskies, 20 gins and several ciders, and a separate tea and coffee station with pretty blue and white china cups, teapots and jugs. Also, background music, daily papers and board games. The lawn has plenty of picnic-sets beneath cocktail parasols.

Brunning & Price ~ Manager Andrew Coverley ~ Real ale ~ Open 10.30am-11pm; 12-10.30 Sun ~ Bar food 12-10 (9.30 Sun) ~ Children welcome ~ Dogs allowed in bar ~ Wi-fi

NETHER ALDERLEY SJ8576
Wizard

(01625) 584000 – www.ainscoughs.co.uk
B5087 Macclesfield Road, opposite Artists Lane; SK10 4UB

Bustling pub with interesting food, real ales, a friendly welcome and relaxed atmosphere

After a walk along Alderley Edge, head to this enjoyable pub for refreshment. The various rooms, connected by open doorways, are cleverly done up in a mix of modern rustic and traditional styles. There are beams and open fires, antique dining chairs (some prettily cushioned) and settles around all sorts of tables, rugs on pale floorboards, prints and paintings on contemporary paintwork and decorative items ranging from a grandfather clock to staffordshire dogs and modern lampshades. Thwaites Wainwright and a guest from Storm plus Jennings Red Rascal and Wells Bombardier on handpump and quite a few wines by the glass; background music and board games. There are plenty of seats in the sizeable back garden. The pub is part of the Ainscoughs group.

Free house ~ Licensee Stacey Wood ~ Real ale ~ Open 12-10 (12-9 Sun) ~ Bar food 12-2.30, 6-9; 12-9 Sat; 12-8 Sun ~ Children welcome ~ Dogs allowed in bar ~ Wi-fi

SANDBACH SJ7560
Old Hall

(01270) 758170 – www.brunningandprice.co.uk/oldhall
1.2 miles from M6 junction 17: A534 – ignore first turn into town and take the second – if you reach the roundabout double back; CW11 1AL

Glorious hall-house with impressive original features, plenty of drinking and dining space, six real ales and imaginative food

This glorious 17th-c manor house is a masterpiece of timbering and fine carved gable-ends. There are many lovely original architectural features, particularly in the room to the left of the entrance hall, which is much as it has been for centuries, with a Jacobean fireplace, oak panelling and priest's hole. This leads into the Oak Room, divided by standing timbers into two dining areas with heavy beams, oak flooring and reclaimed panelling. Other rooms in the original building have hefty beams and oak boards, three open fires and a woodburning stove; the cosy snugs are carpeted. The Garden Room is big and bright, with reclaimed quarry tiling and exposed A-frame oak timbering, and opens on to a suntrap back terrace with teak tables and chairs among flowering tubs. Throughout, the walls are covered with countless interesting prints, there's an appealing collection of antique dining chairs and tables of all sizes, and plenty of rugs, bookcases and plants. From the handsome bar counter, efficient and friendly staff serve Phoenix Brunning & Price Original, Redwillow Feckless and Three Tuns XXX with guests such as Bollington White Nancy, Cheshire Brewhouse Blues Breaker and Titanic Black Ice on handpump, 16 good wines by the glass, 50 malt whiskies, 20 gins and farm cider; board games. There are picnic-sets in front of the building beside rose bushes and clipped box hedging.

Brunning & Price ~ Manager Chris Button ~ Real ale ~ Open 10.30am-11pm; 9am-11pm Sat; 9am-10.30pm Sun ~ Bar food 12-10 (9.30 Sun) ~ Restaurant ~ Children welcome ~ Dogs allowed in bar ~ Wi-fi ~ Live music last Fri of the month

SPURSTOW   SJ5657

Yew Tree

(01829) 260274 – www.theyewtreebunbury.com

Off A49 S of Tarporley; follow Bunbury 1, Haughton 2 signpost into Long Lane; CW6 9RD

Plenty of individuality, smashing food and drinks and an easy-going atmosphere

An eclectic mix of customers enjoy this entertaining pub which creates a cheerful, informal atmosphere – all helped along by the friendly staff. Throughout, there are prettily cushioned dining chairs and built-in wall seats around all sorts of tables on bare boards, beams and timbering, walls hung with lots of prints and big vases of flowers. Some quirky and individual touches include Timorous Beasties' giant bees papered on to the bar ceiling, a stag's head looming out of the wall above a log fire, a magnificent hunting tapestry and a strange angled nook with tartan wallpaper; the doors to the loos are quite a puzzle – which of the many knobs and handles actually work?! Simple chairs line the bar counter where they keep Acorn Barnsley Gold and Calypso IPA, Stonehouse Station Bitter, Tatton Red Red Rye and Wincle Sir Philip on handpump, 40 malt whiskies, 15 wines by the glass from an interesting list and 20 gins; background music. A terrace outside has teak tables under parasols, with more on the lawn.

Free house ~ Licensees Jon and Lindsay Cox ~ Real ale ~ Open 12-11 (10.30 Sun)) ~ Bar food 12-9.30 (10 Fri, Sat; 9 Sun) ~ Well behaved children welcome ~ Dogs welcome ~ Wi-fi ~ Live music last Fri of month

SWETTENHAM   SJ7967

Swettenham Arms

(01477) 571284 – www.swettenhamarms.co.uk

Off A54 Congleton–Holmes Chapel or A535 Chelford–Holmes Chapel; CW12 2LF

Big old country pub in a fine setting with shining brasses, five real ales and tempting food

For over 20 years, the hard-working and welcoming licensees have kept this former nunnery rather special. The three interlinked dark beamed areas are still nicely traditional with individual furnishings on bare floorboards or a sweep of fitted turkey carpet, a polished copper bar, three woodburning stoves, plenty of shiny brasses and a variety of old prints – military, hunting, old ships, reproduction Old Masters and so forth. Friendly efficient staff serve

Black Sheep Best, Hydes Original Bitter, Sharps Doom Bar and Weetwood
Cheshire Cat Blonde Ale on handpump, 12 wines by the glass, 20 malt
whiskies and farm cider; background music. Outside behind, there are tables
on a lawn that merges into a lovely sunflower and lavender meadow; croquet.
There are walks in the pretty surrounding countryside and Quinta Arboretum
is close by. Do visit the interesting village church which dates from the 13th c.

Free house ~ Licensees Jim and Frances Cunningham ~ Real ale ~ No credit cards ~ Open
12-11; 12-3, 6-11 winter ~ Bar food 12-9; closed 3-6pm winter ~ Restaurant ~ Children
welcome ~ Dogs allowed in bar ~ Wi-fi

THELWALL   SJ6587
Little Manor
(01925) 212070 – www.brunningandprice.co.uk/littlemanor
Bell Lane; WA4 2SX

**Restored manor house with plenty of room, lots of interest, well kept
ales and tasty bistro-style food; seats outside**

Linked by open doorways and standing timbers, the six beamed rooms in
this big, handsome 17th-c house are crammed with things to look at; there
are plenty of nooks and crannies too. Flooring ranges from rugs on bare
boards through carpeting to some fine old black and white tiles, and there's
an appealing variety of antique dining chairs around small, large, circular or
square tables, as well as leather armchairs by open fires (note the lovely carved
wooden one); background music. Lighting is from metal chandeliers, wall lights
and standard lamps, and the décor includes hundreds of intriguing prints and
photos, books on shelves and lots of old glass and stone bottles on windowsills
and mantelpieces; plenty of fresh flowers and house plants too. Phoenix
Brunning & Price Original, Coach House Cromwells Best Bitter and Tatton
Blonde and five quickly changing guest beers on handpump, around 15 wines
by the glass, 27 gins and 60 whiskies; the young staff are consistently helpful.
In fine weather you can sit at the chunky teak chairs and tables on the terrace;
some are under a heated shelter.

Brunning & Price ~ Manager Jill Dowling ~ Real ale ~ Open 10.30-11; 12-10.30 Sun ~
Bar food 12-10 (9 Sun) ~ Children welcome ~ Dogs allowed in bar ~ Wi-fi

WHITELEY GREEN   SJ9278
Windmill
(01625) 574222 – www.thewindmill.info
*Brown sign to pub off A523 Macclesfield–Poynton, just N of Prestbury; Hole House Lane;
SK10 5SJ*

**Extensive relaxed country dining bar with big sheltered garden and
enjoyable food**

Most of this pub is given over to dining tables, mainly in a pleasantly informal,
painted base/stripped top style, on bare boards. But the interior spreads
around a big bar counter, its handpumps serving Sharps Doom Bar and local
guests such as Storm Bosley Cloud, Weetwood Best and Wincle Lord Lucan;
also, a dozen wines by the glass served by friendly and helpful staff. One area
has several leather sofas and fabric-upholstered easy chairs; another by a log
fire in a huge brick fireplace has more easy chairs and a suede sofa. Background
music, daily papers and cribbage. The pub is up a long quiet lane in deepest leafy
Cheshire countryside, and its spreading lawns, surrounded by a belt of young

trees, provide plenty of room for well spaced tables and picnic sets, and even a maze to baffle children. Middlewood Way (a sort of linear country park) and Macclesfield Canal (Bridge 25) are just a stroll away.

Mitchells & Butlers ~ Lease Peter and Jane Nixon ~ Real ale ~ Open 12-11 (10.30 Sun) ~ Bar food 12-2.30, 5-9.30; 12-9.30 Sat; 12-8 Sun ~ Children welcome ~ Dogs allowed in bar ~ Wi-fi ~ Live acoustic music second Fri and live bands last Fri of month

DOG FRIENDLY HOTELS, INNS AND B&Bs

BEESTON   SJ5559

Wild Boar Hotel

(01829) 260309 – www.wildboarhotel.com
Whitchurch Road, Beeston, Tarporley, Cheshire CW6 9NW

From £85; 38 comfortably modern rooms. Striking timbered 17th-c former hunting lodge, much extended over the years, with manicured lawns and fine views, beams and standing timbers in relaxed bars and lounges, original features mixed in with bold contemporary furnishings, all manner of attractive chairs and tables and sofas on carpeting, a sleek brasserie, good bistro-style meals and friendly, helpful service; lots of nearby walks. Dogs allowed in some bedrooms; £20 per stay.

BURWARDSLEY   SJ5256

Pheasant

(01829) 770434 – www.thepheasantinn.co.uk
Burwardsley, Chester, Cheshire CH3 9PF

£115; 12 attractive rooms in main building or ivy-clad stable wing. 17th-c half-timbered, sandstone pub with fantastic views across the Cheshire plains and a great stop if you're walking the scenic Sandstone Trail along the Peckforton Hills; the airy, modern-feeling spreading rooms have low beams, comfortable leather armchairs and nice old chairs on wooden floors, a log fire in a huge see-through fireplace, local beers and ciders and enjoyable varied food using local produce (snacks served all day); garden with seating; sister pubs are the Fishpool in Delamere and Bears Paw in Warmingham. Dogs allowed in all bedrooms and anywhere in the pub.

CHOLMONDELEY   SJ5550

Cholmondeley Arms

(01829) 720300 – www.cholmondeleyarms.co.uk
Cholmondeley, Malpas, Cheshire SY14 8HN

£85; 6 attractive rooms in former headmaster's house. Imaginatively converted Victorian former schoolhouse with lofty ceilings, stripped-brick walls, sofas, a massive stag's head above the cosy fire, huge old radiators, big mirrors, assorted school paraphernalia (hockey sticks, tennis rackets and so forth), rugs on bare boards, fresh flowers and church candles; real ales, 330 different gins, wines by the glass, well presented modern food and hearty breakfasts; sizeable lawn with seating, and handy for Cholmondeley Castle Gardens; same owners as the Three

Greyhounds in Allostock, and Bulls Head and Church Inn in Mobberley. Dogs allowed in some bedrooms and anywhere in the pub; dog beer; £10.

POTT SHRIGLEY   SJ9479
Shrigley Hall
(01625) 575757 – www.thehotelcollection.co.uk
Shrigley Park, Pott Shrigley, Macclesfield, Cheshire SK10 5SB

£90-£150; 148 smart and well equipped rooms, some with country views. In over 260 acres of parkland on the edge of the Peak District National Park, this impressive country house has many original features, a splendid entrance hall with several elegant rooms and the Courtyard bar leading off, enjoyable food in the Oakridge restaurant and good service from friendly staff; championship golf course, fishing, tennis, spa, sauna, indoor pool and beauty treatment rooms. Dogs can walk in grounds and in National Trust's Lyme Park (but must not chase deer). Dogs allowed in about ten bedrooms and some public areas; £15.

TARPORLEY   SJ5562
Swan
(01829) 733838 – www.theswantarporley.co.uk
50 High Street, Tarporley, Cheshire CW6 0AG

£115; 16 comfortable rooms, including six in converted coach house. Elegant Georgian-fronted inn (building actually dates from the 16th c) with a good mix of individual tables and chairs in attractive bar, four real ales, decent wines and quite a few malt whiskies, traditional british food with some french touches, nice breakfasts and afternoon teas, beer garden and friendly staff. Dogs allowed in coach-house bedrooms and back bar; £15.

WARMINGHAM   SJ7061
Bears Paw
(01270) 526317 – www.thebearspaw.co.uk
School Lane, Warmingham, Sandbach, Cheshire CW11 3QN

£115; 17 well equipped rooms. Refurbished Victorian inn with a maze of rooms of individual character – two little panelled sitting rooms with fashionable wallpaper, comfortable leather furniture and woodburning stoves in magnificent fireplaces; light, airy dining areas with an eclectic mix of wooden furniture on stripped floorboards and lofty windows; half a dozen real ales, ten wines by the glass and well liked food served by cheerful staff; seats in a small front garden; sister pub to the Pheasant in Burwardsley and the Fishpool at Delamere. Dogs allowed in all bedrooms and bar.

Cornwall

MAP 1

DOG FRIENDLY PUBS

BLISLAND   SX1073
Blisland Inn

(01208) 850739 – www.bodminmoor.co.uk
Village signposted off A30 and B3266 NE of Bodmin; PL30 4JF

A fine choice of real ales, beer-related memorabilia, friendly staff, pubby food and seats outside

The genuinely welcoming landlord in this traditional, old-fashioned pub keeps around six real ales tapped from the cask or on handpump: two named for the pub by Sharps – Blisland Special and Bulldog – as well as quickly changing beers from west country breweries such as Atlantic, Bude, Otter, Padstow, Skinners and St Austell; also, farm cider, fruit wines and real apple juice. Service is good. Every inch of the beams and ceiling is covered with beer badges (or their particularly wide-ranging collection of mugs), and the walls are filled with beer-related posters and the like. The carpeted lounge has several barometers on the walls, toby jugs on beams and a few standing timbers, while the family room has pool, table skittles, euchre, cribbage and dominoes; background music. Plenty of picnic-sets outside. The popular Camel Trail cycle path is close by – though the hill up to Blisland is pretty steep. As with many pubs in this area, the approach by car involves negotiating several single-track roads.

Free house ~ Licensees Gary and Margaret Marshall ~ Real ale ~ Open 11.30-11.30 (midnight Sat); 12-10.30 Sun ~ Bar food 12-2, 6.30-9; not Sun evening ~ Restaurant ~ Children in family room only ~ Dogs welcome ~ Regular live music

BOSCASTLE   SX0991
Cobweb

(01840) 250278 – http://cobwebinn.com
B3263, just E of harbour; PL35 0HE

Plenty of interest in cheerful pub, several real ales and friendly staff

This bustling pub is very near the tiny steeply cut harbour and pretty village. The two interesting bars have quite a mix of seats (from settles and carved chairs to more pubby furniture), heavy beams hung with hundreds of bottles and jugs, lots of pictures of bygone years and cosy log fires. They keep four real ales such as St Austell Proper Job and Tribute, Sharps Doom Bar and a guest beer on handpump and a local cider, and the atmosphere is cheerful and bustling, especially at peak times; games machine, darts and pool. The restaurant is upstairs. There are picnic-sets and benches outside (some under cover); dogs must be on a lead. A self-catering apartment is for rent.

Free house ~ Licensee Adrian Bright ~ Real ale ~ Open 10.30am-11pm (midnight Sat); 12-10.30 Sun ~ Bar food 11.30-2.30, 6-9.30 ~ Restaurant ~ Children welcome ~ Dogs allowed in bar

DEVORAN SW 7938

Old Quay

(01872) 863142 – www.theoldquayinn.co.uk
Devoran from new Carnon Cross roundabout A39 Truro–Falmouth, left on old road, right at mini roundabout; TR3 6NE

Light and airy bar rooms in friendly pub with four real ales, good wine and imaginative food and seats on pretty back terraces; bedrooms

At this bustling, cheerful pub you'll get a warm welcome from both the staff and friendly locals. The roomy bar has an interesting 'woodburner' set halfway up one wall, a cushioned window seat, wall settles and a few bar stools around just three tables on stripped boards, and bar chairs by the counter. Bass, Exmoor Gold, Otter Bitter and Skinners Porthleven on handpump and good wines by the glass; you can buy their own jams and chutneys. Off to the left is an airy room with pictures by local artists (for sale), built-in cushioned wall seating, plush stools and a couple of big tables on the dark slate floor. To the other side of the bar is another light room with more settles and farmhouse chairs, attractive blue and white striped cushions and more sailing photographs; darts and board games. As well as benches outside at the front looking down through the trees to the water, there's a series of snug little back terraces with picnic-sets and chairs and tables. Nearby parking is limited unless you arrive early. There is wheelchair access through a side door. The pub is next to the coast-to-coast Portreath to Devoran Mineral Tramway cycle path.

Punch ~ Tenants John and Hannah Calland ~ Real ale ~ Open 11-11 ~ Bar food 12-3, 6-9 ~ Restaurant ~ Children welcome ~ Dogs allowed in bar ~ Wi-fi ~ Quiz Tues winter ~ Bedrooms: £75

HELFORD SW 7526

Shipwrights Arms

(01326) 231235 – www.shipwrightshelford.co.uk
Off B3293 SE of Helston, via Mawgan; TR12 6JX

17th-c waterside inn with seats on terraces, cheerfully decorated bars, friendly service and tasty food

The terraces that drop down from this thatched pub to the water's edge give a lovely view of the beautiful wooded creek (at its best at high tide); seats on various levels make the most of this. Inside, there's quite a nautical theme, with navigation lamps, models of ships, paintings of fishing boats, drawings of fish and shellfish and even the odd figurehead; plenty of blue paintwork and blue patterned wallpaper add to the seaside feel. Painted high-backed dining chairs with attractive seats, leather wall banquettes and scatter cushions on window seats are grouped around wooden tables of varying sizes. Stools line the counter where they keep Harbour Light and Amber and St Austell Tribute on handpump, several wines by the glass and good rums; a winter open fire. There are good surrounding walks – including a long-distance coast path that goes right past the door.

Free house ~ Licensees David and Vicky Harford ~ Real ale ~ Open 11-11 ~ Bar food 12-9 ~ Restaurant ~ Children welcome ~ Dogs welcome ~ Wi-fi ~ Live jazz Sun lunchtime

LOSTWITHIEL

SX1059

Globe

(01208) 872501 – www.globeinn.com
North Street (close to medieval bridge); PL22 0EG

Traditional local with interesting food and drink, friendly staff and suntrap back courtyard

Good, enjoyable food and a friendly atmosphere continue to draw in customers here. The unassuming bar, which is long and narrow, has a mix of pubby tables and seats, local photographs on pale green plank panelling at one end and nice, mainly local prints (for sale) on canary yellow walls above a coal-effect stove at the snug inner end; there's also a small red-walled front alcove. The ornately carved bar counter, with comfortable chrome and leatherette stools, dispenses Sharps Doom Bar, Skinners Betty Stogs and a guest such as Tintagel Arthurs Ale on handpump, 11 reasonably priced wines by the glass, 20 malt whiskies and two local ciders; background music, darts, board games and TV. The sheltered back courtyard is not large but has some attractive and unusual plants, and is a real suntrap (with an extendable awning and outside heaters). You can park in several of the nearby streets or the (free) town car park. The 13th-c church is worth a look and the ancient river bridge, a few metres away, is lovely.

Free house ~ Licensee William Erwin ~ Real ale ~ Open 12-11 (midnight Fri, Sat) ~ Bar food 12-2, 6.30-9 ~ Restaurant ~ Children welcome but no pushchairs in restaurant ~ Dogs allowed in bar ~ Wi-fi ~ Live music Fri, quiz Sun ~ Bedrooms: £75

MYLOR BRIDGE

SW8137

Pandora

(01326) 372678 – www.pandorainn.com
Restronguet Passage: from A39 in Penryn, take turning signposted Mylor Church, Mylor Bridge, Flushing and go straight through Mylor Bridge following Restronguet Passage signs; or from A39 further N, at or near Perranarworthal, take turning signposted Mylor, Restronguet, then follow Restronguet Weir signs, but turn left downhill at Restronguet Passage sign; TR11 5ST

Beautifully placed waterside inn with lots of atmosphere in beamed and flagstoned rooms, and all-day food

You must get to this medieval pub early to bag a seat outside as the idyllic position draws in the crowds on a sunny day, and the seats at the front and on the long floating jetty are snapped up when the doors open. Inside, there's a back cabin bar with pale farmhouse chairs, high-backed settles and a model galleon in a big glass cabinet. Several other rambling, interconnecting rooms have low beams, beautifully polished big flagstones, cosy alcoves, cushioned built-in wall seats and pubby tables and chairs, three large log fires in high hearths (to protect them against tidal floods) and maps, yacht pictures, oars and ships' wheels; church candles help with the lighting. St Austell HSD, Proper Job, Trelawny and Tribute on handpump, 17 wines by the glass and 18 malt whiskies served by friendly, efficient staff. Upstairs, the attractive dining room has exposed oak vaulting, dark tables and chairs on pale oak flooring and large brass bells and lanterns. Because of the pub's popularity, parking is extremely difficult at peak times; wheelchair access.

St Austell ~ Tenant John Milan ~ Real ale ~ Open 10.30am-11pm ~ Bar food 10.30-9.30 ~ Restaurant ~ Children welcome away from bar area ~ Dogs allowed in bar ~ Wi-fi

PENZANCE   SW4730

Turks Head

(01736) 363093 – www.turksheadpenzance.co.uk

At top of main street, by big domed building turn left down Chapel Street; TR18 4AF

Cheerful pub with a good, bustling atmosphere and popular food beer

There's always a lively mix of both regulars and visitors in this well run town pub and a friendly welcome is offered to all. The bar has old flatirons, jugs and so forth hanging from the beams, pottery above the wood-effect panelling, wall seats and tables and a couple of elbow-rests around central pillars; background music and board games. Sharps Doom Bar, Skinners Betty Stogs and guests such as Greene King Abbot and Wadworths 6X on handpump, a dozen wines by the glass and 12 malt whiskies. The suntrap back garden has big urns of flowers. There's been a Turks Head here for over 700 years – though most of the original building was destroyed by a Spanish raiding party in the 16th c.

Punch ~ Lease Jonathan and Helen Gibbard ~ Real ale ~ Open 11.30am-midnight; 12-11 Sun ~ Bar food 12-2.30, 6-10 ~ Restaurant ~ Children welcome ~ Dogs allowed in bar ~ Wi-fi

PERRANUTHNOE   SW5329

Victoria

(01736) 710309 – www.victoriainn-penzance.co.uk

Signed off A394 Penzance–Helston; TR20 9NP

Carefully furnished inn with interesting food, a friendly welcome, local beers and seats in pretty garden; bedrooms

The imaginative food is the main draw to this enthusiastically run, busy inn, but they do keep Sharps Doom Bar and guests from Cornish Crown and Skinners on handpump and over ten wines by the glass. The L-shaped bar has various cosy corners, exposed joists, a woodburning stove and an attractive array of dining chairs around wooden tables on oak flooring. The restaurant is separate; background music and board games. The pub spaniel is called Monty. The pretty tiered garden has seats and tables. The inn is a minute from the South West Coast Path and just over a mile from the beaches of Mount's Bay.

Free house ~ Licensee Nik Boyle ~ Real ale ~ Open 12-11.30; 12-6 Sun ~ Bar food 12-2, 6-9; not Sun evening ~ Restaurant ~ Children welcome ~ Dogs allowed in bar ~ Wi-fi ~ Bedrooms: £75

PHILLEIGH   SW8739

Roseland

(01872) 580254 – www.roselandinn.co.uk

Between A3078 and B3289, NE of St Mawes just E of King Harry Ferry; TR2 5NB

Character bars and back dining room in attractive pub, local ales, good food and seats on the attractive front terrace

This 16th-c pub is just a mile up the road from the King Harry Ferry, and Trelissick Garden (National Trust) is just across the river. The two character bar rooms (one with flagstones, the other carpeted) have farmhouse and other dining chairs and built-in red cushioned seats, a woodburning stove, old photographs, brass spoons and horsebrasses, and some giant beetles and butterflies in glass cases. The tiny lower area is liked by regulars and there's a back restaurant too. Skinners Betty Stogs, Sharps Doom Bar and a guest beer on handpump and several decent wines by the glass; staff are friendly and helpful. There are seats outside on a pretty paved front courtyard.

Punch ~ Tenant Philip Heslip ~ Real ale ~ Open 11-3, 5.30-11; 11-11 Sat; 11-10.30 Sun ~ Bar food 12-2.30, 6-9 ~ Restaurant ~ Children welcome ~ Dogs allowed in bar ~ Wi-fi ~ Folk night first Weds of month

POLKERRIS
SX0952

Rashleigh

(01726) 813991 – www.therashleighinnpolkerris.co.uk
Signposted off A3082 Fowey–St Austell; PL24 2TL

Lovely beachside spot, with heaters on sizeable sun terrace, five real ales and quite a choice of food

The front terrace here has outside heaters, so you can make the most of the wonderful views towards the far side of St Austell and Mevagissey bays, even in cooler weather. The cosy bar has comfortably cushioned chairs around dark wooden tables at the front, and similar furnishings, local photographs and a winter log fire at the back. Otter Bitter, Skinners Betty Stogs, Timothy Taylors Landlord and a guest from Padstow or Rebel on handpump, several wines by the glass, two farm ciders and organic soft drinks. All the tables in the restaurant have a sea view. A fine beach with a restored jetty is just a few steps away and the local section of the South West Coast Path is renowned for its striking scenery. There's plenty of parking in either the pub's own car park or the large village one.

Free house ~ Licensees Jon and Samantha Spode ~ Real ale ~ Open 11-11 ~ Bar food 12-3, 6-9 ~ Restaurant ~ Children welcome ~ Dogs allowed in bar

POLPERRO
SX2050

Blue Peter

(01503) 272743 – www.thebluepeter.co.uk
Quay Road; PL13 2QZ

Friendly pub overlooking harbour with a good mix of customers, fishing paraphernalia, real ales and carefully prepared food

The cosy low-beamed bar in this chatty little harbourside pub has a relaxed atmosphere, traditional furnishings that include a small winged settle and a polished pew, wooden flooring, fishing regalia, photographs and pictures by local artists, lots of candles and a solid wood bar counter. St Austell Tribute and guests from local breweries such as Bays, Cornish Crown and Harbour on handpump served by the friendly, long-serving licensees. One window seat looks down on the harbour, while another looks out past rocks to the sea; families must use the upstairs room. Background music and board games. There are a few seats outside on the terrace and more in an amphitheatre-style area upstairs. The pub gets busy at peak times. Usefully, they have a cash machine (there's no bank in the village).

Free house ~ Licensees Steve and Caroline Steadman ~ Real ale ~ Open 11-11; 12-11 Sun ~ Bar food 12-3, 6-9; all day in summer peak season ~ Restaurant ~ Children in upstairs family room only ~ Dogs allowed in bar ~ Wi-fi ~ Live music Fri and Sat evenings in summer

PORTHLEVEN

SW6225

Ship

(01326) 564204 – www.theshipinncornwall.co.uk
Mount Pleasant Road (harbour) off B3304; TR13 9JS

Friendly harbourside pub with fantastic views, pubby furnishings, real ales and tasty food and seats on terrace

In kind weather there are tables in the terraced garden here that make the most of the fine sea view, and the harbour is interestingly floodlit at night. Both the bustling bar and candlelit dining room share this view and there are open fires in stone fireplaces, quite a mix of chairs and tables on flagstones or bare boards, beer mats and brasses on the ceiling and walls, and various lamps and pennants. Sharps Cornish Coaster and Doom Bar, Skinners Porthleven and Rebel Gold on handpump; background music. They also have a cosy, traditionally furnished and separate function room. Seats in the terraced garden look over the water.

Free house ~ Licensee Oliver Waite ~ Real ale ~ Open 11am-midnight ~ Bar food 12-2.30, 6-9 ~ Well behaved children welcome ~ Dogs welcome ~ Wi-fi ~ Live music monthly

PORTHTOWAN

SW6948

Blue

(01209) 890329 – www.blue-bar.co.uk
Beach Road, East Cliff; car park (fee in season) advised; TR4 8AW

Informal, busy bar by a stunning beach with modern food and wide choice of drinks

Of course, this isn't a traditional pub – it's a bustling bar with a wide mix of cheerful customers who've come hungry and thirsty straight off the wonderful beach next door. They all pile in here throughout the day and the atmosphere is easy and informal; big picture windows look across the terrace to the huge expanse of sand and sea. The front bays have built-in pine seats, while the rest of the large room has wicker and white chairs around pale tables on grey-painted floorboards, cream or orange walls, several bar stools and plenty of standing space around the counter; ceiling fans, some big ferny plants and fairly quiet background music. St Austell Tribute, Sharps Doom Bar and a guest from Skinners on handpump, several wines by the glass, cocktails and shots, and all kinds of coffees, hot chocolates and teas.

Free house ~ Licensees Tara Roberts and Luke Morris ~ Real ale ~ Open 10am-11pm (midnight Fri, Sat); 10am-10.30pm Sun ~ Bar food 10-9 ~ Children welcome ~ Dogs welcome ~ Wi-fi ~ Live music Sat evening

ROCK

SW9375

Mariners

(01208) 863679 – www.themarinersrock.com
Rock Road; PL27 6LD

Modern pub with huge glass windows taking in the estuary views, highly popular food, three real ales and wines by the glass, friendly service and seats on front terrace

To make the most of the lovely view over the Camel estuary there's a front terrace here with lots of seats and tables (people often sit on the wall too), a much coveted small terrace leading from the first-floor restaurant, and huge windows and folding glass doors; it gets packed in warm weather. The bar is light and spacious with contemporary metal chairs and wall seats around pale wooden-topped tables on slate flooring; walls are partly bare stone and partly painted and hung with old black and white photos, modern prints and blackboards listing food and drink items. There's an open kitchen. Atlantic Ale, Sharps Doom Bar and a guest beer on handpump and good wines by the glass; background music and TV. The upstairs restaurant offering robust, seasonal food is similarly furnished and, if anything, the views are even better from here.

Free house ~ Licensee Nathan Outlaw ~ Real ale ~ Open 11am-midnight ~ Bar food 12-9; 12-4.30, 6-9 Sun ~ Children welcome ~ Dogs welcome ~ Wi-fi

ST IVES   SW5441

Queens

(01736) 796468 – www.queenshotelstives.com
High Street; TR26 1RR

Bustling inn just back from the harbour with a spacious bar, open fire, real ales and tasty food; bedrooms

Plenty of regulars and visitors crowd into the spreading bar here to enjoy the local ales and popular food. This open-plan bar has a relaxed atmosphere, all sorts of wooden chairs around scrubbed tables on bare floorboards, tartan banquettes on either side of the Victorian fireplace, a wall of barometers above a leather chesterfield sofa and some brown leather armchairs; fresh flowers and candles on tables and on the mantelpiece above the open fire. Red-painted bar chairs line the white marble-topped counter where they serve St Austell Cornish Best, HSD, Proper Job and Tribute on handpump, 15 wines by the glass, a good choice of gins and rums and farm cider; background music, board games and TV for sports events. The window boxes and hanging baskets are quite a sight in summer.

St Austell ~ Tenant Neythan Hayes ~ Real ale ~ Open 11-11 (10.30 winter) ~ Bar food 12-2.30, 6-9; 12-9 (6 winter) ~ Children welcome ~ Dogs allowed in bar ~ Wi-fi ~ Bedrooms: £79

ST MAWGAN   SW8765

Falcon

(01637) 860225 – www.thefalconinnstmawgan.co.uk
NE of Newquay, off B3276 or A3059; TR8 4EP

Friendly inn with compact, simply furnished bar and dining room, four ales, good food and seats in garden; bedrooms

The hub of the village, this 16th-c pub is a genuinely welcoming place to both loyal regulars and holidaymakers. The bar has a big fireplace with stone bottles to either side (a log fire in winter and fresh flowers in summer), farmhouse chairs and cushioned wheelbacks around an assortment of tables on patterned carpet, antique coaching prints and falcon pictures, and Colchester No 1, Sharps Perfect Storm, Tintagel Harbour Special and a changing guest on handpump; good wines by the glass. The compact stone-floored dining room has similar furnishings. Plenty of picnic-sets (some painted blue) in the pretty garden, a wishing well and a cobbled front courtyard too.

St Austell ~ Managers David Carbis and Sarah Lawrence ~ Real ale ~ Open 11-3, 5.30-11 (midnight Fri); 11am-midnight Sat; 12-11 Sun ~ Bar food 12-2.30, 6-9.30 ~ Restaurant ~ Children welcome away from the bar ~ Dogs allowed in bar ~ Wi-fi ~ Bedrooms: £94

ST MERRYN   SW8874
Cornish Arms
(01841) 532700 – www.rickstein.com/eat-with-us/the-cornish-arms
Churchtown (B3276 towards Padstow); PL28 8ND

**Bustling pub with lots of cheerful customers, bar and dining rooms,
real ales, good pubby food, friendly service and seats outside**

Holidaymakers crowd into this busy roadside pub during peak season – locals
enjoy it more during less busy months. It's well run and friendly, and the main
door leads into a sizeable informal area with a pool table and plenty of cushioned
wall seating; to the left, a light, airy dining room overlooks the terrace. There's
an unusual modern upright woodburner (with tightly packed logs on each side),
photographs of the sea and former games teams, and pale wooden dining chairs
around tables on quarry tiles. This leads to two more linked rooms with ceiling
joists; the first has pubby furniture on huge flagstones, while the end room has more
cushioned wall seating, contemporary seats and tables and parquet flooring. There's
also a new dining room to the back. St Austell Proper Job, Trelawny and Tribute on
handpump, 17 wines by the glass, a farm cider, friendly service, background music,
board games and TV; they hold a beer and mussel festival every March. The window
boxes are pretty and there are picnic-sets on a side terrace – with more on grass.

St Austell ~ Tenant Siebe Richards ~ Real ale ~ Open 11.30-11 ~ Bar food 12-2.30,
5.30-8.30; 12-8 Sun ~ Children welcome ~ Dogs welcome ~ Wi-fi ~ Quiz Sun winter

ST TUDY   SX0676
St Tudy Inn
(01208) 850656 – www.sttudyinn.com
Off A391 near Wadebridge; PL30 3NN

**Refurbished pub with several bars and dining rooms, good wines
by the glass, enjoyable food and seats outside**

Of course, most customers are here to enjoy the marvellous food cooked by the
landlady, but they do keep a good choice of drinks such as Sharps Doom Bar
and a beer named for the pub on handpump, 25 wines by the glass and a couple of
ciders. It's a welcoming and attractive place and the main bar has a leather armchair
beside a log fire in a raised fireplace (fairy lights on the bressumer beam), beer-cask
seats, chairs and cushioned window seats by a mix of tables on floor slates, and
stools against the wooden counter. The dining rooms are relaxed and informal with
dark farmhouse, wheelback and elegant wooden chairs and tables on bare boards
or rugs, a second fireplace, fresh flowers and candlelight; background music. There
are picnic-sets under parasols at the front and more seats in the garden.

Free house ~ Licensee Emily Scott ~ Real ale ~ Open 11am-midnight; 11-5 Sun; closed
Mon ~ Bar food 12-2.30, 6.30-9; not Sun evening ~ Restaurant ~ Children welcome ~
Dogs allowed in bar ~ Wi-fi

TREBURLEY   SX3477
Springer Spaniel
(01579) 370424 – www.thespringerspaniel.co.uk
A388 Callington–Launceston; PL15 9NS

**Cosy, friendly pub with highly popular, first class food, friendly staff
and a genuine welcome for all**

Food is king here (the owner is a former *MasterChef* winner), but this is no restaurant, it's a proper pub with locals and their dogs (they keep a jar of dog biscuits) and a friendly, easy-going atmosphere. The small beamed bar has antlers and a few copper pans on an exposed stone wall above a woodburning stove, books on shelves, pictures of springer spaniels, a rather fine high-backed settle and other country kitchen chairs and tables and old parquet flooring. A little dining room has more bookcases, candles and similar tables and chairs, and stairs lead up to the main restaurant; a second woodburner is set into a slate wall with a stag's head above it. Dartmoor Jail Ale and St Austells Tribute on handpump and ten good wines by the glass (including sparkling); background music. Outside in the small enclosed, paved garden are picnic-sets.

Free house ~ Licensees Anton and Clare Piotrowski ~ Real ale ~ Open 12-11 ~ Bar food 12-3, 6-9; snacks all day weekends and peak season ~ Restaurant ~ Children welcome ~ Dogs allowed in bar

WADEBRIDGE   SW9972
Ship
(01208) 813845 – www.shipinnwadebridge.co.uk
Gonvena Hill, towards Polzeath; PL27 6DF

One of the oldest pubs in town, with beams and open fires, carefully refurbished bars, real ales and good, seasonally changing food

This 16th-c pub was once owned by a shipbuilding family, so it makes sense that it has plenty of nautical memorabilia on the rough whitewashed walls. Seating in the bar area ranges from leather button-back wall banquettes to all sorts of wooden dining chairs, stools and window seats topped with scatter cushions plus flagstone or bare-board flooring, books on shelves, church candles and open fires; background music. High chairs line the counter where attentive staff serve Padstow Pride and Sharps Atlantic and Doom Bar on handpump and 12 wines by the glass (they hold a wine club on the first Tuesday of the month). There are two dining areas, one with high rafters and brass ship lights. The small, sunny decked terrace outside has seats and chairs.

Punch ~ Tenants Rupert and Sarah Wilson ~ Real ale ~ Open 12-2.30, 5-11; 12-10 Sun ~ Bar food 12-2 (3 Sun), 5-9 (9.30 Fri, Sat); no food Sun evening except peak season ~ Children welcome ~ Dogs allowed in bar ~ Wi-fi ~ Folk club last Tues of month

WAINHOUSE CORNER   SX1895
Old Wainhouse
(01840) 230711 – www.oldwainhouseinn.co.uk
A39; EX23 0BA

Cheerful pub, open all day, with friendly staff and a good mix of customers, plenty of seating spaces, real ales and tasty food

As this is the only pub on a 20-mile stretch of the A39 and also close to the South West Coast Path, it gets busy at peak times – best to book a table in advance. The main bar has an easy-going, cheerful atmosphere, an attractive built-in settle, stripped rustic farmhouse chairs and dining chairs around a mix of tables on enormous old flagstones, a large woodburner with stone bottles on the mantelpiece above it, and beams hung with scythes, saws, a horse collar and other tack, spiles, copper pans and brass plates; do note the lovely photograph of a man driving a pig across a bridge. Off here is a simpler room with similar furniture, a pool table and background music. The dining room to the left of the main door has elegant high-backed dining chairs around pale wooden tables, another woodburner and more horse tack. Sharps Cornish Coaster and Doom Bar on handpump and friendly service. Outside, a grass area to one side of the building has picnic-sets.

Enterprise ~ Lease Bryony Self ~ Real ale ~ Open 10am-midnight ~ Bar food 10-9 ~ Restaurant ~ Children welcome ~ Dogs welcome ~ Wi-fi ~ Live music first Sun of month ~ Bedrooms: £95

DOG FRIENDLY HOTELS, INNS AND B&Bs

BOSCASTLE   SX1291

Old Rectory

(01840) 250225 – www.stjuliot.com
St Juliot, Boscastle, Cornwall PL35 0BT

£110; 4 pretty, light and airy rooms. Carefully restored Victorian house (run along the warmly welcoming owners' green policies) where Thomas Hardy met his wife; a comfortable lounge with a winter woodburning stove and french windows opening on to the verandah, a dining room with Hardy memorabilia, and a conservatory for evening meals (by arrangement); delicious breakfasts using their rare-breed pigs for the bacon and sausages, home-grown fruit, own honey and free-range eggs (they have chickens and ducks); three acres of lovely gardens with seats. Dogs allowed in stable bedroom; £10 per stay.

CADGWITH   SW7214

Cadgwith Cove Inn

(01326) 290513 – www.cadgwithcoveinn.com
Cadgwith, Ruan Minor, Helston, Cornwall TR12 7JX

£100; 7 simply furnished rooms overlooking the sea. Bustling local inn at the bottom of a fishing cove village with fine coastal walks in either direction; plainly furnished and cosy front rooms with lots of local photos, cases of naval hat ribands and fancy ropework, ships' shields on beams and a log fire, a back bar with a big colourful fish mural, real ales on handpump, pubby food and breakfasts using their own jams. Dogs allowed in all bedrooms and anywhere in pub; bowl and treats; £10.

CAMELFORD   SX1486

Pendragon Country Hotel

(01840) 261131 – www.pendragoncountryhouse.com
Davidstow, Camelford, Cornwall PL32 9XR

£105; 7 very comfortable, thoughtfully equipped rooms; also 3 self-catering cottages. Recently revamped, former Victorian rectory with charming, helpful young owners, two lounges with antiques, leather chesterfields by open fires, books and board games, an honesty bar, a downstairs games room with a full-size pool table, and seats in the garden; very good evening meals using local produce, fully licensed and smashing breakfasts with home-made bread and preserves; beaches and walks nearby. Dogs allowed in downstairs bedroom, two cottages and one lounge; £5.

CARNE BEACH

SW9038

Nare

(01872) 501279 – www.narehotel.co.uk
Carne Beach, Veryan, Truro, Cornwall TR2 5PF

£380; 37 lovely rooms to suit all tastes – some stylish ones look over the gardens and out to sea. Attractively decorated and furnished hotel run by staff who really care, in magnificent cliff-top position with secluded gardens, outdoor and indoor swimming pools, sauna and hot tub, tennis, croquet, sailboarding and fishing; antiques, fresh flowers and log fires in the airy, spacious day rooms, very good food in two restaurants (one less formal with a more relaxed atmosphere), wonderful breakfasts; there's a safe sandy beach below. Dogs allowed in all bedrooms and gardens; outside kennels; from £16 including chef's special dog meals (free in kennels).

CONSTANTINE

SW7328

Trengilly Wartha

(01326) 340332 – www.trengilly.co.uk
Constantine, Falmouth, Cornwall TR11 5RP

£90; 11 cottagey rooms. Tucked-away inn with six acres of pretty gardens including a large pond, with a sociable, low-beamed main bar with wooden settles and patterned carpet, cricket team photos, real ales, 14 wines by the glass, 60 malt whiskies and a woodburning stove, a bright family conservatory, enjoyable food served by courteous staff in the cosy bistro and smashing breakfasts; resident dog Whisky; nearby walks. Dogs allowed in all bedrooms and bar; £3.

CONSTANTINE BAY

SW8674

Treglos Hotel

(01841) 520727 – www.tregloshotel.com
Constantine Bay, Padstow, Cornwall PL28 8JH

£209; 42 light rooms, some with dramatic coastal views; also 4 self-catering apartments. Quiet and relaxed hotel close to a good sandy beach, and in the same family for over 40 years, with comfortable traditional furnishings in light, airy lounges and bar, open fires, enjoyable food using plenty of local fish and shellfish in attractive restaurant and friendly helpful staff; indoor swimming pool, spa and treatment rooms, games room, sheltered garden, 18-hole golf course and lovely surrounding walks. Closed mid November to February. Dogs allowed in some bedrooms and on lead in grounds; not in public areas; blanket, towel and bowl; £12.

COVERACK

SW7818

Bay Hotel

(01326) 280464 – www.thebayhotel.co.uk
North Corner, Coverack, Helston, Cornwall TR12 6TF

From £180; 14 airy, restful rooms with fine sea views over Coverack Bay. Family-run hotel by a beach on the Lizard Peninsula, with a well stocked cosy bar, a comfortable lounge with an open gas fire and books, very good modern food (delicious local fish and shellfish) in candlelit conservatory/dining room,

tasty cornish breakfasts and afternoon cream teas on the terrace; plenty
of walks and coast path nearby. Dogs allowed in three bedrooms; not
in public rooms; £10.

FALMOUTH   SW7932

Penmere Manor

(01326) 211411 – www.penmere.co.uk
Mongleath Road, Falmouth, Cornwall TR11 4PN

£142; 37 spacious rooms. Quietly set, family-run Georgian manor house in
5 acres of gardens and woodland, with an indoor swimming pool, Jacuzzi,
sauna and gym; a convivial and informal bar, comfortable, relaxing lounge
and sun terrace, friendly staff, and enjoyable food using local produce in
smart restaurant. Closed Christmas week. Dogs allowed in some bedrooms
only; blanket; £10.

FALMOUTH   SW8131

Rosemary

(01326) 314669 – www.therosemary.co.uk
22 Gyllyngvase Terrace, Falmouth, Cornwall TR11 4DL

£90; 10 well equipped, pretty rooms, many looking over the water. Family-run
Edwardian house (designed by England's first female architect) with sea views
and two-minute walk to the beach; helpful, welcoming owners, comfortable
lounge with books and magazines, a small, cosy bar, enjoyable hearty breakfasts
(cream teas and picnics too on request) and seats on sundeck in south-facing
garden. Closed mid December to February. Well behaved dogs allowed in some
bedrooms (not June-September); £5.

GURNARDS HEAD   SW4337

Gurnards Head

(01736) 796928 – www.gurnardshead.co.uk
Near Zennor, St Ives, Cornwall TR26 3DE

£130; 7 comfortable bedrooms, views of the rugged moors or the sea. Civilised,
easy-going inn 500 metres from the Atlantic and surrounded by glorious walks in
dramatic National Trust countryside; bar rooms (and bedrooms) painted in bold,
strong colours, with work by local artists, books and fresh flowers; local real
ales, 14 wines by the glass, a couple of ciders and good creative food; large back
garden with plenty of seats. Sister pub is the Old Coastguard in Mousehole. Dogs
allowed in all bedrooms, bar and snug; bowl and treats.

HELSTON   SW6522

Halzephron

(01326) 240406 – www.halzephron-inn.co.uk
Gunwalloe, Helston, Cornwall TR12 7QB

£94; 2 bedrooms. Well known as a one-time smugglers' haunt, this busy inn
near Gunwalloe fishing cove has an informal, friendly atmosphere; the neatly
kept bar and dining areas have fishing memorabilia, comfortable seating, a warm
winter fire in a woodburning stove, local real ales, several wines by the glass,

41 malt whiskies and tasty pub food; seats outside look across National Trust fields and countryside, Church Cove with its sandy beach is nearby and there are lovely coastal walks in both directions. Dogs allowed in both bedrooms and elsewhere except dining area.

LANLIVERY SX0759

Crown

(01208) 872707 – www.wagtailinns.com
Lanlivery, Bodmin, Cornwall PL30 5BT

£90; 7 rooms, in converted outbuildings. Pretty, white-painted 12th-c inn in tranquil gardens and close to the Eden Project; traditional rambling rooms with pubby furniture on big flagstones, a log fire in the huge fireplace, a lit-up well with a glass top, popular food in the dining conservatory and quite a choice of drinks including local real ales. Dogs allowed in all bedrooms and bar.

LOOE SX2251

Talland Bay Hotel

(01503) 272667 – www.tallandbayhotel.co.uk
Porthallow, Looe, Cornwall PL13 2JB

£200; 20 charming rooms with sea or country views, including 3 cottages. Down a little lane between Looe and Polperro, this restful, partly 16th-c country house has lovely subtropical gardens just above the sea, a comfortable, contemporary sitting room with log fire, a cosy brasserie with outdoor terrace, quite a choice of good, modern food (lots of local fish) in an elegant oak-panelled dining room, and courteous, friendly service; coastal and beach walks. Dogs allowed in most bedrooms and elsewhere except main dining room; welcome pack, bedding and treats; £12.50.

MAWNAN SMITH SW7828

Meudon Hotel

(01326) 250541 – www.meudon.co.uk
Maenporth Road, Mawnan Smith, Falmouth, Cornwall TR11 5HT

£175; 29 newly refurbished rooms, mostly modern in style; also self-catering cottage. Old mansion, with a newer wing, set in beautiful subtropical gardens laid out 200 years ago by RW Fox; lovely views of Falmouth Bay from dining room, comfortable lounge with log fire and fresh flowers, cosy bar, seating outside, helpful staff and enjoyable food; walks in own grounds and along coastal footpath at bottom of garden. Closed December-February. Dogs allowed in some bedrooms, but not public rooms; £12.

MITHIAN SW7450

Rose in Vale Hotel

(01872) 552202 – http://roseinvalehotel.co.uk
Mithian, St Agnes, Cornwall TR5 0QD

£175; 23 well equipped comfortable rooms. Secluded and quietly set Georgian house in ten acres of neatly kept gardens, with comfortable sofas and open fires, a friendly atmosphere and enjoyable modern food in dining room that overlooks the grounds; ponds with ducks, a trout stream and a heated outdoor swimming pool; walks and beaches nearby. Closed November, January. Dogs allowed in some bedrooms and lounge; £7.50.

MORWENSTOW   SS2015
Bush

(01288) 331242 – www.thebushinnmorwenstow.com
Crosstown, Morwenstow, Bude, Cornwall EX23 9SR

£90; 4 rooms with lovely views; self-catering too. This 13th-c pub is near one of the grandest parts of the Cornish coast – super walks and surfing; a busy, characterful bar with real ales, a woodburning stove in a big stone fireplace and lots of horse tack and copper knick-knacks, and airy dining rooms with carefully sourced produce for well liked, all-day food; garden with picnic-sets. Dogs allowed in one bedroom and bar; £6.50.

MOUSEHOLE   SW4726
Old Coastguard

(01736) 731222 – www.oldcoastguardhotel.co.uk
The Parade, Mousehole, Penzance, Cornwall TR19 6PR

£160; 14 comfortable rooms, most with sea views. Lovely setting for this easy-going, carefully refurbished inn, with tropical palms in the garden, a path leading down to rock pools, and a terrace overlooking the sea to St Michael's Mount and the Lizard; boldly coloured walls hung with paintings of sailing boats and local scenes, stripped floorboards and an atmosphere of informal but civilised comfort; the Upper Deck houses the bar and the restaurant (serving impressive food), while the Lower Deck has windows running the length of the building, deep sofas and armchairs, books and games; real ales, wines by the glass and a farm cider; sister pub to the Gurnards Head near Zennor. Dogs allowed in all bedrooms and bar; blanket, bowl, treats and walks leaflet.

MOUSEHOLE   SW4626
Ship

(01736) 731234 – www.shipinnmousehole.co.uk
Harbourside, Mousehole, Penzance, Cornwall TR19 6QX

£120; 8 light bedrooms above the pub or in the cottage next door, some overlooking the water. A friendly harbourside local pub at the heart of a lovely fishing village; opened-up main bar with black beams and panelling, built-in wooden wall benches, sailors' fancy ropework, granite flagstones and a cosy open fire; local real ales and fairly priced pubby food; traffic can be a bit of a nightmare in summer, so it may be best to park at the top of the village and walk down. Dogs allowed in all bedrooms and bar; £10.

MULLION   SW6618
Mullion Cove Hotel

(01326) 240328 – www.mullion-cove.co.uk
Mullion Cove, Helston, Cornwall TR12 7EP

£155; 30 comfortable rooms, many with sea views; also self-catering apartments. Sizeable cliff-top Victorian hotel overlooking fishing cove and harbour with wonderful uninterrupted sea views; several lounges, a convivial bar, genuinely friendly staff, good daily changing food in bistro and restaurant and extensive breakfast choice; seats in garden and solar-heated swimming pool. Dogs allowed in some ground- and first-floor bedrooms and one lounge; welcome pack with helpful information; £7 (free low season).

MULLION   SW6718
Polurrian Bay Hotel

(01326) 240421 – www.polurrianhotel.com
Mullion, Helston, Cornwall TR12 7EN

£195; 41 appealing rooms, some with memorable sea views. White cliff-top hotel in 12 acres of lovely gardens with a path down to the sheltered private cove; comfortable contemporary lounges and bar, good food using fresh local ingredients in airy restaurant (stunning sea views), and enjoyable breakfasts; gym, indoor and outdoor swimming pools, spa treatments, tennis and coastal path walks. Dogs allowed in most bedrooms; blanket and bowl; £15.

PADSTOW   SW9175
St Petroc's Hotel & Bistro

(01841) 532700 – www.rickstein.com/stay/st-petrocs-hotel
New Street, Padstow, Cornwall PL28 8EA

£195; 10 pretty little rooms. Attractive white Georgian hotel (part of the Rick Stein empire) with a stylish lounge looking over a small courtyard, an airy dining room, good food quickly served from a short bistro-type menu (plenty of fish), a sensible wine list and a friendly, informal atmosphere. Dogs allowed in some bedrooms and bar; bowl and big fleece blanket; £20 first night (then £5).

PORT ISAAC   SX0080
Port Gaverne Hotel

(01208) 880244 – www.portgavernehotel.co.uk
Port Gaverne, Port Isaac, Cornwall PL29 3SQ

£150; 15 character rooms (up steep stairs). Bustling early 17th-c inn with a low beamed and flagstoned bar, chatty customers, real ales and log fires, interesting antiques in comfortable lounge, quite a choice of reliably good food in the 'Captain's Cabin' (a little room where everything is shrunk to scale) and restaurant, seats at the front and in the terraced garden, and splendid cliff-top and beach walks. Dogs allowed in all bedrooms and bar, but not dining room; £10.

PORTSCATHO   SW8736
Rosevine

(01872) 580206 – www.rosevine.co.uk
Porthcurnick Beach, Portscatho, Cornwall TR2 5EW

£235; 15 stylish apartments and suites; also self-catering cottage. Imposing house now a charming boutique hotel set above a fine beach with an attractive, semi-tropical garden, a club-like bar with leather armchairs, a relaxing drawing room with sofas placed in front of a woodburning stove, and sunny dining room serving modern food ranging from brunches through tapas to full evening meals; friendly staff; indoor swimming pool and walks all around. Closed November to mid February except Christmas. Dogs allowed in three Slate Rooms; £15.

ST MAWES   SW8432
Hotel Tresanton

(01326) 270055 – www.tresanton.com
Lower Castle Road, St Mawes, Truro, Cornwall TR2 5DR

£360; 30 contemporary rooms, all with individual furnishings and sea views. Hidden away behind a discreet entrance, with elegant terraces (heating for cool weather), a little lower bar (specially for dogs), steps up to the main building and its stylish lounge with very comfortable sofas and armchairs, big bowls of flowers, log fire, daily papers and sophisticated but relaxed atmosphere; good modern food in airy restaurant, a fine wine list and friendly informal service; several boats for hire including the beautiful 48-ft yacht *Pinuccia*. Closed two weeks January. Dogs allowed in four bedrooms and dogs' bar; bed/blanket, bowl and treats; £25.

TREVAUNANCE COVE   SW7251
Driftwood Spars

(01872) 552428 – www.driftwoodspars.com
Trevaunance Cove, St Agnes, Cornwall TR5 0RT

£90; 15 comfortable, attractive rooms, some with sea views. Friendly old inn with plenty of history, just up the road from a beach and its dramatic cove; timbered bars with massive ships' spars, lots of nautical and wreck memorabilia, a woodburning stove, six real ales (including their own brews), good wines by the glass, helpful staff, wholesome pub food and also a seafood bistro; seats in the garden and the coastal footpath passes the door. Dogs allowed in all bedrooms and bar, but not on furniture; £6.

TRURO   SW8345
Alverton

(01872) 276633 – https://thealverton.co.uk
Tregolls Road, Truro, Cornwall TR1 1ZQ

£149; 50 stylish rooms including 9 suites (15 new rooms opened in 2016). Elegant sandstone hotel, formerly a convent, in six acres of pretty grounds and close to the city centre; comfortable public rooms including a great hall, library and former chapel, friendly service and enjoyable food using local, seasonal produce served in the smart restaurant; outdoor terrace with seating. Dogs allowed in all bedrooms; £10.

ISLES OF SCILLY

ST MARTIN'S   SV9116

Karma St Martin's

(01720) 422368 – www.karmastmartins.com
Lower Town, St Martin's, Isles of Scilly TR25 0QW

£330; 30 recently refurbished rooms (including 3 suites), most with fine sea
views. Stone-built hotel in idyllic position on a white sand beach, with stunning
sunsets; comfortable, light and airy split-level bar-lounge with doors opening on
to a terrace, genuinely friendly professional staff, sophisticated food in the main
restaurant (lighter lunches in the bar) and a fine wine list; spa with treatments;
fantastic walks (the island is car-free), boat trips to other islands and good bird-
watching; two resident golden retrievers. Closed October-Easter. Dogs allowed in
most bedrooms and bar; blanket, bowl and treats; £10.

Cumbria

DOG FRIENDLY PUBS

AMBLESIDE   NY3704

Golden Rule

(015394) 32257 – www.goldenrule-ambleside.co.uk
Smithy Brow; follow Kirkstone Pass signpost from A591 on N side of town; LA22 9AS

Simple town local with a cosy, relaxed atmosphere and real ales

This no-frills town local doesn't change at all – which is just how its regular customers like it. The bar area has built-in wall seats around cast-iron-framed tables (one with a local map set into its top), horsebrasses on black beams, assorted pictures on the walls, a welcoming winter fire and a relaxed atmosphere. Robinsons Dizzy Blonde, Double Hop, Hartleys Cumbria Way and XB and White Label Blonde Rye on handpump and Weston's cider; they also offer various teas and good coffee all day. A brass measuring rule hangs above the bar (hence the pub's name). There's also a back room with TV (not much used), a room on the left with darts and a games machine, and another room, down a couple of steps on the right, with lots of seating. The backyard has benches and a covered heated area, and the window boxes are especially colourful. The scotch eggs and pies (if they have them) run out fast.

Robinsons ~ Tenant John Lockley ~ Real ale ~ Open 11am-midnight ~ Children welcome away from bar before 9pm ~ Dogs welcome ~ Wi-fi

AMBLESIDE   NY3703

Wateredge Inn

(015394) 32332 – www.wateredgehotel.co.uk
Borrans Road, off A591; LA22 0EP

Family-run inn by lake with plenty of room both inside and out, six ales on handpump and enjoyable all-day food; comfortable bedrooms

The sizeable garden here is right by Lake Windermere and in warm weather the picnic-sets get snapped up pretty quickly. The modernised bar (originally two 17th-c cottages) has a wide mix of customers, an easy-going, bustling atmosphere, leather tub chairs around wooden tables on flagstones and several different areas leading off with similar furniture, exposed stone or wood-panelled walls and interesting old photographs and paintings. A cosy and much favoured room has beams and timbering, sofas, armchairs and an open fire. The six real ales on handpump served by friendly, cheerful staff come from breweries such as Barngates, Cumberland, Jennings, Theakstons, Tirril and Watermill and they offer 17 wines by the glass, and quite a choice of coffees. Background music and TV. They have their own moorings.

Free house ~ Licensee Derek Cowap ~ Real ale ~ Open 10am (10.30am Sun)-11pm ~ Bar food 12-9 ~ Children welcome ~ Dogs allowed in bar ~ Wi-fi ~ Live music Fri, Sat ~ Bedrooms: £125

BRIGSTEER   SD4889
Wheatsheaf
(015395) 68938 – www.thewheatsheafbrigsteer.co.uk
Off Brigsteer Brow; LA8 8AN

Bustling pub with interestingly furnished and decorated rooms, a good choice of food and drink, and seats outside; luxury bunkhouse bedrooms

The various rooms here have an easy-going, friendly feel and there's plenty of character throughout. The bar has a two-way log fire, carved wooden stools against the counter and Bowness Bay Swan Blonde, Hawkshead Bitter, Thwaites Wainwright and a changing guest beer on handpump, 16 wines by the glass and eight malt whiskies. There's an appealing variety of cushioned dining chairs, carved and boxed settles and window seats set around an array of tables on either flagstones or floorboards, walls with pale-painted woodwork or wallpaper hung with animal and bird sketches, cartoons or interesting clock faces, and the lighting is both old-fashioned and contemporary. Outside there are seats and tables along the front of the building and picnic-sets arranged on raised terracing.

Individual Inns ~ Managers Nicki Higgs and Tom Roberts ~ Real ale ~ Open 10am-11pm ~ Bar food 12-3, 5.30-9; snacks 3-5.30; 12-7.30 Sun ~ Restaurant ~ Children welcome ~ Dogs allowed in bar ~ Wi-fi ~ Bedrooms: £70

BROUGHTON MILLS   SD2190
Blacksmiths Arms
(01229) 716824 – www.theblacksmithsarms.com
Off A593 N of Broughton-in-Furness; LA20 6AX

Friendly little pub with rewarding food, local beers and open fires; fine nearby walks

After a day on the fells, this charming little 18th-c pub is just the place to head for. The four small bars have warm log fires, beams, a relaxed, friendly atmosphere and are simply but attractively decorated with straightforward chairs and tables on ancient slate floors. Three real ales from breweries such as Cross Bay, Strands and Tirril on handpump, ten wines by the glass and summer farm cider; darts, board games and dominoes. The hanging baskets and tubs of flowers in front of the building are very pretty in summer, and there are seats and tables under parasols on the back terrace.

Free house ~ Licensees Mike and Sophie Lane ~ Real ale ~ Open 12-2.30, 5-11; 12-11 Sat, Sun; closed Mon lunchtime ~ Bar food 12-2, 6-9; not Mon ~ Restaurant ~ Children welcome ~ Dogs welcome

CARLETON   NY5329

Cross Keys

(01768) 865588 – www.thecrosskeyspenrith.co.uk
A686, off A66 roundabout at Penrith; CA11 8TP

Friendly refurbished pub with several connected seating areas, real ales and popular food

This well run pub is at its busiest at lunchtime when walkers, cyclists and others crowd in for refreshment. The beamed main bar has a friendly feel, pubby tables and chairs on light wooden floorboards, modern metal wall lights and pictures on bare stone walls, and Tirril 1823 and a guest such as Shepherd Neame Spitfire on handpump. Steps lead down to a small area with high bar stools around a high drinking table and then upstairs to the restaurant: a light, airy room with big windows, large wrought-iron candelabras hanging from the vaulted ceiling, solid pale wooden tables and chairs and doors to a verandah. At the far end of the main bar are yet another couple of small connected bar rooms with darts, games machine, pool, juke box and dominoes; TV and background music. There are fell views from the garden. This is under the same ownership as the Highland Drove in Great Salkeld.

Free house ~ Licensee Paul Newton ~ Real ale ~ Open 12-2.30, 5-1am; 12-2am Sat; 12-1am Sun ~ Bar food 12-2.30, 6-9 (8.30 Sun); 12-2.30, 5.30-9 Fri, Sat ~ Restaurant ~ Children welcome ~ Dogs allowed in bar ~ Wi-fi

CROSTHWAITE   SD4491

Punch Bowl

(015395) 68237 – www.the-punchbowl.co.uk
Village signed off A5074 SE of Windermere; LA8 8HR

Smart dining pub with a proper bar and other elegant rooms, real ales, a fine wine list, impressive food and friendly staff; stylish bedrooms

There's a relaxed and nicely uncluttered feel throughout this civilised inn. The public bar has rafters, a couple of eye-catching rugs on flagstones, bar stools by the slate-topped counter, Barngates Tag Lag and Bowness Bay Swan Blonde on handpump, 16 wines and two sparkling wines by the glass, 15 malt whiskies and local damson gin. To the right are two linked carpeted and beamed rooms with well spaced country pine furniture of varying sizes, including a big refectory table, and walls that are painted in restrained neutral tones with an attractive assortment of prints; winter log fire, woodburning stove, lots of fresh flowers and daily papers. On the left, the wooden-floored restaurant area (also light, airy and attractive) has comfortable high-backed leather dining chairs; background music. Tables and seats on a terrace are stepped into the hillside and overlook the pretty Lyth Valley.

Free house ~ Licensee Richard Rose ~ Real ale ~ Open 12-11 ~ Bar food 12-8.45; 12-4, 5.30-8.45 weekends ~ Restaurant ~ Children welcome ~ Dogs allowed in bar ~ Wi-fi ~ Bedrooms: £130

GREAT SALKELD   NY5536

Highland Drove

(01768) 898349 – www.highlanddroveinnpenrith.co.uk
B6412, off A686 NE of Penrith; CA11 9NA

Bustling place with cheerful customers, good food and fair choice of drinks, and fine views from the upstairs verandah; bedrooms

A father and son team continue to run this enjoyable pub with enthusiasm and friendliness. The spotlessly kept, chatty main bar has sandstone flooring, stone walls, cushioned wheelback chairs around a mix of tables and an open fire in a raised stone fireplace. The downstairs eating area has more cushioned dining chairs around wooden tables on pale wooden floorboards, stone walls and ceiling joists, and a two-way fire in a raised stone fireplace that separates this room from the coffee lounge with its comfortable leather chairs and sofas. There's also an upstairs restaurant – it's best to book to be sure of a table. A beer named for the pub from Eden, Theakstons Lightfoot Bitter and a guest ale on handpump, a dozen wines by the glass and 28 malt whiskies; background music, darts, pool and dominoes. The lovely views over the Eden Valley and the Pennines are best enjoyed from seats on the upstairs verandah; there are also seats on the back terrace. This is under the same ownership as the Cross Keys in Carleton.

Free house ~ Licensees Donald and Paul Newton ~ Real ale ~ Open 12-3, 6-1am; 12-1am Sat; 12-midnight Sun; closed Mon lunchtime ~ Bar food 12-2, 6-9 (8.30 Sun) ~ Restaurant ~ Children welcome ~ Dogs allowed in bar ~ Wi-fi ~ Bedrooms: £80

HAWKSHEAD

NY3501

Drunken Duck

(015394) 36347 – www.drunkenduckinn.co.uk
Barngates; the pub is signposted from B5286 Hawkshead–Ambleside, opposite the Outgate Inn and from north first right after the wooded caravan site; LA22 0NG

Stylish little bar, several restaurant areas, own-brewed beers and bar meals as well as innovative restaurant choices; stunning views and lovely bedrooms

The own-brewed ales in the smart little bar attract walkers at lunchtime (which is when this civilised inn is at its most informal). From their Barngates brewery they offer Cat Nap, Chesters Strong & Ugly, Cracker Ale, Pride of Westmorland, Red Bull Terrier and Tag Lag on handpump and a new own-brew lager called Vienna – as well as 16 wines by the glass from a fine list, 25 malt whiskies and 16 gins. There's an easy-going atmosphere, leather bar stools by the slate-topped counter, leather club chairs, beams and oak floorboards, photographs, coaching prints and hunting pictures on the walls, and horsebrasses and some kentish hop bines as decoration. The three restaurant areas are elegant. Sit at the wooden tables and benches on grass opposite the building for spectacular views across the fells; the numerous spring and summer bulbs are lovely.

Own brew ~ Licensee Steph Barton ~ Real ale ~ Open 11.30-11; 12-10.30 Sun ~ Bar food 12-4, 6.30-9 ~ Restaurant ~ Children welcome ~ Dogs allowed in bar ~ Wi-fi ~ Bedrooms: £105

LEVENS

SD4987

Strickland Arms

(015395) 61010 – www.thestricklandarms.com
4 miles from M6 junction 36, via A590; just off A590, by Sizergh Castle gates; LA8 8DZ

Friendly, open-plan pub with popular food, local ales and a fine setting; seats outside

A s this particularly well run pub is by the entrance to Sizergh Castle (owned by the National Trust and open from April to October, Sunday to Thursday afternoons), it's advisable to book a table in advance. The bar on the right has oriental rugs on flagstones, a log fire, Bowness Bay Swan Blonde, Cross

Bay Halo, Lancaster Amber, Old School Junior and Thwaites Wainwright on handpump, several malt whiskies and nine wines by the glass. On the left are polished boards and another log fire, and throughout there's a nice mix of sturdy country furniture, candles on tables, hunting scenes and other old prints on the walls, curtains in heavy fabric and some staffordshire china ornaments. Two of the dining rooms are upstairs; background music and board games. The flagstoned front terrace has plenty of seats; disabled access and facilities. The pub is part of the Ainscoughs group.

Free house ~ Licensee Nicola Harrison ~ Real ale ~ Open 12-11 (10.30 Sun) ~ Bar food 12-2.30, 6-9; 12-9 Sat; 12-8 Sun ~ Children welcome ~ Dogs welcome ~ Wi-fi

LITTLE LANGDALE   NY3103
Three Shires
(015394) 37215 – www.threeshiresinn.co.uk
From A593 3 miles W of Ambleside take small road signposted The Langdales, Wrynose Pass; then bear left at first fork; LA22 9NZ

Fine valley views from seats on the terrace, local ales and quite a choice of food; comfortable bedrooms

This is a reliably well run and friendly inn. The view from seats on the terrace down over the valley to the partly wooded hills below is stunning; there are more seats on a neat lawn behind the car park, backed by a small oak wood, and award-winning summer hanging baskets. The comfortably extended back bar has green Lakeland stone and homely red patterned wallpaper, stripped timbers and a stripped beam-and-joist ceiling, antique oak carved settles, country kitchen chairs and stools on big dark slate flagstones and cumbrian photographs. The four real ales on handpump come from local breweries such as Bowness Bay, Coniston, Cumbrian Legendary and Hawkshead, and they also have over 50 malt whiskies and a decent wine list. The front restaurant has chunky leather dining chairs around solid tables on wood flooring, wine bottle prints on dark red walls and fresh flowers; a snug leads off here. Darts, TV and board games. The three shires are the historical counties of Cumberland, Westmorland and Lancashire, which meet at the top of nearby Wrynose Pass.

Free house ~ Licensee Ian Stephenson ~ Real ale ~ Open 11-10.30 (11 Fri, Sat); 12-10.30 Sun; closed 3 weeks Jan ~ Bar food 12-2, 6-8.45; snacks in afternoon ~ Restaurant ~ Children welcome ~ Dogs allowed in bar ~ Wi-fi ~ Bedrooms: £118

LOWESWATER   NY1421
Kirkstile Inn
(01900) 85219 – www.kirkstile.com
From B5289 follow signs to Loweswater Lake; OS Sheet 89 map reference 140210; CA13 0RU

Lovely spot for this well run, popular inn with busy bar, own-brewed beers, good food and friendly welcome; bedrooms

This friendly little pub is surrounded by marvellous walks of all levels. Downstairs, the bustling main bar has a cosy atmosphere, thanks to the roaring log fire, low beams and carpeting, comfortably cushioned small settles and pews, partly stripped stone walls, board games and a slate shove-ha'penny board. As well as their own-brewed Cumbrian Legendary Esthwaite, Langdale and Loweswater Gold, they often keep a guest such as Watermill Collie Wobbles on handpump, as well as nine wines by the glass and 20 malt whiskies. The stunning views of the peaks can be enjoyed from picnic-sets on the lawn, from the very attractive covered verandah in front of the building and from the bow windows in one of the rooms off the bar; you might spot a red squirrel. Dogs are allowed only in the bar and not during evening food service.

Own brew ~ Licensee Roger Humphreys ~ Real ale ~ Open 11-11 ~ Bar food 12-2, 6-9; light meals and tea in afternoon ~ Restaurant ~ Children welcome ~ Dogs allowed in bar ~ Bedrooms: £103

NEWBY BRIDGE   SD3686
Swan
(015395) 31681 – www.swanhotel.com
Just off A590; LA12 8NB

Bustling bar in riverside hotel, a fine choice of drinks, bold fabrics and décor and seats on a waterside terrace; comfortable bedrooms

Beside a five-arch bridge on the banks of the River Leven at the southern tip of Lake Windermere, this family-run, extended coaching inn has been offering hospitality to travellers since the 17th c. Its heart remains the bar, where you'll find locals, hotel guests and boating folk all mingling happily. There are low ceilings, cheerful floral print upholstered dining chairs around scrubbed tables on bare floorboards, window seats, a log fire in a little iron fireplace, pictures and railway posters on the pink walls, and stools at the long bar counter. Jennings Cumberland, Cumbrian Legendary Loweswater Gold and a changing guest beer on handpump, served by smart, friendly staff; background music. Towards the back is another log fire with a sofa and upholstered pouffes around a low table, and a similarly furnished further room; the front snug is cosy. Original features mix well with the bold fabrics and wallpaper, fresh flowers, nice old pieces of china and modern artwork – it's all been done with a great deal of thought and care. In the main hotel off to the left is a sizeable restaurant. Plenty of pretty iron-work tables and chairs line the riverside terrace.

Free house ~ Licensee Lindsay Knaggs ~ Real ale ~ Open 10am-11pm (midnight Sat) ~ Bar food 10-9.30 ~ Restaurant ~ Children welcome until 7pm ~ Dogs allowed in bar ~ Wi-fi ~ Bedrooms: £129

RAVENSTONEDALE   NY7204
Kings Head
(015396) 23050 – www.kings-head.com
Pub visible from A685 W of Kirkby Stephen; CA17 4NH

Riverside inn with beamed bar and adjacent dining room, attractive furnishings, three real ales and interesting food; comfortable bedrooms

Nicely opened up inside, this is a civilised but easy-going inn by a bridge over the River Lune. The beamed bar rooms have lovely big flagstones, assorted rugs, a wing chair by a log fire in a raised fireplace, an attractive array of fine wooden chairs and cushioned settles around various tables, a few prints on grey-painted walls and an old yoke above a double-sided woodburner and bread oven. Jennings Cumberland, Tirril Old Faithful and a changing guest on handpump and eight wines by the glass, served by friendly staff; background music and a games room with darts and local photographs. The dining room is similarly furnished, but with some upholstered chairs on stone floors, tartan curtains, fresh flowers and a few prints. There are picnic-sets by the river in a fenced-off area, and plenty of good surrounding walks.

Free house ~ Licensee Leigh O'Donoghue ~ Real ale ~ Open 12-11 (10.30 Sun) ~ Bar food 12-9 ~ Restaurant ~ Children welcome ~ Dogs allowed in bar ~ Wi-fi ~ Bedrooms: £98

STAVELEY   SD4798

Beer Hall at Hawkshead Brewery

(01539) 825260 – www.hawksheadbrewery.co.uk
Staveley Mill Yard, Back Lane; LA8 9LR

Hawkshead Brewery showcase plus a huge choice of bottled beers, brewery memorabilia and knowledgeable staff

They keep the full range of Hawkshead Brewery ales here and from the 14 handpumps there might be Bitter, Brodie's Prime, Cumbrian Five Hop, Dry Stone Stout, Lakeland Gold, Lakeland Lager, Red, Windermere Pale and seasonal beers; regular beer festivals. Also, 40 bottled beers and 56 whiskies with an emphasis on independent producers. It's a spacious and modern glass-fronted building and the main bar is on two levels with the lower level dominated by the stainless-steel fermenting vessels. There are high-backed chairs around light wooden tables, benches beside long tables, nice dark leather sofas around low tables (all on oak floorboards) and a couple of walls are almost entirely covered with artistic photos of barley, hops and the brewing process. You can buy T-shirts, branded glasses and polypins and there are brewery tours. Note that parking can be tricky at peak times.

Own brew ~ Licensee Chris Ramwell ~ Real ale ~ Open 12-6 Mon-Thurs; 12-11 Fri, Sat; 12-8 Sun ~ Bar food 12-3; 12-8.30 Fri, Sat; 12-6 Sun ~ Children welcome ~ Dogs allowed in bar ~ Wi-fi ~ Live music Sun from 5pm

STAVELEY   SD4797

Eagle & Child

(01539) 821320 – www.eaglechildinn.co.uk
Kendal Road; just off A591 Windermere–Kendal; LA8 9LP

Welcoming inn with warming log fires, a good range of local beers and enjoyable food; bedrooms

After a walk along the Dales Way, head here for lunch – though you might find lots of people with the same thought, so it's best to book ahead. The L-shaped flagstoned main area of the bar has a log fire beneath an impressive mantelbeam and plenty of separate parts furnished with pews, banquettes, bow window seats and high-backed dining chairs around polished dark tables. Also, police truncheons and walking sticks, some nice photographs and interesting prints, a delft shelf of bric-a-brac, a few farm tools and another log fire. Cumberland Legendary Loweswater Gold, Yates Bitter and guests from Barngates, Hawkshead and Ulverston on handpump, several wines by the glass, 20 malt whiskies and farm cider; background music, darts and board games. An upstairs barn-themed dining room has its own bar for functions.

There are picnic-sets under cocktail parasols in a sheltered garden by the River Kent, with more on a good-sized back terrace and a second garden behind. This is a lovely spot with more walks that fan out from the recreation ground just across the road.

Free house ~ Licensees Richard and Denise Coleman ~ Real ale ~ Open 11-11; 12-10.30 Sun ~ Bar food 12-2.30, 6-9; 12-9 weekends ~ Restaurant ~ Children welcome ~ Dogs allowed in bar ~ Wi-fi ~ Bedrooms: £85

STONETHWAITE   NY2513

Langstrath

(017687) 77239 – www.thelangstrath.com
Off B5289 S of Derwentwater; CA12 5XG

Nice little place in a lovely spot, popular food with a modern twist, real ales and good wines, and seats outside; bedrooms

Walking from this friendly and civilised small inn is very popular as both the Cumbrian Way and the Coast to Coast path are close by. The neat, simple bar – at its pubbiest at lunchtime – has a welcoming log fire in a big stone fireplace, rustic tables, plain chairs and cushioned wall seats, and walking cartoons and attractive Lakeland mountain photos on its textured white walls. Jennings Cumberland Ale and Cocker Hoop, Keswick Gold and Theakstons Old Peculier on handpump, 30 malt whiskies and several wines by the glass; background music and board games. The restaurant has fine views. Outside, a big sycamore shelters several picnic-sets with views up to Eagle Crag.

Free house ~ Licensees Guy and Jacqui Frazer-Hollins ~ Real ale ~ Open 12-10.30; closed Mon, all Dec, Jan ~ Bar food 12-4, 6-9 ~ Restaurant ~ Children welcome but must be over 10 in bedrooms ~ Dogs allowed in bar ~ Wi-fi ~ Bedrooms: £110

WINSTER   SD4193

Brown Horse

(015394) 43443 – www.thebrownhorseinn.co.uk
A5074 S of Windermere; LA23 3NR

Traditional coaching inn, recently refurbished, with character bar and dining room, own-brewed ales, good food and seats outside; bedrooms

As well as an extraordinary list of 107 gins from all over the world, this refurbished 19th-c coaching inn brews its own Winster Valley ales: Best Bitter, Cartmel Chaser, Dark Horse, Hurdler, Lakes Blonde, Lakes Lager and Old School. Also, several wines by the glass and quite a few malt whiskies. The chatty beamed and flagstoned bar has church pews, a lovely tall settle and mate's chairs around a mix of tables, while the candlelit dining room has a medley of painted and antique chairs and tables, old skis, carpet beaters, hunting horns and antlers. The gents' is upstairs. There are seats outside among flowering tubs, with more on a raised terrace. This is a pretty valley with good walks nearby.

Free house ~ Licensees Karen and Steve Edmondson ~ Real ale ~ Open 11-11 ~ Bar food 12-2, 6-9 ~ Restaurant ~ Children welcome ~ Dogs allowed in bar ~ Wi-fi ~ Bedrooms: £110

YANWATH
NY5128

Gate Inn

(01768) 862386 – www.yanwathgate.co.uk

2.25 miles from M6 junction 40; A66 towards Brough, then right on A6, right on B5320, then follow village signpost; CA10 2LF

Emphasis on imaginative seasonal food but with local beers and thoughtfully chosen wines, a pubby atmosphere and a warm welcome from helpful staff

Plenty of locals do drop in for a drink and a chat, but most customers are here for the excellent food. It remains a civilised and immaculately kept 17th-c pub and the cosy bar of charming antiquity has country pine and dark wood furniture, lots of brasses on beams, church candles on all tables and a woodburning stove in an attractive stone inglenook. Barngates Pale, Hesket Newmarket Red Pike and Yates Bitter on handpump, a dozen or so good wines by the glass, 12 malt whiskies and Weston's Old Rosie cider; staff are courteous and helpful. The restaurant has been refurbished and has oak floors, panelled oak walls and heavy beams; background music. There are new seats on the terrace and in the garden.

Free house ~ Licensees Simon Prior and Caryl Varty ~ Real ale ~ Open 12-midnight ~ Bar food 12-2.30, 6-9 ~ Restaurant ~ Well behaved children welcome ~ Dogs allowed in bar ~ Wi-fi

DOG FRIENDLY HOTELS, INNS AND B&Bs

ALSTON
NY7546

Lovelady Shield Country House Hotel

(01434) 381203 – www.lovelady.co.uk

Nenthead Road, Alston, Cumbria CA9 3LX

£140; 12 rooms; also 3 self-catering cottages. In a lovely setting with the River Nent running along the bottom of the three-acre garden, this handsome country house has a tranquil atmosphere, courteous staff, log fires in the comfortable bar, lounge and library, and delicious modern british food (excellent breakfasts too) in the elegant, formal dining room; fine walks from the door. Dogs allowed in some bedrooms only; treats; £10.

AMBLESIDE
NY3703

Regent Hotel

(015394) 32254 – www.regentlakes.co.uk

Waterhead Bay, Ambleside, Cumbria LA22 0ES

£129; 32 well equipped, contemporary rooms. Family-run hotel opposite a slipway on to Lake Windermere with pretty gardens, a bar/lounge with sofas, a quiet snug with books, a split-level restaurant with good brasserie-style food, marvellous breakfasts and helpful staff; lots to do nearby and plenty of walks. Dogs allowed in ten courtyard bedrooms; bowl; £10.

BARBON

SD6282

Barbon Inn

(015242) 76233 – www.barbon-inn.co.uk
Barbon, Carnforth, Cumbria LA6 2LJ

£99; 9 simple but comfortable rooms. Small, friendly 17th-c village inn in a quiet spot below the fells, with relaxing bar and traditional lounge, open log fires, hearty meals in candlelit dining room and helpful service; lots of good tracks and paths all around. Dogs allowed in some bedrooms and bar; £10.

BASSENTHWAITE LAKE

NY2032

Armathwaite Hall

(017687) 76551 – www.armathwaite-hall.com
Bassenthwaite Lake, Cockermouth, Cumbria CA12 4RE

£205; 46 lovely rooms with views of the lake, gardens or park. Turreted 17th-c mansion in 400 acres of deer park and woodland and with its own wildlife park (not open to dogs), with handsome public rooms, fine panelling, antiques and flowers, log fires in handsome fireplaces, a bustling bar/brasserie with all-day food, good french and english cooking using local seasonal produce in more formal restaurant, a super wine list and helpful staff; well equipped spa with indoor swimming pool, gym, steam room, sauna, outdoor hot tub and treatments, lots of outdoor activities including fishing and shooting and numerous surrounding walks; resident labradors. Dogs allowed in some bedrooms only; bed and treats; £15.

BASSENTHWAITE LAKE

NY1930

Pheasant

(017687) 76234 – www.the-pheasant.co.uk
Bassenthwaite Lake, Cockermouth, Cumbria CA13 9YE

£160; 15 comfortable rooms. Smart hotel with delightfully old-fashioned pubby bar serving real ales and light lunches, plus restful lounges with open fires, antiques, fresh flowers and comfortable armchairs, a front bistro and more formal back restaurant with first class food, and interesting gardens merging into surrounding fellside woodland; lots of walks all around. Dogs allowed in four bedrooms, bar and lounge; £10.

BOUTH

SD3285

White Hart

(01229) 861229 – www.whitehart-lakedistrict.co.uk
Bouth, Ulverston, Cumbria LA12 8JB

£65; 5 comfortable rooms; also self-catering cottage. Cheerful, bustling inn with Lakeland feel, bars with sloping ceilings and floors, old local photos, farm tools, stuffed animals and a collection of long-stemmed clay pipes, two woodburning stoves, six real ales and 25 malt whiskies, and generously served food using local lamb and beef; seats in the garden and fine surrounding walks. Dogs allowed in all bedrooms and public areas except restaurant; £5.

BOWLAND BRIDGE
SD4189
Hare & Hounds
(015395) 68333 – www.hareandhoundsbowlandbridge.co.uk
Bowland Bridge, Grange-over-Sands, Cumbria LA11 6NN

£135; 5 comfortable rooms. Friendly 17th-c inn not far from Lake Windermere and with fine valley views from spacious garden; log fire, daily papers and interesting ales in little bar, appealing furniture and more open fires in other rooms, very good food using meat from local farms, and super breakfasts; seating outside in terrace and garden; resident collie called Murphy. Dogs allowed in three bedrooms and bar; treats and bowl.

BRAMPTON
NY5760
Farlam Hall
(01697) 746234 – www.farlamhall.co.uk
Hallbankgate, Brampton, Cumbria CA8 2NG

£310 including dinner; 12 smart, comfortable rooms; also self-catering cottage. Very civilised, mainly 19th-c country house with log fires in ornate Victorian lounges, excellent attentive service, good country house-style dinner (served at 8pm) in friendly but formal restaurant, marvellous breakfasts and peaceful, spacious grounds with croquet lawn and small pretty lake; plenty of nearby walks. Dogs allowed in all bedrooms (must not left be unattended) and elsewhere except restaurant.

BUTTERMERE
NY1716
Bridge Hotel
(017687) 70252 – www.bridge-hotel.com
Buttermere, Cockermouth, Cumbria CA13 9UZ

£159; 21 comfortable rooms; also 6 self-catering apartments. Surrounded by some of the best steep countryside in the county and run by the same family for 30 years, this friendly hotel has a lounge and a walkers' bar, local ales, open fires, deep armchairs and books in residents' lounge, hearty food in a separate restaurant and an easy-going atmosphere. Dogs allowed in some bedrooms and walkers' bar; £10.

CARTMEL
SD3879
Aynsome Manor
(01539) 536653 – www.aynsomemanorhotel.co.uk
Cartmel, Grange-over-Sands, Cumbria LA11 6HH

£99; 12 attractive rooms. Lovely old manor house, in the same family for 30 years and surrounded by Vale countryside with plenty of surrounding walks; relaxing, homely sitting room with sofas by a log fire, a cosy, well stocked bar, interesting daily changing food in the oak-panelled restaurant, and a warm, friendly atmosphere throughout. Closed January. Dogs allowed in all bedrooms (must not be left unattended), not in public rooms; £6.

CARTMEL   SD3978

Uplands

(01539) 536848 – www.uplandscartmel.co.uk
Haggs Lane, Cartmel, Grange-over-Sands, Cumbria LA11 6HD

£80; 8 pretty rooms. Comfortable Edwardian house in two acres of grounds (plenty of wildlife) with views over to Morecambe Bay; large, attractively decorated lounge, welcoming owners, an informal atmosphere, very good modern food (including light lunches and afternoon teas) in the restaurant and super breakfasts; walks from the front door. Dogs allowed in five bedrooms only; £10.

CARTMEL FELL   SD4189

Masons Arms

(015395) 68486 – www.masonsarmsstrawberrybank.co.uk
Cartmel Fell, Grange-over-Sands, Cumbria LA11 6NW

£85 without breakfast; 5 stylish suites and 2 cottages. Well run pub in an unrivalled setting with wonderful views and good surrounding walks; a beamed and flagstoned main bar with much character and several real ales, other small rooms with Jacobean panelling, oak furniture and an open range, and inventive, enjoyable food in the upstairs dining room; heated and covered terraces with seating. Dogs allowed in two suites, both cottages and bar (after 9pm).

CLIFTON   NY5326

George & Dragon

(01768) 865381 – www.georgeanddragonclifton.co.uk
Clifton, Penrith, Cumbria CA10 2ER

£95; 11 smart rooms. Carefully restored 18th-c coaching inn with attractive bars, leather or farmhouse chairs around wooden tables on flagstones, bright rugs here and there, open fires, sheep and fell pictures on grey and yellow walls, and real ales and wines by the glass; a sizeable restaurant serving imaginative food from the open kitchen and using rare-breed meat from nearby Lowther Estate; resident patterdale terrier, Porter. Dogs allowed in all bedrooms and public areas except restaurant; blanket, treat and walks leaflet; £10.

CONISTON   SD3097

Sun

(015394) 41248 – www.thesunconiston.com
Coniston, Cumbria LA21 8HQ

£84; 8 quiet, comfortable bedrooms. Splendidly sited 16th-c inn, surrounded by dramatic bare fells and with fine views from the terrace and big tree-sheltered garden; cheerful bar with beams, timbers, exposed stone walls, flagstones, old settles and several Donald Campbell photographs (this was his HQ during his final attempt on the world water-speed record) and a good mix of customers – often with their dogs; other rooms include a large side lounge leading into the dining conservatory; fine range of local ales, 20 malt whiskies, well liked food and friendly staff. Dogs allowed in all bedrooms and everywhere except conservatory; £10.

CROOK   SD4395
Wild Boar
(015394) 45225 – www.englishlakes.co.uk
Crook, Windermere, Cumbria LA23 3NF

From £108; 34 individually decorated rooms, some with woodburning stoves
and brass baths. Open-plan rooms with painted beams and timbers, ladderback chairs and leather tub armchairs around dark tables, big log fires, rugs on
floorboards, own-brewed ales and 120 malt whiskies, helpful, friendly service
and interesting bistro-style food using their own smokehouse, and very nice
breakfasts. Dogs allowed in all bedrooms except bridal suite and public areas
except restaurant; bed, bowl and treats; £20.

DERWENTWATER   NY2618
Lodore Falls Hotel
(017687) 77285 – www.lodorefallshotel.co.uk
Borrowdale, Keswick, Cumbria CA12 5UX

£230; 69 rooms with lakeside or fell views. Imposing hotel in 40 acres of
gardens and overlooking Derwentwater and with fantastic walks from the
front door; courteous, friendly staff, comfortable lounges, bar and café with
lake views and open fire, and imaginative food, morning coffee and afternoon
tea; you can hire kayaks, canoes and sailing boats; works starts on a new
extension in 2017. Dogs allowed in some bedrooms and side lounges; bowl
and basket; £10.

ELTERWATER   NY3204
Britannia
(015394) 37210 – http://thebritanniainn.com
Elterwater, Ambleside, Cumbria LA22 9HP

£105; 9 comfortable rooms. Simple, charmingly traditional pub in fine
surroundings close to the central lakes and tracks over the fells; small front
and back bars with coal fires, oak benches and settles, fine selection of ales
and whiskies, a comfortable lounge and a dining room with generously
served, honest food; smashing breakfasts; access to nearby spa with pool,
gym, sauna and steam room. Dogs allowed in all bedrooms and public areas
except dining room.

ENNERDALE BRIDGE   NY0615
Shepherds Arms
(01946) 861249 – www.shepherdsarms.com
Ennerdale, Cleator, Cumbria CA23 3AR

£96; 8 rooms. Set on the popular Coast to Coast path and with wonderful
surrounding walks, this welcoming inn has a convivial bar, a woodburning stove,
a main bar with a coal fire and traditional seats and tables, a conservatory,
cheerful staff, well kept ales and substantial bar food. Dogs allowed in two
bedrooms and bar (until 6pm).

FAR SAWREY

SD3795

Cuckoo Brow

(015394) 43425 – www.cuckoobrow.co.uk
Far Sawrey, Ambleside, Cumbria LA22 0LQ

£99; 14 comfortable rooms. Friendly, attractively renovated hotel well placed at the foot of Claife Heights and surrounded by lovely scenery and walks, with nice wooden tables and chairs on bare boards, open fires and woodburning stoves, local ales and hearty food using the best local produce and good breakfasts; seats outside; resident dog, Poppy. Dogs allowed in all bedrooms and elsewhere as long as well behaved; £10.

GRASMERE

NY3308

Swan

(01539) 435742 – www.macdonaldhotels.co.uk
Keswick Road, Grasmere, Ambleside, Cumbria LA22 9RF

£120; 37 rooms, most with fine views. Smart and friendly 17th-c former coaching inn in beautiful fell-foot surroundings, with beams and winter log fires in inglenooks, comfortable lounges, a walkers' bar, a wide range of enjoyable food in an elegant dining room and seats in an attractive sheltered garden; lovely walks close by. Dogs allowed in 20 bedrooms and public areas except restaurant; £15.

INGS

SD4498

Watermill

(01539) 821309 – www.lakelandpub.co.uk
Ings, Kendal, Cumbria LA8 9PY

£85; 8 comfortable rooms. Bustling, cleverly converted pub with a fantastic range of real ales including their own brews, 40 malt whiskies and scrumpy cider; lively bars with traditional furnishings, open fires and interesting photos and cartoons, and popular food using their own-reared beef; good walking country. Dogs allowed in all bedrooms and main bar; biscuits; £5 (£1 goes to a dog charity).

IREBY

NY2434

Overwater Hall

(017687) 76566 – www.overwaterhall.co.uk
Ireby, Carlisle, Cumbria CA7 1HH

£180; 11 individually decorated rooms with fell or garden views. Turreted Georgian hotel in 18 acres of gardens and woodland – lots of nearby walks too; log fire in traditionally furnished, comfortable lounge, a well stocked, mahogany-panelled bar, good food in cosy dining room, hearty breakfasts, tasty afternoon teas and genuinely helpful, friendly service; two resident chocolate labradors and one cat. Closed two weeks from New Year. Dogs allowed in all bedrooms, bar and one lounge; dog-sitting available.

LANGDALE

NY2806

Old Dungeon Ghyll

(015394) 37272 – www.odg.co.uk
Great Langdale, Ambleside, Cumbria LA22 9JY

£116; 12 rooms. Friendly, simple and cosy walkers' and climbers' inn dramatically surrounded by fells, with wonderful views and terrific walks straight from the front door; half a dozen local ales, cosy residents' lounge and popular food in dining room – best to book for dinner if not a resident. Dogs allowed in all bedrooms and bar; £5.

LORTON

NY1522

New House Farm

07841 159818 – www.newhouse-farm.co.uk
Lorton, Cockermouth, Cumbria CA13 9UU

£120; 5 rooms with wonderful hillside views; also self-catering. Friendly 17th-c guesthouse in 15 acres of grounds, with beams, rafters, flagstones, farming artefacts and open fires in residents' lounges, very good three- or five-course traditional meals served in the dining room and smashing breakfasts with croissants and freshly squeezed orange juice; one resident terrier; lots of walks nearby. Dogs allowed in all bedrooms only (one dog per room); £20.

LUPTON

SD5581

Plough

(015395) 67700 – www.theploughatlupton.co.uk
Cow Brow, Lupton, Carnforth, Cumbria LA6 1PJ

£115; 6 well equipped, lovely rooms. Stylish 18th-c inn with fine walks all around; spreading open-plan rooms with leather sofas and armchairs in front of a big woodburning stove, antique tables and chairs, hunting prints and cartoons, rugs on bare boards, real ales, daily papers and top class food served all day by helpful staff; very good breakfasts. Dogs allowed in five bedrooms and bar.

MUNGRISDALE

NY3630

Mill Inn

(017687) 79632 – www.robinsonsbrewery.com
Mungrisdale, Penrith, Cumbria CA11 0XR

£75; 7 rooms. Friendly 17th-c Lakeland inn with seats in the garden by the water and marvellous surrounding walks; neatly kept bar with old millstone built into the counter, a log fire in a stone fireplace, traditional dark wooden furnishings, hunting pictures, good real ales and tasty food in the separate dining room. Dogs allowed in all bedrooms and bar; £10.

NEAR SAWREY

SD3795

Tower Bank Arms

(015394) 36334 – www.towerbankarms.com
Near Sawrey, Ambleside, Cumbria LA22 0LF

£97; 4 nice rooms. Busy little inn, backing on to Beatrix Potter's farm (the pub features in *The Tale of Jemima Puddle-Duck*), with genuinely welcoming staff in the low-beamed main bar with a slate floor, a log fire, a grandfather clock, fresh flowers and lots of rustic charm; popular food using local produce and particularly good breakfasts. Dogs allowed in all bedrooms and bar.

NEWBIGGIN-ON-LUNE

NY7005

Brownber Hall

(01539) 623208 – www.brownberhall.co.uk
Newbiggin-on-Lune, Kirkby Stephen, Cumbria CA17 4NX

£95; 10 comfortable rooms. Victorian country house (with new owners since spring 2016) in mature grounds with marvellous spreading views, a relaxing atmosphere, many original features in two traditionally furnished sitting rooms; honesty bar, good breakfasts, and inns and restaurants nearby for evening meals; seats on the terrace look over the countryside. Dogs allowed in two bedrooms and sitting rooms; £5 per stay.

RAVENSTONEDALE

NY7204

Black Swan

(015396) 23204 – www.blackswanhotel.com
Ravenstonedale, Kirkby Stephen, Cumbria CA17 4NG

£85; 16 stylish rooms. Smart, neatly kept Victorian hotel with thriving bar and a happy mix of customers; lots of original period features, plush furnishings and fresh flowers, real ales and more than 30 malt whiskies, enjoyable food using seasonal local produce, and tables in sheltered streamside garden; this is serious walking country and they have leaflets describing the routes. Dogs allowed in five bedrooms, bar and lounge; bowl and treats; £10 per stay.

SCALES

NY3426

Scales Farm

(01768) 779660 – www.scalesfarm.com
Scales, Threlkeld, Cumbria CA12 4SY

£86; 6 comfortable, well equipped rooms. Converted 17th-c farmhouse with wide-stretching views and fine walks all around; a friendly welcome, homely beamed lounge with a woodburning stove, traditional english breakfasts in large dining room (good pub next door for evening meals) and packed lunches on request. Dogs allowed in three bedrooms and lounge; £5.

SEATOLLER

NY2413

Seatoller House

(017687) 77218 – www.seatollerhouse.co.uk
Borrowdale, Keswick, Cumbria CA12 5XN

£170 including dinner; 10 spotless, comfortable rooms. Friendly house-party atmosphere in 17th-c house – a guesthouse for over 100 years – with two-acre garden and many walks from the doorstep (the house is at the foot of Honister Pass); comfortable sitting room and library, a bar for hot and cold drinks, snacks and a daily home-made cake, and a dining room with two large tables for the four-course evening meal (7pm) and for breakfasts; no TVs. Closed December-February. Dogs allowed in all bedrooms only.

SKELWITH BRIDGE

NY3403

Skelwith Bridge Hotel

(015394) 32115 – www.skelwithbridgehotel.co.uk
Skelwith Bridge, Ambleside, Cumbria LA22 9NJ

£104; 28 attractive rooms with fine views; self-catering cottage too. Carefully extended 17th-c former farmhouse in quiet countryside (only two miles to Ambleside) with beams and other original features, open fire in comfortable sitting room, antiques and fresh flowers, oak-panelled Library bar and convivial little Talbot bar, and enjoyable food in restaurant overlooking gardens and river. Dogs allowed in all bedrooms (must not be left unattended); £10.

TIRRIL

NY5026

Queens Head

(01768) 863219 – www.queensheadinn.co.uk
Tirril, Penrith, Cumbria CA10 2JF

£80; 7 rooms. Early 18th-c pub (once owned by Wordsworth) a couple of miles from Ullswater with several bars, an open fire in an inglenook fireplace, low beams, black panelling and flagstones, an attractive mix of tables and chairs, and real ales; speciality pies (and other food choices) are served in two dining rooms; they also run the village shop. Dogs allowed in all bedrooms and bars; £5.

ULVERSTON

SD3177

Bay Horse

(01229) 583972 – www.thebayhorsehotel.co.uk
Canal Foot, Ulverston, Cumbria LA12 9EL

£120; 9 rooms, most with bay views. Civilised and nicely placed hotel overlooking Morecambe Bay with a relaxed, smart bar, comfortable seating, an open fire in the handsomely marbled, grey slate fireplace, a huge stone horse's head and lots of horsebrasses, real ales and 16 wines by the glass; interesting lunchtime bar food (conservatory restaurant only in evening); walks on beach. Dogs allowed in all bedrooms and lounge bar; free-£7.

WASDALE HEAD
NY1808

Wasdale Head

(019467) 26229 – www.wasdale.com
Wasdale Head, Seascale, Cumbria CA20 1EX

£118; 10 simple but warmly comfortable rooms, plus 4 more luxurious ones in farmhouse annexe; also 7 self-catering apartments and camping. Old flagstoned and gabled walkers' and climbers' inn in magnificent setting surrounded by steep fells and wonderful walks; civilised day rooms, residents' lounge with books and games, popular home cooking, good wine list, huge breakfasts and cheerfully busy public bar. Dogs allowed in ten bedrooms and public areas except restaurant; biscuits and towels; £10.

WINDERMERE
NY3902

Holbeck Ghyll

(015394) 32375 – www.holbeckghyll.com
Holbeck Lane, Windermere, Cumbria LA23 1LU

£260; 25 opulent rooms including 6 in lodge. Luxurious country house hotel in 15 acres of grounds and close to Lake Windermere – lots of walks; amazing views from two gracious, comfortable lounges, antiques, panelling and log fires, and highly regarded food in oak-panelled restaurant; health spa and tennis. Dogs allowed in lodge bedrooms only; £25 per stay (free if staying two or more nights).

WINDERMERE
SD4095

Linthwaite House

(015394) 88600 – www.linthwaite.com
Crook Road, Windermere, Cumbria LA23 3JA

£224; 30 light rooms decorated in both contemporary and traditional styles. Edwardian house set in 14 acres of grounds with lovely views over Lake Windermere and their own fishing tarn; an attractive, airy conservatory and sunny terrace overlooking the water, a cosy lounge with roaring fire and afternoon teas, a convivial bar, imaginative modern cooking, an eclectic wine list and warmly friendly, helpful service; croquet, lovely walks from the door and plenty to see nearby. Dogs allowed in two rooms; bed, mat, bowl, biscuits and tennis ball; £10 per stay.

WITHERSLACK
SD4482

Derby Arms

(015395) 52207 – www.thederbyarms.co.uk
Witherslack, Grange-over-Sands, Cumbria LA11 6RH

£70; 6 stylish, comfortable rooms. Bustling country inn with sporting prints, big rugs on floorboards, hops strung over the counter where they keep six real ales on handpump, and an open fire, a larger room with local castle prints, another open fire and quite a bit of china, and two further similarly furnished rooms; highly regarded food served by friendly staff; Levens Hall, Sizergh Castle and plenty of good walks nearby. Dogs allowed in all bedrooms and in bar.

Derbyshire

MAP 7

DOG FRIENDLY PUBS

BRASSINGTON   SK2354

Olde Gate

(01629) 540448 – www.oldgateinnbrassington.co.uk
Village signed off B5056 and B5035 NE of Ashbourne; DE4 4HJ

Lovely old interior, candlelit at night, with tasty, fairly priced food, real ales and country garden

Like a step back in time, you almost expect a Dickens character to pop into this unspoilt old pub. It's full of character with mullioned windows, a 17th-c kitchen range with gleaming copper pots, a venerable wall clock, rush-seated old chairs and antique settles (note the ancient one in black solid oak), beams hung with pewter mugs and shelves lined with embossed Doulton stoneware flagons. There's a panelled Georgian room and, to the left of a small hatch-served lobby, a cosy beamed room with stripped panelled settles, scrubbed-top tables and a blazing fire under a huge mantelbeam. Marstons Pedigree and up to three guests on handpump; cribbage, dominoes and cards. The inviting garden has tables that look out to idyllic silvery-walled pastures, and there are benches in the small front yard. The large car park has level access into the pub.

Marstons ~ Lease Melanie Cachart ~ Real ale ~ No credit cards ~ Open 12-3, 5-11; 5-11 Mon; 12-midnight Fri, Sat; 12-11 Sun; closed Mon lunchtime ~ Bar food 12-3, 6-9 ~ Restaurant ~ Well behaved children welcome ~ Dogs allowed in bar ~ Wi-fi

CHELMORTON   SK1170

Church Inn

(01298) 85319 – www.thechurchinn.co.uk
Village signposted off A5270, between A6 and A515 SE of Buxton; keep on up through village towards church; SK17 9SL

Cosy, convivial, traditional inn beautifully set in High Peak walking country; good value food; bedrooms

The hospitable licensees have been here for nearly 20 years now – in fact, the landlady was born in the village. They've created a warmly friendly old inn and our readers enjoy their visits very much, returning regularly. The chatty, low-ceilinged bar has an open fire and is traditionally furnished with built-in cushioned benches and simple chairs around polished cast-iron-framed tables (a couple still with their squeaky sewing treadles). Shelves of books, Tiffany-style lamps and house plants in the curtained windows, atmospheric Dales photographs and prints and a coal-effect stove in the stripped-stone end wall all add a cosy feel. Abbeydale Moonshine, Adnams Southwold, Marstons Pedigree and guests such as Leatherbritches Ashbourne IPA and Thornbridge Jaipur on handpump and nine wines by the glass; darts in a tile-floored games area on the left; TV and board games. The inn is opposite a mainly 18th-c church and is prettily tucked into woodland with fine views over the village and hills beyond from good teak tables on a two-level terrace.

Free house ~ Licensees Julie and Justin Satur ~ Real ale ~ Open 12-3.30, 6-11; 12-11 Sat; 12-11 Sun ~ Bar food 12-2.30, 6-8.30; 12-8.30 Fri-Sun ~ Children welcome ~ Dogs allowed in bar ~ Wi-fi ~ Quiz night Mon 9pm ~ Bedrooms: £80

CHINLEY
SK0382

Old Hall

(01663) 750529 – www.old-hall-inn.co.uk
Village signposted off A6 (very sharp turn) E of New Mills; also off A624 N of Chapel-en-le-Frith; Whitehough Head Lane, off B6062; SK23 6EJ

Fine range of ales and ciders in splendid building with lots to look at and good country food; comfortable bedrooms

Do poke your nose into the dining room here (even if you only want a drink) as it's surprisingly grand, with a great stone chimney soaring into high eaves, refectory tables on a parquet floor, lovely old mullioned windows and a splendid minstrels' gallery. The warm bar – basically four small friendly rooms opened into a single area tucked behind a massive central chimney – contains open fires, broad flagstones, red patterned carpet, sturdy country tables and a couple of long pews and various other seats. Marstons Burton Bitter and guests from breweries such as Marble, Howard Town, Peak, Redwillow, Storm, Thornbridge and Whim on handpump, as well as some interesting lagers on tap, 20 malt whiskies, eight cask ciders, a rare range of bottled ciders and around 50 bottled (mostly belgian) beers. They hold a beer festival with music in September. Also, around a dozen new world wines by the glass and friendly, helpful service. The pretty walled garden has picnic-sets under sycamore trees.

Free house ~ Licensee Daniel Capper ~ Real ale ~ Open 12-midnight ~ Bar food 12-2, 5-9 (9.30 Fri, Sat); 12-7.30 Sun ~ Restaurant ~ Children welcome ~ Dogs allowed in bar ~ Wi-fi ~ Bedrooms: £89

GREAT LONGSTONE
SK1971

Crispin

(01629) 640237 – www.thecrispingreatlongstone.co.uk
Main Street; village signed from A6020, N of Ashford in the Water; DE45 1TZ

Spotless traditional pub with emphasis on good, fairly priced pubby food; good drinks choice too

There's always quite a collection of customers here – walkers, cyclists and families – who've been enjoying the beautiful surrounding countryside; the pub is helpfully open all day. Décor throughout is traditional: brass or copper implements, decorative plates, a photo collage of regulars, horsebrasses on the beams in the red ceiling, cushioned built-in wall benches and upholstered chairs and stools around polished tables on red carpet, and a fire. A corner area is snugly partitioned off and there's a separate, more formal dining room on the right; darts, board games and maybe faint background music. Robinsons Dizzy Blonde, Double Hop, Red Jester, Unicorn and White Label Porter on handpump, Weston's Old Rosie cider and quite a choice of wines and whiskies. There are picnic-sets out in front (one under a heated canopy).

Robinsons ~ Tenant Paul Rowlinson ~ Real ale ~ Open 12-3, 6-midnight; 12-midnight Sat; 12-10.30 Sun ~ Bar food 12-2.30, 6-9 ~ Restaurant ~ Children welcome ~ Dogs welcome ~ Wi-fi

HASSOP   SK2272

Eyre Arms

(01629) 640390 – www.eyrearms.com
B6001 N of Bakewell; DE45 1NS

Comfortable, family-run 17th-c former farmhouse with decent food and beer, and pretty views from the garden

It's especially appealing here in warm weather: the hanging baskets are lovely and the delightful garden (with its gurgling fountain) looks straight out to fine Peak District countryside. Inside, the low-ceilinged beamed rooms are snug and cosy with log fires and traditional furnishings that include cushioned oak settles, comfortable plush chairs, a longcase clock, old pictures and lots of brass and copper. The small public bar has an unusual collection of teapots, as well as Bradfield Farmers Blonde, Peak Swift Nick and a guest such as Brampton Best Bitter on handpump, eight wines by the glass and 20 malt whiskies; darts, board games and background music. The dining room is dominated by a painting of the Eyre coat of arms above the stone fireplace.

Free house ~ Licensees Nick and Lynne Smith ~ Real ale ~ Open 11-3, 6-11; 12-10.30 Sun; closed Mon evenings in winter ~ Bar food 12-2, 6-8.30; 12-3, 6-9 Sat; 12-8 Sun ~ Children welcome ~ Dogs allowed in bar ~ Wi-fi

HAYFIELD   SK0388

Lantern Pike

(01663) 747590 – www.lanternpikeinn.co.uk
Glossop Road (A624 N) at Little Hayfield, just N of Hayfield; SK22 2NG

Relaxing retreat from the surrounding moors of Kinder Scout, with reasonably priced food; bedrooms

It's quite possible that the interior hasn't changed much since the late Tony Warren (the creator of *Coronation Street*) used to visit this homely place; he based his characters on some of the locals. The traditional red plush bar proudly displays photos of the original cast, many of whom were also regulars here. There's a warm fire, an array of antique clocks and a montage of local photographs. Copper Dragon Golden Pippin and Timothy Taylors Landlord on handpump; TV and background music. The tables on the stone-walled terrace look over a big-windowed weaver's house towards Lantern Pike Hill. Dogs may be allowed in at the licensees' discretion, and if clean; good walks in the Peak District National Park.

Enterprise ~ Lease Stella and Tom Cuncliffe ~ Real ale ~ Open 12-3, 5-11; 12-11 Sat, Sun; closed Mon lunchtime ~ Bar food 12-2.30, 5-8.30; all day weekends ~ Restaurant ~ Children welcome ~ Dogs allowed in bar ~ Wi-fi ~ Bedrooms: £72

HAYFIELD

SK0387

Royal Hotel

(01663) 742721 – www.theroyalathayfield.com
Market Street; SK22 2EP

Big, bustling inn with fine panelled rooms, friendly service and thoughtful choice of drinks and food; bedrooms

Very much the centre of local life and with a genuinely pubby feel, this traditional stone building is enjoyed just as much by visitors. The oak-panelled bar and lounge areas have open fires, a fine collection of seats from long settles with pretty scatter cushions through elegant upholstered dining chairs to tub chairs and chesterfields, around an assortment of solid tables on rugs and flagstones; house plants and daily papers. Thwaites Original and guests such as Dark Star Hophead, Happy Valley Kinder Falldown, High Peak Pale Ale and Howard Town Longdendale Lights on handpump (they hold a beer festival in October), nine wines by the glass and three farm ciders; background music, TV and board games. The sunny front terrace is spacious.

Free house ~ Licensees Mark Miller and Lisa Davis ~ Real ale ~ Open 11-11 (11.30 Fri, Sat); 11-10.30 Sun ~ Bar food 12-2.30, 6-8.30; 12-9 Sat; 12-7 Sun ~ Children welcome ~ Dogs welcome ~ Wi-fi ~ Irish folk band most Thurs evenings ~ Bedrooms: £80

HURDLOW

SK1265

Royal Oak

(01298) 83288 – www.peakpub.co.uk
Monyash–Longnor Road, just off A515 S of Buxton; SK17 9QJ

Bustling, carefully renovated pub in rural spot with beamed rooms, friendly staff and tasty, all-day food

Attractively presented food is served all day in this hospitable pub, which is a huge bonus for the walkers, cyclists and horse riders who crowd in. Friendly, helpful staff serve Sharps Doom Bar, Whim Hartington Bitter and a guest or two such as Thornbridge Lord Marples on handpump, seven wines by the glass and two farm ciders. The two-roomed beamed bar has an open fire in a stone fireplace, lots of copper kettles, bed warming pans, horsebrasses and country pictures, cushioned wheelback chairs and wall settles around dark tables, and stools against the counter; background music. The attractive dining room has country dining chairs, wheelbacks, a cushioned pine settle in one corner on bare floorboards, pretty curtains and another open fire. For large groups, there's also a flagstoned cellar room with benches on either side of long tables. The terraced garden has plenty of seats and picnic-sets on the grass. The self-catering barn with bunk bedrooms and the campsite are both very popular.

Free house ~ Licensee Paul White ~ Real ale ~ Open 10am-11pm; 8.30am-midnight Sat; 8.30am-11pm Sun ~ Bar food 10-9 ~ Children welcome ~ Dogs welcome ~ Wi-fi

INGLEBY

SK3427

John Thompson

(01332) 862469 – www.johnthompsoninn.com
NW of Melbourne; turn off A514 at Swarkestone Bridge or in Stanton by Bridge; can also be reached from Ticknall (or from Repton on B5008); DE73 7HW

Own-brew pub that strikes the right balance between attentive service, roomy comfort and good value lunchtime food

This is the longest established microbrewery in the country. The John Thompson brews launched in 1977 and friendly staff now serve JTS XXX, Rich Porter, St Nicks and Summer Gold. The simple but comfortable and immaculately kept modernised lounge has ceiling joists, some old oak settles, button-back leather seats, sturdy oak tables, antique prints and paintings and a log-effect gas fire; background music. A couple of smaller, cosier rooms open off; piano, games machine, board games, darts, TV, and pool in the conservatory. There are lots of tables by flower beds on the neat lawns or you can sit on the partly covered terrace, surrounded by pretty countryside. Breakfast is left in your fridge if you stay in one of the self-catering chalet lodges. Dogs are allowed in the conservatory.

Own brew ~ Licensee Nick Thompson ~ Real ale ~ Open 11.30-2.30, 6-10 (11 Fri); 11.30-11 Sat; 12-10.30 Sun; evening opening 6.30 in winter; closed Mon except bank holidays ~ Bar food 12-2 ~ Restaurant ~ Children until 9pm ~ Dogs allowed in bar ~ Wi-fi

KIRK IRETON   SK2650

Barley Mow

(01335) 370306
Village signed off B5023 S of Wirksworth; DE6 3JP

Welcoming old inn that focuses on real ale and conversation; bedrooms

Once you've found this quite unspoilt and unchanging mid 18th-c pub, you won't want to leave – especially given the genuine welcome you'll get from the long-serving, kindly landlady, who's been here 40 years. The small main bar is relaxed and pubby with chatty locals, a roaring coal fire, antique settles on tiles or built into panelling, four slate-topped tables and shuttered mullioned windows. Another room has built-in cushioned pews on oak parquet and a small woodburning stove; a third has more pews, low beams and big landscape prints. In casks behind a modest wooden counter are five well kept ales from breweries such as Abbeydale, Blue Monkey, Burton Bridge, Peak, Storm and Whim; french wines and farm cider too. There are also two pub dogs. Outside you'll find a good-sized garden, a couple of benches at the front and a shop in what used to be the stable. This hilltop village is very pretty and within walking distance of Carsington Water. The four bedrooms are comfortable and breakfasts good; there are also decent evening meals (no choice) for overnight guests. Dogs may be allowed in bedrooms at the owners' discretion, but not at breakfast.

Free house ~ Licensee Mary Short ~ Real ale ~ No credit cards ~ Open 12-2, 7-11 (10.30 Sun) ~ Bar food lunchtime rolls only ~ Well behaved, supervised children lunchtime only ~ Dogs allowed in bar ~ Bedrooms: £65

OLD BRAMPTON   SK3171

Fox & Goose

(01246) 566335 ~ www.thefoxandgooseinn.com
Off A619 Chesterfield–Baslow at Wadshelf; S42 7JJ

Fine panoramic views for bustling pub with a restful bar, inventive food in light and airy restaurant, helpful staff and seats outside

It's believed that there was a resting place here 500 years ago on the old London–Manchester road, and this carefully restored pub still welcomes travellers today – but in much more comfort and style. The character beamed bar has a woodburning stove in a big stone fireplace, mate's chairs and button-back wall seating surrounding a mix of wooden tables on large flagstones, and Bradwell Farmers Blonde and Peak Bakewell Best Bitter and Chatsworth

Gold on handpump and a dozen wines by the glass served by friendly staff. A small snug leads off with heavy beams, button-back wall seats, beige carpeting and a small fireplace, and there's also a dining room with double-sided plush banquette seating. If eating, most customers head for the airy Orangery restaurant with contemporary high-backed plush chairs around polished tables and lovely panoramic views through big picture windows. Outside, there are plenty of seats and tables under parasols on a terrace and decked area, and picnic-sets on gravel.

Free house ~ Licensee Craig Lynch ~ Real ale ~ Open 12-9; 12-11 Sat ~ Bar food 12-3, 5-9; 12-9 Fri, Sat; 12-6 Sun; not Mon Jan, Feb ~ Restaurant ~ Children welcome ~ Dogs allowed in bar ~ Wi-fi ~ Live music Sat evening

STANTON IN PEAK   SK2364
Flying Childers

(01629) 636333 – www.flyingchilders.com
Village signposted from B6056 S of Bakewell; Main Road; DE4 2LW

Top notch beer and inexpensive simple bar lunches in a warm-hearted, unspoilt pub – a delight

In a beautiful steep stone village, this cottagey pub is named after an unbeatable racehorse of the early 18th c. The friendly landlord keeps Wells Bombardier and a couple of guests from breweries such as Abbeydale and Storm on handpump, and several wines by the glass. The best room in which to enjoy them is the snug little right-hand bar, virtually built for chat with its dark beam-and-plank ceiling, dark wall settles, single pew, plain tables, a hot coal and log fire, a few team photographs, dominoes and cribbage; background music. There's a bigger, equally unpretentious bar on the right. Simple lunchtime-only food cooked by the landlady includes filled rolls and toasties, home-made soups and weekend dishes such as liver and bacon, casseroles and local sausages. As well as seats out in front, there are picnic-sets in the well tended back garden. The surrounding walks are very fine and both walkers and their dogs are warmly welcomed; they keep doggie treats behind the bar.

Free house ~ Licensees Stuart and Mandy Redfern ~ Real ale ~ No credit cards ~ Open 12-2 (3 weekends), 7-11; closed Mon and Tues lunchtimes ~ Bar food 12-2 ~ Children in lounge bar only ~ Dogs allowed in bar ~ Live acoustic music and quiz nights

DOG FRIENDLY HOTELS, INNS AND B&Bs

ASHBOURNE   SK1746
Callow Hall

(01335) 300900 – www.callowhall.co.uk
Mappleton Road, Ashbourne, Derbyshire DE6 2AA

£210; 16 lovely, individually furnished rooms. Quietly smart and friendly Victorian mansion up a long drive through 35 acres of grounds and surrounded by marvellous countryside walks; heavy drapes, antiques, open fires and fresh flowers, plenty of original features, a comfortable drawing room and informal bar, extremely good modern food in the elegant restaurant, delicious breakfasts and kind staff. Dogs allowed in two bedrooms, but not in public areas; £25 per stay.

ASHOVER SK3462

Old Poets Corner

(01246) 590888 – www.oldpoets.co.uk
Butts Road, Ashover, Chesterfield, Derbyshire S45 0EW

£75; 5 attractive rooms; also self-catering cottage. Characterful village pub with enthusiastic licensees and cosy lived-in feel in friendly bar, three roaring fires, lots of knick-knacks and hops, and a pile of board games by the piano; ten interesting real ales (some own-brewed), a dozen each of farm ciders and fruit wines, and 20 malt whiskies; generous helpings of honest food; newspapers and vintage comics in smaller room, regular live acoustic, folk and blues music, quiz nights, morris dancers, and beer festivals in March and October; miles of walks from doorstep; resident cocker spaniels, Rosy and Lilly, and Ruby the brewery cat. Dogs allowed in bedrooms and bar, but not main dining room; £5.

BEELEY SK2667

Devonshire Arms

(01629) 733259 – www.devonshirebeeley.co.uk
The Beeches, Beeley, Matlock, Derbyshire DE4 2NR

£179; 14 stylishly comfortable rooms. Handsome stone inn on the fringes of the Chatsworth Estate; various bar rooms with contemporary colours contrasting well with attractive traditional furnishings, lots of prints and floral arrangements, black beams and flagstones, log burners, six real ales and well chosen wines, and inventive food in modern brasserie using seasonal produce from the Estate. Dogs allowed in four bedrooms and in bar, not restaurant; £10.

BIGGIN-BY-HARTINGTON SK1559

Biggin Hall

(01298) 84451 – www.bigginhall.co.uk
Biggin-by-Hartington, Buxton, Derbyshire SK17 0DH

£105; 21 spacious rooms with antiques, some in converted 18th-c stone courtyard building and in bothy. Cheerfully run 17th-c house in eight acres of quiet grounds with a very relaxed atmosphere, two comfortable sitting rooms, one with a library, the other with a woodburning stove in the inglenook fireplace, and an attractive dining room serving interesting country house-style food using local and free-range produce; two resident collies, one cat, geese, chickens and horses; plenty of trails and dales to walk. Dogs allowed in courtyard and bothy bedrooms, but not public areas.

GRINDLEFORD SK2478

Maynard

(01433) 630321 – www.themaynard.co.uk
Main Road, Nether Padley, Grindleford, Hope Valley, Derbyshire S32 2HE

£134; 10 rooms. Comfortable hotel with log fire and good Peak District views from the first-floor lounge, a welcoming bar, interesting modern food in the smart restaurant, generous breakfasts, afternoon cream teas and particularly attentive service; walks in the garden and nearby Padley Gorge. Dogs allowed in some bedrooms, bar and lounge; £10.

HATHERSAGE

SK2380

Plough

(01433) 650319 – www.theploughinn-hathersage.co.uk
Leadmill Bridge, Hathersage, Hope Valley, Derbyshire S32 1BA

£105; 6 rooms in converted barn. Immaculately kept old dining pub with traditional dark wooden tables and chairs on tartan and oriental patterned carpets, a big log fire and a woodburner, decorative plates and paintings of local scenes, a fine choice of drinks, enterprising food and friendly staff; the nine acres of gardens slope down to the River Derwent and the inn is usefully placed for exploring the Peak District. Dogs allowed in all bedrooms and anywhere in the pub; £15.

LADYBOWER RESERVOIR

SK2084

Yorkshire Bridge

(01433) 651361 – www.yorkshire-bridge.co.uk
Ashopton Road, Bamford, Derbyshire S33 0AZ

£96; 14 rooms. A short stroll from the Ladybower Dam and with wonderful walks from the front door, this friendly, family-run place has a cosy bar with red walls, a woodburning stove, tankards hanging from beams, china plates, photos, paintings and horsebrasses, plus several other rooms including a light and airy garden room with fine valley views; amiable staff, local real ales and tasty pubby food. Dogs allowed in some bedrooms, but not in the bar at mealtimes; £10.

MATLOCK BATH

SK2958

Hodgkinsons Hotel

(01629) 582170 – www.hodgkinsons-hotel.co.uk
150 South Parade, Matlock Bath, Matlock, Derbyshire DE4 3NR

£105; 8 comfortable rooms with fine views (the ones at the back are the quietest). Dating from 1770 and keeping many original features, this warmly friendly hotel is traditionally furnished and has an open fire, portraits and figurines in the lounge, a good choice of drinks in the small bar, and good, modern cooking and excellent breakfasts in the restaurant; this is a pretty village with fine surrounding walks. Dogs allowed in three bedrooms, but not in bar or restaurant; bedding, bowl; £10.

MONSAL HEAD

SK1871

Monsal Head Hotel

(01629) 640250 – www.monsalhead.com
Monsal Head, Buxton, Derbyshire DE45 1NL

£110; 7 good rooms, some with outstanding views. Comfortable and enjoyable small hotel in marvellous setting high above the River Wye, with a horsey theme in the little bar (converted from old stables), enjoyable food using seasonal produce in popular restaurant, open fires, well kept real ales and good service; resident dog; lots of trails and walks from the hotel. Dogs allowed in some bedrooms and bar, not restaurant; £10.

OVER HADDON

SK2066

Lathkil Hotel

(01629) 812501 – www.lathkil.co.uk

School Lane, Over Haddon, Bakewell, Derbyshire DE45 1JE

£90; 4 rooms. Comfortable traditional inn popular with cyclists and walkers, with stunning views and plenty of surrounding walks; woodburning stove in carved fireplace, old-fashioned settles and upholstered chairs, a delft shelf of plates, and some original prints and photos; well kept real ales served in airy bar, plus a beer garden and a sunny, spacious dining area that doubles as an evening restaurant serving good, popular food. Dogs allowed in two bedrooms and bar; £10.

ROWSLEY

SK2565

Peacock at Rowsley

(01629) 733518 – www.thepeacockatrowsley.com

Rowsley, Matlock, Derbyshire DE4 2EB

£270; 15 comfortable rooms. Smart 17th-c country-house stone hotel by rivers Derwent and Wye (private fishing in season), with neat gardens (where dogs may walk) and close to the moors; friendly staff, an interesting and pleasant old-fashioned bar, a spacious and comfortable lounge, and very popular restaurant using meat from Haddon Estate. Closed three weeks January. Dogs allowed in some bedrooms, not public areas; £10.

Devon

MAP 1

DOG FRIENDLY PUBS

BRAMPFORD SPEKE
SX9298

Lazy Toad

(01392) 841591 ~ www.thelazytoadinn.co.uk
Off A377 N of Exeter; EX5 5DP

Well run dining pub in pretty village with particularly good food, real ales, friendly service and pretty garden

The friendly licensees here work hard to ensure that both drinkers and diners enjoy this 18th-c inn. The interconnected bar rooms have beams, standing timbers and slate floors, a comfortable sofa by an open log fire and cushioned wall settles and high-backed wooden dining chairs around a mix of tables; the cream-painted brick walls are hung with lots of pictures. Hanlons Yellowhammer, Otter Bitter and St Austell Tribute on handpump and several wines by the glass are served by attentive staff; the irish terrier is called Rufus. The courtyard (once used by the local farrier and wheelwright) has green-painted picnic-sets, with more in the walled garden. It's worth wandering around this charming village of thatched cottages and there are fine walks beside the River Exe and on the Exe Valley Way and Devonshire Heartland Way.

Free house ~ Licensees Harriet and Mike Daly ~ Real ale ~ Open 12-3, 6-11; 12-4 Sun; closed Sun evening, Mon ~ Bar food 12-2, 6.30-9; 12-2.30 Sun ~ Children welcome ~ Dogs allowed in bar ~ Wi-fi

BUCKLAND MONACHORUM
SX4968

Drake Manor

(01822) 853892 ~ www.drakemanorinn.co.uk
Off A386 via Crapstone, just S of Yelverton roundabout; PL20 7NA

Nice little village pub with snug rooms, popular food, quite a choice of drinks and pretty back garden; bedrooms

This is a charming little pub and the long-serving landlady offers a genuine welcome to both visitors and regulars. The heavily beamed public bar on the left has a chatty, easy-going feel, brocade-cushioned wall seats, prints of the village from 1905 onwards, horse tack and a few ship badges and a woodburning stove in a very big stone fireplace; a small door leads to a low-beamed cubbyhole. The snug Drakes Bar has beams hung with tiny cups and big brass keys, a woodburning stove in another stone fireplace, horsebrasses and stirrups, and a mix of seats and tables (note the fine stripped-pine high-backed settle with hood).

On the right is a small beamed dining room with settles and tables on flagstones. Darts, euchre and board games. Dartmoor Jail Ale, Otter Amber and Sharps Doom Bar on handpump, ten wines by the glass, 15 malt whiskies and apple juice using apples from the village. There are picnic-sets in the prettily planted and sheltered back garden and the front floral displays are much admired; morris men perform regularly in summer. Buckland Abbey (National Trust) is close by.

Punch ~ Lease Mandy Robinson ~ Real ale ~ Open 11.30-2.30, 6.30-11; 11.30-11.30 Fri, Sat; 12-11 Sun ~ Bar food 12-2 (2.30 Sun), 6.30-9.30; 11.30-2.30, 6.30-10 Fri, Sat ~ Restaurant ~ Children allowed in restaurant and area off main bar ~ Dogs allowed in bar ~ Wi-fi ~ Bedrooms: £90

COCKWOOD   SX9780

Anchor

(01626) 890203 – www.anchorinncockwood.com
Off, but visible from, A379 Exeter–Torbay, after Starcross; EX6 8RA

Busy dining pub specialising in seafood (other choices available), with up to six real ales

Even in midwinter, this ex-seamen's mission remains immensely popular, and you must arrive early to be sure of a table – and even a parking space. It's in a fine spot fronting the little harbour with its bobbing boats, swans and ducks, and tables on a sheltered verandah overlook the water. As well as an extension made up of mainly reclaimed timber and decorated with over 300 ship emblems, brass and copper lamps and nautical knick-knacks, there are several small, low-ceilinged, rambling rooms with black panelling and good-sized tables in various nooks; the snug has a cheerful winter coal fire. Otter Ale, St Austell Tribute and Tintagel Castle Gold plus a couple of guests such as Caledonian Deuchars IPA and Exeter Avocet on handpump (beer festivals at Easter and Halloween), eight wines by the glass and 40 malt whiskies; background music, darts, cards and board games.

Heavitree ~ Lease Malcolm and Katherine Protheroe, Scott Hellier ~ Real ale ~ Open 11-11; 11.30-10.30 Sun ~ Bar food 12-9 (10 Fri, Sat) ~ Restaurant ~ Children welcome if seated and away from bar ~ Dogs allowed in bar

COLEFORD   SS7701

New Inn

(01363) 84242 – www.thenewinncoleford.co.uk
Just off A377 Crediton–Barnstaple; EX17 5BZ

Ancient thatched inn with interestingly furnished areas, well liked food and real ales and welcoming licensees; bedrooms

At 600 years old, this warmly friendly place is one of the oldest 'new' inns in the country. The U-shaped building has the servery in the 'angle' with interestingly furnished areas leading off it: ancient and modern settles, cushioned stone wall seats, some character tables (a pheasant worked into the grain of one) and carved dressers and chests. Also, paraffin lamps, antique prints on the white walls, landscape-decorated plates on one beam and pewter tankards on another. Captain, the chatty parrot, may greet you with a 'hello' or even a 'goodbye'. Otter Ale and Sharps Doom Bar on handpump, local cider, 15 wines by the glass and a dozen malt whiskies; background music, darts and board games. There are chairs and tables on decking beneath a pruned willow tree by the babbling stream, and more in a covered dining area.

Free house ~ Licensees Carole and George Cowie ~ Real ale ~ Open 12-3, 6-11 (10.30 Sun) ~ Bar food 12-2, 6.30-9.30 ~ Restaurant ~ Children welcome ~ Dogs allowed in bar ~ Wi-fi ~ Monthly quiz, summer hog roasts and bi-annual sea shanty singers ~ Bedrooms: £89

DALWOOD

ST2400

Tuckers Arms

(01404) 881342 – www.thetuckersarms.co.uk

Village signposted off A35 Axminster–Honiton; keep on past village; EX13 7EG

13th-c thatched inn with friendly, hard-working licensees, real ales and interesting bar food

A lovely sight in summer with colourful window boxes, hanging baskets and tubs, this pretty thatched longhouse is reached down narrow high-hedged lanes in hilly pasture country. The beamed and flagstoned bar has a bustling, friendly atmosphere, traditional furnishings including assorted dining chairs, window seats and wall settles, and a log fire in an inglenook fireplace with numerous horsebrasses on the wall above. The back bar has an enormous collection of miniature bottles and there's also a more formal dining room; lots of copper implements and platters. Branscombe Vale Branoc and Otter Bitter and Amber on handpump, several wines by the glass and up to 20 malt whiskies; background music and a double skittle alley. There are seats in the garden. Apart from the church, this is the oldest building in the parish.

Free house ~ Licensee Tracey Pearson ~ Real ale ~ Open 11.30-3, 6.30-11.30 ~ Bar food 12-2, 6.30-9 ~ Restaurant ~ Well behaved children in restaurant ~ Dogs allowed in bar ~ Wi-fi ~ Bedrooms: £69.50

DODDISCOMBSLEIGH

SX8586

Nobody Inn

(01647) 252394 – www.nobodyinn.co.uk

Off B3193; EX6 7PS

Busy old pub with plenty of character, a fine range of drinks, well liked bar food and friendly staff; bedrooms

In summer, try to bag one of the picnic-sets in the pretty garden with views of the surrounding wooded hill pastures. Inside, the beamed lounge bar of two character rooms contains handsomely carved antique settles, windsor and wheelback chairs, all sorts of wooden tables, guns and hunting prints in a snug area by one of the big inglenook fireplaces, and fresh flowers; board games. An extraordinary range of drinks includes a beer named for the pub from Branscombe Vale and two changing guests such as Bays Topsail and Piddle Martyrs Relief on handpump, 30 wines by the glass from a list of 200, 270 malt whiskies and three farm ciders. The restaurant is more formal. Do visit the local church, which has some of the best medieval stained glass in the west country.

Free house ~ Licensee Susan Burdge ~ Real ale ~ Open 11-11; 12-10.30 Sun ~ Bar food 12-2.30, 6-9 (9.30 Fri, Sat); 12-3, 6-9 Sun ~ Restaurant ~ Children welcome away from main bar; no under-5s in restaurant ~ Dogs allowed in bar ~ Wi-fi ~ Bedrooms: £99

EXETER   SX9192

Fat Pig

(01392) 437217 – www.fatpig-exeter.co.uk
John Street; EX1 1BL

**Lively pub with own-brew beers, home-distilled spirits, big-flavoured
food and a buoyant atmosphere**

Run with enthusiasm and with a genuine, cheerful welcome to all, this
renovated Victorian pub has hit the ground running. They brew their own
beers, have a newly opened distillery and only use local produce for their
enjoyable, hearty food. The big-windowed bar is simply furnished: elegant stools
against a tiled counter, more stools and long cushioned pews by sturdy pale
wooden tables on bare boards, an open fire in a pretty fireplace, blackboards
listing food choices and lots of mirrors. There's also a red-painted and red quarry-
tiled conservatory with a happy jumble of hops and house plants, books and old
stone bottles on shelves, more mirrors, and long benches and settles scattered
around rustic tables. They source their rare-breed meat from nearby farms, shoot
local game and make their own sausages, black pudding and dry-cured ham,
and their smokehouse is put to good use. Fat Pig John Street Ale, Pigmalion and
Steam Hammer on handpump, good wines by the glass, around 100 malt whiskies
and their Exeter Distillery gins (they have three), vodka and apple pie moonshine.

Free house ~ Licensee Paul Timewell ~ Real ale ~ Open 5-11; 4-11.30 Fri; 12-11 Sat; 12-6
Sun ~ Bar food 5-9 (10 Fri); 12-10 Sat; 12-4 Sun ~ Restaurant ~ Children allowed until 6pm
~ Dogs welcome ~ Wi-fi

EXETER   SX9293

Rusty Bike

(01392) 214440 – www.rustybike-exeter.co.uk
Howell Road; EX4 4LZ

**Bustling, quirky pub tucked away in a backstreet, with ales from
own-brew sister pub, hearty food and lively atmosphere**

Although only open from 5pm (except on Sundays when it's open midday to
7pm), this lively and interesting place draws in customers of all ages, keen
to enjoy the good food (which uses carefully sourced and very local produce),
thoughtful choice of drinks and regular events. The large open-plan bar has
bench seating, long wall pews and church chairs around a medley of tables on
stripped boards, big modern art pieces on the walls, table football, books piled
on to shelves and windowsills, and a lovely carved counter where they dispense
Fat Pig John Street Ale, Nelsons Fanny and Pigmalion on handpump (brewed at
their sister pub, the Fat Pig – see above), their own Exeter Distillery vodka, gin
and apple pie moonshine, 18 wines by the glass, 80 malt whiskies and farm cider;
board games. The Snug is similarly furnished and has a vast, ornate mirror on one
wall, and there's also a separate restaurant with elegant chairs around chunky
tables and doors to an outside terrace.

Free house ~ Licensee Paul Timewell ~ Real ale ~ Open 5-11 (midnight Sat); closed
lunchtimes except Sun ~ Bar food 6-10; 12-7 Sun ~ Restaurant ~ Children welcome until
8pm ~ Dogs welcome ~ Wi-fi

GEORGEHAM   SS4639

Rock

(01271) 890322 – www.therockinn.biz
Rock Hill, above village; EX33 1JW

Beamed pub with good food, five real ales, plenty of room inside and out and a relaxed atmosphere

The bustling bar in this 17th-c pub is the heart of the place. It's sizeable and heavy beamed and divided in two by a step. The pubby top part has half-planked walls, an open woodburning stove in a stone fireplace and captain's and farmhouse chairs around wooden tables on quarry tiles; the lower area has panelled wall seats, some built-in settles forming a cosy booth, old local photographs and ancient flatirons. Leading off here is a red-carpeted dining room with attractive black and white photographs of North Devon folk. Friendly young staff serve local Braunton #2 Bitter alongside Exmoor Gold, St Austell Tribute, Sharps Doom Bar and Timothy Taylors Landlord on handpump and more than a dozen wines by the glass; background music and board games. The light and airy back dining conservatory has high-backed wooden or modern dining chairs around tables under a vine, with a little terrace beyond. There are picnic-sets at the front beside pretty hanging baskets and tubs; wheelchair access.

Punch ~ Lease Daniel Craddock ~ Real ale ~ Open 11am-11.30pm (midnight Sat); 12-11.30 Sun ~ Bar food 12-2.30, 6-9; 12-8.30 Sun ~ Restaurant ~ Children welcome ~ Dogs allowed in bar ~ Wi-fi

MARLDON   SX8663

Church House

(01803) 558279 – www.churchhousemarldon.com
Off A380 NW of Paignton; TQ3 1SL

Pleasant inn with spreading bar rooms, particularly good food, fine choice of drinks and seats on three terraces

Customers very much enjoy dining in this traditional 15th-c pub – but the friendly welcome from the licensees is quite a draw too. The attractively furnished, spreading bar with its woodburning stove has several different areas radiating off the big semicircular bar counter: unusual windows, some beams, dark pine and other nice old dining chairs around solid tables and yellow leather bar chairs. Leading off here is a cosy little candlelit room with four tables on bare boards, a dark wood dado and stone fireplace. There's also a restaurant with a large stone fireplace and, at the other end of the building, a similarly interesting room, split into two, with a stone floor in one part and a wooden floor (and big woodburning stove) in the other. The old barn holds yet another restaurant, with displays by local artists. Otter Ale, Dartmoor Legend and Teignworthy Neap Tide on handpump, 18 wines by the glass, ten malt whiskies and a farm cider; background music. There are picnic-sets on three carefully maintained grassy terraces behind the pub, and the village cricket field is opposite.

Enterprise ~ Lease Julian Cook ~ Real ale ~ Open 11.30-3, 5.30-11 (11.30 Fri, Sat; 12-3, 5.30-10.30 Sun ~ Bar food 12-2, 7-9.30 (9 Sun) ~ Restaurant ~ Children welcome ~ Dogs allowed in bar

MORETONHAMPSTEAD SX7586

Horse

(01647) 440242 – www.thehorsedartmoor.co.uk
George Street; TQ13 8NF

Attractive mediterranean-style courtyard behind simply furnished town pub, with a good choice of drinks and excellent food

This interesting place is run by a genuinely friendly landlady and her chef husband. The bar has leather chesterfields and deep armchairs in front of a woodburning stove, all manner of wooden chairs, settles and tables on carpet or wooden floorboards, rustic tools and horse tack alongside military and hunting prints on the walls and a dresser offering home-made cakes and local cider and juice for sale. There are stools by the green-planked counter where they serve Dartmoor Legend, Marstons Pedigree New World and a couple of guest beers on handpump, a dozen wines by the glass, ten malt whiskies, two farm ciders and quite a few coffees. A long light room leads off from here, and there's also a high-ceilinged barn-like back dining room; do look at forthcoming events as there's always something going on, from live bands to art shows. The sheltered inner courtyard, with metal tables and chairs, is popular in warm weather.

Free house ~ Licensees Nigel Hoyle and Malene Graulund ~ Real ale ~ Open 12-3.30, 5-midnight; closed Mon lunchtime ~ Bar food 12.30-2.30, 6.30-9 ~ Restaurant ~ Children welcome ~ Dogs allowed in bar ~ Wi-fi ~ Live folk last Mon of month

POSTBRIDGE SX6780

Warren House

(01822) 880208 – www.warrenhouseinn.co.uk
B3212 0.75 miles NE of Postbridge; PL20 6TA

Straightforward old pub, relaxing for a drink or straightforward meal after a Dartmoor hike

As a refuge for walkers crossing Dartmoor, this isolated pub is invaluable. There's a lot of local character and the place was built to serve the once busy tin mining community. The cosy bar is straightforward, with simple furnishings such as easy chairs and settles beneath the beamed ochre ceiling, old pictures of the inn on partly panelled stone walls and dim lighting (powered by the pub's own generator); one of the open fires is said to have been kept alight since 1845. There's also a family room. Otter Ale plus guests such as Butcombe Bitter, Cotleigh 25 and Ringwood Old Thumper on handpump, local farm cider and malt whiskies; background music and board games. The picnic-sets on both sides of the road have moorland views.

Free house ~ Licensee Peter Parsons ~ Real ale ~ Open 11-11; 12-10.30 Sun; 11-3 Mon, Tues in winter ~ Bar food 12-9 (8.30 Sun); 12-2.30 Mon, Tues in winter ~ Restaurant ~ Children in family room only ~ Dogs allowed in bar

RATTERY SX7461

Church House

(01364) 642220 – www.thechurchhouseinn.co.uk
Village signposted from A385 W of Totnes, and A38 S of Buckfastleigh; TQ10 9LD

Ancient place with friendly landlord plus a good range of drinks, popular bar food and peaceful views

The craftsmen who built the Norman church were probably housed in the original building here, and parts of it still survive – notably the spiral stone steps behind a little stone doorway on your left. The rooms have plenty of character: massive oak beams and standing timbers in the homely open-plan bar, large fireplaces (one with a cosy nook partitioned around it), traditional pubby chairs and tables on patterned carpet, some window seats and prints and horsebrasses on plain white walls. The dining room is separated by heavy curtains and there's a lounge too. Drinks include Dartmoor Jail Ale, Hanlons Stormstay, Otter Bitter and a changing guest on handpump, 19 malt whiskies and a dozen wines by the glass. The garden has picnic-sets on the large hedged-in lawn and peaceful views of the partly wooded surrounding hills.

Free house ~ Licensees John and William Edwards ~ Real ale ~ Open 11-11 ~ Bar food 12-2.30, 6.30-9 ~ Restaurant ~ Children welcome ~ Dogs allowed in bar ~ Wi-fi

SALCOMBE   SX7439

Victoria

(01548) 842604 – www.victoriainn-salcombe.co.uk
Fore Street; TQ8 8BU

Friendly, bustling town-centre pub with plenty of character, west country ales, good seasonal food and back garden; bedrooms

Genuinely welcoming to all, this is a well run place with hands-on, hard-working licensees. It's an attractive 19th-c pub on two floors opposite the harbour car park, with pretty flowering summer window boxes and a large, sheltered, tiered back garden with a play area for children and maybe chickens. The beamed bar has an open fire in a big stone fireplace, huge flagstones and traditional furnishings that take in mate's chairs, built-in wall seats with scatter cushions and upholstered stools around sturdy tables. St Austell Proper Job, Tribute and a beer named for the pub and a guest such as Exmoor Fox on handpump, 19 wines by the glass, a prosecco menu and six gins; background music and board games. Several bright dining rooms lead off with all manner of painted and wooden cushioned dining chairs around polished tables on stripped floorboards, lots of prints and mirrors above a blue dado, bookcase and china plate wallpaper and quite a collection of nautical items – lanterns, oars, glass balls, ropework and so forth. Upstairs has similar tables and chairs and button-back leather chesterfields and armchairs.

St Austell ~ Licensee Tim and Liz Hore ~ Real ale ~ Open 11-11 ~ Bar food 12-9 ~ Children welcome ~ Dogs allowed in bar ~ Wi-fi ~ Bedrooms: £70

SIDBURY   SY1496

Hare & Hounds

(01404) 41760 – www.hareandhounds-devon.co.uk
3 miles N of Sidbury, at Putts Corner; A375 towards Honiton, crossroads with B3174; EX10 0QQ

Large, well run pub with log fires, beams and attractive layout, popular daily carvery and a big garden

This large roadside place is so popular that you must book a table in advance at lunchtime, when most customers are here for the exceptionally highly thought-of carvery. They also keep Otter Ale and Bitter and St Austell Tribute tapped from the cask and eight wines by the glass. There are two log fires (and rather unusual wood-framed leather sofas complete with pouffes), heavy beams, fresh flowers, and red plush cushioned dining chairs, window seats and leather sofas around plenty of tables on carpeting or bare boards. The newer dining extension, with a central open fire, leads on to a decked area; the seats here, and the picnic-sets in the big garden, have marvellous views down the Sid Valley to the sea at Sidmouth.

Heartstone Inns ~ Managers Graham Cole and Lindsey Chun ~ Real ale ~ Open 10am-11pm ~ Bar food 12-9 ~ Children welcome but no under-12s in bar ~ Dogs allowed in bar ~ Wi-fi

SOUTH ZEAL   SX6593

Oxenham Arms

(01837) 840244 – www.theoxenhamarms.com
Off A30/A382; EX20 2JT

Wonderful 15th-c inn with lots of history, character bars, real ales, enjoyable food and big garden; bedrooms

This ancient place is just the spot to unwind after the busy A30. First licensed in 1477, it was built to combat the pagan power of the Neolithic standing stone that still forms part of the wall in the room behind the bar (there are actually six metres of stone below the floor). The heavily beamed and partly panelled front bar has elegant mullioned windows and Stuart fireplaces, all sorts of chairs and built-in wall seats with scatter cushions around low oak tables on bare floorboards, and bar stools against the counter where friendly staff serve Exeter 'fraidNot, Hunters Crispy Pig, a Red Rock beer named for the pub and a guest from Dartmoor on handpump; also, seven wines by the glass, 65 malt whiskies, 25 ports and three farm ciders. A small room has beams, wheelback chairs around polished tables, decorative plates and another open fire. The imposing curved stone steps lead up to the four-acre garden where there are plenty of seats and fine views; there are also seats under parasols out in front. Charles Dickens, snowed up one winter, wrote a lot of *The Pickwick Papers* here. You can walk straight from the door on to the moor and they provide details of walking tours.

Free house ~ Licensees Simon and Lyn Powell ~ Real ale ~ Open 11-11 ~ Bar food 12-2.30, 6-9; 12-5 afternoon tea and sandwiches ~ Restaurant ~ Children welcome ~ Dogs allowed in bar ~ Wi-fi ~ Bedrooms: £115

SPARKWELL   SX5857

Treby Arms

(01752) 837363 – www.thetrebyarms.co.uk
Off A38 at Smithaleigh, W of Ivybridge, Sparkwell signed from village; PL7 5DD

Village pub offering carefully crafted food, real ales, good wines and a friendly welcome

The food cooked by 2012 *MasterChef* winner Anton Piotrowski is so delicious that most customers come to this little village pub to eat. But there's a bar area used by locals for a pint and a chat, which keeps the atmosphere nicely informal. This small room has stools against the counter, simple wooden dining chairs and tables, a built-in cushioned window seat and a woodburning stove in a stone fireplace with shelves of cookery and guidebooks piled up on either side. Dartmoor Jail Ale and Hanlon Yellowhammer on handpump, several good wines by the glass from a list with helpful notes, 20 malt whiskies and local cider served by friendly, competent staff. Off to the right is the dining room with another woodburning stove, old glass and stone bottles on the mantelpiece and captain's and wheelback chairs around rustic tables; there's another carpeted dining room upstairs. The sunny front terrace has seats and tables.

Free house ~ Licensees Anton and Clare Piotrowski ~ Real ale ~ Open 12-3, 6-11; 12-11 Fri, Sat; 12-10.30 Sun; closed Mon ~ Bar food 12-2, 6-9 ~ Restaurant ~ Children welcome ~ Dogs allowed in bar ~ Wi-fi

SPREYTON   SX6996

Tom Cobley

(01647) 231314 – www.tomcobleytavern.co.uk
Dragdown Hill; W out of village; EX17 5AL

Huge range of quickly changing real ales and ciders and wide choice of traditional food in friendly and busy village pub

Up to 14 real ales are well kept on handpump or tapped from the cask here by the engaging landlord and his cheerful staff. These change all the time, but the main breweries are Dartmoor, Hanlon, Hunters, Otter, St Austell and Teignworthy; also, up to 14 farm ciders and perries and quite a range of malt whiskies. The comfortable little bar has straightforward pubby furnishings and an open fire, and local photographs and country scenes on the walls. A large back dining room has beams and background music. There are seats in the tree-shaded garden and more out in front by the quiet street.

Free house ~ Licensees Roger and Carol Cudlip ~ Real ale ~ Open 12-3, 6-11 (midnight Sat); 12-4, 7-11 Sun; closed Mon lunchtime ~ Bar food 12-2, 7-9 ~ Restaurant ~ Children welcome ~ Dogs allowed in bar ~ Bedrooms: £80

UGBOROUGH   SX6755

Anchor

(01752) 690388 – www.anchorinnugborough.co.uk
Off A3121; PL21 0NG

A wide mix of customers for well run, gently civilised old inn, beamed rooms, good food and drink and seats outside; bedrooms

This 17th-c pub is a good base for exploring nearby Dartmoor National Park. Throughout, the décor is light and contemporary with modern art on pale-painted walls and a relaxed and friendly atmosphere. The beamed bar has an open fire, leather sofas and dining chairs around a mix of tables on wooden flooring, and stools against the planked bar counter where they keep Sharps Doom Bar and Quercus Devon Amber on handpump and several wines by the glass; background music, TV and board games. The two-level beamed restaurant has elegant rattan dining chairs and wooden tables on flagstones in one part and more traditional dark wooden furniture on the lower area; there's a woodburning stove in a big fireplace.

Free house ~ Licensee Sarah Cuming ~ Real ale ~ Open 11-11 ~ Bar food 12-3, 6.30-9; 12-3, 6-9 Fri, Sat; 12-3, 6-8 Sun ~ Restaurant ~ Children welcome ~ Dogs allowed in bar ~ Wi-fi ~ Bedrooms: £75

WIDECOMBE   SX7276

Rugglestone

(01364) 621327 – www.rugglestoneinn.co.uk
Village at end of B3387; pub just S – turn left at church and NT church house, OS Sheet 191 map reference 720765; TQ13 7TF

Charming local with a couple of bars, cheerful customers, friendly staff, four real ales and traditional pub food

A complete contrast to the busy tourist village just down the road, this remains a tucked-away gem. The unspoilt bar has just four tables, a few window and wall seats, a one-person pew built into the corner beside a nice old stone fireplace (with a woodburner) and a good mix of customers. The rudimentary bar counter dispenses Bays Gold, Dartmoor Legend, Otter Amber and a beer named for the pub (from Teignworthy) tapped from the cask; local farm cider and a decent small wine list. The room on the right is slightly bigger and lighter in feel, with beams, another stone fireplace, stripped-pine tables and a built-in wall bench; there's also a small dining room. To reach the picnic-sets in the garden you have to cross a bridge over a little moorland stream.

Free house ~ Licensees Richard and Vicki Palmer ~ Real ale ~ Open 11.30-3, 6-11.30; 11.30-3, 5-midnight Fri; 11.30am-midnight Sat; 11.30-11 Sun ~ Bar food 12-2, 6.30-9 ~ Restaurant ~ Children allowed away from bar area ~ Dogs welcome

WOODBURY SALTERTON   SY0189
Diggers Rest
(01395) 232375 – www.diggersrest.co.uk
3.5 miles from M5 junction 30: A3052 towards Sidmouth, village signposted on right about 0.5 miles after Clyst St Mary; also signposted from B3179 SE of Exeter; EX5 1PQ

Bustling village pub with real ales, well liked food and country views from the terraced garden

There are walks around Woodbury Common and in the surrounding Otter Valley, so this thatched former cider house makes a good pit stop. The main bar has antique furniture, local art on the walls and a cosy seating area by the open fire. The modern extension is light and airy and opens on to the garden. Exeter Lighterman, Otter Ale and a guest from Powder Keg on handpump, 13 wines by the glass and Weston's cider; service is attentive and efficient. Background music, darts, TV and board games. The window boxes and flowering baskets are pretty in summer.

Heartstone Inns ~ Licensee Marc Slater ~ Real ale ~ Open 11-3, 5.30-11; 11-11 Sat; 12-10.30 Sun ~ Bar food 12-2.15, 6-9 ~ Restaurant ~ Children welcome ~ Dogs welcome ~ Wi-fi ~ Live music, check website for dates

DOG FRIENDLY HOTELS, INNS AND B&Bs

ASHPRINGTON   SX8156
Watermans Arms
(01803) 732214 – www.thewatermansarms.net
Tuckenhay Road, Bow Bridge, Ashprington, Totnes, Devon TQ9 7EG

£100; 15 comfortable rooms. Bustling pub in quiet spot by Bow Creek with plenty of riverside seats; several beamed, rambling rooms with lots to look at (stone bottles, copper implements, stuffed fish, fishing rods, oars and so forth), a log fire, a woodburning stove, all manner of tables and chairs and a good choice of drinks; friendly staff serve tasty food using local free-range produce and enjoyable breakfasts; lots of nearby walks. Dogs allowed in 13 bedrooms and anywhere in the pub except dining rooms.

ASHWATER
SX3696

Blagdon Manor

(01409) 211224 – www.blagdon.com
Ashwater, Beaworthy, Devon EX21 5DF

£150; 6 pretty rooms. Standing in rolling countryside, this carefully restored and tranquil 17th-c manor has 20 acres of grounds including three acres of gardens; beams and flagstones, antiques and paintings, log fires and fresh flowers in the bar and lounge, a comfortable library, delicious, beautifully presented food using the best local produce in smart but informal restaurant, big breakfasts in airy conservatory, and a genuinely warm welcome; three resident chocolate labradors, Cassia, Mace and Saffron. Closed two weeks January. Dogs allowed in all bedrooms and away from restaurant; blanket, towel, bowl and biscuits; £8.50.

BAMPTON
SS9221

Bark Guest House

(01398) 351236 – www.thebarkhouse.co.uk
Oakford Bridge, Bampton, Devon EX16 9HZ

£95; 5 cottagey rooms; self-catering cottage too. Charming guesthouse with lovely rural views, a garden with croquet and plenty of surrounding walks; hospitable owners, open fires and low beams in comfortable homely sitting and dining rooms, very good food in tea room using local produce (evening meals on request), a thoughtful wine list and super breakfasts. Well behaved dogs allowed in one bedroom only; rug and mat.

BIGBURY-ON-SEA
SX6544

Henley Hotel

(01548) 810240 – www.thehenleyhotel.co.uk
Folly Hill, Bigbury-on-Sea, Kingsbridge, Devon TQ7 4AR

£140; 5 rooms. Renovated Edwardian cottage with fine views of the Avon estuary, Burgh Island and beyond; lounge and conservatory dining room with magnificent sea views, deep Lloyd Loom chairs and polished furniture, binoculars and books, good, enjoyable food from a small menu, super breakfasts and steep private path down the cliff to a sandy bay where dogs may walk. Dogs allowed in bedrooms, but not in dining room; £5.

BOVEY TRACEY
SX8078

Edgemoor Hotel

(01626) 832466 – www.edgemoor.co.uk
Haytor Road, Bovey Tracey, Newton Abbot, Devon TQ13 9LE

£140; 17 charming rooms. Family-run, ivy-covered country house (a former grammar school) in neatly kept gardens on the edge of Dartmoor, with a comfortable lounge and cosy bar, log fires, good modern english cooking using seasonal local produce in elegant restaurant, afternoon teas; walks in grounds and on Dartmoor. Dogs allowed in six Woodland Wing bedrooms with back door leading to private terrace; blanket, towel, ball and treats.

BRANSCOMBE

SY2088

Masons Arms

(01297) 680300 – www.masonsarms.co.uk
Main Street, Branscombe, Devon EX12 3DJ

£95; 27 comfortable, modern bedrooms, above the inn or in converted cottages overlooking the garden. Popular pub in a pretty village near the sea; the rambling main bar is the heart of the place with comfortable seats and chairs on slate floors, ancient ships' beams and a log fire in a massive hearth; also another bar with a two-sided woodburning stove, two smartly furnished dining rooms and a quiet, flower-filled front terrace with thatched-roof tables; real ales and popular food that makes much use of local produce. Dogs allowed in some cottage bedrooms and bar; £10.

BURRINGTON

SS6218

Northcote Manor

(01769) 560501 – www.northcotemanor.co.uk
Burrington, Umberleigh, Devon EX37 9LZ

£170; 16 individually decorated rooms. Country house hotel in the Taw Valley in 20 acres of grounds with far-reaching views and surrounding walks; comfortable lounges with big murals and lots of house plants, a well stocked bar, open fires, rugs on floorboards, interesting modern, well presented food in the elegant restaurant (more large murals), and genuinely helpful, courteous staff. Dogs allowed in some bedrooms and bar, but not in lounge or restaurant; bowl and treats; £10.

CHAGFORD

SX7188

Easton Court

(01647) 433469 – www.easton.co.uk
Easton Cross, Chagford, Newton Abbot, Devon TQ13 8JN

£90; 8 rooms – under new ownership, with revamp and new bedrooms planned. Extended Tudor thatched longhouse in nearly four acres of gardens and paddocks, with a relaxed and informal atmosphere; hearty breakfasts in guest lounge/breakfast room and plenty of surrounding pubs and restaurants for evening meals; lots to do nearby. Dogs allowed in some bedrooms.

CHAGFORD

SX7087

Three Crowns

(01647) 433444 – www.threecrowns-chagford.co.uk
High Street, Chagford, Devon TQ13 8AJ

£135; 21 stylish, well equipped bedrooms. A stunning thatched 13th-c former manor house on the edge of Dartmoor that blends ancient and modern features with great effectiveness; there's a bar with a log fire, dining lounges with an assortment of furniture, including a conservatory-style area, and a courtyard with sturdy seating among box topiary; throughout are painted beams and standing timbers, flagstones and rugs, lots of copper items and exposed stone walls hung with photographs and prints; good choice of food and drinks, including generous breakfasts. Dogs allowed in six bedrooms, bar and snug, not restaurant; £10.

CHILLINGTON
SX7942

Whitehouse

(01548) 580505 – www.whitehousedevon.com
Chillington, Devon TQ7 2JX

£190; 6 individually decorated, well equipped rooms. Georgian house with a peaceful back garden, an easy-going, friendly atmosphere, comfortable leather sofas and armchairs on bare boards in the sitting room, a snug study with daily papers, magazines and an open fire, a small bar, good, modern food in an airy dining room overlooking the terrace, and delicious breakfasts; guests get free access to pool, gym, sauna and spa at Dart Marina Hotel (below). Dogs allowed in all bedrooms and in public rooms; £10.

COUNTISBURY
SS7449

Blue Ball

(01598) 741263 – www.blueballinn.com
Countisbury, Lynton, Devon EX35 6NE

£80; 14 rooms. 13th-c inn surrounded by fine scenery and nearby coastal walks – the website has details of four circular routes; rambling, heavy beamed rooms, three ales including one brewed for the pub, handsome log fires, generous local food in bar and restaurant and friendly service; two residents dogs, Molly and Ruby. Dogs allowed in all bedrooms; home-made treats for sale; £8.

CULMSTOCK
ST1013

Culm Valley

(01884) 840354 – www.theculmvalleyinn.co.uk
Culmstock, Cullompton, Devon EX15 3JJ

£95 without breakfast; 5 rooms. Quirky, friendly dining pub with an enjoyable and informal atmosphere, lots of chatty locals and visitors, a hotchpotch of modern and unrenovated furnishings, knick-knacks, a big fireplace and a really interesting choice of drinks including real ales and local ciders; there's also a dining room, a small conservatory and an oak-floored room with views into the kitchen; imaginative, highly enjoyable food; seats overlook the River Culm. Dogs allowed in one bedroom, bar and conservatory.

DARTMOUTH
SX8752

Dart Marina Hotel

(01803) 832580 – www.dartmarina.com
Sandquay Road, Dartmouth, Devon TQ6 9PH

£260; 49 stylish, well equipped rooms, all with river views; self-catering apartments too. Well run hotel beside the River Dart with a contemporary bar/lounge, genuinely friendly, helpful staff, first class food using the best local seasonal produce in light, airy restaurant (panoramic views, white tablecloths, crystal and candlelight) and lovely breakfasts; seats on the terrace, luxury spa, gym and swimming pool. Dogs allowed in ground-floor bedrooms and bar/lounge, not restaurant; £10 per stay.

DARTMOUTH   SX8752

Royal Castle Hotel

(01803) 833033 – www.royalcastle.co.uk
11 The Quay, Dartmouth, Devon TQ6 9PS

£160; 24 charming rooms, many with harbour views. 17th-c hotel at the heart
of a lovely town, with a lot of character, many original features and a thriving
atmosphere; two quite different bars – the Galleon Bar is traditional with fine
antiques and maritime pieces and a Tudor fireplace, while the Harbour Bar is
contemporary and rather smart with regular live acoustic music; the more formal
restaurant overlooks the water, and particularly friendly staff serve enjoyable,
all-day food; real ales and several wines by the glass. Dogs allowed in all
bedrooms and anywhere in the hotel except restaurant; bed, toy and treats; £20.

EXETER   SX9292

Hotel du Vin

(01392) 790120 – www.hotelduvin.com
Magdalen Street, Exeter, Devon EX2 4HY

£150; 59 beautifully furnished rooms with lovely bathrooms. Cleverly converted
Victorian eye hospital with a lounge, modern furnishings and a stunning botanical
wall painting, a library with lots of books and an open fire, excellent imaginative
food from the theatre-style kitchen in the stylish open-plan restaurant, morning
coffee and afternoon tea, spa with an inside-out swimming pool, and plenty of
seats on the terrace in the walled garden. Note: it joined the Hotel du Vin chain
in 2016, so refurbishments are planned and changes are likely. Dogs allowed in
bedrooms, lounge and bar; bed and bowl; £10.

EXMINSTER   SX9686

Turf

(01392) 833128 – www.turfpub.net
Exminster, Exeter, Devon EX6 8EE

£100; 2 nice rooms. Remote, friendly, family-run pub reached on towpath beside
the ship canal, by bicycle or by boat (from Topsham quay); enormously popular
in fine weather and plenty of seating in the big garden – the summer barbecues
are very good indeed; simply furnished rooms with pine tables and chairs, a
woodburning stove, local beers, cider and wine, and enjoyable food using their
own produce; lots of walks nearby; two resident jack russells. Closed October to
mid February. Dogs allowed in both bedrooms and anywhere in the pub.

FROGMORE   SX7742

Globe

(01548) 531351 – www.theglobeinn.co.uk
Hillside, Frogmore, Kingsbridge, Devon TQ7 2NR

£90; 8 well equipped, airy bedrooms. Extended and neatly refurbished inn
on Frogmore creek and surrounded by lovely countryside; there's a bar with a
double-sided woodburner with horsebrass-decorated stone pillars on either side,
another fireplace filled with logs, assorted furniture – and a copper diving helmet,
a comfortable dining lounge, a games room with pool and darts, a two-level back

terrace with seating and very pretty window boxes in summer; real ales, popular traditional food and generous breakfasts. Dogs allowed in most bedrooms and part of bar; £5.

GULWORTHY

SX4473

Horn of Plenty

(01822) 832528 – www.thehornofplenty.co.uk
Gulworthy, Tavistock, Devon PL19 8JD

£125; 16 lovely rooms with personal touches – 4 with traditional design in main house, 12 with contemporary design in coach house annexe with french windows to walled gardens. Luxury small country house hotel in six acres of gardens and orchards with wonderful views over the Tamar Valley (direct access to Tamar Valley trails); drawing room with log fires and fresh flowers, separate bar/lounge, delicious modern cooking (and super breakfasts) using produce from Devon and Cornwall in smart, airy restaurant and a friendly, relaxed atmosphere. Dogs allowed in some coach house rooms; blanket, bowl and treats; £10.

HAWKCHURCH

SY3499

Fairwater Head Hotel

(01297) 678349 – www.fairwaterheadhotel.co.uk
Hawkchurch, Axminster, Devon EX13 5TX

£145; 16 rooms, most with country views. Edwardian hotel in quiet, flower-filled gardens with genuinely friendly, attentive staff, an open fire in the comfortable lounge hall, a well stocked bar and wine cellar and enjoyable brasserie-style food in the bustling restaurant; walks directly from the door; resident springer/cocker spaniel, Mocca, and labradors, Lolly and Barney. Closed January. Dogs allowed in all bedrooms and anywhere except restaurant; welcome biscuits and info pack.

HAYTOR VALE

SX7777

Rock

(01364) 661305 – www.rock-inn.co.uk
Haytor Vale, Newton Abbot, Devon TQ13 9XP

£100; 9 individual rooms; also self-catering cottage. Civilised former coaching inn on the edge of Dartmoor National Park that's at its most informal at lunchtime; two neatly kept, linked, partly panelled bars have courteous staff, lots of dark wood and red plush, candles, fresh flowers and warming log fires; there's a thoughtful choice of drinks, a residents' lounge, a spacious dining room serving extremely good food and a pretty garden opposite; super breakfasts. Dogs allowed in some bedrooms, and public rooms with tiled floors; bed and bowl; £10.

HORNDON

SX5280

Elephants Nest

(01822) 810273 – www.elephantsnest.co.uk
Horndon, Mary Tavy, Tavistock, Devon PL19 9NQ

£97.50; 3 attractively furnished, comfortable rooms. Isolated old inn surrounded by lots of Dartmoor walks with a warmly friendly landlord; simply furnished bar with farm ciders, real ales and several wines by the glass, two other rooms with modern dark wood tables and chairs on flagstones, three woodburning stoves, bare stone walls and spreading pretty garden with seating; changing bar food using local produce and super breakfasts (devilled kidneys and kedgeree); resident glen of imaal terrier, Bertie. Dogs allowed in all bedrooms and anywhere in pub; towel; £5.

HORNS CROSS   SS3723

Hoops

(01237) 451222 – www.hoopsinn.co.uk
Horns Cross, Bideford, Devon EX39 5DL

£110; 13 well equipped rooms. Striking thatched inn, a former smugglers' haunt, with plenty of character and a cheerful mix of customers; bars have traditional furniture, log fires in sizeable fireplaces, standing timbers and partitioning, a more formal restaurant has another open fire, real ales, wines by the glass and enterprising food served all day from midday plus breakfasts; two acres of gardens. Dogs allowed in coach house bedrooms and bar; £5.

IDDESLEIGH   SS5608

Duke of York

(01837) 810253 – www.dukeofyorkdevon.co.uk
Iddesleigh, Winkleigh, Devon EX19 8BG

£80; 8 charming, timbered rooms, including 3 in separate building. Originally four cottages built for craftsmen rebuilding the church, this inn is long, thatched and dates from the 15th c; the unspoilt bar has a homely character, rocking chairs and built-in wall benches, banknotes pinned to beams, a log fire in a big fireplace and chatty customers, while the separate dining room has an inglenook and serves honest, fairly priced food; seats in a small back garden. Dogs allowed in all bedrooms and bar; £5.

ILFRACOMBE   SS5146

Strathmore

(Q1271) 862248 – www.the-strathmore.co.uk
57 St Brannocks Road, Ilfracombe, Devon EX34 8EQ

£75; 8 rooms. Traditionally furnished Victorian guesthouse close to the town centre and beach with a comfortable and well stocked lounge bar, hearty breakfasts in dining room, welcoming owners and staff, and a terraced garden; plenty of nearby walks. Dogs allowed in seven bedrooms; welcome letter, sausage for breakfast; £6.50.

ILSINGTON   SX7876

Ilsington Country House

(01364) 661452 – www.ilsington.co.uk
Ilsington, Newton Abbot, Devon TQ13 9RR

£120; 25 country-style rooms. Family-run extended hotel in ten acres of gardens surrounded by Dartmoor National Park with its rolling hills and ancient woodland; a friendly, easy-going atmosphere throughout the traditionally decorated public rooms (fine views too), interesting modern food using the best local produce in the green carpeted restaurant, informal meals in the Blue Tiger Inn and helpful, courteous service; indoor swimming pool and spa. Closed one week January. Dogs allowed in eight bedrooms, bar and conservatory; info pack; £8.

LEWDOWN
SX4586

Lewtrenchard Manor

(01566) 783256 – www.lewtrenchard.co.uk
Lewdown, Okehampton, Devon EX20 4PN

£180; 14 luxurious rooms with period furniture. Lovely family-run Jacobean manor house in gardens with a fine dovecote and surrounded by a peaceful estate; dark panelling, ornate ceilings, antiques, fresh flowers and log fires in the public rooms, a relaxed atmosphere, a friendly welcome, and a candlelit restaurant with very good imaginative food; very good afternoon teas and breakfasts too; resident dog, Spencer; walks in the grounds and on many nearby footpaths. Dogs allowed in all bedrooms and on leads in public rooms except restaurant; bedding and treats; £15.

LIFTON
SX3885

Arundell Arms

(01566) 784666 – www.arundellarms.com
Fore Street, Lifton, Devon PL16 0AA

£160; 25 well equipped rooms; also self-catering cottage. Carefully renovated old coaching inn with 20 miles of its own waters – salmon and trout fishing and a long-established fly-fishing school; also shooting and deer stalking; comfortable sitting room, log fires, super food in both bar and elegant restaurant, carefully chosen wines, and kind service from local staff; attractive terraced garden (where dogs may walk) and walks in nearby playing fields. Dogs allowed in some bedrooms and anywhere except restaurant; bed, bowl and treats; £15.

MALBOROUGH
SX7037

Soar Mill Cove Hotel

(01548) 561566 – www.soarmillcove.co.uk
Malborough, Salcombe, Devon TQ7 3DS

£199; 22 comfortable rooms that open on to the garden; also self-catering cottages. Neatly kept, single-storey, family-run hotel in idyllic spot by a peaceful and very beautiful cove on National Trust coast – lovely views and ten acres of grounds; bars, a coffee shop and lounge with an informal, easy-going atmosphere (and lovely views), good, enjoyable food in the restaurant (more fine views) and well trained, kind staff; excellent walks all around and they also have a dog-walks map; spa, indoor pool, snooker, pitch and putt and tennis. Dogs allowed in all bedrooms and coffee shop; treats; £10.

MOLLAND

SS8028

London

(01769) 550269 – www.londoninnmolland.co.uk
Molland, South Molton, Devon EX36 3NG

£75; 2 cottagey rooms (1 with spiral staircase). A proper Exmoor inn tucked away down narrow lanes and hardly changed in 50 years; two small linked rooms with local stag-hunting pictures, plain furniture, a friendly, easy-going atmosphere, real ales and tasty, reasonably priced food using seasonal game; look out for the particularly good game bird prints in the panelled dining room and the original Victorian mahogany and tiling in the lavatories; the cottagey garden has picnic-sets and the church next door has some untouched early 18th-c box pews. Dogs allowed in both bedrooms and bar; £10.

MORETONHAMPSTEAD

SX7386

Great Sloncombe Farm

(01647) 440595 – www.greatsloncombefarm.co.uk
Moretonhampstead, Newton Abbot, Devon TQ13 8QF

£85; 3 comfortable country rooms. Lovely 13th-c farmhouse on a working stock farm, with friendly owners, carefully polished old-fashioned furniture in oak-beamed lounge with woodburning stove in an inglenook, games and books, hearty breakfasts with sausages from their pigs and eggs from their hens, and a relaxed atmosphere; they will make up picnics and have bikes for hire – good nearby walking and bird-watching – and three resident scottish terriers, a bearded collie and a dachshund. Dogs allowed in all bedrooms and lounge; £5.

NORTHAM

SS4528

Yeoldon House

(01237) 474400 – www.yeoldonhousehotel.co.uk
Durrant Lane, Northam, Bideford, Devon EX39 2RL

£125; 10 individually decorated rooms, 5 with water views. Quietly set hotel in one acre of grounds by the River Torridge, with a warmly friendly and relaxed atmosphere, an open fire and fresh flowers in the comfortable lounge, breakfast but no evening meals – lots of pubs and restauarnts nearby; plenty of walks and lots to do nearby. Closed Feburary. Small or medium-size dogs allowed in some bedrooms (not to be left unattended) – must phone in advance; £5.

POSTBRIDGE

SX6578

Lydgate House

(01822) 880209 – www.lydgatehouse.co.uk
Postbridge, Yelverton, Devon PL20 6TJ

£120; 7 pleasant rooms; also self-catering cottage. Friendly and relaxed Victorian country house in 36 acres of grounds in a secluded wild Dartmoor valley spot, lots of wildlife and good walks from the door; there's a log fire in the comfortable sitting room, good, simple modern cooking in the candlelit conservatory dining room, and fine breakfasts (and picnic lunches on request); resident dogs and cats; no under-12s. Dogs allowed in all bedrooms; £3.

SANDFORD

SS8202

Lamb

(01363) 773676 – www.lambinnsandford.co.uk
Sandford, Crediton, Devon EX17 4LW

£85; 7 well equipped, comfortable modern rooms. Bustling 16th-c village inn with much genuine character, beams and standing timbers in bar and connected dining room, red leather sofas in front of a log fire (there's also a woodburner), cushioned settles and window seats, interesting animal paintings (done by the landlord's wife), real ales, decent wines and 20 malts; a skittle alley doubles as a free cinema, there's a cobbled three-level garden, the food is highly enjoyable and the breakfasts nice, and staff are cheerful and helpful; resident dog called Eager. Dogs allowed in all bedrooms and anywhere in the pub; £5.

SANDY PARK

SX7189

Mill End Hotel

(01647) 432282 – www.millendhotel.com
Sandy Park, Chagford, Newton Abbot, Devon TQ13 8JN

£150; 20 charming, peaceful rooms – 4 with direct garden access. Quietly set former flour mill, with original waterwheel, in 15 acres of neatly kept grounds below Dartmoor and beside River Teign – wonderful surrounding walks; three lounges with comfortable sofas, fresh flowers and open fires, excellent british cooking in elegant restaurant, fine breakfasts and cream teas on the lawn, good service and helpful to dog-owners. Dogs allowed in some bedrooms and anywhere in hotel except restaurant; walks map; £8.

SHEEPWASH

SS4806

Half Moon

(01409) 231376 – www.halfmoonsheepwash.co.uk
Sheepwash, Beaworthy, Devon EX21 5NE

£95; 13 rooms – 4 in converted stables. Civilised heart-of-Devon hideaway with 12 miles of private salmon, sea trout and brown trout fishing on the River Torridge and plenty of walks; simply furnished main bar, lots of beams and a big log fire, real ales and wines by the glass, enjoyable food in extended dining room and a friendly atmosphere. Dogs allowed in stable bedrooms and bar; £5.

SIDFORD

SY1389

Salty Monk

(01395) 513174 – www.saltymonk.co.uk
Church Street, Sidford, Sidmouth, Devon EX10 9QP

£135; 6 cottagey rooms, some with spa baths. 16th-c former salt house (monks trading in salt stayed here on their way to Exeter) with comfortable sofas and fresh flowers in sitting room, good food using local produce cooked by the owners in restful restaurant, nice breakfasts and cream teas, and seats in the quiet garden; yoga suite/fitness room and mini spa; two resident spinones, Isca and Sorrel; fantastic walks all around and near the famous donkey sanctuary. Closed one week November, all January. Dogs allowed in two bedrooms and lounge (on lead); bowl, treats and maps; £20.

SLAPTON
SX8245

Tower

(01548) 580216 – www.thetowerinn.com
Slapton, Kingsbridge, Devon TQ7 2PN

£90; 3 cosy, refurbished rooms. 14th-c century inn built for masons erecting the next-door chantry; a low-ceilinged, beamed bar with a friendly, relaxed atmosphere, log fire, settles and scrubbed oak tables on flagstones or bare boards, well kept beers, wines by the glass and impressive food including fresh fish; seats in pretty back garden and resident cockapoo, Bella, and westie, Tavi; fine beaches and nature reserve nearby. Closed first two weeks January. Dogs allowed in one bedroom and everywhere in pub; £5.

STAVERTON
SX7964

Sea Trout

(01803) 762274 – www.theseatroutinn.co.uk
Staverton, Totnes, Devon TQ9 6PA

£110; 11 cottagey rooms. Comfortable, partly 15th-c pub in quiet hamlet near River Dart with fishing flies and stuffed fish on the walls of the neatly kept beamed lounge, a simpler locals' bar with more stuffed fish, a stag's head, lots of horsebrasses and a woodburning stove, a smarter panelled restaurant and conservatory with very popular, enjoyable food, and an attractive back garden with seating; plenty of walks and lots to do nearby including fishing on the river (daily permits available). Dogs allowed in some bedrooms and bar; blanket, map and bowl; £7.50.

THURLESTONE
SX6742

Thurlestone Hotel

(01548) 560382 – www.thurlestone.co.uk
Thurlestone, Kingsbridge, Devon TQ7 3NN

£260; 64 lovely, comfortable rooms, all with sea or country views. Owned by the same family since 1896, this well run hotel sits in 19 acres of subtropical gardens and is just a five-minute walk from the sea; stylish and spacious lounges, a convivial bar, imaginative food in the light, attractive restaurant with views over Bigbury Bay, enjoyable light lunches, afternoon teas and first class breakfasts, and courteous helpful staff; they also own the local pub; outdoor heated swimming pool, tennis, squash and badminton courts, a golf course and a spa with an indoor pool and sauna; plenty of nearby beaches and walks. Dogs allowed in most bedrooms and foyer; welcome pack with info on local walks; £9.

TORQUAY
SX9365

Cary Arms

(01803) 327110 – www.caryarms.co.uk
Beach Road, Babbacombe, Torquay, Devon TQ1 3LX

£295; 10 lovely New England-style rooms and suites in main hotel and 8 stylish separate 'beach huts' (new in 2016), all with sea views; also self-catering cottages. Charming and unusual higgledy-piggledy boutique hotel at the bottom of a tortuously steep lane – glorious sea views; a beamed, grotto-effect bar with alcoves, rustic hobbit-style red leather cushioned chairs around carved wooden tables on slate or bare boards, an open woodburning stove, local beers and cider, and enjoyable, interesting food; comfortable residents' lounge, smashing breakfasts and wonderful terraces with steps leading down to the quay; spa (new in 2016) with treatment rooms. Dogs allowed in some bedrooms, some beach huts and bar; bed, bowl and treats; £20.

TWO BRIDGES   SX6274
Prince Hall
(01822) 890403 – www.princehall.co.uk
Two Bridges, Yelverton, Devon PL20 6SA

£190; 9 attractive, spacious rooms. Surrounded by Dartmoor National Park, this tranquil 18th-c country house is run by caring, friendly owners and their helpful staff; lovely views from convivial bar, a comfortable sitting room, a smart, cosy dining room, open fires, inventive food using local seasonal produce, enjoyable breakfasts and delicious cream teas; lots of fine walks; Polo and Timber are the resident dogs, and dogs are made very welcome. Dogs allowed in all bedrooms and anywhere in hotel except dining room; two dogs free, three dogs and above £15.

Dorset

DOG FRIENDLY PUBS

BOURTON   ST7731
White Lion
(01747) 840866 – www.whitelionbourton.co.uk
High Street, off old A303 E of Wincanton; SP8 5AT

Stone inn built in 1723, with beamed bar and dining room, pleasing food and ales and seats in the garden; bedrooms

An early 18th-c former coaching inn, this is a handsome place with a welcoming landlord and friendly, efficient staff. The bar is traditionally furnished and the two-level dining room has nice old wooden chairs around a medley of tables. Throughout, there are beams, bare boards, fine flagstones, stripped stone and half-panelling, bow window seats, church candles and a log fire in an inglenook fireplace. Otter Amber and a couple of guest beers such as Isle of Purbeck Fossil Fuel and Keystone Bedrock on handpump and several wines by the glass; background music. The back terrace and raised lawn have picnic-sets. Stourhead (National Trust) is close by.

Free house ~ Licensee William Stuart ~ Real ale ~ Open 11.30-11 (10.30 Sun) ~ Bar food 12-2 (3 Sat), 6-9; 12-3, 7-9 Sun ~ Restaurant ~ Children welcome ~ Dogs welcome ~ Wi-fi ~ Bedrooms: £80

CHETNOLE   ST6008
Chetnole Inn
(01935) 872337 – www.thechetnoleinn.co.uk
Village signed off A37 S of Yeovil; DT9 6NU

Attractive country pub with beams and huge flagstones, real ales, popular food and seats in the back garden; bedrooms

The bar at this nicely run beamed inn has a relaxed country kitchen feel with wheelback chairs and pine tables on huge flagstones and a woodburning stove. Friendly staff serve Butcombe Rare Breed, Wriggle Valley Gold, Yeovil Star Gazer and a weekly guest beer on handpump and there's a fair choice of wines. Popular with locals, the snug has a leather sofa near another woodburner and stools against the counter; dogs are allowed in here. The airy dining room has more wheelback chairs around pale wooden tables on stripped floorboards and a small open fire. At the back, a delightful garden has picnic-sets and a view over fields.

Free house ~ Licensees Simon and Maria Hudson ~ Real ale ~ Open 11-3, 6-11; 11-11 Sat;
12-4 Sun ~ Bar food 12-2, 6.30-9 ~ Restaurant ~ Children welcome ~ Dogs allowed in bar ~
Wi-fi ~ Bedrooms: £105

CHIDEOCK   SY4191

Anchor

(01297) 489215 – www.theanchorinnseatown.co.uk
Off A35 from Chideock; DT6 6JU

**Stunning beach position for carefully renovated inn, lots of character,
well kept ales and popular food and seats on front terrace; light, airy
bedrooms**

What really distinguishes this thoughtfully refurbished old pub is its splendid
position, almost straddling the Dorset Coast Path and nestling beneath the
617-ft Golden Cap pinnacle. Just a few steps from the beach, seats and tables
on the spacious front terrace are ideally placed for views, but you'll have to
get there early in summer to bag a spot. Inside, plenty of original character
has been kept in the three smallish, light rooms: padded wall seating, nice old
wooden chairs and stools around scrubbed tables on bare boards, a couple of
woodburning stoves (one under a huge bressumer beam), tilley lamps, model
ships and lots of historic photographs of the pub, the area and locals. From the
wood-panelled bar they serve Palmers 200, Best, Copper and Dorset Gold on
handpump, seven wines by the glass and cocktails; background music. You can
park for free in front of the pub or across the road for £4 (refundable against a
spend of £20 or more in the pub).

Palmers ~ Tenant Paul Wiscombe ~ Real ale ~ Open 10am-11pm ~ Bar food 12-9; 12-3, 6-9
Mon-Thurs Nov-Mar ~ Children welcome ~ Dogs allowed in bar ~ Wi-fi ~ Bedrooms: £130

CHIDEOCK   SY4292

George

(01297) 489419 – www.georgeinnchideock.co.uk
A35 Bridport–Lyme Regis; DT6 6JD

**Comfortably traditional local with a thriving feel and well liked food
and drink**

A cheerful mix of both holidaymakers and locals crowd into this heavily
thatched old village inn creating a lively atmosphere. The cosy, low-ceilinged,
carpeted bar is nicely traditional, with Palmers 200, Copper, Dorset Gold, IPA and
a guest beer on handpump, six wines by the glass and farm cider, warm log fires
and brassware and pewter tankards hanging from dark beams. There are wooden
pews and long built-in tongue-and-groove banquettes, cream walls hung with old
tools and high shelves of bottles, plates and mugs; background music, TV, bar
billiards, darts and board games. The garden room opens on to a pretty walled
garden with a terrace and a much used wood-fired oven.

Palmers ~ Tenant Jamie Smith ~ Real ale ~ Open 12-3, 6-11 ~ Bar food 12-2.30, 6-9.30 ~
Restaurant ~ Children welcome except in snug bar ~ Dogs allowed in bar ~ Wi-fi

CRANBORNE   SU0513

Inn at Cranborne

(01725) 551249 – www.theinnatcranborne.co.uk
Wimborne Street (B3078 N of Wimborne); BH21 5PP

**Neatly refurbished old inn with a friendly atmosphere, good choice of
drinks, highly rated food and seats outside; comfortable bedrooms**

This is a well run all-rounder. The rambling bars have heavy beams, open
doorways, the odd standing timber and a chatty, relaxed atmosphere.
The main bar area, divided into two by a partition, is a favourite place to sit:
grey-planked and tartan-cushioned built-in wall seats and assorted chairs
(farmhouse, wheelback, ladderback) on parquet flooring, flagstones or rugs,
nightlights on each table and a woodburner in an inglenook fireplace. Badger
First Call and a guest such as Tanglefoot on handpump and several wines by
the glass served by friendly, helpful staff; background music, TV, darts and
board games. The dining areas spread back from here, with similar furnishings
and a little brick fireplace; there's also a second bar with white-painted or
wooden furniture and another woodburning stove. Plenty of coaching prints on
grey walls above a darker grey dado, and church candles. Outside, you'll find
benches, seats and tables on neat gravel. Thomas Hardy visited the pub while
writing *Tess of the D'Urbervilles*.

Badger ~ Tenant Jane Gould ~ Real ale ~ Open 11-11; 11-10 Sun ~ Bar food 12-2, 6-9;
12-2.30, 6-9.30 Fri, Sat; 12-2.30, 6-9 Sun ~ Restaurant (evening only) ~ Children welcome ~
Dogs welcome ~ Wi-fi ~ Bedrooms: £99

KINGSTON   SY9579

Scott Arms

(01929) 480270 – www.thescottarms.com
West Street (B3069); BH20 5LH

**Wonderful views from a large garden, rambling character rooms, real
ales and interesting food and an easy-going atmosphere; bedrooms**

The views of Corfe Castle and the Purbeck Hills from the big, attractive
garden are quite magnificent; there's also rustic-style seating and an
outside summer kitchen with a jerk shack for caribbean-style food (the
landlady is jamaican). Inside, the bar areas and more formal dining room
are on several levels with stripped stone and brickwork, flagstones and bare
boards, beams and high rafters, seats ranging from sofas and easy chairs
through all manner of wooden chairs around tables of varying sizes and
open fires; stairs lead up from the bar to a small minstrels' gallery-like area
with sofas facing one another across a table. Bath Gem, Butcombe Bitter,
Dorset Jurassic and Ringwood Best on handpump, 11 wines by the glass
and local cider; background music, board games and darts. The surrounding
area has many good walks.

Greene King ~ Lease Ian, Simon and Cynthia Coppack ~ Real ale ~ Open 11-11 ~ Bar food
12-2.30, 6-8.30 ~ Children welcome ~ Dogs allowed in bar ~ Wi-fi ~ Bedrooms: £10

NETTLECOMBE

Marquis of Lorne

(01308) 485236 – www.themarquisoflorne.co.uk
Off A3066 Bridport–Beaminster, via West Milton; DT6 3SY

Attractive country pub with enjoyable food and drink, friendly licensees and seats in big garden; bedrooms

The big mature garden here really comes into its own in warm weather with its pretty herbaceous borders, picnic-sets under apple trees and a rustic-style play area. The comfortable, bustling main bar has a log fire, mahogany panelling, old prints and photographs and neatly matching chairs and tables. Two dining areas lead off, the smaller of which has another log fire. The wooden-floored snug (liked by locals) has board games, table skittles and background music, and they keep Palmers Copper, Dorset Gold and IPA on handpump, with ten wines by the glass from a decent list. Eggardon Hill, one of Dorset's most spectacular Iron Age hill forts with views over the coast and surrounding countryside, is within walking distance.

Palmers ~ Tenants Stephen and Tracey Brady ~ Real ale ~ Open 11.30-2.30, 6-10.30 ~ Bar food 12-2, 6-9 ~ Restaurant ~ Children welcome ~ Dogs allowed in bar ~ Wi-fi ~ Bedrooms: £95

PLUSH

Brace of Pheasants

(01300) 348357 – www.braceofpheasants.co.uk
Village signposted from B3143 N of Dorchester at Piddletrenthide; DT2 7RQ

16th-c thatched pub with friendly service, generously served food and pleasant garden; comfortable bedrooms

The friendly licensees of this 16th-c inn make sure both locals and visitors receive a genuine welcome. The bustling, beamed bar has windsor chairs around good solid tables on patterned carpeting, a few standing timbers, a huge heavy-beamed inglenook at one end with cosy seating inside, and a good warming log fire at the other. Flack Manor Double Drop, Ringwood Best and Sunny Republic Dolphin Amber are tapped from the cask and they offer a fine choice of wines with 18 by the glass, and two proper farm ciders. Food is very good, with local suppliers listed. A decent-sized garden includes a terrace and a lawn sloping up towards a rockery. The pub is well placed for walks – a pleasant bridleway behind the building leads to the left of the woods and over to Church Hill.

Free house ~ Licensees Phil and Carol Bennett ~ Real ale ~ Open 12-3, 7-11 (10.30 Sun) ~ Bar food 12-2, 7-9 ~ Children welcome ~ Dogs allowed in bar ~ Wi-fi ~ Bedrooms: £115

SHERBORNE

Digby Tap

(01935) 813148 – www.digbytap.co.uk
Cooks Lane; park in Digby Road and walk round corner; DT9 3NS

Regularly changing ales in simple alehouse, open all day with very inexpensive beer and food

Handy for the glorious golden-stone Sherborn Abbey, this is an old-fashioned, unchanging alehouse with a lively, chatty and warmly welcoming atmosphere and is much loved by customers of all ages and from every walk of life. The straightforward flagstoned bar, with its cosy corners, is full of understated character; the small games room has a pool table and a quiz machine, and there's also a TV room; mobile phones are banned. The food (lunchtime only) is extraordinarily good value and the fine range of ales includes Black Sheep Bitter, Cottage Conquest, Otter Bitter and Wriggle Valley Ryme Rambler on handpump. Also, several wines by the glass and a choice of malt whiskies.

Free house ~ Licensees Oliver Wilson and Nick Whigham ~ Real ale ~ No credit cards ~ Open 11-11; 12-11 Sun ~ Bar food 12-2; not Sun ~ Children welcome until 6pm ~ Dogs allowed in bar ~ Wi-fi

TRENT   ST5818
Rose & Crown
(01935) 850776 – www.roseandcrowntrent.co.uk
Opposite the church; DT9 4SL

Character thatched pub with a friendly licensee, cosy rooms, open fires, a good choice of drinks and well thought-of food; bedrooms

The cosy little bar on the right has big comfortable sofas and stools around a low table in front of an open fire, fresh flowers and candlelight. The bar opposite is furnished with nice old wooden tables and chairs on quarry tiles, and stools against the counter where they serve Wadworths Bishops Tipple, IPA, 6X and Horizon and a guest beer on handpump and 14 wines by the glass; board games. Two other connected rooms have similar wooden tables and chairs, settles and pews, a grandfather clock, pewter tankards and more fireplaces. Throughout are all sorts of pictures, including Stuart prints commemorating the fact that Charles II sought refuge in this village after the Battle of Worcester. The simply furnished back dining room leads out to the garden with seats and tables and fine views (and sunsets); there are some picnic-sets at the front. The church opposite is lovely.

Wadworths ~ Tenant Nick Lamb ~ Real ale ~ Open 11-11 ~ Bar food 12-2.30, 6-9 ~ Children welcome ~ Dogs welcome ~ Wi-fi ~ Bedrooms: £85

WEST BAY   SY4690
West Bay
(01308) 422157 – www.thewestbayhotel.co.uk
Station Road; DT6 4EW

Relaxed seaside inn with emphasis on seafood; bedrooms

There are two unspoilt beaches on either side of the busy little harbour (much visited since the two *Broadchurch* TV series were filmed here) and you can watch the comings and goings of the boats while enjoying a pint or a fresh fish meal. The fairly simple front part of the building, with bare boards, a coal-effect gas fire and a mix of sea and nostalgic prints, is separated by an island servery from the cosier carpeted dining area, which has more of a country kitchen feel; background music and board games. Although it's spacious enough never to feel crowded, booking is essential in season. Palmers 200, Best, Copper, Dorset Gold and a seasonal guest are served on handpump alongside good house wines (including eight by the glass) and several malt whiskies. There are tables in a small side garden and more in the large main garden. Several local teams meet to play in the pub's 100-year-old skittle alley.

Palmers ~ Tenant Samuel Good ~ Real ale ~ Open 12-11 (midnight Sat, 10 Sun); 12-3, 6-11
Nov-Mar in winter ~ Bar food 12-2 (3 weekends), 6-9; 12-3, 6-8 Sun~ Children welcome until
8pm ~ Dogs allowed in bar ~ Wi-fi ~ Bedrooms: £115

WEST STOUR   ST7822
Ship

(01747) 838640 – www.shipinn-dorset.com
A30 W of Shaftesbury; SP8 5RP

**Civilised and pleasantly updated roadside dining inn offering a wide
range of food and ales; bedrooms**

The friendly landlord here keeps his ale well and we get warm feedback
on the food too. The neatly kept rooms include a smallish but airy bar
on the left with cream décor, a mix of chunky farmhouse furniture on dark
boards and big sash windows that look beyond the road and car park to
rolling pastures. The smaller flagstoned public bar has a good log fire and low
ceilings. Butcombe Bitter, Ringwood Best and Waylands Sixpenny 6d Original
on handpump, 14 wines by the glass and four farm ciders. During their summer
beer festival they showcase a dozen beers and ten ciders, all from the west
country. On the right, two carpeted dining rooms with stripped pine dado,
stone walls and shutters are similarly furnished in a pleasantly informal style,
and have some attractive contemporary cow prints; TV, numerous board games
and background music. The bedlington terriers are called Douglas and Toby.
Good surrounding walks.

Free house ~ Licensee Gavin Griggs ~ Real ale ~ Open 12-3, 6-11.30; 12-midnight Sat; 12-
10.30 Sun ~ Bar food 12-2.30, 6-9; not Sun evening ~ Restaurant ~ Well behaved children in
restaurant and lounge ~ Dogs allowed in bar ~ Wi-fi ~ Bedrooms: £90

WIMBORNE MINSTER   SZ0199
Green Man

(01202) 881021 – www.greenmanwimborne.com
Victoria Road, at junction with West Street (B3082/B3073); BH21 1EN

Cosy, warm-hearted town tavern with simple food at very fair prices

This is a cheery, traditional town pub with customers dropping in and out
all day. The four small linked areas have maroon plush banquettes and
polished dark pub tables, copper and brass ornaments, red walls, Wadworths
6X, IPA and Swordfish on handpump and a farm cider. One room has a log
fire in a sizeable brick fireplace, another has a coal-effect gas fire, and there
are two dartboards, a silenced games machine, background music and TV;
the Barn houses a pool table. Their little border terrier is called Cooper. In
summer, the award-winning flowering tubs, hanging baskets and window
boxes are quite amazing – there are more on the heated back terrace.
Bargain-priced food is served at lunchtime only.

Wadworths ~ Tenant Andrew Kiff ~ Real ale ~ Open 10am-11.30pm (midnight Sat) ~
Bar food 10-2 ~ Restaurant ~ Children welcome until 7.30pm ~ Dogs allowed in bar

WORTH MATRAVERS   SY9777

Square & Compass

(01929) 439229 - www.squareandcompasspub.co.uk
At fork of both roads signposted to village from B3069; BH19 3LF

Unchanging country tavern with masses of character, in the same family for many years; lovely sea views and fine nearby walks

At peak times you'll find a queue of customers at the serving hatches in this much loved gem, but the charming Newman family (who've run the pub for over a century) cope with warm friendliness and efficiency. It remains quite unchanging and totally unspoilt. A couple of simple rooms have straightforward furniture on flagstones and wooden benches around the walls, a woodburning stove, a stuffed albino badger and a loyal crowd of chatty locals. Bristol Beer Factory Milk Stout, Butcombe Haka, Hattie Brown New Moonlite, Otter Head and Palmers Copper tapped from the cask, and home-produced and ten other farm ciders are passed through the two serving hatches to customers in the drinking corridor; also, 20 malt whiskies. Darts and shove-ha'penny. Bar food is limited to home-made pasties and pies. From the local stone benches out in front there's a fantastic view over the village rooftops down to the sea. There may be free-roaming chickens and other birds clucking around and the small (free) museum exhibits local fossils and artefacts, mostly collected by the current landlord and his father. Wonderful walks lead to some exciting switchback sections of the coast path above St Aldhelm's Head and Chapman's Pool – you'll need to park in the public car park (£2 honesty box) 100 metres along the Corfe Castle road.

Free house ~ Licensees Charlie Newman and Kevin Hunt ~ Real ale ~ No credit cards ~ Open 12-11 ~ Bar food all day ~ Children welcome ~ Dogs welcome ~ Live music Fri and Sat evenings, Sun lunchtime

DOG FRIENDLY HOTELS, INNS AND B&Bs

BEAMINSTER   ST4801

Bridge House

(01308) 862200 - www.bridge-house.co.uk
Prout Bridge, Beaminster, Dorset DT8 3AY

£160; 13 attractive rooms, including 4 in the adjacent coach house. Originally a house for priests, this 700-year-old stone building is a friendly place with an open fire in the cosy, comfortable sitting room, a convivial bar, a breakfast room overlooking the attractive walled garden (where dogs may walk), good, modern cooking in the Georgian dining room and an informal, relaxed atmosphere. Dogs allowed in bedrooms in coach house and in some public areas; £15.

BOURNEMOUTH
SZ1491
White Topps

(01202) 428868 – www.whitetopps.co.uk
45 Church Road, Southbourne, Bournemouth, Dorset BH6 4BB

£84; 5 rooms with shared bathrooms. Homely Edwardian house that is 100 per cent dog oriented and guests must bring at least one dog in order to stay; two lounges, one with a bar and one with a fridge for guests (used for storing dog food), traditional meals (and vegetarian choices) in dining room, and lots of doggie pictures and ornaments; three resident dogs; walks on nearby beach. Closed November-February. Dogs welcome everywhere; ground-floor bedroom is for elderly or disabled dogs.

BRIDPORT
SY4691
Britmead House

(01308) 422941 – www.britmeadhouse.co.uk
West Bay Road, Bridport, Dorset DT6 4EG

£84; 9 clean rooms. Extended Victorian guesthouse with lots to do nearby, a comfortable lounge overlooking the garden, attractive dining room serving good breakfasts, and kind helpful service; resident dog; fields at back of the grounds to walk dogs and a nearby beach. Closed December and January. Dogs allowed in some bedrooms (must not be left unattended) by prior arrangement; £5.

CERNE ABBAS
ST6601
New Inn

(01300) 341274 – www.thenewinncerneabbas.co.uk
14 Long Street, Cerne Abbas, Dorchester, Dorset DT2 7JF

£95; 12 lovely, well equipped rooms, in main building or converted stable block. 16th-c former coaching inn with character bar and dining room, featuring mullioned windows, heavy oak beams, attractive old furniture on slate or polished wooden floors, various nooks and crannies and a woodburning stove; local ales and cider, friendly licensees and excellent, inventive food; you can walk from the village up and around the prehistoric Cerne Abbas Giant chalk carving and on to other nearby villages. Dogs allowed in some bedrooms and in bar areas; treats.

EAST KNIGHTON
SY8185
Countryman

(01305) 852666 – www.thecountrymaninndorset.com
East Knighton, Dorchester, Dorset DT2 8LL

£85-£125; 9 cosy rooms. Attractively converted pair of old cottages, with open fires and plenty of character in the main bar which opens into several smaller areas; real ales, an extensive menu including a popular carvery and nice breakfasts in the large restaurant, and courteous staff; two resident dogs; walks in garden and nearby. Dogs allowed in bedrooms and bar; treats, bowls and meals; £10 per stay.

EVERSHOT

ST5704

Acorn

(01935) 83228 – www.acorn-inn.co.uk
28 Fore Street, Evershot, Dorchester, Dorset DT2 0JW

£115; 10 comfortable, individually decorated rooms, each with a Thomas Hardy name. Immortalised as the Sow & Acorn in Hardy's *Tess of the D'Urbervilles*; two bars with opens fires, wood panelling, copper and brass items, beer mats on beams, pretty knick-knacks, flagstones and quarry tiles, real ales, 39 wines by the glass and over 100 malt whiskies; good seasonal food in bistro-style dining room and slightly more formal restaurant; walled garden with seats under a fine beech tree and numerous nearby walks; breakfasts are first class and guests get a discount on the gym/spa facilities at Summer Lodge hotel (see below). Dogs allowed in bedrooms and all public areas; towel, bowl, treats and guide; £10.

EVERSHOT

ST5704

Summer Lodge

(01935) 482000 – www.summerlodgehotel.com
9 Fore Street, Evershot, Dorchester, Dorset DT2 0JR

£235–£675; 24 beautifully decorated rooms, including 4 suites. Spotlessly kept and peacefully set former dower house with an airy conservatory, a cosy whisky bar, a smart, elegant dining room, a carefully chosen wine list, excellent english cooking with contemporary touches and using home-grown and best quality local produce, delicious breakfasts and afternoon teas; personal, caring service; spa with gym and indoor swimming pool, tennis, croquet and giant chess; dogs can walk in garden on a lead and there are other walks nearby. Dogs allowed in some bedrooms and some public rooms; bed, bowl, towel, washing area and food menu; £20.

FARNHAM

ST9515

Museum Inn

(01725) 516261 – www.museuminn.co.uk
Farnham, Blandford Forum, Dorset DT11 8DE

£110; 8 attractive rooms, including 4 in converted stables; also large self-catering cottage. Rather smart 17th-c thatched inn with comfortably cushioned furnishings in the bustling, beamed and flagstoned small bar, various dining areas including one with an inglenook fireplace and fine antique dresser, another with a glass roof, plus outdoor seating; real ales, excellent wine list, particularly good modern cooking and attentive service; walks in the surrounding fields. Dogs allowed in stable bedrooms, cottage and public areas except restaurant; bedding, bowl and treats; £10 per stay.

HAZELBURY BRYAN

ST7409

Old Causeway Bakery

(01258) 817228 – www.oldcausewaybakery.co.uk
Hazelbury Bryan, Sturminster Newton, Dorset DT10 2BH

£90; 2 comfortable rooms, plus self-catering. Plenty of antiques, paintings and guidebooks in comfortable sitting room/dining room, bold coloured walls, friendly, helpful owners and good, generous breakfasts; resident dogs Henry the black labrador and Bertie the working cocker spaniel; adjacent field, lots of nearby walks and beaches. Dogs allowed anywhere except on beds.

LOWER BOCKHAMPTON
SY7290
Yalbury Cottage
(01305) 262382 – www.yalburycottage.com
Lower Bockhampton, Dorchester, Dorset DT2 8PZ

£120; 8 rooms overlooking garden or fields. Very attractive, family-run 16th-c thatched house with a relaxed friendly atmosphere, candlelight, low beams, exposed stone walls and woodburning stoves in inglenook fireplaces in comfortable lounge and restaurant, carefully cooked and beautifully served imaginative food, good wines; outdoor seating on pretty terrace overlooking fields. Dogs allowed in some bedrooms and lounge, but not restaurant; £7.50.

MIDDLEMARSH
ST6607
Hunters Moon
(01963) 210966 – www.hunters-moon.org.uk
Middlemarsh, Sherborne, Dorset DT9 5QN

£85; 8 comfortable rooms. Cheerfully run former coaching inn with friendly hands-on licensees, a pubby atmosphere in the comfortably traditional beamed bars, quite a variety of tables and chairs on red patterned carpets, plenty of bric-a-brac, children's books and toys, board games, three log fires, local beers and good food; seats on a neat lawn. Dogs allowed in some bedrooms and bar (well behaved and on leads); £10 per stay.

STUDLAND
SZ0383
Knoll House
(01929) 450450 – www.knollhouse.co.uk
Studland, Swanage, Dorset BH19 3AH

£220; 80 simply decorated rooms including singles and suites. Spacious, well run hotel owned by the same family for over 50 years and set in 100 acres with marvellous views of Studland Bay and direct access to the fine three-mile beach; comfortable spreading lounges with open fires, paintings and plenty of armchairs and sofas, a cocktail bar, enjoyable meals in airy restaurant and lots to do – tennis, table tennis, pool and table football, heated outdoor pool and health spa, adventure playground, small private golf course and nearby sea fishing, riding, walking, sailing and windsurfing; resident dogs. Closed January-late March. Dogs allowed in all bedrooms and public areas, except dining rooms, pool and spa; bedding; £5.

STURMINSTER NEWTON
ST7711
Plumber Manor
(01258) 472507 – www.plumbermanor.co.uk
Hazelbury Bryan Road, Plumber, Sturminster Newton, Dorset DT10 2AF

£240; 16 very comfortable rooms, 6 in the house and 10 in the restored stone barn with river and garden views. Handsome 17th-c house (owned and run by the same family since it was built) in quiet countryside, with a convivial well stocked bar, antiques, fresh flowers and open fires in the lounge, good interesting english/french food in three dining rooms, smashing breakfasts, a relaxed atmosphere and exceptionally friendly, helpful service; two resident black labradors; tennis, croquet; dogs allowed in gardens and plenty of walks nearby. Closed February. Dogs allowed in some bedrooms in barn, but not in main house; £10 per stay.

TARRANT MONKTON   ST9408

Langton Arms

(01258) 830225 – www.thelangtonarms.co.uk
Tarrant Monkton, Blandford Forum, Dorset DT11 8RX

£100; 6 comfortable rooms. Charming thatched pub next to a 15th-c church in a pretty village with nearby walks, a beamed bar with modern paintwork, wooden tables and chairs, lots of black and white photos and an inglenook fireplace; local beers; the attractive restaurant and conservatory are in a converted barn and the well liked food is carefully prepared using some own-grown produce and meat from the pub's own butchery; seats in the pleasant back garden and a children's play area. Dogs allowed in bedrooms and one bar; £5.

Essex

DOG FRIENDLY PUBS

CHRISHALL
TL4439

Red Cow

(01763) 838792 ~ www.theredcow.com
High Street; off B1039 Wendens Ambo–Great Chishill; SG8 8RN

Bustling, well run local with beamed rooms, four real ales, well liked food and seats in attractive garden

Popular and welcoming, this 16th-c thatched pub is run by hands-on licensees and their friendly staff. The atmospheric bar and dining room are heavily beamed and timbered, there's a woodburning stove and an open fire, all sorts of wooden dining chairs around tables of every size on bare floorboards, and a comfortable sofa and armchairs. The drinks list includes Adnams Southwold, Morlands Old Speckled Hen, Timothy Taylors Landlord and Woodfordes Wherry on handpump, eight wines by the glass, Aspall's cider and cocktails; they hold a music and beer festival in May. Terracing has picnic-sets and the garden is pretty. The pub is handy for the Icknield Way.

Free house ~ Licensees Toby and Alexis Didier Serre ~ Real ale ~ Open 12-3, 6 (5 Fri)-11; 12-11 Sat; 12-8 Sun; closed Mon ~ Bar food 12-2, 6-9; 12-9 Sat; 12-3 Sun ~ Restaurant ~ Children welcome ~ Dogs allowed in bar ~ Wi-fi ~ Live music last Fri of month

FEERING
TL8720

Sun

(01376) 570442 ~ www.suninnfeering.co.uk
Just off A12 Kelvedon bypass; Feering Hill (B1024 just W of Feering proper); CO5 9NH

Striking 16th-c pub with six real ales, well liked food and pleasant garden

Always deservedly busy, the spreading slate-floored bar is relaxed, unpretentious and civilised, with two big woodburning stoves – one in the huge central inglenook fireplace, another by an antique winged settle on the left. Throughout, the timbered and jettied pub has handsomely carved black beams and timbers galore, and attractive wild-flower murals in a frieze above the central timber divider. Half a dozen ales on handpump include Shepherd Neame Bishops Finger, Goldings, Master Brew Bitter, Spitfire and Whitstable Bay Pale, plus a guest beer – and they hold summer and winter beer festivals; also, 11 wines by the glass, ten malt whiskies and 14 gins served by cheerful staff.

A brick-paved back courtyard has tables, heaters and a shelter; in the garden beyond, tall trees shade green picnic-sets.

Shepherd Neame ~ Tenant Andy Howard ~ Real ale ~ Open 12-3, 5.30-11; 12-midnight Sat; 12-10.30 Sun ~ Bar food 12-2.30, 6-9 (9.30 Fri, Sat); 12-8 Sun ~ Children welcome away from bar ~ Dogs welcome ~ Wi-fi

FULLER STREET
TL7416

Square & Compasses

(01245) 361477 – www.thesquareandcompasses.co.uk
Back road Great Leighs–Hatfield Peverel; CM3 2BB

Neatly kept country pub with two woodburning stoves, four ales and enjoyable food

This gently civilised pub is in attractive countryside and handy for the Essex Way long-distance footpath. As well as a small extension for walkers and dogs, the L-shaped beamed bar has two woodburning stoves in inglenook fireplaces, and friendly staff serve Colchester No.1, Crouch Vale Essex Boys Best Bitter and Mighty Oak Captain Bob tapped from the cask, Bertie's dry cider and 18 wines by the glass; background jazz. The dining room features shelves of bottles and decanters against timbered walls, and an appealing variety of dining chairs around dark wooden tables set with linen napkins, on carpeting. Tables out in front on decking offer gentle country views.

Free house ~ Licensee Victor Roome ~ Real ale ~ Open 11.30-11; 12-midnight Sat; 12-11 Sun ~ Bar food 12-2 (2.30 Sat), 6.30-9.30; 12-6 Sun ~ Restaurant ~ Well behaved children welcome ~ Dogs allowed in bar

GOLDHANGER
TL9008

Chequers

(01621) 788203 – www.thechequersgoldhanger.co.uk
Church Street; off B1026 E of Heybridge; CM9 8AS

Cheerful and neatly kept pub with six real ales, traditional furnishings, friendly staff and tasty food

You can be sure of a genuinely warm and friendly welcome here. The nice old corridor with its red and black floor tiles leads to six rambling rooms, including a spacious lounge with dark beams, black panelling and a huge sash window overlooking the graveyard, a traditional dining room with bare boards and carpeting and a games room with bar billiards; woodburning stove, open fires, TV and background music. Youngs IPA and five guests from breweries such as Adnams, Crouch Vale, St Austell and Sharps on handpump; they also hold spring and autumn beer festivals. Also, 16 wines by the glass, ten malt whiskies and several farm ciders. There are picnic-sets under umbrellas in the courtyard with its grapevine. Do look at the fine old church next door.

Punch ~ Lease Philip Glover and Dominic Davies ~ Real ale ~ Open 11-11; 12-11 Sun ~ Bar food 12-3, 6.30-9; not Sun evening or Mon bank holiday evening ~ Restaurant ~ Children welcome except in tap room ~ Dogs allowed in bar ~ Wi-fi

HATFIELD BROAD OAK

TL5416

Dukes Head

(01279) 718598 – www.thedukeshead.co.uk
B183 Hatfield Heath–Takeley; High Street; CM22 7HH

Relaxed, well run dining pub with enjoyable food in an attractive layout of nicely linked separate areas

In warm weather, head for the back garden with its sheltered terrace and chairs around teak tables under cocktail parasols; there are also picnic-sets at the front corner of the building which has some nice pargeting. Rambling around the central woodburner and side servery are various cosy seating areas: good solid wooden dining chairs around a variety of chunky stripped tables with a comfortable group of armchairs and a sofa at one end, and a slightly more formal area at the back on the right. Cheerful prints on the wall and some magenta panels in the mostly cream décor make for a buoyant mood. Greene King IPA, Sharps Doom Bar and Timothy Taylors Landlord on handpump and 30 wines by the glass from a good list, served by cheerful staff; background music and board games. Sam and Zac the pub dogs welcome other canines and there are always dog biscuits behind the bar.

Enterprise ~ Lease Liz Flodman ~ Real ale ~ Open 11.30-11; 10.30-11 Sat; 10.30-10 Sun ~ Bar food 12-2.30, 6-9.30; 10.30-10 Sat; 10.30-9 Sun ~ Restaurant ~ Children welcome ~ Dogs allowed in bar ~ Wi-fi

LITTLEY GREEN

TL6917

Compasses

(01245) 362308 – www.compasseslittleygreen.co.uk
Village signposted off B1417 Felsted road in Hartoft End (opposite former Ridleys Brewery), about a mile N of junction with B1008 (former A130); CM3 1BU

Charming brick tavern – a prime example of what is now an all too rare breed; bedrooms

They keep a fantastic choice of drinks in the companionable bar here: Bishop Nick Ridleys Rite (brewed in Felsted by the landlord's brother) as well as guests from brewers such as Adnams, Crouch Vale, Mighty Oak, Red Fox, Skinners, Tyne Bank and two weekend guest ales, all tapped from casks in a back cellar. In summer and at Christmas they hold beer festivals featuring dozens of beers, alongside festivities that may include vintage ploughing in the field opposite. Also, Fosseway and Tumpy Ground farm ciders, perries from Cornish Orchards and Gwynt y Ddraig and eight wines by the glass. The bar has very traditional brown-painted panelling and wall benches, plain chairs and tables on quarry tiles, with chat and laughter rather than piped music. There's a piano, darts and board games in one side room, and decorative mugs hanging from beams in another. There are picnic-sets out on the sheltered side grass and the garden behind, with a couple of long tables on the front cobbles by the quiet lane.

Free house ~ Licensee Jocelyn Ridley ~ Real ale ~ Open 12-3, 5.30-11.30; 12-11.30 Thurs-Sun ~ Bar food 12-2.30 (4 Sat, 5 Sun), 7-9.30 ~ Children welcome ~ Dogs welcome ~ Wi-fi ~ Live folk music every third Mon ~ Bedrooms: £70

MARGARETTING TYE   TL6801

White Hart

(01277) 840478 – www.thewhitehart.uk.com

From B1002 (just S of A12/A414 junction) follow Maldon Road for 1.3 miles, then turn right immediately after river bridge, into Swan Lane, keeping on for 0.7 miles; The Tye; CM4 9JX

Cheery pub with a fine choice of ales, good food, plenty of customers and a family garden; bedrooms

The open-plan but cottagey rooms have walls and wainscoting painted in chalky traditional colours that match well with the dark timbers and mix of old wooden chairs and tables; a stuffed deer head is mounted on the chimney breast above a woodburning stove. Tapped straight from the cask, the fine range of ales includes Adnams Southwold and Broadside, Mighty Oak IPA and Oscar Wilde and a couple of guests such as Farmers Ales Pucks Folly and Woodfordes Wherry; they hold beer festivals in July and November. Also, a german wheat beer, interesting bottled beers, quite a range of spirits and winter mulled wine. The neat carpeted back conservatory is similar in style to the other rooms, and the front lobby has a bookcase of charity paperbacks. Darts, board games and background music. There are plenty of picnic-sets out on grass and terracing around the pub, with a sturdy play area, a fenced duck pond and views across the fields; lovely sunsets.

Free house ~ Licensee Elizabeth Haines ~ Real ale ~ Open 11.30-3.30, 5.30-midnight; 11.30-midnight Sat; 12-midnight Sun; 11.30-3.30, 6-11 weekdays in winter; closed Mon ~ Bar food 12-2.30, 6-9 (9.30 Fri); 12-3.30, 6-9.30 Sat; 12-7.30 Sun ~ Restaurant ~ Well behaved children welcome ~ Dogs allowed in bar ~ Wi-fi ~ Bedrooms: £80

SAFFRON WALDEN   TL5338

Eight Bells

(01799) 522790 – www.8bells-pub.co.uk

Bridge Street; B184 towards Cambridge; CB10 1BU

Beautiful bar and dining rooms, helpful, courteous staff, enjoyable food and drink and seats in the garden

The very good food continues to draw plenty of customers to this handsomely timbered black and white Tudor inn – but they also keep Fullers London Pride, St Austell Tribute and Woodfordes Wherry on handpump, ten wines by the glass and several malt whiskies. Staff are friendly and the atmosphere is relaxed and gently civilised. The open-plan beamed bar area has leather armchairs, chesterfield sofas and old wooden settles on bare floorboards, a coal-effect gas fire in a brick fireplace and interesting old photographs. The back dining part is in a splendidly raftered and timbered barn with modern dark wood furniture and upholstered wall banquettes, a woodburning stove built into a log-effect end wall and display cabinets with old books, candlesticks and so forth; background music. There are seats and tables outside and a raised decked area. Audley End (English Heritage) is nearby, as are some decent walks.

Cozy Pub Company ~ Lease Leanne Langman ~ Real ale ~ Open 10am-11pm (midnight Sat); 10am-10.30pm Sun ~ Bar food 12-9.30; 12-6 Sun ~ Restaurant ~ Children welcome ~ Dogs allowed in bar ~ Wi-fi

SOUTH HANNINGFIELD   TQ7497
Old Windmill
(01268) 712280 – www.brunningandprice.co.uk/oldwindmill
Off A130 S of Chelmsford; CM3 8HT

Extensive, invitingly converted pub with interesting food and a good range of drinks

Cosy, rambling areas are created by a forest of stripped standing timbers and open doorways here and there's always an abundance of chatty, cheerful customers. An agreeable mix of highly polished old tables and chairs are spread throughout as are frame-to-frame pictures on cream walls, woodburning stoves and homely pot plants. Deep green or dark red dado and a few old rugs dotted on the glowing wood floors provide splashes of colour; other areas are more subdued with beige carpeting. Phoenix Brunning & Price Original and five guests such as Milton Pegasus, Mighty Oak Kings, Slaters Rye IPA, Trumans Swift and XT Three on handpump, with a dozen wines by the glass, 70 malt whiskies and a good range of spirits; background music. A back terrace has tables and chairs under parasols and there are picnic-sets on the lawn, and a few more seats out in front.

Brunning & Price ~ Manager Nick Clark ~ Real ale ~ Open 11.30-11; 12-10.30 Sun ~ Bar food 12-10 (9.30 Sun) ~ Restaurant ~ Children welcome ~ Dogs allowed in bar ~ Wi-fi

STOCK   TQ6999
Hoop
(01277) 841137 – www.thehoop.co.uk
B1007; from A12 Chelmsford bypass take Galleywood, Billericay turn-off; CM4 9BD

Happy weatherboarded pub with interesting beers, nice food and a large garden

This is a refreshingly unmodern village pub with Adnams Bitter and guests from Billericay, Harveys and Youngs on handpump or tapped from the cask; they also hold a beer festival at the end of May featuring 100 real ales, 80 ciders, a hog roast and a barbecue. The open-plan bar has beams and standing timbers (hinting at the original layout when it was once three weavers' cottages), pubby tables and chairs and a happy bustle of cheery locals and visitors. The dining room up in the timbered eaves is a fine room with an open fire in a big brick-walled fireplace, napery and elegant high-backed wooden chairs on bare boards. Prettily bordered with flowers, the large sheltered back garden has picnic-sets and a covered seating area. Parking is limited, so it's worth arriving early.

Free house ~ Licensee Michelle Corrigan ~ Real ale ~ Open 11-11; 12-10.30 Sun ~ Bar food 12-2.30, 6-9; 12-9.30 Sat; 12-5 Sun ~ Restaurant ~ Children welcome on left-hand side of bar ~ Dogs allowed in bar ~ Wi-fi

DOG FRIENDLY HOTELS, INNS AND B&Bs

BURNHAM-ON-CROUCH   TQ9595
White Harte
(01621) 782106 – www.whiteharteburnham.co.uk
The Quay, Burnham-on-Crouch, Essex CM0 8AS

£95–£105; 19 simply decorated rooms including 8 with shared bathroom, many overlooking the water; no disabled rooms. Comfortably old-fashioned red-brick hotel overlooking the River Crouch with picnic-sets on the jetty and riverside walks from the door; informal bars with assorted nautical bric-a-brac and real ales, and other traditionally furnished high-ceilinged rooms with oak furniture on polished parquet flooring, sea pictures, big log fires in winter and pubby food; chatty, friendly staff. Dogs allowed everywhere except restaurant; £5.

GREAT CHESTERFORD   TL5042
Crown House
(01799) 530515 – www.crownhousehotel.com
Great Chesterford, Saffron Walden, Essex CB10 1NY

£99.50; 18 traditionally styled rooms, some in former stable block. Carefully restored, imposing Georgian coaching inn set in lovely gardens, with plenty of original features, an open fire and comfortable leather seating in the attractive lounge bar, good, bistro-style food in the smart panelled restaurant, and pleasant, efficient staff. Dogs allowed in ground-floor annexe bedrooms and bar; £5.

HORNDON-ON-THE-HILL   TQ6783
Bell
(01375) 642463 – www.bell-inn.co.uk
High Road, Horndon-on-the-Hill, Stanford-le-Hope, Essex SS17 8LD

£70–£140; 27 attractive rooms of varying sizes, in pub and two other nearby buildings. Lovely Tudor inn, run by the same family for more than 75 years, with a heavily beamed bar, antique high-backed settles and benches on polished oak floorboards and flagstones, a curious collection of ossified hot-cross buns hanging along a beam, an impressive range of drinks and quite an emphasis on the excellent food; seats in pretty flower-filled courtyard; resident black labrador, Floyd, and shar pei, Stella. Dogs allowed in some bedrooms and bar; bowls; £10.

LITTLE WALDEN   TL5441
Crown
(01799) 522475 – www.thecrownlittlewalden.co.uk
Little Walden, Essex CB10 1XA

£75; 3 rooms. Bustling 18th-c cottage pub that's very much the hub of the community and particularly well run by the friendly, helpful landlord and his courteous staff; low ceilings, red walls, bare boards and traditional furnishings, a chatty atmosphere, cosy warm fires and an unusual walk-through fireplace; three changing beers tapped straight from casks racked up behind the bar; hearty and fairly priced food; tables on the terrace have views over the surrounding tranquil countryside. The breakfasts are excellent. Dogs allowed in bedrooms and bar.

MISTLEY   TM1131

Mistley Thorn

(01206) 392821 – www.mistleythorn.com
High Street, Mistley, Manningtree, Essex CO11 1HE

£100–£115; 12 stylish, well equipped rooms including a new suite, 4 with Stour estuary views. 18th-c former coaching inn with a contemporary open-plan interior, modern paintwork and art on the walls, a convivial small bar, and a smart dining area with a woodburning stove in a brick fireplace; quite a choice of top notch food (including local oysters and plenty of fish/seafood) and good breakfasts; they also run a pizzeria in town (Lucca); walks on the nearby Essex Way. Dogs welcome in some bedrooms; dog biscuits; £10.

Gloucestershire

DOG FRIENDLY PUBS

BLEDINGTON   SP2422

Kings Head

(01608) 658365 – www.kingsheadinn.net
B4450 The Green; OX7 6XQ

16th-c inn with atmospheric furnishings, super wines by the glass, real ales and delicious food; smart bedrooms

This former cider house is friendly, civilised and a thoroughly good all-rounder. The main bar is the beating heart of the place. It's full of ancient beams and other atmospheric furnishings (high-backed wooden settles, gate-leg or pedestal tables) and has a warming log fire in a stone inglenook; sporting memorabilia of rugby, racing, cricket and hunting. To the left, a drinking area has built-in wall benches, stools and dining chairs around wooden tables, rugs on bare boards and a woodburning stove. Hook Norton Best and guests from breweries such as Butcombe, Flying Monk, Hook Norton and Purity on handpump, a super wine list with ten by the glass, 20 malt whiskies and an extensive gin collection; background music, board games and cards. There are seats out in front and rattan-style armchairs around tables in the lovely back courtyard garden with a pagoda; maybe free-ranging bantams and ducks. This is a lovely place to stay and the setting – opposite the green in a tranquil village – is very pretty.

Free house ~ Licensees Nicola and Archie Orr-Ewing ~ Real ale ~ Open 11-11 ~ Bar food 12-2, 6.30-9 ~ Restaurant ~ Children welcome ~ Dogs allowed in bar ~ Wi-fi ~ Bedrooms: £100

BROCKHAMPTON   SP0322

Craven Arms

(01242) 820410 – www.thecravenarms.co.uk
Village signposted off A436 Andoversford–Naunton – look out for inn sign at head of lane in village; can also be reached from A40 Andoversford–Cheltenham via Whittington and Syreford; GL54 5XQ

Friendly village pub with a convivial landlord, tasty bar food, real ales and seats in a big garden; bedrooms

With a warm welcome and a happy, chatty atmosphere, this is all you could wish for in an attractive old country pub. The character bars have low beams, roughly coursed thick stone walls and some tiled flooring; although it's largely been opened out to give a sizeable eating area off the smaller bar servery, there's a feeling of several communicating rooms. The furniture is mainly pine, with comfortable leather sofas, wall settles and tub chairs; also, gin traps, various stuffed animal trophies and a woodburning stove. There's Otter Bitter, Butcombe Legless Bob (named for the landlord, with 20p per pint going to Diabetes UK) and Ramsbury Bitter on handpump, eight wines by the glass and a farm cider, served by attentive staff; board games. The large garden has plenty of seats and the views are lovely. Good surrounding walks.

Free house ~ Licensee Barbara Price ~ Real ale ~ Open 12-3, 6-11; 12-11 Sat; 12-5 Sun; closed Sun evening, Mon ~ Bar food 12-2 (2.30 Sat), 6.30-9; 12.30-3 Sun ~ Restaurant ~ Children welcome ~ Dogs allowed in bar ~ Wi-fi ~ Bedrooms: £80

CHIPPING CAMPDEN SP1539
Eight Bells

(01386) 840371 – www.eightbellsinn.co.uk
Church Street (one-way – entrance off B4035); GL55 6JG

Lovely inn with massive timbers and beams, log fires, quite a choice of bar food, real ales and seats in a large terraced garden; bedrooms

The candlelit bars have heavy oak beams, massive timber supports and stripped-stone walls with cushioned pews, sofas and solid dark wood furniture on broad flagstones, and log fires in up to three restored stone fireplaces; the atmosphere throughout is cheerful and bustling. A glass panel in the dining room floor reveals the passage from the church by which Roman Catholic priests escaped the Roundheads. Hook Norton Hooky, Goffs Jouster, Purity Pure UBU and Wye Valley HPA on handpump from the fine oak bar counter, seven wines by the glass and two farm ciders; background music and board games. There's a large terraced garden with plenty of seats, and striking views of the almshouses and church. The Cotswold Way, which leads to Bath, is nearby.

Free house ~ Licensee Neil Hargreaves ~ Real ale ~ Open 12-11 (10.30 Sun) ~ Bar food 12-2, 6.30-9; 12-2.30, 6.30-9.30 Fri, Sat; 12-9 Sun ~ Restaurant ~ Well behaved children welcome in dining room but not in bar after 7pm; must be over 6 in bedrooms ~ Dogs allowed in bar ~ Wi-fi ~ Bedrooms: £115

COOMBE HILL SO8926
Gloucester Old Spot

(01242) 680321 – www.thegloucesteroldspot.co.uk
Exit M5 junction 11 and use satnav GL51 9SY; access from junction 10 is restricted; GL51 9SY

The country local comes of age – a model for today's country pubs

As this cheerful, carefully restored country pub is close to Cheltenham Racecourse, it gets pretty packed on race days and it's best to book a table in advance then. The quarry-tiled beamed bar has chapel chairs and other seats around assorted tables (including one in a bow-windowed alcove) and opens into a lighter, partly panelled area with cushioned settles and stripped kitchen tables. Purity Mad Goose, Timothy Taylors Landlord and Wye Valley Butty Bach on handpump, seven decent wines by the glass and farm cider and perry – all served by young, friendly staff. Decoration is in unobtrusive good taste, with winter log fires. A handsome separate dining room has similar country furniture, high stripped-brick walls, dark flagstones and candlelight. Outside, there are chunky benches and tables under parasols on a terrace, with some oak barrel tables on brickwork and pretty flowers in vintage buckets and baskets; heaters for cooler weather.

Free house ~ Licensees Simon Daws and Hayley Flaxman ~ Real ale ~ Open 10am-11pm
(10.30pm Sun) ~ Bar food 12-2, 6-9; 12-8 Sun ~ Restaurant ~ Children welcome ~ Dogs
allowed in bar ~ Wi-fi

COWLEY   SO9714

Green Dragon

(01242) 870271 – www.green-dragon-inn.co.uk

Off A435 S of Cheltenham at Elkstone, Cockleford sign; OS Sheet 163 map reference
970142; GL53 9NW

17th-c inn with character bars, separate restaurant, popular food,
real ales and seats on terraces; bedrooms

Customers come here from far and wide to enjoy the good food and thoughtful
range of drinks. It's an attractive, stone-fronted old inn and the two beamed
bars have plenty of character and a cosy, nicely old-fashioned feel. There are big
flagstones and wooden floorboards, candlelit tables and winter log fires in two
stone fireplaces, and staff are consistently friendly and helpful. Hook Norton Old
Hooky, Sharps Doom Bar and guests such as Butcombe Bitter and Sharps Atlantic
on handpump, 12 wines by the glass and ten malt whiskies; background music.
The furniture and the bar itself in the upper Mouse Bar were made by Robert
Thompson – little mice run over the hand-carved tables, chairs and mantelpiece;
there's also a small upstairs restaurant and a separate skittle alley. There are seats
outside on terraces and this is good walking country.

Buccaneer Holdings ~ Managers Simon and Nicky Haly ~ Real ale ~ Open 11-11; 12-10.30
Sun ~ Bar food 12-2.30 (3 Sat), 6-10; 12-3.30, 6-9 Sun ~ Restaurant ~ Children welcome ~
Dogs allowed in bar ~ Wi-fi ~ Bedrooms: £95

DURSLEY   ST7598

Old Spot

(01453) 542870 – www.oldspotinn.co.uk

Hill Road; by bus station; GL11 4JQ

Unassuming and cheery town pub with a fine range of ales, regular beer
festivals and good value lunchtime food

This is one of those pubs that has a healthy local following but also attracts
serious pub-goers from far and wide. The front door opens into a deep-
pink small room with stools on shiny quarry tiles beside a pine-boarded bar
counter, and old enamel beer signs on the walls and ceiling; there's a profusion
of porcine paraphernalia. A small room leads off on the left and the little
wood-floored room to the right has a stone fireplace. A step goes down to a
cosy Victorian tiled snug and (to the right) a meeting room. A fine choice of
drinks includes up to eight real ales, 30 malt whiskies, three farm ciders, half
a dozen wines by the glass and artisan spirits. The beers on handpump include
Otter Bitter and Uley Old Ric, with guests such as Otter Bright, Palmers Copper
and 200, and a couple from Flying Monk; they hold two annual beer festivals.
Staff are cheerful and enthusiastic. The heated and covered garden has
seats. Wheelchair access. Sister pub is the Old Badger in Eastington.

Free house ~ Licensee Ellie Sainty ~ Real ale ~ Open 11-11 (midnight Sat); 12-11 Sun ~ Bar
food 12-3; 12-4 Sun ~ Children welcome away from bar area before 9pm ~ Dogs allowed in
bar ~ Wi-fi

EASTINGTON   SO7705

Old Badger

(01453) 822892 – www.oldbadgerinn.co.uk
Alkerton Road, a mile from M5 junction 13; GL10 3AT

Friendly, traditionally furnished pub with plenty to look at, five real ales, tasty food and seats in attractive garden

The fine choice of drinks here, served by helpful and chatty staff, might include real ales from breweries such as Castle Combe, Moles, Otter, Sarah Hughes, Strands, Uley and Wye Valley on handpump, ten wines by the glass, a dozen malt whiskies and farm cider; they hold beer and cider festivals with local musicians and brewery trips. The split-level connected rooms have an informal, easy-going feel and feature two open fires and traditional furnishings such as built-in planked and cushioned wall seats, settles and farmhouse chairs around all sorts of tables, quarry tiles and floorboards. There are stone bottles, bookshelves, breweriana on red or cream walls and even a stuffed badger. The nicely landscaped garden has benches and picnic-sets on a terrace, a lawn and under a covered gazebo; the flowering tubs and window boxes are pretty. Wheelchair access to top bar/dining area only; disabled loos are shared with baby-changing facilities. Sister pub is the Old Spot in Dursley.

Free house ~ Licensees Ellie Sainty and Julie Gilborson ~ Real ale ~ Open 12-11 ~ Bar food 12-2.30, 6-9; 12-3 Sun ~ Children welcome away from bar area ~ Dogs welcome ~ Wi-fi ~ Live music monthly Sat

FORD   SP0829

Plough

(01386) 584215 – www.theploughinnford.co.uk
B4077 Stow–Alderton; GL54 5RU

16th-c inn in horse-racing country with a bustling atmosphere, first class service, good food and well kept beer; bedrooms

Customers return to this honey-coloured stone pub on a regular basis. You can be sure of a genuine welcome from the helpful, friendly licensees whether you're a visitor or a regular – the inn is opposite a well known racehorse trainer's yard so many of the customers belong to the racing fraternity. The beamed and stripped-stone bar has a chatty atmosphere, racing prints and photos, old settles and benches around big tables on uneven flagstones, oak tables in a snug alcove and open fires and woodburning stoves. Darts, TV (for the races) and background music. Donnington BB and SBA on handpump, eight wines by the glass and a dozen malt whiskies. There are picnic-sets under parasols and pretty hanging baskets at the front, and a large back garden with a children's play fort. It gets packed on race days. Cotswold Farm Park is nearby.

Donnington ~ Tenant Rebecca Chanin ~ Real ale ~ Open 9am-10.30pm ~ Bar food 12.15-2.15, 6-9.15; all day Fri-Sun ~ Restaurant ~ Children welcome ~ Dogs allowed in bar ~ Wi-fi ~ Bedrooms: £80

KILCOT

SO6925

Kilcot Inn

(01989) 720707 – www.kilcotinn.com

2.3 miles from M50 junction 3; B4221 towards Newent; GL18 1NG

Attractively reworked small country inn, kind staff, enjoyable local food and drink; bedrooms

The open-plan bar and dining areas have stripped beams, bare boards and dark flagstones, sunny bay-window seats, homely armchairs by one of the two warm woodburning stoves, tables with padded dining chairs and daily papers. Stools line the brick counter where the hard-working landlord and his courteous staff serve Wye Valley Butty Bach and a changing guest ale on handpump, four draught ciders and perry (with more by the bottle), 20 malt whiskies, local wine and organic fruit juice; TV and maybe background music. The front terrace has picnic-sets under cocktail parasols, with more out behind. There's a smart shed for bicycle storage.

Free house ~ Licensee Mark Lawrence ~ Real ale ~ Open 9am-11pm; reduced Sun openings Jan/Feb in winter ~ Bar food 12-2.30, 6-9 (9.30 Thurs-Sat); 12-3 Sun ~ Restaurant ~ Children welcome ~ Dogs allowed in bar ~ Wi-fi ~ Bedrooms: £85

NAILSWORTH

ST8699

Weighbridge

(01453) 832520 – www.weighbridgeinn.co.uk

B4014 towards Tetbury; GL6 9AL

Bustling pub with cosy old-fashioned bar rooms, a fine choice of drinks and food, friendly service and sheltered garden

The famous two-in-one pies here continue to draw in customers – but the friendly welcome and real ales play their part too. The relaxed bar has three cosily old-fashioned rooms with open fires, stripped-stone walls and antique settles, country chairs and window seats. The black-beamed ceiling of the lounge bar is thickly festooned with black ironware – sheep shears, gin traps, lamps and a large collection of keys, many from the old Longfords Mill opposite the pub. Upstairs is a raftered hayloft with an engaging mix of rustic tables. No noisy games machines or background music. Uley Old Spot, Wadworths 6X and a couple of guest beers such as Bath Gem and Great Western Maiden Voyage on handpump, 18 wines (and champagne and prosecco) by the glass, farm cider, 12 malt whiskies and 20 gins. A sheltered landscaped garden at the back has picnic-sets under umbrellas. Good disabled access and facilities.

Free house ~ Licensee Mary Parsons ~ Real ale ~ Open 12-11 (10.30 Sun) ~ Bar food 12-9 ~ Restaurant ~ Children allowed away from the bars ~ Dogs welcome ~ Wi-fi

NETHER WESTCOTE

SP2220

Feathered Nest

(01993) 833030 – www.thefeatherednestinn.co.uk

Off A424 Burford to Stow-on-the-Wold; OX7 6SD

Caring service, a happy atmosphere, attractive surroundings and exceptional food and drink; lovely bedrooms

The food here is accomplished and beautifully presented, and for many customers it's the main reason for their visit – but it would be a shame to miss out on the companionable bar. This is cosy and friendly with Purity Pure UBU and a guest beer on handpump, 22 wines by the glass from an impressive list and some pubby dining choices too; service is exemplary. Softly lit, this largely stripped-stone bar has real saddles as bar stools (some of the country's best racehorse trainers live locally), a carved settle among other carefully chosen seats, dark flagstones and low beams. This opens into an ochre-walled high-raftered room with deeply comfortable sofas by a vast log fire; background music and TV. Two attractively decorated dining rooms, both on two levels, have a pleasing mix of antique tables in varying sizes, and a lively, up-to-date atmosphere. A flagstoned terrace and heated shelter have teak tables and wicker armchairs, and a spreading lawn bounded by floodlit trees has groups of rustic seats, with the Evenlode Valley beyond.

Free house ~ Licensee Amanda Timmer ~ Real ale ~ Open 11-11 (7.30 Sun); closed Mon except bank holidays ~ Bar food 12-2.30, 6-9.30; 12-3.30 Sun; not Sun evening except bank holidays ~ Restaurant ~ Children welcome ~ Dogs allowed in bar ~ Wi-fi ~ Bedrooms: £195

NEWLAND   SO5509
Ostrich

(01594) 833260 – www.theostrichinn.com
Off B4228 in Coleford; or can be reached from the A466 in Redbrook, by turn-off at the England/Wales border – keep bearing right; GL16 8NP

Super range of beers in welcoming country pub, with spacious bar, open fire and good interesting food

Parts of this friendly old inn date back to the 13th c, though much of what you see inside is 17th-c. The low-ceilinged bar is spacious but cosily traditional, with a chatty, relaxed atmosphere, a roaring log fire, creaky floors, window shutters, candles in bottles on the tables, miners' lamps on uneven walls, and comfortable furnishings that include cushioned window seats, wall settles and rod-backed country kitchen chairs. The charming, warmly friendly landlady and her helpful staff keep a fine choice of real ales on handpump from breweries such as Bath, Cotswold Lion, Otter, RHC, Wye Valley and a couple of changing guests. Also, several wines by the glass and a couple of farm ciders; newspapers to read, perhaps quiet background jazz and board games. The walled garden has picnic-sets, with more out in front, and the pub is popular with walkers and their dogs. The church, known as the Cathedral of the Forest, is worth a visit.

Free house ~ Licensee Kathryn Horton ~ Real ale ~ Open 12-3, 6.30-11; 12-3, 6-midnight Sat; 12-4, 6.30-10.30 Sun ~ Bar food 12-2.30, 6.30 (6 Sat)-9.30 ~ Restaurant ~ Children welcome ~ Dogs allowed in bar

OAKRIDGE LYNCH   SO9103
Butchers Arms

(01285) 760371 – www.butchersarmsoakridge.com
Off Eastcombe–Bisley Road E of Stroud; GL6 7NZ

Bustling country pub with nice old bars and dining room, real ales, food cooked by the landlady and seats in a big garden

Attractive, friendly and relaxed, the beamed bar in this well run 18th-c pub has an open fire in a big stone fireplace with large copper pans to each side, an attractive medley of chapel and other country chairs around tables of various sizes on wooden floorboards, and modern art on exposed stone walls. Stools line the central counter where they keep Wadworths 6X and IPA and a changing guest beer on handpump and several wines by the glass. The dining room is similarly furnished, with hunting prints and old photos on pale walls above a grey dado, a longcase clock and stone bottles on windowsills. The big garden with valley views has picnic-sets and other seats and tables. They have a self-catering cottage next to the pub. This is a small village surrounded by lovely countryside and good walks.

Wadworths ~ Tenants Philip and Alison McLaughlin ~ Real ale ~ Open 12-3, 6-11; 12-11 Sat, Sun; may close earlier Sun in winter; closed Mon except bank holidays ~ Bar food 12-2, 6-9; not Sun evening, Mon ~ Restaurant ~ Children welcome ~ Dogs allowed in bar ~ Wi-fi

OLDBURY-ON-SEVERN   ST6092

Anchor

(01454) 413331 – www.anchorinnoldbury.co.uk
Village signposted from B4061; BS35 1QA

Friendly country pub with tasty bar food, a thoughtful range of drinks and a pretty garden with hanging baskets

You can walk to the River Severn and along numerous footpaths and bridleways and then come to this bustling village pub to enjoy the fine choice of drinks: Bass, Butcombe Bitter, Great Western Maiden Voyage and St Austell Trelawny on handpump, a dozen wines by the glass, three farm ciders and around 80 malt whiskies with helpful tasting notes. The neat lounge has black beams and stonework, cushioned window seats and a range of other wooden chairs, gate-leg tables, oil paintings of local scenes and a big log fire. The Village Bar has old and farming photographs on the walls, and there's a contemporary dining room towards the back of the building. The garden is pretty in summer, with lovely hanging baskets and window boxes and seats under parasols and trees. Wheelchair access to the dining room and a disabled lavatory. Nearby St Arilda's church is interesting, set on an odd little knoll.

Free house ~ Licensees Michael Dowdeswell and Mark Sorrell ~ Real ale ~ Open 11.30-2.30, 6-10.30; 11.30-11 Fri, Sat; 12-10 Sun ~ Bar food 12-2 (2.30 Sat), 6-9; 12-3, 6-8 Sun ~ Restaurant ~ Children in dining room only ~ Dogs allowed in bar ~ Wi-fi ~ Bedrooms: £75

SHEEPSCOMBE   SO8910

Butchers Arms

(01452) 812113 – www.butchers-arms.co.uk
Village signed off B4070 NE of Stroud; or A46 N of Painswick (but narrow lanes); GL6 7RH

Country pub with open fire and woodburner, plenty to look at, several real ales and enjoyable food; fine views

Tucked away down narrow lanes, this is a busy rural pub with a welcome for all. One half of the bar has parquet flooring, the other has old quarry tiles – as well as a woodburning stove, farmhouse chairs and stools around scrubbed tables, two big bay windows with cushioned seats and low beams clad with horsebrasses; also, delft shelves lined with china, brass and copper cups, lamps and blow torches (there's even a pitchfork) and walls decorated with hunting prints and photos of the village and surrounding area. Leading off here is a high-ceilinged room with exposed-stone walls hung with maps of local walks (there are many) and wheelback and mate's chairs around tables on bare boards. The more formal restaurant is carpeted and has an open log fire. Otter Ale, Prescott Hill Climb and Wye Valley HPA on handpump, ten wines by the glass and Weston's cider; daily papers, chess, cribbage and draughts. The view over the lovely steep beechwood valley is terrific, and the seats outside make the most of it. The area was apparently once a hunting ground for Henry VIII.

Free house ~ Licensees Mark and Sharon Tallents ~ Real ale ~ Open 11.30-3, 6.30-11; 11.30-11.30 Sat; 12-10.30 Sun ~ Bar food 12-2.30, 6.30-9.30; all day Sat; 12-8 (6 in winter) Sun ~ Restaurant ~ Children welcome ~ Dogs allowed in bar ~ Wi-fi

UPPER ODDINGTON   SP2225

Horse & Groom

(01451) 830584 – www.horseandgroom.uk.com
Village signposted from A436 E of Stow-on-the-Wold; GL56 0XH

16th-c Cotswold inn with enterprising food, lots of wines by the glass, local beers and comfortable, character bars; bedrooms

Reliably well run, this pretty place is always deservedly busy. The hard-working, hands-on landlord always has a genuine welcome for all his customers. The bar has pale polished flagstones, a handsome antique oak box settle among other more modern seats, some nice armchairs at one end, oak beams in the ochre ceiling, stripped-stone walls and a log fire in the inglenook fireplace; the comfortable lounge is similarly furnished. Goffs Lancer, Purity Mad Goose and Wye Valley Bitter on handpump, 25 wines (including champagne and sweet wines) by the glass, 20 malt whiskies and gin, vodka, lager and cider from the local Cotswold Brewing Company. There are seats and tables under green parasols on the terrace and in the pretty garden.

Free house ~ Licensees Simon and Sally Jackson ~ Real ale ~ Open 12-3, 5.30-11; 12-3, 6.30-10.30 Sun; closed first two weeks Jan ~ Bar food 12-2, 6.30 (7 Sun)-9 ~ Children welcome ~ Dogs allowed in bar ~ Wi-fi ~ Bedrooms: £110

DOG FRIENDLY HOTELS, INNS AND B&Bs

ARLINGHAM   SO6911

Old Passage

(01452) 740547 – www.theoldpassage.com
Passage Road, Arlingham, Gloucestershire GL2 7JR

£120; 2 airy rooms with river views. Civilised seafood restaurant-with-rooms overlooking the River Severn, with sofas and magazines in the small lounge, local artwork on green walls and plenty of dining space; simple, innovative cooking using sustainably sourced fish plus set lunches midweek and excellent breakfasts; seats in the garden and terrace. Dogs allowed in bedrooms and on terrace, but not in restaurant; £10.

BARNSLEY   SP0705

Village Pub

(01285) 740421 – www.thevillagepub.co.uk
Barnsley, Cirencester, Gloucestershire GL7 5EF

£149; 6 individually decorated rooms. Smart, civilised country pub attracting a wide mix of customers (often with their dogs); low-ceilinged bar rooms with contemporary paintwork, polished candlelit tables on flagstones or oak floorboards, heavy swagged curtains, three open fires and country magazines; real ales and an extensive wine list, super breakfasts with their own conserves, home-made bread and local produce, and extremely good, imaginative food; seats in sheltered back courtyard with parasols and heaters. Dogs allowed in bedrooms and anywhere in the pub; bedding, bowl and blanket.

BIBURY SP1106
Swan
(01285) 740695 – www.cotswold-inns-hotels.co.uk
Bibury, Cirencester, Gloucestershire GL7 5NW

£180; 22 very pretty, individually decorated rooms including 4 suites in garden cottages. Handsome creeper-covered hotel on the River Coln, with private fishing and attractive formal garden (where dogs may walk); lovely flowers and log fires in carefully furnished comfortable lounges, a cosy parlour, an opulent dining room, stylish modern brasserie-bar, modern european cooking, excellent breakfasts and attentive staff; country walks nearby. Dogs allowed in some bedrooms and public rooms, but not restaurant; £10.

CHELTENHAM SO9421
Montpellier Chapter
(01242) 527788 – www.themontpellierchapterhotel.com
Bayshill Road, Cheltenham, Gloucestershire GL50 3AS

£225; 60 large, stylish and well equipped rooms. White-painted Regency hotel with contemporary furnishings throughout; bar, restaurant and garden room, lots of art on pale walls, log fires, enjoyable modern cooking from an open-plan kitchen including first class breakfasts, light lunches and afternoon teas; friendly, willing staff; seats on the terrace and in the courtyard. Dogs allowed in some bedrooms by prior arrangement and in bar; bowl, bedding and treats.

CIRENCESTER SP0202
Fleece
(01285) 658507 – www.thefleececirencester.co.uk
Market Place, Cirencester, Gloucestershire GL7 2NZ

£115; 28 attractive, well equipped bedrooms (some with much character). Carefully renovated inn with assorted areas for drinking and dining; contemporary pale paintwork, bare floorboards, good lighting, wooden tables and a variety of chairs, prints, fresh flowers, shelves of glassware and pottery; french windows open on to a terrace with white metal tables and chairs under parasols; efficient, courteous staff; real ales, good coffees and teas, hearty breakfasts and enjoyable all-day food; a good base for exploring the lovely town and surrounding countryside. Dogs allowed in all bedrooms and everywhere except restaurant; bedding; £15 per stay.

COLN ST ALDWYNS SP1405
New Inn
(01285) 750651 – www.new-inn.co.uk
Main Street, Coln St Aldwyns, Cirencester, Gloucestershire GL7 5AN

£110–£140; 15 strikingly decorated rooms. Partly 16th-c ivy-covered inn with a cheerful bar with an easy-going, chatty atmosphere, comfortable sofas and chairs and woodburning stoves in bar; a wide choice of enjoyable food in the attractive restaurant and new outdoor kitchen, good breakfasts and friendly staff; seats on the terrace and in the garden, and walks in the surrounding countryside; resident chocolate labrador called Tilda. Dogs allowed in some bedrooms and bar; treats; £20.

CORSE LAWN   SO8330
Corse Lawn House
(01452) 780771 – www.corselawn.com
Corse Lawn, Gloucester, Gloucestershire GL19 4LZ

£180; 18 well equipped, colourful, chintzy rooms. Handsome Queen Anne building surrounded by 12 acres of gardens and fields and in the same family for almost 40 years; a friendly, relaxed atmosphere in two comfortable drawing rooms; a large bistro, a distinguished restaurant and a new bar, with quite a choice of highly regarded french-influenced dishes (meals in the bistro are simpler) and a carefully chosen wine list; good breakfasts served by helpful, long-serving staff; heated indoor pool, tennis, croquet and table tennis; two resident black labradors, Bubble and Squeak, with walks in the grounds. Dogs allowed in bedrooms and in public areas (on leads) except restaurant and bistro.

DIDMARTON   ST8187
Kings Arms
(01454) 238245 – www.kingsarmsdidmarton.co.uk
The Street, Didmarton, Badminton, Gloucestershire GL9 1DT

£95; 6 individually furnished bedrooms; also 2 self-catering cottages in a converted stable block. Thoughtfully refurbished 17th-c former coaching inn with several knocked-through beamed bar rooms with grey-painted half panelling, church candles, antlers, prints and fresh flowers, armchairs by a log fire and a mix of farmhouse chairs and benches around wooden tables of all shapes and sizes; good food using prime local ingredients and real ales; there's also a restaurant with another open fire and a pleasant back garden with seats and picnic-sets; the resident jack russell is called Spoof and the pub is handy for Westonbirt Arboretum. Dogs allowed in all bedrooms and bar; bed, treats and dog beer; £10.

ENGLISH BICKNOR   SO5714
Dryslade Farm
(01594) 860259 – www.drysladefarm.co.uk
English Bicknor, Coleford, Gloucestershire GL16 7PA

£70; 3 homely rooms. 18th-c farmhouse owned by same family for 100 years and part of a working farm; friendly and relaxed atmosphere, cosy guest lounge with a winter log fire, and traditional breakfasts in light, airy conservatory (cake and tea on arrival); resident springer spaniel; plenty of walks nearby. Well behaved dogs allowed in bedrooms.

FOSSEBRIDGE

SP0711

Inn at Fossebridge

(01285) 720721 – www.cotswolds-country-pub-hotel.co.uk
Fossebridge, Cheltenham, Gloucestershire GL54 3JS

£110; 9 smart rooms named after local towns; also 2 self-catering cottages.
Partly Tudor and partly Georgian inn with four acres of riverside gardens,
a 15th-c bar with chatty locals, cider and real ales; other rooms with beams,
arches, stripped-stone walls and polished flagstones, a happy mix of chairs and
tables, copper implements, open fires, candles and fresh flowers; reliably good
food; lots of nearby walks. Dogs allowed in all bedrooms and in bar; must be on
leads in the grounds (free-range fowl); treats; £15.

GREAT RISSINGTON

SP1917

Lamb

(01451) 820388 – www.thelambinn.com
Great Rissington, Cheltenham, Gloucestershire GL54 2LN

£99–£180; 14 rooms, each with a teddy bear and views of village or fields.
Civilised golden-stone inn overlooking the Windrush Valley with surrounding
walks in stunning countryside; two-roomed bar with a woodburning stove in
the stone fireplace and some interesting things to look at (a wellington bomber
crashed in the garden in 1943); there's another woodburner and agricultural
tools in the restaurant serving bistro-style food using local produce; the village
church is idyllic; circular walk from pub door. Dogs allowed in all bedrooms and
anywhere in pub except restaurant; £7.

KEMPSFORD

SU1596

Kempsford Manor

(01285) 810131 – www.kempsfordmanor.com
High Street, Kempsford, Fairford, Gloucestershire GL7 4EQ

£80; 4 antiques-filled rooms. Lovely 17th-c house surrounded by beautiful
gardens leading to a canal walk; warmly friendly owners, a restful atmosphere
in gracious sitting room with panelling, comfortable seats on rug-covered
floorboards and an open fire, and a well stocked library; delicious breakfasts and
suppers (by arrangement) using home-grown produce; resident whippet; cricket
field and walks nearby. Dogs allowed in all bedrooms; £10.

LOWER SLAUGHTER

SP1522

Slaughters Manor House

(01451) 820456 – www.slaughtersmanor.co.uk
Copsehill Road, Lower Slaughter, Stow-on-the-Wold, Gloucestershire GL54 2HP

From £175; 19 luxurious rooms. Grand 17th-c manor house in four neatly kept
acres of gardens and grounds with a 15th-c dovecote, all-weather tennis court
and croquet; sitting rooms with open fires, decorative plaster ceilings, antiques
and paintings; excellent modern cooking in the elegant stylish dining room, fine
breakfasts and afternoon teas, and attentive welcoming staff; ground floor was
refurbished in 2016. Dogs allowed in eight bedrooms in Coach House; bedding
and bowl; £10.

LOWER SLAUGHTER $\qquad$ SP1622
Slaughters Country Inn

(01451) 822143 – www.theslaughtersinn.co.uk
Lower Slaughter, Stow-on-the-Wold, Gloucestershire GL54 2HS

£155; 31 individually decorated, spacious rooms, including 6 cottage suites. Honey-coloured stone hotel in a lovely Cotswold village, beside the little River Eye in four acres of neat grounds where dogs may walk (nearby local walks too); comfortable and charming lounges and spreading bar, beams, stone mullioned windows, open fires, persian rugs on polished parquet floors; thoroughly professional and efficient service; delicious modern cooking in light airy restaurant including super breakfasts, light bar lunches and afternoon teas. Dogs allowed in ground-floor bedrooms and anywhere in hotel except restaurant; £10.

MORETON-IN-MARSH $\qquad$ SP2032
Manor House

(01608) 650501 – www.cotswold-inns-hotels.co.uk
High Street, Moreton-in-Marsh, Gloucestershire GL56 0LJ

£130; 35 luxurious rooms. 16th-c manor house with pretty gardens and a chic, contemporary interior that blends well with the lovely original features; a convivial bar, comfortable lounge and library, elegant restaurant serving first class, inventive food, plus an airy conservatory for lighter brasserie meals (breakfasts are excellent too); courteous, helpful staff; walks in the grounds and other local walks. Dogs allowed in some bedrooms, library and lounge; £10.

MORETON-IN-MARSH $\qquad$ SP2032
White Hart Royal

(01608) 650731 – www.whitehartroyal.co.uk
High Street, Moreton-in-Marsh, Gloucestershire GL56 0BA

£119; 28 stylish rooms, some in converted stable block. Partly 14th-c former coaching inn with interesting Civil War history; cosy pubby bar with exposed stone walls, quarry tiles and open fire; comfortable beamed lounge areas with armchairs, big gilt mirrors and paintings; also a separate restaurant with attractive wall tapestries; real ales; bistro-style food and an easy-going atmosphere; seats in pleasant courtyard; lots of surrounding Cotswold walks. Dogs allowed in ground-floor bedrooms and everywhere in hotel except restaurant; welcome pack.

NORTH CERNEY $\qquad$ SP0208
Bathurst Arms

(01285) 832150 – www.bathurstarms.co.uk
North Cerney, Cirencester, Gloucestershire GL7 7BZ

£80; 6 comfortable, recently refurbished rooms. Handsome pink-painted old inn (under new ownership) with a beamed and panelled bar, a good mix of visitors, an open fire and a woodburning stove at each end of the room, nice old furniture on flagstones, real ales; there's also an oak-floored room, a restaurant with another woodburner and enjoyable food; appealing garden with picnic-sets next to the little River Churn; Cerney House Gardens are worth a visit and there are lots of nearby walks (leaflets available). Dogs allowed in two bedrooms and most of pub except one dining area; £10.

NORTHLEACH

SP1114

Wheatsheaf

(01451) 860244 – www.cotswoldswheatsheaf.com

West End, Northleach, Cheltenham, Gloucestershire GL54 3EZ

£130; 14 stylish, well equipped rooms. Handsome 17th-c former coaching inn by fine market square in lovely Cotswold town; big-windowed linked rooms with antique and contemporary artwork, church candles, fresh flowers, attractive chairs and tables on flagstones or wooden floors, three open fires, a fantastic wine list, local beers and cider, enterprising food and excellent breakfasts; seats in the pretty back garden and they can arrange fishing on the River Coln; lots of nearby walks; dogs are genuinely welcomed – they keep a jar of pigs' ears behind the bar for them. Dogs allowed in three bedrooms and anywhere in the pub; bed, bowl and treats; £10.

PARKEND

SO6108

Edale House

(01594) 562835 – www.edalehouse.co.uk

Folly Road, Parkend, Lydney, Gloucestershire GL15 4JF

£72; 6 rooms. Georgian house opposite a cricket green and backing on to RSPB Nagshead nature reserve, with a comfortable, homely sitting room, honesty bar, good food in the attractive dining room and a relaxed atmosphere; resident dog; nearby walks in the Forest of Dean. Dogs allowed in two ground-floor rooms, but not public areas; £10 per stay.

STOW-ON-THE-WOLD

SP1925

Old Stocks

(01451) 830666 – www.oldstockshotel.co.uk

The Square, Stow-on-the-Wold, Gloucestershire GL54 1AF

£139–£189; 16 stylish, contemporary rooms. Overlooking the market square, this 16th-c Cotswold-stone hotel has been updated (spring 2015) with bright fashionable modern furnishings; there's a cosy welcoming small bar with beams, a comfortable lounge with books and games, a restaurant serving good british food, a separate café at the front of the hotel, and a walled garden with a pizza oven and seating; friendly staff; a young bichon cavalier cross called Ralph; nearby walks. Dogs allowed in three garden bedrooms and public areas, but not restaurant; bedding and bowl; £10.

STOW-ON-THE-WOLD

SP1925

Porch House

(01451) 870048 – www.porch-house.co.uk

Digbeth Street, Stow-on-the-Wold, Gloucestershire GL54 1BN

£99; 13 individually designed, comfortable bedrooms. This historic building (the oldest part was a hospice built in 947) has been beautifully restored to create plenty of space for both drinking and dining, with beams, flagstones or bare boards, exposed stone walls and open fireplaces; there's also a dining room, a conservatory and tables outside on a raised terrace; real ales, good wines by the glass, home-brewed ginger ale and home-made lemonade are served by courteous, helpful staff; rewarding food includes particularly good breakfasts, and the atmosphere throughout is informal and gently civilised. Dogs allowed in four bedrooms, bar and conservatory; £15.

TETBURY
ST8993
Royal Oak

(01666) 500021 – www.theroyaloaktetbury.co.uk
Cirencester Road, Tetbury, Gloucestershire GL8 8EY

£110; 6 character bedrooms. Carefully renovated golden-stone former coaching inn with an easy-going, friendly atmosphere and genuine welcome from helpful, courteous staff; there's an open-plan rambling bar with a roaring log fire and several snug areas, plus an upstairs dining room with a fine raftered ceiling, dark polished furniture, creamy yellow paintwork, fresh flowers and candlelight; real ales, interesting spirits, highly enjoyable food and extremely good breakfasts; outside, there are seats and tables on terraces and a lawn; walks from the door. Closed first week January. Dogs allowed in three bedrooms and bar; £10.

THORNBURY
ST6390
Thornbury Castle

(01454) 281182 – www.thornburycastle.co.uk
Castle Street, Thornbury, Bristol BS35 1HH

£235; 29 opulent rooms, some with big Tudor fireplaces or fine oriel windows. Impressive and luxuriously renovated early 16th-c castle with antiques, tapestries, huge fireplaces and mullioned windows in the baronial public rooms, two dining rooms and a lounge, fine modern cooking using home-grown and local produce, an extensive wine list (including wine from their own vineyard) and thoughtful friendly service; 14 acres of grounds including the oldest Tudor gardens in England, archery and croquet (falconry can be arranged); nearby fields for walks. Dogs allowed in most bedrooms and in public areas except dining rooms; £15.

WESTONBIRT
ST8690
Hare & Hounds

(01666) 880233 – www.cotswold-inns-hotels.co.uk
Westonbirt, Tetbury, Gloucestershire GL8 8QL

£130; 43 attractive country-style rooms. Cotswold-stone hotel in lovely gardens and woodland with two tennis courts and plenty of nearby walks; a contemporary, convivial bar with an open fire and high-backed brown leather dining and nice old wooden chairs around a mix of tables on flagstones or wooden flooring, a comfortable lounge with plenty of sofas and armchairs and another log fire, enjoyable light lunches and afternoon teas, and an elegant restaurant with original features serving interesting modern food using the best local seasonal produce. Dogs allowed in some bedrooms, grounds and public areas; bedding, bowl and treats; £10.

WESTON SUBEDGE

SP1241

Seagrave Arms

(01386) 840192 – www.seagravearms.com

Friday Street, Weston Subedge, Chipping Camden, Gloucestershire GL55 6QH

£105; 8 well equipped, modern bedrooms, in the main house and in converted stables. Handsome 400-year-old country inn with a lot of character and friendly staff; there's a cosy little bar with a chatty atmosphere, an open fire, ancient flagstones, half-panelled walls and padded window seats, as well as two dining rooms; real ales, 14 wines (plus prosecco and champagne) by the glass and impressive food cooked by the landlord that includes fine daily specials, set lunches and good breakfasts; seats outside on gravel at the front of the building and in the back garden; the Cotswold Way is nearby, so the pub is popular with walkers and their dogs, especially at lunchtime. Dogs allowed in two stable bedrooms and bar; bed, bowls and treats; £10.

WINCHCOMBE

SP0228

Lion

(01242) 603300 – www.thelionwinchcombe.co.uk

North Street, Winchcombe, Gloucestershire GL54 5PS

£110; 8 individually decorated, country-style bedrooms (no TVs). Stylish historic coaching inn with plenty of rustic-chic furnishings and an appealing and relaxed atmosphere; exposed golden-stone walls, portraits and gilt-edged mirrors on pale paintwork, flagstones, armchairs, wall seats, fresh flowers and big stubby candles; highly rewarding modern food and wide choice of real ales served by smiling, courteous staff; the garden is charming with plenty of seating on grass and various terraced areas among shrubs and climbers; Sudeley Castle is within walking distance and Cheltenham Racecourse is not far. Dogs allowed in all bedrooms and bar; bed, bowl and treats; £15.

Hampshire

MAP 2

DOG FRIENDLY PUBS

AMPORT
SU2944

Hawk Inn

(01264) 710371 – www.hawkinnamport.co.uk

Off A303 at Thruxton interchange; at Andover end of village just before Monxton; SP11 8AE

Relaxed rambling pub with contemporary furnishings in front bar and dining areas, helpful staff and well thought-of food; bedrooms

This very pleasing, rambling old place is handy for visitors to the famous Hawk Conservancy Trust, which is just down the road. The comfortable front bar is open-plan and modern, with brown leather armchairs and plush grey sofas by a low table, a log fire in a brick fireplace and sisal matting on bare boards. To the left, a tucked-away snug room has horse-racing photographs, shelves of books and a TV. Two dining areas have smart window blinds, black leather cushioned wall seating and elegant wooden chairs (some carved) around pale tables, big oil paintings on pale walls above a grey dado, and a woodburning stove. Black-topped stools line the counter, where courteous staff serve Upham Punter, Stakes Ale and Tipster and a guest ale on handpump and quite a few wines by the glass. The sunny sandstone front terrace has picnic-sets looking across the lane to more seating on grass that leads down to Pill Hill brook.

Free house ~ Licensee Becky Anderson ~ Real ale ~ Open 7.30am-11pm; 8.30am-11pm Sat; 8.30am-10.30pm Sun ~ Bar food 12-2.30, 6-9 (9.30 Fri, Sat) ~ Children welcome ~ Dogs allowed in bar ~ Wi-fi ~ Bedrooms: £90

BANK
SU2806

Oak

(023) 8028 2350 ~ www.oakinnlyndhurst.co.uk

Signposted just off A35 SW of Lyndhurst; SO43 7FE

New Forest pub with a good mix of customers, popular food and interesting décor

There's a warm welcome for all from the friendly staff at this bustling pub. The L-shaped bar has bay windows with built-in red-cushioned seats, and two or three little pine-panelled booths with small built-in tables and bench seats. The rest of the bare-boarded bar has low beams and joists, candles in brass holders on a row of stripped old and newer blond tables set against the wall and all manner of bric-a-brac: fishing rods, spears, a boomerang, old ski poles, brass platters, heavy knives and guns. There are cushioned milk churns along the bar counter and little red lanterns among hop bines above the bar. Fullers London Pride, HSB and Gales Seafarers and a changing local guest on handpump and 14 wines by the glass; background music. The pleasant side garden has picnic-sets and long tables and benches by big yew trees.

Fullers ~ Manager Carlos Dias ~ Real ale ~ Open 11.30-3, 5.30-11; 11.30-11 Sat; 12-10.30 Sun ~ Bar food 12-2.30, 6-9 (9.30 Fri); 12-5, 6-9.30 (9 Sun) Sat ~ Children welcome until 6pm; must be over 10 after 6pm ~ Dogs allowed in bar ~ Wi-fi

BAUGHURST   SU5860

Wellington Arms

(0118) 982 0110 – www.thewellingtonarms.com
Baughurst Road, S of village; RG26 5LP

Small, pretty country pub-with-rooms, exceptional cooking and a friendly welcome; bedrooms

As always, this delightful little country inn is run with great care by the friendly licensees and their courteous staff. Of course, most people are here for the excellent food but they do keep a couple of ales such as Longdog Bunny Chaser and West Berkshire Good Old Boy on handpump, ten wines by the glass and a farm cider; background music. The dining room is attractively decorated with an assortment of cushioned oak dining chairs around a mix of polished tables on terracotta tiles, pretty blinds, brass candlesticks, flowers and windowsills stacked with cookery books. The garden has teak furniture and herbaceous borders.

Free house ~ Licensees Simon Page and Jason King ~ Real ale ~ Open 9-3, 6-11; 9-4 Sun ~ Bar food 12-1.30, 6.30-8.30 (9 Fri, Sat); 12-4 Sun ~ Children welcome ~ Dogs welcome ~ Wi-fi ~ Bedrooms: £100

BEAULIEU   SU3902

Montagu Arms

(01590) 614986 – www.montaguarmshotel.co.uk
Almost opposite Palace House; SO42 7ZL

Separate Monty's Bar, open all day for both drinks and food

The solidly built and civilised Montagu Arms hotel has a separate little bar called Monty's with its own entrance. Usefully open all day, this simply furnished bar has panelling, bare floorboards, bay windows and a mix of pale tables surrounded by tartan-cushioned dining chairs; winter log fire. There are still a couple of stools against the bar counter where they keep Ringwood Best and Fortyniner and a seasonal guest on handpump and several wines by the glass, served by cheerful, helpful bar staff. Across the entrance hall is a smarter panelled dining room. Do visit the hotel's tucked-away back garden, which is quite charming in warm weather.

Free house ~ Licensee Sunil Kanjanghat ~ Real ale ~ Open 11-11 (10.30 Sun); 11-3, 6-11 in winter ~ Bar food 12-2.30 (3 weekends), 6.30-9.30 ~ Restaurant ~ Children welcome ~ Dogs allowed in bar ~ Wi-fi ~ Bedrooms: £159

BIGHTON   SU6134

English Partridge

(01962) 732859 – www.englishpartridge.co.uk
Bighton Dean Lane; village signed off B3046 N of Alresford; SO24 9RE

Character bars in friendly country pub with good wines and beers and highly enjoyable food

Although this charming little country pub is extremely popular locally, you can be sure that visitors are just as warmly welcomed. At the front, a small simple room to the left of the door is just right for walkers and their dogs, with a warm open fire, a few chairs and tables and stools against the counter. The main bar has a wonderful ancient parquet floor, a black dado with hunting prints, local shoot photographs and game bird pictures on the walls above, a stuffed pheasant in a glass cabinet, a woodburning stove in a brick inglenook, a fireplace filled with candles, and all sorts of dining chairs and tables. Flowerpots Perridge Pale and Triple fff Altons Pride and Moondance on handpump, ten wines by the glass, eight gins, farm cider and Somerset cider brandy; darts, board games and maybe unobtrusive background music. Through an open doorway, the back dining room has long built-in wall seats with scatter cushions, similar chairs and tables (each set with a candle in a candlestick), a huge deer's head and a boar's head, antlers, shooting and hunting photographs and fish and bird prints. The garden has a terrace with tables and chairs under parasols.

Free house ~ Licensee David Young ~ Real ale ~ Open 12-3, 5-11; 12-11 Sat; 12-8 Sun; closed Mon, Tues except summer school holidays ~ Bar food 12-2.30, 6.30-9.30; 12-3 Sun ~ Children welcome ~ Dogs allowed in bar ~ Wi-fi

BRANSGORE   SZ1997

Three Tuns

(01425) 672232 – www.threetunsinn.com
Village signposted off A35 and off B3347 N of Christchurch; Ringwood Road, opposite church; BH23 8JH

Pretty thatched pub with proper old-fashioned bar and good beers, a civilised main dining area and inventive food

Run by helpful, friendly licensees, this 17th-c thatched pub has a good choice of beers and inventive food. On the right is a separate traditional regulars' bar that seems almost taller than it is wide, with an impressive log-effect stove in a stripped-brick hearth, some shiny black panelling and individualistic pubby furnishings. The roomy low-ceilinged and carpeted main area has a fireside 'codgers' corner', as well as a good mix of comfortably cushioned low chairs around a variety of dining tables. Otter Amber, Ringwood Fortyniner and Razorback plus guests such as Skinners Betty Stogs and Cornish Knocker Ale on handpump, a dozen wines by the glass and farm cider; they hold a beer festival in September. The hanging baskets are lovely in summer and there are picnic-sets on an attractive, extensive, shrub-sheltered terrace with more tables on the grass looking over pony paddocks; pétanque. The Grade II listed barn is popular for parties – and they hold a civil ceremonies licence.

Enterprise ~ Lease Nigel Glenister ~ Real ale ~ Open 11-11; 12-10.30 Sun ~ Bar food 12-2.15, 6.30-9.15; 12-9.15 weekends and bank holidays ~ Restaurant ~ Children welcome ~ Dogs allowed in bar ~ Wi-fi

CADNAM   SU2913

White Hart

(023) 8081 2277 – www.brunningandprice.co.uk/whitehartcadnam
Old Romsey Road, handy for M27 junction 1; SO40 2NP

Extended New Forest pub with busy bar and dining rooms, a warm welcome, good choice of drinks and tasty food

Smartly done up and extended, this bustling place is always full of both locals and visitors. The bar with its long curved counter is at the heart of things, with an open fire, stools and tables on parquet flooring, Phoenix Brunning & Price, Cottage Conquest Session IPA and Duchess, Hop Back Golden Best, Upham Punter and a guest or two on handpump and good wines by the glass served by helpful, friendly staff. There's also a cosy area with a woodburning stove in a nice old brick fireplace, rugs and comfortable leather armchairs. Various dining rooms lead off with more rugs on carpet or tiles, all manner of cushioned dining chairs and wooden tables, painted wooden dados with frame-to-frame country pictures and photographs on pale walls above, house plants on windowsills, mirrors and elegant metal chandeliers. The back terrace and garden have plenty of chairs and tables and there's a children's play area with a painted tractor.

Brunning & Price ~ Manager Sorrel Taylor ~ Real ale ~ Open 10.30am-11pm (10.30pm Sun) ~ Bar food 12-10 (9 Sun) ~ Restaurant ~ Children welcome ~ Dogs allowed in bar ~ Wi-fi

DROXFORD   SU6018

Bakers Arms

(01489) 877533 – www.thebakersarmsdroxford.com
High Street; A32 5 miles N of Wickham; SO32 3PA

Welcoming, opened-up and friendly pub with good beers, interesting cooking and cosy corners

Bowman brewery is just a mile away and their ales and maybe a couple of guests are well kept on handpump here. It's a friendly pub with an easy-going atmosphere and is attractively laid out with the central bar as the main focus: Bowman Swift One and Wallops Wood and Ringwood Old Thumper on handpump, local cider and 15 wines by the glass from a short, carefully chosen list. Well spaced tables on carpet or neat bare boards are spread around the airy L-shaped open-plan bar, with low leather chesterfields and an assortment of comfortably cushioned chairs at one end; a dark panelled dado, dark beams and joists and a modicum of country oddments emphasise the freshness of the crisp white paintwork; good log fire and board games. To one side, with a separate entrance, is the village post office. There are picnic-sets outside. There are some lovely walks along and around the nearby River Meon.

Free house ~ Licensees Adam and Anna Cordery ~ Real ale ~ Open 12-3, 6-11; 12-4 Sun ~ Bar food 12-2.30, 6.30-9.30; 12-3 Sun ~ Well behaved children welcome ~ Dogs allowed in bar ~ Wi-fi

EAST STRATTON   SU5339

Northbrook Arms

(01962) 774150 – www.thenorthbrookarms.com
Brown sign to pub off A33 4 miles S of A303 junction; SO21 3DU

Half a dozen beers and tasty food in pretty pub on family estate; bedrooms

There's been some redecoration for this attractive brick-built village pub. The traditional tiled-floor beamed bar on the right has beams and standing timbers, quite a mix of chairs and tables and up to five real ales on handpump such as Branscombe Vale Best Bitter, Butcombe Bitter, Triple fff Altons Pride and Sharps Cornish Coaster; quite a few wines by the glass too. The left-hand carpeted part is slightly more formal, ending in a dining room giving a little central hall; background music. The skittle alley is in the former stables. You can sit in the pretty country garden to the side or on the village green opposite. Fine nearby walks.

Free house ~ Licensee Ian Ashton ~ Real ale ~ Open 11-11 (10.30 Sun) ~ Bar food 12-3, 6-9; 12-9 Sat; 12-6 Sun ~ Restaurant ~ Children welcome ~ Dogs welcome ~ Wi-fi ~ Bedrooms: £90

EASTON

SU5132

Chestnut Horse

(01962) 779257 – www.thechestnuthorse.com

3.6 miles from M3 junction 9: A33 towards Kings Worthy, then B3047 towards Itchen Abbas; Easton signposted on right – bear left in village; SO21 1EG

This smart 16th-c pub is the hub of this pretty village of thatched cottages – and the hands-on landlady offers a friendly welcome to all

The interior, although open-plan, has a pleasantly rustic and cosy feel with a series of intimate separate areas; the snug décor takes in candles and fresh flowers on the tables, log fires in open fireplaces and comfortable furnishings. The black beams and joists are hung with all sorts of jugs, mugs and chamber-pots, and there are pictures of wildlife and the local area. Badger First Call and K&B Sussex Bitter and a guest beer on handpump, up to a dozen wines by the glass and 20 malt whiskies. The smallish sheltered decked area has seats and tables and colourful flowering tubs and baskets, and there are picnic-sets at the front. There are plenty of walks in the nearby Itchen Valley.

Badger ~ Tenant Karen Wells ~ Real ale ~ Open 12-4, 5.30-11; 12-11 Fri-Sun ~ Bar food 12-2.30, 6-9.30; 12-8 Sun ~ Restaurant ~ Children welcome ~ Dogs allowed in bar ~ Wi-fi

FRITHAM

SU2314

Royal Oak

(023) 8081 2606

Village signed from M27 junction 1; SO43 7HJ

Rural New Forest spot with traditional rooms, log fires, seven real ales and simple lunchtime food

The appeal of this charming brick and cob thatched pub lies in its simple rural rusticity. It's in a lovely spot right in the middle of the New Forest and part of a working farm, so there are ponies and pigs out on the green and plenty of livestock nearby. The three neatly kept black-beamed rooms are straightforward but full of proper traditional character, with prints and pictures involving local characters on the white walls, restored panelling, antique wheelback, spindleback and other old chairs and stools with colourful seats around solid tables on oak floors, and two roaring log fires. The back bar has several books; darts and board games. Up to seven real ales are tapped from the cask including one named for the pub (from Bowman), Bowman Swift One, Eight Arch Parabolic, Flack Manor Double Drop, Hop Back Summer Lightning, Stonehenge Danish Dynamite and a guest ale from Kingstone. Also, nine wines by the glass (mulled wine in winter), 14 country wines, local cider and a September beer festival; service remains friendly and efficient even when packed (which it often is). Summer barbecues may be held in the neatly kept big garden, which has a marquee for poor weather and a pétanque pitch. They have three shepherd's huts to rent for overnight stays.

Free house ~ Licensees Neil and Pauline McCulloch ~ Real ale ~ Open 11-11; 12-10.30 Sun; 11-3, 5.30-11 weekdays in winter ~ Bar food 12-2.30 (3 weekends) ~ Children welcome ~ Dogs welcome

HOOK

SU7153

Hogget

(01256) 763009 – www.thehogget.co.uk

1.1 miles from M3 junction 5; A287 N, at junction with A30 (car park just before traffic lights); RG27 9JJ

Well run and accommodating, a proper pub moving with the times and giving good value

There are plenty of visitors as well as lots of regular customers at this very cheerful and chatty place. The various rooms ramble around the central servery so there's plenty of space for all; the wallpaper, lighting and carpet pattern, plus high-backed stools and bar tables on the right at the back, give an easy-going and homely feel – as does the way the layout provides several smallish distinct areas. Ringwood Fortyniner and Razorback and Wychwood Dirty Tackle on handpump, 13 wines by the glass plus prosecco and plenty of neatly dressed staff; daily papers, background music and books (often cookbooks) on shelves. A sizeable terrace has sturdy tables and chairs, including some in a heated covered area.

Marstons ~ Lease Tom and Laura Faulkner ~ Real ale ~ Open 12-3, 6-11; 12-11 Sat; 12-6 Sun ~ Bar food 12-2.30, 6.30-9; all day Sat; 12-6 Sun ~ Restaurant ~ Children welcome but not after 7pm Fri and Sat ~ Dogs allowed in bar ~ Wi-fi

HORDLE

SZ2996

Mill at Gordleton

(01590) 682219 – www.themillatgordleton.co.uk

Silver Street; SO41 6DJ

Charming tucked-away country inn with friendly bar, exceptional food and pretty waterside gardens; comfortable bedrooms

This place is on the edge of the New Forest, so there are plenty of nearby walks. The little panelled bar on the right is popular with locals (often with a dog) and has leather armchairs and Victorian-style mahogany dining chairs on parquet flooring, a feature stove, a pretty corner china cupboard, Ringwood Best and Upham 1st Drop on handpump, 18 good wines by the glass, 22 malt whiskies and a rack of daily papers. This overflows into a cosy lounge, and there's also a spacious second bar by the sizeable beamed restaurant extension (an attractive room with contemporary art and garden outlook). The gardens are really lovely, featuring an extensive series of interestingly planted areas looping about pools and a placid winding stream, dotted with intriguing art objects and with plenty of places to sit, from intimate pairs of seats to teak or wrought-iron tables on the main waterside terrace (which is beautifully lit up at night).

Upham ~ Tenant Thomas Lyon-Shaw ~ Real ale ~ Open 11-11; 12-10.30 Sun ~ Bar food 12-2.15, 7-9.15; 12-3, 6.30-8.15 Sun ~ Restaurant ~ Children welcome ~ Dogs allowed in bar ~ Wi-fi ~ Bedrooms: £150

HURSLEY

SU4225

Kings Head

(01962) 775208 – www.kingsheadhursley.co.uk

A3090 Winchester–Romsey; SO21 2JW

Creeper-covered pub with an easy, friendly atmosphere, interestingly furnished rooms, well kept ales, good wines and enjoyable food; lovely bedrooms

With welcoming, helpful staff, character rooms and a thoughtful choice of both drinks and food, this former coaching inn is a winner. The bar to the left has shutters by a cushioned window seat, high-backed plush green chairs and chunky leather stools around scrubbed tables on black floor slates, one high table with equally high chairs, a raised fireplace with church candles on the mantelpiece and stools against the S-shaped, grey-painted counter. Bowman Swift One, Flack Manor Double Drop, Ringwood Best, Sharps Doom Bar and Upham Sprinter on handpump and 21 wines by the glass; background music, a piano, daily papers and board games. A character lower room has a fine end brick wall, a woodburning stove and wall banquettes with leather and tartan upholstery, and cushioned settles on floorboards. You can hire out the atmospheric downstairs skittle alley. The smartly updated courtyard garden has wooden or metal seats and tables on brickwork or gravel, parasols and heaters. The ancient village church is opposite.

Free house ~ Licensees Mark and Penny Thornhill ~ Real ale ~ Open 11-11; 12-10.30 Sun ~ Bar food 12-3, 6-9; 12-9.30 Sat; 12-8 Sun ~ Restaurant ~ Children welcome ~ Dogs allowed in bar ~ Wi-fi ~ Bedrooms: £100

LITTLETON
SU4532
Running Horse
(01962) 880218 – www.runninghorseinn.co.uk
Main Road; village signed off B3049 NW of Winchester; SO22 6QS

Carefully renovated country pub with several dining areas, woodburning stove in the bar, enjoyable food and cabana in garden; pretty bedrooms

Staff here are courteous and friendly and the atmosphere is chatty and easy-going. Spreading dining areas are attractively furnished with an appealing variety of chairs and tables on big flagstones or bare boards, there are button-backed banquettes in a panelled alcove, a much prized cushioned seat in a bay window plus wooden armchairs around a table, and polo photographs on red walls. Also, unusual wine-bottle ceiling lights, old books on rustic bookshelves, antlers and big mirrors. A brick fireplace holds a woodburning stove, and leather-topped stools line the bar counter where they keep Upham Punter and Tipster and a changing guest on handpump, 14 wines by the glass and a farm cider. The front and back terraces have green metal tables and chairs, and there are picnic-sets on the back grass by a spreading sycamore, and a popular cabana with cushioned seats. Breakfasts are open to non-residents. This is sister pub to the Thomas Lord in West Meon.

Upham ~ Licensee Anita Peel ~ Real ale ~ Open 11-11 (10.30 Sun) ~ Bar food 12-2.30, 6.30-9.30; 12-3.30, 6.30-9 Sun ~ Restaurant ~ Children welcome ~ Dogs allowed in bar ~ Wi-fi ~ Bedrooms: £105

LOWER WIELD
SU6339
Yew Tree
(01256) 389224 – www.the-yewtree.org.uk
Turn off A339 NW of Alton at 'Medstead, Bentworth 1' signpost, then follow village signposts; or off B3046 S of Basingstoke, signposted from Preston Candover; SO24 9RX

Bustling country pub with a delightful, hard-working landlord, relaxed atmosphere and super choice of wines and food; sizeable garden

Customers enthuse about their visits to this very well run pub – with particular praise for the charming, hands-on landlord and his staff and the very fair prices. A small flagstoned bar area on the left has pictures above a stripped-brick dado, a ticking clock and a log fire. There's carpet around to the right of the serving counter (with a couple of stylish wrought-iron bar chairs); throughout there's a mix of tables, including quite small ones for two, and miscellaneous chairs. Drinks include 13 wines by the glass from a well chosen list (with summer rosé and Louis Jadot burgundies), a beer named for the pub (from Triple fff) and Bowman South Sea Spice on handpump, local Silverback gin and a locally made lager from Andwell. Outside, there are solid tables and chunky seats on the front terrace, picnic-sets in a sizeable side garden, pleasant views and a cricket field across the quiet lane; nearby walks.

Free house ~ Licensee Tim Gray ~ Real ale ~ Open 12-3, 6-11; 12-10.30 Sun; closed Mon, closed first two weeks Jan ~ Bar food 12-3, 6.30-9 ~ Children welcome ~ Dogs allowed in bar ~ Wi-fi

LYMINGTON
SZ3295

Angel & Blue Pig

(01590) 672050 – www.angel-lymington.com
High Street; SO41 9AP

Bustling, friendly inn with plenty of space in several connected rooms, four real ales, enjoyable food and helpful staff; bedrooms

To guarantee a table you must book in advance at this well run, busy pub as it's in the middle of a very popular tourist town. To the right of the door, a cosy front room has comfortable sofas and armchairs around a big chest, rugs on bare boards and an open fire; this leads into a pubby, flagstoned area with high tables and chairs and built-in leather wall seats. The two interconnected rooms to the left of the entrance – one carpeted, one with rugs on quarry tiles – have beams and timbers, upholstered dining chairs around a variety of tables, an old range in a brick fireplace, a large boar's head, lots of books on shelves and a bookshelf mural; throughout are numerous hunting prints and porcine bits and pieces. At the back, overlooking the terrace where there are seats and tables under blue parasols, is yet another area with some nice old leather armchairs beside a woodburning stove and the serving counter where they keep Banks's Sunbeam, Blonde Angel (named for the pub from Ringwood) and Ringwood Razorback on handpump, 16 wines by the glass and a choice of coffees; service is cheerful and helpful.

Free house ~ Licensee Matt England ~ Real ale ~ Open 9.30am-11pm (midnight Fri, Sat); 9.30am-10.30pm Sun ~ Bar food 12-10 (9 Sun) ~ Restaurant ~ Children welcome ~ Dogs allowed in bar ~ Wi-fi ~ Live music last Fri of month ~ Bedrooms: £90

NORTH WALTHAM
SU5645

Fox

(01256) 397288 ~ www.thefox.org
3 miles from M3 junction 7: A30 southwards, then turn right at second North Waltham turn, just after Wheatsheaf; pub also signed from village centre; RG25 2BE

Traditional flint country pub, very well run, with tasty food and drink and a nice garden

In summer, the colourful garden here is a big draw. A pergola walkway leads to the pub from a gate on the lane, the flower boxes and baskets are immaculate and there are picnic-sets under cocktail parasols in three separate areas. Inside, the low-ceilinged bar on the left has Andwell Gold Muddler, Brakspears Bitter, West Berkshire Good Old Boy and a guest beer on handpump, lots of bottled ciders plus Aspall's cider on draught; 13 wines by the glass, 22 malt whiskies and quite a collection of miniatures. The big woodburning stove, parquet floor, simple padded country kitchen chairs, and 'Beer is Best' and poultry prints above the dark dado – all give a comfortably old-fashioned feel, in which perhaps the vital ingredient is the polite and friendly efficiency of the hands-on landlord. The separate dining room, with high-backed leather chairs on a blue tartan carpet, is larger. Walks include a pleasant one to Jane Austen's church at Steventon.

Free house ~ Licensees Rob and Izzy MacKenzie ~ Real ale ~ Open 11-11 (10.30 Sun) ~ Bar food 12-2.30, 6.30-9.30; 12-3, 6.30-8.30 Sun ~ Restaurant ~ Children welcome ~ Dogs allowed in bar ~ Wi-fi

NORTH WARNBOROUGH   SU7352

Mill House

(01256) 702953 – www.brunningandprice.co.uk/millhouse
A mile from M3 junction 5: A287 towards Farnham, then right (brown sign to pub) on to B3349 Hook Road; RG29 1ET

Converted mill with an attractive layout, inventive modern food, good choice of drinks and lovely waterside terraces

Handy for the M3, this sizeable raftered mill building is especially well run by efficient, courteous staff. Several linked areas on the main upper floor have heavy beams, plenty of well spaced tables in a variety of sizes and styles, rugs on polished boards or beige carpet, coal-effect gas fires in pretty fireplaces and a profusion of (often interesting) pictures. A section of floor is glazed to reveal the rushing water and mill wheel below, and a galleried section on the left looks down into a dining room, given a more formal feel by panelling. The well stocked bar has Phoenix Brunning & Price Original, Fuzzy Duck Cunning Stunt, Hogs Back TEA, Triple fff Altons Pride and West Berkshire Tamesis on handpump, a fine range of 50 malt whiskies, 18 wines by the glass and local farm cider; background music and board games. The extensive back garden has lots of solid tables and chairs on terraces, even more picnic-sets on grass and attractive landscaping around the sizeable millpond; there's a couple of swings too.

Brunning & Price ~ Lease Ben Walton ~ Real ale ~ Open 11-11 ~ Bar food 12-10 (9.30 Sun) ~ Restaurant ~ Children welcome ~ Dogs allowed in bar ~ Wi-fi

PETERSFIELD   SU7423

Old Drum

(01730) 300544 – www.theolddrum.co.uk
Chapel Street; GU32 3DP

Restored 18th-c inn with friendly staff and atmosphere in bars and dining room, interesting ales and food and seats in back garden; bedrooms

Right in the centre of town, this bustling, friendly pub is the oldest in the area. The airy L-shaped bar has all manner of antique dining chairs and tables on bare boards, with a comfortable chesterfield and armchair by an open fire (there are three fires in all) and prettily upholstered stools against the counter. Bowman Swift One and Wallops Wood, Dark Star American Red and Hophead and Suthwyk Liberation on handpump, 16 wines by the glass, ten malt whiskies and farm cider and perry; background jazz and board games. A cosy beamed dining room leads off, with more interesting old cushioned chairs and tables on bare boards; and throughout there are prints and mirrors and the odd stag's head on pale paintwork or exposed bricks, modern lighting and fresh flowers. The back courtyard garden has chairs and tables and plants in raised flower beds.

Free house ~ Licensee Maria Solovieth ~ Real ale ~ Open 10am-11pm; 10-8 Sun ~ Bar food 12-3, 6-9; 12-4 Sun ~ Restaurant ~ Children welcome until 8pm ~ Dogs allowed in bar ~ Wi-fi ~ Bedrooms: £120

PETERSFIELD   SU7227

Trooper

(01730) 827293 – www.trooperinn.com

From A32 (look for staggered crossroads) take turning to Froxfield and Steep; pub 3 miles down on left in big dip; GU32 1BD

Courteous landlord, popular food, decent drinks, persian knick-knacks and local artists' work; attractive bedrooms

This place remains popular for its good food and the genuine welcome from the charming landlord and his friendly staff. The bar has a log fire in a stone fireplace, all sorts of cushioned dining chairs around dark wooden tables, old film star photos, paintings by local artists (for sale), little persian knick-knacks here and there, several ogival mirrors, lit candles and fresh flowers; there's also a sun room with lovely downland views, carefully chosen background music, board games, newspapers and magazines. Bowman Swift One, Ringwood Best and Triple fff Moondance on handpump, good wines by the glass and several gins. The attractive raftered restaurant has french windows to a paved terrace with views across the open countryside, and there are lots of picnic-sets on an upper lawn. The horse rail in the car park is reserved 'for horses, camels and local livestock'. The inn backs on to Ashford Hangers nature reserve.

Free house ~ Licensee Hassan Matini ~ Real ale ~ Open 12-3, 6-11; 12-4 Sun; closed Sun evening, Mon lunchtime except bank holidays ~ Bar food 12-2, 6.30-9; 12-2.30 Sun ~ Restaurant ~ Children welcome ~ Dogs allowed in bar ~ Wi-fi ~ Bedrooms: £99

PETERSFIELD   SU7129

White Horse

(01420) 588387 – www.pubwithnoname.co.uk

Up on an old downs road about halfway between Steep and East Tisted, near Priors Dean – OS Sheet 186 or 197 map reference 715290; GU32 1DA

Much-loved old place with a great deal of simple character, friendly licensees and fantastic range of beers

Up to ten real ales are kept on handpump in this unspoilt old pub. One or two are named for the pub plus Adnams Ghost Ship, Belvoir Rare Breed, Butcombe Bitter, Fullers London Pride, Ringwood Boondoggle and Fortyniner and quickly changing guests; lots of country wines, a dozen wines by the glass, 20 malt whiskies and two farm ciders. They hold a beer festival in June and a cider festival in September. The two parlour rooms remain charming and idiosyncratic: open fires, oak settles and a mix of dark wooden dining chairs, nice old tables (including some drop-leaf ones), various pictures, farm tools, rugs, a longcase clock, a couple of fireside rocking chairs and so forth. The beamed dining room is smarter with lots of pictures on the white or pink walls. There are some rustic seats outside and camping facilities.

Gales (Fullers) ~ Managers Georgie and Paul Stuart ~ Real ale ~ Open 12-11 ~ Bar food 12-2.30, 7-9; all day weekends ~ Restaurant ~ Children welcome ~ Dogs allowed in bar

PORTSMOUTH

SZ6399

Old Customs House

(023) 9283 2333 – www.theoldcustomshouse.com

Vernon Buildings, Gunwharf Quays; follow brown signs to Gunwharf Quays car park; PO1 3TY

Well converted historic building in a prime waterfront development with real ales and well liked food

Spacious, rambling and usefully open all day, this fine Grade I listed building is very handy for shopping in the extensive modern waterside complex (of which it is part). The big-windowed high-ceilinged rooms have nautical prints and photographs on pastel walls, coal-effect gas fires, nice unobtrusive lighting and well padded chairs around sturdy tables of varying sizes on bare boards; the sunny entrance area has leather sofas. Broad stairs lead up to a carpeted restaurant with similar décor. Fullers ESB, HSB, London Pride and Gales Seafarers and a couple of changing guests on handpump, a decent range of wines by the glass and good coffees and teas. Staff are efficient, the background music well reproduced and the games machines silenced. Picnic-sets out in front are just metres from the water; the bar has disabled access and facilities. The graceful Spinnaker Tower (170 metres high with staggering views from its observation decks) is just around the corner.

Fullers ~ Manager Marc Duvauchelle ~ Real ale ~ Open 9.30am-11pm ~ Bar food 9.30am-9pm ~ Children welcome ~ Dogs allowed in bar ~ Wi-fi

ROCKBOURNE

SU1118

Rose & Thistle

(01725) 518236 – www.roseandthistle.co.uk

Signed off B3078 Fordingbridge–Cranborne; SP6 3NL

Homely cottage with hands-on landlord and friendly staff, informal bars, real ales and good food, and seats in garden

This is just the place to come after visiting the nearby Roman villa. It's a 16th-c, warm and cosy thatched pub (originally two cottages) with beams, timbers and old flagstones. The bar has homely dining chairs, stools and benches around a mix of old pubby tables, Butcombe Gold, Sharps Doom Bar and a changing local ale on handpump, ten wines by the glass and three farm ciders; board games. The restaurant has a log fire in each of its two rooms (one in a big brick inglenook), old engravings and cricket prints and an informal and relaxed atmosphere. There are benches and tables under lovely hanging baskets at the front of the building, with picnic-sets under parasols on grass; good nearby walks. This is a pretty village on the edge of the New Forest.

Free house ~ Licensee Chris Chester-Sterne ~ Real ale ~ Open 11-3, 6-10.30; 11-10.30 Sat; 12-8 Sun ~ Bar food 12-2.15, 7-9.15; 12-2.15 Sun ~ Restaurant ~ Children welcome ~ Dogs allowed in bar ~ Wi-fi

ST MARY BOURNE

SU4250

Bourne Valley

(01264) 738361 – www.bournevalleyinn.com

Upper Link (B3048); SP11 6BT

Bustling country inn with plenty of space, an easy-going atmosphere and enjoyable food and drink; good bedrooms

This is an attractively updated old red-brick inn with plenty of space in rambling, characterful rooms. It's very popular locally but there's a warm welcome for visitors too, and dogs and children are very much part of the scene at lunchtime. The bar areas have sofas, all manner of wooden dining chairs and tables on coir or bare boards, empty wine bottles lining shelves and windowsills, and a warm log fire; at one end a deli counter serves coffee and cake, afternoon tea and picnic hampers. Ringwood Best, Sharps Doom Bar, Upham 1st Drop and a guest beer on handpump and lots of wines by the glass served by helpful, friendly staff; background music and TV. The large barn extension, complete with rafters and beams, rustic partioning and movable shelves made from crates, has big tables surrounded by leather, cushioned and upholstered chairs, more coir carpeting and a second open fire and doors that lead out to a terrace with picnic-sets and other seating. Good nearby walks.

Free house ~ Licensee Ryan Stacey ~ Real ale ~ Open 8.30am-11pm ~ Bar food 12-3, 6-9 (9.30 weekends) ~ Children welcome ~ Dogs welcome ~ Wi-fi ~ Bedrooms: £85

STEEP   SU7525

Harrow

(01730) 262685 – www.harrow-inn.co.uk
Take Midhurst exit from Petersfield bypass, at exit roundabout take first left towards Midhurst, then first turning on left opposite garage, and left again at Sheet church; follow over dual carriageway bridge to pub; GU32 2DA

Unchanging, simple place with long-serving landladies, beers tapped from the cask, unfussy food and cottage garden; no children inside

This place has been in the same family for 87 years and remains quite unspoilt and unchanging, with no pandering to modern methods – no credit cards, no waitress service, no restaurant, no music and the rose-covered loos are outside. Everything revolves around village chat and the friendly locals are likely to involve you in light-hearted conversation. Adverts for logs sit next to calendars of local views (on sale in support of local charities) and news of various quirky competitions. The small public bar has hops and dried flowers (replaced every year) hanging from the beams, built-in wall benches on the tiled floor, stripped-pine wallboards, a good log fire in the big inglenook and wild flowers on scrubbed deal tables; dominoes. Bowman Swift One, Dark Star Hophead, Flack Manor Double Drop, Hop Back GFB, Langham Hip Hop and Ringwood Best are tapped straight from casks behind the counter, and they have local wine and apple juice; staff are polite and friendly, even when under pressure. The big garden has seats on paved areas surrounded by cottage garden flowers and fruit trees. The Petersfield bypass doesn't intrude much on this idyll, though you'll need to follow the directions above to find the pub. No children inside and dogs must be on leads. They sell honesty-box flowers outside for Macmillan nurses.

Free house ~ Licensees Claire and Denise McCutcheon ~ Real ale ~ No credit cards ~ Open 12-2.30, 6-11; 11-3, 6-11 Sat; 12-3, 7-10.30 Sun; closed Sun evening in winter ~ Bar food 12-2, 7-9; not Sun evening ~ Dogs allowed in bar

WEST MEON   SU6424

Thomas Lord

(01730) 829244 – www.thethomaslord.co.uk
High Street; GU32 1LN

Cricketing knick-knacks in character bar rooms, a smarter dining room, helpful staff, local beers, well thought-of food and pretty garden

Cyclists and walkers enjoy this village pub after spending time in the lovely nearby countryside of the Meon Valley. The relaxed, friendly bar has a leather chesterfield and armchairs beside a log fire, wooden chairs, animal-hide stools and corner settles on parquet flooring, and Timothy Taylors Landlord, Upham Punter, Sprinter, Stakes Ale and Tipster on handpump, a dozen wines by the glass and seasonal cocktails, served by chatty, helpful staff. There's plenty of cricketing memorabilia as the place is named after the founder of Lord's Cricket Ground: bats, gloves, balls, shoes, stumps, photographs and prints, and even stuffed squirrels playing the game in a display cabinet above the counter. A small room leads off the bar with similar furnishings, a brace of pheasant in the fireplace and antlers above; background music and board games. The dining room is slightly more formal, with long wide tartan benches beside long tables, green cushioned chairs, a big clock above another fireplace and ruched curtains; another little room has a large button-back banquette, tables and a rustic mural. Plenty of candles throughout – in nice little teacups with saucers, in candlesticks, in silver glassware, in moroccan-style lanterns and in fireplaces. The sizeable garden has picnic-sets, herbaceous borders, an outdoor pizza oven, a barbecue area, a chicken run and a kitchen garden. Sister pub is the Running Horse in Littleton.

Upham ~ Licensee Clare Winterbottom ~ Real ale ~ Open 12-11 (midnight Sat); 12-10.30 Sun ~ Bar food 12-2.30, 6-9.30 (10 Fri, Sat); 12-4, 6-9 Sun ~ Restaurant ~ Children welcome ~ Dogs allowed in bar ~ Wi-fi

DOG FRIENDLY HOTELS, INNS AND B&Bs

BROCKENHURST   SU2904

New Park Manor Hotel

(01590) 623467 – www.newparkmanorhotel.co.uk
Lyndhurst Road, Brockenhurst, Hampshire SO42 7QH

£215; 25 comfortable, individually decorated rooms. Handsome 17th-c royal hunting lodge in the heart of the New Forest (plenty of nearby walks), now a family-oriented hotel with appealing contemporary furnishings in comfortable lounges, bar and light, bright dining rooms with enjoyable modern british cooking; plenty of family facilities including a crèche, children's room with toys and a cinema; badminton, croquet, bike hire, outdoor pool, spa with indoor pool, steam room, sauna and outdoor hot tub. Dogs allowed in all bedrooms and public areas except dining room and spa; bed, bowls and treats; £15.

BUCKLER'S HARD   SU4000

Master Builders

(01590) 616253 – www.hillbrookehotels.co.uk
Buckler's Hard, Beaulieu Estate, Brockenhurst, Hampshire SO42 7XB

£90–£220; 26 lovely, recently refurbished rooms; also 2 self-catering cottages. Sizeable hotel with character bar in lovely spot overlooking the Beaulieu River in charming hamlet; a small gate at the bottom of the garden leads to a walkway beside the river; the original yachtsman's bar is on two levels with a warm winter log fire, benches and cushioned wall seats around long tables, rugs on bare boards, mullioned windows, real ales and steps down to a lower room with a fireplace at each end; some sort of bar food served all day (book in advance for afternoon cream teas), more elaborate restaurant food with tables outside in summer, and good breakfasts. Dogs allowed in five annexe bedrooms, cottages, bar and some public areas (on leads); bed, bowl, treats and food menu; £20 per stay.

CHERITON   SU5828
Flower Pots

(01962) 771318 – www.flowerpots-inn.co.uk
Brandy Mount, Cheriton, Alresford, Hampshire SO24 0QQ

£85; 2 rooms. Unspoilt and quietly comfortable village local run by a very friendly family, with two pleasant little bars, log fire, decent bar food, super own-brew beers and old-fashioned seats on pretty lawns; resident dog; lots of walks nearby; no children. Dogs allowed in bedrooms and bars if well behaved and on a lead.

EAST TYTHERLEY   SU2927
Star

(01794) 340225 – www.thestarinn.co
East Tytherley Road, Lockerley, Romsey, Hampshire SO51 0LW

£70; 3 rooms in a cottage overlooking the cricket pitch. Spic and span country pub with friendly licensees, a bar with comfortable sofas and tub armchairs, a log fire, well kept beers and cider, popular traditional food in an attractive restaurant, tasty breakfasts and seats outside; lots of nearby walks. Dogs allowed in bedrooms by prior arrangement and (on a lead) in bar.

HIGHCLERE   SU4358
Yew Tree

(01635) 253360 – www.theyewtree.co.uk
Hollington Cross, Andover Road, Highclere, Hampshire RG20 9SE

£99; 8 well equipped, cottage-style bedrooms (named after trees). This 17th-c country inn with a heavy-beamed character bar has an atmosphere of easy informality; there are antlers, stuffed squirrels, books piled on shelves and church candles, while seating includes leather tub chairs and sofas, wall seats and a mix of wooden and painted dining chairs around nice old tables on red and black tiles or carpet; the dining rooms are to the left of the bar, and the garden has an outside bar and elegant metal and teak furniture on gravel or raised decking; Highclere Castle is just a few minutes away. Dogs allowed in all bedrooms and everywhere in the pub; £10 per stay.

HURSTBOURNE TARRANT   SU4054
Esseborne Manor

(01264) 736444 – www.esseborne-manor.co.uk
Hurstbourne Tarrant, Andover, Hampshire SP11 0ER

£135; 17 individually decorated rooms. Small stylish family-run Victorian manor with a relaxed friendly atmosphere, a comfortable lounge and snug little bar, good contemporary cooking and log fires in the smart dining room and courteous staff; three acres of neat gardens (where dogs may walk, also paths nearby) with croquet; the hotel also has a special arrangement with a local golf club and health and leisure centre. Dogs allowed in four ground-floor bedrooms in annexe.

LONGSTOCK

SU3537

Peat Spade

(01264) 810612 – www.peatspadeinn.co.uk
Longstock, Stockbridge, Hampshire SO20 6DR

£145; 7 stylish, contemporary rooms. Fishermen from far and wide come to this attractive, well run former coaching inn to try their luck on the River Test just 100 metres away; the new owners have expanded the bar and restaurant area (spring 2016); you'll find a nice, bustling atmosphere, lots of stuffed fish and hunting pictures on green walls and several old wine bottles dotted here and there, imaginative food and real ales; there's also an upstairs room with comfortable sofas and armchairs, and seats outside on the terrace and in the garden; plenty of surrounding walks. Dogs allowed in bedrooms and bar; £5.

LOWER FROYLE

SU7643

Anchor

(01420) 23261 – www.anchorinnatlowerfroyle.co.uk
Lower Froyle, Alton, Hampshire GU34 4NA

£120; 5 stylish rooms. Civilised but informal pub with blazing fires, a good bustle of cheerful customers, various bars with low beams and standing timbers, contemporary paintwork mixing well with nice old chairs and tables, genuinely interesting knick-knacks, copper items, horsebrasses and lots of pictures and prints; separate restaurant with extremely good modern food served by helpful staff, first class breakfasts; back garden with seating; Chawton Cottage (Jane Austen's house) is ten minutes away and there are walks nearby. Dogs allowed in two bedrooms and bar; bowl, bedding and treats.

LYMINGTON

SZ3094

Efford Cottage

(01590) 642315 – www.effordcottage.co.uk
Milford Road, Everton, Lymington, Hampshire SO41 0JD

£70; 3 comfortable rooms. Spacious Georgian cottage in an acre of garden that has a special dog-friendly area marked out; marvellous breakfasts with home-baked bread and home-made preserves served in charming dining room, and friendly, helpful owners; good parking; walks on nearby beach, footpaths and in the New Forest. Dogs allowed in bedrooms but must not be left unattended; £2.

LYMINGTON

SZ3295

Stanwell House

(01590) 677123 – www.stanwellhouse.com
High Street, Lymington, Hampshire SO41 9AA

£145; 29 lovely rooms, including 7 suites. Boutique hotel set in a handsome townhouse with an attractively furnished lounge, a cosy little bar, contemporary european food in the stylish bistro overlooking the walled back garden, and steak and english tapas in the recently refurbished main restaurant; the New Forest is nearby for walks. Dogs allowed in garden bedrooms; blanket and treats; £15.

OWER   SU3318
Ranvilles Farm House
(02380) 814481 – www.ranvilles.com
Pauncefoot Hill, Romsey, Hampshire SO51 6AA

£85; 4 attractively decorated, cottagey rooms; also self-catering. Dating from the
14th c when Richard de Ranville came from Normandy and settled with his family,
this Grade II listed house is in five quiet acres of gardens and paddock; warmly
friendly owners, lots of antiques and paintings in the very comfortable two-level
sitting room, and enjoyable breakfasts (no evening meals); two resident dogs;
walks in the grounds and in the nearby New Forest. Dogs allowed in bedrooms;
bedding, bowl, treats and large outside kennel; first dog free, second dog £5.

PETERSFIELD   SU7023
Langrish House
(01730) 266941 – www.langrishhouse.co.uk
Langrish, Petersfield, Hampshire GU32 1RN

£138–£158; 13 pretty themed rooms with country views. Family home dating
from the 17th c, traditionally decorated with lots of antiques and set in three
acres of lovely gardens; genuinely helpful and friendly staff, a drawing room for
afternoon tea, a vaulted, candlelit bar and imaginative, prettily presented food
in a small cosy restaurant with a log fire; resident dog, cats and fowl. Closed
two weeks early January. Dogs allowed in bedrooms and public areas except for
restaurant; blanket, bowl and treats; £15.

SPARSHOLT   SU4431
Lainston House
(01962) 776088 – www.lainstonhouse.co.uk
Woodman Lane, Sparsholt, Winchester, Hampshire SO21 2LT

£295; 50 sumptuous rooms. Close to Winchester, this elegant William and Mary
hotel stands in 63 acres of parkland, with tennis court, croquet, falconry and a small
gym (fishing, archery and clay pigeon shooting can be arranged); there's a cosy
panelled bar with leather seating, an open fire and a fine view down the avenue of
lime trees, a relaxing, deeply comfortable drawing room with fresh flowers and
paintings where the delicious afternoon teas are taken, and an elegant restaurant
serving first class food using produce from the kitchen garden. Dogs allowed in
some ground-floor bedrooms; bedding, bowl, treats and food menu; £50 per stay.

STUCKTON   SU1613
Three Lions
(01425) 652489 – www.thethreelionsrestaurant.co.uk
Stuckton, Fordingbridge, Hampshire SP6 2HF

£125; 7 rooms, including 4 in courtyard block. Friendly, family-run restaurant-
with-rooms on the edge of the New Forest with two-acre gardens and paddock
where dogs may walk, plus woods and fields; a cosy bar, comfortable little lounge,
airy conservatory, particularly good english/french food in cottagey restaurant
and enjoyable breakfasts; hot tub and sauna; resident cat. Closed last two weeks
February. Dogs allowed in all bedrooms and dining conservatory; £10.

TOTFORD

SU5737

Woolpack

(01962) 734184 – www.thewoolpackinn.co.uk
Totford, Northington, Hampshire SO24 9TJ

£100; 7 comfortable, well equipped rooms named after game birds. Handsome and comfortable flint and brick roadside inn (recently refurbished) with an easy-going and gently civilised atmosphere; rugs on flagstones, exposed brick and stone work, church candles, lots of photographs, a raised open fire with guns, bellows and other country knick-knacks above it, and an assortment of seating from leather button-back armchairs and wall seats to wooden chairs around a medley of tables; also a smart split-level dining room, an outdoor kitchen with pizza oven and seating on a terrace, on gravel and on grass; real ales, good food from bar snacks to restaurant dishes, excellent breakfasts, efficient service and good walks nearby; resident dog. Dogs allowed in bedrooms and bar; bed and bowl.

WINCHESTER

SU4729

Hotel du Vin

(01962) 896329 – www.hotelduvin.com
14 Southgate Street, Winchester, Hampshire SO23 9EF

£170–£240; 24 smart clubby rooms. This is the original Hotel du Vin – an engaging early 18th-c townhouse in the middle of Winchester, with a comfortable sitting room, lots of prints on panelled walls, all manner of dark wooden tables and chairs on bare floorboards, two relaxed and pretty eating areas with imaginative bistro-style cooking and an exceptional wine list; seats under parasols in the pretty walled garden. Dogs in some bedrooms and anywhere in hotel except bistro; bedding, bowl and treats; £10.

WINCHESTER

SU4829

Wykeham Arms

(01962) 853834 – www.wykehamarmswinchester.co.uk
75 Kingsgate Street, Winchester, Hampshire SO23 9PE

£149; 14 individually styled rooms, some with four-posters. Very well run and smart old city inn, between Winchester Cathedral and Winchester College, with all sorts of interesting collections dotted about in several bustling rooms, three log fires, 19th-c oak desks retired from the college, five real ales, lots of wines by the glass, several malt whiskies, ports and sherries and an excellent collection of teas; there's also a snug back room, a panelled room and tables on a covered back terrace and in a small courtyard; imaginative food and smashing breakfasts; water meadows for walking nearby. Dogs allowed in two bedrooms and bar; £7.50.

Herefordshire

DOG FRIENDLY PUBS

CAREY   SO5631

Cottage of Content
(01432) 840242 – www.cottageofcontent.co.uk
Village signposted from good back road betweeen Ross-on-Wye and Hereford E of A49,
through Hoarwithy; HR2 6NG

**Country furnishings in a friendly rustic cottage with interesting food,
real ales and seats on terraces; bedrooms**

Nicely tucked away in a tranquil spot near the River Wye, this medieval inn was
once three labourers' cottages. The place has much character and you can be
sure of a warm welcome from the helpful, friendly licensees. There's a multitude
of beams and country furnishings such as stripped-pine kitchen chairs, long
pews beside one big table and various old-fashioned tables on flagstones or bare
boards. Hobsons Best and Wye Valley Butty Bach on handpump and local cider
and perry during the summer; background music. Picnic-sets sit on the flower-
filled front terrace and in the rural-feeling garden at the back.

Free house ~ Licensees Richard and Helen Moore ~ Real ale ~ Open 12-2.30, 6.30 (6 Weds,
5.30 Fri)-11; 12-3.30 Sun; closed Sun evening, Mon, winter Tues, one week Feb, one week
Oct ~ Bar food 12-2, 6.30-9; 12-2 Sun ~ Restaurant ~ Children welcome ~ Dogs allowed in
bar ~ Bedrooms: £85

EARDISLEY   SO3149

Tram
(01544) 327251 – www.thetraminn.co.uk
Corner of A4111 and Woodseaves Road; HR3 6PG

**Character pub with welcoming licensees, a cheerful mix of customers
and good food and beer**

As this handsome old place is always deservedly busy, you'd be best to book
a table in advance. There's a cheerful mix of both drinkers and diners (all
genuinely welcomed by the convivial licensees and their smiling staff) and the
beamed bar on the left has warm local character, especially in the cosy back
section behind sturdy standing timbers. Here, regulars congregate on the bare
boards by the counter, which serves Clun Pale Ale, Hobsons Best and Wye Valley
Butty Bach on handpump and three local organic ciders. Elsewhere there are
antique red and ochre floor tiles, a handful of nicely worn tables and chairs, a pair

of long cushioned pews enclosing one much longer table, a high-backed settle, old country pictures and a couple of pictorial Wye maps. There's a small dining room on the right, a games room (with pool and darts) in a converted brewhouse and a covered terrace; background music. The outside gents' is extremely stylish; the sizeable, neatly planted garden has picnic-sets on the lawn; pétanque. The famous black and white village is a big draw too.

Free house ~ Licensees Mark and Kerry Vernon ~ Real ale ~ Open 12-3, 6-midnight; 12-4, 7-10.30 Sun; closed Mon except bank holidays ~ Bar food 12-3, 6-9; 12-3 Sun ~ Restaurant ~ Children welcome ~ Dogs allowed in bar ~ Wi-fi

KILPECK   SO4430
Kilpeck Inn

(01981) 570464 – www.kilpeckinn.com
Village and church signposted off A465 SW of Hereford; HR2 9DN

Imaginatively extended country inn in fascinating and peaceful village

Green values matter a lot to the licensees here: they have hi-spec insulation, underfloor heating run by a wood pellet boiler, solar heating panels and a rainwater recycling system; food and drinks are sourced as locally as possible. The beamed bar with dark slate flagstones rambles happily around to provide several tempting corners, with an antique high-backed settle in one and high stools around a matching chest-high table in another. This opens into two cosily linked dining rooms on the left, with high panelled wainscoting. Wobbly Gold and Wye Valley Butty Bach on handpump, seven wines by the glass and farm cider; background music. The neat back grass has picnic-sets. If you stay overnight, you can make the most of the interesting nearby castle ruins and the unique romanesque church.

Free house ~ Licensee Ross Williams ~ Real ale ~ Open 12-3, 5.30-11; 12-11 Sat; 12-4 Sun; closed Sun evening, Mon ~ Bar food 12-2, 6.30-9; 12.30-3 Sun ~ Restaurant ~ Children welcome ~ Dogs allowed in bar ~ Wi-fi ~ Bedrooms: £90

MICHAELCHURCH ESCLEY   SO3133
Bridge Inn

(01981) 510646 – www.thebridgeinnmichaelchurch.co.uk
Off back road SE of Hay-on-Wye, along Escley Brook valley; HR2 0JW

Character riverside inn with warm, simply furnished bar and dining rooms, local drinks, hearty food and seats by the water; bedrooms

In warm weather, you can sit outside this remote inn – delightfully tucked away down a steep lane in an attractive valley – and watch ducks and maybe brown trout on the river. There's a relaxed homely atmosphere in the simply furnished bar, which has hops on dark beams, pine pews and dining chairs around rustic tables, a big woodburning stove and Wye Valley Butty Bach and Country Pale Ale on handpump, good wines by the glass and local cider served by the friendly landlord. Background music. Two dining areas, with contemporary paintwork, have prints on the walls. Stunning nearby walks.

Free house ~ Licensee Glyn Bufton ~ Real ale ~ Open 12-3, 5.30-11; 6.30-11 Mon; 12-11 Sat; 12-10.30 Sun; closed Mon lunchtime ~ Bar food 12-2.30, 5.30 (6.30 Mon)-8.30; 12-3, 5.30-9.30 Sat; 12-4, 5.30-8.30 Sun ~ Restaurant ~ Children welcome ~ Dogs allowed in bar ~ Wi-fi ~ Live bands monthly (see website) ~ Bedrooms: £95

SYMONDS YAT

SO5616

Saracens Head

(01600) 890435 – www.saracensheadinn.co.uk
Symonds Yat E; HR9 6JL

Lovely riverside spot with seats on waterside terraces, a fine range of drinks and interesting food; comfortable bedrooms

With Wye Valley views and nearby Forest of Dean walks, this busy 17th-c inn is extremely popular with lovers of the outdoors. The hands-on, welcoming landlord and his able, friendly staff keep a close eye on things – even at peak times, it all runs along smoothly. There's a buoyant atmosphere and plenty of chatty customers in the flagstoned bar, where they serve Sharps Doom Bar, Wye Valley Butty Bach and HPA and guests such as Bespoke Over a Barrel, Kingstone Classic Bitter and Wadworths 6X on handpump, a dozen wines by the glass, 20 malt whiskies and several ciders. TV, background music and board games. There's also a cosy lounge and a modernised bare-boards dining room, as well as fine old photos of the area and fresh flowers in jugs. The terraces by the River Wye have plenty of seats, though you'll need to arrive early in fine weather to bag one. One way to reach the inn is on the little hand ferry (pulled by one of the staff). Disabled access to the bar and terrace.

Free house ~ Licensees P K and C J Rollinson ~ Real ale ~ Open 11-11; 11-10.30 Sun ~ Bar food 12-2.30, 6.30-9 ~ Restaurant ~ Children welcome but not in bedrooms ~ Dogs allowed in bar ~ Wi-fi ~ Bedrooms: £89

TILLINGTON

SO4645

Bell

(01432) 760395 – www.thebelltillington.com
Off A4110 NW of Hereford; HR4 8LE

Relaxed and friendly pub with a snug character bar opening into civilised dining areas – good value

The Williams family run this popular pub extremely well and it's always deservedly busy. The snug parquet-floored bar on the left has assorted bucket armchairs around low chunky mahogany-coloured tables, brightly cushioned wall benches, team photographs and shelves of books; the black beams are strung with dried hops. Hobson Town Crier, Wye Valley Bitter and a guest beer on handpump, cider made on site, several wines by the glass and locally produced spirits from Chase, all served by notably cheerful staff; daily papers, unobtrusive background music. The bar opens into a comfortable bare-boards dining lounge with stripy plush banquettes and a coal fire. Beyond that is a pitched-ceiling restaurant area with more banquettes and big country prints; through slatted blinds you can see a sunken terrace with contemporary tables, and a garden with teak tables, picnic-sets and a play area.

Free house ~ Licensee Glenn Williams ~ Real ale ~ Open 11-11 (midnight Sat); 12-10.30 Sun ~ Bar food 12-2.30, 6-9; all day Sat; 12-3 Sun ~ Restaurant ~ Children welcome ~ Dogs allowed in bar ~ Wi-fi

UPPER COLWALL   SO7643

Chase

(01684) 540276 – www.thechaseinnmalvern.co.uk
Chase Road, brown sign to pub off B4218 Malvern–Colwall, first left after hilltop on bend going W; WR13 6DJ

Gorgeous sunset views from cheerful country tavern's garden, good drinks and cost-conscious food

It's particularly worth visiting this nicely traditional pub on a clear day: the seats and tables on the steep series of small, pretty back terraces look across Herefordshire and even as far as the Black Mountains and the Brecon Beacons. Inside, the atmosphere is chatty and companionable. There's an array of gilt cast-iron-framed and treadle sewing tables, a great variety of seats (from a wooden-legged tractor seat to a carved pew), an old black kitchen range and plenty of decorations – china mugs, blue glass flasks, lots of small pictures; bar billiards. Four well kept ales are tapped from the cask, such as Bathams Best, Brains Rev James, Ringwood Fortyniner and Woods Beauty, and friendly staff also serve several wines by the glass. Plenty of good surrounding walks.

Free house ~ Licensee Duncan Ironmonger ~ Real ale ~ Open 12-3, 5-11; 12-11 Sat; 12-10.30 Sun ~ Bar food 12-2 (2.30 weekends), 6.30-9 ~ Children welcome ~ Dogs allowed in bar ~ Wi-fi

WALFORD   SO5820

Mill Race

(01989) 562891 – www.millrace.info
B4234 Ross-on-Wye to Lydney; HR9 5QS

Contemporary furnishings in uncluttered rooms, good quality food, real ales served by attentive staff, and terrace tables

Many customers visit this whitewashed pub for a meal before or after a walk (the pub has leaflets describing pleasant ones nearby). It's all very civilised and stylish, with a row of strikingly high arched windows, comfortable leather armchairs and sofas on flagstones, and smaller chairs around broad pedestal tables. Photographs of the local countryside hang on the mainly cream or red walls and there's good unobtrusive lighting. One wall, stripped back to the stonework, contains a woodburning stove that's open to the comfortable, compact dining area on the other side; background music. From the granite-topped modern bar counter, friendly staff serve Wye Valley Bitter and a changing guest such as Hillside Legless Cow on handpump, farm cider and 22 fairly priced wines by the glass. There are seats on the terrace with views towards Goodrich Castle (English Heritage), and more seats and tables in the garden. Much of the produce for the good food comes from their own farm and woodlands (cattle, rare-breed pigs, turkeys, geese, pheasant and ducks) or from other local suppliers.

Free house ~ Licensee Luke Freeman ~ Real ale ~ Open 11.30-3, 6-11; 11.30-11.30 Sat; 12-11 Sun ~ Bar food 12-2 (3 Sat), 6.30-9; 12-3, 4-8 Sun ~ Restaurant ~ Children welcome ~ Dogs allowed in bar ~ Wi-fi

WOOLHOPE

SO6135

Butchers Arms

(01432) 860281 – www.butchersarmswoolhope.com

Off B4224 in Fownhope; HR1 4RF

Pleasant country inn in peaceful setting, with an inviting garden, interesting food and a fine choice of real ales

With enjoyable food cooked by the landlord, local ales and a friendly welcome, it's not surprising this half-timbered pub is so popular. The bar has very low beams, built-in cushioned wall seats, farmhouse chairs and stools around a mix of old tables (some set for dining) on carpet, hunting and horse pictures on cream walls and an open fire in a big fireplace; there's also a little beamed dining room, similarly furnished. Wye Valley Bitter and Butty Bach and Ledbury Gold on handpump, six wines by the glass from a good list, 14 malt whiskies and a couple of farm ciders. There are picnic-sets in a pretty, streamside garden. To really appreciate the surroundings, turn left as you come out of the pub and take the tiny left-hand road at the end of the car park; this turns into a track and then a path, and the view from the top of the hill is quite something.

Free house ~ Licensee Philip Vincent ~ Real ale ~ Open 11-3, 6-11; 12-3.30 Sun; closed Sun evening, Mon except bank holidays ~ Bar food 12-2.30, 6-9; 12-2.30 Sun ~ Restaurant ~ Children welcome ~ Dogs allowed in bar ~ Wi-fi

DOG FRIENDLY HOTELS, INNS AND B&Bs

BODENHAM

SO5451

Englands Gate

(01568) 38797286 – www.englandsgate.co.uk

Bodenham, Hereford, Herefordshire HR1 3HU

£70–£82; 7 smart, modern rooms in converted coach house. Comfortable 16th-c inn with a rambling, open-plan interior, heavy beams and joists, an attractive mix of furnishings on well worn flagstones, open fires, real ales on handpump, a wide choice of good pubby food, and seats under parasols on the terrace and in the large garden. Small dogs allowed in one bedroom and part of the bar; £10.

GLEWSTONE

SO5622

Glewstone Court

(01989) 770367 – www.glewstonecourt.com

Glewstone, Ross-on-Wye, Herefordshire HR9 6AW

£129; 9 smart, chintzy rooms. Elegant, partly Georgian and partly Regency country house hotel set in beautiful grounds with a fine cedar of Lebanon and views over Ross-on-Wye; under new ownership since late 2014; comfortable and relaxing bar and lounges, paintings, chandeliers and open fires, and good food using local produce in antiques-filled dining room; walks in the grounds and in surrounding countryside. Dogs allowed in some bedrooms; blanket and mat; £10.

LEDBURY

SO7137

Feathers

(01531) 635266 – www.feathers-ledbury.co.uk
25 High Street, Ledbury, Herefordshire HR8 1DS

£155; 22 carefully decorated rooms making the most of the old beams and timbers; also self-catering. Very striking, mainly 16th-c black and white hotel with convivial back bar-brasserie, cosy leather sofas and armchairs by the fire at one end, contented diners in the main part and comfortable bays of banquettes and other seats; masses of hop bines on long beams, prints and antique sale notices on stripped panelling, real ales, wines by the glass from an extensive list and 40 malts; a sedate lounge has daily papers, a big log fire and good afternoon teas while the more formal restaurant serves enjoyable bistro-style food; spa with indoor pool and steam room. Dogs allowed in bedrooms and bar.

ROSS-ON-WYE

SO5924

Kings Head

(01989) 763174 – www.kingshead.co.uk
8 High Street, Ross-on-Wye, Herefordshire HR9 5HL

£85; 15 good rooms. Market-town hotel dating from the 14th c with traditional pubby furnishings on stripped boards, a log-effect fire and real ales in little beamed and panelled bar, a beamed library with some timbering and soft leather seating, and a big carpeted dining room serving good value lunches, afternoon snacks and more elaborate evening meals; good breakfasts; can walk along nearby river paths. Dogs allowed in bedrooms, bar and library.

ROSS-ON-WYE

SO5824

Wilton Court

(01989) 562569 – www.wiltoncourthotel.com
Wilton Lane, Wilton, Ross-on-Wye, Herefordshire HR9 6AQ

£145; 11 pretty, old-fashioned chintzy rooms. 16th-c riverside building with friendly owners and two acres of grounds, lots of original features such as leaded windows, heavy beams and sloping floors, a comfortable sitting room, a bar with an open fire and river views, lovely breakfasts and imaginative food using local seasonal produce in pretty, country-style restaurant. Dogs allowed in all bedrooms; £10 per stay.

SYMONDS YAT

SO5417

Norton House

(01600) 890046 – www.norton-house.com
Whitchurch, Symonds Yat, Herefordshire HR9 6DJ

£80; 3 attractive, homely rooms. 300-year-old farmhouse with charming, friendly owners, plenty of original features, flagstones, beams, inglenook fireplaces and stripped pine shutters and doors, a residents' sitting room and a homely lounge, fine breakfasts taken around an antique mahogany table in the beamed dining room with its farmhouse dresser, and cake and tea on arrival. Dogs allowed in bedrooms; £15 per stay.

TITLEY

SO3259

Stagg

(01544) 230221 – www.thestagg.co.uk
Titley, Kington, Herefordshire HR5 3RL

£110; 7 rooms, above pub and in nearby Georgian vicarage. One of Britain's top dining pubs but still very much a pub rather than a pure restaurant; a small hospitable bar with 200 jugs hanging from the ceiling, real ales, local potato and apple vodkas and gins, and fine wines; an extensive dining rooms with truly excellent, inventive food using their own-grown produce and eggs, and first class breakfasts; welcoming, courteous staff; there's also a two-acre garden and lovely surrounding countryside (lots of walks). Closed first two weeks November, one week January/February. Dogs allowed in pub bedrooms and bar.

Hertfordshire

DOG FRIENDLY PUBS

BARNET   TQ2599
Duke of York
(020) 8449 0297 – www.brunningandprice.co.uk/dukeofyork
Barnet Road (A1000); EN5 4SG

Big place with reasonably priced bistro-style food and nice garden

The spreading rooms in this rather grand place have been cleverly divided up using open doorways and stairs, and big windows and mirrors keep everything light and airy. There's a friendly, easy-going atmosphere and an eclectic mix of furniture on tiled or wooden flooring, hundreds of prints and photos on cream walls, fireplaces and thoughtful touches such as table lamps, books, rugs, fresh flowers and pot plants. Stools line the impressive counter where friendly staff serve Phoenix Brunning & Price Original plus guests such as Mighty Oak Fools Gold and Oscar Wilde, Portobello American Pale Ale and Trumans Zephyr on handpump, 20 wines by the glass, 70 whiskies and farm cider; background music. The garden is particularly attractive, with seats, tables and picnic-sets on a tree-surrounded terrace and lawn, and a tractor in the good play area.

Brunning & Price ~ Manager John Johnston ~ Real ale ~ Open 11.30-11; 11.30-10.45 Sun ~ Bar food 12-10 (9 Sun) ~ Children welcome ~ Dogs allowed in bar ~ Wi-fi

BERKHAMSTED   SP9807
Highwayman
(01442) 285480 – www.highwaymanberkhamsted.com
High Street; HP4 1AQ

Bustling town pub, newly refurbished, with plenty of room for both drinking and dining

As this attractively refurbished town pub is usefully open all day, customers are constantly popping in and out – after shopping, to meet friends for lunch or for a chat and a pint after work. Food does play a major part, but the relaxed bar is a social place with Fullers London Pride and Sharps Doom Bar plus guests such as St Austell Tribute and Tring Drop Bar Pale Ale on handpump and good wines by the glass. There are upholstered and leather chairs around all sorts of tables, lots of church candles in stubby holders and big windows overlooking the street; young staff are cheerful and helpful. The dining room has dark green leather wall seating, cushioned dining chairs around tables with barley twist legs on bare boards and a bookcase mural at one end. Up some stairs, a mezzanine with rustic wooden walls offers more seating. There are seats and tables arranged outside on the back terraced garden.

White Brasserie Company ~ Manager Mike White ~ Real ale ~ Open 11-11; 9am-11pm Sat; 9am-10.30pm Sun ~ Bar food 12-10 (10.30 Fri); 9-11am, 12-10.30 Sat; 9-9 Sun ~ Restaurant ~ Children welcome ~ Dogs allowed in bar ~ Wi-fi ~ Live music monthly

FLAUNDEN   TL0101
Bricklayers Arms

(01442) 833322 – www.bricklayersarms.com
4 miles from M25 junction 18; village signposted off A41 – from village centre follow Boxmoor, Bovingdon road and turn right at Belsize, Watford signpost into Hogpits Bottom; HP3 0PH

Cosy country restaurant with fairly elaborate food; very good wine list

In an inviting, peaceful spot, this is a civilised 18th-c dining pub. The mainly open-plan interior has stubs of knocked-through oak-timbered walls that indicate the original room layout, and the well refurbished low-beamed bar is snug and comfortable, with a roaring log fire in winter. Stools line the brick counter where they keep Sharps Doom Bar and guests like Paradigm Win-Win and Tring Side Pocket for a Toad on handpump, and an extensive wine list with 25 by the glass; background music. The terrace and lovely old-fashioned garden has seats and tables. Just up the Belsize road, a path on the left leads through delightful woods to a forested area around Hollow Hedge. The pub is just 15 minutes by car from the Warner Bros Studios where the *Harry Potter* films were made; you can tour the studios but must book in advance.

Free house ~ Licensee Alvin Michaels ~ Real ale ~ Open 12-11.30 (12.30am Sat); 12-9.30 Sun ~ Bar food 12-2.30, 6.30-9.30; 12-7 Sun ~ Restaurant ~ Children welcome ~ Dogs allowed in bar ~ Wi-fi

FRITHSDEN   TL0109
Alford Arms

(01442) 864480 – www.alfordarmsfrithsden.co.uk
A4146 from Hemel Hempstead to Water End, then second left (after Red Lion) signed Frithsden, then left at T junction, then right after 0.25 miles; HP1 3DD

Thriving dining pub with a chic interior, good food from imaginative menu and a thoughtful wine list

Lovely National Trust woodland surrounds this pretty Victorian pub, so many of the lunchtime customers are walkers – at other times, there's a cheerful mix of both locals and diners. The elegant, understated interior has simple prints on pale cream walls, with blocks picked out in rich heritage colours, and an appealing mix of antique furniture (from Georgian chairs to old commode stands) on bare boards and patterned quarry tiles. Sharps Doom Bar and a couple of guests such as Chiltern Beechwood and Tring Side Pocket for a Toad on handpump; also, 24 wines by the glass from a european list (quite a few sweet ones too) and a good choice of spirits; background jazz and darts. There are plenty of tables outside.

Salisbury Pubs ~ Lease Darren Johnston ~ Real ale ~ Open 11-11; 12-10.30 Sun ~ Bar food 12-2.30, 6.30-9.30; 12-3, 6-10 Fri, Sat; 12-9 Sun ~ Restaurant ~ Children welcome ~ Dogs allowed in bar ~ Wi-fi

HARPENDEN   TL1312

White Horse

(01582) 469290 – www.thewhitehorseharpenden.co.uk
Redbourn Lane, Hatching Green (B487 just W of A1081 roundabout); AL5 2JP

Smart up-to-date dining pub with civilised bar side

Behind this extended, white-weatherboarded pub is a huge sunny terrace with plenty of contemporary seats and tables under parasols. Inside, the chatty bar is split-level (one part was once the stables) with prints on burnt orange-painted plank panelling, stools around tables with taller ones against the counter, and an open fire. Haresfoot Wild Boy, Sharps Doom Bar and Tring Bring Me Sunshine on handpump and several wines by the glass, served by friendly, helpful staff; background music and board games. The airy, stylish dining room has tartan-upholstered dining chairs, cushioned wall seats and settles around pale wooden tables on floorboards, and black and white photographs on the walls.

Peach Pub Company ~ Manager Alex Callinan ~ Real ale ~ Open 9.30am-11pm (11.30pm Sat, 10.30pm Sun) ~ Bar food 12-9.30 (8.30 Sun) ~ Restaurant ~ Children welcome ~ Dogs allowed in bar ~ Wi-fi

HERTFORD HEATH   TL3510

College Arms

(01992) 558856 – www.thecollegearmshertfordheath.com
London Road; B1197; SG13 7PW

Light and airy rooms with contemporary furnishings, friendly service, good, interesting food and real ales; seats outside

On the edge of a village and backed by woodland, this is a popular and civilised place for a drink or a meal. The bar has long cushioned wall seats and pale leather dining chairs around tables on rugs or wooden floorboards, and a modern bar counter where they serve Adnams Ghost Ship and Titanic Plum Porter on handpump and 20 wines by the glass; background jazz. Another area has more long wall seats and an open fireplace piled with logs, and there's a charming little room with brown leather armchairs, a couple of cushioned pews, a woodburning stove in an old brick fireplace, hunting-themed wallpaper and another rug on floorboards. The elegant, partly carpeted dining room contains a real mix of antique dining chairs and tables. The back terrace has tables, seats and a long wooden bench among flowering pots and a children's play house.

Punch ~ Lease Andy Lilley ~ Real ale ~ Open 11-11 (midnight Sat); 12-8 Sun ~ Bar food 12-3, 6-9 (9.30 Fri); 12-4, 6-9.30 Sat; 12-7 Sun ~ Restaurant ~ Children welcome ~ Dogs allowed in bar ~ Wi-fi ~ Live music last Fri of month

PRESTON   TL1824

Red Lion

(01462) 459585 – www.theredlionpreston.co.uk
Village signposted off B656 S of Hitchin; The Green; SG4 7UD

Homely village local with changing beers, fair-priced food and neat colourful garden

A few picnic-sets on the grass in front of this community-owned village pub face lime trees on the peaceful village green opposite – while the pergola-covered back terrace and good-sized sheltered garden, with its colourful herbaceous border, have seats and picnic-sets (some shade is provided by a tall ash tree). The main room on the left, with grey wainscot, has sturdy, well varnished furniture including padded country kitchen chairs and cast-iron-framed tables on patterned carpet, a generous window seat, a log fire in a brick fireplace and fox-hunting prints. The somewhat smaller room on the right has steeplechase prints, varnished plank panelling and brocaded bar stools on flagstones around the servery; darts and dominoes. Fullers London Pride and Youngs Bitter on handpump with guests such as Oakham Akhenaten, Oldershaw Grantham Dark and Tring Drop Bar Pale Ale; also, four farm ciders, 11 wines by the glass (including an english house wine), a perry and winter mulled wine.

Free house ~ Licensee Raymond Lambe ~ Real ale ~ Open 12-2.30, 5.30-11; 12-midnight Sat; 12-10.30 Sun ~ Bar food 12-2, 6.30-8.30; not Sun evening, Mon ~ Children welcome ~ Dogs welcome ~ Wi-fi

REDBOURN   TL1011
Cricketers

(01582) 620612 – www.thecricketersofredbourn.co.uk
3.2 miles from M1 junction 9; A5183 signed Redbourn/St Albans, at second roundabout follow B487 for Hemel Hempstead, first right into Chequer Lane, then third right into East Common; AL3 7ND

Good food and beer in attractively updated pub with a bar and two restaurants

This nicely placed village pub has a relaxed front bar with country-style décor: comfortable tub chairs, cushioned bench seating and high-backed bar stools on pale brown carpet, and a woodburning stove. They serve five quickly changing ales on handpump such as St Austell Tribute and Tring Side Pocket for a Toad with guests such as Sharps Doom Bar and Tring Brock Bitter, 16 wines by the glass, farm cider, several malt whiskies and good coffee; well reproduced background music. This bar leads back into an attractive, comfortably refurbished and unusually shaped modern restaurant; there's also an upstairs contemporary restaurant for private parties or functions. The side garden has plenty of seating and summer barbecues; there are lots of nearby walks and cycle routes. They can help with information on the museum next door.

Free house ~ Licensees Colin and Debbie Baxter ~ Real ale ~ Open 12-11 (midnight Sat); 12-10.30 Sun ~ Bar food 12-3, 6-9; 12-5 Sun ~ Restaurant ~ Children welcome ~ Dogs allowed in bar ~ Wi-fi

SARRATT   TQ0499
Cricketers

(01923) 270877 – www.brunningandprice.co.uk/cricketers
The Green; WD3 6AS

Plenty to look at in rambling rooms, up to six real ales, nice wines, enjoyable food and friendly staff; seats outside

Once three charming old cottages, this cleverly refurbished pub has interlinked rooms with numerous little snugs and alcoves – perfect for a quiet drink. There's all manner of antique dining chairs and tables on rugs or stripped floorboards, comfortable armchairs or tub seats, cushioned pews, wall seats and two open fires in raised fireplaces. Also, cricketing memorabilia, fresh flowers, large plants and church candles, Phoenix Brunning & Price Original, Paradigm

Win-Win, Tring Side Pocket for a Toad and a couple of guests on handpump, good wines by the glass, 27 gins and 50 malt whiskies; background music and board games. Several sets of french windows open on to the back terrace where there are tables and chairs, with picnic-sets on grass next to a colourfully painted tractor; seats at the front overlook the village green and duck pond.

Brunning & Price ~ Licensee David Stowell ~ Real ale ~ Open 10am-11pm; 9am-11pm (10.30pm Sun) Sat ~ Bar food 12-9.30 ~ Restaurant ~ Children welcome ~ Dogs allowed in bar ~ Wi-fi

ST ALBANS

TL1407

Verulam Arms

(01727) 836004 – www.the-foragers.com
Lower Dagnall St; AL3 4QE

Unusual pub with foraged ingredients for both food and drink

The foragers who run this unusual town pub are a team of hunters and gatherers using wild game, fruit and fungi for their interesting food. They also brew their own ale with wild ingredients and make home-made liqueurs and cocktails such as woodruff and apple vodka or a martini that uses sloe gin, vermouth and douglas fir syrup (a sort of christmas tree-with-grapefruit taste); you can also buy tickets to join them on their foraging walks. Furnishings and décor are simple: scrubbed tables surrounded by all manner of old dining chairs on floorboards, fireplaces with big gilt-edged mirrors above, a few prints on sage green paintwork, large blackboards with daily specials listed, frosted windows and candles. High chairs line the counter where they serve their own Foragers Sling Shot and two guests plus ales from local breweries such as Oakham and Tring on handpump; also, beers from all over the world, tapped from the cask and in bottles, and cider. The gravelled garden has brightly painted picnic-sets and a heated awning where they grow hops and grapes.

Free house ~ Licensee George Fredenham ~ Real ale ~ Open 12-11 (midnight Fri, Sat) ~ Bar food 12-3, 6.30-9 (10 Fri, Sat); 12-4 Sun ~ Restaurant ~ Well behaved children welcome ~ Dogs welcome ~ Wi-fi

WATTON-AT-STONE

TL3019

Bull

(01920) 831032 – www.thebullwatton.co.uk
High Street; SG14 3SB

Bustling old pub with beamed rooms, candlelight and fresh flowers, real ales served by friendly staff and enjoyable food

As it's open all day and in a pretty village, this well run old pub has a good mix of customers dropping in and out. The huge inglenook fireplace is in the middle with a leather button-back chesterfield and armchairs on either side, a leather banquette beside a landscape-patterned wall, and solid dark wooden dining chairs and plush-topped stools around all sorts of tables on bare boards. The atmosphere is relaxed and friendly, there are fresh flowers, and friendly staff serve Adnams Ghost Ship, St Austell Proper Job and Sharps Doom Bar on handpump and good wines by the glass; background music. Near the entrance are some high bar chairs along counters by the windows; from here, it's a step up to a charming little room with just four tables, wooden dining chairs, a wall banquette, decorative logs in a fireplace, books on shelves, board games and an old typewriter. At the other end of the building is an elegantly furnished dining room with carpet and a slate floor. Paintwork throughout is contemporary. Outside there are church chairs and tables on a covered terrace, picnic-sets on grass and a small, well equipped play area.

Punch ~ Lease Alastair and Anna Bramley ~ Real ale ~ Open 9.30am-11pm; 12-6 Sun; closed Sun evening ~ Bar food 12-3 (4 Sat), 6-10; 12-4 Sun ~ Restaurant ~ Children welcome ~ Dogs allowed in bar ~ Wi-fi

DOG FRIENDLY HOTELS, INNS AND B&Bs

ASHWELL   TL2739
Three Tuns
(01462) 743343 – www.thethreetunsashwell.co.uk
6 High Street, Ashwell, Hertfordshire SG7 5NL

£100; 3 attractive rooms. Built in the reign of Queen Anne, this pretty red-brick building was converted to an inn in 1806; it has a friendly and relaxed bar with pale walls above a blue dado, an open fire, bare floorboards, a long settle and cushioned wooden dining chairs and real ales; there's also a long Victorian-style dining room with a woodburning stove, and seats on the terrace and in the substantial garden with apple trees; food is first rate and inventive food (good breakfasts too) and this is a charming village. Dogs allowed in one bedroom and bar; £10 per stay.

REDCOATS GREEN   TL2026
Redcoats Farmhouse
(01438) 729500 – www.redcoats.co.uk
Redcoats Green, Hitchin, Hertfordshire SG4 7JR

£110; 13 comfortable rooms – 4 in main house, 9 in converted stables. Small, friendly hotel in a handsome old red-brick farmhouse (parts date from the 15th c) – in the same family since the early 1900s and a hotel since the 1960s; atmospheric timbered bar (good wine selection) and cosy sitting rooms with open fires, and conservatory restaurant serving seasonal menus using produce from the kitchen garden and local beef and game; large garden and plenty of walks nearby (they can provide a map). Dogs allowed in stable bedrooms, bar and 'old kitchen'; £7.50.

Isle of Wight

MAP 2

DOG FRIENDLY PUBS

BEMBRIDGE   SZ6587
Crab & Lobster
(01983) 872244 – www.crabandlobsterinn.co.uk
Foreland Fields Road, off Howgate Road (which is off B3395 via Hillway Road);
PO35 5TR

Clifftop views from terrace and delicious seafood; bedrooms

The fine view over the Solent from this busy pub perched on a coastal bluff are best enjoyed from picnic-sets on the terrace – but you'll need to arrive early on a sunny day to bag one. The interior is roomier than you might expect and decorated in a parlour-like style, with lots of yachting memorabilia, old local photographs and a blazing winter fire; darts, dominoes and cribbage. Helpful, cheerful staff serve Goddards Fuggle-Dee-Dum, Sharps Doom Bar and Upham Punter on handpump, a dozen wines by the glass, 16 malt whiskies and good coffee. The shore is just a stroll away.

Enterprise ~ Lease Caroline and Ian Quekett ~ Real ale ~ Open 11-11; 12-10.30 Sun ~ Bar food 12-2.30, 6-9; 12-9 weekends ~ Children welcome ~ Dogs allowed in bar ~ Wi-fi ~ Bedrooms: £115

HULVERSTONE   SZ3984
Sun
(01983) 741124 – www.sun-hulverstone.com
B3399; PO30 4EH

Fine setting and views over the sea for picture-postcard pub, a good mix of walkers and cyclists in bustling bar, real ales and tasty traditional food and plenty of outside seats

With lovely views over the Channel, this pretty thatched pub has lots of picnic-sets in a secluded, split-level cottagey garden looking across to the sea. The low-ceilinged bar has a nice mix of character furniture (including a fine old settle) on flagstones and floorboards, brick and stone walls, and horsebrasses and ironwork around a woodburning stove. Brakspears Bitter, Greene King Abbot, Sharps Doom Bar and Youngs Special on handpump and several wines by the glass. Large windows in the traditionally furnished and carpeted dining room take in the fine view.

Enterprise ~ Lease Rob Benwell ~ Real ale ~ Open 11.30-11 (10 Sun) ~ Bar food 12-9 (8.30 Sun) ~ Restaurant ~ Children welcome ~ Dogs allowed in bar ~ Live music Fri/Sat evenings

SHALFLEET   SZ4089

New Inn

(01983) 531314 – www.thenew-inn.co.uk
A3054 Newport–Yarmouth; PO30 4NS

Bustling pub with seafood specialities and good beers and wines

---

Only a stroll from the quay, this is an 18th-c former fishermen's haunt with quite an emphasis on fish and seafood dishes. The rambling rooms have plenty of character, with warm fires, yachting photographs and pictures, boarded ceilings and scrubbed pine tables on flagstone, carpet or slate floors. Goddards Scrumdiggity, Ringwood Best and Sharps Doom Bar on handpump, 11 wines by the glass and farm cider; background music. There may be double sittings in summer. Dogs are only allowed in areas with stone floors.

Enterprise ~ Lease Martin Bullock ~ Real ale ~ Open 10am-11pm; 10am-10.30pm Sun ~ Bar food 12-2.30, 6-9.30 ~ Children welcome ~ Dogs allowed in bar ~ Wi-fi

SHORWELL   SZ4582

Crown

(01983) 740293 – www.crowninnshorwell.co.uk
B3323 SW of Newport; PO30 3JZ

Popular pub with an appealing streamside garden and play area, pubby food and several real ales

---

In warm weather, the peaceful tree-sheltered garden here is just the place to head for. There's a little stream that broadens into a small trout-filled pool, plenty of closely spaced picnic-sets and white garden chairs and tables on grass, and a decent children's play area. Four opened-up rooms spread around a central bar with carpet, tiles or flagstones, and there's a warm welcome for all. Adnams Broadside, Goddards Fuggle-Dee-Dum, Sharps Doom Bar, St Austell Proper Job and Timothy Taylors Landlord on handpump, 11 wines by the glass and a farm cider. The beamed, knocked-through lounge has blue and white china on an attractive carved dresser, country prints on stripped-stone walls and a winter log fire with a fancy tilework surround. Black pews form bays around tables in a stripped-stone room off to the left, with another log fire; background music and board games. This is an attractive rural setting.

Enterprise ~ Lease Nigel and Pam Wynn ~ Real ale ~ Open 11.30-11 ~ Bar food 12-9.30 ~ Children welcome ~ Dogs welcome ~ Wi-fi

DOG FRIENDLY HOTELS, INNS AND B&Bs

SEAVIEW   SZ6390

Priory Bay Hotel

(01983) 613146 – www.priorybay.co.uk
Priory Croft, Priory Road, Seaview, Isle of Wight PO34 5BU

£180; 18 individually furnished rooms, including 10 in modern cottages; also self-catering and yurts. Former Tudor farmhouse with Georgian and more recent additions in a 70-acre estate that leads to a lovely sandy private beach; lovely day rooms with comfortable sofas, books and magazines on coffee tables, and pretty flower arrangements, imaginative food in the classically decorated Island Restaurant, delicious fish and shellfish in the more contemporary Priory Oyster restaurant, excellent breakfasts; outdoor swimming pool, tennis, croquet and a nine-hole par three golf course; resident dog called Whisper. Dogs allowed in cottages in grounds; £20 per stay.

SEAVIEW   SZ6291

Seaview Hotel

(01983) 612711 – www.seaviewhotel.co.uk
High Street, Seaview, Isle of Wight PO34 5EX

£155; 28 attractively decorated rooms including 5 suites, some with sea views; also self-catering cottage. Friendly and spotlessly kept hotel with fine naval photographs and artefacts in the chatty and relaxed front lounge bar, an interesting old-fashioned back bar with real ales and a pubby feel, and a pretty restaurant serving good imaginative food using local produce. Dogs allowed in some bedrooms and in public areas except restaurant; treats; £10.

TOTLAND   SZ3286

Sentry Mead

(01983) 753212 – www.sentrymead.co.uk
Madeira Road, Totland Bay, Isle of Wight PO39 0BJ

£105; 10 bright, modern rooms. Victorian country-house guesthouse in flower-filled gardens overlooking the Solent and very near the beach; traditionally furnished lounge, bar area and an airy conservatory; caring, attentive staff; super breakfasts using local produce and home-made jams and marmalade; good nearby walks. Dogs in bedrooms and anywhere except dining area; must be on lead; £10 per stay plus £3 per night.

Kent

MAP 3

DOG FRIENDLY PUBS

BIDBOROUGH   TQ5643

Kentish Hare

(01892) 525709 ~ www.thekentishhare.com
Bidborough Ridge; TN3 0XB

Plenty of drinking and dining space in well run pub with local ales, good wines, enjoyable food and attentive staff

The easy-going and friendly atmosphere here is appealing to both drinkers and diners. The main bar has leather armchairs grouped around an open fire with antlers above, some unusual stools made of corks, bookcase wallpaper and carved stools against the counter where they keep a beer named for them from Tonbridge plus Coppernob (also from Tonbridge) and Harveys Best on handpump, 30 wines by the glass, a locally brewed lager, cocktails and a farm cider. A cosy middle room has a modern two-way woodburner at one end with leather sofas and armchairs beside it, old photographs of the pub, local people and the area, lamps made from fire extinguishers, and wallpaper depicting old leather suitcases. On the other side of the woodburner is a second bar, with attractive chunky wooden chairs and cushioned settles around various tables on wide dark floorboards; some in small booths. The airy back restaurant is similarly furnished with industrial-style lights hanging from painted joists, pots of fresh flowers and candles, exposed brick walls and an open kitchen; background music. A decked terrace with contemporary tables and chairs overlooks a lower terrace that is laid out with picnic-sets.

Free house ~ Licensees Chris and James Tanner ~ Real ale ~ Open 11-3, 5-11; 11-11 Sat; 11-6 Sun; closed Sun evening, Mon ~ Bar food 12-2.30, 6-9.30; 12-4 Sun ~ Restaurant ~ Children welcome (under-5s eat free) ~ Dogs allowed in bar ~ Wi-fi

BIDDENDEN   TQ8238

Three Chimneys

(01580) 291472 ~ www.thethreechimneys.co.uk
Off A262 at pub sign, a mile W of village; TN27 8LW

Pubby beamed rooms of considerable individuality, log fires, imaginative food and big, pretty garden; comfortable bedrooms

The small, low-beamed bar and dining rooms of this fine old pub are civilised but informal with plenty of character. They're simply done out with plain wooden furniture and old settles on flagstones and coir matting, some harness and sporting prints on the stripped-brick walls and good log fires. The public bar on the left is quite down to earth, with darts, dominoes and cribbage. Well trained, attentive staff serve Adnams Southwold, Harveys Best and a guest such as Westerham British Bulldog tapped from the cask, 15 wines plus sparkling wine and champagne by the glass, local Biddenden cider and 13 malt whiskies. A candlelit bare-boards restaurant has rustic décor and french windows that open into a conservatory; the excellent food uses the best local, seasonal produce. There are seats in the pretty garden. Sissinghurst gardens (National Trust) are nearby.

Free house ~ Licensee Craig Smith ~ Real ale ~ Open 11.30-11 ~ Bar food 12-9; lighter afternoon menu ~ Restaurant ~ Children welcome ~ Dogs allowed in bar ~ Wi-fi ~ Bedrooms: £120

CHIDDINGSTONE CAUSEWAY   TQ5146

Little Brown Jug

(01892) 870318 – www.thelittlebrownjug.co.uk
B2027; TN11 8JJ

Bustling pub with interconnected bar and dining rooms, open fires, five real ales and enjoyable food; seats outside

Set in rolling countryside, this is a friendly pub with seats and tables on a terrace, picnic-sets on grass, several 'dining huts' (bookable in advance for £25) and a children's play area. Inside, the beamed front bar has rugs on bare boards or tiled floors, a roaring log fire, leather chesterfield sofas and chunky stools in one corner and high chairs against the carved counter where they keep Greene King IPA and Abbot, Harviestoun Bitter & Twisted and Larkins Traditional on handpump and good wines by the glass; background music and board games. Throughout, various dining areas merge together with open doorways and timbering, more open fires, hundreds of prints, framed old cigarette cards, maps and photos on painted walls, books on shelves, houseplants, old stone bottles and candles on windowsills, big mirrors and all manner of cushioned wooden dining chairs, wall seats and settles with scatter cushions and polished dark wood or rustic tables.

Whiting & Hammond ~ Lease Duke Chidgey ~ Real ale ~ Open 10am-11.30pm; 9am-midnight Fri, Sat; 9am-10.30pm Sun ~ Bar food 12-9.30; 9am-9.30pm Fri-Sun ~ Restaurant ~ Children welcome ~ Dogs allowed in bar ~ Wi-fi

CHIPSTEAD   TQ5056

George & Dragon

(01732) 779019 – www.georgeanddragonchipstead.com
Near M25 junction 5; 39 High Street; TN13 2RW

Excellent food in popular village dining pub with three real ales, friendly, efficient service and seats in garden

Most customers are here for the particularly good food, but drinkers who want a pint and a chat are made just as welcome. The opened-up bar has heavy black beams and standing timbers, grey-green panelling, framed articles on the walls about their suppliers, and an easy-going, friendly atmosphere; background music. In the centre, a comfortable sofa and table sit in front of a log fire, with a tiny alcove to one side housing a built-in wall seat and just one table and chair. Westerham Grasshopper and Georges Marvellous Medicine and a weekly changing guest such as Westerham Puddledock Porter on handpump and 21 wines by the glass served by courteous, helpful staff. Up a step to each side are two small dining areas with more panelling, an attractive assortment of nice old chairs around various tables on bare floorboards and two more (unused) fireplaces. Upstairs is a sizeable timbered dining room with similar furnishings and a cosy room that's just right for a private party. The back garden has benches, modern chrome and wicker chairs and tables under parasols, and raised beds for flowers, herbs and vegetables. Wheelchair access to garden only.

Free house ~ Licensee Ben James ~ Real ale ~ Open 11-11 (10.30 Sun) ~ Bar food 12-3 (4 weekends), 6-9.30 (8.30 Sun) ~ Restaurant ~ Children welcome ~ Dogs allowed in bar ~ Wi-fi

ICKHAM   TR2258

Duke William

(01227) 721308 – www.thedukewilliamickham.com
Off A257 E of Canterbury; The Street; CT3 1QP

Friendly and gently civilised country pub with character rooms, good food and ales and seats in pretty garden; bedrooms

This is a well run country pub. The spreading bar has huge oak beams and stripped joists, seats that range from country kitchen to cushioned settles with animal-skin throws, all manner of tables on stripped wooden floors and a log fire with a low barrel table in front of it. Seats line the bar where friendly staff serve Shepherd Neame Whitstable Bay Pale Ale, Tonbridge Rustic and a local guest from breweries such as Old Dairy, Pig & Porter and Romney Marsh on handpump, eight wines by the glass and several gins. The low-ceilinged dining room is similarly furnished, there's a snug with a TV and table football, and a conservatory overlooking the garden and fields beyond. Throughout, paintwork is contemporary, tables are set with fresh flowers and candles in stone bottles and there are interesting paintings, prints and china plates on the walls; background music and board games. Modern seats and tables are set under parasols on the partly covered terrace, with picnic-sets and a children's play area on grass. Canterbury is just ten minutes by car.

Free house ~ Licensee Mark Sargeant ~ Real ale ~ Open 11-11 (midnight Sat); 11-10.30 Sun ~ Bar food 12-3, 5.30 (6.30 Sat)-9.30; 11-5 Sun ~ Restaurant ~ Live music every second Weds ~ Dogs allowed in bar ~ Wi-fi ~ Bedrooms: £100

LANGTON GREEN   TQ5439

Hare

(01892) 862419 – www.brunningandprice.co.uk/hare
A264 W of Tunbridge Wells; TN3 0JA

Interestingly decorated Edwardian pub with a fine choice of drinks and imaginative brasserie-style food

This is a particularly well run and highly popular pub that's always deservedly busy. The high-ceilinged rooms are light and airy, with rugs on bare boards, built-in wall seats, stools and old-style wooden tables and chairs, dark dados below pale-painted walls covered in old photographs and prints, old romantic pastels and a huge collection of chamber-pots hanging from beams. Greene King IPA and London Glory, Hardys & Hansons Olde Trip and two changing guest ales on handpump, 30 wines by the glass, 75 malt whiskies, 25 gins and a farm cider; background music and board games. French windows open on to a big terrace with pleasant views of the tree-ringed village green. Parking in front of the pub is limited but you can park in the lane to one side.

Brunning & Price ~ Manager Tina Foster ~ Real ale ~ Open 11-11; 11am-midnight Fri, Sat;
12-10.30 Sun ~ Bar food 12-9.30 (10 Fri, Sat, 9 Sun) ~ Restaurant ~ Children welcome ~
Dogs allowed in bar ~ Wi-fi

MATFIELD   TQ6541

Wheelwrights Arms

(01892) 722129 – www.thewheelwrightsarmsfreehouse.co.uk
The Green; TN12 7JX

**Cosy, character village pub with friendly staff, good food cooked by the
landlord, up to seven real ales and decent wines; seats on a front terrace**

Run by enthusiastic and hard-working licensees, this attractive weatherboarded
pub is extremely popular locally but offers a genuine welcome to visitors too.
There are hop-strung beams, traditional dark pubby tables and chairs on bare
floorboards (one bench has a half wheel as its back), church candles and leather
armchairs in front of a woodburning stove; background music. Canterbury Ales
The Pardoner's Ale, Dark Star Antares, Greene King Abbot, Larkins Traditional,
Westerham Finchcocks Original and Whitstable Native on handpump, 13 good
wines by the glass, local lager, cider brewed in the village and several whiskies
and gins; helpful, courteous service. The dining room leads off the bar with a
decorative woodburner in an inglenook fireplace, horsetack, old soda siphons
and other knick-knacks dotted about, and some old photos of the pub and village
along with cricketing prints and cartoons on the walls. At the front are hanging
baskets and modern seats and tables.

Free house ~ Licensees Rob and Gem Marshall ~ Real ale ~ Open 12-11; 12-9 Sun; closed
Mon except bank holidays ~ Bar food 12-2.15, 6.30-8.45; 12-3.45 Sun~ Restaurant ~ Well
behaved children welcome ~ Dogs allowed in bar ~ Wi-fi

MEOPHAM   TQ6364

Cricketers

(01474) 812163 – www.thecricketersinn.co.uk
Wrotham Road (A227); DA13 0QA

**Busy village pub with friendly staff, plenty to look at, several real ales,
good wines and well thought-of food**

Opposite the village green, this is a busy, well run village pub with plenty
of space for both drinking and dining. The bar has cushioned wall settles,
a medley of old-style wooden dining chairs and tables, a raised fireplace,
newspapers to read and Bexley Bob, Sharps Doom Bar, Tring Robin Redbreast
and a guest ale on handpump and around a dozen wines by the glass. Glass
partitioning separates an end room that has bookshelves either side of another
fireplace, rugs on bare floorboards and big house plants. Down steps to one side
of the bar is a sizeable dining room with another raised fireplace and similar
chairs and tables on more rugs and boards. Throughout, there are frame-to-frame
photos, prints and paintings, and church candles on each table; background
music. A family room at the end has doors that open to sizeable outdoor seating
areas with contemporary black rattan-style seats under parasols overlooking a
windmill; there are a few seats out in front too.

Whiting & Hammond ~ Manager Scott Hawkes ~ Real ale ~ Open 9am-11pm (midnight
Fri, Sat) ~ Bar food 12-9.30; 9am-9.30pm Fri, Sat; 9am-9pm Sun ~ Restaurant ~ Children
welcome ~ Dogs allowed in bar ~ Wi-fi

PENSHURST   TQ5142

Bottle House

(01892) 870306 – www.thebottlehouseinnpenshurst.co.uk
Coldharbour Lane; leaving Penshurst SW on B2188 turn right at Smarts Hill signpost, then bear right towards Chiddingstone and Cowden; keep straight on; TN11 8ET

Country pub with friendly service, a good choice of drinks, tasty food and sunny terrace; nearby walks

After enjoying a walk in the surrounding rolling countryside, come to this cottagey place for lunch. The bars have all sorts of joists and beams (a couple of particularly low ones are leather padded) and the open-plan rooms are split into cosy areas by numerous standing timbers. Pine wall boards and bar stools are ranged along the timber-clad copper-topped counter where they keep Dark Star American Pale Ale, Larkins Traditional and Tonbridge Coppernob on handpump and 19 wines by the glass from a good list. There's also a hotchpotch of wooden tables (with fresh flowers and candles), fairly closely spaced chairs on dark boards or coir, a woodburning stove and photographs of the pub and local scenes; background music. Some of the walls are of stripped stone. The sunny, brick-paved terrace has teak chairs and tables under parasols, and olive trees in white pots. There is limited parking.

Free house ~ Licensee Paul Hammond ~ Real ale ~ Open 11-11; 11-10.30 Sun ~ Bar food 12-10 (9 Sun) ~ Restaurant ~ Children welcome ~ Dogs allowed in bar

PLUCKLEY   TQ9243

Dering Arms

(01233) 840371 – www.deringarms.com
Pluckley station, which is signposted from B2077; or follow Station Road (left turn off Smarden Road in centre of Pluckley) for about 1.3 miles S, through Pluckley Thorne; TN27 0RR

Handsome building with stylish main bar, carefully chosen wines, three ales, good fish dishes and roaring log fire; comfortable bedrooms

This fine building with an imposing frontage, mullioned arched windows and dutch gables was originally built as a hunting lodge on the Dering Estate. The high-ceilinged, stylishly plain main bar has a solid country feel with a variety of wooden furniture on flagstones, a roaring log fire in a great fireplace, country prints and some fishing rods. The smaller half-panelled back bar has similar dark wood furnishings, plus an extension with a woodburning stove, comfortable armchairs, sofas and a grand piano; board games. Goachers Gold Star and a beer named for the pub from Goachers on handpump, 11 good wines by the glass from a fine list, local cider, 30 malt whiskies and 20 cognacs. The good food focuses on fish and shellfish, though non-fishy dishes are offered as well. Classic car meetings (the landlord James has a couple of classic motors) are held here on the second Sunday of the month.

Free house ~ Licensee James Buss ~ Real ale ~ Open 11.30-3.30, 6-11; 12-4 Sun; closed Sun evening, Mon ~ Bar food 12-2.30 (3 Sat), 6.30-9; 12-3 Sun ~ Restaurant ~ Children welcome ~ Dogs allowed in bar ~ Bedrooms: £95

SEVENOAKS   TQ5055

Kings Head

(01732) 452081 – www.kingsheadbesselsgreen.co.uk
Bessels Green; A25 W, just off A21; TN13 2QA

Bustling pub with open-plan, character rooms, quite a choice of ales, good food and seats in garden

The little bar here is liked by chatty locals and has black and white floor tiles, stools against the counter and friendly staff who serve Caledonian Deuchars IPA and Fullers London Pride, as well as guests such as Blackjack Jabberwocky, Dark Star Hophead, Old Dairy Blue Top and St Austell Tribute on handpump and a dozen wines by the glass. An attractive small room with a two-way open fire leading off here is dog-friendly. Spreading dining areas fan out from the bar with a wide mix of cushioned dining chairs, button-back wall seats and settles with scatter cushions around rustic or dark wooden tables on bare board or tile floors. Also, open fires, frame-to-frame prints, old photos and maps on painted walls, house plants, church candles and old bottles on windowsills, and bookshelves; background music. Outside there are teak tables and chairs on a terrace, picnic-sets on grass and one or two circular 'dining huts' (these are bookable in advance for £25).

Whiting & Hammond ~ Manager Jamie Owen ~ Real ale ~ Open 11-11 (midnight Sat); 11-10.30 Sun ~ Bar food 12-9.30 (9 Sun); breakfast 9-11.30am weekends ~ Children welcome ~ Dogs allowed in bar ~ Wi-fi

SEVENOAKS   TQ5352

White Hart

(01732) 452022 – www.brunningandprice.co.uk/whitehart
Tonbridge Road (A225 S, past Knole); TN13 1SG

Well run coaching inn with lots to look at in character rooms, rewarding food and friendly, helpful staff

Service with a smile, well liked food and a thoughtful choice of drinks keep customers coming back on a regular basis to this carefully renovated old place. The many rooms (with open fires and woodburning stoves) are connected by open doorways and steps. All manner of nice wooden dining chairs around tables of every size sit on rugs or bare floorboards, cream walls are hung with lots of prints and old photographs (many of local scenes or schools) and there are fresh flowers and plants, daily papers, board games and plenty of chatty, cheerful customers. Phoenix Brunning & Price Original and Old Dairy Blue Top plus guests from breweries such as Empire, Harveys, Timothy Taylors, Tonbridge and Westerham on handpump, 20 good wines by the glass, 50 malt whiskies and a farm cider. At the front are picnic-sets under parasols, with wooden benches and chairs around tables under more parasols on the back terrace.

Brunning & Price ~ Manager Chris Little ~ Real ale ~ Open 11-11; 12-10.30 Sun ~ Bar food 12-10 (9 Sun) ~ Children welcome away from bar until 7pm ~ Dogs allowed in bar ~ Wi-fi

SHIPBOURNE TQ5952
Chaser
(01732) 810360 – www.thechaser.co.uk
Stumble Hill (A227 N of Tonbridge); TN11 9PE

Busy country pub with lots to look at in rambling rooms, log fires, good choice of drinks, enjoyable food and seats outside

The comfortably opened-up bar and dining areas here have a gently civilised and friendly feel – helped along by the courteous, obliging staff. There are stripped wooden floors, frame-to-frame pictures, maps and old photos on the walls above pine wainscoting, house plants and antique glass bottles on windowsills, several roaring log fires, shelves of books and an eclectic mix of solid wood tables (each set with a church candle) surrounded by prettily cushioned dining chairs. Greene King IPA, Larkins Traditional, Sharps Cornish Coaster and York Guzzler on handpump, good wines by the glass, 20 malt whiskies and two farm ciders; background music. A striking, school chapel-like room at the back has wooden panelling and a high timber-vaulted ceiling. French windows open on to an enclosed central courtyard with wicker-style tables and chairs on large flagstones and plants in wall pots; this has a retractable awning and a woodburning stove and creates extra family dining space. A side garden with hedges and shrubs has picnic-sets and is overlooked by the church. You can use the small back car park or park in the lane opposite by the green-cum-common; local walks.

Whiting & Hammond ~ Manager Craig White ~ Real ale ~ Open 11-11; 9am-midnight (10.30 Sun) Sat ~ Bar food 12-9.30; 9am-9.30pm Thurs, Sat; 9-9 Sun ~ Children welcome ~ Dogs allowed in bar ~ Wi-fi

SISSINGHURST   TQ7937
Milk House
(01580) 720200 – www.themilkhouse.co.uk
The Street; TN17 2JG

Bustling village inn of character with well kept ales, enjoyable food and seats in big garden; restful bedrooms

Handy for Sissinghurst Castle (National Trust) and its beautiful gardens, this is just the place to head for afterwards. Through the notable entrance hall, turn right for the companiable bar. This has grey-painted beams, a grey plush sofa by a handsome Tudor fireplace and candles in hurricane jars; unusual touches include the book mural wallpaper, milk churns on windowsills, wickerwork used on the bar counter and for lampshades, and a wire cow. Daily papers, board games and background music. Dark Star American Pale Ale, Harveys Best and a guest from local breweries such as Old Dairy, Tonbridge and Westerham on handpump, 14 wines by the glass, local cider and gin and several malt whiskies, all served by friendly, helpful staff. The restaurant to the left is similarly furnished and there's also a small room leading off, just right for a private party. A large terrace outside the bar has sturdy tables and chairs under green parasols, there's an outdoor pizza/flatbread oven, picnic-sets and a children's play hut beside a fenced-in pond. Tea, coffee and cake are served from 9am.

Mint Pub Company ~ Managers Dane and Sarah Allchorne ~ Real ale ~ Open 9am-11pm; 9am-midnight Fri, Sat ~ Bar food 12-3, 6-9; light snacks in afternoon ~ Restaurant ~ Children welcome ~ Dogs allowed in bar ~ Wi-fi ~ Live music winter Weds from 6pm ~ Bedrooms: £120

SPELDHURST   TQ5541

George & Dragon

(01892) 863125 – www.speldhurst.com
Village signed from A264 W of Tunbridge Wells; TN3 0NN

**Handsome old pub with beams, flagstones and huge fireplaces, local
beers, good food and attractive outside seating areas**

Based around a 13th-c manorial hall, this is a lovely half-timbered building with
some fine original features: heavy beams (installed during 'modernisation' in
1589 – until then, the room went up to the roof), some of the biggest flagstones
you'll ever see and a massive stone fireplace. To the right of the rather splendid
entrance hall, a half-panelled room is set for dining with a mix of old wheelback and
other dining chairs and a cushioned wall pew around several tables, small pictures
on the walls and horsebrasses on one huge beam. A doorway leads to another
dining room with similar furnishings and a second big inglenook. Those wanting a
drink and a chat tend to head to the room on the left of the entrance (you can eat
in here too), where there's a woodburning stove in a small fireplace, high-winged
cushioned settles and various wooden tables and dining chairs on a stripped
wood floor; background music. The restaurant is upstairs. Harveys Best, Larkins
Traditional and a guest beer on handpump, 16 wines by the glass and a farm cider,
served by friendly, efficient staff. Teak tables, chairs and benches sit on a nicely
planted gravel terrace in front of the pub, while at the back is a covered area with
church candles on tables and a lower terrace with seats around a 200-year-old olive
tree; more attractive planting here and some modern garden design.

Free house ~ Licensee Julian Leefe-Griffiths ~ Real ale ~ Open 12-11 ~ Bar food 12-2.30
(3 Sat), 6.30-9.30; 12-4 Sun ~ Restaurant ~ Children welcome ~ Dogs allowed in bar ~ Wi-fi

STALISFIELD GREEN   TQ9552

Plough

(01795) 890256 – www.theploughinnstalisfield.co.uk
Off A252 in Charing; ME13 0HY

**Ancient country pub with rambling rooms, open fires, interesting local
ales and smashing food**

The imaginative food here (cooked by the landlord) is very highly regarded,
but drinkers are made just as welcome and the atmosphere is easy-going
and friendly. The hop-draped rooms ramble around, up and down, with open
fires in brick fireplaces, interesting pictures, books on shelves, farmhouse and
other nice old dining chairs around a mix of pine or dark wood tables on bare
boards, and the odd milk churn dotted about; background music. Hopdaemon
Incubus, Old Dairy Blue Top, Westerham Finchcocks Original and a guest beer
on handpump, 14 wines by the glass, a dozen malt whiskies, four local ciders
and a fair choice of gins, vodkas and bourbons. The pub appears to perch on
its own amid downland farmland, and picnic-sets on a simple terrace overlook
the village green below.

Free house ~ Licensees Richard and Marianne Baker ~ Real ale ~ Open 12-3, 6-11; 12-3,
5-11 Weds, Fri; 12-11 Sat; 12-6 Sun; closed Sun evening, Mon; first week Jan ~ Bar food 12-2
(2.30 Sat), 6-9; 12-3.30 Sun ~ Restaurant ~ Children welcome in designated areas ~ Dogs
allowed in bar ~ Live music every two months

STODMARSH TR2160

Red Lion

(01227) 721339 – www.theredlionstodmarsh.com
High Street; off A257 just E of Canterbury; CT3 4BA

Interesting country pub with lots to look at, good choice of drinks and well liked food; bedrooms

This friendly country pub is handy for Stodmarsh National Nature Reserve. The bar rooms have country kitchen chairs and tables, books on shelves and windowsills, tankards hanging from beams, a big log fire and plenty of candles and fresh flowers. Greene King IPA and a guest such as Wychwood Goddess tapped from the cask, eight wines by the glass and a farm cider; background music. There are seats and tables in the back garden.

Free house ~ Licensee Jeremy Godden ~ Real ale ~ Open 11.30-11; 11.30-midnight Fri, Sat; 12-10.30 Sun ~ Bar food 12-3, 6-9.30; 12-9.30 Sat, Sun ~ Children welcome ~ Dogs allowed in bar ~ Wi-fi ~ Bedrooms: £95

STONE IN OXNEY TQ9428

Ferry

(01233) 758246 – www.oxneyferry.com
Appledore Road; N of Stone-cum-Ebony; TN30 7JY

Bustling small cottage with character rooms, candlelight, open fires, real ales and popular food

In a lovely marshland setting, this pretty 17th-c cottage has plenty of room inside for both diners and drinkers. The main bar has hop-draped painted beams, a green dado and stools against the counter where they serve a beer named for the pub (from Westerham), Harveys Best, Sharps Doom Bar and a guest from the local Three Legs Brewing Company on handpump, eight wines by the glass and farm ciders. To the right is a cosy eating area with wheelback chairs and a banquette around a few long tables, a log fire in an inglenook and candles in wall sconces on either side. To the left of the main door is a dining area with big blackboards on red walls, a woodburning stove beneath a large bressumer beam and high-backed light wooden dining chairs around assorted tables; up a couple of steps, a smarter dining area has modern chandeliers. Throughout, there are wooden floors, all sorts of pictures and framed maps, a stuffed fish, beer flagons, an old musket and various brasses. Background music, TV, games machine, darts and pool in the games room. In warm weather the tables and benches on the front terrace and seats in the back garden are much prized; a river runs along the bottom and sunsets can be lovely. Disabled access in the bar and on the terrace.

Free house ~ Licensee Paul Withers Green ~ Real ale ~ Open 11-11; 12-10 Sun ~ Bar food 12-3, 6-9; 12-9 Sat; 12-8 Sun ~ Restaurant ~ Children welcome in restaurant and games room ~ Dogs allowed in bar ~ Wi-fi

TUNBRIDGE WELLS TQ5839

Black Pig

(01892) 523030 – www.theblackpig.net
Grove Hill Road; TN1 1RZ

Busy town pub with real ales, rewarding food, friendly service and seats outside

Very popular locally but with a genuine welcome for visitors too, this is a
bustling town pub with cheerful staff. The long narrow bar has a woodburning
stove in a brick fireplace with leather sofas to each side, bookshelves, a large
antelope head and some unusual friesian cow wallpaper, and a few tables and
chairs on bare boards; an overflow room up some steps to the right has wooden
chairs around heavy, dark tables and more books on shelves. Harveys Best on
handpump and good wines by the glass. If dining, most customers head for the
character room to the left of the bar: a mix of contemporary wallpaper and
panelling, oriental paintings, large flower arrangements and candles, button-
back wall banquettes and an assortment of wooden tables and chairs on more
floorboards and an open kitchen. A back terrace has seats and tables on gravel.

Free house ~ Licensee Ajay Sandhu ~ Real ale ~ Open 12-11 (10 Sun, Mon) ~ Bar food
12-2.30, 7-9.30 (10 Fri); 12-3, 6-10 Sat; 12-9 Sun ~ Restaurant ~ Children welcome ~
Dogs allowed in bar ~ Wi-fi

TUNBRIDGE WELLS   TQ5839
Sankeys

(01892) 511422 – www.sankeys.co.uk
Mount Ephraim (A26 just N of junction with A267); TN4 8AA

**Pubby street-level bar, real ales, decent food, cheerful feel;
downstairs brasserie (wonderful fish and shellfish) and seats
on sunny back terrace**

Light and airy with a cheerful atmosphere, the pubby bar here has
comfortably worn leather sofas and pews around all sorts of tables on bare
boards, a fine collection of rare enamel signs and antique brewery mirrors, and
old prints, framed cigarette cards and lots of old wine bottles; a big flat-screen
TV (for rugby only) and background music. There's a constantly changing
range of real ales, craft beers, fruit beers, lagers and ciders, and they always
feature local Larkins Traditional and Tonbridge Coppernob on handpump; also,
16 wines by the glass and a wide choice of spirits. Straightforward pub food is
available in the bar. Downstairs is the informal fish restaurant with bistro-style
décor; from here, french windows lead on to an inviting suntrap deck with
wicker and chrome chairs around wooden tables.

Free house ~ Licensee Matthew Sankey ~ Real ale ~ Open 12-1am; 12-11 Sun ~
Bar food 12-3, 6-10; 12-10 Sat; 12-8 Sun ~ Restaurant ~ Children welcome ~ Dogs allowed
in bar ~ Wi-fi

ULCOMBE   TQ8550
Pepper Box

(01622) 842558 – www.thepepperboxinn.co.uk
*Fairbourne Heath; signposted from A20 in Harrietsham, or follow Ulcombe signpost from
A20, then turn left at crossroads with sign to pub, then right at next minor crossroads;
ME17 1LP*

**Friendly country pub with lovely log fire, well liked food, fair choice
of drinks and seats in a pretty garden**

With attentive and convivial licensees welcoming both locals and visitors,
this well run country pub is always deservedly busy. The homely bar has
standing timbers and a few low beams (some hung with hops), copper kettles
and pans on windowsills, and nice horsebrasses on the fireplace's bressumer

beam; two leather sofas are set beside the splendid inglenook fireplace with its lovely log fire. A side area, furnished more functionally for eating, extends into the opened-up beamed dining room with a range in another inglenook and more horsebrasses. Shepherd Neame Master Brew and guests such as Early Bird and Whitstable Bay Pale Ale on handpump and 15 wines by the glass; background music. In summer, the hop-covered terrace and shrub-filled garden (looking out over a great plateau of rolling arable farmland) is just the place to relax after a walk along the nearby Greensand Way footpath. The village church is worth a look.

Shepherd Neame ~ Tenant Sarah Pemble ~ Real ale ~ Open 11-3, 6-11; 12-5 Sun ~ Bar food 12-2.15, 6.30-9.30; 12-3 Sun ~ Restaurant ~ Children over 7 only ~ Dogs allowed in bar

WHITSTABLE
TR1066

Pearsons Arms

(01227) 773133 – www.pearsonsarmsbyrichardphillips.co.uk
Sea Wall off Oxford Street after road splits into one-way system; public parking on left as road divides; CT5 1BT

Seaside pub with an emphasis on imaginative food, several local ales and good mix of customers

This is a rewarding place for either a drink or an enjoyable meal. It's a weatherboarded, beachside pub with two front bars, divided by a central chimney: cushioned settles, captain's chairs and leather armchairs on a stripped-wood floor, driftwood walls and big flower arrangements on the bar counter. Nethergate Growler, Sharps Doom Bar, Timothy Taylors Landlord and Whitstable East India Pale Ale on handpump, 14 wines by the glass and an extensive choice of cocktails; background music. A cosy lower room has a bookcase mural and a couple of big chesterfields and dining chairs around plain tables on a stone floor. Up a couple of flights of stairs, the restaurant has sea views, mushroom-coloured paintwork, contemporary wallpaper, more driftwood and church chairs and pine tables on nice wide floorboards.

Enterprise ~ Lease Jake Alder ~ Real ale ~ Open 12-midnight (11 Sun) ~ Bar food 12-2.30, 6.30-9.30 ~ Restaurant ~ Children welcome ~ Dogs allowed in bar ~ Wi-fi ~ Live music Tues, Sun evenings

WYE
TR0546

Kings Head

(01233) 812418 – www.kingsheadwye.co.uk
Church Street; TN25 5BN

Simply furnished, bustling pub – good food, ales and wines by the glass – and bright bedrooms

At the top of the handsome high street close to the church, this is a bustling, friendly inn with a good mix of locals and visitors. The bare-boards bar is divided by a two-way log fire, with a long brown button-back wall banquette in one part and armchairs beside the fire on the other side by a glass-topped trunk table. There are low-backed button-back pale grey chairs around all sorts of tables and pale-painted high chairs beside the counter where they keep Shepherd Neame Spitfire and Whitstable Bay Pale Ale on handpump and six good wines by the glass, plus an array of olives, cheese straws, cupcakes and so forth; service is efficient and helpful. In one corner, there's a dresser where they sell flavoured olive oils and jams. The dining room has one long wall banquette and painted kitchen chairs around pine tables and an open fire at one end with a pile of logs to one side. Throughout, there are rustic, bare-board walls, church candles, photographs of the local area, daily papers and background jazz. There are seats in a small back courtyard.

Shepherd Neame ~ Tenant Scott Richardson ~ Real ale ~ Open 7.30am-10pm; 7.30am-11pm Fri, Sat ~ Bar food 12-3, 6-9; 12-10 Sat; 12-7 Sun ~ Restaurant ~ Children welcome ~ Dogs welcome ~ Wi-fi ~ Live music Weds evening ~ Bedrooms: £90

DOG FRIENDLY HOTELS, INNS AND B&Bs

BOUGHTON LEES   TR0147

Eastwell Manor

(01233) 213000 – www.eastwellmanor.co.uk
Eastwell Park, Boughton Lees, Ashford, Kent TN25 4HR

£125; 23 traditionally decorated rooms in hotel and 39 in courtyard cottages (some have their own garden and can also be booked on a self-catering basis). Fine Jacobean-style manor (actually rebuilt in the 1920s) in 62 acres of grounds and surrounded by a 3,000-acre estate – lots of walks; grand oak-panelled rooms, open fires, comfortable leather seating, antiques and fresh flowers, courteous helpful service and extremely good, creative food in several restaurants; health and fitness spa with indoor pool – plus croquet, tennis, boules, golf and heated outdoor swimming pool. Dogs allowed in mews cottages only; £10.

CANTERBURY   TR1457

Canterbury Hotel

(01227) 453227 – www.thecanterburyhotel.co.uk
140 Wincheap, Canterbury, Kent CT1 3RY

£160; 15 contemporary rooms. Thoughtfully managed and warmly welcoming hotel (formerly the Thanington) with elegant little rooms, a good-sized bar with a huge choice of malt whiskies, two elegant dining rooms serving enjoyable breakfasts, a suntrap walled garden and an indoor swimming pool and sauna. Dogs allowed in some bedrooms; £20.

PENSHURST   TQ5243

Leicester Arms

(01892) 871617 – www.theleicesterarmshotel.com
High Street, Penshurst, Kent TN11 8BT

£85; 12 comfortable bedrooms. Attractively refurbished old place in a lovely village, with beamed and timbered bar rooms with open woodburning stoves, wonky brick floor and wide floorboards, church candles, fresh flowers and a huge ornate gilt mirror, lots of suspended saddles and horsey wallpaper; also an airy dining room with half panelling, contemporary paintwork and bookshelves wallpaper, and a more formal purple-painted and panelled restaurant; friendly staff, local ales and reliably good food; Penshurst Place is nearby, and plenty of walks. Dogs allowed in all bedrooms and bar.

ST MARGARET'S AT CLIFFE
TR3444

Wallett's Court

(01304) 852424 – www.wallettscourt.com
Dover Road, Westcliffe, Dover, Kent CT15 6EW

£195; 14 rooms, some in converted stables and barns. Fine, family-run old manor house in wild landscape, with 13th-c cellars, beams, antiques, comfortable seating and an open fire in the lounge, good, interesting food using the best local produce in the conservatory and restaurant (light meals all day and afternoon teas); particularly friendly and helpful service; outdoor terrace with seating; indoor swimming pool, spa and gym, tennis, croquet and boules; handy for the ferries. Dogs allowed in some bedrooms and lounge; £10.

THURNHAM
TQ8057

Black Horse

(01622) 737185 – www.wellieboot.net
Pilgrims Way, Thurnham, Maidstone, Kent ME14 3LD

£90; 27 rooms in separate annexe. Family-run 18th-c inn beneath the North Downs (good nearby walks) with a characterful bar with hops, beams, real ales, daily papers and an open log fire; a wide choice of enjoyable food in the neat, airy restaurant; friendly staff and a pleasant garden with partly covered back terrace, water features and nice views. Dogs allowed in bedrooms; welcome pack; £10.

TUNBRIDGE WELLS
TQ5839

Hotel du Vin

(01892) 526455 – www.hotelduvin.com
Crescent Road, Tunbridge Wells, Kent TN1 2LY

£150; 34 well equipped, chic rooms including 3 suites. Handsome sandstone Georgian building with a relaxed atmosphere and comfortable, attractive décor in lobby, lounge and bar; good modern cooking in the airy, high-ceilinged and informal bistro (including french-style Sunday brunch) and particularly good wines; seats on the terrace and in garden. Dogs allowed in three bedrooms; bowl and bed available for £10.

Lancashire
with Greater Manchester and Merseyside

MAP 7

DOG FRIENDLY PUBS

BAY HORSE   SD4952
Bay Horse
(01524) 791204 – www.bayhorseinn.com
1.2 miles from M6 junction 33: A6 southwards, then off on left; LA2 0HR

18th-c former coaching inn with log fires, comfortable bar and restaurant, rewarding food, local ales and friendly staff

This civilised family-run dining pub is handy if you want to explore the area or need to break a journey while on the nearby motorway. The cosily pubby beamed bar has cushioned wall banquettes in bays, lamps on windowsills, and a good log fire. Moorhouses Pendle Witches Brew, Thwaites Wainwright and Timothy Taylors Golden Best on handpump and ten wines by the glass served by friendly, efficient staff. The smarter restaurant has cosy corners, fresh flowers, a woodburning stove and lovely views over the garden – where there are plenty of seats and tables.

Mitchells ~ Tenant Craig Wilkinson ~ Real ale ~ Open 12-3, 6-11; closed Mon, Tues; second week Jan, second week Nov ~ Bar food 12-2, 6-9; 12-3, 6-8 Sun ~ Restaurant ~ Children welcome ~ Dogs allowed in bar

BISPHAM GREEN   SD4813
Eagle & Child
(01257) 462297 – www.ainscoughs.co.uk
Maltkiln Lane (Parbold–Croston road, off B5246); L40 3SG

Gently civilised pub with antiques, enterprising food, an interesting range of beers and appealing rustic garden

Facing the village green, this is a bustling all-rounder. The largely open-plan bar is carefully furnished with several handsomely carved antique oak settles (the finest made in part, it seems, from a 16th-c wedding bed-head), a mix of small old oak chairs, an attractive oak coffer, old hunting prints and engravings and hop-draped low beams. Also, red walls, coir matting, oriental rugs on ancient flagstones in front of a fine old stone fireplace and counter; the pub dogs are called Betty and Doris. Friendly young staff serve Bowland Hen Harrier, Coniston Bluebird Bitter, Hawkshead Windermere Pale, Southport Carousel, Thwaites Original and Wainwright and Wychwood Hobgoblin on handpump, farm cider, ten wines by the glass and around 30 malt whiskies. A popular beer festival is usually held on the early May Bank Holiday weekend. The spacious garden has a well tended but unconventional bowling green; beyond is a wild area that's home to crested newts and moorhens. They also run a shop in a handsome side barn selling interesting wines and pottery, plus a proper butcher and a deli. This is part of the Ainscoughs group.

Free house ~ Licensee Peter Robinson ~ Real ale ~ Open 12-11 (10.30 Sun) ~ Bar food 12-2, 5.30-9; 12-9 Sat; 12-8 Sun ~ Children welcome ~ Dogs welcome ~ Live music monthly Fri evening

DOWNHAM   SD7844

Assheton Arms

(01200) 441227 – www.seafoodpubcompany.com/the-assheton-arms
Off A59 NE of Clitheroe, via Chatburn; BB7 4BJ

Fine old inn with plenty of dining and drinking space, a friendly welcome, several real ales and creative food; bedrooms

This is a genuinely friendly old place with helpful staff and an easy-going atmosphere. A small front bar, with a hatch to the kitchen, has tweed-upholstered armchairs and stools on big flagstones around a single table, a woodburning stove surrounded by logs, and drawings of dogs and hunting prints on grey-green walls. Off to the right, a wood-panelled partition creates a cosy area where there are similarly cushioned pews and nice old chairs around various tables on a rug-covered wooden floor, and a couple of window chairs. The main bar, up a couple of steps, has old photographs of the pub and the village on pale walls and a marble bar counter where they serve Moorhouses White Witch, Thwaites Wainwright and Timothy Taylors Landlord on handpump, a dozen wines by the glass and farm cider; background music and board games. A two-level restaurant has carpet or wooden flooring, two fireplaces (one with a woodburning stove and the other with a lovely old kitchen range) and hunting prints. The setting at the top of a steep hill is very pretty, and picnic-sets and tables and chairs make the most of this. Do note the lovely church opposite. This is part of the Seafood Pub Company.

Free house ~ Licensee Jocelyn Neve ~ Real ale ~ Open 12-11 (midnight Sat, 10.30 Sun) ~ Bar food 12-9 (10 Fri, Sat, 8 Sun) ~ Restaurant ~ Children welcome ~ Dogs allowed in bar ~ Wi-fi

FORMBY   SD3109

Sparrowhawk

(01704) 882350 – www.brunningandprice.co.uk/sparrowhawk
Southport Old Road; brown sign to pub just off A565 Formby bypass, S edge of Ainsdale; L37 0AB

Light and airy pub with interesting décor, good food and drinks choices and wooded grounds

You'll find plenty of space for drinking and dining in the open-plan linked areas that spread out from the central bar here, and there's a bustling atmosphere at any time of day. The various rooms have plenty of interest, from attractive prints on pastel walls, church candles, flowers and snug leather fireside armchairs in library corners through tables with rugs on dark boards by big bow windows and a comfortably carpeted conservatory dining room; background music. A wide choice of drinks includes 21 wines by the glass, 89 malt whiskies, 49 gins and Phoenix Brunning & Price Original, Salopian Oracle, Titanic Plum Porter and a couple of guest beers on handpump. A flagstoned side terrace has sturdy tables, and several picnic-table sets are nicely spread on the woodside lawns by a set of swings and an old Fergie tractor (painted green instead of the usual grey). A walk from the pub to coastal nature reserves might just yield red squirrels, still hanging on in this area.

Brunning & Price ~ Manager Iain Hendry ~ Real ale ~ Open 10.30am-11pm; 10.30-10.30 Sun ~ Bar food 12-10 (9.30 Sun) ~ Children welcome ~ Dogs allowed in bar ~ Wi-fi

GREAT MITTON   SD7138

Aspinall Arms

(01254) 826555 – www.brunningandprice.co.uk/aspinallarms
B6246 NW of Whalley; BB7 9PQ

Cleverly refurbished and extended riverside pub with cheerful, friendly service and a fine choice of drinks and food

The setting by the River Ribble for this well run pub is lovely, and in warm weather the picnic-sets on grass overlooking the water and seats and tables on the terrace make the most of the view. Various rambling rooms and snugger corners inside have a chatty, easy-going atmosphere, with customers dropping in and out all day. Seating ranges from attractively cushioned old-style dining chairs through brass-studded leather ones to big armchairs and sofas around an assortment of dark tables. Floors are flagstoned, carpeted or wooden and topped with rugs, while the pale-painted or bare stone walls are hung with an extensive collection of prints and local photographs. Dotted about are large mirrors, house plants, stone bottles and bookshelves and there are both open fires and a woodburning stove. From the central servery, friendly and helpful staff serve Phoenix Brunning & Price Original, Hawkshead Lakeland Gold, Lancaster Blonde, Moorhouses Aspinall Witch (named for the pub) and Phoenix Monkeytown Mild on handpump, 15 wines by the glass, 50 gins, an amazing 150 malt whiskies and a farm cider; background music and board games.

Brunning & Price ~ Manager Chris Humphries ~ Real ale ~ Open 10.30am-11pm; 10.30-10.30 Sun ~ Bar food 12-10 (9.30 Sun) ~ Restaurant ~ Children welcome ~ Dogs allowed in bar ~ Wi-fi

MANCHESTER   SJ8297

Wharf

(0161) 220 2960 – www.brunningandprice.co.uk/thewharf
Blantyre Street/Slate Wharf; M15 4SW

Big wharf-like pub with large terrace overlooking the water and a fine range of drinks and food

Although this huge place is open-plan and on several levels, there are enough cosy nooks and alcoves to keep some sense of cosiness. Downstairs is more pubby and informal with groups of high tables and chairs, while the restaurant upstairs has table service. Throughout there's an appealing variety of pre-war-style dining chairs around quite a choice of dark wooden tables on rugs and shiny floorboards, hundreds of interesting prints and posters on bare-brick or painted walls, old stone bottles, church candles, house plants and fresh flowers on windowsills and tables, bookshelves and armchairs here and there, and large mirrors over open fires. Despite the crowds, the hard-working staff remain unfailingly helpful and friendly. They serve Phoenix Brunning & Price Original and Weetwood Cheshire Cat plus up to eight quickly changing guest ales on handpump, such as Beartown Polar Eclipse, Cotleigh Redfire, Milestone Raspberry Wheat Beer, Mobberley HedgeHopper, Pennine Real Blonde, Tatton White Queen and Three Castles Try Me, as well as farm cider, 19 wines by the glass and over 50 malt whiskies. The large front terrace has plenty of wood and chrome tables and chairs around a fountain, and picnic-sets overlooking the canal basin.

Brunning & Price ~ Manager Siobhan Youngs ~ Real ale ~ Open 10.30am-11pm (midnight Sat); 10.30-10.30 Sun ~ Bar food 12-10; 9am-10pm Sat; 9am-9.30pm Sun ~ Restaurant ~ Children welcome ~ Dogs allowed in bar ~ Wi-fi ~ Live music Fri evening

THORNTON HOUGH   SJ2979

Red Fox

(0151) 353 2920 – www.brunningandprice.co.uk/redfox
Liverpool Road; CH64 7TL

Big spreading pub with character rooms, a fine choice of beers, wines, gins and whiskies, courteous staff serving enjoyable food and large back garden

With its own drive and grounds, this is a substantial brick and sandstone pub on the edge of a village of striking mock-Elizabethan estate workers' houses. The big, spacious main bar is reached up stairs from the entrance: large central pillars divide the room into smaller areas with high stools and tables in the middle, dark wooden tables and chairs to each side and deep leather armchairs and fender seats by the large fireplace. This leads into a long, airy carpeted dining room with two rows of painted iron supports, hefty leather and wood chairs around highly polished tables and a raised fire pit; doors from here lead out to a terrace. Two additional dining rooms are similarly furnished, one with an elegant chandelier hanging from a fine moulded ceiling, the other with a huge metal elephant peeping through large house plants. Throughout there are photographs, prints and pictures covering the walls, big plants, stone bottles and shelves of books. Friendly, cheerful staff serve Phoenix Brunning & Price Original and Facers Sunlight Sunny Bitter with guests such as Brightside The Optimist, Castle Rock Red Riding Hood, Cheshire Brew Brothers Earls Eye Amber and Merlin Castle Black Stout on handpump, 21 wines by the glass, 165 malt whiskies, 100 gins and seven farm ciders; background music and board games. At the back, terraces have good quality wooden chairs and tables under parasols with steps down to picnic-sets around a fountain on a spreading lawn, and country views.

Brunning & Price ~ Manager David Green ~ Real ale ~ Open 10.30am-11pm (10.30pm Sun) ~ Bar food 12-10 (9.30 Sun) ~ Restaurant ~ Children welcome ~ Dogs allowed in bar ~ Wi-fi

UPPERMILL   SD0006

Church Inn

(01457) 820902 – www.churchinnsaddleworth.co.uk
From the main street (A607), look out for the sign for Saddleworth Church, and turn off up this steep narrow lane – keep on up; OL3 6LW

Community pub with big range of own-brew beers at unbeatable bargain prices and tasty food; children very welcome

Cheerful, friendly and well run – and with fantastic own brews to boot – this is a first class pub and always deservedly busy. The big, unspoilt, L-shaped main bar has high beams and some stripped stone, settles, pews, a good individual mix of chairs, lots of attractive prints, staffordshire and other china on a high delft shelf, jugs, brasses and so forth. They keep up to 11 of their own Saddleworth beers – though, if the water levels from the spring aren't high enough for brewing, they bring in guests such as Black Sheep and Copper Dragon. Some of their own seasonal ales are named after the licensee's children, only appearing around their birthdays; two home-brewed lagers on tap too. TV (for sporting events) and unobtrusive background music. A conservatory opens on to the terrace. The local bellringers arrive on Wednesdays to practise with a set of handbells kept here; anyone can join the morris dancing on Thursdays. Children enjoy all the animals, including rabbits, chickens, dogs, ducks, geese, alpacas, horses, 14 peacocks in the next-door field and some cats that live in an adjacent barn; dogs are made to feel very welcome. It's next to an isolated church, with fine views down the valley.

Own brew ~ Licensee Christine Taylor ~ Real ale ~ Open 12-midnight (1am Sat) ~ Bar food 12-3, 5-9; 12-9 Fri-Sun and bank holidays ~ Restaurant ~ Children welcome ~ Dogs allowed in bar ~ Wi-fi

WADDINGTON
SD7243
Lower Buck
(01200) 423342 – www.lowerbuck.co.uk
Edisford Road; BB7 3HU

Hospitable village pub with reasonably priced food and five real ales

Close to Ribble Valley walks and tucked away behind the church, this little stone building is a proper chatty local. The several small, neatly kept cream-painted bars and dining rooms, each with a warming coal fire, have plenty of cheerful customers, good solid chairs and settles on carpet or wooden floors and lots of paintings. Welcoming staff serve up to five real ales on handpump, such as Bowland Hen Harrier, IPA and Pheasant Plucker, Moorhouses Premier Bitter and Timothy Taylors Landlord, and ten wines by the glass; darts and pool. There are picnic-sets out on cobbles at the front and in the sunny back garden.

Free house ~ Licensee Andrew Warburton ~ Real ale ~ Open 11-11; 11-midnight Fri, Sat ~ Bar food 12-2.30, 5-9; 12-9 Sat, Sun and bank holidays ~ Children welcome ~ Dogs allowed in bar ~ Wi-fi

WORSLEY
SD7401
Worsley Old Hall
(0161) 703 8706 – www.brunningandprice.co.uk/worsleyoldhall
A mile from M60 junction 13: A575 Walkden Road, then after roundabout take first left into Worsley Park; M28 2QT

Very handsomely converted landmark building, now a welcoming pub scoring high on all counts

If you want a break from the nearby M60, come to this civilised and grand timbered mansion. It's been carefully restored and has some lovely original architectural features: a gracefully arched inglenook and matching window alcove, handsome staircase, heavy beams and glowing mahogany panelling. The relaxed and chatty main area spreads generously around the feature central bar, where exceptionally well trained staff serve 17 good wines by the glass, over 100 malt whiskies, 38 gins and Phoenix Brunning & Price Original and

Brightside Brindley Blonde on handpump with guests such as Battlefield 1066, Merlin Dark Magic, Weetwood Eastgate Ale, George Wright Blonde Moment. There's also the usual abundance of well chosen prints, fireside armchairs and a wide collection of cushioned dining chairs and wooden tables, and rugs on oak parquet; board games and background music. A big flagstoned terrace has heavy teak tables and a barbecue area, while the neat lawn beyond has a fountain among the picnic-table sets. The Worsley Bridgewater Canal heritage area is a ten-minute walk away.

Brunning & Price ~ Manager David Green ~ Real ale ~ Open 9am-11pm (10.30pm Sun) ~ Bar food 12-10 (9.30 Sun) ~ Restaurant ~ Children welcome ~ Dogs allowed in bar ~ Wi-fi

DOG FRIENDLY HOTELS, INNS AND B&Bs

BASHALL EAVES   SD6943
Red Pump
(01254) 826227 – www.theredpumpinn.co.uk
Clitheroe Road, Bashall Eaves, Clitheroe, Lancashire BB7 3DA

£120; 8 individually decorated, comfortable bedrooms; also 'glamping' yurts. The chatty, helpful licensees at this beautifully placed country inn create a cheerful atmosphere; there are two pleasantly up-to-date dining rooms and a traditional, cosy central bar with log fires; changing regional beers, highly regarded food and generous breakfasts; views from seats in the terraced gardens (where they grow their own herbs) are splendid, residents can fish in the nearby river and the pub is surrounded by lovely Forest of Bowland countryside; resident black lab cross, Charlie. Dogs allowed in two bedrooms, bar and snug; £12.50.

BLACKPOOL   SD3037
Imperial Hotel
(01253) 623971 – www.thehotelcollection.co.uk/hotels/imperial-hotel-blackpool
North Promenade, Blackpool, Lancashire FY1 2HB

£90; 180 well equipped rooms, many with sea views. Extensive Victorian hotel overlooking the sea, with spacious and comfortable lounges, a bustling, convivial bar, lots of period features, enjoyable food and fine wines in a smart restaurant, and a full health and leisure club with indoor swimming pool, gym, sauna and beauty treatments; dogs can walk in the grounds on leads and on the nearby beach. Dogs allowed in most bedrooms, but not near food areas; £10.

COWAN BRIDGE   SD6475
Hipping Hall
(01524) 271187 – www.hippinghall.com
Cowan Bridge, Kirkby Lonsdale, Carnforth, Lancashire LA6 2JJ

£269 with dinner; 15 rooms decorated in pretty, pale colours, some overlooking the garden, some in restored stable block. Relaxed country house atmosphere in sensitively furnished hotel – open fires, big portraits and plenty of comfortable armchairs and sofas in lounges, a lovely beamed Great Hall with minstrels' gallery, an elegant 15th-c dining room with an open fire, stripped bare boards, chandeliers and excellent, beautifully presented food (dinner included in price) and a carefully chosen wine list; four acres of walled gardens and walks from the front door. Dogs allowed in some bedrooms; welcome basket; £25 per stay.

HURST GREEN   SD6837

Shireburn Arms

(01254) 826678 – www.shireburnarmshotel.co.uk
Whalley Road, Hurst Green, Clitheroe, Lancashire BB7 9QJ

£95; 18 comfortable rooms. Smartly updated 17th-c hotel with Ribble Valley views, a beamed and flagstoned lounge bar with armchairs, sofas and a log fire, well kept ales, wines by the glass, daily papers, enjoyable food from traditional to contemporary dishes in the light and airy restaurant, friendly staff and a lovely, neatly kept garden with an attractive terrace; pretty walks nearby. Dogs allowed in some bedrooms and everywhere except main restaurant.

MANCHESTER   SJ8498

Malmaison

(0161) 641 1883 – www.malmaison.com
Piccadilly, Manchester M1 3AQ

£222; 167 chic modern rooms, including 13 suites. Stylishly contemporary hotel in a former warehouse near Piccadilly station, with comfortable furniture, exotic flower arrangements, bright paintings, efficient service, an opulent cocktail bar, a grill serving brasserie-style food, generous breakfasts and a spa. Dogs allowed in three bedrooms and lobby area; £10.

MORECAMBE   SD4264

Midland

(01524) 424000 – www.englishlakes.co.uk
Marine Road West, Morecambe, Lancashire LA4 4BU

£116–£158; 44 boutique-style rooms. Famous art deco showpiece hotel overlooking Morecambe Bay, carefully restored with chic minimalist decor; an airy modern restaurant with a glass frontage to make the most of the sea views and serving contemporary food using the best local produce (also lighter lunches and afternoon teas), plus an informal terrace café serving drinks, coffees and snacks all day; genuinely friendly, helpful staff and a bustling, informal atmosphere; beauty spa. Dogs allowed in bedrooms and public areas except restaurant; £20.

SAWLEY   SD7746

Spread Eagle

(01200) 441202 – www.spreadeaglesawley.co.uk
Sawley, Clitheroe, Lancashire BB7 4NH

£95; 7 smart, comfortable bedrooms. Attractive old coaching inn near the River Ribble and close to the substantial ruins of a 12th-c cistercian abbey, with a pleasing mix of nice old and quirky modern furniture, low ceilings, a warming fire, cottagey windows and a grey rustic stone floor; the dining areas are more formal with modern stripes and a bookshelf mural; real ales and a wide choice of good food; plenty of exhilarating walks nearby in the Forest of Bowland. Dogs allowed in two bedrooms and bar.

WADDINGTON   SD7243
Waddington Arms

(01200) 423262 – www.waddingtonarms.co.uk
Clitheroe Road, Waddington, Clitheroe, Lancashire BB7 3HP

£85; 6 attractive rooms. Classic pub with plenty of character and a friendly atmosphere in four linked rooms; low beams, a woodburning stove in huge fireplace, ancient flagstones, antique prints, vintage motor-racing posters, carefully chosen furniture, a good choice of drinks and enjoyable country cooking; seats on the front terrace look across to the attractive church; good walks nearby – the pub is on the edge of the Forest of Bowland. Dogs allowed in bedrooms and bar.

WHITEWELL   SD6546
Inn at Whitewell

(01200) 448222 – www.innatwhitewell.com
Dunsop Road, Whitewell, Clitheroe, Lancashire BB7 3AT

£150; 23 individually decorated, luxurious rooms, many with open fires; also self-catering. A first class all-rounder, this is an elegant old manor house on the River Hodder with several miles of trout, salmon and sea trout fishing and six acres of grounds with valley views; several bars with antique settles, oak tables and sonorous clocks, big attractive prints on powder blue walls, a pubby main room with roaring log fires, daily papers, local maps and guidebooks, an extraordinary wine list and several real ales; well presented bar food, a more elaborate restaurant menu and hearty breakfasts; resident working labradors and spaniels. Dogs allowed in all bedrooms and bar, but not restaurant.

Leicestershire
and Rutland

DOG FRIENDLY PUBS

BREEDON ON THE HILL   SK4022

Three Horseshoes

(01332) 695129 – www.thehorseshoes.com
Main Street (A453); DE73 8AN

Comfortable pub with friendly licensees and emphasis on popular food

This thoughtfully run 18th-c dining pub has been nicely restored and decorated to make the most of its attractive structure. The clean-cut central bar has a stylishly simple feel with heavy worn flagstones, green walls and ceilings, a log fire, pubby tables and a dark wood counter. Marstons Pedigree and a guest beer on handpump and decent house wines served by chatty, helpful staff. Beyond the bar is a dining room with maroon walls, dark pews and tables, while a two-room dining area on the right has a comfortably civilised and chatty feel with big antique tables set quite closely together on coir matting, and colourful modern country prints and antique engravings on canary yellow walls. Even at lunchtime there are lit candles in elegant modern holders. The farm shop sells their own and other local produce: eggs, jams, meat, smoked foods and chocolates. Look out for the quaint conical village lock-up opposite.

Free house ~ Licensees Ian Davison, Jennie Ison, Stuart Marson ~ Real ale ~ Open 11.30-2.30, 5.30-10.30 (11 Sat); 12-3 Sun; closed Sun evening, Mon ~ Bar food 12-2, 5.30-9; 12-3 Sun ~ Restaurant ~ Children welcome ~ Dogs allowed in bar ~ Wi-fi

BUCKMINSTER   SK8822

Tollemache Arms

(01476) 860477 – www.tollemache-arms.co.uk
B676 Colsterworth–Melton Mowbray; Main Street; NG33 5SA

Emphasis on good food in stylishly updated pub; bedrooms

There's plenty to do nearby this impressive 19th-c stone-built country pub. Table and standard lamps, big bunches of flowers and the smell of baking bread from the kitchen create a homely feel, and there's plenty of wood throughout – floors, hand-made pews, chairs and tables, with leather armchairs beside an open fire in the bar. Next to the main restaurant is a library with shelves of books and leather sofas and armchairs; background music. Grainstore Rutland

Bitter, Marstons Pedigree and Oakham JHB on handpump, a good choice of wines by the glass and several malt whiskies. There are plenty of teak tables and chairs in the sizeable garden. This is a lovely village.

Free house ~ Licensee Sarah Turner ~ Real ale ~ Open 11-3, 6 (5 Fri)-11; 11-11 Sat; 12-5 Sun; closed Sun evening, Mon ~ Bar food 12-3, 6-9; 12-9 Sat; 12-4 Sun ~ Restaurant ~ Children welcome ~ Dogs allowed in bar ~ Wi-fi ~ Bedrooms: £75

COLEORTON   SK4117

George

(01530) 834639 – www.georgeinncoleorton.co.uk
Loughborough Road (A512 E); LE67 8HF

Attractively traditional homely pub with dining area, honest food and drink and large garden

There's a good welcoming atmosphere in this attractive pub, and the bar on the right is nicely laid out to give the feel of varied and fairly small separate areas. As well as a dark panelled dado with lots of local photographs on the walls above, there are shelves of books, pews and wall seats with scatter cushions, a leather sofa and tartan-upholstered tub chairs by the woodburning stove and church candles on tables. Leatherbritches Goldings, Marstons Pedigree and Tollgate Billy's Best Bitter on handpump and ten wines by the glass served by friendly staff. A bigger room on the left has another woodburning stove and plenty to look at; background music. The spreading back garden has sturdy tables and chairs.

Free house ~ Licensees Mark and Janice Wilkinson ~ Real ale ~ Open 12-3, 5.30-11; 12-11 Fri, Sat; 12-9 Sun ~ Bar food 12-2, 6-9; 12-7 Sun ~ Restaurant ~ Well behaved children welcome ~ Dogs allowed in bar ~ Wi-fi

GREETHAM   SK9314

Wheatsheaf

(01572) 812325 – www.wheatsheaf-greetham.co.uk
B668 Stretton–Cottesmore; LE15 7NP

Warmly friendly stone pub with interesting food, real ales, a dozen wines, and seats in front and back gardens

The welcoming and helpful licensees of this particularly well run pub create a cheerful atmosphere that their many customers enjoy very much. The linked L-shaped rooms have both a log fire and a blazing open stove, traditional settles and cushioned captain's chairs around tables of varying sizes, and Brewsters Decadence, Greene King IPA and Nene Valley DXB on handpump, a dozen wines by the glass and home-made cordials; background music. A games room has TV, darts, pool and board games. The pub dogs are a dachshund and a labradoodle, and visiting dogs are welcome in the bar. There are chunky picnic-sets on the front lawn and more seats on a back terrace by a pretty stream with a duck house; pétanque. They sell their own pickles, chutneys and chocolates; there is a ramp for wheelchairs.

Punch ~ Lease Scott and Carol Craddock ~ Real ale ~ Open 12-3, 6-11; 12-11 Fri, Sat; 12-10.30 Sun; closed Mon except bank holidays; two weeks Jan ~ Bar food 12-2 (2.15 Sat), 6.30-9; 12-3 Sun ~ Restaurant ~ Children welcome ~ Dogs allowed in bar ~ Wi-fi

OAKHAM   SK8509

Grainstore

(01572) 770065 – www.grainstorebrewery.com
Station Road, off A606; LE15 6RE

Super own-brewed beers in a converted railway grain warehouse, cheerful customers and pubby food

The ten own-brews in this former Victorian grain store are the reason so many customers are here, and staff will usually offer a sample or two to help you decide which to drink. They're served traditionally on handpump at the left end of the bar counter and through swan necks with sparklers on the right. Following the traditional tower system of production, the beer is brewed on the upper floors of the building directly above the down-to-earth bar; during working hours, you'll hear the busy noises of the brewery rumbling overhead. They offer beer takeaways and hold a beer festival (with over 80 real ales and live music) on the August Bank Holiday weekend; there's also a farm cider, several wines by the glass and 15 malt whiskies. Décor is plain and functional, with well worn wide floorboards, bare ceiling boards above massive joists supported by red metal pillars, a long brick-built bar counter with cast-iron stools, tall cask tables and simple elm chairs; games machine, darts, board games, giant Jenga and bottle-walking. In summer, the huge glass doors are pulled back, opening on to a terrace with picnic-sets. You can book a brewery tour (though not on Friday or Saturday evenings) – tickets are available online. Disabled access.

Own brew ~ Licensee Peter Atkinson ~ Real ale ~ Open 12-11 (midnight Fri); 9am-midnight Sat; 9am-11pm Sun ~ Bar food 12-3, 6-9; 9-9 Sat; 9-5 Sun ~ Children welcome ~ Dogs welcome ~ Wi-fi ~ Live music twice a month, comedy monthly

OAKHAM   SK8608

Lord Nelson

(01572) 868340 – www.kneadpubs.co.uk
Market Place; LE15 6DT

Splendidly restored and full of interest, usefully open all day, real ales and ciders and enjoyable food

There are half a dozen rooms in this handsome place spread over two floors. You can choose from cushioned church pews, leather elbow chairs, long oak settles, sofas, armchairs – or, to watch the passing scene, a big bow-window seat; carpet, bare boards and ancient red and black tiles, plus paintwork in soft shades of ochre, canary yellow, sage or pink and William Morris wallpaper. There's plenty to look at too, from intriguing antique *Police News* and other prints – plenty of Nelson, of course – to the collections of mullers, copper kettles and other homely bric-a-brac in the heavy-beamed former kitchen with its Aga. But the main thing is simply the easy-going, good-natured atmosphere. Castle Rock Harvest Pale and Fullers London Pride with guests such as Navigation Last Knight, North Yorkshire Archbishop Lee's Ruby Ale and Warwickshire Duck Soup on handpump; also three farm ciders and 17 wines by the glass. Background music and TV.

Knead Pubs ~ Managers Danielle Usher and Lee Jones ~ Real ale ~ Open 10am-11pm; 12-11 Sun ~ Bar food 12-2.30, 6-9; 12-5, 6-9 Sat; 12-8 Sun ~ Children welcome ~ Dogs allowed in bar ~ Wi-fi

PEGGS GREEN

SK4117

New Inn

(01530) 222293 – www.thenewinnpeggsgreen.co.uk
Signposted off A512 Ashby–Shepshed at roundabout, then turn immediately left down Zion Hill towards Newbold; pub is 100 metres on the right, with car park on opposite side of road; LE67 8JE

Intriguing bric-a-brac in unspoilt pub, friendly welcome, well liked food at fair prices and real ales; cottagey garden

Since 1978 this cheerful pub has been run by the same friendly family who have been collecting old bric-a-brac since then; it covers almost every inch of the walls and ceilings in the two cosy tiled front rooms, and is worth close inspection. The little room on the left, a bit like an old kitchen parlour (called the Cabin), has china on the mantelpiece, lots of prints and photographs, three old cast-iron tables, wooden stools and a small stripped kitchen table. The room to the right has attractive stripped panelling and more appealing bric-a-brac. The small back 'Best' room has a stripped-wood floor and a touching display of old local photographs including some colliery ones. Bass, Marstons Pedigree and a quickly changing guest beer on handpump; background music and board games. There are plenty of seats in front of the pub, with more in the peaceful back garden. Do check the unusual opening and food service times carefully.

Enterprise ~ Lease Maria Christina Kell ~ Real ale ~ Open 12-2.30, 5.30-11; 12-3, 6.30-11 Sat; 12-3, 7-10.30 Sun; closed Tues-Thurs lunchtimes ~ Bar food 12-2, 6-8 Mon; 12-2 Fri, Sat; filled rolls might be available at other times ~ Well behaved children welcome ~ Dogs welcome ~ Wi-fi ~ Live folk club second Mon of month, quiz Thurs

SILEBY

SK6015

White Swan

(01509) 814832 – www.whiteswansileby.co.uk
Off A6 or A607 N of Leicester; in centre turn into King Street (opposite church), then after mini roundabout turn right at Post Office signpost into Swan Street; LE12 7NW

Exemplary town local, a boon to its chatty regulars, with tasty home cooking and a friendly welcome

The very good value food and the genuine can-do attitude of the helpful staff make this honest local a special place. It's been run for over 30 years by Mrs Miller. It has all the touches that mark the best of between-the-wars estate pub design, such as an art deco-tiled lobby, polychrome-tiled fireplaces, shiny red Anaglypta ceiling and a comfortable layout of linked but separate areas including a small restaurant (now lined with books). Packed with bric-a-brac from bizarre hats to decorative plates and lots of prints, it quickly draws you in thanks to the genuinely bright and cheerful welcome. Sharps Doom Bar and maybe a guest beer on handpump and six wines by the glass. The pub is especially popular with walkers from Cossington Meadows and those moored at Sileby Marine.

Free house ~ Licensee Theresa Miller ~ Real ale ~ Open 6-10 Tues-Thurs; 12-2, 6-11 Fri; 6-11 Sat; 12-3 Sun; closed Sun evening, all day Mon, lunchtimes Tues-Thurs, Sat ~ Bar food 6-8.30 Tues-Thurs, Sat; 12-1.30, 6-8.30 Fri; 12-1.30 Sun ~ Children welcome ~ Dogs allowed in bar ~ Wi-fi

STATHERN
SK7731

Red Lion

(01949) 860868 – www.theredlioninn.co.uk

Off A52 W of Grantham via the brown-signed Belvoir road (keep on towards Harby; Stathern is signposted on left); or off A606 Nottingham–Melton Mowbray via Long Clawson and Harby; LE14 4HS

Country-style dining pub with fine range of drinks and imaginative food; good garden with a play area

New owners have taken over this bustling place and some refurbishments have taken place. The lounge bar on the right has a woodburning stove and leads to a more traditional flagstoned bar with an open fire, beams, oak doors, comfortable seating and photos of the village. The small snug, with tables set for eating, connects to a long, narrow restaurant and then out to a suntrap terrace and lawn where there are good quality seats and tables. Fullers London Pride and a changing guest from Brewsters on handpump, 25 wines and champagnes by the glass, and a fine choice of spirits. Behind the car park is an unusually big play area with swings and climbing frames.

Free house ~ Licensees Mark Barbour and Karen Hammond ~ Real ale ~ Open 12-11 ~ Bar food 12-9; 12-6 Sun ~ Restaurant ~ Children welcome ~ Dogs allowed in bar ~ Wi-fi

SUTTON CHENEY
SK4100

Hercules Revived

(01455) 699336 – www.herculesrevived.co.uk

Off A447 3 miles S of Market Bosworth; CV13 0AG

Attractively furnished bar and upstairs dining rooms, highly thought-of food, real ales and helpful staff

You'll feel equally warmly welcomed in this 18th-c former coaching inn whether you're popping in for a pint and a chat or for a very good meal. The long bar is easy-going and has brown leather wall seating with attractive scatter cushions, upholstered brown and white checked or plain wooden church chairs around various tables, rugs on wooden flooring, fresh flowers, prints and ornamental plates on creamy yellow walls and a big open fire; background music. There are high leather chairs against the rough hewn counter, where they serve Church End What the Foxs Hat and Sharps Doom Bar on handpump and ten wines by the glass. Upstairs, each of the interlinked, grey-carpeted dining rooms (one wall is a giant map of the area) have their own colour scheme and tartan dining chairs around dark wooden tables. There are picnic-sets with parasols on the little back terrace, with views across a meadow to the church.

Free house ~ Licensee Oliver Warner ~ Real ale ~ Open 12-3.30, 6-11; 12-11 Sat; 12-9.30 Sun ~ Bar food 12-2.30, 6-9 (8 Sun) ~ Restaurant ~ Children welcome ~ Dogs allowed in bar

SWITHLAND
SK5512

Griffin

(01509) 890535 – www.griffininnswithland.co.uk

Main Street; between A6 and B5330, between Loughborough and Leicester; LE12 8TJ

A good mix of cheerful customers and well liked food in a well run, busy pub

After a walk in Bradgate Park or Swithland Wood, come to this bustling country pub for lunch. It's a friendly place with a warm welcome for all. The three beamed communicating rooms are cosy and traditional with some panelling, leather armchairs and sofas, cushioned wall seating, a woodburner, a nice mix of wooden tables and chairs and lots of bird prints. Stools line the counter where Adnams Southwold, Everards Original and Tiger and a guest such as Wadworths Bishops Tipple are well kept on handpump; also, a couple of farm ciders, several malt whiskies and wines by the glass from a good list; background music. The terrace, screened by plants, has wicker seats, and there are more seats in the streamside garden overlooking open fields, as well as painted picnic-sets outside the Old Stables. They also have a café/deli selling local produce and artisan products. Good wheelchair access and disabled facilities.

Everards ~ Tenant John Cooledge ~ Real ale ~ Open 12-11 (10.30 Sun) ~ Bar food 12-2, 5.30-9; 12-9 Sat; 12-8 Sun ~ Restaurant ~ Children welcome ~ Dogs allowed in bar ~ Wi-fi

WYMONDHAM   SK8518
Berkeley Arms

(01572) 787587 ~ www.theberkeleyarms.co.uk
Main Street; LE14 2AG

Well run village pub with interesting food, interlinked beamed rooms, a relaxed atmosphere and sunny terrace

The hands-on, hard-working licensees keep their friendly golden-stone inn in tip top form. There's a welcoming, relaxed atmosphere, knick-knacks, magazines, table lamps and cushions – and at one end (in front of a log fire), two wing chairs on patterned carpet beside a low coffee table. The red-tiled or wood-floored dining areas, dense with stripped beams and standing timbers, are furnished in a kitchen style with light wood tables and red-cushioned chunky chairs. Marstons Pedigree and guests such as Batemans XB, Castle Rock Harvest Pale, and Timothy Taylors Golden Best on handpump, 11 wines by the glass and local cider. Outside, on small terraces to either side of the front entrance, picnic-sets get the sun nearly all day long. Good surrounding walks.

Free house ~ Licensee Louise Hitchen ~ Real ale ~ Open 12-3, 6-11; 12-5 Sun; closed Sun evening, Mon; first two weeks Jan, two weeks summer ~ Bar food 12-1.45, 6.30-9; 12-3 Sun ~ Restaurant ~ Children welcome ~ Dogs allowed in bar

DOG FRIENDLY HOTELS, INNS AND B&Bs

BREEDON ON THE HILL   SK4022
Breedon Hall

(01332) 864935 – www.breedonhall.co.uk
Breedon on the Hill, Leicestershire, DE73 8AN

£120; 5 charming rooms; also self-catering. Friendly, family-run B&B in a handsome red-brick Georgian house with a lovely walled garden, charming drawing room with antiques and comfortable furnishings; good home cooking including delicious breakfasts and evening meals on request (dog-friendly pubs nearby too); resident cocker spaniel, Bullet, and ginger cat, Mr Bingo. Dogs (well behaved and vaccinated) allowed in all bedrooms and public areas; £5.

CLIPSHAM

SK9616

Olive Branch

(01780) 410355 – www.theolivebranchpub.com
Main Street, Clipsham, Oakham, Rutland LE15 7SH

£175; 6 lovely rooms in Beech House opposite. Civilised inn made up of former labourers' cottages with various small and charmingly attractive rooms, rustic chairs around candlelit tables, dark joists and beams, a log fire in a stone inglenook, an interesting mix of pictures (some by local artists) and lots of books (sometimes for sale), a carefully chosen range of drinks including real ales, spirits, cocktails and an enticing wine list, extremely highly thought-of food and delicious breakfasts; efficient and genuinely friendly service; outside there are seats on a pretty terrace with more on a neat lawn. Dogs allowed in ground-floor bedrooms and bar; £10.

EXTON

SK9110

Barnsdale Lodge

(01572) 724678 – www.barnsdalelodge.co.uk
The Avenue, Exton, Oakham, Leicestershire LE15 8AH

£125; 45 individually decorated rooms; also 12 self-catering lodges. Updated 18th-c former farmhouse on the north shore of Rutland Water, with a relaxed atmosphere in the comfortable lounge and bar, garden room, conservatory and smart main dining room, very good food from smashing breakfasts, quick bites and light lunches to more formal evening choices using home-grown vegetables, their own eggs and top quality, seasonal local produce; friendly, helpful staff; seats under parasols on the terrace; fishing, cycle hire and lots of walks nearby. Dogs allowed in ground-floor bedrooms; welcome pack; £10.

EXTON

SK9211

Fox & Hounds

(01572) 812403 – www.afoxinexton.co.uk
19 The Green, Exton, Oakham, Rutland LE15 8AP

£140; 4 spotlessly clean rooms. Well run and friendly, this handsome 17th-c village inn has been refurbished by new owners; high-ceilinged candlelit lounge with a winter log fire in a big stone fireplace and comfortable seating; real ales and wines served by helpful staff, and excellent food in the bar and a more formal restaurant; the sheltered walled garden overlooks pretty paddocks, and Rutland Water and Barnsdale Gardens are both nearby. Dogs allowed in one bedroom and bar; food menu (summer).

HINCKLEY

SP4292

Sketchley Grange

(01455) 251133 – www.sketchleygrangehotel.co.uk
Sketchley Lane, Hinckley, Leicestershire LE10 3HU

£114; 95 rooms, some contemporary in style, others more traditional. In its own grounds with country views, this mock-Tudor hotel is a friendly, relaxed place with a lounge and bar for morning coffees, light lunches, afternoon teas and evening cocktails, a main restaurant overlooking the garden with a wide range of cosmopolitan food, and a leisure club with a sauna, spa and indoor swimming pool. Small dogs allowed in bedrooms; £10.

LYDDINGTON   SP8797
Marquess of Exeter

(01572) 822477 – www.marquessexeter.co.uk
52 Main Street, Lyddington, Oakham, Leicestershire LE15 9LT

£99.50; 17 modern pretty rooms. Carefully reworked inside, this friendly stone inn has attractive historic features such as flagstones, thick walls, beams and exposed stonework, while the spacious open-plan areas have stylish furnishings and several open fires; real ales, a dozen wines by the glass and excellent food cooked by the landlord; seats in the tree-sheltered gardens seem to merge with the countryside beyond; the charming village is worth strolling around. Dogs allowed in some bedrooms and bar; £10.

MELTON MOWBRAY   SK7319
Sysonby Knoll

(01664) 563563 – www.sysonby.com
Asfordby Road, Melton Mowbray, Leicestershire LE13 0HP

£110.50; 30 individually styled rooms. Family-run Edwardian brick house on the edge of a bustling market town, with period-style furnishings in the reception and lounge areas, winter open fires, friendly owners and excellent service, a wide choice of brasserie-style food in the airy restaurant or bar, and five acres of landscaped gardens and meadows (dogs can walk here) leading down to the River Eye where guests can fish; walks from the door too; resident miniature daschunds, Twiglet and Tilly. Dogs allowed in most bedrooms and in public areas except restaurant; £5.

ROTHLEY   SK5712
Rothley Court

(0116) 237 4141 – www.oldenglishinns.co.uk
Westfield Lane, Rothley, Leicestershire LE7 7LG

£85; 30 rooms of individual character, some in court annexe. Mentioned in the Domesday Book, this carefully run manor house with its beautifully preserved 13th-c chapel has some fine oak panelling, open fires, stained-glass windows, suits of armour, a comfortable bar and lounge, a conservatory, a restaurant with beams and a huge stone fireplace, a wide choice of good food, and courteous staff; seats out on the terrace and in the neatly kept gardens; walks in nearby Charnwood Forest. Dogs allowed in ground-floor and annexe rooms; £10.

STAPLEFORD   SK8118
Stapleford Park

(01572) 787000 – www.staplefordpark.com
Stapleford, Melton Mowbray, Leicestershire LE14 2EF

£160; 55 individually designed rooms, including 6 in cottages. Luxurious country house, extravagantly restored, in 500 acres of grounds with riding, shooting, falcony, tennis and an 18-hole championship golf course; lots of opulent furnishings including splendid wallpapers and fabrics, fine oil paintings and an impressive library, delicious food in the smart restaurant or more informal dining areas; warmly welcoming staff; health spa with treatment rooms and pool complex. Dogs allowed in some bedrooms (not to be left unattended) and most public areas; bowl, bedding and treats; £20.

UPPINGHAM   SP8699

Falcon Hotel

(01572) 823535 – www.falcon-hotel.co.uk
Market Place, Uppingham, Rutland LE15 9PY

£160; 25 comfortable rooms. Carefully renovated historic coaching inn overlooking the marketplace, with a traditional restaurant, a lounge with sofas and a woodburner and a cosy bar with real ales; it's worth exploring this charming market town, there are walks nearby and Rutland Water is not far. Dogs allowed in four bedrooms and front bar; £10.

WING   SK8902

Kings Arms

(01572) 737634 – www.thekingsarms-wing.co.uk
Top Street, Wing, Oakham, Rutland LE15 8SE

£100; 8 comfortable rooms in the Old Bake House (the village's former bakery) or Orchard House (just up the private drive). Neatly kept former farmhouse with lots of chatty customers, an attractive low-beamed bar with two big log fires (one in a copper-canopied central hearth) and various nooks and crannies, stripped-stone walls and flagstone or wood-strip floors, real ales, local cider, home-made liqueurs and a dozen malt whiskies; modern, inventive cooking (they have their own smokehouse – you can also buy produce to take away) and excellent breakfasts; seats out in front and more in the sunny yew-sheltered garden; there's a medieval turf maze just up the road and walks nearby. Dogs allowed in four bedrooms, bar, snug, reception; bowl, treats and food menu; £10.

Lincolnshire

MAP 8

DOG FRIENDLY PUBS

BASTON   TF1113
White Horse
(01778) 560923 – www.thewhitehorsebaston.co.uk
Church Street; PE6 9PE

Blue-painted and refurbished village pub with four real ales, friendly staff and good, popular food

Carefully restored, this 18th-c village pub is run by a friendly family. Using reclaimed farm materials (the bricks in the bay window, the boards in the ceiling, some of the beams and the huge piece of sycamore that acts as the counter in the snug bar), it's an interesting place with a good mix of customers. The main bar has built-in wall seats with scatter cushions, windsor and farmhouse chairs and stools around all sorts of tables on wooden flooring, a woodburning stove in a brick fireplace (with big logs piled into another) and horse-related items on pale paintwork; background music, TV, darts and board games. The dining area is similarly furnished. Stools line the blue-painted counter where they keep Adnams Southwold, Castle Rock Harvest Pale, Grainstore Calcutta and Hopshackle American Pale Ale on handpump, a dozen wines by the glass, several gins and ten malt whiskies; the resident springer spaniel is called Audrey. There are seats and tables on a side terrace.

Free house ~ Licensees Ben and Germaine Larter ~ Real ale ~ Open 4-11 Mon, Tues; 12-11 Wed, Thurs; 12-midnight Fri, Sat; 12-10.30 Sun ~ Bar food 5.30-9 Tues; 12-2.30, 5.30-9 Wed-Fri; 12-9 Sat; 12-6 Sun ~ Restaurant ~ Children welcome until 9pm only ~ Dogs allowed in bar ~ Wi-fi

GEDNEY DYKE   TF4125
Chequers
(01406) 366700 – www.the-chequers.co.uk
Off A17 Holbeach–Kings Lynn; PE12 0AJ

Smart dining pub with small bar, stylish restaurant rooms and imaginative food

Much emphasis is placed on the first class food in this stylish and friendly fenland village pub – but there's a warm welcome for those just wanting a chat and a pint too. The beamed bar has seats against the counter where they serve Greene King Abbot and Woodfordes Wherry on handpump, 12 wines and champagne by the glass and a wide range of spirits. There are several high chairs around equally high tables and an open fire. The smart, linked, carpeted dining rooms and conservatory have high-backed cream or black dining chairs around white-clothed tables, and throughout there's bare brick here and there and good lighting; service is helpful and courteous. The back terrace and fenced-off garden have plenty of seats and tables.

Free house ~ Licensee Gareth Franklin ~ Real ale ~ Open 11.30-3, 5-11 (midnight Sat); 12-5 Sun; closed Sun evening, Mon, Tues; first week Jan ~ Bar food 12-2, 6-9; 12-3 Sun ~ Restaurant ~ Children welcome ~ Dogs allowed in bar ~ Wi-fi

GREAT LIMBER

TA1308

New Inn

(01469) 569998 – www.thenewinngreatlimber.co.uk
High Street; DN37 8JL

Rather grand but with a civilised and easy-going atmosphere in bar and dining rooms, marvellous food, fine wines and large back garden; bedrooms

Part of the Brocklesby Estate, this handsome place is thriving following its reopening and refurbishment. The focus is on the excellent food (using organic produce from the Estate's kitchen garden) and fine bedrooms, but there's a proper working bar liked by locals for a pint and a chat, quiz evenings or a game of darts. Here, there are windsor chairs, red button-back wall seating, some upholstered tub seats and oak tables on pale floorboards, neatly stacked logs to either side of one fireplace and shelves of books by another, and chairs against the counter where efficient, friendly staff serve Batemans XXXB, Tom Woods Old Codger and Wadworth IPA on handpump and a dozen wines by the glass. A snug little corner has a curved high-backed wall seat just right for a small group. The dining room is split into two, with cushioned wooden chairs in one part and comfortable red chairs and long wall seats with pretty scatter cushions in another. Throughout, the walls are hung with modern art, black and white photos and big mirrors; background music and TV. The landscaped back garden has both picnic-sets and tables and chairs. Breakfasts are available for non-residents and are highly regarded.

Free house ~ Licensee Alex Carter ~ Real ale ~ Open 12-11.30; 12-10.30 Sun ~ Bar food 12-2.30, 6.30-9; 12-6 Sun; not Mon lunchtime ~ Restaurant ~ Dogs allowed in bar ~ Wi-fi ~ Bedrooms: £96

HEIGHINGTON

TF0369

Butcher & Beast

(01522) 790386 – www.butcherandbeast.co.uk
High Street; LN4 1JS

Traditional village pub with terrific range of drinks, pubby food and a pretty garden by stream

The award-winning hanging baskets and tubs outside this cheerful village pub make quite a show in summer, and for warmer weather there are picnic-sets on a lawn that runs down to a stream. The simply decorated bar has button-back wall banquettes, pubby furnishings and stools along the counter where the hard-working, hands-on licensees keep half a dozen ales such as Batemans XB, XXXB and a seasonal guest plus Bass and changing beers from Everards and Hop Back; also two farm ciders, eight wines by the glass, 30 gins and 20 malt whiskies; occasional TV. The Snug has red-cushioned wall settles and high-backed wooden dining chairs, and the beamed dining room (extended this year) is neatly set with an attractive medley of wooden or painted chairs around chunky tables on floorboards, and a woodburning stove; throughout, the cream or yellow walls are hung with old village photos and country pictures.

Batemans ~ Tenants Mal and Diane Gray ~ Real ale ~ Open 12-11 (10.30 Sun) ~ Bar food 12-2, 5-8.30; 12-2.30, 6-8 Sun ~ Restaurant ~ Children welcome away from bar ~ Dogs allowed in bar ~ Wi-fi

KIRKBY LA THORPE   TF0945
Queens Head
(01529) 305743 – www.thequeensheadinn.com
Village and pub signposted off A17, just E of Sleaford, then turn right into Boston Road cul-de-sac; NG34 9NU

Reliable dining pub very popular for its good food and helpful, efficient service

Gently traditional and neatly comfortable, this is highly regarded locally but draws in plenty of visitors too. There are open fires, elaborate flower arrangements and plenty of courteous dark-waistcoated staff, and the carpeted bar has stools along the counter, button-back banquettes, sofas and captain's chairs around shiny dark tables. The smart, beamed restaurant has high-backed orange-upholstered dining chairs around linen-set tables on carpet, heavy curtains and a woodburning stove; there's also a popular dining conservatory. Nice decorative touches take in thoughtful lighting, big prints, china plates on delft shelves and handsome longcase clocks (it's quite something when they all chime at midday). Batemans XB and a guest such as Black Sheep on handpump; background music. Easy disabled access.

Free house ~ Licensee John Clark ~ Real ale ~ Open 12-3, 6-11; 12-10.30 Sun ~ Bar food 12-2.30, 6-9.30; 12-8.30 Sun ~ Restaurant ~ Children welcome until 7pm ~ Dogs allowed in bar ~ Wi-fi

STAMFORD   TF0307
Tobie Norris
(01780) 753800 – www.kneadpubs.co.uk
St Paul's Street; PE9 2BE

A warren of ancient rooms, a good period atmosphere, a fine choice of drinks, enjoyable food and seats outside

The best has been made of this building's great age: worn flagstones, meticulously stripped stonework, a huge hearth for one room's woodburning stove and steeply pitched rafters in one of the two upstairs rooms – it's been beautifully restored. The charming series of little rooms are full of character and have a wide variety of furnishings from pews and wall settles to comfortable armchairs and a handsomely panelled shrine to Nelson and the Battle of Trafalgar. Attentive, friendly staff serve Adnams Mosaic, Castle Rock Harvest Pale Ale and guests such as St Austell Tribute and Thornbridge Jaipur on handpump, farm cider and several wines by the glass. A snug end conservatory opens to a narrow but sunny two-level courtyard with seats and tables.

Free house ~ Licensees Tim Chantrell and Gemma Rogerson ~ Real ale ~ Open 11-11 (midnight Fri, Sat) ~ Bar food 12-2.30, 6-9; 12-5, 6-9 Sat ~ Children welcome until 8pm; no pushchairs ~ Dogs welcome ~ Wi-fi

DOG FRIENDLY HOTELS, INNS AND B&Bs

STAMFORD   TF0306

George of Stamford

(01780) 750750 – www.georgehotelofstamford.com
71 St Martins, Stamford, Lincolnshire PE9 2LB

£195; 45 comfortable, attractive rooms. Historic former coaching inn with
plenty of genuine character; civilised and relaxed, with a surprisingly pubby bar,
various other rooms with leather, cane and antique wicker seats and soft sofas
and armchairs, a particularly striking central lounge with heavy beams, sturdy
timbers, broad flagstones and massive stonework; real ales, 30 malt whiskies, an
excellent wine list and quite a choice of impressive food served by professional
staff in the sedate oak-panelled formal restaurant, less formal garden room
and lovely, partly covered courtyard; good morning coffees, afternoon teas and
breakfasts; the walled garden is immaculately kept and there's a sunken lawn
and croquet. Dogs allowed in all bedrooms and public areas except restaurant.

STAMFORD   TF0306

William Cecil

(01780) 750070 – www.hillbrookehotels.co.uk
St Martins, Stamford, Lincolnshire PE9 2LJ

£155; 27 chic rooms. Handsome golden-stone hotel dating from the 17th c,
stylishly updated with smart contemporary décor; colourful rugs, dark wood
furniture and a particularly grand fireplace in the bar, a bright restaurant with
tasty, seasonal, modern british food, and also a small conservatory; outdoor
seating; this is a lovely market town with riverside meadow walks; next door
is Burghley House and its extensive parkland (free admission, dogs must be
kept on a lead because of the deer). Dogs allowed in seven bedrooms, bar and
conservatory; bed, bowls and dog food menu; £20 per stay.

WASHINGBOROUGH   TF0170

Washingborough Hall

(01522) 790340 – www.washingboroughhall.com
Church Hill, Washingborough, Lincoln, Lincolnshire LN4 1BE

£135; 12 stylish rooms of varying sizes. Lovely and elegant family-run Georgian
house in three acres of gardens, with carefully restored rooms; convivial bar,
deeply comfortable reception/lounge, open fires and woodburning stoves,
enjoyable food in charming dining overlooking the gardens, and seats under
parasols on the terrace. Dogs allowed in three bedrooms, reception, bar and
front grounds; £10.

WINTERINGHAM SE9322

Winteringham Fields

(01724) 733096 – www.winteringhamfields.co.uk
1 Silver Street, Winteringham, Scunthorpe, Lincolnshire DN15 9ND

£180; 15 attractive rooms. Family-run restaurant-with-rooms in 16th-c manor house with attractive furnishings, beams and woodburning stove, excellent, inventive and beautifully presented food, super breakfasts and an admirable wine list; friendly service; miles of walks directly from the door. Dogs allowed in three courtyard bedrooms (must be caged in the room); bedding, treats and bowls; £25.

WOODHALL SPA TF1963

Petwood

(01526) 352411 – www.petwood.co.uk
Stixwould Road, Woodhall Spa, Lincolnshire LN10 6QG

£140; 53 smart rooms. Sizeable mock-Tudor Edwardian house in 30 acres of mature woodland and gardens, with a croquet lawn; many original features including a fine main staircase, an informal bar where light lunches are served overlooking the terrace and grounds, a traditionally furnished restaurant, comfortable lounge and a bar with RAF memorabilia (the 'Dambusters' 617 Squadron were based here); enjoyable food from breakfasts to afternoon teas and evening meals; helpful, courteous service. Dogs allowed in some bedrooms, some public rooms and grounds; £20 per night (not per dog).

WOOLSTHORPE SK8334

Chequers

(01476) 870701 – www.chequersinn.net
Main Street, Woolsthorpe, Grantham, Lincolnshire NG32 1LU

£70; 4 simply furnished rooms in converted stables. 17th-c former coaching inn with views of Belvoir Castle from seats outside; a heavily beamed main bar with bare stone walls, two huge oak tables surrounded by handsome leather chairs and banquettes, and a big boar's head above a log fire in a brick fireplace; real ales, seasonal cocktails, 50 malt whiskies, 20 gins and 30 wines by the glass, and interesting modern food in both the dining room (once the village bakery) and the restaurant; resident springer spaniels, Hector and Ruby; miles of open country walks on the Belvoir Estate. Dogs allowed in three bedrooms and bar; £5.

Norfolk

DOG FRIENDLY PUBS

BAWBURGH   TG1508
Kings Head
(01603) 744977 – www.kingshead-bawburgh.co.uk
Harts Lane; A47 just W of Norwich then B1108; NR9 3LS

Busy, small-roomed pub with five real ales, good wines by the glass, interesting food and friendly service; bedrooms

This 17th-c pub in a pretty village has friendly, helpful staff and a cheerful atmosphere. The small rooms have plenty of low beams and standing timbers, leather sofas and an attractive assortment of old dining chairs and tables on wood-strip floors; also, a knocked-through open fire and a couple of woodburning stoves in the restaurant areas. Adnams Southwold and Broadside, Tring Moongazer and Woodfordes Reedlighter and Wherry on handpump, ten wines by the glass and 12 malt whiskies; service is friendly and helpful. Background music, TV and board games. There are seats in the garden and the pub is opposite a little green.

Free house ~ Licensee Anton Wimmer ~ Real ale ~ Open 11-11; 12-10.30 (8 in winter) Sun ~ Bar food 12-2, 5.30-9; 12-3, 6-9 Sun; no food Sun evenings Nov-Mar ~ Restaurant ~ Children welcome ~ Dogs allowed in bar ~ Wi-fi ~ Bedrooms: £110

BURSTON   TM1383
Crown
(01379) 741257 – www.burstoncrown.com
Village signposted off A140 N of Scole; Mill Road; IP22 5TW

Friendly, relaxed village pub usefully open all day, with a warm welcome, real ales and well liked bar food

On a chilly day, the best place to sit here is the heavily beamed, quarry-tiled bar room with its comfortably cushioned sofas in front of a woodburning stove in a huge brick fireplace; there are also stools by a low chunky wooden table, and newspapers and magazines. Locals tend to gather in an area by the bar counter where they serve Adnams Broadside and Southwold and guests such as Castle Rock Starling and Cottage Pacific on handpump or tapped from the cask, six wines by the glass and nine malt whiskies. The public bar on the left has a nice long table and panelled settle on an old brick floor in one alcove, a pool table, and more tables and chairs towards the back near a dartboard. Both rooms are hung with paintings by local artists; background music and board games. The simply furnished, beamed dining room has another big brick fireplace. Outside, there's a smokers' shelter, seats and tables on a terrace and in the secluded garden where there's also a play area for children.

Free house ~ Licensees Bev and Steve Kembery ~ Real ale ~ Open 12-11; 10.30am-11pm
Sat; 12-10.30 Sun ~ Bar food 12 (10.30 Sat)-2, 6.30-9; 12-4 Sun; not Mon ~ Restaurant ~
Children welcome ~ Dogs allowed in bar ~ Wi-fi ~ Live music Thurs 8.30pm, every second
Sun from 5pm

CASTLE ACRE   TF8115

Ostrich

(01760) 755398 – www.ostrichcastleacre.com
Stocks Green; PE32 2AE

**Friendly old village pub with original features, fine old fireplaces,
real ales and tasty food; bedrooms**

Although largely rebuilt during the 18th c, there are still features to search
out that date back a couple of hundred years earlier – such as the original
masonry, beams and trusses. The L-shaped, low-ceilinged front bar (on two levels)
has a woodburning stove in a huge old fireplace, lots of wheelback chairs and
cushioned pews around pubby tables on a wood-strip floor and gold patterned
wallpaper; it's a step up to an area in front of the bar counter where there are
similar seats and tables and a log fire in a brick fireplace. Greene King Abbot,
IPA, Speckled Hen and a beer named for the pub on handpump, around a dozen
wines by the glass and several malt whiskies. There's a separate dining room with
another brick fireplace. The sheltered garden has picnic-sets under parasols and
the inn faces the tree-lined village green; nearby are the remains of a Norman
castle and a Cluniac monastery (English Heritage).

Greene King ~ Tenant Tiffany Turner ~ Real ale ~ Open 10am-11pm; 10am-midnight Sat ~
Bar food 12-3, 6-9 ~ Restaurant ~ Children welcome ~ Dogs allowed in bar ~ Wi-fi ~ Live
music last Sun of month ~ Bedrooms: £85

KING'S LYNN   TF6119

Bank House

(01553) 660492 – www.thebankhouse.co.uk
Kings Staithe Square via Boat Street and along the quay in one-way system; PE30 1RD

**Georgian bar-brasserie with plenty of history and character, airy rooms,
real ales and imaginative food from breakfast onwards; bedrooms**

This is a splendid quayside spot and the Corn Exchange theatre and arts centre
is just five minutes away. Usefully open all day, the various stylish rooms are
busy with customers popping in and out for drinks and meals. The elegant bar
(once the bank manager's office – the building was Barclays Bank's first opening
in 1780) has sofas and armchairs, a log fire with fender seating and Adnams
Broadside and Southwold and Wychwood Hobgoblin on handpump, 26 wines
by the glass, ten whiskies and cocktails; background music. The restaurant has
fine antique chairs and tables on bare boards, an airy brasserie has sofas and
armchairs around low tables and a big brick fireplace, and two other areas (one
with fine panelling, the other with a half-size billiards table) have more open fires.
The atmosphere throughout is bustling and welcoming and service is helpful and
courteous. An outside area is flanked by magnificent wrought-iron gates, with fire
pits for warmth on chillier evenings, and the riverside terrace (lovely sunsets) has
an open-air bar. Sister pub is the Rose & Crown in Snettisham.

Free house ~ Licensee Anthony Goodrich ~ Real ale ~ Open 11-11 (10.30 Sun); 12-9.30
Sat; 12-8.30 Sun ~ Bar food 12-9.30 (8.30 Sun) ~ Restaurant ~ Children welcome ~
Dogs allowed in bar ~ Wi-fi ~ Bedrooms: £115

MORSTON
TG0043

Anchor

(01263) 741392 – www.morstonanchor.co.uk
A149 Salthouse–Stiffkey; The Street; NR25 7AA

Quite a choice of rooms filled with bric-a-brac and prints, real ales and highly regarded food using local produce

The friendly hands-on licensees run this bustling place with great enthusiasm – they really care about their pub and their customers, and it shows. Three traditional rooms on the right have straightforward seats and tables on original wooden floors, coal fires, local 1950s beach photographs and lots of prints and bric-a-brac. Adnams Old Ale, local Winters Golden and Woodfordes Wherry on handpump, 22 wines by the glass and 13 gins; background music, darts and board games. The contemporary airy extension on the left, with comfortable benches and tables, leads into the more formal restaurant where local art is displayed on the walls. You can sit outside at the front of the building. If parking is tricky at the pub, there's an overflow around the corner off-road and a National Trust car park five minutes' walk away. The surrounding area is wonderful for bird-watching and walking, and you can book seal-spotting trips here.

Free house ~ Licensees Harry Farrow and Rowan Glennie ~ Real ale ~ Open 9am-11pm; 9am-10pm Sun; closed Sun evening Jan-Apr ~ Bar food 12-3, 6-9 ~ Restaurant ~ Children welcome ~ Dogs allowed in bar ~ Wi-fi

NORTH CREAKE
TF8538

Jolly Farmers

(01328) 738185 – www.jollyfarmersnorfolk.co.uk
Burnham Road; NR21 9JW

Friendly village local with three cosy rooms, open fires and woodburners, well liked food and several real ales

Nothing is too much trouble for the thoughtful licensees in this well run former coaching inn. There are three cosy and relaxed rooms, including the main bar with a large open fire in a brick fireplace, a mix of pine farmhouse and high-backed leather dining chairs around scrubbed pine tables on quarry tiles and pale yellow walls. Beside the wooden bar counter are some high bar chairs, and they keep Woodfordes Nelsons Revenge and Wherry tapped from the cask, 11 wines by the glass and a dozen malt whiskies; service is helpful and friendly. There's also a cabinet of model cars. A smaller bar has pews and a woodburning stove, while the red-walled dining room has similar furniture to the bar and another woodburner. There are seats outside on the terrace.

Free house ~ Licensees Adrian and Heather Sanders ~ Real ale ~ Open 12-2.30, 7-11; 12-7 Sun; closed Mon, Tues ~ Bar food 12-2, 7-9; 12-5.30 Sun ~ Children welcome ~ Dogs allowed in bar

NORWICH
TG2109

Fat Cat

(01603) 624364 – www.fatcatpub.co.uk
West End Street; NR2 4NA

A place of pilgrimage for beer lovers and open all day

A visit to this lively pub is akin to coming to a private beer festival. There's usually an extraordinary range of up to 32 quickly changing ales and the knowledgeable landlord and his helpful staff can guide you through the choices. On handpump or tapped from the cask in a stillroom behind the bar – big windows reveal all – are their own beers (Fat Cat Bitter, Hell Cat, Honey Ale, Marmalade Cat, Stout Cat and Wild Cat), as well as guests from breweries such as Crouch Vale, Fullers, Oakham and Timothy Taylors – and many more choices from across the country. You'll also find imported draught beers and lagers, over 50 bottled beers from around the world and 20 ciders and perries. The no-nonsense furnishings include plain scrubbed pine tables and simple solid seats, lots of brewery memorabilia, bric-a-brac and stained glass. There are tables outside. Lunchtime-only food consists of rolls and good pies (not Sunday).

Own brew ~ Licensee Colin Keatley ~ Real ale ~ No credit cards ~ Open 12-11 (midnight Fri); 11-midnight Sat ~ Children allowed until 6pm ~ Dogs allowed in bar ~ Wi-fi

SALTHOUSE   TG0743

Dun Cow

(01263) 740467 – www.salthouseduncow.com
A149 Blakeney–Sheringham (Purdy Street, junction with Bard Hill); NR25 7XA

Relaxed village pub, a good all-rounder and with enterprising food

On a sunny day, the picnic-sets on the front grass looking across the bird-filled salt marshes towards the sea are the perfect place to be; there are more seats in a sheltered back courtyard and an orchard garden beyond. Inside, the flint-walled bar consists of a pair of high-raftered rooms opened up into one area, with stone tiles around the counter where regulars congregate, and a carpeted seating area with a fireplace at each end. Also, scrubbed tables, one very high-backed settle, country kitchen chairs and elegant little red-padded dining chairs, with big sailing ship and other prints. Adnams Broadside, Norfolk Brewhouse Moon Gazer Golden Ale and Woodfordes Reedlighter and Wherry on handpump, 19 wines by the glass, 14 malt whiskies and a good relaxed atmosphere. They have self-catering bedrooms.

Punch ~ Lease Daniel Goff ~ Real ale ~ Open 11-11 ~ Bar food 12-9 ~ Children welcome ~ Dogs welcome ~ Wi-fi

STANHOE   TF8037

Duck

(01485) 518330 – www.duckinn.co.uk
B1155 Docking–Burnham Market; PE31 8QD

Smart candlelit country dining pub with popular food, real ales and appealing layout; bedrooms

With such good food on offer in this neatly kept pub, most customers are here to dine. But drinkers are made just as welcome and there's an entrance bar where those wanting just a chat and a pint can feel at home. This bar has pale grey paintwork, cushioned Edwardian-style chairs around wooden tables on dark floor slates, and stools against the panelled counter where they serve Adnams Ghost Ship and Elgoods Cambridge on handpump from a fine slab-topped counter and a dozen wines by the glass. A small wooden-floored area leads off, with a woodburning stove in an old brick fireplace and modern artwork, and this in turn opens into two dining rooms: cushioned chairs and farmhouse tables on more slates or coir carpeting, scatter cushions on wall seating and local seascapes on the walls. The small garden has picnic-sets under a fruit tree, and seats and tables in a garden room with fairy lights and candles; more seats and tables on the front gravel. Good disabled access and loo.

Elgoods ~ Tenants Sarah and Ben Handley ~ Real ale ~ Open 11-11; 12-10.30 Sun ~ Bar food 12-2.30, 6-9; 12-8 Sun ~ Restaurant ~ Children welcome ~ Dogs allowed in bar ~ Wi-fi ~ Bedrooms: £135

WIVETON   TG0442
Wiveton Bell
(01263) 740101 – www.wivetonbell.co.uk
Blakeney Road; NR25 7TL

Busy dining pub where drinkers are welcomed too, local beers, consistently enjoyable food and seats outside; bedrooms

The mainly open-plan rooms here have some fine old beams, an attractive mix of dining chairs around wooden tables on a stripped-wood floor, a log fire and prints on yellow walls. The sizeable conservatory has smart beige dining chairs around wooden tables on coir flooring. Friendly, attentive staff serve Norfolk Brewhouse Moon Gazer Amber Ale and Dark Mild, Woodfordes Wherry and Yetmans Amber on handpump, and a dozen wines by the glass. Picnic-sets on the front grass look across to the church; at the back, stylish wicker tables and chairs on several decked areas are set among decorative box hedging.

Free house ~ Licensee Berni Morritt ~ Real ale ~ Open 12-11 (10.30 Sun) ~ Bar food 12-2.15, 6-9.15 ~ Children welcome ~ Dogs allowed in bar ~ Wi-fi ~ Bedrooms: £130

DOG FRIENDLY HOTELS, INNS AND B&Bs

BLAKENEY   TG0244
Blakeney Hotel
(01263) 740797 – www.blakeneyhotel.co.uk
Blakeney, Holt, Norfolk NR25 7NE

£234; 60 comfortable rooms, many with views over the salt marshes and some with their own little terrace. Overlooking the harbour and the estuary, this friendly hotel has light, airy, appealing public rooms, good food served in the bar, restaurant and on the terrace, and very pleasant staff; indoor swimming pool, sauna, steam room and mini gym. Dogs allowed in 12 bedrooms; £10.

BRANCASTER STAITHE   TF8044
White Horse
(01485) 210262 – www.whitehorsebrancaster.co.uk
Main Road, Brancaster Staithe, King's Lynn, Norfolk PE31 8BY

£180; 15 modern rooms – 8 with their own terrace and access to the Norfolk Coast Path. Set beside the salt marshes (the sunsets are wonderful), this well run, recently revamped hotel has an informal locals' bar at the front serving real ales, a middle area with comfortable sofas and newspapers, and a spacious dining conservatory with enjoyable food (plenty of fish dishes) and good breakfasts; helpful, friendly staff. Dogs allowed in ground-floor bedrooms; blanket and treats; £10.

BURNHAM MARKET   TF8342

Hoste Arms

(01328) 738777 – www.thehoste.com
Market Place, Burnham Market, King's Lynn, Norfolk PE31 8HD

£185; 62 stylish, comfortable rooms – 37 in the main hotel with views over the garden or village green, the rest in buildings nearby; also self-catering cottages. Handsome and civilised 17th-c inn – most emphasis is on the smart hotel and dining side of the business, but there's also a proper bustling bar with panelling, a log fire, nice watercolours, real ales and an exceptional wine list; a conservatory with comfortable leather sofas and armchairs, a lounge for afternoon tea and several restaurants serving delicious modern food from simple bar lunches upwards; the pretty walled garden has lots of seats; beauty treatments; lovely beaches close by for walks. Dogs allowed in bedrooms, bar, lounge and conservatory; £15.

CLEY-NEXT-THE-SEA   TG0443

George

(01263) 740652 – www.thegeorgehotelatcley.co.uk
High Street, Cley, Holt, Norfolk NR25 7RN

£120; 10 refurbished rooms, some with fine views. Busy pub in quiet village overlooking the salt marshes (fantastic bird-watching); small public bar with photos of wherries and local scenes, simple seats and tables, good local beers and plenty of wines by the glass; two dining rooms with candlelight, pale wooden cushioned dining chairs and banquettes around a mix of tables, a woodburning stove and enjoyable food using local produce. Dogs allowed in some bedrooms, bar and front restaurant; £10.

EAST RUDHAM   TF8228

Crown

(01485) 528530 – www.crowninnnorfolk.co.uk
The Green, East Rudham, King's Lynn, Norfolk PE31 8RD

£110; 6 comfortable rooms. Civilised and friendly inn at the head of the village green with stylish open-plan areas, winter log fires, all manner of seating from comfortable sofas through leather dining chairs to pubby built-in cushioned wall benches, a cosy back sitting room, interesting décor, first class contemporary cooking, hearty breakfasts and friendly young staff. Dogs allowed in bedrooms and anywhere in the pub; bed, towel and treats; £10 per stay.

ERPINGHAM   TG1732

Saracens Head

(01263) 768909 – www.saracenshead-norfolk.co.uk
Wolterton, Erpington, Norwich, Norfolk NR11 7LZ

£100; 6 comfortable, modern rooms. Remote inn with an easy-going atmosphere, a two-roomed bar with a good mix of seats and tables, fresh flowers, woodburning stoves, real ales, a six-table parlour with another big open fire, and inventive, popular food; seats outside in a charming, old-fashioned gravelled stable yard. Closed two weeks February/March. Dogs allowed in bedrooms and back bar.

GREAT BIRCHAM
TF7632
Kings Head
(01485) 578265 – www.thekingsheadhotel.co.uk
Great Bircham, King's Lynn, Norfolk PE31 6RJ

£140; 12 contemporary rooms. Rather grand-looking Edwardian hotel with a bustling and attractively modern bar with a log fire and comfortable sofas, good innovative food in the light, airy restaurant, hearty breakfasts, friendly staff, and seats out in front and at the back with rustic views. Dogs allowed in all bedrooms and bar; £10.

GREAT MASSINGHAM
TF7922
Dabbling Duck
(01485) 520827 – www.thedabblingduck.co.uk
11 Abbey Road, Great Massingham, King's Lynn, Norfolk PE32 2HN

£100; 9 rooms, most named after famous local sportsmen and airmen from the World War II air base in Massingham. Bustling inn overlooking a sizeable village green with big duck ponds; relaxed bars with leather sofas and armchairs, woodburning stoves, antique dining chairs and tables on flagstones or stripped wooden floors, quirky 18th- and 19th-c prints and cartoons and seats on front terrace and in enclosed back garden; local beers, imaginative food using local produce and nice breakfasts. Dogs allowed in six bedrooms and bar; £10.

HOLKHAM
TF8943
Victoria
(01328) 711008 – www.victoriaatholkham.co.uk
Park Road, Holkham, Wells-next-the-Sea, Norfolk NR23 1RG

£200; 20 individually decorated, comfortable rooms – 10 in inn, 10 in historic, recently refurbished building opposite. Stylish hotel (part of the Holkham Estate) just a few minutes from vast Holkham Beach, upmarket yet informal and friendly, with an eclectic mix of furnishings in the engaging bar – deep sofas, chunky candles, an open log fire, fresh flowers and real ales; an airy dining room serving enjoyable food with an emphasis on game and beef from the estate, fresh fish and shellfish and other seasonal local produce; friendly staff, and seats in the sheltered courtyard; walks to the nature reserve, salt marshes and the sea. Dogs allowed in bedrooms in the inn and on ground floor; bed, bowl and treats; kennels; £10 per stay.

MORSTON
TG0043
Morston Hall
(01263) 741041 – www.morstonhall.com
The Street, Morston, Holt, Norfolk NR25 7AA

£340 including dinner; 13 comfortable rooms with country views – 7 in the main house, 6 in the pavilion. Attractive 17th-c flint-walled house with lovely quiet gardens, two small lounges (one with an antique fireplace), a conservatory and hard-working friendly owners; exceptional modern cooking (they also run cookery demonstrations and courses), a thoughtful short wine list, and super breakfasts and afternoon teas; croquet; coastal path for walks right outside. Closed January. Dogs allowed in most bedrooms; kennels; £10.

MUNDFORD

TL8093

Crown Hotel

(01842) 878233 – www.the-crown-hotel.co.uk
Crown Road, Mundford, Thetford, Norfolk IP26 5HQ

£85; 40 good rooms. Unassuming old pub, warmly welcoming, with heavy beams and huge fireplace, interesting local memorabilia, real ales, over 50 malt whiskies, sensibly priced and enjoyable food in two dining areas, and seats on a back terrace and in the garden with a wishing well. Well behaved dogs allowed in some bedrooms and in public bar; £10.

NORTH WALSHAM

TG2730

Beechwood Hotel

(01692) 403231 – www.beechwood-hotel.co.uk
Cromer Road, North Walsham, Norfolk NR28 0HD

£130; 18 traditional-style rooms. Creeper-covered Georgian house, once Agatha Christie's Norfolk hideaway, now a traditional hotel with comfortable lounge and bar, charming owners and super staff; good, imaginative modern cooking in attractive dining room and nice breakfasts; lovely garden where dogs may walk – there's also a park nearby and beaches too. Dogs allowed in some bedrooms, lounge and bar; £12.

OXBOROUGH

TF7401

Bedingfeld Arms

(01366) 328300 – www.bedingfeldarms.co.uk
The Green, Oxborough, Norfolk PE33 9PS

£69; 9 lovely rooms – 4 in the inn, 5 in the coach house annexe. Attractively furnished Georgian inn with a relaxed, wood-floored bar with an open fire in a marble fireplace with a large gilt mirror above, an airy dining room, a new covered verandah extension (using local oak trees) and a garden with seating and a view of the church; fresh flowers and candles throughout, real ales, courteous, helpful staff, tempting food using lamb and game from their farm, some home-grown vegetables and other local seasonal produce and very good breakfasts; Oxburgh Hall (National Trust) is opposite and there are plenty of walks and cycling routes nearby. Dogs allowed in two bedrooms and bar; £8.

RINGSTEAD

TF7040

Gin Trap

(01485) 525264 – www.thegintrapinn.co.uk
6 High Street, Ringstead, Hunstanton, Norfolk PE36 5JU

£120; 4 comfortable rooms; also a self-catering cottage. Bustling 17th-c coaching inn with friendly licensees, a beamed bar with pubby furniture, yellow tartan window seats, horse tack, coach lamps and a woodburning stove, as well as a quarry-tiled room with similar furnishings, a conservatory and a character back snug with red-painted walls; real ales, good wines by the glass, around 30 gins and popular food; the back garden has picnic-sets and a children's play area, and the Peddars Way is nearby. Dogs allowed in all bedrooms and bar.

SEDGEFORD
TF7136

King William IV

(01485) 571765 – www.thekingwilliamsedgeford.co.uk
Heacham Road, Sedgeford, Hunstanton, Norfolk PE36 5LU

£100; 9 comfortable rooms. Carefully run inn with enthusiastic owners, a
homely, relaxed bar, several cosy dining areas and a separate restaurant, log fires,
paintings of the north Norfolk coast, high-backed leather dining chairs around
pine tables on slate tiles, real ales, popular food and rather special breakfasts;
lots of seats outside plus a covered dining area; several nearby beaches, fantastic
bird-watching, walks on the Peddars Way and Sandringham Estate. Dogs allowed
in five bedrooms and bar/sitting area; £7.50.

SNETTISHAM
TF6834

Rose & Crown

(01485) 541382 – www.roseandcrownsnettisham.co.uk
Old Church Road, Snettisham, King's Lynn, Norfolk PE31 7LX

£120; 16 modern rooms decorated in seaside colours. Particularly well run old
pub with three bars, log fires and interesting furnishings, old quarry tiles and coir
carpeting, beams, nice old prints of King's Lynn and Sandringham and photos of
the pub's cricket team, an airy garden room, a thoughtful choice of drinks and
interesting, highly regarded food served by neat, courteous staff; seats in walled
garden with colourful borders, outdoor heaters and children's wooden galleon
play fort. This is sister pub to the Bank House in King's Lynn. Dogs allowed in all
bedrooms and bars; £15.

STIFFKEY
TF9643

Red Lion

(01328) 830552 – www.stiffkey.com
44 Wells Road, Stiffkey, Wells-next-the-Sea, Norfolk NR23 1AJ

£119; 10 airy, eco-friendly rooms with own balcony or terrace plus 2 suites.
Cheerful local pub with an appealing layout and a perky atmosphere, cushioned
pews and settles and other pubby seats, candlelit tables, two back dining rooms
(one almost a flint-walled conservatory), local landscape photos, good wines by
the glass, two dozen malts and local beers, tasty food and chatty, helpful staff;
nice coastal walks nearby. Dogs allowed in ten bedrooms and anywhere in the
pub; £5 per stay.

SWAFFHAM
TF8109

Strattons Hotel

(01760) 723845 – www.strattonshotel.co.uk
Ash Close, Swaffham, Norfolk PE37 7NH

£140; 14 individually designed, opulent rooms, including 7 suites; also
self-catering. Handsome Palladian-style red-brick villa with individual and
comfortably decorated rooms filled with sculptures, ornaments, original
paintings and log fires; imaginative seasonal food using local organic produce,
good breakfasts using their own eggs and home-baked bread, a separate café-deli

and eco-friendly approach; small garden and plenty of nearby walks; resident cats. Dogs allowed in three annexe bedrooms; bowl and walks map; £10.

THORNHAM
TF7343

Lifeboat

(01485) 512236 – www.lifeboatinnthornham.com
Ship Lane, Thornham, Hunstanton, Norfolk PE36 6LT

£140; 13 smart rooms, many with sea views. Rambling inn facing coastal sea flats and with numerous surrounding walks; under new ownership and recently refurbished; several character bars and a more formal restaurant; beams, open fires and woodburning stoves, reed-slashers and other antique farm tools on the walls, seats ranging from low settles and pews to more ornate dining chairs, fresh flowers and candles; real ales and wines by the glass, and enjoyable food using seasonal local produce; steps up from the conservatory lead to a sunny terrace. Dogs allowed in all bedrooms, bar and lounge; £10.

THORNHAM
TF7343

Orange Tree

(01485) 512213 – www.theorangetreethornham.co.uk
Church Street, Thornham, Hunstanton, Norfolk PE36 6LY

£99; 10 contemporary rooms – 6 in courtyard, 4 in former bakery. Friendly village-centre pub with a mix of seats from red leather chesterfields to wooden dining chairs and stripy plush wall seats, wood or quarry-tiled floors, white-painted beams in low ceilings, a log fire, real ales, plenty of wines by the glass and a chatty atmosphere; the two-part dining area is cheerfully contemporary in style and the top notch food is interesting and inventive; front garden with lavender beds and climbing roses, seating under parasols, outdoor heaters and a small smart corner pavilion, plus another outdoor area at the back with children's play equipment. Dogs allowed in some bedrooms and bar; £10.

THORPE MARKET
TG2434

Gunton Arms

(01263) 832010 – www.theguntonarms.co.uk
Cromer Road, Thorpe Market, Norwich, Norfolk NR11 8TZ

£130; 8 stylish rooms with original fittings. Stately and traditional place in a 1,000-acre deer park with impressive rooms and an easy-going atmosphere; huge entrance hall, pubby bar with simple furnishings, a log fire, pool table and beers served from a large mahogany counter; dining room with vast antlers on the walls and a second huge log fire (they often cook over this), a lounge with comfortable leather sofas and armchairs in front of yet another fire, and a formal restaurant; robust and contemporary food uses their own venison, local fish, foraged plants and seashore vegetables. Dogs allowed in three bedrooms and bar; bedding and bowl; £10.

TITCHWELL
TF7543

Titchwell Manor Hotel

(01485) 210221 – www.titchwellmanor.com
Main Road, Titchwell, King's Lynn, Norfolk PE31 8BB

£155; 27 light rooms in various buildings, some simply designed, others with bright colours. Comfortable hotel, handy for nearby RSPB Titchwell Marsh reserve, and with lots of walks and footpaths nearby; roaring log fire, magazines and good naturalists' records of the wildlife; a cheerful bar, attractive brasserie with french windows on to lovely sheltered walled garden plus more formal conservatory restaurant, good breakfasts and modern take on afternoon tea; particularly helpful licensees and staff. Dogs allowed in some bedrooms and bar; towel, bowl, biscuits and walks map; £10.

WARHAM
TF9441

Three Horseshoes

(01328) 710547 – www.warhamhorseshoes.co.uk
The Street, Warham, Wells-next-the-Sea, Norfolk NR23 1NL

£70; 5 rooms in former post office next to the pub with its own residents' lounge. Basic but cheerful flint and brick local with marvellously unspoilt traditional atmosphere in its three friendly gas-lit rooms, simple furnishings, open fires in Victorian fireplaces, very tasty generous bar food, decent wines and very well kept real ales; plenty of surrounding walks – in field opposite pub, on Warham marshes and nearby Holkham Beach. Dogs allowed in all bedrooms and anywhere in the pub; blanket.

WELLS-NEXT-THE-SEA
TF9143

Globe

(01328) 710206 – http://theglobeatwells.co.uk
The Buttlands, Wells-next-the-Sea, Norfolk NR23 1EU

£160; 7 airy rooms; also self-catering. Handsome whitewashed Georgian inn just a short walk from the quay, with several opened-up rooms with contemporary furnishings, comfortable sofas and armchairs in relaxed front bar, quirky fish and shellfish drawings on driftwood, good ales and wines and enjoyable seasonal cooking; seats in attractive back courtyard. Closed two weeks January. Dogs allowed in three bedrooms (advance notice essential) and front bar; £15.

WINTERTON-ON-SEA
TG4919

Fishermans Return

(01493) 393305 – www.fishermans-return.com
The Lane, Winterton-on-Sea, Great Yarmouth, Norfolk NR29 4BN

£90; 6 modern rooms (3 reached by a tiny staircase); also self-catering lodge. Traditional, 300-year-old pub in quiet village, close to the beach (fine walking), with warmly welcoming and helpful owners, a relaxed lounge bar with well kept real ales and open fire, and a new extension for functions; good home-made food including local fish dishes and enjoyable breakfasts; sheltered garden. Dogs allowed in bedrooms and bar; blanket, bowl and treats.

WOLTERTON   TG1732
Saracens Head
(01263) 768909 – www.saracenshead-norfolk.co.uk
Wolterton, Erpingham, Norfolk NR11 7LZ

£100; 6 comfortable rooms. Civilised Georgian inn hidden away down country lanes with a simple but stylish two-room bar with high ceilings, light terracotta walls and tall windows with cream and gold curtains, plus a pretty parlour and a charming old-fashioned gravel stableyard with plenty of chairs, benches and tables; log fires, flowers, real ales and extremely good, interesting food using the best local produce. Dogs allowed in all bedrooms and back bar.

Northamptonshire

DOG FRIENDLY PUBS

ASHBY ST LEDGERS   SP5768

Olde Coach House

(01788) 890349 – www.oldecoachhouse.co.uk
*Main Street; 4 miles from M1 junction 18; A5 S to Kilsby, then A361 S towards Daventry;
village also signed off A5 N of Weedon; CV23 8UN*

**Much character in ex-farmhouse with real ales, good wines, well liked
food and plenty of outside seating; bedrooms**

In an attractive village ancient enough to be mentioned in the Domesday Book,
this carefully updated inn has an opened-up bar on the right that's full of original
charm, with stools against the counter where they keep Wells Bombardier, Youngs
Bitter and a guest beer on handpump and 16 wines by the glass, served by friendly
staff. Several dining areas, all very relaxed, take in paintwork ranging from white
and light beige to purple, and flooring that includes stripped wooden boards,
original red and white tiles and beige carpeting. All manner of pale wooden tables
are surrounded by assorted church chairs, high-backed leather dining chairs and
armchairs, with comfortable squashy leather sofas and pouffes in front of a log
fire. There are hunting pictures, large mirrors, an original old stove and fresh
flowers; background music and TV. The back garden has picnic-sets among shrubs
and trees, modern tables and chairs out in front under pretty hanging baskets, and
a dining courtyard. The nearby church is of interest.

Quicksilver Management ~ Lease Mark Butler ~ Real ale ~ Open 12-11 ~ Bar food 12-2.30,
6-9.30 ~ Restaurant ~ Children welcome ~ Dogs allowed in bar ~ Wi-fi ~ Bedrooms: £75

FARTHINGHOE   SP5339

Fox

(01295) 713965 – www.foxatfarthinghoe.co.uk
Just off A422 Brackley–Banbury; Baker Street; NN13 5PH

**Bustling stone inn with a neat bar and dining rooms, tasty food, helpful
service and seats in the garden; bedrooms**

Carefully restored and spruced-up, this golden-stone pub has plenty of space
for both drinking and eating. The dark beamed bar has stools and a log fire in
a stripped-stone fireplace, and the dining areas have seats ranging from leather
tub chairs to banquettes, cushioned wall seats with scatter cushions and quite
a range of wooden dining chairs – all around rustic wooden tables; mirrors and
country prints on pastel walls. You'll find Courage Directors and Youngs Bitter on

handpump, nine wines by the glass and a good choice of gins; background music. The terrace and lawn have picnic-sets under a giant parasol.

Charles Wells ~ Lease Neil Bellingham ~ Real ale ~ Open 12-11; 12-10.30 Sun ~ Bar food 12-2.30, 6-9.30; 12-4, 6-8 Sun ~ Restaurant ~ Children welcome ~ Dogs allowed in bar ~ Wi-fi ~ Bedrooms: £75

FARTHINGSTONE   SP6155
Kings Arms
(01327) 361604
Off A5 SE of Daventry; village signed from Litchborough; NN12 8EZ

Individual place with cosy traditional interior, carefully prepared food and lovely garden

The hard-working landlord in this little gem of a pub keeps his ever-changing beers in top condition and sources interesting choices from far and wide. It's a traditional pub with a wide mix of chatty customers and the cosy flagstoned bar has a huge log fire, comfortable homely sofas and armchairs near the entrance, whisky-water jugs hanging from oak beams, and lots of pictures and decorative plates on the walls. A games room at the far end has darts, dominoes, cribbage, table skittles and board games. Dent Aviator Ale, Wickwar BOB and Woodfordes Wherry on handpump and a short but decent wine list. Look out for the interesting newspaper-influenced décor in the outside gents'. The handsome gargoyled stone exterior is nicely weathered and very pretty in summer when the hanging baskets are at their best; there are seats on a tranquil terrace among plant-filled, painted tractor tyres and recycled art, and they've recorded over 200 species of moth and 20 different butterflies. This is a picturesque village and good walks nearby include the Knightley Way. It's worth ringing ahead to check the opening and food times.

Free house ~ Licensees Paul and Denise Egerton ~ Real ale ~ Open 7-11 Mon-Thurs; 6.30-midnight Fri; 12-11.30 Sat; 12-6, 9-11 Sun; closed Mon, weekday lunchtimes ~ Bar food 12-2.30 weekends; maybe evening snacks ~ Children welcome ~ Dogs allowed in bar ~ Wi-fi

FOTHERINGHAY   TL0593
Falcon
(01832) 226254 – www.thefalcon-inn.co.uk
Village signposted off A605 on Peterborough side of Oundle; PE8 5HZ

Upmarket dining pub with a good range of drinks and modern british food, and attractive garden

Both drinkers and diners are warmly welcomed in this stylish pub and the gently civilised atmosphere appeals to all. There are winter log fires in stone fireplaces, fresh flowers, cushioned slatback armchairs, bucket chairs and comfortably cushioned window seats and bare floorboards. The Orangery restaurant opens on to a charming lavender-surrounded terrace with lovely views of the huge church behind and of the attractively planted garden; plenty of seats under parasols. The thriving little locals' tap bar has a fine choice of drinks including Fullers London Pride, Greene King IPA and a guest such as Nobbys Swift Nick on handpump, 16 good wines by the glass and several malt whiskies; darts team and board games. This is a lovely village (Richard III was born here) with plenty of moorings on the River Nene; the ruins of Fotheringhay Castle, where Mary, Queen of Scots was executed, is nearby.

Free house ~ Licensee Sally Facer ~ Real ale ~ Open 12-11; 12-5 Sun (12-10 Sun
June-Sept) ~ Bar food 12-2, 6-9; 12-3 Sun (12-3, 5-8.30 Sun June-Sept) ~ Restaurant ~
Children welcome ~ Dogs allowed in bar ~ Wi-fi

GREAT BRINGTON   SP6664
Althorp Coaching Inn
(01604) 770651 – www.althorp-coaching-inn.co.uk
Off A428 NW of Northampton, near Althorp Hall; until recently known as the
Fox & Hounds; NN7 4JA

**Friendly golden-stone thatched pub with some fine architectural
features, tasty popular food, well kept real ales and sheltered garden**

The fine range of well kept real ales on handpump in this 16th-c former
coaching inn might include Greene King IPA, Phipps NBC India Pale Ale,
St Austell Tribute, Sharps Doom Bar and a couple of guest beers; the extended
dining area gives views of the 30 or so casks racked in the cellar. Also, eight wines
by the glass and a dozen malt whiskies. The ancient bar has all the traditional
features you'd wish for, from a dog or two sprawled by the huge log fire, to old
beams, sagging joists and an appealing mix of country chairs and tables (maybe
with fresh flowers) on broad flagstones and bare boards. There are snug alcoves,
nooks and crannies with some stripped-pine shutters and panelling, two fine log
fires and an eclectic medley of bric-a-brac from farming implements to an old
clocking-in machine and country pictures. A function room in a converted stable
block is next to the lovely cobbled and paved courtyard (also accessible by the
old coaching entrance) with sheltered tables and tubs of flowers; there's more
seating in the charming garden.

Free house ~ Licensee Michael Krempels ~ Real ale ~ Open 11am-midnight; 12-11 Sun ~
Bar food 12-3, 6-9.30; 12-8.30 Sat; 12-8 Sun ~ Restaurant ~ Children welcome ~
Dogs allowed in bar ~ Wi-fi

LOWICK   SP9780
Snooty Fox
(01832) 733434 ~ www.thesnootyfoxlowick.com
Off A6116 Corby–Raunds; NN14 3BH

**Bustling village pub with plenty of seating space, real ales, quite a choice
of food and friendly staff**

At the heart of a peaceful village, this solidly built 17th-c pub is popular for its
highly thought-of food. The spacious lounge bar has a woodburning stove in a
sizeable fireplace, handsomely moulded dark oak beams, leather sofas, stools and
bucket armchairs on big terracotta tiles, and stripped stonework. A formidable
carved counter has a beer named for the pub (from Marstons), Digfield Fools
Nook, Marstons Pedigree and Wychwood Hobgoblin on handpump, lots of wines
by the glass and a farm cider. The more formal dining rooms have high-backed
leather and other dining chairs around quite a choice of chunky tables on pale
wooden floorboards; background music. There are picnic-sets under parasols on
the front grass and a children's play area.

Free house ~ Licensee Carmen Sharpe ~ Real ale ~ Open 12-3, 5-11; 12-11 Sat, Sun;
closed Mon ~ Bar food 12-2 (3 Sun), 6-9 (9.30 Sat) ~ Restaurant ~ Children welcome ~
Dogs allowed in bar ~ Wi-fi

NORTHAMPTON
SP7559

Malt Shovel

(01604) 234212 – www.maltshoveltavern.com

Bridge Street (approach road from M1 junction 15); no parking in nearby street,
best to park in Morrisons central car park, far end – passage past Europcar straight
to back entrance; NN1 1QF

Friendly, well run real ale pub with bargain lunches and over
a dozen varied beers

Of course, everyone comes to this lively tavern for the fantastic ales but it's a genuine place with a cheerful feel, fairly priced food and knowledgeable, enthusiastic staff. Up to 13 real ales are served from a battery of handpumps lined up on the long counter: Frog Island Best Bitter, Fullers London Pride, Greene King New Horizons IPA and XX Mild, Hook Norton Old Hooky, JW Lees Moonraker, Nobbys Best, Oakham Bishops Farewell and JHB, and Phipps NBC India Pale Ale. They also stock belgian draught and bottled beers, 50 malt whiskies, 17 rums, 17 vodkas and 17 gins and Cheddar Valley farm cider; regular beer festivals. It's also home to quite an extensive collection of carefully chosen brewing memorabilia – look out for the rare Northampton Brewery Company star, displayed outside the pub, and some high-mounted ancient beer engines; darts, daily papers and background music. The secluded backyard has tables and chairs and a smokers' shelter; disabled facilities.

Free house ~ Licensee Mike Evans ~ Real ale ~ Open 11.30-3, 5-11; 11.30-11 Fri, Sat; 12-10.30 Sun ~ Bar food 12-2; not Sun ~ Well behaved children welcome in bar ~ Dogs allowed in bar ~ Wi-fi ~ Blues Weds evening

SPRATTON
SP7170

Kings Head

(01604) 847351 – www.kingsheadspratton.co.uk

Brixworth Road, off A5199 N of Northampton; NN6 8HH

Part brasserie and part bar with contemporary furnishings, an easy-going
atmosphere, real ales and rewarding food; seats outside

'Three in one' is how this enterprising place describes itself – bar, restaurant and coffee shop. It works well. There are pale flagstones and ancient stripped stonework mixing well with handsome new wood flooring and up-to-date décor, plus leather chesterfields, an antique settle, café chairs around stripped brasserie-style tables and a woodburning stove in a brick fireplace. Friendly staff serve St Austell Tribute, Sharps Doom Bar and a guest such as Phipps NBC India Pale Ale on handpump, eight wines by the glass and artisan spirits; background music and darts. The back coffee shop has a glass wall overlooking a courtyard with modern metal and wood tables and chairs.

Free house ~ Licensee Natalie Tompkins ~ Real ale ~ Open 12-3, 6-11; 12-11.30 Fri, Sat; 12-10.30 Sun ~ Bar food 12-2.30, 6-9 (9.30 Fri, Sat); 12-5 Sun; coffee shop 8.30-5; 12-5 Sun ~ Restaurant ~ Children welcome ~ Dogs allowed in bar ~ Wi-fi

DOG FRIENDLY HOTELS, INNS AND B&Bs

OUNDLE   TL0388
Ship
(01832) 273918 – www.theshipinn-oundle.co.uk
18 West Street, Oundle, Peterborough, Northamptonshire PE8 4EF

£69 (breakfast not provided); 14 rooms. Bustling, down-to-earth town pub with a genuinely welcoming and lively atmosphere; with interesting beers and a good range of malt whiskies; heavily beamed bar with leather and other seats around sturdy tables, and a warming log fire in a stone inglenook; also a wooden-floored public bar with a cheerful, chatty feel and a terrace bar with pool, darts and board games; good value traditional food. Dogs allowed in bedrooms and bar; £6.50.

Northumbria (County Durham, Northumberland and Tyneside)

MAP 10

DOG FRIENDLY PUBS

CRASTER   NU2519
Jolly Fisherman
(01665) 576461 – www.thejollyfishermancraster.co.uk
Off B1339, NE of Alnwick; NE66 3TR

Stunning views, very good food and plenty of seasonal visitors

The surrounding coastal walks are very much worth exploring – including one from this well run inn along the cliff to Dunstanburgh Castle (English Heritage). The bustling bar, full of locals and ramblers, has a winter fire, leather button-back wall banquettes and upholstered and wooden dining chairs around hefty tables on bare boards, a few stools scattered here and there, and photographs and paintings in gilt-edged frames on the walls. Black Sheep, Mordue Workie Ticket, Timothy Taylors Landlord and a changing guest on handpump served by friendly staff. From big windows in the upstairs dining room you look down on the pretty harbour and out to sea. Seats and tables in the garden have the same outlook – and get snapped up pretty quickly. They're known for their crab sandwiches and crab soup. They have a couple of fishermen's cottages and an apartment for rent and have opened a café and gift shop opposite the pub.

Punch ~ Lease David Whitehead ~ Real ale ~ Open 11-11 (midnight Fri); 11am-1am Sat; 12-10.30 Sun ~ Bar food 11-3, 5.30-9; 12-3, 5-9 Sun; not Sun evening in winter ~ Restaurant ~ Children welcome ~ Dogs allowed in bar ~ Wi-fi

GILSLAND　　　　　　　　　　　　　　　　　　　　NY6366
Samson
(016977) 47880 – www.thesamson.co.uk
B6318, E end of village; CA8 7DR

Friendly village pub in wonderful countryside, cheerful atmosphere in cosy bar, local ales and enjoyable food; bedrooms

---

This is a charming little pub in all aspects. The cosy bar has a chatty, easy-going atmosphere, red-patterned carpeting, swagged curtains, woodburning stoves, cushioned settles, traditional chairs and stools around sewing machine-treadle and other pubby tables and plush stools at the carved wooden counter. Allendale Pennine Pale and a guest from Hesket Newmarket on handpump and several wines by the glass served by friendly staff; throughout the year they hold quiz nights, themed evenings and live music events. In the dining room are beige tartan-upholstered chairs around white-clothed tables on wide floorboards and prints on red or yellow walls. There are picnic-sets on the back lawn. Hadrian's Wall and Hadrian's Wall National Trail and Cycleway are nearby.

Free house ~ Licensees Liam McNulty and Lauren Harrison ~ Real ale ~ Open 12-10.30 ~ Bar food 12-2.30, 6-8.30 ~ Children welcome ~ Dogs allowed in bar ~ Wi-fi ~ Acoustic night second Sun of month ~ Bedrooms: £80

MICKLETON　　　　　　　　　　　　　　　　　　　NY9724
Crown
(01833) 640381 – www.thecrownatmickleton.co.uk
B6277; DL12 0JZ

Bustling, friendly pub with hands-on owners, an easy-going atmosphere in connected rooms and seats in garden

---

Set in lovely countryside, this well run pub has a good mix of both locals and visitors and a warm welcome is offered to all by the friendly family in charge. The simply furnished bars and dining areas have a mix of cushioned settles, upholstered, leather and wooden dining chairs around all sorts of tables on polished floorboards, country prints and photographs on the walls and a woodburning stove flanked by two leather armchairs. Stools line the bar counter where they keep Jennings Bitter, Banks's Bitter and local guests such as Pennine Hair of the Dog and Sonnet 43 Steam Beer Amber Ale on handpump, and good wines by the glass. There are rustic picnic-sets in the front garden with fine views. They have two self-catering properties for rent and a campsite.

Free house ~ Licensee Joyce Rowbotham ~ Real ale ~ Open 12-midnight; 12-9 Sun ~ Bar food 12-9; 12-6 Sun ~ Children welcome ~ Dogs welcome ~ Wi-fi ~ Bedrooms: £75

NEWTON　　　　　　　　　　　　　　　　　　　　NZ0364
Duke of Wellington
(01661) 844446 – www.thedukeofwellingtoninn.co.uk
Off A69 E of Corbridge; NE43 7UL

Big stone pub with modern and traditional furnishings, five real ales, good wines by the glass and highly thought-of food; bedrooms

---

The bustling bar of this welcoming pub has leather chesterfields, built-in cushioned wall seats, farmhouse chairs and tables on honey-coloured flagstones, a woodburning stove with a shelf of books to one side, and rustic stools against the counter where they keep Greene King Old Speckled Hen and Hadrian & Border Tyneside Blonde with guests from local breweries such as Anarchy, Mordue and Wylam on handpump, a dozen wines by the glass and 12 malt whiskies; TV, darts, dominoes and daily papers. The L-shaped restaurant has elegant tartan and wood dining chairs around pale tables on bare boards, modern art on exposed stone walls, and french windows that lead out to the terrace. Paintwork throughout is contemporary. Seats on the back terrace have lovely views across the Tyne Valley. They hold regular wine-tasting evenings and quiz and music nights. Breakfasts are served to non-residents too.

Free house ~ Licensee Rob Harris ~ Real ale ~ Open 11-11 ~ Bar food 12-9; 12-6 (5 in winter) Sun ~ Restaurant ~ Children welcome ~ Dogs allowed in bar ~ Wi-fi ~ Bedrooms: £120

NEWTON-BY-THE-SEA   NU2424

Ship

(01665) 576262 – www.shipinnnewton.co.uk
Low Newton-by-the-Sea, signed off B1339 N of Alnwick; NE66 3EL

In a charming square of fishermen's cottages with good simple food and own-brew beers; best to check winter opening times

You can walk along the massive stretch of empty, beautiful beach with views all the way to Dunstanburgh Castle from this row of converted fishermen's cottages; tables outside the pub look across the sloping village green and down to the sea. Their own-brew ales on handpump remain a big draw as well; these usually include five at any one time from a choice of 26 – maybe Ship Inn Dolly Daydream, Hop Monster, Red Herring, Sandcastles at Dawn and Squid Ink. The plainly furnished but cosy bare-boards bar on the right has nautical charts on dark pink walls, while another simple room on the left has beams, hop bines, some bright modern pictures on stripped-stone walls and a woodburning stove in a stone fireplace; darts, dominoes. It can get extremely busy at peak times, so it's best to book in advance – and there might be a queue for the bar. No nearby parking from May to September, but there's a car park up the hill.

Own brew ~ Licensee Christine Forsyth ~ Real ale ~ Open 11-11; 12-10 Sun; check website or phone for winter variations ~ Bar food 12-2.30, 7-8; not Sun-Tues evenings ~ Children welcome ~ Dogs welcome ~ Wi-fi ~ Live folk last Mon of month, other live music last Sun of month

NORTH SHIELDS   NZ3668

Staith House

(0191) 270 8441 – www.thestaithhouse.co.uk
Fish Quay/Union Road; NE30 1JA

Smashing food and real ales in refurbished dining pub with friendly staff and seats outside

Most customers are here for the particularly good food (cooked by the landlord, a former *MasterChef* finalist), but you will also find Caledonian Deuchars IPA, Robinsons Dizzy Blonde and Theakstons Lightfoot Bitter on handpump and ten wines by the glass, served by enthusiastic staff. The attractive interior blends stripped wood, brickwork and stone with upholstered armchairs and dining chairs, captain's chairs and tartan wall seating, a medley of wooden tables and slate flooring and bare boards; to one end are some high bar chairs around equally high tables. Above the white woodburning stove are candles on a big mantlebeam and a large, rustic mirror, while the walls have ships' lamps and old photographs of the Tyne. Picnic-sets and solid benches and tables sit on side terraces and the hanging baskets look pretty against the blue-painted pub walls.

Free house ~ Licensee John Calton ~ Real ale ~ Open 12-10; 12-11.30 Sat; 12-9 Sun ~ Bar food 12-3, 6-9 (9.30 Sat); 12-4.30 Sun ~ Children welcome ~ Dogs allowed in bar ~ Wi-fi ~ Live music Sun 3pm

DOG FRIENDLY HOTELS, INNS AND B&Bs

BLANCHLAND   NY9650

Lord Crewe Arms

(01434) 675469 – www.lordcrewearmsblanchland.co.uk
The Square, Blanchland, Consett, County Durham DH8 9SP

£170; 21 smart, well equipped bedrooms. Particularly good food, real ales, a genuine welcome and a remarkable history (it was built in 1235 as a monastery guesthouse) make this fine hotel somewhere pretty special. The unique Crypt bar is a medieval vaulted room with thick stone walls, family crests on the ceiling and candlelight; there's also a sitting area with a leather sofa and tartan armchairs in front of a large open fire, a grand yet informal restaurant with leather dining chairs, oak tables, fresh flowers, antlers on the walls and a big central candelabra, and a large walled garden with tables under parasols; plenty of surrounding walks and Derwent Reservoir is nearby. Dogs allowed in some bedrooms and bar; bed, bowl and treats; £10.

CARTERWAY HEADS   NZ0452

Manor House Inn

(01207) 255268 – www.themanorhouseinn.com
Carterway Heads, Shotley Bridge, County Durham DH8 9LX

£85; 4 modern rooms. Simple slate-roofed stone inn with stunning views over Derwent Reservoir and lots of nearby walks; the plain, heart-warming locals' bar has an original boarded ceiling, wooden tables and chairs and an old-fashioned feel, the carpeted lounge has a woodburning stove, and picture windows make the most of the lovely setting; several real ales, 20 malt whiskies and good food using local game and meat. Dogs allowed in bedrooms and bar; treats and dog beer; £10.

CORNHILL-ON-TWEED   NT8842

Tillmouth Park

(01890) 882255 – www.tillmouthpark.co.uk
Cornhill-on-Tweed, Northumberland TD12 4UU

£155; 14 spacious, pretty rooms with period furniture. Solid stone-built country house in 15 acres of parkland, with comfortable, relaxing panelled lounges, antiques, stained-glass windows, open fires and a galleried hall; good, thoughtfully prepared food in the candlelit restaurant, hearty breakfasts, afternoon teas, a carefully chosen wine list and over 60 malt whiskies; nearby golf and shooting, plenty of walks. Closed January-Easter. Dogs allowed in all bedrooms, bar and grounds; £12 per stay.

COTHERSTONE

NZ0119

Fox & Hounds

(01833) 650241 – www.cotherstonefox.co.uk

Cotherstone, Barnard Castle, County Durham DL12 9PF

£80; 3 bedrooms. In an attractive spot by the village green and surrounded by fine walks, this Georgian country inn has a cheerful, simply furnished beamed bar with a log fire, thickly cushioned wall seats, local photographs and country pictures in various alcoves, real ales, around 15 malt whiskies from smaller distilleries, tasty traditional food and seats outside on a terrace; don't be surprised by the unusual loo attendant – an african grey parrot called Reva. Dogs allowed in all bedrooms and side bar; £5.

CROOKHAM

NT9138

Coach House

(01890) 820293 – http://coachhousecrookham.com

Crookham, Cornhill-on-Tweed, Northumberland TD12 4TD

£100; 10 individual rooms with nice views. 17th-c farm buildings around a sunny courtyard, with helpful and friendly staff, an airy beamed lounge with comfortable sofas, big arched windows and open fire, good breakfasts, complimentary afternoon tea and enjoyable dinners using local seasonal produce; paddocks and footpaths for walking and lots to do nearby. Dogs allowed in some bedrooms.

DURHAM

NZ2742

Victoria

(0191) 386 5269 – www.victoriainn-durhamcity.co.uk

86 Hallgarth Street, Durham, County Durham DH1 3AS

£83; 6 rooms. Lovingly preserved inn run by the same friendly family for over 40 years; three small rooms lead off a central bar with typical Victorian décor that takes in mahogany, etched and cut glass and mirrors, colourful William Morris wallpaper over a high panelled dado, plush seating and narrow drinkers' tables; coal fires in handsome iron and tile fireplaces, lots of period prints and engravings of Queen Victoria, and staffordshire figurines of her and the Prince Consort; local ales, 85-plus whiskies (scottish and irish); no credit cards except for accommodation, no food; dog exercise area 20 metres away. Dogs allowed in bedrooms and anywhere in the pub.

ELLINGHAM

NU1625

Pack Horse

(01665) 589292 – www.packhorseinn-ellingham.co.uk

Ellingham, Chathill, Northumberland NE67 5HA

£80; 5 bedrooms. Set in a peaceful village, this delightful little pub makes a good base for exploring the lovely coastline and nearby castles; there's a flagstoned bar with masses of jugs hanging from beams, pubby furniture and a log fire, as well as a snug with a woodburner in a big stone fireplace with a stag's head above and a restaurant with high-backed black leather chairs on tartan carpet; real ales, very good food, picnic-sets in the enclosed garden and their own veg patch. Closed first two weeks February. Dogs allowed in all bedrooms, bar and snug; £10 per stay.

GRETA BRIDGE
NZ0813

Morritt

(01833) 627232 – www.themorritt.co.uk
Greta Bridge, Barnard Castle, County Durham DL12 9SE

£85; 26 rooms. Striking 17th-c country house hotel where Charles Dickens stayed in 1838 to research for *Nicholas Nickleby* – one of the interesting bars has a colourful Dickensian mural by John Gilroy; comfortable lounges with sofas and open fires, enjoyable, attractively presented food in the smart restaurant served by knowledgeable staff, and seats in the pleasant garden; lots of surrounding walks, coarse fishing and adjacent spa. Dogs allowed in some rooms, lounge, bar and garden.

HEADLAM
NZ1818

Headlam Hall

(01325) 730238 – www.headlamhall.co.uk
Headlam, Darlington, County Durham DL2 3HA

£160; 38 comfortable, attractive rooms – in the main house, coach house, mews building and spa. Peaceful, recently refurbished, family-run Jacobean mansion in four acres of carefully kept gardens with an ornamental canal, tennis court and croquet lawn; elegantly updated rooms, a fine carved oak fireplace in the main hall, stylish food in the restaurant's three individually decorated rooms and attentive staff; spa with swimming pool, sauna, gym and treatment rooms, and nine-hole golf course and driving range; resident dogs Purdy (labrador), Mabel (jack russell) and Hector (terrier); walks in grounds and surrounding footpaths. Dogs allowed in mews bedrooms and (on lead) in lounge, bar and gardens; mat, bowl and treats.

LONGHORSLEY
NZ1596

Macdonald Linden Hall

(0344) 879 9084 – www.macdonaldhotels.co.uk/lindenhall
Longhorsley, Morpeth, Northumberland NE65 8XF

£191; 50 comfortable, contemporary rooms. Georgian hotel in 450 acres of landscaped parkland with an 18-hole golf course; open fires and fresh flowers, a clubby pub room, a friendly cocktail bar, an airy drawing room, and good modern cooking served by courteous staff in the smart, plush restaurant; spa and health club with indoor pool. Dogs allowed in ground-floor bedrooms, lounge and parkland; £10.

ROMALDKIRK
NY9922

Rose & Crown

(01833) 650213 – www.rose-and-crown.co.uk
Romaldkirk, Barnard Castle, County Durham DL12 9EB

£160; 14 charming, stylish rooms, in main building, courtyard or cottage. Smart and interesting 18th-c coaching inn with a cosily traditional beamed bar-brasserie with old-fashioned seats facing a warming log fire, a Jacobean oak settle, a grandfather clock and plenty of farm tools and black and white pictures of Romaldkirk, as well as an oak-panelled restaurant and an interestingly decorated hall; imaginative food using local seasonal produce – super breakfasts too; the exceptional Bowes Museum and High Force waterfall are close by; walks along nearby disused railway line. Dogs allowed in 12 bedrooms and bar; towel and treats.

STANNERSBURN

NY7286

Pheasant

(01434) 240382 – www.thepheasantinn.com
Stannersburn, Hexham, Northumberland NE48 1DD

£99; 8 courtyard rooms. Beautifully located, unpretentious 17th-c stone inn close to Kielder Water and its quiet forests; it's been updated recently but the traditional comfortable low-beamed lounge still has old local photos on stripped stone and panelling, open fires and straightforward furnishings; there's also a simpler public bar and a further cosy seating area with more beams and panelling; local beers, 38 malts and courteous staff; bar food is good, breakfasts are tasty and there are seats in the streamside garden. Dogs allowed in bedrooms only; £5.

STANNINGTON

NZ1881

St Marys Inn

(01670) 293293 – www.stmarysinn.co.uk
St Mary's Lane, St Mary's Park, Morpeth, Stannington, Northumberland NE61 6BL

£100; 11 airy, modern, comfortable bedrooms. This spacious red-brick building with gables and a clock tower (once part of a Victorian asylum) has been recently refurbished; regulars (and a dog or two) enjoy the bar with its daily papers, board games, woodburner, real ales, 15 wines by the glass and 50 malt whiskies served by friendly staff; a wide range of enjoyable food is served all day in several dining rooms with contemporary paintwork or flowery wallpaper, more woodburning stoves, brightly coloured blinds, copper kettles and pans and interesting artwork; seats in the courtyard garden; the inn is handy for the A1. Dogs allowed in two bedrooms and bar; bedding, bowl and treats.

WARK

NY8676

Battlesteads

(01434) 230209 – www.battlesteads.com
Wark, Hexham, Northumberland NE48 3LS

£120; 22 comfortable bedrooms. A pretty stone inn with a nicely restored carpeted bar featuring low beams, a woodburning stove, leather sofas, easy chairs and old *Punch* country life cartoons on the terracotta walls above a dark dado, as well as a restaurant, a spacious conservatory and tables on the terrace; four changing local ales, several malt whiskies and interesting, fair value food; the eco-conscious owners grow their own produce, have a charging point for electric cars and use a biomass boiler; resident black labrador is called Winston. Dogs allowed in nine bedrooms and bar; bedding, bowl, treats and dog food; £10.

WELDON BRIDGE

NZ1398

Anglers Arms

(01665) 570271 – www.anglersarms.com
Weldon Bridge, Longframlington, Morpeth, Northumberland NE65 8AX

£95; 7 rooms. Sizeable place with a comfortable two-part bar at its heart; oak panelling, beams hung with copper pans, a profusion of fish memorabilia, some nice old prints, a shelf of staffordshire cats, a sofa by a coal fire, large helpings of traditional food served in bar and dining room, and friendly staff; fishing on the River Coquet. Dogs allowed in bedrooms and bar; £10.

Nottinghamshire

MAP 7

DOG FRIENDLY PUBS

CAYTHORPE
SK6845
Black Horse

(0115) 966 3520 – www.caythorpebrewery.co.uk

Turn off A6097 0.25 miles SE of roundabout junction with A612, NE of Nottingham;
into Gunthorpe Road, then right into Caythorpe Road and keep on; NG14 7ED

Quaintly old-fashioned little pub brewing its own beer, simple interior
and enjoyable homely food; no children, no credit cards

The same friendly family have run this old country local for three generations.
It's a homely place and the uncluttered carpeted bar has just five tables, along
with brocaded wall banquettes and settles, decorative plates on a delft shelf, a
few horsebrasses attached to the ceiling joists and a coal fire. Cheerful regulars
might occupy the few bar stools to enjoy Caythorpe Bitter and a seasonal ale
brewed in outbuildings here and served alongside a couple of guests such as
Caythorpe Dover Beck and Greene King Abbot Ale on handpump; nine wines by
the glass too. Off the front corridor is a partly panelled inner room, with a wall
bench running all the way round three unusual, long, copper-topped tables; there
are several old local photographs, darts and board games. Down on the left, an
end room has just one huge round table. There are seats outside. The pub is close
to the River Trent where there are waterside walks.

Own brew ~ Licensee Sharron Andrews ~ Real ale ~ No credit cards ~ Open 12-3, 6-11;
12-5, 8-11 Sun; closed Mon except bank holidays ~ Bar food 12-2, 6-8.30; not Sat evening,
Sun ~ Dogs allowed in bar

DOG FRIENDLY HOTELS, INNS AND B&BS

LANGAR
SK7234
Langar Hall

(01949) 860559 – www.langarhall.com

Church Lane, Langar, Nottingham, Nottinghamshire NG13 9HG

£130; 12 individually decorated, pretty rooms. Fine family-run country house
in spacious grounds and with 30 acres of surrounding fields for walks; a friendly,
informal atmosphere, a convivial bar, a homely drawing room and library with
antiques, comfortable sofas and armchairs and fresh flowers, a conservatory

offering light meals and afternoon teas, and a pillared, candlelit restaurant with imaginative meals served by willing young staff. Small dogs allowed in two bedrooms; £20.

NOTTINGHAM   SK5639

Hart's

(0115) 988 1900 – www.hartsnottingham.co.uk
Standard Hill, Park Row, Nottingham, Nottinghamshire NG1 6GN

£198; 32 well appointed, quiet rooms with fine views. Adjacent to the well known restaurant of the same name, this is a smart and stylish purpose-built hotel in a traffic-free cul-de-sac on the site of the city's medieval castle; charming, friendly staff, an airy, recently refurbished bar, and excellent modern british cooking in Hart's restaurant next door (the very good breakfasts are served here); small gym, and seats in the courtyard garden. Dogs allowed in some bedrooms (not to be left unattended), bar and garden; £5.

Oxfordshire

MAPS 2 & 4

DOG FRIENDLY PUBS

ASTHALL   SP2811

Maytime

(01993) 822068 – www.themaytime.com
Off A40 at W end of Witney bypass, then first left; OX18 4HW

Carefully renovated Cotswold-stone inn with individually furnished bar and dining rooms, good food and seats outside; smart bedrooms

A 17th-c former coaching inn with its own smithy, this is now a carefully refurbished inn of much character. The lofty bar has exposed roof trusses, flagstones, leather sofas, cushioned wall seats and stools against the counter where friendly staff serve Dark Star Hophead and Mantle Cwrw Teifi on handpump, good wines by the glass and a fine collection of 69 gins; background music and board games. Several white-painted beamed rooms lead off on several levels with cushioned window seats, a mix of tartan upholstered and traditional wooden chairs around tables of varying size on black slates or bare boards, and pictures on painted or stone walls; one room has a glass ceiling. The pub springer is called Alfie. Seats and tables sit under parasols on the back terrace with more seats in the extended garden overlooking the River Windrush. There are good walks from the door.

Free house ~ Licensee Dominic Wood ~ Real ale ~ Open 11-11 ~ Bar food 12-2.30 (3 weekends), 6-9.30 ~ Restaurant ~ Children welcome but not in bedrooms ~ Dogs allowed in bar ~ Wi-fi ~ Live music 3-5pm every second Sun ~ Bedrooms: £95

BANBURY   SP4540

Olde Reindeer

(01295) 270972 – www.yeoldereindeer.co.uk
Parsons Street, off Market Place; OX16 5NA

Interesting town pub with a friendly welcome, real ales and simple food

T his is a splendid old inn, full of history and with a chatty mix of shoppers and regulars. The front bar has a good, bustling atmosphere, heavy 16th-c beams, very broad polished oak floorboards, a magnificent carved overmantel for one of the two roaring log fires and traditional solid furnishings; some interesting breweriana too. It's worth looking at the handsomely proportioned Globe Room used by Oliver Cromwell as his base during the Civil War. Quite a sight, it still has some very fine 17th-c carved dark oak panelling. Hook Norton Hooky, Cotswold Lion, Old Hooky, Hooky Mild and a couple of guest beers on handpump, 12 wines

by the glass, fruit wines and several malt whiskies. The little back courtyard has
tables and benches under parasols, aunt sally and pretty flowering baskets.

Hook Norton ~ Tenant Jeremy Money ~ Real ale ~ Open 11-11 (midnight Fri, Sat); 12-10.30
Sun ~ Bar food 12-3, 6-9; 12-3 Sun ~ Children welcome until 8pm ~ Dogs allowed in bar ~
Live music Sat from 9pm; jam night Sun

BESSELS LEIGH   SP4501
Greyhound

(01865) 862110 – www.brunningandprice.co.uk/greyhound
A420 Faringdon–Botley; OX13 5PX

**Cotswold-stone inn with rambling rooms, up to half a dozen real ales,
lots of wines by the glass and enjoyable food**

The knocked-through rooms in this handsome pub have plenty of character
and interest: the half-panelled walls are covered in all manner of old
photographs and pictures, individually chosen cushioned dining chairs,
leather-topped stools and dark wooden tables are grouped on carpeting or rug-
covered floorboards, and there are books on shelves, glass and stone bottles
on windowsills, big gilt mirrors, three fireplaces (one housing a woodburning
stove) and sizeable pot plants. Wooden bar stools line the counter where they
serve Phoenix Brunning & Price Original, Cottage Black Diamond, Loddon
Ferrymans Gold, Prescott Summer Seasons Best and White Horse Village Idiot
on handpump, 14 wines by the glass, 102 malt whiskies and a farm cider. By the
back dining extension is a white picket fence-enclosed garden with picnic-sets
under parasols; the summer window boxes and hanging baskets are very pretty.

Brunning & Price ~ Manager Darren Snell ~ Real ale ~ Open 11-11; 11.30-10.30 Sun ~ Bar
food 12-10 (9.30 Sun) ~ Well behaved children welcome ~ Dogs allowed in bar ~ Wi-fi

BRIGHTWELL BALDWIN   SU6594
Lord Nelson

(01491) 612497 – http://thenelsonbrightwell.co.uk
Off B480 Chalgrove–Watlington, or B4009 Benson–Watlington; OX49 5NP

**Attractive inn with several character bars, real ales, good wines
by the glass and enjoyable well thought-of food; bedrooms**

The atmosphere in this bustling 300-year-old inn is relaxed and friendly – and
helped along by the cheerful mix of both drinkers and diners. The bar has
candles and fresh flowers, wine bottles on windowsills, horsebrasses on standing
timbers, lots of paintings on white or red walls, wheelback and other dining chairs
around assorted dark tables and a big brick inglenook fireplace. One cosy room
has cushions on comfortable sofas, little lamps on dark furniture, ornate mirrors
and portraits in gilt frames; background music. Rebellion IPA and Roundhead on
handpump, 20 wines (including champagne) by the glass, a dozen malt whiskies
and winter mulled wine. There are seats and tables on the back terrace and in the
willow-draped garden.

Free house ~ Licensees Roger and Carole Shippey ~ Real ale ~ Open 12-3, 6-11; 12-5 Sun;
12-5 in winter ~ Bar food 12-2, 6-10; 12-4 Sun ~ Restaurant ~ Children welcome ~
Dogs allowed in bar ~ Wi-fi ~ Bedrooms: £100

CHURCHILL
SP2824
Chequers
(01608) 659393 ~ www.thechequerschurchill.com
Church Road; B4450 Chipping Norton to Stow-on-the-Wold (and village signed off A361 Chipping Norton–Burford); OX7 6NJ

Simple furnishings in spacious bars and dining rooms, a friendly relaxed atmosphere, up to six ales and popular food

This busy village inn is Cotswold stone at its most golden. There's a relaxed and friendly bar with plenty of chatty customers, an armchair and other comfortable chairs around an old trunk in front of an inglenook fireplace, some exposed stone walls, cushioned wall seats, and a mix of wooden and antique leather chairs around nice old tables on bare floorboards. Rugs are dotted about and stools line the counter presided over by a big stag's head: a beer named for the pub (from Chadlington) plus Butcombe Bitter, Crate Rye, Hook Norton Hooky, JW Lees Manchester Pale Ale and Sharps Cornish Coaster on handpump, 12 wines by the glass, 11 malt whiskies, mocktails and a farm cider; darts and background music. At the back is a large extension with soaring rafters, big lantern lights, long button-back leather banquettes and other seating, while upstairs is another similarly and simply furnished dining area and a room for a private party. The terraced back garden has been enlarged recently and has good quality wooden chairs and tables. The church opposite is impressive.

Free house ~ Licensee Peter Creed ~ Real ale ~ Open 11am-midnight ~ Bar food 12-3, 6-9.30 ~ Restaurant ~ Children welcome ~ Dogs welcome ~ Wi-fi

EAST HENDRED
SU4588
Eyston Arms
(01235) 833320 ~ www.eystonarms.co.uk
Village signposted off A417 E of Wantage; High Street; OX12 8JY

Attractive bar areas with low beams, flagstones, log fires and candles, imaginative food and helpful service

Always busy and welcoming, this is a well run place and although many customers are here to enjoy the very good food, locals do pop in for just a drink and a chat. There are seats at the bar and they keep a few tables free for drinkers keen to try the Hook Norton Hooky, Wadworths 6X and a guest ale on handpump, ten wines by the glass and 15 malt whiskies. Several candlelit areas have contemporary paintwork and modern country-style furnishings, low ceilings and beams, stripped timbers and the odd standing upright, nice tables and chairs on flagstones and carpet, some cushioned wall seats and an inglenook fireplace; background music. Picnic-sets outside overlook the pretty lane and there are seats in the back courtyard garden.

Free house ~ Licensees George Dailey and Daisy Barton ~ Real ale ~ Open 9am-11pm (10pm Sun) ~ Bar food 12-9 (light menu 2-5); 12-8 Sun (light menu 4-8) ~ Restaurant ~ Children welcome ~ Dogs allowed in bar ~ Wi-fi

FILKINS

SP2304

Five Alls

(01367) 860875 – www.thefivealsfilkins.co.uk
Signed off A361 Lechlade–Burford; GL7 3JQ

Thoughtfully refurbished inn with creative food, quite a range of drinks, a friendly welcome and seats outside; bedrooms

Impressive food can be enjoyed in the elegant and individually furnished dining rooms here – but there's also a beamed bar liked by locals. This has a cosy area with three leather chesterfields grouped around a table by an open fire, an informal dining space with farmhouse chairs and cushioned pews around tables on bare boards and a nice little window seat for two. Stools line the bar where friendly staff serve a beer named for the pub (from Wychwood), Brakspears Bitter and Oxford Gold and Butcombe Bitter on handpump, 16 wines by the glass and six malt whiskies. Décor in the dining room includes some unusual postage-stamp wallpaper, an attractive mix of chairs and tables on rugs, floorboards and flagstones, plus chandeliers, church candles, fresh flowers and modern artwork on pale-painted walls; background music and TV. The back terrace has chunky tables and chairs under parasols and there are a few picnic-sets at the front.

Free house ~ Licensee Sebastian Snow ~ Real ale ~ Open 12-11; 12-9 Sun ~ Bar food 12-3, 6-10; not Sun evening ~ Restaurant ~ Children welcome ~ Dogs allowed in bar ~ Wi-fi ~ Bedrooms: £120

HIGHMOOR

SU6984

Rising Sun

(01491) 640856 – www.risingsunwitheridgehill.co.uk
Witheridge Hill, signposted off B481; OS Sheet 175 map reference 697841; RG9 5PF

Friendly village pub with a welcoming landlord, character bars and eating areas, and good food and drink; seats in garden

To be sure of a table, it's best to book in advance as this charming 17th-c pub is always full of chatty customers – all made welcome by the friendly landlord. The cosy bar has beams, old red and white floor tiles, a comfortable sofa, lots of walking sticks in a pot by the woodburning stove, books on the windowsill and leather stools against the counter where they serve Brakspears Bitter and a couple of guests such as Marstons Pedigree and Ringwood Best on handpump and a dozen wines by the glass; background music. The three interlinked eating areas have rugs on bare boards, pictures on dark red walls and seating that includes captain's and farmhouse chairs, chunky benches and cushioned wall seats around an assortment of tables; one section has a log fire in a small brick fireplace. There are picnic-sets and white metal chairs and tables in the pleasant back garden. Good surrounding walks.

Brakspears ~ Tenant Simon Duffy ~ Real ale ~ Open 12-3, 5-11; 12-11 Sat; 12-9 Sun ~ Bar food 12-2, 6-9; 12-2.30, 6-9.30 Sat; 12-3 Sun ~ Restaurant ~ Children welcome ~ Dogs allowed in bar ~ Wi-fi

KELMSCOTT

SU2499

Plough

(01367) 253543 – www.theploughinnkelmscott.com
NW of Faringdon, off B4449 between A417 and A4095; GL7 3HG

Lovely spot for tranquil pub with character bar and dining rooms, attractive furnishings and friendly owners; bedrooms

This pretty 17th-c country pub is in a peaceful hamlet by the upper Thames; moorings are just a few minutes away. The small traditional beamed front bar has ancient flagstones and stripped stone walls, along with a good log fire and the relaxed chatty feel of a real village pub. Butcombe Bitter, Hook Norton Hooky and Sharps Doom Bar on handpump, good wines by the glass and maybe farm cider. The dining room has elegant wooden or painted dining chairs around all sorts of tables, striped and cushioned wall seats, cartoons on exposed stone walls, rugs on the floor and plants on windowsills. The garden has seats and tables (some under cover). The Oxfordshire Cycleway runs close by and the inn is handy for Kelmscott Manor.

Free house ~ Licensee Sebastian Snow ~ Real ale ~ Open 12-11 ~ Bar food 12-2.30, 6-9.30 (not Mon evening); 12-3, 6-10 Sat; 12-7 Sun ~ Restaurant ~ Children welcome ~ Dogs allowed in bar ~ Wi-fi ~ Bedrooms: £90

KIRTLINGTON

SP4919

Oxford Arms

(01869) 350208 – www.oxford-arms.co.uk
Troy Lane, junction with A4095 W of Bicester; OX5 3HA

Civilised and friendly stripped-stone pub with enjoyable food using local produce and good wine choice

This sturdy 19th-c stone pub, in a lovely village, is a popular spot. The long line of linked rooms is divided by a central stone hearth with a great round stove, and by the servery itself – where you'll find Black Sheep and Hook Norton Hooky on handpump, an interesting range of 13 wines by the glass, nine malt whiskies, farm cider and organic soft drinks. Past the bar area with its cushioned wall pews, creaky beamed ceiling and age-darkened floor tiles, dining tables on parquet have neat red chairs; beyond that, leather sofas cluster round a log fire at the end. Also, church candles, fresh flowers and plenty of stripped stone. A sheltered back terrace has teak tables under giant parasols with heaters – as well as white metal furniture and picnic-sets on neat gravel. The geranium-filled window boxes are pretty.

Punch ~ Lease Bryn Jones ~ Real ale ~ Open 12-3, 6-11; 12-3 Sun; closed Sun evening, bank holiday Mon evening ~ Bar food 12-2.30, 6.30-9; 12-3 Sun ~ Restaurant ~ Well behaved children welcome ~ Dogs welcome

LONGWORTH

SU3899

Blue Boar

(01865) 820494 – www.blueboarlongworth.co.uk
Tucks Lane; OX13 5ET

Smashing old pub with good wines and beer, and enjoyable food

This handsome country pub is close to the Thames, and there's also a circular two-mile walk from the front door. Inside, it's warmly traditional and the three low-beamed, characterful small rooms have a bustling but easy-going atmosphere and a good mix of locals and visitors. There are brasses, hops and assorted knick-knacks (skis, an old clocking-in machine) on the walls and ceilings, scrubbed wooden tables and benches, faded rugs and floor tiles, fresh flowers on the bar and two blazing log fires (the one by the bar is noteworthy). The main eating area is the red-painted room at the end and there's a quieter restaurant extension too. Brakspears Bitter and Otter Ale on handpump, 20 malt whiskies and a dozen wines by the glass. There are tables outside in front and on the back terrace.

Free house ~ Licensee Paul Dailey ~ Real ale ~ Open 12-11; 12-10 Sun ~ Bar food 12-2.30, 6.30-9.30 (10 Fri, Sat); 12-3, 6.30-9 Sun ~ Restaurant ~ Children allowed lunchtime only ~ Dogs allowed in bar ~ Wi-fi

MILTON-UNDER-WYCHWOOD   SP2618

Hare

(01993) 835763 – www.themiltonhare.co.uk
High Street; OX7 6LA

Renovated stone inn with linked bar and dining rooms, attractive contemporary furnishings, real ales, pleasing food and seats in the garden

Locals are thrilled that this village pub (closed for several years) has now been reopened and completely refurbished. There's a bar and a couple of little drinking areas warmed by a woodburning stove and various dining areas leading off: wooden floors, dark grey painted or exposed stone walls, painted beams, big gilt-edged mirrors and seating that includes stools, wooden or leather dining chairs, long button-back wall seats and cushioned settles around tables of every size – each set with a little glass oil lamp. Splashes of bright colour here and there brighten things considerably. Throughout, there's all manner of hare paraphernalia – photos, paintings, statues, a large glass case with stuffed boxing hares, motifs on scatter cushions and so forth. Stools line the counter where friendly, well trained staff serve Hook Norton Hooky and guests such as Bath Summers Hare and North Cotswold Shagweaver on handpump and good wines by the glass; on Fridays at 5pm it's champagne happy hour. The garden has tables, benches and chairs on a terrace and on a lawn.

Free house ~ Licensees Sue and Rachel Hawkins ~ Real ale ~ Open 12-3, 5.30-11; 11-11 Sat, Sun ~ Bar food 12-2.30, 6-9 (9.30 Sat); 12-9 Sun ~ Restaurant ~ Children welcome but not in the bar at weekends ~ Dogs allowed in bar ~ Wi-fi ~ Live acoustic music Sun evening

OXFORD   SP5106

Bear

(01865) 728164 – www.bearoxford.co.uk
Alfred Street/Wheatsheaf Alley; OX1 4EH

Delightful pub with friendly staff, two cosy rooms, six real ales and well liked bar food

The oldest drinking house in the city, this is a charming little tavern tucked away from the tourist trail. The two small rooms are beamed, partly panelled and have a chatty, bustling atmosphere (in term time it's often packed with students), winter coal fires, thousands of vintage ties on the walls and up to six real ales from handpumps on the fine pewter bar counter: Fullers ESB, HSB, London Pride and Olivers Island and a guest from Shotover. Staff are friendly and helpful; board games. There are seats under parasols in the large terraced back garden where summer barbecues are held.

Fullers ~ Manager James Vernede ~ Real ale ~ Open 11-11 (midnight Fri, Sat); 11.30-10.30 Sun ~ Bar food 12-4, 5-8 (8.30 Thurs); 12-9 Fri-Sun ~ Children welcome but no pushchairs inside ~ Dogs welcome ~ Wi-fi

OXFORD   SP4907
Perch

(01865) 728891 – www.the-perch.co.uk
Binsey Lane, on right after river bridge leaving city on A420; OX2 0NG

A fine mix of customers for beautifully set inn with riverside gardens, local ales, popular food and friendly service

In summer, this thatched 17th-c limestone pub is a special place with a lovely garden running down to the Thames Path where there are moorings. A partly covered terrace has seats and tables, there are picnic-sets on the lawn, a summer bar and an attractively furnished marquee. The heavily beamed bar has red leather chesterfields in front of a woodburning stove, a very high-backed settle, little stools around tables and fine old flagstones. Hook Norton Hooky and guests such as Loose Cannon Gunners Gold and White Horse Bitter on handpump and plenty of wines by the glass. Leading off here are the dining areas with bare floorboards, scatter cushions on built-in wall seats, wheelbacks and other chairs around light tables, a second woodburner with logs piled to the ceiling next to it, and a fine brass chandelier. Service is helpful and friendly; they hold an annual beer and cider festival, outdoor film evenings in summer and a folk festival.

Free house ~ Licensee Jon Ellse ~ Real ale ~ Open 10.30am-11pm ~ Bar food 12-10 (9 Sun) ~ Restaurant ~ Children welcome ~ Dogs welcome ~ Wi-fi

OXFORD   SP5005
Punter

(01865) 248832 – www.thepunteroxford.com
South Street, Osney (off A420 Botley Road via Bridge Street); OX2 0BE

Easy-going atmosphere in bustling pub overlooking the water with plenty of character and enjoyable food

There's a boathouse feel to this cheerful place – which is apt given its position on Osney Island with views over the Thames. Run by an enthusiastic landlord and his friendly staff, the lower area has attractive rugs on flagstones and an open fire, while the upper room has more rugs on bare boards and a single big table surrounded by oil paintings – just right for a private group. Throughout are all manner of nice old dining chairs around an interesting mix of tables, art for sale on whitewashed walls and a rather fine stained-glass window. Greene King Fireside, Morlands Original and Old Golden Hen on handpump from the tiled counter and several wines by the glass; board games.

Greene King ~ Lease Tom Rainey ~ Real ale ~ Open 12-midnight; 12-11.30 Sun ~ Bar food 12-3, 6-10; 12-10 Sat; 12-9 Sun ~ Children welcome ~ Dogs welcome ~ Wi-fi

RAMSDEN   SP3515
Royal Oak

(01993) 868213 – www.royaloakramsden.com
Village signposted off B4022 Witney–Charlbury; OX7 3AU

Busy pub with long-serving licensees, large helpings of varied food, carefully chosen wines and seats outside; bedrooms

For nearly 30 years now, the same licensees have run their village pub with enthusiasm and care. The unpretentious rooms are relaxed and friendly with all manner of wooden tables, chairs and settles, cushioned window seats, exposed stone walls, bookcases with old and new copies of *Country Life* and, when the weather gets cold, a cheerful log fire. Butts Barbus Barbus, Hook Norton Hooky and Loose Cannon Recoil on handpump, 40 wines by the glass from a carefully chosen list and three farm ciders. Folding doors from the restaurant give easy access to the back terrace and there are some tables and chairs out in front. The village church is opposite.

Free house ~ Licensee Jon Oldham ~ Real ale ~ Open 11.30-3, 6.30-11; 11.30-11 Sat; 12-10.30 Sun ~ Bar food 12-2.30, 7-10; 12-10 Sat; 12-9 Sun ~ Restaurant ~ Children welcome ~ Dogs allowed in bar ~ Wi-fi ~ Bedrooms: £85

SHILTON SP2608

Rose & Crown

(01993) 842280 – www.shiltonroseandcrown.com
Just off B4020 SE of Burford; OX18 4AB

Simple and appealing little pub with particularly good food cooked by the landlord-chef, real ales and fine wines

Consistently high standards keep this pretty, 17th-c stone pub as popular as ever. It's a friendly place and the small front bar has an unassuming but civilised feel, low beams and timbers, exposed stone walls, a log fire in a big fireplace and half a dozen or so farmhouse chairs and tables on the red tiled floor. There are usually a few locals at the planked counter where they serve Butcombe Rare Breed, Hook Norton Old Hooky and Youngs Bitter on handpump, along with ten wines by the glass, seven malt whiskies and farm cider. A second room, similar but bigger, is used mainly for eating, and has another fireplace. An attractive side garden has picnic-sets. This is a lovely village.

Free house ~ Licensee Martin Coldicott ~ Real ale ~ Open 11.30-3, 6-10.30; 11.30-11 Sat; 12-10 Sun ~ Bar food 12-2 (2.45 weekends and bank holidays), 7-9 ~ Children welcome lunchtime only ~ Dogs allowed in bar

SPARSHOLT SU3487

Star

(01235) 751873 – www.thestarsparsholt.co.uk
Watery Lane; OX12 9PL

Delicious food, real ales and good wines by the glass, helpful friendly staff and seats in the garden; bedrooms

Of course, most customers come to this inviting and compact 16th-c pub for the excellent food – but they do have a simply furnished bar where they keep Purity Gold and Sharps Doom Bar on handpump and several wines by the glass; staff are efficient and friendly. The dining rooms have pale farmhouse chairs around chunky tables on floorboards or big flagstones, hops on beams, an open fire and old stone bottles and plants dotted about. The atmosphere is easy-going and informal; background music and board games. The two pub dogs are called Minnie and Ella. There are seats in the back garden and a new kitchen garden. You can enjoy walks along the Ridgeway and a carpet of spring snowdrops in the churchyard.

Free house ~ Licensee Caron Williams ~ Real ale ~ Open 12-11 (midnight Sat); 12-11 Sun ~ Bar food 12-2.30, 6.30-9 (9.30 Fri, Sat); 12-8 Sun ~ Restaurant ~ Children welcome ~ Dogs welcome ~ Wi-fi ~ Bedrooms: £95

STANFORD IN THE VALE   SU3393

Horse & Jockey

(01367) 710302 – www.horseandjockey.org
A417 Faringdon–Wantage; Faringdon Road; SN7 8NN

**Bustling, traditional village local with real character, highly thought-of
and good value food and well chosen wines; bedrooms**

The friendly, hard-working licensees in this charming pub offer a warm welcome
to all. It's an interesting place and since this is racehorse-training country
(and given the pub's name) there are big Alfred Munnings racecourse prints, card
collections of Grand National winners and other horse and jockey pictures on the
walls. The place is split into two sections: a contemporary dining area and an older
part with flagstones, wood flooring, low beams and raftered ceilings. There are old
high-backed settles and leather armchairs, a woodburning stove in a big fireplace
and an easy-going atmosphere. A beer named for the pub (from Greene King),
Greene King Molecule of Life and St Austell Tribute on handpump, carefully chosen
wines by the glass and a dozen malt whiskies; background music. As well as tables
under a heated courtyard canopy, there's a separate enclosed and informal garden.

Greene King ~ Lease Charles and Anna Gaunt ~ Real ale ~ Open 11-3, 5-midnight; 11am-
12.30am Sat; 11-11 Sun ~ Bar food 12-2.30, 6.30-9 (9.30 Fri, Sat) ~ Restaurant ~ Children
welcome ~ Dogs allowed in bar ~ Wi-fi ~ Open mike first Weds of month ~ Bedrooms: £80

STONESFIELD   SP3917

White Horse

(01993) 891063 – www.whitehorsestonesfield.co.uk
Village signposted off B4437 Charlbury–Woodstock; Stonesfield Riding; OX29 8EA

**Neatly kept little pub with a relaxed atmosphere and enjoyable food
and beer**

As this attractively upgraded small country pub is on the Oxfordshire Way
long-distance path, it's just the place for a weekend lunch. There's a friendly,
uncluttered feel – just a few pieces of contemporary artwork on green and cream
paintwork, and the cosy bar has a woodburning stove, country-style chairs and
plush or leather stools around solid tables on bare boards, Ringwood Best Bitter on
handpump and six wines by the glass; background music. The pink-walled dining
room has similar but more elegant furnishings and an open fire; a nice touch is the
inner room with just a pair of Sheraton-style chairs around a single mahogany table.
Doors open on to a neat walled garden with picnic-sets and interesting plants in
pots and they've redesigned the courtyard this year. It's handy for the Roman villa at
nearby North Leigh (English Heritage) but do note the pub's restricted opening hours.

Free house ~ Licensees John and Angela Lloyd ~ Real ale ~ Open 5-11; 12-3, 6-11 Sat; 12-3
Sun; closed Sun evening, Mon, lunchtimes Tues-Fri; first week Jan ~ Bar food 6.30-9 Fri;
12-2, 6.30-9 Sat; 12-2 Sun ~ Restaurant ~ Children welcome ~ Dogs allowed in bar ~ Wi-fi

SWERFORD   SP3830

Masons Arms

(01608) 683212 – www.masons-arms.com
A361 Banbury–Chipping Norton; OX7 4AP

**Well liked food and fair choice of drinks in bustling dining pub with
relaxed atmosphere and country views**

The friendly bar here is welcoming at any time of year with a big brown leather sofa facing a couple of armchairs in front of a log fire in a stone fireplace, rugs on pale wooden floors, Brakspears Bitter and Jennings Cumberland on handpump and 12 wines by the glass. The light and airy dining extension has pastel-painted dining chairs around nice old tables on beige carpet, and steps lead down to a cream-painted room with chunky tables and contemporary pictures. Around the other side of the bar is another spacious dining room with great views by day, candles at night and a civilised feel; background music. In warm weather, head for the picnic-sets on grass in the neat back garden and enjoy the pretty views over the Oxfordshire countryside.

Free house ~ Licensee Louise Davies ~ Real ale ~ Open 11-3, 6-11; 11-6 Sun ~ Bar food 12-2.15, 6-9 (9.30 Sat); 11-6 Sun ~ Restaurant ~ Children welcome ~ Dogs allowed in bar ~ Wi-fi

SWINBROOK   SP2812

Swan

(01993) 823339 – www.theswanswinbrook.co.uk
Back road a mile N of A40, 2 miles E of Burford; OX18 4DY

Smart old pub with handsome oak garden rooms, antiques-filled bars, local beers and contemporary food; bedrooms

The outdoor seats and circular picnic-sets make the best of this 400-year-old stone pub's position by a bridge over the River Windrush. It's a civilised place and owned by the Devonshire Estate – there are plenty of interesting Mitford family photographs blown up on the walls. The little bar has simple antique furnishings, settles and benches, an open fire and (in an alcove) a stuffed swan; locals drop in here for a pint and a chat. A small dining room leads off from the bar to the right of the entrance, and there are also two garden rooms with high-backed beige and green dining chairs around pale wood tables and views across the garden and orchard. Hook Norton Hooky and a couple of changing guests from breweries such as Cotswold Lion and Flying Monk on handpump, nine wines by the glass, farm ciders and local draught lager; background music, board games and TV.

Free house ~ Licensees Archie and Nicola Orr-Ewing ~ Real ale ~ Open 11-11 ~ Bar food 12-2, 7-9; 12-3, 7-8.30 Sun ~ Restaurant ~ Children welcome ~ Dogs allowed in bar ~ Wi-fi ~ Bedrooms: £125

WOLVERCOTE   SP4809

Jacobs Inn

(01865) 514333 – www.jacobs-inn.com
Godstow Road; OX2 8PG

Cheerful pub with enthusiastic staff, simple furnishings, inventive cooking and seats in the garden

The robust, interesting food, lively and informal atmosphere and slightly quirky décor are all enjoyed here. The simply furnished bar has leather armchairs and chesterfields, some plain tables and benches, wide floorboards, a small open fire and high chairs at the counter where they keep Brakspears Bitter, Wychwood Dirty Tackle and Hobgoblin and a guest beer on handpump, 13 wines by the glass, a good choice of spirits and lots of teas and coffees; background music. You can eat at plain wooden tables in a grey panelled area with an open fire or in the smarter knocked-through dining room; the food features big rustic flavours and uses home-reared pigs, free-range eggs and other local, seasonal produce. This has standing timbers in the centre, a fire at each end and shiny, dark wooden chairs and tables on floorboards; there are standard lamps, stags' heads, a reel-to-reel tape recorder, quite a few mirrors, and deli items for sale. Several seating areas outside have good quality tables and chairs under parasols, picnic-sets on decking, and deckchairs and more picnic-sets on grass.

Marstons ~ Lease Damion Farah and Johnny Pugsley ~ Real ale ~ Open 9am-11pm ~ Bar food 9am-10pm ~ Restaurant ~ Children welcome ~ Dogs allowed in bar ~ Wi-fi

WOODSTOCK   SP4416
Kings Arms

(01993) 813636 – www.kings-hotel-woodstock.co.uk
Market Street/Park Lane (A44); OX20 1SU

Bustling town-centre hotel with well liked food, a wide choice of drinks and an enjoyable atmosphere; comfortable bedrooms

This stylish town-centre pub has an unfussy bar with a cheerful mix of locals and visitors, an appealing variety of old and new furnishings including brown leather seats on the stripped-wood floor, smart blinds and black and white photographs; at the front is an old wooden settle and a modern woodburning stove. The neat restaurant has high-backed black leather dining chairs around a mix of tables on black and white floor tiles, and piles of neatly stacked logs on either side of another woodburning stove; background music. Brakspears Bitter, Jennings Cumberland and Thwaites Lancaster Bomber on handpump, 11 wines (plus champagne) by the glass and 35 malt whiskies. There are seats and tables on the street outside.

Free house ~ Licensees David and Sara Sykes ~ Real ale ~ Open 7am-11pm ~ Bar food 12-2.30, 6-9; 12-5, 6-9 Sun ~ Restaurant ~ Children welcome in bar and restaurant but no under-12s in bedrooms ~ Dogs allowed in bar ~ Wi-fi ~ Bedrooms: £150

DOG FRIENDLY HOTELS, INNS AND B&Bs

BURFORD   SP2412
Lamb

(01993) 823155 – www.cotswold-inns-hotels.co.uk
Sheep Street, Burford, Oxfordshire OX18 4LR

£175; 17 attractive, comfortable rooms. Lovely 500-year-old Cotswold inn with a classic, cosy bar, high-backed settles and old chairs on flagstones, a log fire and an extensive choice of drinks; also a roomy beamed main lounge with plenty of antiques, rugs on wide flagstones or polished floorboards, fresh flowers and winter log fire; impeccable service, good enjoyable food including smashing breakfasts; neatly kept lawns and terracing and suntrap garden, and walks in surrounding countryside. Dogs allowed in some bedrooms and anywhere except restaurant; bowls and treats; £10.

BURFORD   SP2512
Highway

(01993) 823661 – www.thehighwayinn.co.uk
High Street, Burford, Oxfordshire, OX18 4RG

£130; 10 comfortable, country house-style bedrooms. In a charming Cotswold town, this is a friendly pub with old float glass windows overlooking the pretty High Street; the main bar has closely set tables with stag candlesticks, beams and well worn floorboards, walls of stripped stone and modern filigree wallpaper, dark leather chairs and a nice old station clock above a big log fire in a pleasingly simple stone fireplace; there's also a second bar room and a cellar bar (open for tapas at weekends), a good choice of drinks (they hold a beer festival and barbecue in June) and interesting food including good breakfasts; tables outside on the pavement and in a small courtyard. Closed first two weeks January. Dogs allowed in two bedrooms and main bar; £10 per stay.

GORING   SU5980
Miller of Mansfield
(01491) 872829 – www.millerofmansfield.com
High Street, Goring, Oxfordshire RG8 9AW

£100; 13 individually decorated bedrooms including 2 suites. A handsome 18th-c coaching inn run by hands-on professional licensees with an atmosphere of easy, friendly informality backed up by excellent seasonal food (cooked by the chef-owner) and a carefully chosen choice of drinks; décor in the beamed bars is simple and unfussy – plain wooden tables, bare floorboards, exposed stone and brick walls and a few prints and gilt-edged mirrors – and there are also dining rooms painted in yellow or cream and a multi-level terraced garden with seating among flowering tubs; this is a lovely village surrounded by pretty countryside and woodland walks. Dogs allowed in all bedrooms and bar; £10.

KINGHAM   SP2523
Mill House
(01608) 658188 – www.millhousehotel.co.uk
Station Road, Kingham, Chipping Norton, Oxfordshire OX7 6UH

£140; 21 light rooms with country views. Carefully renovated, family-run 17th-c flour mill in 40 acres of grounds with a trout stream and plenty of original features; a bright, bustling bar, a comfortable spacious lounge with books and magazines, and an elegant restaurant where helpful, friendly staff serve inventive modern dishes, popular afternoon teas and hearty breakfasts. Dogs allowed in some bedrooms; £10 per stay.

KINGHAM   SP2624
Plough
(01608) 658327 – www.thekinghamplough.co.uk
The Green, Kingham, Chipping Norton, Oxfordshire OX7 6YD

£195; 6 pretty rooms. Friendly restaurant-with-rooms combining an informal pub atmosphere with upmarket food; a properly pubby bar with nice old high-backed settles and brightly cushioned chapel chairs, candles on stripped tables, cheerful country prints, a log fire at one end and a woodburner at the other, and good bar food; spacious and raftered two-part dining room serving highly enjoyable and inventive modern british food (smashing breakfasts too) and a thoughtful choice of drinks; resident jack russell, Ooti. Dogs allowed in two bedrooms and bar; bed, bowl and treats; £10 per stay.

MINSTER LOVELL

SP3211

Old Swan & Minster Mill

(01993) 774441 – www.oldswanandminstermill.com
Old Minster, Minster Lovell, Witney, Oxfordshire OX29 0RN

£195; 52 luxurious rooms and suites – 36 contemporary ones in Mill and 16 traditional ones in Old Swan; also a private cottage. Lovingly restored old place with much emphasis on the hotel and restaurant side but with a restful and unchanging bar at its heart; several attractive low-beamed rooms lead off here with big log fires in huge fireplaces, lots of sofas, armchairs and wooden dining chairs on bare boards or ancient flagstones, interesting antiques (bed-warming pans, swords, hunting horns and even a suit of armour) and fresh flowers; excellent, elaborate food using produce from their kitchen garden and other local suppliers, and delicious breakfasts; spa (new for 2016) with pool, sauna, steam and treatment rooms; seats (and walks) in 65 acres of grounds – they have a mile of fishing on the River Windrush, chickens, ducks and resident cat. Dogs allowed in some bedrooms and snug; bed, bowl and dog menu; occasional puppy training classes; £20.

SHILLINGFORD

SU5991

Shillingford Bridge Hotel

(01865) 858567 – www.shillingfordbridgehotel.com
Shillingford Road, Shillingford, Wallingford, Oxfordshire OX10 8LZ

£129; 40 rooms. Thames-side hotel with its own river frontage, terraced gardens, fishing and moorings; spacious comfortable bars and airy restaurant (all with fine views) with leather sofas and oak tables and chairs on tiled floor; enjoyable food served by helpful staff; walks along the Thames. Dogs allowed in all bedrooms only; £10.

SHIPLAKE

SU7779

Baskerville

(0118) 940 3332 – www.thebaskerville.com
Station Road, Lower Shiplake, Henley-on-Thames, Oxfordshire RG9 3NY

£110; 4 spotless rooms. Particularly well run and friendly village pub with emphasis on the imaginative food – but with a proper public bar, too; pale wooden tables and chairs and plush banquettes, sporting memorabilia and pictures, log fires in brick fireplaces, fresh flowers and house plants and a very good choice of drinks served by well trained staff; the separate restaurant offers impressive food using organic produce and sustainably sourced fish, and the breakfasts are very good; pretty garden with smart teak furniture under huge parasols and fun statues made from box hedges; walks nearby including on Thames Path. Dogs allowed in all bedrooms and on lead in bar and garden; £10.

SHIPTON-UNDER-WYCHWOOD

SP2717

Shaven Crown

(01993) 830500 – www.theshavencrown.co.uk
High Street, Shipton-under-Wychwood, Chipping Norton, Oxfordshire OX7 6BA

£115; 7 character rooms. Densely beamed, ancient stone hospice built around a striking medieval courtyard with seating by a lily pool and roses; impressive medieval hall with a magnificent lofty ceiling, a sweeping stairway and old stone walls, a comfortable bar with log fire, a residents' lounge, an intimate candlelit restaurant, good friendly service and a warm relaxed atmosphere; inventive food including fine breakfasts and weekend brunch; bowling green and lots of walks not far away. Closed Christmas and New Year. Dogs allowed in all bedrooms and anywhere except restaurant; £5.

TADPOLE BRIDGE   SP3300
Trout
(01367) 870382 – www.troutinn.co.uk
Buckland Marsh, Faringdon, Oxfordshire SN7 8RF

£130; 6 spacious modern rooms. Recently refurbished, smart country inn by the River Thames with walks along the Thames Path and seats in waterside gardens; L-shaped bar with exposed stone walls, beams and standing timbers, flagstones, leather armchairs, two woodburning stoves, fresh flowers, interesting prints, helpful staff and a friendly, civilised feel; well kept ales, carefully chosen wines and an appealing, candlelit restaurant serving inventive and deservedly popular food (particularly good breakfasts); pretty garden with seating under parasols. Dogs allowed in three bedrooms and anywhere in the pub; bedding, bowl and treats; £15 per stay.

WOODSTOCK   SP4416
Feathers
(01993) 812291 – www.feathers.co.uk
Market Street, Woodstock, Oxfordshire OX20 1SX

£150; 21 individually decorated rooms, including 5 suites. Lovely old brick building given a tasteful contemporary makeover with bold coloured furnishings, comfortable sofas and armchairs on pale wooden flooring or rugs on flagstones, prints and pictures, open fires and courteous staff; imaginative modern food from good breakfasts through light lunches to afternoon teas and excellent evening meals, a bar specialising in gins, and a sunny courtyard with attractive seating; Blenheim Palace and plenty of walks nearby. Dogs allowed in five bedrooms and all public areas except restaurant; £15.

Shropshire

DOG FRIENDLY PUBS

BRIDGNORTH   SO7192
Old Castle
(01746) 711420 ~ www.oldcastlebridgnorth.co.uk
West Castle Street; WV16 4AB

Cheerful town pub, relaxed and friendly, with generous helpings of good value pubby food, well kept ales and good-sized suntrap terrace

A big plus for this traditional pub (once two cottages) is the sunny back terrace with picnic-sets, lovely hanging baskets, big pots of flowers, shrub borders and decking at the far end that gives an elevated view over the west side of town; children's playthings. The low-beamed open-plan bar is properly pubby with some genuine character: you'll find tiles and bare boards, cushioned wall banquettes and settles around cast-iron-framed tables, and bar stools arranged along the counter where the friendly landlord and his staff serve Hobsons Town Crier, Sharps Doom Bar, Thwaites Lancaster Bomber and Wye Valley HPA on handpump. The good pubby food is fairly priced. A back conservatory extension has darts, pool and a games machine; background music and big-screen TV for sports events. Do walk up the street to see the ruined castle – its 20-metre Norman tower tilts at such an extraordinary angle that it makes the leaning tower of Pisa look like a model of rectitude.

Punch ~ Tenant Bryn Charles Masterman ~ Real ale ~ Open 11.30-11; 11.30-10.30 Sun ~ Bar food 12-3, 6.30-8.30 ~ Children welcome ~ Dogs welcome ~ Wi-fi

CARDINGTON   SO5095
Royal Oak
(01694) 771266 ~ www.at-the-oak.com
Village signposted off B4371 Church Stretton–Much Wenlock, pub behind church; also reached via narrow lanes from A49; SY6 7JZ

Heaps of character in well run and friendly rural pub with tasty seasonal bar food and real ales

Tucked away in a lovely spot, this is said to be Shropshire's oldest continuously licensed pub. The rambling low-beamed traditional bar has a roaring winter log fire, a cauldron, black kettle and pewter jugs in a vast inglenook fireplace, aged standing timbers from a knocked-through wall, and red and green tapestry seats solidly capped in elm; board games and dominoes. Ludlow Best and Sharps Doom Bar with guests such as Hobsons Town Crier and Wye Valley Butty Bach on handpump, eight wines by the glass, ten gins, several malt whiskies and farm cider. A comfortable dining area has exposed old beams and studwork. This is glorious country for walks, such as the one to the summit of Caer Caradoc, a couple of miles to the west (ask for directions at the pub), and the front courtyard makes the most of its beautiful position.

Free house ~ Licensees Steve and Eira Oldham ~ Real ale ~ Open 12-2.30, 6-11; 12-11 Sat, Sun; 12-4 Sun in winter; closed Mon except bank holidays ~ Bar food 12-2.30, 6-9 ~ Restaurant ~ Children welcome ~ Dogs allowed in bar ~ Wi-fi

CHETWYND ASTON   SJ7517
Fox

(01952) 815940 – www.brunningandprice.co.uk/fox
Village signposted off A41 and A518 just S of Newport; TF10 9LQ

Civilised dining pub with generous helpings of well liked food and a fine array of drinks served by ever attentive staff

Although this handsome Edwardian pub is large and spreading, there are cosy corners too – all filled with a cheerful crowd of customers. The linked rooms (one with a broad arched ceiling) has plenty of tables in varying shapes and sizes, some quite elegant, and a loosely matching diversity of comfortable chairs on parquet, polished boards or attractive floor tiles. Masses of prints and photographs line the walls, there are three open fires, and big windows and careful lighting contribute to the relaxed atmosphere; board games. Bar stools line the long bar counter where courteous, efficient staff keep around 18 wines by the glass, 40 malt whiskies, 20 gins and Phoenix Brunning & Price Original, Three Tuns XXX, Woods Shropshire Lad and three quickly changing guests from breweries such as Purple Moose, Rowton and Woods on handpump. The large back garden is quite lovely, with a sunny terrace, picnic-sets tucked into the shade of mature trees and extensive views across quiet country fields. Good disabled access.

Brunning & Price ~ Manager Samantha Forrest ~ Real ale ~ Open 11am-11.30pm; 11-11 Sun ~ Bar food 12-10; 12-9.30 Sun ~ Children welcome ~ Dogs allowed in bar ~ Wi-fi

COALPORT   SJ7002
Woodbridge

(01952) 882054 – www.brunningandprice.co.uk/woodbridge
Village signposted off A442 1.5 miles S of A4169 Telford roundabout; down in valley, turn left across narrow bridge into Coalport Road, pub immediately left; TF8 7JF

Superb Ironbridge Gorge site for extensive handsomely reworked pub, an all-round success

Big windows here look out on a lovely section of a wooded gorge and the many tables and chairs on the big raised deck look over the River Severn. The spreading series of linked rooms are comfortable and civilised with log fires and Coalport-style stoves, rugs on broad boards as well as tiles or carpet, black beams in the central part and plenty of polished tables and cosy armchair corners. A mass of mainly 18th- and 19th-c prints line the walls and the historic pictures, often of local scenes, are well worth a look; background music. Phoenix Brunning & Price Original and guests such as Hobsons Twisted Spire, Three Tuns XXX, Timothy Taylors Landlord and Woods Parish Bitter on handpump, 16 wines by the glass, 45 malt whiskies and 15 gins; tasty food; service is quick and friendly.

Brunning & Price ~ Manager Vrata Krist ~ Real ale ~ Open 11.30-11; 11.30-midnight Fri, Sat;
11.30-10.30 Sun ~ Bar food 12-10 (9.30 Sun) ~ Restaurant ~ Children welcome ~
Dogs allowed in bar ~ Wi-fi

HODNET   SJ6128

Bear

(01630) 685214 – www.bearathodnet.co.uk
Drayton Road (A53); TF9 3NH

**Black and white timbered former coaching inn with beamed rooms,
four real ales, enjoyable food and seats outside; bedrooms**

This nice old village inn is run by a professional, hands-on landlord. The
rambling, open-plan main room has heavy 16th-c beams and timbers
creating separate areas, wooden tables and chairs on rugs or flagstones, and a
woodburning stove in a large stone fireplace (there are three other open fires as
well); there's a former bear pit under the floor. The smaller, beamed and quarry-
tiled bar has Black Sheep, Rowton Portly Stout and Salopian Shropshire Gold on
handpump, 14 wines by the glass, 30 malt whiskies and around 20 gins served by
friendly staff; the pub jack russell is called Jack. The garden has picnic-sets and a
play area. Hodnet Hall Gardens are opposite and the inn is handy for Hawkstone
Park; good walks in lovely surrounding countryside.

Free house ~ Licensees Gregory and Pia Williams ~ Real ale ~ Open 12-11; 12-9 Sun ~
Bar food 12-3, 6-9; 12-4 Sun ~ Restaurant ~ Children welcome ~ Dogs allowed in bar ~
Wi-fi ~ Bedrooms: £120

MAESBURY MARSH   SJ3125

Navigation

(01691) 672958 – www.thenavigation.co.uk
Follow Maesbury Road off A483 S of Oswestry; by canal bridge; SY10 8JB

**Versatile and friendly canalside pub with cosy bar and local seasonal
produce in a choice of dining areas**

Picnic-sets outside this 18th-c wharf building are arranged beside the
Montgomery Canal, and windows in the dining room also overlook the water.
As well as running a traditional pub, the friendly hands-on licensees have a book
exchange, a shop where you can buy fresh local produce (including fish and
shellfish) and a two-pint takeaway service. The quarry-tiled bar on the left has
squishy brown leather sofas by a traditional black range blazing in a big red-brick
fireplace, little upholstered cask seats around three small tables, and dozens of
wrist- and pocket-watches hanging from the beams. A couple of steps lead up
to a carpeted area beyond a balustrade, with armchairs and sofas around low
tables, and a piano; off to the left is a dining area with paintings by local artists.
The main beamed dining room, with some stripped stone, is beyond another small
bar (they serve cocktails here) with a coal-effect gas fire – and an amazing row of
cushioned carved choir stalls complete with misericord seats. Salopian Darwin's
Origin and Stonehouse Cambrian Gold on handpump, 11 wines by the glass, nine
malt whiskies (one from Wales) and a farm cider (in summer); quiet background
music and board games.

Free house ~ Licensees Brent Ellis and Mark Baggett ~ Real ale ~ Open 12-2, 6-11; 12-6 Sun;
closed Sun evening, all day Mon, lunchtime Tue, first two weeks Jan ~ Bar food 12-2, 6-8.30;
12-2 Sun ~ Restaurant ~ Children welcome ~ Dogs allowed in bar ~ Wi-fi ~ Folk music last
Weds of month

SHIPLEY   SO8095

Inn at Shipley

(01902) 701639 – www.brunningandprice.co.uk/innatshipley
Bridgnorth Road; A454 W of Wolverhampton; WV6 7EQ

Light and airy country pub – a good all-rounder

Carefully extended, this is a handsome 18th-c building with rambling rooms and a civilised atmosphere. Several woodburning stoves and log fires surround the central bar – one in a big inglenook in a cosy, traditionally tiled black-beamed end room and another by a welcoming set of wing and other leather armchairs. All sorts of dining chairs are grouped around a variety of well buffed tables, rugs are set on polished boards, attractive pictures are hung frame to frame and big windows let in plenty of daylight; church candles, careful spotlighting and chandeliers add atmosphere. The various areas are interconnected but manage to also feel distinct and individual; upstairs is a separate private dining room. Phoenix Brunning & Price Original, Holdens Golden Glow, Salopian Oracle, Three Tuns XXX, Titanic Plum Porter and Woods Shropshire Lad on handpump, 17 wines by the glass, 80 malt whiskies, 70 gins and two farm ciders; good neatly dressed staff, background music and board games. There are plenty of sturdy tables outside, some on a sizeable terrace with a side awning, others by weeping willows on the main lawn behind the car park, more on smaller lawns around the building.

Brunning & Price ~ Manager Marc Eeley ~ Real ale ~ Open 10.30am-11pm; 10.30-10.30 Sun ~ Bar food 12-10 (9.30 Sun) ~ Restaurant ~ Children welcome ~ Dogs allowed in bar ~ Wi-fi

SHREWSBURY   SJ4812

Armoury

(01743) 340525 – www.brunningandprice.co.uk/armoury
Victoria Quay, Victoria Avenue; SY1 1HH

Vibrant atmosphere in interestingly converted riverside warehouse with tempting all-day food

They certainly keep a fine range of drinks in this 18th-c former warehouse – Phoenix Brunning & Price Original, Longden The Golden Arrow, Salopian Oracle, Woods Shropshire Lad and a couple of guest beers on handpump, 17 wines by the glass, 100 malt whiskies, a dozen gins, lots of rums and vodkas, a variety of brandies and a farm cider. The spacious open-plan interior has long runs of big arched windows with views across the broad River Severn – but, despite its size, it also has a personal feel, helped by the eclectic décor, furniture layout and cheerful bustle. A mix of wood tables and chairs are grouped on stripped-wood floors, the huge brick walls display floor-to-ceiling books or masses of old prints mounted edge to edge, and there's a grand stone fireplace at one end. Colonial-style fans whirr away on the ceilings, which are supported by green-painted columns, and small wall-mounted glass cabinets display smokers' pipes. The hanging baskets are quite a sight in summer. The pub doesn't have its own car park, but there are plenty of parking places nearby.

Brunning & Price ~ Manager Emily Waring ~ Real ale ~ Open 12-11 (10.30 Sun) ~ Bar food 12-10 (9.30 Sun) ~ Children welcome ~ Dogs allowed in bar ~ Wi-fi

DOG FRIENDLY HOTELS, INNS AND B&Bs

BISHOP'S CASTLE   SO3288

Castle Hotel

(01588) 638403 – www.thecastlehotelbishopscastle.co.uk
Market Square, Bishop's Castle, Shropshire SY9 5BN

£110; 12 spacious rooms with fine views. On the site of the old castle keep, this enjoyable 18th-c hotel is surrounded by the Shropshire Hills and Welsh Borders and plenty of good walks; three convivial bars, log fires and a relaxed and friendly atmosphere, an oak-panelled restaurant, real ales and good bar and restaurant food; seats in the garden; resident dachshund, Milly. Closed first two weeks January. Dogs allowed in all bedrooms and back bar; welcome pack, bowl and food fridge.

CLUN   SO2785

New House Farm

(01588) 638314 – www.new-house-clun.co.uk
Clun, Craven Arms, Shropshire SY7 8NJ

£90; 2 rooms with thoughtful extras. Remote 18th-c farmhouse not far from Wales with plenty of surrounding hillside walks and lovely views; a cosy sitting room with a woodburning stove, collections of china and farming artefacts, a dining room for breakfasts that include home-made preserves and muesli, a lovely country garden and helpful, friendly owner. Closed November-Easter. Dogs allowed in bedrooms, but not dining room; must bring own bedding; £5.

CLUN   SO3080

White Horse

(01588) 418128 – www.whi-clun.co.uk
The Square, Clun, Craven Arms, Shropshire SY7 8JA

£65; 4 rooms. Friendly 18th-c pub with a cheerful atmosphere in the low-beamed front bar, a woodburning stove in a cosy inglenook, real ales including their popular own brews and good value traditional food served by attentive staff in separate small dining room with a rare plank and munton screen; small games room; resident weimaraner/collie cross called Dave; fine walking nearby in Shropshire Hills. Dogs allowed in all bedrooms and anywhere in pub except dining room; bed, blanket and bowl.

HOPTON HEATH   SO3877

Hopton House

(01547) 530885 – www.shropshirebreakfast.co.uk
Hopton Heath, Craven Arms, Shropshire SY7 0QD

£120; 3 large, airy and very comfortable rooms. Friendly converted granary with several walks from the door in lovely countryside; a comfortable sun room with seating facing the garden and shelves of books and games, and a dining room with an open fire, delicious breakfasts (served until 10am) using local sausages, their own eggs and home-made fruit compotes; two places nearby for evening meals or you can bring in takeaways to eat in the dining room; resident dogs, Mitsi and Murphy. Well-behaved dogs (free-range chickens on site) allowed in one bedroom; towel and bowl on request, biscuits; £5 per stay.

HOPTON WAFERS
SO6376

Crown

(01299) 270372 – www.crownathopton.co.uk
Hopton Wafers, Cleobury Mortimer, Shropshire DY14 0NB

£125; 19 charming rooms, including 9 in modern annexe. Attractive stone inn in pleasant countryside with nearby walks; an open fire, beams and stonework in the interestingly furnished bar, three dining areas serving enjoyable food, decent house wines and well kept real ales, friendly efficient service and a streamside garden. Dogs allowed in all bedrooms and bar; £15 per stay.

IRONBRIDGE
SJ6703

Golden Ball

(01952) 432179 – www.goldenballironbridge.co.uk
New Bridge Road, Ironbridge, Telford, Shropshire TF8 7BA

£65; 4 bedrooms. Friendly inn tucked away in a steep little hamlet of other ancient buildings, with low beams, worn boards, red-cushioned pews, a dresser of decorative china, a woodburning stove, real ales, belgian bottled ales and a farm cider; tasty pubby food and good breakfasts; a pretty fairy-lit pergola path leads to the door and a sheltered side courtyard has tables under parasols; you can walk down to the River Severn in the Ironbridge Gorge, and beyond – though it's pretty steep getting back up. Dogs allowed in one bedroom and bar; £10 per stay.

LUDLOW
SO5174

Church Inn

(01584) 872174 – www.thechurchinn.com
Buttercross, Ludlow, Shropshire SY8 1AW

£80; 8 simple rooms, including 3 with balconies and views. Characterful town-centre inn with cheerful landlord, an impressive ten real ales on handpump and three appealingly decorated areas with hops on heavy beams, banquettes in cosy alcoves and pews from the nearby church; a long central area has a winter fire, daily papers and old black and white local photos, and the civilised upstairs lounge bar has views of the church and surrounding countryside; straightforward, tasty food and good breakfasts. Dogs allowed in bedrooms and bar; treats.

LUDLOW
SO5074

Dinham Hall

(01584) 876464 – www.dinhamhall.co.uk
Dinham, Ludlow, Shropshire SY8 1EJ

£139; 13 individually decorated rooms, including 2 in cottage. Late 18th-c manor house in quiet walled gardens opposite the ruins of Ludlow Castle, with restful lounges, open fires and period furnishings, modern british cooking in the glass-roofed restaurant, good breakfasts in the Georgian morning room with Teme Valley views, friendly staff, and seats on pretty terraces; pool, sauna and treatment rooms at their nearby sister hotel. Dogs allowed in some bedrooms, but not in public areas; £15.

NORTON
SJ7200
Hundred House
(01952) 580240 – www.hundredhouse.co.uk
Bridgnorth Road, Norton, Bridgnorth, Shropshire TF11 9EE

£79; 9 colourful rooms with antiques, chandeliers and a swing hanging from the beams. Family-run mainly Georgian inn with quite a sophisticated feel, a neatly kept bar with old quarry-tiled floors, beamed ceilings, oak panelling and handsome fireplaces; hearty breakfasts, good pubby lunches and interesting evening meals using own-grown veg, fruit and herbs (50 different varieties), and friendly service; delightful gardens (dogs allowed here under control) and walks nearby in Ironbridge Gorge and along the Severn Way. Dogs allowed in all bedrooms and reception; £10.

RHYDYCROESAU
SJ2430
Pen-y-Dyffryn
(01691) 653700 – www.peny.co.uk
Rhydycroesau, Oswestry, Shropshire SY10 7JD

£74; 12 comfortable rooms, including 4 in coach house with patios. Handsome stone-built Georgian rectory in five acres with lovely views of the Shropshire and Welsh hills, log fires in two comfortable lounges, excellent modern food using the best local ingredients, delicious breakfasts, helpful staff and a relaxed friendly atmosphere; trout fishing, riding (shooting can be arranged) and 100-acre woodland next door for walks; resident spaniel, Phoebe. Closed mid December to mid January. Dogs allowed in all bedrooms and (before 6pm) in public areas; welcome pack with bowl, towel and treats.

SHREWSBURY
SJ4917
Albright Hussey
(01939) 290571 – www.albrighthussey.co.uk
Ellesmere Road, Broad Oak, Shrewsbury, Shropshire SY4 3AF

£120; 26 traditionally decorated rooms, including 4 suites. Fine moated medieval manor house, partly timber-framed and partly stone and brick, in four acres of landscaped gardens, with particularly good, interesting food in panelled formal restaurant with an open fire, comfortable sitting room and excellent service; walks from the door. Dogs allowed in all bedrooms, reception and lounge; £10.

WEM
SJ5430
Soulton Hall
(01939) 232786 – www.soultonhall.co.uk
Soulton, Wem, Shropshire SY4 5RS

£130; 8 large, comfortable rooms, some in carriage house and lodge; also self-catering. Red-brick Tudor manor house in the same family since 1556 and at the heart of a 500-acre working farm – plenty of walks here and nearby; charming, friendly owners, a relaxed atmosphere, a lounge, study and dining room with much genuine character, fine original features, antiques and open fires, and enjoyable, beautifully presented evening meals, generous breakfasts and afternoon teas using their own produce; resident german shepherd, Max. Dogs allowed in four bedrooms; not in public rooms; £10.

WREKIN   SJ6309

Buckatree Hall

(01952) 641821 – www.buckatreehallhotel.com
Wrekin, Telford, Shropshire TF6 5AL

£100; 62 well appointed rooms, several with own balconies and many with lake views. Extended former hunting lodge dating from 1820 in large wooded estate at the foot of the Wrekin, with a comfortable bar and lounge, dark red leather sofas and armchairs on carpet, enjoyable food in the plush Lakeside restaurant, and helpful attentive service. Dogs allowed in some bedrooms, bar and lounge; welcome pack with treats; £10.

WROCKWARDINE   SJ6212

Church Farm

(01952) 251927 – www.churchfarm-shropshire.co.uk
Wrockwardine, Telford, Shropshire TF6 5DG

£85; 5 individual, well equipped rooms, most ensuite. Recently redecorated Georgian farmhouse on very ancient site overlooking an attractive garden and church and surrounded by footpaths; a friendly, relaxed atmosphere, beams and a log fire in the lounge, and super breakfasts and good food using local seasonal produce in the traditionally furnished dining room; two resident dogs. Dogs allowed in all bedrooms, but not in breakfast room; £10 (£5 for subsequent nights).

Somerset

DOG FRIENDLY PUBS

ASHCOTT   ST4337
Ring o' Bells
(01458) 210232 – www.ringobells.com
High Street; pub well signed off A39 W of Street; TA7 9PZ

Friendly village pub with homely décor in several bars, separate restaurant, tasty bar food and changing local ales

As the RSPB reserve Ham Wall is nearby, this traditional 18th-c pub is a popular lunch spot for bird-watchers. It's been run for many years by the same family and the three main bars, on different levels, are all comfortable, with maroon plush-topped stools, cushioned mate's chairs and dark wooden pubby tables on patterned carpet, horsebrasses along the bressumer beam above a big stone fireplace and a growing collection of handbells; background music. Black Rock Pale and Flowerpots Bitter on handpump, eight wines by the glass and local farm cider. There's also a separate restaurant, a skittle alley/function room, and plenty of picnic-sets out on the terrace and in the garden.

Free house ~ Licensees John and Elaine Foreman and John Sharman ~ Real ale ~ Open 12-2.30, 7-11; 12-3, 7-10.30 Sun ~ Bar food 12-2, 7-10 ~ Restaurant ~ Children welcome ~ Dogs allowed in bar ~ Wi-fi

BABCARY   ST5628
Red Lion
(01458) 223230 – www.redlionbabcary.co.uk
Off A37 S of Shepton Mallett; 2 miles or so N of roundabout where A37 meets A303 and A372; TA11 7ED

Thatched pub with comfortable rambling rooms, interesting food and local beers and seats outside; bedrooms

Several distinct areas in this busy thatched inn work their way around the bar counter. To the left is a longish room with dark red walls, a squashy leather sofa and two winged armchairs around a low table by an open fire – plus a few well spaced tables and captain's chairs. There are elegant rustic wall lights, clay pipes in a display cabinet, local papers or magazines to read and board games. A more dimly lit public bar with lovely dark flagstones has a high-backed old settle and other more straightforward chairs; table skittles and background music. In the good-sized dining room a big stone lion's head sits on a plinth above a large open fire, and tables and chairs are set on polished boards. There's Lyme Regis Cobb Bitter, Otter

Ale and Teignworthy Reel Ale on handpump, 18 wines by the glass and cocktails. The Den, set in a pretty courtyard, has light modern furnishings, a summer wood-fired pizza oven and a brasserie-style menu, and doubles as a party, wedding and conference venue. The long informal garden has a play area and plenty of seats. The pub is handy for the Fleet Air Arm Museum at Yeovilton, the Haynes Motor Museum in Sparkford and for shopping at Clarks Village in Street. Wheelchair access.

Free house ~ Licensee Charles Garrard ~ Real ale ~ Open 12-3, 6-midnight ~ Bar food 12-2.30, 6.30-9.30 (9 Sun) ~ Restaurant ~ Children welcome ~ Dogs allowed in bar ~ Wi-fi ~ Bedrooms: £110

BATH ST7465

Chequers

(01225) 360017 – www.thechequersbath.com
Rivers Street; BA1 2QA

City-centre pub with friendly staff, pretty upstairs restaurant and enjoyable food and beers

Located in the centre of Bath, this bustling 19th-c pub is a popular spot. The bar has velvet-cushioned wall pews, chapel, farmhouse and kitchen chairs around all sorts of tables (each set with flowers) on parquet flooring, wedgwood blue paintwork and some fine plasterwork and a coal-effect gas fire in a white-painted fireplace. Bath Gem and Butcombe Bitter on handpump and several wines by the glass. The recently refurbished and attractive little restaurant upstairs has leather-seated chapel chairs and wall pews around candlelit tables, a wooden floor and a huge window into the kitchen. In warm weather there are picnic-sets under awnings on the pavement.

Bath Pub Company ~ Lease Joe Cussens ~ Real ale ~ No credit cards ~ Open 12-11 ~ Bar food 6-9.30 Mon-Fri; 12-2, 6-10 Sat; 12-4, 6-9 Sun ~ Restaurant ~ Children welcome ~ Dogs allowed in bar ~ Wi-fi

BATH ST7467

Hare & Hounds

(01225) 482682 – www.hareandhoundsbath.com
Lansdown Road, Lansdown Hill; BA1 5TJ

Lovely views from back terrace with plenty of seating, relaxed bar areas, real ales, nice food (including breakfast) and helpful staff

One of the big pluses here is the wonderful extended view down over villages and fields from windows in the bar and from seats and tables on the decked back terrace; if you head down some steps from the terrace there's a garden with more seats and tables. The atmosphere in the single long bar is relaxed and friendly, helped along by cheerful staff. There are chapel chairs and long cushioned wall settles around pale wood-topped tables on bare boards, minimal decoration on pale walls above a blue-grey dado and an attractively carved counter where they serve a beer named for the pub (from Caledonian), Butcombe Bitter and Theakstons Vanilla Stout on handpump and several wines by the glass; background music. There's a bronze hare and hound at one end of the mantelpiece over a log fire, and a big mirror above. A little side conservatory is similarly furnished, with dark slate flagstones.

Bath Pub Company ~ Lease Joe Cussens ~ Real ale ~ Open 8.30am-11pm (10.30pm Sun) ~ Bar food 8.30-11, 12-3, 5.30-9; 8.30-11, 12-8 Sun ~ Children welcome ~ Dogs welcome ~ Wi-fi

BATH   ST7465
Marlborough
(01225) 423731 – www.marlborough-tavern.com
35 Marlborough Buildings/Weston Road; BA1 2LY

Open all day and with plenty of customers; candles, fresh flowers, cheerful staff and good food

This easy-going place is very central, and usefully open every day for coffee from 8am (9am weekends). The U-shaped bar is always busy and the cheerful staff keep things buzzing along nicely. There are bare boards throughout, church candles in sizeable jars on windowsills and on the mantelpiece above a fireplace strung with fairy lights and plenty of tea-lights; each table has a single flower in a vase. Seating ranges from thick button-back wall seats to chapel, kitchen and high-backed cushioned dining chairs; background music. Chunky bar stools line the counter, where they serve Butcombe Bitter and guests such as Box Steam Piston Broke and Butcombe Moxee IPA on handpump and several wines by the glass. The little courtyard side garden is a suntrap in summer and there are benches and chairs around tables among the various plantings.

Free house ~ Licensees Joe Cussens and Justin Sleath ~ Real ale ~ Open 9am-11pm ~ Bar food 12-2.30 (3 Sat), 6-9.30; 12-7 Sun ~ Children welcome ~ Dogs welcome ~ Wi-fi

BATH   ST7565
Star
(01225) 425072 – www.abbeyales.co.uk/www.star-inn-bath.co.uk
Vineyards; The Paragon (A4), junction with Guinea Lane; BA1 5NA

Quietly chatty and unchanging old town local, the brewery tap for Abbey Ales

In quiet steep streets of undeniably handsome if well worn stone terraces, yet handy for the main shopping area, this old pub gives a strong sense of the past. The four small linked rooms have many original features such as traditional wall benches (one is known as Death Row), panelling, dim lighting and open fires. Abbey Bellringer plus guests such as Abbey Black Friar, Banfield Tunnel Vision, Bass and St Austell Proper Job tapped from the cask, several wines by the glass, 30 malt whiskies and Cheddar Valley cider; darts, shove-ha'penny, cribbage and board games – and complimentary snuff. Food consists of filled rolls. The place gets particularly busy at weekends and is around five minutes' walk from the city centre.

Punch ~ Lease Paul Waters and Alan Morgan ~ Real ale ~ Open 12-2.30, 5.30-midnight; noon-1am Fri, Sat; 12-midnight Sun ~ Bar food ~ Children welcome ~ Dogs welcome ~ Wi-fi ~ Singing session Sun evening, irish folk Fri evening, quiz first Sun of month

BISHOPSWOOD   ST2512
Candlelight
(01460) 234476 – www.candlelight-inn.co.uk
Off A303/B3170 S of Taunton; TA20 3RS

Friendly, hard-working licensees in neat dining pub with real ales and farm cider, enjoyable imaginative food and seats in the garden

Always friendly thanks to the personable landlord at the helm, this is a gently civilised pub that's handy for the A303. The neatly kept, more or less open-plan rooms are separated into different areas by standing stone pillars and open doorways. The beamed bar has high chairs by the counter where they serve a fine range of drinks: Bass and Otter Bitter with guests such as Teignworthy Gun Dog and Yeovil Star Gazer tapped from the cask, eight wines by the glass, a couple of farm ciders and winter drinks such as hot Pimms, whisky toddies and hot chocolate. Also, captain's chairs, pews and cushioned window seats around a mix of wooden tables on sanded floorboards, and a small ornate fireplace. To the left is a comfortable area with a button-back sofa beside a big woodburner, wheelback chairs and cushioned settles around wooden tables set for dining, with country pictures, photos, a hunting horn and bugles on the granite walls; background music and shove-ha'penny. On the other side of the bar is a similarly furnished dining room. Outside, a decked area has picnic-sets and a neatly landscaped garden has a paved path winding through low walls set with plants.

Free house ~ Licensees Tom Warren and Debbie Lush ~ Real ale ~ Open 12-2.30 (3 Sat), 6-11; 12-11 Sun; closed Mon, first week Nov ~ Bar food 12-2, 7-9; 12-2.30, 7-9.30 Fri, Sat ~ Well behaved children welcome away from bar area ~ Dogs allowed in bar ~ Wi-fi

CHARLTON HORETHORNE   ST6623

Kings Arms

(01963) 220281 – www.thekingsarms.co.uk
B3145 Wincanton–Sherborne; DT9 4NL

Bustling inn with relaxed bars and more formal restaurant, good ales and wines and enjoyable food; bedrooms

The hands-on landlord here remains as enthusiastic as ever and his staff are friendly and efficient. It's a smart place and the main bar has an appealing assortment of local art (all for sale) on dark mulberry or cream walls, nice old carved wooden dining chairs and pine pews around a mix of tables, a slate floor and a woodburning stove. Leading off is a cosy room with sofas and newspapers on low tables. Butcombe Bitter, Wadworths 6X and a guest beer on handpump are served from the rather fine granite bar counter; they also keep 14 wines by the glass, nine malt whiskies and local farm cider. To the left of the main door is an informal dining room with Jacobean-style chairs and tables on a pale wooden floor and more local artwork. The back restaurant (past the open kitchen which is fun to peek into) has decorative wood and glass mirrors, wicker or black leather high-backed dining chairs around chunky, polished, pale wooden tables on coir carpeting, and handsome striped curtains. The attractive courtyard at the back of the inn has chrome and wicker chairs around teak tables under green parasols; a smokers' shelter overlooks a croquet lawn.

Free house ~ Licensee Tony Lethbridge ~ Real ale ~ Open 7am-11pm ~ Bar food 12-2.30, 7-9.30; 12-2.30, 7-10 Fri, Sat; 12-2.30, 7-9 Sun ~ Restaurant ~ Children welcome ~ Dogs allowed in bar ~ Wi-fi ~ Bedrooms: £135

CHURCHILL   ST4459

Crown

(01934) 852995
The Batch; in village, turn off A368 into Skinners Lane at Nelson Arms; BS25 5PP

Unchanging small cottage with friendly customers and staff, super range of real ales and homely lunchtime food

For those keen on more modern comforts, this rural cottage might not appeal. It's an untouched, simple old pub and for lovers of the unspoilt – it's perfect.

There are seven real ales tapped from the cask, including Bath Gem, Butcombe Bitter, Otter Bitter, Palmers IPA, RCH IPA, St Austell Tribute and a quickly changing guest; several wines by the glass and five local ciders too. The small and rather local-feeling stone-floored and cross-beamed room on the right has a big log fire in a large stone fireplace, chatty and friendly customers and steps that lead up to another seating area. The left-hand room – with a slate floor, window seats and a log burner – leads through to the Snug. There's no noise from music or games (except perhaps dominoes). The outside lavatories are basic. There are garden tables at the front, more seats on the back lawn and hill views; the Mendip morris men visit in summer and some of the best walking on the Mendips is nearby. There isn't a pub sign outside, but no one seems to have a problem finding the place.

Free house ~ Licensee Brian Clements ~ Real ale ~ No credit cards ~ Open 11-11; 12-10.30 Sun ~ Bar food 12-2.30 ~ Children welcome away from bar ~ Dogs allowed in bar ~ Wi-fi

CLAPTON-IN-GORDANO   ST4773
Black Horse
(01275) 842105 – www.thekicker.co.uk
4 miles from M5 junction 19; A369 towards Portishead, then B3124 towards Clevedon; in North Weston opposite school, turn left signposted Clapton, then in village take second right, may be signed 'Clevedon, Clapton Wick'; BS20 7RH

Unpretentious old pub with lots of cheerful customers, friendly service, real ales, cider and simple lunchtime food; pretty garden

Customers of all ages enjoy this old-fashioned 14th-c tavern where, thankfully, nothing changes. The partly flagstoned, partly red-tiled main room has winged settles and built-in wall benches around narrow, dark wooden tables, window seats, a big log fire with stirrups and bits on the mantelbeam, and amusing cartoons and photographs of the pub. A window in an inner snug retains metal bars from the days when this room was the petty sessions gaol; also, high-backed settles – one with a marvellous carved and canopied creature, another with an art nouveau copper insert reading 'East, West, Hame's Best' – lots of mugs hanging from black beams and numerous small prints and photographs. A simply furnished room is the only place that families are allowed; background music. Bath Gem, Butcombe Bitter, Courage Best, Exmoor Gold and Otter Bitter on handpump or tapped from the cask, six wines by the glass and three farm ciders. There are rustic tables and benches in the garden, with more to one side of the car park – the summer flowers are quite a sight. Paths from the pub lead up Naish Hill or to Cadbury Camp (National Trust) and there's access to local cycle routes.

Enterprise ~ Lease Nicholas Evans ~ Real ale ~ Open 11-11; 12-9.30 Sun ~ Bar food 12-2.30; not evenings or Sun ~ Children in family room only ~ Dogs welcome ~ Wi-fi

CROSCOMBE   ST5844
George
(01749) 342306 – www.thegeorgeinn.co.uk
Long Street (A371 Wells–Shepton Mallet); BA5 3QH

Warmly welcoming, family-run coaching inn with charming canadian landlord, enjoyable food, good local beers and attractive garden; bedrooms

As well as four farm ciders, they keep King George the Thirst (from Blindmans), Butcombe Rare Breed, Cotleigh Osprey and Yeovil Summerset on handpump or tapped from the cask, ten wines by the glass and home-made elderflower cordial. It's a very well run and genuinely friendly inn and the main bar has a good mix of locals and visitors, stripped stone, dark wooden tables and chairs and more comfortable seats, a settle by one of the log fires in the inglenook fireplaces, and the family's grandfather clock; a snug area has a woodburning stove. The attractive dining room has more stripped stone, local artwork and family photographs on burgundy walls and high-backed cushioned dining chairs around a mix of tables. The back bar has canadian timber and a pew reclaimed from the local church, and there's a family room with games and books for children. Darts, a skittle alley, board games, shove-ha'penny and a canadian wooden table game called crokinole. The pub dog Tessa has been joined by Pixy the labrador/spaniel cross. The attractive, sizeable garden has seats on a heated and covered terrace, flower borders, a grassed area, a wood-fired pizza oven (used on Fridays) and chickens; children's swings.

Free house ~ Licensees Peter and Veryan Graham ~ Real ale ~ Open 10-3, 6-11; 11-11 Sat, Sun ~ Bar food 12-2.30, 6-9; 12-8 Sun ~ Restaurant ~ Children welcome ~ Dogs allowed in bar ~ Wi-fi ~ Bedrooms: £80

DULVERTON   SS9127

Woods

(01398) 324007 – www.woodsdulverton.co.uk
Bank Square; TA22 9BU

Smartly informal place with exceptional wines, real ales, first rate food and a good mix of customers

This place continues to be highly praised by its customers. There are satisfied diners to the right and happy lunchtime drinkers nursing their pints to the left; as the pub is on the edge of Exmoor, there are plenty of good sporting prints on salmon pink walls, antlers and other hunting trophies, stuffed birds and a couple of salmon rods. By the bar counter are bare boards, daily papers, tables partly separated by stable-style timbering and masonry dividers, and (on the right) a carpeted area with a woodburning stove in a big fireplace; maybe unobjectionable background music. The marvellous drinks choice includes Otter Ale and St Austell Cornish Best and Proper Job tapped from the cask, farm cider, many sherries and some unusual spirits – but it's the stunning wine list that draws the most attention. Mr Groves, the landlord, reckons he could put 1,000 different wines up on the bar and will open any of them (with a value of up to £100) for just a glass. He is there every night and will happily chat to tables of restaurant customers about any wines they might be interested in. Big windows look on to the quiet town centre (there's also a couple of metal tables on the pavement) and a small suntrap back courtyard has a few picnic-sets.

Free house ~ Licensee Patrick Groves ~ Real ale ~ Open 12-3, 6-11.30; 12-4, 7-11.30 Sun ~ Bar food 12-2, 6 (7 Sun)-9.30 ~ Restaurant ~ Children welcome ~ Dogs welcome ~ Wi-fi

HINTON ST GEORGE   ST4212

Lord Poulett Arms

(01460) 73149 – www.lordpoulettarms.com
Off A30 W of Crewkerne and off Merriott road (declassified – former A356, off B3165) N of Crewkerne; TA17 8SE

Thatched 17th-c stone inn with top class food, good choice of drinks and pretty garden; attractive bedrooms

The several attractive and cosy linked bar areas in this civilised inn have hop-draped beams, walls made of honey-coloured stone or painted in bold Farrow & Ball colours, and rugs on bare boards or flagstones; also, open fires (one in an inglenook, another in a raised fireplace that separates two rooms), antique brass candelabra, fresh flowers and candles, and some lovely old farmhouse, windsor and ladderback chairs around fine oak or elm tables. Branscombe Vale Bitter, Otter Ale and St Austell Trelawny on handpump, 13 wines by the glass, home-made cordial, some interesting spirits and local bottled cider and perry; background music, chess and backgammon. The pub cat is called Honey. Outside, beneath a wisteria-clad pergola, are white metalwork tables and chairs in a mediterranean-style, lavender-edged gravelled area, and picnic-sets in a wild flower meadow; boules. This is a peaceful and attractive village with nice surrounding walks.

Free house ~ Licensees Steve Hill and Michelle Paynton ~ Real ale ~ Open 12-11 ~ Bar food 12-2.30, 6.30-9.15; 12-3, 7-9.15 Sun ~ Children welcome ~ Dogs allowed in bar ~ Wi-fi ~ Live music summer Sun afternoons ~ Bedrooms: £95

HUISH EPISCOPI   ST4326
Rose & Crown
(01458) 250494
Off A372 E of Langport; TA10 9QT

17th-c pub with local cider and real ales, simple food and a friendly welcome from long-serving licensees

The same friendly family have run this unspoilt thatched inn for more than 146 years; it's known locally as 'Eli's' after the licensees' grandfather. There's no bar as such, just a central flagstoned still room where drinks are served: Teignworthy Reel Ale and a couple of guests such as Glastonbury Mystery Tor and Hop Back Summer Lightning, local farm cider and Somerset cider brandy. The casual little front parlours, with their unusual pointed-arch windows, have family photographs, books, cribbage, dominoes, shove-ha'penny and bagatelle and attract a good mix of both locals and visitors. A much more orthodox big back extension has pool, a games machine and a juke box. There are plenty of seats and tables in the extensive outdoor area and two lawns – one is enclosed and has a children's play area; you can camp (by arrangement to pub customers) on the adjoining paddock. There's also a separate skittle alley, a large car park, morris men (in summer) and fine nearby river walks; the site of the Battle of Langport (1645) is not far.

Free house ~ Licensees Maureen Pittard, Stephen Pittard and Patricia O'Malley ~ Real ale ~ No credit cards ~ Open 11.30-2.30, 5.30-11; 11.30-11.30 Fri, Sat; 12-10.30 Sun ~ Bar food 12-2, 5.30-7.30; not Sun evening ~ Children welcome ~ Dogs welcome ~ Wi-fi ~ Live music last Thurs of month, folk singaround third Sat of month (except June-Aug)

MELLS   ST7249
Talbot
(01373) 812254 – www.talbotinn.com
W of Frome, off A362 or A361; BA11 3PN

Carefully refurbished and interesting old coaching inn, real ales and good wines, inventive food and seats in courtyard; lovely bedrooms

The bustling candlelit bar is nicely informal with various wooden tables and chairs on big quarry tiles, a woodburning stove in a stone fireplace, and stools (much used by locals) against the counter where friendly, helpful staff serve a beer named for the pub (from Keystone), Butcombe Bitter and a couple of guests such as Butcombe Big IPA and Hop Back Citra on handpump, several good wines by the glass and a farm cider. The two interconnected dining rooms have brass-studded leather chairs around wooden tables, a log fire with candles in fine clay cups on the mantelpiece above and lots of coaching prints on the walls;

quiet background music and board games. There's a mediterranean air to the courtyard with its pale green metalwork chairs and tables. Off here, in separate buildings, are the enjoyable, rustic-feeling sitting room with sofas, chairs and tables, smart magazines, a huge mural and vast glass bottles (free films or popular TV programmes are shown here on Sunday evenings), and the grill room, where food is cooked simply on a big open fire overlooked by 18th-c portraits. Until the dissolution of the monasteries in the early 16th c, this village was owned by Glastonbury Abbey – do visit the lovely church where Siegfried Sassoon is buried; the walled gardens opposite the inn are very pretty.

Free house ~ Licensee Matt Greenlees ~ Real ale ~ Open 8am-11pm ~ Bar food 12-3, 6-9.30 ~ Restaurant ~ Children welcome ~ Dogs welcome ~ Wi-fi ~ Bedrooms: £100

MIDFORD   ST7660
Hope & Anchor
(01225) 832296 – www.hopeandanchormidford.co.uk
Bath Road (B3110); BA2 7DD

Welcoming old pub with popular food and several real ales

Parts of this friendly place date from the 17th c and as it's at the heart of the Cam Valley it makes a fine spot for a lunch break. Open-plan and neatly kept by the long-serving licensees, it has a civilised bar plus a heavy-beamed restaurant with a long cushioned settle against red-patterned wallpaper, a mix of dark wooden dining chairs and tables on flagstones and a woodburning stove. The back conservatory is modern, stylish and popular with families. Otter Amber, Sharps Doom Bar and a guest on handpump, 11 wines by the glass and a farm cider are served by courteous staff. Outside, there are seats on the sheltered back terrace which has an upper tier. The pub is on the Colliers Way cycling/walking path and near walks on the disused Somerset & Dorset Railway.

Free house ~ Licensee Richard Smolarek ~ Real ale ~ Open 11.30-3, 6-11; 11.30-11 Sat, Sun ~ Bar food 12-2 (3 weekends), 6-9.30 ~ Restaurant ~ Children welcome ~ Dogs allowed in bar ~ Wi-fi

MILVERTON   ST1225
Globe
(01823) 400534 – www.theglobemilverton.co.uk
Fore Street; TA4 1JX

Bustling and friendly inn with a welcome for all, good ales, quite a choice of tasty seasonal food and seats outside; bedrooms

Although locals do pop in for a pint of Otter Bitter, Quantock Ale or a guest beer on handpump served by cheerful, helpful staff, most customers are here for the very good food. This is a handsome former coaching inn and the opened-up rooms have solid rustic tables surrounded by an attractive mix of wooden or high-backed black leather chairs, artwork on pale-painted walls above a red dado, and a big gilt-edged mirror above a woodburning stove in an ornate fireplace; background music and board games. Bar chairs line the counter where they keep ten wines by the glass and local farm cider. The sheltered outside terrace has raffia-style chairs and tables and cushioned wall seating under parasols.

Free house ~ Licensees Mark and Adele Tarry ~ Real ale ~ Open 12-3, 6-11 (11.30 Sat); 12-3 Sun; closed Sunday evening, Mon lunchtime ~ Bar food 12-2, 6.30-9 ~ Restaurant ~ Children welcome ~ Dogs allowed in bar ~ Wi-fi ~ Bedrooms: £65

MONKSILVER

ST0737

Notley Arms

(01984) 656095 – www.notleyarmsinn.co.uk
B3188; TA4 4JB

Bustling friendly pub with a good mix of regulars and visitors, enjoyable food and drink, and seats in streamside garden; bedrooms

Very well run by friendly licensees, this pub is in a lovely village on the edge of Exmoor National Park. Each of the open-plan bar rooms has its own atmosphere: two open fires plus two woodburning stoves (the one in the lounge is fronted by chesterfield sofas), cushioned window seats and settles, an appealing collection of old dining chairs around mixed wooden tables on slate tiles or flagstones, original paintings on cream walls and panelling, and fresh flowers, church candles and big stone bottles; background music. Tractor seats line the bar where they keep Exmoor Ale, St Austell Tribute and Sleaford Pleasant Pheasant on handpump, 30 wines by the glass, 20 malt whiskies and farm cider; staff are courteous and helpful. At the bottom of the neat garden is a clear-running stream and plenty of picnic-sets on grass; a heated, circular wooden pavilion is just right for a party of 12; boules.

Free house ~ Licensees Simon and Caroline Murphy ~ Real ale ~ Open 8am-11pm ~ Bar food 12-2, 6-9 ~ Restaurant ~ Children welcome ~ Dogs welcome ~ Wi-fi ~ Bedrooms: £64

MONKTON COMBE

ST7761

Wheelwrights Arms

(01225) 722287 – www.wheelwrightsarms.co.uk
Just off A36 S of Bath; Church Cottages; BA2 7HB

18th-c stone pub with cheerful customers, helpful landlord and staff, good food and seats outside; comfortable bedrooms

Bath is nearby and the peaceful village here is surrounded by picturesque hills and valleys, so it's not surprising that this friendly place gets booked up pretty quickly. At one end of the bar-dining room is an open fire in a raised fireplace with logs piled on either side, cushioned and wood-planked built-in wall seats, rush-seated or cushioned high-backed dining chairs around tables (each set with a small lamp), parquet flooring or carpet, and old photographs and oil paintings (the one above the fireplace of a dog is particularly nice). The middle room has some pretty frieze work, a high shelf of wooden wader birds and stools against the green-painted counter where they keep Butcombe Bitter and Otter Bitter on handpump, 15 wines by the glass and farm cider; background jazz and board games. A small end room is just right for a group. The gravelled terraces have wood and metal tables and chairs and picnic-sets.

Free house ~ Licensee David Munn ~ Real ale ~ Open 8am-11pm ~ Bar food 12-2, 6-9.30 ~ Children welcome ~ Dogs allowed in bar ~ Wi-fi ~ Bedrooms: £160

ODCOMBE

ST5015

Masons Arms

(01935) 862591 – www.masonsarmsodcombe.co.uk
Off A3088 or A30 just W of Yeovil; Lower Odcombe; BA22 8TX

Own-brew beers and tasty food in pretty thatched cottage; bedrooms

This is a popular place with own-brew beers served by friendly staff. The simple little bar has joists and a couple of standing timbers, a mix of cushioned dining chairs around all sorts of tables on cream and blue patterned carpet, and a couple of tub chairs and a table in the former inglenook fireplace. Up a step is a similar area, while more steps lead down to a dining room with a squashy brown sofa and a couple of cushioned dining chairs in front of a woodburning stove; the sandstone walls are hung with black and white local photographs and country prints. Their own ales are Odcombe No.1, Roly Poly and seasonal beers on handpump, they make their own sloe and elderflower cordials, have 11 wines by the glass and serve farm cider. There's a thatched smokers' shelter and picnic-sets in the garden, plus a vegetable patch and chicken coop and a campsite.

Own brew ~ Licensees Drew Read and Paula Tennyson ~ Real ale ~ Open 8am-3pm, 6-midnight ~ Bar food 12-2, 6.30-9.30 ~ Children welcome ~ Dogs welcome ~ Wi-fi ~ Bedrooms: £90

PITNEY   ST4527

Halfway House

(01458) 252513 – www.thehalfwayhouse.co.uk
Just off B3153 W of Somerton; TA10 9AB

Bustling, friendly local with nine real ales, local ciders and good simple food

An unpretentious village local with a fine range of up to ten regularly changing beers. The atmosphere is chatty and easy-going and there's a good cross-section of cheerful customers in the three old-fashioned rooms which have communal tables, roaring log fires and a homely feel underlined by a profusion of books, maps and newspapers. Tapped from the cask, the ales might include Bays Gold, Branscombe Vale Summa This, Butcombe Rare Breed, Dark Star American Pale Ale, Exmoor Gold, Hop Back Summer Lightning, Otter Bright, Teignworthy Reel Ale and Whitstable East India Pale Ale; also, four farm ciders, a dozen malt whiskies and several wines by the glass; board games. There are tables outside.

Free house ~ Licensee Mark Phillips ~ Real ale ~ Open 11.30-3, 4.30-11; 11.30-3, 4.30-midnight Fri, Sat; 12-11 Sun ~ Bar food 12-2.30, 7-9.30; 1-5 Sun ~ Children welcome ~ Dogs welcome ~ Wi-fi

PRIDDY   ST5250

Queen Victoria

(01749) 676385 – www.thequeenvicpriddy.co.uk
Village signed off B3135; Pelting Drove; BA5 3BA

Stone-built country pub with open fires and woodburners, friendly atmosphere, real ales and honest food; seats outside

There's plenty of room for all here, both inside and out; it's very popular locally and also with cyclists and walkers – and their dogs. The various dimly lit rooms and alcoves have a lot of character and plenty of original features, and customers are chatty and cheerful. One room leading off the main bar has a log fire in a big old stone fireplace with a huge cauldron to one side. There are flagstoned or slate floors, bare stone walls (the smarter dining room is half panelled and half painted), horse tack, farm tools and photos of Queen Victoria. Furniture is traditional: cushioned wall settles, farmhouse and other solid chairs around all manner of wooden tables, a nice old pew beside a screen settle making a cosy alcove, and high chairs next to the bar counter where they serve Butcombe Bitter and Rare Breed and Fullers London Pride on handpump, two farm ciders, eight malt whiskies and nine wines by the glass. There are seats in the front courtyard and more across the lane where there's also a children's playground. Wheelchair access.

Butcombe ~ Tenant Mark Walton ~ Real ale ~ Open 12-11; 12-10.30 Sun ~ Bar food 12-2, 6-9 (all day end May-Sept); 12-9 Sat; 12-8 Sun ~ Children welcome ~ Dogs welcome ~ Wi-fi ~ Live folk second Mon of month; folk festival July

STANTON WICK   ST6162
Carpenters Arms
(01761) 490202 – www.the-carpenters-arms.co.uk
Village signposted off A368, just W of junction with A37 S of Bristol; BS39 4BX

Bustling, friendly dining pub on country lane with enjoyable food, helpful staff and fine choice of drinks; nice bedrooms

This attractive little stone pub is in peaceful countryside with good nearby walks. You can be sure of a warm welcome from the landlord and his attentive staff. Coopers Parlour on the right has a couple of beams, seats around heavy tables on a tartan carpet and attractive curtains; in the angle between here and the bar area is a wide woodburning stove in an opened-through fireplace. The bar has wall settles with cushions, stripped-stone walls and a big log fire in an inglenook. There's also a snug inner room (brightened by mirrors in arched recesses) and a restaurant with leather sofas, easy chairs and a lounge area at one end. Bath Gem, Butcombe Bitter and Sharps Doom Bar on handpump, ten wines by the glass (and some interesting bin ends) and several malt whiskies; TV in the snug. There are picnic-sets on the front terrace along with pretty flower beds, hanging baskets and tubs.

Buccaneer Holdings ~ Manager Simon Pledge ~ Real ale ~ Open 11-11; 12-10.30 Sun ~ Bar food 12-2.30, 6-9.30 (10 Fri, Sat); 12-9 Sun ~ Restaurant ~ Children welcome ~ Dogs allowed in bar ~ Wi-fi ~ Bedrooms: £110

WEDMORE   ST4348
Swan
(01934) 710337 – www.theswanwedmore.com
Cheddar Road, opposite Church Street; BS28 4EQ

Bustling place with a friendly, informal atmosphere, lots of customers, efficient service and tasty food; bedrooms

There's a lively, buoyant atmosphere here as customers drop in and out all day – for breakfasts, morning coffee and afternoon tea and lunchtime and evening bar food. Mirrors dotted about give the open-plan layout a feeling of even more space and the main bar has all sorts of wooden tables and chairs on floorboards, a wall seat with attractive scatter cushions, a woodburning stove, suede stools against the panelled counter and a rustic central table with daily papers; background music. Bath Gem, Cheddar Potholer, Otter Bitter and a guest beer on handpump, 20 wines by the glass and two farm ciders are served by quick, friendly staff. At one end of the room, a step leads down to an area with rugs on huge flagstones, a leather chesterfield, armchairs and brass-studded leather chairs, then down another step to more sofas and armchairs. The airy dining room has attractive high-backed chairs, tables set with candles in glass jars and another woodburner. There are plenty of seats and tables outside on the terrace and lawn, and the metal furniture among flowering tubs at the front of the building gives a continental feel.

Free house ~ Licensee Natalie Zvonek-Little ~ Real ale ~ Open 9am-11pm (10.30 Sun) ~ Bar food 9am-10pm; snacks in afternoon ~ Restaurant ~ Children welcome ~ Dogs allowed in bar ~ Wi-fi ~ Bedrooms: £100

WRAXALL   ST4971

Battleaxes

(01275) 857473 – www.flatcappers.co.uk
Bristol Road B3130, E of Nailsea; BS48 1LQ

Bustling pub with relaxed dining and drinking areas, helpful staff and good food; big bedrooms with contemporary bathrooms

The spacious interior in this interesting stone-built Victorian pub is split into separate areas: polished floorboards or flagstones, portraits and pictures on walls above painted and panelled dados, mirrors on boldly patterned wallpaper, fresh flowers and house plants, books on windowsills and church candles. The bar has leather-topped stools against the counter where they keep a beer named for the pub (from Three Castles), Butcombe Bitter and a guest ale on handpump and several wines by the glass; background music. Throughout there are long pews with scatter cushions, church chairs and a medley of other wooden dining chairs around chunky tables and groups of leather armchairs; it's all very easy-going. There are picnic-sets outside. Tyntesfield (National Trust) is nearby. Wheelchair access using ramps.

Flatcappers ~ Manager Ben Paxton ~ Real ale ~ Open 8am-11pm ~ Bar food 8am-10pm (9pm Sun) ~ Children welcome ~ Dogs allowed in bar ~ Wi-fi ~ Bedrooms: £80

WRINGTON   ST4762

Plough

(01934) 862871 – www.theploughatwrington.co.uk
2.5 miles off A370 Bristol–Weston, from bottom of Rhodiate Hill; BS40 5QA

Welcoming pub with bustling bar and two dining rooms, appealing food, well kept beer and seats outside

As this neatly kept and well run village pub is so popular, it's best to book a table in advance. The bar is chatty and convivial, with locals perched on stools against the counter where they keep Butcombe Bitter (the brewery is in the village), Black Sheep and Youngs Special on handpump and 18 wines by the glass served by friendly and efficient staff. The two dining rooms (the one at the back has plenty of big windows overlooking the gazebo and garden) have open doorways and throughout you'll find (three) winter fires, slate or wooden floors, beams and standing timbers, plenty of pictures on the planked, red or yellow walls and all manner of high-backed leather or wooden dining or farmhouse chairs around tables of many sizes. Also, fresh flowers, table skittles and a chest of games. There are picnic-sets at the front and on the back grass; boules. They hold a farmers' market on the second Friday of the month.

Youngs ~ Tenant Jason Read ~ Real ale ~ Open 12-3, 5-11; 12-midnight Fri, Sat; 12-11 Sun ~ Bar food 12-2.30, 6-9.30; 12-5 Sun ~ Restaurant ~ Children welcome ~ Dogs welcome ~ Wi-fi

DOG FRIENDLY HOTELS, INNS AND B&Bs

ALLERFORD   SS9047

West Lynch Farm

(01643) 862816 – www.exmoorfalconry.co.uk
West Lynch, Allerford, Somerset TA24 8HJ

£80; 2 rooms with country views. Listed 15th-c National Trust farmhouse in six acres of landscaped gardens and paddocks on the edge of Exmoor – no walking in the grounds but lots in surrounding countryside; plenty of original features, antiques and persian rugs, homely lounge/dining room with woodburning stove, super breakfasts with their own honey and home-made marmalade; lots of animals and also a small bird of prey centre with falconry tuition and hawking all year and horse-riding. Dogs allowed in bedrooms; towel, bowl and cover for bed on request; £5.

ASHILL   ST3016

Square & Compass

(01823) 480467 – www.squareandcompasspub.com
Windmill Hill, Ashill, Ilminster, Somerset TA19 9NX

£95; 8 spacious, comfortable rooms. Friendly simple pub tucked away in the Blackdown Hills with long-serving owners, chatty customers in little beamed bar, upholstered window seats taking in the fine country views, heavy hand-made furniture, an open winter fire, maybe the pub cat, Lily, good ales and wines and well liked, generously served food; seats on a glass-covered walled terrace and in the garden. Dogs allowed in all bedrooms and anywhere (on lead) in the pub.

BABINGTON   ST7051

Babington House

(01373) 812266 – www.babingtonhouse.co.uk
Babington, Frome, Somerset BA11 3RW

From £330; 33 individually decorated, well equipped contemporary rooms, including 12 in coach house, 5 in stable block, 3 in lodge, 2 in cabin. Georgian mansion (part of the Soho House members' club) in 18 acres of lovely grounds with lake, cricket and football pitches, indoor and outdoor swimming pools, walled kitchen garden, tennis courts and croquet; unusually decorated lounges, comfortable sofas and an open fire in the bar, a library with books and games, a snooker room, a wide range of modern food in the Deli Bar, Log Room and Orangery, a particularly relaxed, informal atmosphere and helpful, friendly young staff; free cinema with films five days a week and Cowshed spa with steam room, sauna, gym and treatments. Dogs allowed in ground-floor coach house rooms, stable block, lodge and cabin; bed and bowl.

BARWICK   ST5613

Little Barwick House

(01935) 423902 – www.littlebarwickhouse.co.uk
Barwick, Yeovil, Somerset BA22 9TD

£121; 7 attractive rooms. Georgian dower house in three-plus acres, now a carefully run restaurant-with-rooms; two cosy sitting rooms with log fires, an elegant restaurant with imaginative food using local produce, a thoughtful wine list, super breakfasts, nice afternoon teas, a relaxed atmosphere and particularly good service; resident dog, Ellie, plus three cats and two horses; walks in grounds and nearby. Closed four weeks December/January. Dogs allowed in all bedrooms and sitting rooms, but not restaurant; £15 per stay.

BATH   ST7365

Bath Priory Hotel

(01225) 331922 – www.thebathpriory.co.uk
Weston Road, Bath, Somerset BA1 2XT

£350; 33 individually decorated rooms. Just a short stroll from the city centre, this Georgian hotel has the feeling of a country house in four acres of gardens; the elegant lounge and sitting room are full of antiques, chandeliers, oil paintings and fresh flowers, with french windows opening on to the garden; the atmosphere is welcoming and warm, the modern european cooking is excellent and served in two restaurants (one light and spacious, the other cosy and sumptuous), the breakfasts are delicious, and the dedicated staff are courteous and helpful; indoor and outdoor swimming pools, spa and fitness centre. Closed one to two weeks January. Dogs allowed in two bedrooms only; mat and bowl; £10.

BATH   ST7465

Royal Crescent Hotel

(01225) 823333 – www.royalcrescent.co.uk
16 Royal Crescent, Bath, Somerset BA1 2LS

£400; 45 luxurious rooms. Elegant Georgian hotel in a glorious curved terrace and made up of five buildings; comfortable antiques-filled drawing rooms, open fires and lovely flowers, excellent and imaginative modern cooking in the Dower House restaurant overlooking an acre of secluded gardens, a lighter all-day menu, delicious afternoon teas and breakfasts and impeccable service; spa with sauna, steam room and treatments, gym and croquet. Dogs allowed in six bedrooms, main building and garden; bed, bowl, blanket and treats; £35 per stay.

BRISTOL   ST5873

Hotel du Vin

(0117) 925 5577 – www.hotelduvin.com
Narrow Lewins Mead, Bristol BS1 2NU

£185; 40 rooms with spacious bathrooms, including loft-style suites. Attractively converted former sugar refinery with big pillars and arched cellars, wine prints, posters and empty bottles, comfortable armchairs on stripped wooden floors and a bustling but relaxed dining room; good, imaginative bistro-style cooking, helpful efficient staff and an interesting wine list. Dogs allowed in some bedrooms and bar; mat and bowl; £10 per stay.

COMBE HAY
ST7360

Wheatsheaf

(01225) 833504 – www.wheatsheafcombehay.co.uk
Combe Hay, Bath, Somerset BA2 7EG

£120; 3 stylishly simple, spacious rooms. Smart, cheerful flint and brick dining pub perched prettily above a steep wooded valley with walks from the front door; a small bar with sofas on dark flagstones and a big log fire, and other fresh, bright areas with stylish high-backed dining chairs around chunky modern dining tables on parquet or coir matting, contemporary artwork, mirrors and lots of interest on the sills of the many shuttered windows; a very good choice of drinks, first class food using game and fish caught by the landlord and locally foraged produce; friendly, informal staff; resident springer spaniel, Brie, and cocker spaniels, Gloria and Margaux. Dogs allowed in all bedrooms and anywhere in the pub.

CORTON DENHAM
ST6322

Queens Arms

(01963) 220317 – www.thequeensarms.com
Corton Denham, Sherborne, Somerset DT9 4LR

£125; 8 comfortable rooms with country views. Civilised honey-coloured stone inn with friendly young staff, a plain high-beamed bar with a woodburner in the inglenook, rugs on flagstones, old pews, barrel seats and a sofa, church candles, fresh flowers and a super choice of drinks; the enterprising food, served in the bustling dining room, uses their own pork and eggs, local game and other produce and home-made preserves for breakfast; some fine surrounding walks and the pub has a list of walking and running routes. Dogs allowed in one bedroom and bar; bed and bowl; £15.

DUNSTER
SS9943

Luttrell Arms

(01643) 821555 – www.luttrellarms.co.uk
High Street, Dunster, Somerset TA24 6SG

£140; 28 lovely bedrooms – some with four-posters, antiques and carved fireplaces. A rather special hotel with some fine medieval features, in an interesting and pretty town on the edge of Exmoor National Park; the main bar – popular locally – has a huge fireplace and all sorts of items on display (swords and guns, horsebrasses, copper kettles, plates and warming pans, animal furs, a stag's head, an antler chandelier and various country knick-knacks); also other bars, a deeply comfortable sitting room and a smart restaurant; courteous staff serve real ales, good wines by the glass, farm ciders and enjoyable food including first class breakfasts; lovely garden on several levels and a little galleried courtyard. Dogs allowed in most bedrooms; bed and welcome letter; £10–£20.

EXFORD
SS8538

Crown

(01643) 831554 – www.crownhotelexmoor.co.uk
Exford, Minehead, Somerset TA24 7PP

£155; 17 attractive rooms. Comfortably upmarket coaching inn on the village green in Exmoor National Park with a delightful water garden – a lovely summer spot with trout stream, gently sloping lawns, tall trees and plenty of tables; brightly furnished lounge with a very relaxed feel, smart cushioned benches, hunting prints on grey walls and old photographs of the area; real ales, a good wine list, and enjoyable modern cooking in candlelit dining room with simpler meals in the bar; a good base for walking and they can arrange riding, fishing, shooting, hunting, wildlife-watching, cycling and trekking. Dogs allowed in all rooms and public areas except restaurant; £20 per stay.

FROME   ST77478

Archangel

(01373) 456111 – www.archangelfrome.com
King Street, Frome, Somerset BA11 1BH

£90; 10 richly decorated, well equipped bedrooms. Dating back to the Domesday Book, this old place opened its doors as an inn in 1311; they've kept the ancient beams and walls and added contemporary artwork and furniture and touches of glass, steel, slate and leather to create a striking restaurant/bar-with-rooms; as well as a bustling bar with a good mix of customers, there's a high-raftered restaurant with a free-floating glass mezzanine cube, another, smaller dining room, a two-roomed snug area with big leather sofas and an open fire, and a central courtyard with a mediterranean feel; local ales, lots of cocktails and enjoyable food; this is an attractive and historic market town. Dogs allowed in some bedrooms and everywhere except restaurant; £10.

HATCH BEAUCHAMP   ST3020

Farthings

(01823) 480664 – www.farthingshotel.co.uk
Hatch Beauchamp, Taunton, Somerset TA3 6SG

£90; 11 pretty rooms with thoughtful extras. Charming 18th-c house in two acres of pretty gardens with open countryside nearby for walks; open log fires in the comfortable lounge, a convivial, well stocked bar, good varied food using their own-grown and other local produce in three elegant dining rooms, and breakfasts using eggs from their hens; resident dogs, Sasha, Aonghas and Hamish, lambs, pigs and lots of fowl. Dogs allowed in some bedrooms; not in restaurant; £8.

HOLCOMBE   ST6649

Holcombe Inn

(01761) 232478 – www.holcombeinn.co.uk
Stratton Road, Holcombe, Somerset BA3 5EB

£120; 10 lovely rooms, some with peaceful farmland views. A thoroughly enjoyable all-rounder, this well run place continues to be very popular; there's a bar with fine old flagstones, window seats and chunky captain's chairs, a dining room with a two-way woodburning stove and some snug partitioned areas, as well as other cosy sitting areas; enjoyable food and a good drinks list that includes real ales, 21 wines and champagne by the glass, cocktails and local drinks (cider, vodka, sloe gin, juices); a terrace and side lawn have seating, and the sunsets can be stunning; resident dogs and chickens. Dogs allowed in two lodge bedrooms and bar; bed, bowl and treats; £20.

HOLFORD

ST1540

Combe House

(01278) 741382 – www.combehouse.co.uk
Holford, Bridgwater, Somerset TA5 1RZ

£99; 17 pretty rooms. Warmly friendly former tannery (still with a waterwheel) with gardens in a pretty spot with walks in the Quantock Hills; comfortable rooms, log fires, good home-made food using home-grown and other local produce in a light and airy modern dining room, and a relaxed atmosphere. Dogs allowed in some bedrooms and on lead in public areas and bar; £10.

KINGSDON

ST5126

Kingsdon Inn

(01935) 840543 – www.kingsdoninn.co.uk
Kingsdon, Somerton, Somerset TA11 7LG

£95; 3 cottagey bedrooms. Handy for the A303, this charming old thatched pub – a former cider house – has a main bar, a couple of dining areas and an attractive separate restaurant, all with low ceilings, woodburning stoves, a mix of seating around scrubbed kitchen tables, red quarry tiles and fresh flowers; courteous, helpful staff serve real ales and rewarding, italian-influenced modern food that uses local produce (including own-made bread, ice-creams and crackers for cheese). Dogs allowed in all bedrooms and bar; £10 per stay.

LUXBOROUGH

SS9837

Royal Oak

(01984) 641498 – www.theroyaloakinnluxborough.co.uk
Luxborough, Watchet, Somerset TA23 0SH

£90; 8 neat, cottagey rooms. Unspoilt and interesting old pub in idyllic spot, marvellous for exploring Exmoor with many wonderful walks; compact characterful bar with ancient flagstones and a log fire in a huge brick fireplace, plenty of locals (often with their dogs) and a genuinely warm welcome; two dining areas with attractive old pine and more formal chairs around nice tables, and seating in sunny courtyard; real ales, farm ciders and reliably good food using seasonal local game and lamb and beef from nearby farms. Dogs allowed in all bedrooms and bar; £10.

NETHER STOWEY

ST1939

Old Cider House

(01278) 732228 – www.theoldciderhouse.co.uk
25 Castle Street, Nether Stowey, Bridgwater, Somerset TA5 1LN

£75; 5 rooms. Carefully restored Edwardian house (previously used to produce cider – they now brew their own beers) in a secluded garden, with a big comfortable lounge and log fire, delicious breakfasts using their own bread, eggs and preserves, and interesting, candlelit evening meals using home-grown and local produce; plenty of walks and dog-friendly beaches nearby. Well behaved dogs allowed in two bedrooms; not in dining room; welcome pack; £3.

PORLOCK
SS8647

The Café
(01643) 863300 – www.thecafeporlockweir.co.uk
Porlock Weir, Minehead, Somerset TA24 8PB

£110; 5 rooms, most with sea views. Victorian villa overlooking the harbour; country house-style decor, good bistro cooking using first class local produce (lovely fish and seafood), super breakfasts, afternoon teas and a well chosen wine list. Closed Mon, Tues all year, also Wed, Thurs November-February. Dogs allowed in all bedrooms and until 6pm in café; £10 per stay.

SELWORTHY
SS9346

Hindon Organic Farm
(01643) 705244 – www.hindonfarm.co.uk
Selworthy, Minehead, Somerset TA24 8SH

£95; 3 pretty rooms. 18th-c house on an organic Exmoor hill farm of 500 acres with sheep, pigs, cattle and ducks; lovely walks from the door to the heather moors (dogs must be on a lead on the farm until away from stock animals); a quiet, homely sitting room with lots of paintings and antiques, fine breakfasts in the comfortable dining room using their own organic bacon, sausages, eggs and fresh-baked bread, and seats in the garden; own organic farm shop; several resident dogs. Dogs allowed in bedrooms if well house trained; £5.

SOMERTON
ST4928

Lynch Country House
(01458) 272316 – www.thelynchcountryhouse.co.uk
4 Behind Berry, Somerton, Somerset TA11 7PD

£95; 9 prettily decorated rooms, including 4 in coach house; also self-catering. Carefully restored and homely Georgian house in tranquil grounds with a lake with black swans and exotic ducks; a friendly welcome, a comfortable lounge with books, and delicious breakfasts (no evening meals) in the airy Orangery overlooking the gardens; surrounded by woodland and lots of nearby walks. Dogs allowed in one coach house room; £10.

SOMERTON
ST4928

White Hart
(01458) 272273 – www.whitehartsomerton.com
Market Place, Somerton, Somerset TA11 7LX

£85; 8 lovely, well equipped rooms. Attractively renovated, partly 16th-c pub with a light and airy bar, some smaller, cosier rooms, a simply furnished dining room and seating outside on a flower-filled terrace and on grass; throughout there are rugs on parquet flooring, open fires, church candles, contemporary paintwork and interesting lighting – look out for the antler chandelier with its pretty hanging lampshades; real ales, farm ciders, 14 wines by the glass and interesting brasserie-style food, much of it cooked in a wood-fired oven (breakfasts for non-residents too), served by friendly staff; this is a lovely village. Dogs allowed in all bedrooms.

STON EASTON

ST6253

Ston Easton Park

(01761) 241631 – www.stoneaston.co.uk
Ston Easton, Bath BA3 4DF

£179; 23 really lovely rooms. Majestic Palladian mansion of Bath stone with beautifully landscaped 18th-c gardens and 36 acres of parkland; elegant day rooms with antiques and flowers, a library and billiard room, an attractive and elegant restaurant with imaginative food using kitchen garden produce and local game, fine afternoon teas and extremely helpful, friendly and unstuffy service; resident working cocker spaniel, Oscar; walks in the grounds and surrounding countryside. Dogs allowed in all bedrooms and public areas, but not restaurant; £15.

TAUNTON

ST2224

Castle

(01823) 272671 – www.the-castle-hotel.com
Castle Green, Taunton, Somerset TA1 1NF

£150; 44 rooms, some overlooking the garden. Appealingly modernised, partly Norman castle, imaginative food including lighter meals in both the restaurant and brasserie, bar area, good breakfasts, a range of good value wines from a thoughtful list, and efficient friendly service; seats in the pretty garden and walks in the nearby park. Dogs allowed in some bedrooms only; £15.

WATERROW

ST0525

Rock

(01984) 623293 – www.rockinnwaterrow.co.uk
Waterrow, Taunton, Somerset TA4 2AX

£85; 8 modern rooms of varying sizes. Striking 400-year-old timbered inn built into a rock face on the edge of Exmoor National Park, with a civilised and friendly atmosphere, a small bar with a log fire in a stone fireplace, dining chairs and scrubbed kitchen tables on tartan carpet, local beers, farm cider, several malt whiskies and good wines by the glass, and interesting food in elegant dining room with pale grey-painted panelled walls; there are seats under umbrellas out in front. Dogs allowed in most bedrooms and on a lead in bar and dining room; £10.

Staffordshire

DOG FRIENDLY PUBS

ALSTONEFIELD
SK1355
George

(01335) 310205 – www.thegeorgeatalstonefield.com
Village signed from A515 Ashbourne–Buxton; DE6 2FX

Simply furnished and friendly pub in a pretty Peakland village, real ales and enjoyable food and seats outside

In the middle of a quiet farming hamlet and opposite the village green, this is a welcoming stone-built pub run by a long-serving family. There's an easy-going atmosphere in the chatty bar which has low beams and quarry tiles, old Peak District photographs and pictures, a log fire, Marstons Burton Bitter and Pedigree New World Pale Ale and guests such as Brakspears Oxford Gold and Ringwood Best Bitter on handpump and a dozen wines by the glass; service is friendly and helpful. As well as a little snug, there's a neat dining room with a woodburning stove, simple farmhouse furniture, candlelight and fresh flowers. The particularly good food uses local produce, including some grown in their own organic garden. There are picnic-sets at the front with more seats in a big, sheltered back stable yard.

Marstons ~ Tenant Emily Brighton ~ Real ale ~ Open 11.30-3, 6-11; 11.30-11 Fri, Sat; 12-9.30 Sun ~ Bar food 12-2.30, 6.30-9 ~ Restaurant ~ Children welcome ~ Dogs allowed in bar ~ Wi-fi

BREWOOD
SJ8708
Oakley

(01902) 859800 – www.brunningandprice.co.uk/oakley
Kiddemore Green Road; ST19 9BQ

Cleverly extended and refurbished bar and dining areas in substantial pub, with lots to look at, interesting food and drink and seats on long terrace

The spreading terrace behind this newly opened pub has flowering tubs, raised beds and overlooks a lake, so its many seats and benches are quickly snapped up in warm weather. Inside, the open-plan rooms have been furnished with thought and care and the many windows and pastel paintwork keep it all very light and airy. Partitioning and metal standing posts split larger areas into cosier drinking and dining spaces. Throughout there are big house plants in pots with smaller ones on windowsills, mirrors above open fires (some in pretty Victorian fireplaces), books on shelves, elegant metal chandeliers, standard lamps, stubby candles and fresh flowers. Seating ranges from groups of leather armchairs to all manner of cushioned wooden dining chairs around character tables, the walls (some half-panelled) are hung with hundreds of prints, and flooring consists of rugs on big boards and, in the restaurant, carpet. From the long counter, friendly, helpful staff serve Phoenix Brunning & Price Original, Salopian Oracle and Wye Valley Butty Bach with guests such as Stonehouse Station Bitter and Titanic Plum Porter on handpump, a dozen wines by the glass, 86 whiskies, 71 gins and 68 rums; background music. There's a rack outside for cyclists. Disabled parking and loos.

Brunning & Price ~ Manager John Duncan ~ Real ale ~ Open 11-11 (10.30 Sun) ~ Bar food 12-10 (9.30 Sun) ~ Restaurant ~ Children welcome ~ Dogs allowed in bar ~ Wi-fi

CAULDON   SK0749

Yew Tree

(01538) 309876 – www.yewtreeinncauldon.co.uk
Village signposted from A523 and A52 about 8 miles W of Ashbourne; ST10 3EJ

A unique collection of curios in friendly pub with good value snacks and bargain beer; very eccentric

This extraordinary roadside local is a treasure trove of fascinating curiosities and antiques, the most impressive pieces being the working polyphons and symphonions – 19th-c developments of the musical box, some taller than a person, each with quite a repertoire of tunes and elaborate sound-effects. There are also two pairs of Queen Victoria's stockings, an amazing collection of ceramics and pottery including a Grecian urn dating back almost 3,000 years, penny-farthing and boneshaker bicycles and the infamous Acme Dog Carrier. Seats include 18th-c settles, plenty of little wooden tables and a four-person oak church choir seat with carved heads that came from St Mary's church in Stafford. Look out for the array of musical instruments ranging from a one-string violin (phonofiddle) through pianos and sousaphones to the aptly named serpent. Drinks are very reasonably priced, so it's no wonder the place is popular with locals. Burton Bridge Bitter, Rudgate Ruby Mild and a guest or two on handpump, ten interesting malt whiskies, eight wines by the glass and farm cider; they hold a music and beer festival in July and a vintage vehicle rally in September. Darts, table skittles and board games. There are seats outside the front door and in the cobbled stable yard, and they have a basic campsite for pub customers and a small caravan for hire. The pub is almost hidden by a towering yew tree.

Free house ~ Licensee Alan East ~ Real ale ~ Open 12-3, 6-11; 12-midnight Sat; 12-11 Sun; closed weekday lunchtimes in winter ~ Bar food 12-3, 6-9; 12-9 weekends ~ Children allowed in polyphon room ~ Dogs allowed in bar ~ Wi-fi ~ Live folk music first Tues of month

ELLASTONE   SK1143

Duncombe Arms

(01335) 324275 – www.duncombearms.co.uk
Main Road; DE6 2GZ

Nooks and crannies here and there, a thoughtful choice of drinks, friendly staff and lovely food; seats outside

Notably friendly, this stylishly refurbished village pub offers a genuine welcome to all its customers ranging from damp walkers to those out for a special meal – and there's somewhere interesting to sit whatever the occasion. There are beams here and there, bare brick, exposed stone and painted walls, open fires and woodburners, horse prints and photos, big bold paintings of pigs, sheep, cows and chickens, large clocks and fresh flowers, church candles on mantelpieces, in big glass jars and on tables – and flooring that ranges from carpet to flagstones to bare floorboards and brick. Furnishings are just as eclectic: long leather button-back and cushioned wall seats, armchairs, all manner of wooden or upholstered dining chairs and tables made from mahogany, pine and even driftwood. Black Sheep, Marstons Pedigree and a beer named for the pub on handpump, 20 wines by the glass from a fine list, a dozen gins and 18 malt whiskies; background music and board games. An attractive terrace has wooden or rush seats around tables under parasols, braziers for cooler evenings and a view down over the garden to Worthy Island Wood.

Free house ~ Licensees Johnny and Laura Greenall ~ Real ale ~ Open 12-11; 12-midnight Sat; 12-10.30 Sun ~ Bar food 12-2.30, 6-9; 12-2.30, 5.30-10 Fri, Sat; 12-8 Sun ~ Restaurant ~ Children welcome ~ Dogs allowed in bar ~ Wi-fi

LONGDON GREEN   SK0813

Red Lion

(01543) 490410 ~ www.brunningandprice.co.uk/redlion
Hay Lane; WS15 4QF

Large, well run pub with interesting furnishings, a fine range of drinks, enjoyable food and spreading garden

In summer, this handsome pub is especially popular as it has a large garden with seats and tables on a suntrap terrace, picnic-sets on grass, a gazebo and swings and a play tractor for children; you can also watch cricket matches on the village green opposite. The interior has been extended and thoughtfully opened up, but the bar remains the heart of the place, with spreading rooms and nooks and crannies leading off. One dining room has skylights, rugs on nice old bricks, house plants lining the windowsill, an elegant metal chandelier and a miscellany of cushioned dining chairs around dark wooden tables. Similar furnishings fill the other rooms, and the walls are covered with old photos, pictures and prints relating to the local area and big gilt-edged mirrors; background music and board games. Open fires include a raised central fire pit. You'll find Phoenix Brunning & Price Original, Backyard Blonde, Blythe Bagots Bitter, Castle Rock Elsie Mo and Salopian Lemon Dream on handpump, 20 wines by the glass, 50 malt whiskies, 30 gins and two farm ciders. Staff are friendly, courteous and helpful.

Brunning & Price ~ Manager Chloe Turner ~ Real ale ~ Open 10.30am-11pm (10.30pm Sun) ~ Bar food 12-10 (9.30 Sun) ~ Restaurant ~ Children welcome ~ Dogs allowed in bar ~ Wi-fi

SWYNNERTON   SJ8535

Fitzherbert Arms

(01782) 796782 ~ www.fitzherbertarms.co.uk
Off A51 Stone–Nantwich; ST15 0RA

Thoughtfully renovated pub with character rooms, interesting décor, local ales and rewarding food; seats outside with country views

This charming village pub has reopened after a major restoration – the frontage is fun with a stack of old beer barrels between two large glass windows and box topiary. It's on Lord Stafford's estate at the centre of Swynnerton and a circular walk (details on their website) guides you from the pub car park and back again – just in time for lunch; dogs will be greeted with a biscuit and a water bowl. On entering through an impressive glass door, the bar sits at the centre to the right, with a raised fireplace styled like a furnace and blacksmiths' tools and relics. Down a step to the left is the older part of the pub with button-back leather armchairs beside a two-way fireplace, rugs on flagstones, hops and some fine old brickwork. Fitzherbert Best (from Weetwood) and Swynnerton Stout (from Titanic) on handpump with a couple of guests from breweries within a 35-mile radius; also, 15 good wines by the glass, a fantastic array of 30 ports with helpful notes and a farm cider from the Apple County Cider Company. Staff are helpful and friendly. The beamed dining room has similar furnishings to the bar (a nice mix of old dining chairs and tables) plus window seats with scatter cushions, gilt-edged mirrors, black and white photographs and chandeliers; background music and board games. Do look out for the glass-topped giant bellows and anvil tables, door handles made of old smithy's irons, and candles in old port bottles. Outside, a covered oak-timbered terrace has contemporary seats around rustic tables, heaters, fairy-lit shrubs in pots and country views; there are more seats in a small hedged garden too.

Free house ~ Licensee Leanne Wallis ~ Real ale ~ Open 12-11 (10.30 Sun) ~ Bar food 12-9 (9.30 Fri, Sat); 12-8.45 Sun ~ Children welcome but no under 10s after 7pm ~ Dogs allowed in bar ~ Wi-fi

WRINEHILL   SJ7547
Hand & Trumpet
(01270) 820048 – www.brunningandprice.co.uk/hand
A531 Newcastle–Nantwich; CW3 9BJ

All-day food in big attractive dining pub with a good choice of ales and wines by the glass, served by courteous staff

Whether it's a drink and a chat you're after or an enjoyable meal, this substantial pub is just the place. The linked, open-plan areas work their way around the long, solidly built counter, with a mix of dining chairs and sturdy tables on polished tiles or stripped-oak boards with rugs. There are nicely lit prints and mirrors on cream walls between a mainly dark dado, plenty of house plants, open fires and deep red ceilings. Original bow windows and a large skylight keep the place light and airy, and french windows open on to a spacious balustraded deck with teak tables and chairs, and a view down to ducks swimming on a big pond in the sizeable garden. Friendly attentive staff serve Phoenix Brunning & Price Original, Big Shed Engineers Best, Lancaster Northern Hemisphere Hopped Ale, Slaters Haka and a couple of guest beers on handpump, as well as 16 wines by the glass, 20 gins and about 70 whiskies; board games. Good disabled access and facilities.

Brunning & Price ~ Manager John Unsworth ~ Real ale ~ Open 12-11 (10.30 Sun) ~ Bar food 12-9 ~ Children welcome ~ Dogs allowed in bar ~ Wi-fi

DOG FRIENDLY HOTELS, INNS AND B&Bs

HOPWAS   SK1704
Oak Tree Farm
(01827) 56807 – www.oaktreefarmhotel.co.uk
Hints Road, Hopwas, Tamworth, Staffordshire B78 3AA

£95; 14 comfortable, spacious and pretty rooms, including 10 in annexe. Carefully restored farmhouse with an elegant little lounge featuring an inglenook fireplace with a woodburning stove and antiques, plus an attractive adjoining breakfast room; friendly atmosphere and owners, and enjoyable breakfasts; gardens overlooking the River Tame and a seasonal indoor swimming pool. Dogs allowed in five bedrooms.

PENKRIDGE   SJ9113

Mercure Stafford South Hatherton House

(01785) 712459 – www.hotels-stafford.com
Pinfold Lane, Penkridge, Staffordshire ST19 5QP

£85; 51 well equipped rooms. Surrounded by countryside but handy for Stafford, this sizeable, well run hotel has several comfortable lounge areas with leather sofas and armchairs, a bar, an attractive restaurant with interesting modern food, afternoon tea and good buffet-style breakfasts, and helpful, friendly staff; health club with indoor swimming pool, sauna, steam room and gym. Dogs allowed in ground-floor bedrooms; £5.

Suffolk

MAP 5

DOG FRIENDLY PUBS

CHELMONDISTON   TM2037
Butt & Oyster
(01473) 780764 – www.debeninns.co.uk/buttandoyster
Pin Mill – signposted from B1456 SE of Ipswich; continue to bottom of road; IP9 1JW

Chatty old riverside pub with pleasant views, good food and drink and seats on the terrace

From windows in the bar or from seats on the terrace, this simple old bargeman's pub has fine views over the River Orwell; it's named for the flounders and oysters that used to be caught here. The half-panelled little smoke room is pleasantly worn and unfussy with high-backed and other old-fashioned settles on a tiled floor. There's also a two-level dining room with country kitchen furniture on bare boards, and pictures and boat-related artefacts on the walls above the dado. Adnams Southwold and Mosaic and a couple of guests tapped from the cask by friendly, efficient staff, several wines by the glass and local cider; board games. Fish dishes play a big role on the menu, but they have non-fishy choices too. The annual Thames Barge Race (end June/early July) is fun. The car park can fill up pretty quickly.

Adnams ~ Lease Steve Lomas ~ Real ale ~ Open 9am-11pm ~ Bar food 9am-9.30pm ~ Restaurant ~ Children welcome ~ Dogs allowed in bar ~ Wi-fi

EASTBRIDGE   TM4566
Eels Foot
(01728) 830154 – www.theeelsfootinn.co.uk
Off B1122 N of Leiston; IP16 4SN

Country local with hospitable atmosphere, fair value food and Thursday evening folk sessions; bedrooms

As this simple, friendly place borders the freshwater marshes and RSPB Minsmere is nearby, it attracts plenty of bird-watchers and walkers – particularly at lunchtime; a footpath leads directly to the sea. There are light modern furnishings on stripped-wood floors in the upper and lower parts of the bar, a warming fire, Adnams Southwold, Broadside, Ghost Ship, Mosaic and a guest ale on handpump, 11 wines by the glass, several malt whiskies and a farm cider; darts in a side area, board games, cribbage and a neat back dining room. The good quality, home-cooked food includes several gluten-free options. The terrace has seats and tables and there are benches in the lovely big back garden.

Adnams ~ Tenant Julian Wallis ~ Real ale ~ Open 12-3, 6-11; 12-11 Fri; 11.30-11 Sat;
11.30-11.30 Sun ~ Bar food 12-2.30, 6-9; 12-9 Fri-Sun ~ Children welcome ~ Dogs
welcome ~ Wi-fi ~ Live folk music Thurs and last Sun of month ~ Bedrooms: £105

IPSWICH   TM1844

Fat Cat

(01473) 726524 ~ www.fatcatipswich.co.uk
Spring Road, opposite junction with Nelson Road (best bet for parking is up there);
IP4 5NL

**Fantastic range of changing real ales in a well run town pub,
with a garden**

With an extraordinary range of up to 18 real ales from around the country on
handpump or tapped from the cask, this cheery and busy town pub remains
a beer lover's dream. There might be Adnams Southwold, Crouch Vale Brewers
Gold and Yakima Gold, Dark Star Hophead, Earl Soham Albert, Exmoor Gold, Fat
Cat Honey Cat, Hop Back Summer Lightning, Mighty Oak Holly Daze, Navigation
Eclipse, Pheasantry Mikado Mild, St Austell Tribute, Skinners Betty Stogs, Titanic
Plum Porter and Woodfordes Wherry. They also stock quite a few belgian bottled
beers, farm cider and seven wines by the glass. The bars have a mix of café chairs
and stools, unpadded wall benches and cushioned seats around cast-iron and
wooden pub tables, bare floorboards, lots of enamel brewery signs and posters
on canary-yellow walls; board games and shove-ha'penny. There's also a spacious
back conservatory and several picnic-sets on the terrace and lawn. To eat, there
are rolls, spicy scotch eggs and sausage rolls and you can bring in takeaway
food (not Friday or Saturday). Very little nearby parking. Well behaved dogs are
welcome but must be kept on a lead.

Free house ~ Licensees John and Ann Keatley ~ Real ale ~ No credit cards ~ Open 12-11;
11am-midnight Sat; 12-midnight Sun ~ Bar food all day while it lasts ~ Dogs welcome ~ Wi-fi

MIDDLETON   TM4267

Bell

(01728) 648286
Off A12 in Yoxford via B1122 towards Leiston; also signposted off B1125
Leiston–Westleton; The Street; IP17 3NN

**Thatch and low beams, friendly landlord, good beer and popular
good value food – a peaceful spot**

The grand flint tower of the village church overlooks this pretty cream-washed
pub and there are picnic-sets out in front under parasols. On the left, the
traditional bar has a warm welcome from the character landlord, a log fire in a
big hearth, old local photographs, a low plank-panelled ceiling, and bar stools and
pew seating; Adnams Southwold, Broadside and Ghost Ship tapped from the cask
and nine wines by the glass. On the right, an informal two-room carpeted lounge/
dining area has padded mate's and library chairs around dark tables under low
black beams, with pews by a big woodburning stove and modern seaside brewery
prints. Dogs are welcomed with treats and a bowl of water. Camping is available
in the broad meadow behind. RSPB Minsmere is nearby, as are coastal walks.

Adnams ~ Tenants Nicholas and Trish Musgrove ~ Real ale ~ Open 12-3, 6-11 (midnight
Fri); 12-midnight Sat; 12-9 Sun; closed Mon ~ Bar food 12-2, 6-9; 12-5 Sun ~ Restaurant ~
Well behaved children allowed away from bar ~ Dogs allowed in bar ~ Wi-fi

PETTISTREE   TM2954

Greyhound

(01728) 746451 – www.greyhoundinnpettistree.co.uk
*The Street; brown sign to pub off B1438 S of Wickham Market, 0.5 miles N of A12;
IP13 0HP*

Neatly kept village pub with enjoyable food and drink; seats outside

Hard-working, friendly licensees run this bustling pub and there's a welcome for all. It's basically just two smallish rooms with open fires, some rather low beams, chunky farmhouse chairs and cushioned settles around dark wooden tables on bare floorboards and candlelight. Earl Soham Victoria Bitter and guests such as Adnams Ghost Ship and Crouch Vale Brewers Gold on handpump, several wines by the glass and quite a few malt whiskies; it's best to book in advance to be sure of a table. The interesting food, cooked by the landlady, makes the most of local produce. The well kept side garden has picnic-sets under parasols, with more beside the gravelled front car park. The village church is next door.

Free house ~ Licensees Stewart and Louise McKenzie ~ Real ale ~ Open 12-3, 6-11; 12-4 Sun; closed Sun evening, Mon, two weeks Jan ~ Bar food 12-2.30, 6-9; 12-3 Sun ~ Restaurant ~ Children welcome ~ Dogs allowed in bar ~ Wi-fi

SIBTON   TM3570

White Horse

(01728) 660337 – www.sibtonwhitehorseinn.co.uk
Halesworth Road/Hubbard's Hill, N of Peasenhall; IP17 2JJ

Particularly well run inn with nicely old-fashioned bar, good mix of customers, real ales and imaginative food; bedrooms

The licensees running this busy village inn are hands-on and hard-working and offer a genuine welcome to all. The appealing bar has a roaring log fire in a large inglenook fireplace, horsebrasses and tack on the walls, old settles and pews, and they serve Adnams Southwold, Wolf Golden Jackal and Woodfordes Wherry on handpump, nine wines by the glass and 15 malt whiskies from an old oak-panelled counter. Beer festivals are held in June and August and a viewing panel reveals the working cellar and its ancient floor. Steps lead up past an old partly knocked-through timbered wall into a carpeted gallery, and there's also a smart dining room and a secluded (and popular) dining terrace. The notably good food uses local, seasonal produce, with everything made in-house. The big garden has plenty of seats.

Free house ~ Licensees Neil and Gill Mason ~ Real ale ~ Open 12-3, 6-11; 12-3.30, 6.30-11 Sun; closed Mon lunchtime, one week Jan ~ Bar food 12-2, 6.30-9; 12-2.30, 7-8.30 Sun ~ Restaurant ~ Well behaved children welcome but must be over 7 in evening; not in bedrooms ~ Dogs allowed in bar ~ Wi-fi ~ Music and beer festival in summer, barbecue Fri evening in summer ~ Bedrooms: £95

SOUTHWOLD   TM5076

Crown

(01502) 722275 – www.adnams.co.uk/hotels/the-crown
High Street; IP18 6DP

Comfortable hotel with relaxed bars, a fine choice of drinks, interesting food and seats outside; bedrooms

Of course, this isn't a pub in the true sense, it's a civilised hotel – but those in the know head for the back bar. Here, there's an informal, chatty atmosphere with locals and their dogs, oak panelling, some fine antique tables and chairs on bare boards, very well kept Adnams Southwold, Broadside, Ghost Ship and Old Ale on handpump, plenty of wines by the glass from a splendid list, ten malt whiskies and interesting spirits; staff are courteous and friendly. The beamed front bar has a stripped curved high-backed settle and smaller dark varnished settles, kitchen and other chairs and a restored, carved wooden fireplace. Seats in a sunny sheltered corner are very pleasant.

Adnams ~ Manager Jenny Knights ~ Real ale ~ Open 11-11 ~ Bar food 12-2.30, 6.30 (6 in summer)-9 ~ Children welcome ~ Dogs allowed in bar ~ Bedrooms: £205

SOUTHWOLD   TM4975

Harbour Inn

(01502) 722381 – www.harbourinnsouthwold.co.uk
Blackshore, by the boats; from A1095, turn right at the Kings Head, and keep on past the golf course and water tower; IP18 6TA

Great spot down by the boats with lots of outside tables and interesting interior; popular food with emphasis on local seafood

You can walk from here along the Blyth estuary to Walberswick (where the Bell is under the same good management as this pub) via a footbridge and return by the one-man ferry. The back bar is nicely nautical with dark panelling and built-in wall seats around scrubbed tables, and cheerful staff serve 16 wines by the glass, along with Adnams Southwold, Broadside, Ghost Ship and a guest such as Oyster Stout on handpump. The low ceiling is draped with ensigns, signal flags, pennants and a line strung with ancient dried fish, and there's a quaint old stove, rope fancywork, local fishing photographs and even portholes with water bubbling behind them; they have their own weather station for walkers and sailors. The lower front bar, with a tiled floor and panelling, is broadly similar, while the large, elevated dining room has panoramic views of the harbour, lighthouse, brewery and churches beyond the marshes. Picnic-sets on the terrace look over the boats on the estuary; there are also seats and tables behind the pub, which overlook the marshy commons to the town.

Adnams ~ Tenant Nick Attfield ~ Real ale ~ Open 11-11 ~ Bar food 12-9 ~ Children welcome away from top bar ~ Dogs allowed in bar ~ Folk singers Thurs and Sun evenings

STOKE-BY-NAYLAND   TL9836

Crown

(01206) 262001 – www.crowninn.net
Park Street (B1068); CO6 4SE

Smart dining pub with attractive modern furnishings, imaginative food, real ales and a great wine choice; good bedrooms

This is a civilised and easy-going inn. The extensive open-plan dining bar is well laid out to give several distinct-feeling areas: a sofa and easy chairs on flagstones near the serving counter, a couple of armchairs under heavy beams by the big woodburning stove, one sizeable table tucked nicely into a three-sided built-in seat and a lower side room with more beams and cheerful floral wallpaper. Tables are mostly stripped veterans, with high-backed dining chairs, but there are more modern chunky pine tables at the back; also, contemporary artwork (mostly for sale) and daily papers. Served by friendly staff, there's

Adnams Southwold, Crouch Vale Brewers Gold, Woodfordes Wherry and a changing guest such as Lacons Falcon Ale on handpump and Aspall's cider. Wine is a key feature, with 30 by the glass and hundreds more from the glass-walled 'cellar shop' in one corner – you can buy there to take away too. The sheltered flagstoned back terrace has comfortable teak furniture, heaters, big terracotta-coloured parasols and a peaceful view over rolling, lightly wooded countryside. Breakfasts are available for non-residents. Good disabled access. This pretty village is worth exploring and there are plenty of well-marked footpaths.

Free house ~ Licensee Richard Sunderland ~ Real ale ~ Open 11-11; 12-10.30 Sun ~ Bar food 12-2.30, 6-9.30 (10 Fri, Sat); all day Sun ~ Children welcome ~ Dogs allowed in bar ~ Wi-fi ~ Bedrooms: £135

STRATFORD ST MARY
TM0434
Swan
(01206) 321244 – www.stratfordswan.com
Lower Street; CO7 6JR

Excellent food and drink in 16th-c coaching inn; riverside seats

With creative food and a great interest in beers, wines and spirits, this lovely timbered inn is much enjoyed by a wide mix of customers. They keep Adnams Ghost Ship, Swannay Orkney IPA and Oakham JHB on handpump, nine craft ales, 130 bottled beers from around the world, 14 wines by the glass, 53 malt whiskies, 11 vodkas, 19 gins, a farm cider and several interesting bottled ones. There's a log fire in a Tudor brick fireplace in one of the two beamed bars and a coal fire in the other, and an eclectic range of old furniture on parquet or brick floors; board games. The compact and timbered back restaurant is rather elegant; the inventive food is paired with wine and ales. Outside, there are teak tables and chairs under parasols on a terrace, more seats on a big lawn and, across the road, some tables under willow trees by the River Stour (where there's a landing stage).

Free house ~ Licensee Jane Dorber ~ Real ale ~ Open 11-11; closed Mon, Tues ~ Bar food 12-3, 6-9 ~ Restaurant ~ Children welcome ~ Dogs allowed in bar ~ Wi-fi

UFFORD
TM2952
Crown
(01394) 461030 – www.theuffordcrown.com
High Street; IP13 6EL

Bustling pub with a good mix of customers, real ales, enjoyable seasonal food and friendly atmosphere; seats outside

Very much a family business, this is a friendly pub with plenty of room for both drinking and dining. The bar and eating areas have cushioned wooden dining chairs and leather wall banquettes around a medley of dark tables on bare boards or carpeting, books on shelves, modern ceiling lights and open fires in brick fireplaces. Stools line the counter where they serve Adnams Southwold and Earl Soham Victoria Bitter on handpump and a dozen good wines by the glass; maybe daily papers. At the front of the building are some tables and chairs and the back terrace and garden have plenty of picnic-sets under parasols.

Free house ~ Licensees Max and Polly Durrant ~ Real ale ~ Open 12-3, 5 (4 Fri)-11; 12-11 Sat; 12-10.30 Sun; closed Tues ~ Bar food 12-2, 6-9; 12-3, 6-8 Sun ~ Restaurant ~ Children welcome ~ Dogs allowed in bar ~ Wi-fi

WALDRINGFIELD

TM2844

Maybush

(01473) 736215 – www.debeninns.co.uk/maybush
Off A12 S of Martlesham; The Quay, Cliff Road; IP12 4QL

Busy pub with tables outside by the riverbank; nautical décor and a decent choice of drinks and fair value food

This spot is a haven for bird-watchers and ramblers, and river cruises are available nearby (though you have to pre-book). The picnic-sets overlooking the River Deben get snapped up pretty quickly, though some of the tables inside by the windows have the same view. The spacious knocked-through bar is divided into separate areas by fireplaces or steps. There's a nautical theme, with an elaborate ship's model in a glass case and a few more in a light, high-ceilinged extension – as well as lots of old lanterns, pistols and aerial photographs; background music and board games. Adnams Southwold and Ghost Ship on handpump and a fair choice of wines by the glass; board games.

Adnams ~ Lease Steve and Louise Lomas ~ Real ale ~ Open 9am-11pm ~ Bar food 9am-9.30pm ~ Restaurant ~ Children welcome ~ Dogs allowed in bar ~ Wi-fi

WHEPSTEAD

TL8258

White Horse

(01284) 735760 – www.whitehorsewhepstead.co.uk
Off B1066 S of Bury; Rede Road; IP29 4SS

Charming country pub with attractively furnished rooms and well liked food and drink

This is a 17th-c building with several Victorian additions and the dark-beamed bar still has a woodburning stove in a low fireplace, stools around pubby tables on a tiled floor, and Adnams Southwold and a guest from St Peters on handpump. Linked rooms have country kitchen tables and chairs on antique floor tiles and some traditional wall seats and rather fine old farmhouse chairs. The neat sheltered back terrace has seats and tables and there are also picnic-sets on grass. New licensees took over recently and are planning future refurbishments.

Free house ~ Licensees Hana and Lee Saunders ~ Real ale ~ Open 11.30-3, 7-11; 11.30-3 Sun; closed Sun evening ~ Bar food 12-2, 7-9 ~ Restaurant ~ Children welcome ~ Dogs welcome ~ Wi-fi

DOG FRIENDLY HOTELS, INNS AND B&Bs

ALDEBURGH

TM4656

Cross Keys

(01728) 452637
Crabbe Street, Aldeburgh, Suffolk IP15 5BN

£89.50; 3 attractively furnished rooms. Cheerful 16th-c pub near the beach with views from seats on the sheltered back terrace across the promenade to the water; a buoyant atmosphere, low-ceilinged, interconnecting bars with antique and other pubby furniture, the landlord's collection of oils and Victorian watercolours, paintings by local artists and roaring log fires in two inglenook fireplaces; real ales and decent wines by the glass and tasty, traditional food; resident dog Dave. Dogs allowed in all bedrooms and anywhere in the pub (on leads).

ALDEBURGH

TM4657

Wentworth

(01728) 452312 – www.wentworth-aldeburgh.com
Wentworth Road, Aldeburgh, Suffolk IP15 5BD

£190; 35 rooms, some with sea view, including 7 in Darfield House opposite (more spacious but no sea view). Comfortable and tranquil hotel run by the same family since 1920, overlooking the fishing huts, boats and beach (where you can walk); a couple of lounges with log fire, a convivial bar, good enjoyable food (plenty of fish) in the red-walled, candlelit restaurant, hearty breakfasts and a sunny terrace for light lunches. Dogs allowed in all bedrooms, bar and lounges; £2.

BILDESTON

TL9949

Bildeston Crown

(01449) 740510 – www.thebildestoncrown.co.uk
High Street, Bildeston, Ipswich, Suffolk IP7 7EB

£90; 12 pretty, individually furnished rooms. Lovely ochre-coloured timber-framed Tudor inn with log fires and stripped wooden floors in the spacious and convivial beamed bar with hand-painted walls, a comfortable, heavily beamed lounge, elegant restaurant, excellent modern cooking, well kept real ales and welcoming, courteous staff; seats in a central courtyard and on a heated terrace; lots of walks nearby. Dogs allowed in all bedrooms and bar; £10.

BURY ST EDMUNDS

TL8564

Angel

(01284) 714000 – www.theangel.co.uk
3 Angel Hill, Bury St Edmunds, Suffolk IP33 1LT

£130; 77 individually decorated rooms with bold colours and fabrics. Thriving town-centre Georgian hotel given a contemporary makeover, with all manner of artwork on the walls, interesting global curios dotted among comfortable sofas in the log-fire lounge, a relaxed bar with all-day light meals, interesting modern british food using the best local produce in the easy-going and elegant bare-boards restaurant, good breakfasts and friendly, helpful staff; gardens to walk in 50 metres away. Sister hotel is Salthouse in Ipswich. Dogs allowed in some bedrooms and lounge; £15 (£5 subsequent nights).

DUNWICH

TM4770

Ship at Dunwich

(01728) 648219 – www.shipatdunwich.co.uk
St James's Street, Dunwich, Saxmundham, Suffolk IP17 3DT

£115; 16 rooms, some with marsh and sea views. Pleasant old brick pub by the sea with a welcome for regulars and visitors – and dogs, who are given a treat and bowl of water; the traditionally furnished main bar has benches, pews, captain's chairs and wooden tables on floor tiles, a woodburning stove (left open in cold weather) and lots of sea prints, and there's a simple conservatory, two dining rooms, a courtyard and a large garden with an enormous fig tree; local beers, cider and wines by the glass and enjoyable food including good fish and chips; the RSPB Minsmere reserve and Dunwich Museum are nearby – as are lots of coastal walks. Dogs allowed in some bedrooms, bar, conservatory and small dining room; £5.

HADLEIGH
TM0242

Edge Hall

(01473) 822458 – www.edgehall.co.uk
2 High Street, Hadleigh, Ipswich, Suffolk IP7 5AP

£85; 10 pretty rooms including 4 in Lodge; also self-catering. Friendly Georgian house with an attractive walled garden where you can have afternoon tea or play croquet; a comfortable, elegant lounge with chandeliers, traditional english cooking and good breakfasts using home-grown produce in the stately dining room. Dogs allowed in Lodge rooms; £5.

HINTLESHAM
TM0843

Hintlesham Hall

(01473) 652334 – www.hintleshamhall.co.uk
Hintlesham, Ipswich, Suffolk IP8 3NS

£165; 32 lovely rooms. Magnificent mansion, mainly Georgian but dating from Elizabethan times, in 175 acres with big walled gardens, croquet, tennis and 18-hole golf course next door; restful and comfortable day rooms with books, antiques and open fires, fine modern cooking in two smart restaurants (lighter all-day options too), a marvellous wine list, popular afternoon teas (taken on the terrace in fine weather) and exemplary service; new spa with treatment rooms. Dogs allowed in some bedrooms; £15.

HORRINGER
TL8161

Ickworth

(01284) 735350 – www.ickworthhotel.com
Horringer, Bury St Edmunds, Suffolk IP29 5QE

£195; 27 rooms plus 11 apartments in the Lodge. Lovely 18th-c house in marvellous parkland on an 1,800-acre National Trust estate (formerly owned by the Marquess of Bristol), the east wing of which is a luxury hotel; elegant and traditional décor mixes with more contemporary touches, the atmosphere is relaxed and informal, and staff are friendly and helpful; excellent modern cooking in family-oriented dining conservatory and more formal restaurant (lighter bites in lounge) and good, extensive breakfasts; riding, tennis, indoor swimming pool and treatment rooms and lots of surrounding walks; resident border terrier, Brogue. Dogs allowed in some bedrooms and lounge; £10.

IPSWICH
TM1644

Salthouse Harbour Hotel

(01473) 226789 – www.salthouseharbour.co.uk
Neptune Quay, Ipswich, Suffolk IP4 1AX

£139; 70 chic modern rooms. Converted Victorian warehouse overlooking the marina, now a boutique hotel with contemporary furnishings and décor in the open-plan bar and lounge, lots of artwork, attentive, courteous staff, inventive brasserie-style food in the clubby-feeling restaurant, good breakfasts. Sister hotel is Angel in Bury St Edmunds. Dogs allowed in some bedrooms and lounge; £15 (£5 subsequent nights).

LAVENHAM TL9149

Swan at Lavenham

(01787) 247477 – www.theswanatlavenham.co.uk
High Street, Lavenham, Sudbury, Suffolk CO10 9QA

£145; 45 smart rooms. Handsome and comfortable Elizabethan hotel that incorporates several fine half-timbered buildings; lots of cosy seating areas, interesting historic prints and alcoves with beams, timbers, armchairs and settees, an intriguing small bar, good food in lavishly timbered restaurant with a minstrels' gallery (actually built in 1965) or more informal brasserie, afternoon teas, generous breakfasts and friendly helpful staff; garden and spa. Dogs allowed in all bedrooms and anywhere except restaurant and brasserie; £10.

LONG MELFORD TL8645

Bull

(01787) 378494 – www.oldenglishinns.co.uk
Hall Street, Long Melford, Sudbury, Suffolk CO10 9JG

£85; 25 comfortable rooms. An inn since 1580, this fine black and white hotel was originally a medieval manorial hall and has handsome and interesting carved woodwork and timbering, and an old weavers' gallery overlooking the courtyard; old-fashioned front lounge with antique furnishings and a log fire in a huge fireplace, a spacious back bar with sporting prints and real ales, a restaurant with reasonably priced food, and an attractive courtyard with seats; staff are friendly. Dogs allowed in some bedrooms (not on beds); not in food service areas; £5.

ORFORD TM4249

Crown & Castle

(01394) 450205 – www.crownandcastle.co.uk
Orford, Woodbridge, Suffolk IP12 2LJ

£215; 21 thoughtfully designed, stylish rooms. High gabled red-brick Victorian hotel by the Norman castle in this seaside village – they think of themselves as more of a restaurant-with-rooms; a lovely relaxed atmosphere, courteous staff, a small, smartly minimalist bar and an open fire in the comfortable lounge, exceptionally good modern british cooking using the best local ingredients in the informal restaurant (lighter lunches and excellent breakfasts too), 20 wines by the glass; and seats in the garden and lots of nearby walks; resident wire-haired fox terriers called Annie and Teddy. Dogs allowed in five garden bedrooms, bar and at one table in restaurant; home-made treats and towels; £10.

ORFORD
TM4249

Kings Head

(01394) 450271 – www.thekingsheadorford.co.uk
Front Street, Orford, Woodbridge, Suffolk IP12 2LW

£110; 4 cosy rooms. Likeable, partly 700-year-old pub surrounded by fine walks and lovely coastline; plenty of authentic atmosphere in the snug main bar with straightforward furniture on red carpeting, heavy low beams and local beers, a candlelit dining room with stripped brick walls and rugs on ancient bare boards, popular bar food; pub dog called Benjy. Dogs allowed in one bedroom and anywhere in the pub.

ROUGHAM
TL9063

Ravenwood Hall

(01359) 270345 – www.ravenwoodhall.co.uk
Rougham, Bury St Edmunds, Suffolk IP30 9JA

£125; 14 comfortable rooms with antiques (7 in main building, 7 in mews). Tranquil Tudor country house in seven acres of carefully tended gardens and woodland; log fire in comfortable lounge, a cosy bar, good food in the timbered restaurant with big inglenook fireplace (home-preserved fruits and veg, home-smoked meat and fish), a good wine list and helpful service; croquet and heated outdoor swimming pool; lots of animals, resident dogs and walks in the grounds. Dogs allowed in some bedrooms, bar and lounge; £15.

SNAPE
TM4058

Golden Key

(01728) 688510 – www.goldenkeysnape.co.uk
Priory Lane, Snape, Saxmundham, Suffolk IP17 1SA

£75; 3 rooms. 16th-c village pub, surrounded by plenty of walks, with a traditional low-beamed lounge bar, winter log fire, a mix of pubby tables and chairs, local beer and cider and a dozen wines by the glass, a small snug, two dining rooms with open fireplaces, settles and scrubbed pine tables, a terrace with tables and flower tubs, and likeable bar food served by friendly staff. Dogs allowed in all bedrooms and anywhere in the pub; bowl and treats; £5.

SOUTHWOLD
TM5076

Swan

(01502) 722186 – www.adnams.co.uk/hotels/the-swan
Market Place, Southwold, Suffolk IP18 6EG

£185; 42 well appointed rooms, including 17 Lighthouse rooms separate from main hotel. 17th-c hotel on the market square with a comfortable lounge, a convivial bar, interesting, enjoyable food in elegant dining room, fine wines, well kept real ales (the hotel backs on to Adnams Brewery) and polite, helpful staff; garden with seats and it's a short stroll to the beach. Dogs allowed in Lighthouse bedrooms but not main hotel; bedding, bowl and treats.

THORPENESS   TM4759

Dolphin

(01728) 454994 – www.thorpenessdolphin.com
Peace Place, Thorpeness, Leiston, Suffolk IP16 4NB

£115; 3 airy rooms. Neatly kept extended pub in an interesting village – a
fascinating early 20th-c curio built as a small-scale upmarket holiday resort;
scandinavian-feeling main bar with pale wooden tables and chairs on broad
modern quarry tiles, a winter log fire, fresh flowers, local beers, 13 wines by the
glass and several whiskies and bourbons, a smaller public bar, and a sizeable
dining room with enjoyable food; plenty of seats outside in big garden; walks on
beach. Dogs allowed in all bedrooms and everywhere except restaurant; £10.

WALBERSWICK   TM4974

Anchor

(01502) 722112 – www.anchoratwalberswick.com
The Street, Walberswick, Suffolk IP18 6UA

£155; 10 bedrooms including 6 chalet-style rooms in the garden with views of the
water or beach huts and sand dunes. Drinkers and diners are equally well served
at this friendly bustling pub with a simply furnished front bar with big windows,
a two-way open fire and black and white photographs of fishermen, as well as a
small, more modern-feeling lounge and an extensive dining area; helpful, friendly
staff, local ales (beer festival in August) and inventive food using local, seasonal
produce; there's an outdoor bar and wood-fired pizza oven, and plenty of seats in
the attractive garden; walks along the coast path and to Southwold. Dogs allowed
in three bedrooms and bar; £10.

WALBERSWICK   TM4974

Bell

(01502) 723109 – www.bellinnwalberswick.co.uk
Ferry Road, Walberswick, Southwold, Suffolk IP18 6TN

£100; 6 well equipped rooms. Thriving 16th-c inn with a charming, rambling
bar, antique curved settles, cushioned pews and scrubbed tables on bare boards,
flagstones or black and red tiles, two huge fireplaces, good beers and wines
served by friendly staff, and interesting food using free-range lamb and pork and
local fish; the Barn Café (open in summer) serves tea, cakes and takeaways; seats
in the neat garden have a view over dunes to the sea; the rowing-boat ferry to
Southwold is nearby. Dogs allowed in two bedrooms and bar; £5 per stay.

WESTLETON   TM4469

Westleton Crown

(01728) 648777 – www.westletoncrown.co.uk
The Street, Westleton, Saxmundham, Suffolk IP17 3AD

£125; 34 comfortable rooms in main inn or converted stables and cottages.
Stylish old coaching inn with an attractive little bar at its heart – log fire, plenty
of original features, local ales, a thoughtfully chosen wine list and a chatty,
informal atmosphere; also a parlour, a dining room and a conservatory, a nice mix
of wooden dining chairs and tables, and old photos on fine old bare-brick walls,

interesting modern cooking and excellent breakfasts; seats in charming terraced garden; beach and heath walks. Dogs allowed in some bedrooms, bar, snug and lounge; blanket, biscuits, bowl, sausage and walks map; £7.50.

WOODBRIDGE
TM2548

Seckford Hall

(01394) 385678 – www.seckford.co.uk

Seckford Hall Road, Great Bealings, Woodbridge, Suffolk IP13 6NU

£185; 32 well equipped, comfortable rooms including 10 in courtyard. Handsome red-brick Tudor mansion in 34 acres of gardens and parkland with a carp-filled lake and putting; fine linenfold panelling, huge fireplaces, heavy beams, plush furnishings and antiques in comfortable day rooms, good bistro-style food (lovely teas with home-made cakes) in two restaurants and helpful service; indoor heated pool, recently refurbished spa in converted tithe barn. Dogs allowed in courtyard bedrooms; £10.

Surrey

DOG FRIENDLY PUBS

BUCKLAND   TQ2250
Pheasant
(01737) 221355 – www.brunningandprice.co.uk/pheasant
Reigate Road (A25 W of Reigate); RH3 7BG

Busy roadside pub with a thoughtful range of drinks and food served by friendly young staff, character rooms and seats on terrace and lawn

Carefully extended from its 18th-c heart, this is now an attractive weatherboarded pub with a bustling atmosphere and friendly, helpful staff. The various interconnected areas are split up by timbering and painted standing pillars and throughout there are wall-to-wall prints and pictures, gilt-edged mirrors, house plants, old stone bottles and elegant metal chandeliers. A couple of dining rooms at one end, separated by a two-sided open fire, have captain's chairs and cushioned dining chairs around a mix of tables on bare boards and rugs. The busy bar has a long high table with equally high chairs, another two-way fireplace with button-back leather armchairs and sofas in front of it and stools against the counter where they keep Brunning & Price Phoenix Original plus guests such as Harveys Best, Hogs Back TEA, Pilgrim Surrey Bitter, Surrey Hills Shere Drop and Titanic Plum Porter on handpump, 23 wines by the glass, 60 whiskies and 41 gins; background music and board games. Of the two further dining rooms, one has a big open fire pit in the middle. On the terrace is another open fire pit surrounded by built-in seats plus solid tables and chairs, while the lawn has plenty of picnic-sets and a play tractor for children.

Brunning & Price ~ Manager Beth Wells ~ Real ale ~ Open 9am-11pm (10.30pm Sun) ~ Bar food 9am-10pm ~ Restaurant ~ Children welcome ~ Dogs allowed in bar ~ Wi-fi

CHIDDINGFOLD   SU9635
Swan
(01428) 684688 – www.theswaninnchiddingfold.com
Petworth Road (A283 S); GU8 4TY

Open-plan light and airy rooms in well run inn, with local ales, modern food and seats in terraced garden; bedrooms

Especially busy on Goodwood race days, this stylishly updated tile-hung inn is popular with both locals and visitors. The bar has an open fire in an inglenook fireplace with leather armchairs in front and antlers above, wooden tables and chairs and cushioned wall seats on pale floorboards and leather-topped stools against the counter where they keep Upham Tipster and Stakes on handpump, 19 wines by the glass and a good choice of spirits. Staff are helpful and friendly. The dining room leads off here with modern chairs and chunky tables set with fresh flowers on more bare boards. Outside, a three-tiered terraced garden has plenty of seats and tables. There's plenty to do and see nearby.

Upham ~ Managers Zach and Sinead Leach ~ Real ale ~ Open 9am-11pm ~ Bar food 10-3, 6.30-9.30 (9 Sun) ~ Children welcome ~ Dogs allowed in bar ~ Wi-fi ~ Bedrooms: £165

CHILWORTH   TQ0347

Percy Arms

(01483) 561765 – www.thepercyarms.net
Dorking Road; GU4 8NP

Popular, well run pub, liked by families on Sunday lunchtime, with stylish décor, modern paintwork, attentive staff and highly regarded food; lots of outside seating

This extended and attractively decorated pub is popular – it's best to book a table in advance. To the right of the bar is a small room with logs piled neatly above a woodburning stove, a long slate-topped table lined with an equally long pew and cushioned bench and an L-shaped settle with scatter cushions by one other table; TV. The flagstoned bar has similar furnishings plus a high table and chairs in a corner and tartan-cushioned chairs against the counter where very efficient staff serve a beer named for the pub (from Greene King), Greene King IPA, Abbot and a guest beer on handpump and 16 wines by the glass. To the left of the entrance are two dining rooms down steps with upholstered tub and high-backed chairs on bare boards or rugs, and a self-service carvery. Down more steps and leading off the bar, other dining rooms have alcoves with built-in cushioned wall seats, high-backed spindle and other chairs on wooden floors, antler chandeliers and doors out to a decked terrace; another terrace has plenty of picnic-sets. Paintwork is contemporary, pictures have large rustic frames and here and there are antlers and animal skins. The interesting food includes south african specialities, and breakfast is open to non-residents. The two-part garden is connected by a bridge over a small stream and has children's play equipment and lots more picnic-sets.

Greene King ~ Lease Janine Hunter ~ Real ale ~ Open 7am-10pm; 8am-11pm Sat; 8am-10pm Sun ~ Bar food 12-3, 6-10; 12-10 Sat; 12-9 Sun ~ Children welcome ~ Dogs allowed in bar ~ Wi-fi

CHIPSTEAD   TQ2757

White Hart

(01737) 554455 – www.brunningandprice.co.uk/whitehartchipstead
Hazelwood Lane; CR5 3QW

Plenty to look at in open-plan rooms, thoughtful choice of drinks, interesting food and friendly staff

Opposite rugby playing fields with far distant views, this is a well run, busy pub in a pretty village. There's a raftered dining room to the right with elegant metal chandeliers, rough-plastered walls, an open fire in a brick fireplace and a couple of carved metal standing uprights. Helpful staff serve Phoenix Brunning & Price Original, Pilgrim Surrey Bitter and Sharps Doom Bar with guests such as Dark Star Partridge and Twickenham Wolf of the Woods on handpump, 16 wines by the glass, over 25 gins and up to 60 malt whiskies; background music and board games. The long room to the left is light and airy, with wall panelling at one end, a woodburning stove and numerous windows overlooking the seats on the terrace. Throughout, there's a fine mix of antique dining chairs and settles around all sorts of tables, rugs on bare boards or flagstones, hundreds of interesting cartoons, country pictures, cricketing prints and rugby team photographs, large, ornate mirrors and, on the windowsills and mantelpieces, old glass and stone bottles, clocks, books and plants.

Brunning & Price ~ Manager Damien Mann ~ Real ale ~ Open 11.30-11; 12-10.30 Sun ~ Bar food 12-10 (9.30 Sun) ~ Restaurant ~ Children welcome ~ Dogs allowed in bar ~ Wi-fi

CHOBHAM   SU9761
White Hart
(01276) 857580 – www.brunningandprice.co.uk/whitehartchobham
High Street; GU24 8AA

Brick-built village inn with cheerful customers and a thoughtful choice of food and drink

Dating from the early 16th c, this handsome place is one of the oldest buildings in the village. The opened-up bar has white-painted beams, standing pillars, rugs on parquet or wide boards, an assortment of dark wooden dining chairs and tables, and armchairs beside two fireplaces. High chairs line the counter where cheerful, well trained staff serve Phoenix Brunning & Price Original, Dark Star Original, Thurstons Horsell Gold, Tillingbourne Falls Gold and Twickenham Spring Ale on handpump, and a fine choice of wines and around 50 gins and 50 whiskies. An L-shaped dining room has a leather wall banquette and leather and brass-studded dining chairs around a mix of tables and lots of old photos and prints on exposed brick or painted walls. There's also a carpeted, comfortable dining room with similar furniture and a big elegant metal chandelier. The little side garden has seats under parasols.

Brunning & Price ~ Manager Nikki Szabo ~ Real ale ~ Open 11-11; 12-10.30pm Sun ~ Bar food 12-10; 9am-10pm Sat; 9am-9.30pm Sun ~ Restaurant ~ Children welcome ~ Dogs allowed in bar ~ Wi-fi

ELSTEAD   SU9044
Mill at Elstead
(01252) 703333 – www.millelstead.co.uk
Farnham Road (B3001 just W of village, which is itself between Farnham and Milford); GU8 6LE

Fascinating building with big attractive waterside garden, Fullers beers and well liked food

Rising four storeys, this sensitively converted, largely 18th-c watermill is in a rather special setting above the prettily banked River Wey. Picnic-sets are dotted about by the water (floodlit at night) which includes a lovely millpond, swans and weeping willows. A series of rambling linked bar areas on the spacious ground floor have big windows that make the most of the view, and there's a restaurant upstairs. You'll find brown leather armchairs and antique engravings by a longcase clock, neat modern tables and dining chairs on bare boards, big country tables on broad ceramic tiles, iron pillars, stripped masonry and a log fire in a huge inglenook. Fullers London Pride, ESB and Olivers Island with a guest such as Hogs Back Surrey Nirvana on handpump, 15 wines by the glass and several malt whiskies and gins; background music, board games and TV.

Fullers ~ Manager Paul Stephens ~ Real ale ~ Open 11-11; 12-10.30 Sun ~ Bar food 12-3, 5-9; 12-9 Sat; 12-7 Sun ~ Restaurant ~ Children welcome ~ Dogs welcome ~ Wi-fi ~ Quiz night Weds

ENGLEFIELD GREEN   SU9869

Bailiwick

(01784) 477877 – www.brunningandprice.co.uk/bailiwick
Wick Road; TW20 0HN

Fine position by parkland for busy pub, with lots of interest in various bars and dining rooms, well liked food and drink and super staff

The seats and tables on the small front terrace here overlook ancient woodland, and a circular walk from this busy pub follows the south-east corner of Windsor Great Park – you can also see the polo lawns, Virginia Water lake and the vast expanses of landscaped parkland. Smaller than many of the other Brunning & Price pubs, it has an open-plan bar area at the front where dogs are allowed: cushioned dining tables around wooden tables on rugs and bare boards, a pretty Victorian fireplace with a large mirror above and stools against the counter where knowledgable, warmly friendly staff serve Phoenix Brunning & Price Original, Dorking Gold, Trumans Swift and Twickenham Champions Ale on handpump, 21 good wines by the glass and farm cider. Steps lead down to a dining area and on again to a bigger room with caramel-coloured leather dining chairs, banquettes and every size of table. Throughout there are elegant metal chandeliers, prints and black and white photographs, lots of house plants and windowsills full of old stone and glass bottles. There's no car park but there are 20 free spaces in the long lay-by on Wick Road; if full there's a large pay-on-entry car park alongside.

Brunning & Price ~ Manager Paolo Corgiolu ~ Real ale ~ Open 10am-11pm; 9am-11pm Sat, Sun ~ Bar food 12-9.30 (9 Sun) ~ Children welcome but only in downstairs dining room after 6pm; no prams ~ Dogs allowed in bar ~ Wi-fi

ESHER   TQ1566

Marneys

(020) 8398 4444 – www.marneys.com
Alma Road (one-way), Weston Green; heading N on A309 from A307 roundabout, after Lamb & Star pub turn left into Lime Tree Avenue (signposted to All Saints Parish Church), then left at T junction into Chestnut Avenue; KT10 8JN

Country-feeling pub with good value food and attractive garden

A good local following enjoys the chatty low-beamed bar in this charming small pub – and it's handy for Hampton Court Palace. Fullers London Pride, Sharps Doom Bar and Youngs Original on handpump, 16 wines by the glass, ten malt whiskies and perhaps horse-racing on the unobtrusive corner TV. To the left, past a little cast-iron woodburning stove, the dining area has big pine tables, pews, pale country kitchen chairs and cottagey blue-curtained windows; background music. There are seats and wooden tables on the front terrace, which has views over the wooded common, village church and duck pond, and more seats on the decked area in the pleasantly planted sheltered garden.

Free house ~ Licensee Thomas Duxberry ~ Real ale ~ Open 11-11; 12-10.30 Sun ~ Bar food 12-2.30, 6-9; 12-3.30 Sun; not Fri-Sun evenings ~ Restaurant ~ Children welcome away from bar ~ Dogs allowed in bar ~ Wi-fi

MICKLEHAM   TQ1753

Running Horses

(01372) 372279 – www.therunninghorses.co.uk
Old London Road (B2209); RH5 6DU

Country pub with plenty of customers in bar and dining rooms, enjoyable food and drink and seats on big front terrace; bedrooms

On a warm day, the front terrace here is a fine place to sit among the pretty flowering tubs and hanging baskets, and there's a peaceful view of the old church with its strange stubby steeple. Inside, the stylish and spacious bar has cushioned wall settles and other dining chairs around straightforward tables on parquet flooring, racing cartoons and Hogarth prints on the walls, lots of race tickets hanging from a beam and a log fire in an inglenook fireplace; some wood-panelled booths have red leather banquettes. Stools line the counter where friendly, helpful staff serve a beer named for the pub (from Banks's), Brakspears Bitter and Oxford Gold, Fullers London Pride and Ringwood Boondoggle on handpump and around 20 wines by the glass; background music. The panelled restaurant has an attractive mix of upholstered and wooden dining chairs around a medley of tables on tartan carpet. Parking is in a narrow lane (you can also park on the main road).

Brakspears ~ Manager Iain Huddy ~ Real ale ~ Open 12-11 ~ Bar food 12-3, 6-9 (10 Fri, Sat); 12-6 Sun ~ Restaurant ~ Children welcome but must be over 10 in bar area ~ Dogs allowed in bar ~ Wi-fi ~ Bedrooms: £135

MILFORD   SU9542

Refectory

(01483) 413820 – www.brunningandprice.co.uk/refectory
Portsmouth Road; GU8 5HJ

Beamed and timbered rooms of much character, six real ales and other thoughtful drinks and well liked food

Originally a cattle barn, this handsome place then became an antiques shop and tea room before Brunning & Price carefully restored and extended it into this lovely pub. The L-shaped, mainly open-plan rooms are spacious and interesting with exposed stone walls, stalling and standing timbers creating separate seating areas, strikingly heavy beams and a couple of big log fires in fine stone fireplaces. A two-tiered and balconied part at one end has a wall covered with huge brass platters; elsewhere there are nice old photographs and a variety of paintings. Dining chairs and dark wooden tables are grouped on wooden, quarry-tiled or carpeted floors, and there are bookshelves, big pot plants, stone bottles on windowsills and fresh flowers. High wooden bar stools line the long counter where they serve Phoenix Brunning & Price Original, Hogs Back TEA, Dark Star Hophead and three guests from breweries such as Cottage, Langham and Tillingbourne on handpump, a dozen wines by the glass, around 80 malt whiskies and two farm ciders. The back courtyard – adjacent to the characterful pigeonry – has teak tables and chairs. Wheelchair facilities and disabled parking.

Brunning & Price ~ Manager Lee Parry ~ Real ale ~ Open 10.30am-11pm; 12-11 Sun ~ Bar food 12-10 (9.30 Sun) ~ Restaurant ~ Children welcome ~ Dogs allowed in bar ~ Wi-fi

SHAMLEY GREEN TQ0343

Red Lion

(01483) 892202 – www.redlionshamleygreen.com
The Green; GU5 0UB

Pleasant dining pub with popular tasty food and nice gardens

The highly rated food is the main draw to this friendly pub, but they do keep Youngs IPA and a couple of guests such as Greene King Morlands Old Golden Hen and Sharps Doom Bar on handpump, and 11 wines by the glass; staff are helpful and attentive. The two interconnected bars are fairly traditional with a mix of new and old wooden tables, chairs and cushioned settles on bare boards and red carpet, stripped standing timbers, fresh white walls, deep red ceilings and open fires; background music. There are plenty of hand-made rustic tables and benches outside, both at the front and at the back – which is more secluded and has seats on a heated, covered terrace and grassed dining areas.

Punch ~ Lease Debbie Ersser ~ Real ale ~ Open 11.30-11; 12-10 Sun (12-8 in winter) ~ Bar food 12-2.30 (3 weekends), 6.30-9.30; 12-3, 6.30-8.30 Sun; no food Sun evening in winter ~ Restaurant ~ Children welcome ~ Dogs allowed in bar ~ Wi-fi

SUNBURY TQ1068

Flower Pot

(01932) 780741 – www.theflowerpothotel.co.uk
1.6 miles from M3 junction 1; follow Lower Sunbury sign from exit roundabout, then at Thames Street turn right; pub on next corner, with Green Street; TW16 6AA

Former coaching inn with appealing, contemporary bar and dining room, real ales and all-day food; bedrooms

Although not actually on the river, this handsome place with its elegant wrought-iron balconies and pretty summer hanging baskets is in a villagey area with waterside walks. The airy bar has leather tub chairs around copper-topped tables, high chairs upholstered in brown and beige tartan around equally high tables in pale wood, attractive flagstones, contemporary paintwork and stools against the counter; there's also a couple of comfortably plush burgundy armchairs. The bar leads into a dining area with pale blue-painted and dark wooden cushioned dining chairs around an assortment of partly painted tables on bare boards, artwork on papered walls and a large gilt-edged mirror over an open fireplace; candles in glass jars, fresh flowers, background music and newspapers. Brakspears Bitter and Oxford Gold and a guest beer such as Wychwood Dirty Tackle on handpump and 15 wines by the glass. A side terrace has wood and metal tables and chairs. Breakfast is served to non-residents.

Authentic Inns ~ Tenant Simon Bailey ~ Real ale ~ Open 7am-11pm; 8am-11pm Sat, Sun ~ Bar food 7-3, 6-9 (10 Fri, Sat); 8am-9pm Sun ~ Restaurant ~ Children welcome ~ Dogs allowed in bar ~ Wi-fi ~ Live music last Sat of month ~ Bedrooms: £99

WALTON ON THE HILL TQ2255

Blue Ball

(01737) 819003 – www.theblueball.co.uk
Not far from M25 junction 8; Deans Lane, off B2220 by pond; KT20 7UE

Popular pub with spreading drinking and dining areas, helpful staff, well liked food and drink and lots of outside seating

Opposite Banstead Heath, this sizeable pub has been thoughtfully renovated. The entrance bar has a chatty atmosphere, a good welcome from cheerful staff and colourful leather-topped stools at the counter. there are rugs on bare boards, house plants on windowsills, all manner of old pictures and photographs on the walls, antique-style cushioned, farmhouse and high-backed kitchen chairs around tables of every size, and a sizeable wine cage. A beer named for the pub (from Caledonian), Caledonian Deuchars IPA, Courage Directors and Jennings Cumberland on handpump and good wines by the glass. Leading back from here, several dining rooms have multi-coloured button-back leather banquettes, similar chairs and tables on more rugs and wooden floors, bookshelves, gilt-edged mirrors and a big central conical open fire. On our Sunday visit, there were plenty of cheerful family groups enjoying roast lunches; background music. The outside terrace has lots of seats and tables plus a fire pit under a gazebo, and you can hire cabanas for a private group (you must book in advance, especially in warm weather when they're extremely popular).

Whiting & Hammond ~ Manager Martin Slocombe ~ Real ale ~ Open 10am-11pm; 9am-midnight Sat; 9am-10.30pm Sun ~ Bar food 12-9.30; 9am-9.30pm Sat; 9-9 Sun ~ Restaurant ~ Children welcome ~ Dogs allowed in bar ~ Wi-fi

DOG FRIENDLY HOTELS, INNS AND B&Bs

BAGSHOT   SU9062
Pennyhill Park
(01276) 471774 – www.pennyhillpark.co.uk
College Ride, Bagshot, Surrey GU19 5ET

£435 (breakfast extra); 123 individually designed luxury rooms and suites. Impressive Victorian country house in almost 125 acres of well kept gardens and parkland – nine-hole golf course, tennis courts, indoor and outdoor swimming pools, an international rugby pitch and a spa with sauna, steam room and treatments; friendly, courteous staff, a tranquil wood-panelled bar, a comfortable two-level lounge and reading room, open fires and fresh flowers; exceptional, imaginative food in the smart Latymer restaurant and stylish brasserie, indulgent afternoon teas, delicious breakfasts and Sunday lunchtime jazz; seats on the terraces overlooking the golf course. Dogs allowed in some bedrooms and lobby; bedding, treats and dog menu; £50 per stay.

BRAMLEY   TQ0044
Jolly Farmer
(01483) 893355 – www.jollyfarmer.co.uk
High Street, Bramley, Guildford, Surrey GU5 0HB

£80 (breakfast extra); 4 cosy rooms; also self-catering flat. Family-owned pub handy for Winkworth Arboretum (National Trust) and walks up St Martha's Hill; the bars have a homely miscellany of wooden tables and chairs, collections of enamel advertising signs, sewing machines, antique bottles, prints and old tools, and the timbered semi-partitions, mix of brick and timbering and open fireplace give the place a snug, cosy feel; eight real ales, six continental lagers and two ciders and a range of tasty bar food. Dogs allowed in all bedrooms and bar.

CHOBHAM
SU9563

Pembroke House

(01276) 857654 – www.pembrokebandb.co.uk
Valley End Road, Chobham, Surrey GU24 8TB

£130; 6 light, airy rooms (2 are ensuite). Lovely house in extensive pretty gardens surrounded by rolling fields, with a warm welcome from the owners, a rather fine entrance hall, a gracious sitting room and good breakfasts (no evening meals) in a charming dining room with spreading views; tennis court. Dogs allowed in all bedrooms.

CRANLEIGH
TQ0539

Richard Onslow

(01483) 274922 – www.therichardonslow.co.uk
113–117 High Street, Cranleigh, Surrey GU6 8AU

£110; 10 well equipped rooms. Bustling town-centre pub usefully open all day from 7am for excellent breakfasts; public bar with leather tub chairs and sofa and a slate-floored drinking area with real ales, two dining rooms with open fires, local photos and tartan tub chairs, and a sizeable restaurant with pale tables and chairs on wooden flooring and a good choice of interesting modern food served by friendly, efficient staff; walks in the Surrey Hills. Dogs allowed in one bedroom and bar; £10.

WEST END
SU9461

The Inn West End

(01276) 858652 – www.the-inn.co.uk
42 Guildford Road, West End, Surrey GU24 9PW

£90; 12 well equipped, comfortable bedrooms. An airy, bright place with a relaxed, friendly atmosphere and enthusiastic, hard-working licensees; the bar has pale paintwork, wooden benches and elegant chairs, pretty curtains and an unusual clock; there's also an extended restaurant and a lounge area, a charming garden and terrace with plenty of seats for warm weather; wine plays a big part here, with 20 by the glass from a fantastic list of around 500 (Iberia is the speciality) and a wine shop; first class food using local producers and ingredients includes breakfast, morning coffee and afternoon tea; Sunny and Teddy are the pub dogs. No under-5s. Dogs allowed in two bedrooms and bar; mats; £10.

Sussex

DOG FRIENDLY PUBS

ALFRISTON
TQ5203

Star

(01323) 870495 ~ www.thestaralfriston.co.uk
High Street; BN26 5TA

Ancient inn with original features, plenty of space for drinking and dining, helpful staff and enjoyable food; bedrooms

The handsome timbered frontage of this 13th-c inn is decorated with fine medieval carvings, and the striking red lion on the corner – known as Old Bill – was probably the figurehead from a wrecked Dutch ship. The character front bar has heavy dark beams, cushioned settles, stools and captain's chairs around pubby tables on bare floorboards, a log fire in the Tudor fireplace and tankards hanging over the counter where they serve beers from Harveys and Long Man on handpump and ten wines by the glass. Steps down to the left lead into a big two-level bar (one level has a lovely herringbone brick floor) with rustic tables, chapel chairs and both an open fire and woodburning stove; there's a door through to yet another room with book-mural wallpaper, plush burgundy armchairs and sofas, another woodburner and a TV. Some medieval artefacts are hung on the walls. The village is well worth a stroll around, and there are plenty of surrounding walks.

Free house ~ Licensee Julie Garvin ~ Real ale ~ Bar food ~ Restaurant ~ Children welcome ~ Dogs allowed in bar ~ Wi-fi ~ Live music Fri evenings ~ Bedrooms: £92

CHARLTON
SU8812

Fox Goes Free

(01243) 811461 – www.thefoxgoesfree.com
Village signposted off A286 Chichester–Midhurst in Singleton, also from Chichester–Petworth via East Dean; PO18 0HU

Comfortable old pub with beamed bars, popular food and drink and big garden; bedrooms

This is a lovely place to while away a lunchtime – especially in good weather when you can sit at one of the picnic-sets under the apple trees in the attractive back garden with the South Downs as a backdrop; there are rustic benches and tables on the gravelled front terrace too. The bar, the first of several cosy separate rooms, has old irish settles, tables and chapel chairs and an open fire. Standing timbers divide up a larger beamed bar, which has a huge brick fireplace and old local photographs on the walls. A dining area overlooks the garden. The family extension is a clever conversion from horse boxes and the stables where the 1926 Goodwood winner was once housed; darts, board games, TV and background music. A beer named for the pub (from Arundel), Langham Hip Hop and Saison and Listers Best Bitter on handpump, 15 wines by the glass and Addlestone's cider. You can walk up to Levin Down nature reserve, or stroll around the Iron Age hill fort on the Trundle with huge views to the Isle of Wight; the Weald & Downland Open Air Museum and West Dean Gardens are nearby too.

Free house ~ Licensee David Coxon ~ Real ale ~ Open 11am-11pm (midnight Sat); 12-11 Sun ~ Bar food 12-2.30, 6.15-9.45; 12-10 weekends ~ Restaurant ~ Children welcome ~ Dogs allowed in bar ~ Wi-fi ~ Live music first Weds of month ~ Bedrooms: £95

COPTHORNE   TQ3240
Old House
(01342) 718529 ~ www.theoldhouseinn.co.uk
B2037 NE of village; RH10 3JB

Charming old place with plenty of character, real ales, enjoyable food and attentive staff; attractive bedrooms

This is a lovely old inn housed in a timbered higgledy-piggledy building with nooks and crannies in several interconnected rooms. The immediately warming little bar has an easy-going feel, a brown leather chesterfield, armchairs and carved wooden chairs around all sorts of tables, a big sisal mat on flagstones, a decorative fireplace and nightlights. Ringwood Razorback, Sharps Doom Bar and a guest from Copthorne on handpump, several good wines by the glass and a couple of huge glass flagons holding Sipsmith vodka and gin. Off to the left is a charming small room with a woodburning stove in an inglenook fireplace and two leather armchairs in front, white-painted beams in a low ceiling (this is the oldest part, dating from the 16th c), cushioned settles and pre-war-style cushioned dining chairs around varying tables. A teeny back room, like something you'd find on an old galleon, has button-back wall seating up to the roof, a few chairs and heavy ropework. The dining rooms are beamed (some painted) and timbered with parquet, quarry tiles or sisal flooring, high-backed leather and other dining chairs, more wall seating and fresh flowers and candles; background music and board games. The terraced garden has heavy rustic tables and benches. Gatwick Airport is nearby.

Free house ~ Licensee Stephen Godsave ~ Real ale ~ Open 11-11; 12-10 Sun ~ Bar food 12-3, 6-9 (8 Sun) ~ Restaurant ~ Children welcome ~ Dogs allowed in bar ~ Wi-fi ~ Bedrooms: £90

DANEHILL   TQ4128
Coach & Horses
(01825) 740369 ~ www.coachandhorses.co
Off A275, via School Lane towards Chelwood Common; RH17 7JF

Well run dining pub with bustling bars, welcoming staff, very good food and ales and a big garden

In warm weather, the adults-only terrace beneath a huge maple tree is quite a draw, and the big garden has picnic-sets, a children's play area and fine views of the South Downs. Inside, the little bar to the right has half-panelled walls, simple furniture on polished floorboards, a woodburner in a brick fireplace and a big hatch to the bar counter: Harveys Best and a guest from a local brewery such as Long Man on handpump, local Black Pig farmhouse cider and a dozen wines by the glass including prosecco and Bluebell sparkling wine from Sussex. A couple of steps lead down to a half-panelled area with a mix of dining chairs around characterful wooden tables (set with flowers and candles) on a fine brick floor, and changing artwork on the walls; cribbage, dominoes and cards. Down another step is a dining area with stone walls, beams, flagstones and a woodburning stove.

Free house ~ Licensee Ian Philpots ~ Real ale ~ Open 12-3, 5.30-11; 12-11 Sat; 12-10.30 Sun ~ Bar food 12-2, 6.30-9 (9.30 Fri, Sat); 12-3 Sun ~ Restaurant ~ Well behaved children welcome but not on adult terrace ~ Dogs allowed in bar ~ Wi-fi

DIAL POST   TQ1519

Crown

(01403) 710902 ~ www.crowninndialpost.co.uk
Worthing Road (off A24 S of Horsham); RH13 8NH

Tile-hung village pub with interesting food and a good mix of drinkers and diners; bedrooms

The friendly licensees here are equally welcoming to locals and visitors, and this creates a cheerful, bustling atmosphere. The beamed bar has a couple of standing timbers, brown squashy sofas, pine tables and chairs on the stone floor, a small woodburning stove in a brick fireplace, and Greyhound Beer, Long Man Best Bitter and a changing ale from Hammerpot on handpump served from the attractive herringbone brick counter; eight wines by the glass plus prosecco, champagne and a pudding wine. To the right of the bar, the restaurant (with more beams) has an ornamental woodburner in a brick fireplace, a few photographs, chunky pine tables, chairs, a couple of cushioned pews and a shelf of books; steps lead down to an additional dining room; board games. The pub dog is called Chops. The straightforwardly furnished dining conservatory, facing the village green, is light and airy. There are picnic-sets in the garden behind the pub.

Free house ~ Licensees James and Penny Middleton-Burn ~ Real ale ~ Open 12-3, 6-11; 12-4 Sun ~ Bar food 12-2.15, 6-9 (9.30 Fri, Sat); 12-3 Sun ~ Restaurant ~ Children welcome but must be dining after 7pm ~ Dogs welcome ~ Wi-fi ~ Bedrooms: £69

DITCHLING   TQ3215

Bull

(01273) 843147 ~ www.thebullditchling.com
High Street (B2112); BN6 8TA

500-year-old local in centre of village with three bars and dining rooms, a good choice of ales and popular food; bedrooms

This ancient and atmospheric pub is said to get its name from the papal bull designating it as a safe house for pilgrims and travellers to the great monastery at Lewes. The beamed main room on the right is a cosy haven in winter with a log fire in a sizeable inglenook fireplace, and efficient staff greet you at the bar counter where they serve Bedlam Benchmark, Timothy Taylors Landlord and guests such as Dark Star Revelation, Gun Project Babylon and 360° Pale #39 on handpump, 22 wines by the glass and a large choice of spirits. There are benches, scrubbed wooden tables and leather chesterfields on bare boards, and modern artwork and historic photos of the village on the walls; daily papers and background music. Two other rooms lead off to the left from the main entrance. You can sit in the garden under apple trees or on a terrace; the kitchen garden provides fruit, vegetables and herbs for the pub's menu.

Free house ~ Licensee Dominic Worrall ~ Real ale ~ Open 11-11 (10.30 Sun) ~ Bar food 12-2.30, 6-9.30; 12-9.30 Sat; 12-9 Sun ~ Restaurant ~ Children welcome ~ Dogs allowed in bar ~ Wi-fi ~ Quiz night second Sun of month ~ Bedrooms: £140

DUNCTON

SU9517

Cricketers

(01798) 342473 – www.thecricketersduncton.co.uk
Set back from A285; GU28 0LB

Charming old coaching inn with friendly licensees, real ales, popular food and suntrap back garden

Handy for Goodwood, this old inn dates from at least the 1600s and got its present name from the 19th-c owner John Wisden, the cricketer who published the famous *Wisden Cricketers' Almanack*. The traditional bar has a display of cricketing memorabilia, a few standing timbers, simple seating and an open woodburning stove in an inglenook fireplace. Steps lead down to a dining room with farmhouse chairs around wooden tables. Dark Star Partridge, Langham Hip Hop, Triple fff Moondance and a guest from Firebird on handpump, nine wines by the glass and two farm ciders. There are picnic-sets out in front beneath the flowering window boxes and more on decked areas and under parasols on the grass in the picturesque back garden.

Inn Company ~ Manager Martin Boult ~ Real ale ~ Open 11-11; 12-10.30 Sun ~ Bar food 12-2.30, 6-9; 12-9 Sat, Sun; brunch 11-midday (not Sun), hot snacks 3-6 ~ Children welcome ~ Dogs allowed in bar ~ Wi-fi

EARTHAM

SU9309

George

(01243) 814340 – www.thegeorgeeartham.com
Signed off A285 Chichester–Petworth, from Fontwell off A27, from Slindon off A29; PO18 0LT

170-year-old pub in tucked-away village with country furnishings and contemporary touches, local ales and enjoyable food

There are some lovely walks and cycle routes in the rolling South Downs around this well run, friendly pub. The light and airy bar has a cheerful mix of customers and is prettily decorated with scatter cushions on a long wall pew, painted dining chairs around wood-topped tables (each set with fresh flowers and candles) on parquet flooring. There are sofas, armchairs, a dresser with country knick-knacks, beams, timbering, paintings on cream-painted walls above a grey-planked dado, stone bottles and books and three open fires; background music and board games. A beer named for the pub (from Otter) and guests such as Goldmark Liquid Gold, Hogs Back Surrey Nirvana and Langham Decennium 10 on handpump, 13 wines by the glass, 20 gins, 20 malt whiskies and farm cider. The large garden has picnic-sets on grass and seats and tables under a gazebo. Easy disabled access.

Free house ~ Licensees James and Anita Thompson ~ Real ale ~ Open 11.30-11; 12-6 Sun; closed Mon ~ Bar food 12-3, 6-9; 12-4 Sun ~ Restaurant ~ Children welcome ~ Dogs allowed in bar

EAST DEAN

TV5597

Tiger

(01323) 423209 – www.beachyhead.org.uk
Off A259 Eastbourne–Seaford; BN20 0DA

Pretty old pub with two little bars and a dining room, an informal and friendly atmosphere and own-brewed beers; bedrooms

The walks to the coast and along the clifftops of the Seven Sisters and up to Belle Tout Lighthouse and Beachy Head are splendid, so this charming old pub is always packed. The delightful cottage-lined green position is also a big draw and in warm weather customers sit on the grass here or at picnic-sets on the flower-filled terrace. You need to arrive early to be sure of a seat and they only take table reservations from October to March. The focal point of the little beamed main bar is the open woodburning stove in a brick inglenook, surrounded by polished horsebrasses; there are just a few rustic tables with benches, simple wooden chairs, a window seat and a long cushioned wall bench. The walls are hung with fish prints and a stuffed tiger's head, and a couple of hunting horns hang above the long bar counter. Friendly, attentive staff serve their own-brewed Beachy Head Legless Rambler and South Downs Ale (brewery tours available on request), Harveys Best, Long Man Golden Tipple and Long Blonde and St Austell Tribute on handpump, and nine wines by the glass. Down a step on the right is a small room with an exceptionally fine high-backed curved settle, a couple of other old settles and nice old chairs and wooden tables on coir carpeting; on the walls there's an ancient map of Eastbourne and Beachy Head and photographs of the pub. The dining room to the left of the main bar has a cream woodburner and hunting prints.

Free house ~ Licensee Rebecca Vasey ~ Real ale ~ Open 8am-11pm ~ Bar food 12-3, 6-9 ~ Restaurant ~ Children welcome ~ Dogs allowed in bar ~ Wi-fi ~ Bedrooms: £130

ERIDGE GREEN   TQ5535
Nevill Crest & Gun

(01892) 864209 ~ www.brunningandprice.co.uk/nevillcrestandgun
A26 Tunbridge Wells–Crowborough; TN3 9JR

Handsome old building with lots of character, plenty to look at, six real ales and enjoyable modern food

This 500-year-old former farmhouse has been cleverly opened up and extended with standing timbers and doorways keeping some sense of separate rooms. Throughout, there are heavy beams (some carved), panelling, rugs on wooden floors and woodburning stoves and open fires in three fireplaces (the linenfold carved bressumer above one is worth seeking out). Also, all manner of individual dining chairs around dark wood or copper-topped tables, lots of pictures, maps and photographs relating to the local area, and windowsills crammed with toby jugs, stone and glass bottles and plants. Phoenix Brunning & Price Original, Hurst Founders Best Bitter, Larkins Traditional, Long Man Best Bitter, Old Dairy Red Top, Tonbridge Coppernob and Westerham Grasshopper on handpump, 15 wines by the glass and 70 malt whiskies; daily papers, board games and background music. There are a few picnic-sets in front of the building and teak furniture on the back terrace, next to the newer dining extension with its large windows, light oak rafters, beams and coir flooring.

Brunning & Price ~ Manager Ian Huxley ~ Real ale ~ Open 11-11 ~ Bar food 12-9 ~ Children welcome ~ Dogs allowed in bar ~ Wi-fi

FIRLE   TQ4607
Ram

(01273) 858222 ~ www.raminn.co.uk
Village signed off A27 Lewes–Polegate; BN8 6NS

Bustling country pub with three open fires, character rooms, good food and drink and seats in garden; bedrooms

There's usually a cheerful crowd of locals and walkers in this 500-year-old country inn, part of the Firle Estate. The main bar has a log fire, captain's and mate's chairs and a couple of gingham armchairs around dark pubby tables on bare boards or quarry tiles, gilt-edged paintings on dark brown walls, Harveys Best and guest beers such as Dark Star Hophead, Long Man Golden Tipple and Sharps Doom Bar on handpump, 21 wines by the glass and eight malt whiskies; service is welcoming and helpful. A cosy bar leads off here with another log fire, olive green built-in planked and cushioned wall seats and more dark chairs and tables on parquet flooring. Throughout, there are various ceramic ram's heads or skulls, black and white photos of the local area, candles in hurricane jars and daily papers; darts and toad in the hole. The back dining room is up some steps and overlooks the flint-walled garden where there are tables and chairs on a terrace and picnic-sets on grass; more picnic-sets under parasols at the front.

Free house ~ Licensee Hayley Bayes ~ Real ale ~ Open 9am-11pm ~ Bar food 9am-9.30pm ~ Children welcome away from bar ~ Dogs welcome ~ Wi-fi

FLETCHING   TQ4223
Griffin
(01825) 722890 – www.thegriffininn.co.uk
Village signposted off A272 W of Uckfield; TN22 3SS

Busy, gently upmarket inn with a fine wine list, real ales, bistro-style bar food and a big garden; pretty bedrooms

This is a handsome village and this civilised inn is very much its focal point. The beamed and quaintly panelled bar rooms have blazing log fires, old photographs and hunting prints, straightforward close-set furniture including some captain's chairs, and china on a delft shelf. A small bare-boarded serving area is off to one side and there's a cosy separate bar with sofas and a TV. The place gets pretty packed at weekends. Harveys Best and guests such as Beachy Head Legless Rambler and Gun Scaramanga on handpump, plus 20 wines by the glass from a good list (including champagne, prosecco and sweet wine); they hold a monthly wine club with supper (on a Thursday evening). At the bottom of the two-acre garden behind the pub is an outside bar and wood oven, tables and chairs under parasols and a stunning view over Sheffield Park; there are more seats on a sandstone terrace. There are ramps for wheelchairs.

Free house ~ Licensees James Pullan and Samantha Barlow ~ Real ale ~ Open 12-11; 12-midnight Sat; 12-10.30 Sun ~ Bar food 12-2.30 (2.45 weekends), 7-9.30 (9 Sun) ~ Restaurant ~ Children welcome ~ Dogs allowed in bar ~ Wi-fi ~ Piano player Fri and Sat evenings, Sun lunch ~ Bedrooms: £100

FRIDAY STREET   TV6203
Farm at Friday Street
(01323) 766049 – www.farmfridaystreet.com
B2104, Langney; BN23 8AP

Handsome 17th-c house with lots to look at, efficient staff serving popular food and drink and seats outside

There's plenty of both dining and drinking areas in what was once a farmhouse (although houses have replaced the fields that used to surround it) and the atmosphere is friendly and easy-going. The old core has many newer extensions, but it's been done well – the open-plan rooms are split by brick pillars into cosier areas with sofas, stools and all manner of wooden dining chairs and tables on bare boards, creamy coloured flagstones, coir or carpet: Throughout, there are open fires, big house plants, stubby church candles, frame-to-frame prints and pictures and farming implements. Caledonian Deuchars IPA, Langham Best Bitter, Long Man Long Blonde, St Austell Tribute and Sharps Doom Bar on handpump and 14 wines by the glass. The dining room is on two levels with timbered walls, glass partitions, a raised conical roof and an open kitchen. The front lawn has plenty of picnic-sets.

Whiting & Hammond ~ Manager Paul Worman ~ Real ale ~ Open 9am-11pm (10.30pm Sun) ~ Bar food 12-9.30 (9 Sun) ~ Restaurant ~ Children welcome ~ Dogs allowed in bar ~ Wi-fi

HASTINGS

TQ8109

Crown

(01424) 465100 - www.thecrownhastings.co.uk
All Saints Street, Old Town; TN34 3BN

Informal and friendly corner pub with interesting food, local ales and simple furnishings – a good find

With an easy-going and gently quirky feel, this bustling little corner pub in the Old Town is just up from the sea. The simply furnished bar has bare boards, plain chairs around tables inlaid with games and set with posies of flowers, a log fire and plenty of windows to keep everything light (despite the dark paintwork); a snug has leather armchairs in front of another open fire, a couple of tables, and books and house plants on a windowsill and mantelpiece; board games. Stools line the counter where they keep four changing ales from breweries such as Bedlam, Franklins, Old Dairy and Three Legs on handpump, 15 good wines by the glass, 17 gins, 17 whiskies and local cider; service is friendly and helpful. There's a dining area at one end of the bar with scatter cushions on wall seats, mismatched chairs and some sizeable tables. Local art hangs on the walls (some for sale) and on our visit one window was hung with bright neckties and lined with shelves of local pottery, greetings cards and hand-made purses; daily papers and background jazz or blues music. Dogs and children receive a genuinely warm welcome. There are a few picnic-sets at the front.

Free house ~ Licensees Tess Eaton and Andrew Swan ~ Real ale ~ Open 11-11 (10.30 Sun) ~ Bar food 12-10 (9.30 Sun) ~ Children welcome ~ Dogs welcome ~ Wi-fi

HEATHFIELD

TQ5920

Star

(01435) 863570 - www.starinnoldheathfield.co.uk
Church Street, Old Heathfield, off A265/B2096 E; TN21 9AH

Pleasant old pub with bustling, friendly atmosphere, well liked food, a decent choice of drinks and seats in lovely garden

The irregular stonework at the bottom of this pub shows its great age – it was built in 1328 as a resting place for pilgrims on their way along this high ridge across the Weald to Canterbury. There are ancient heavy beams, built-in wall settles and window seats, panelling, inglenook fireplaces and a roaring winter log fire; a doorway leads to a similarly decorated room set up more for eating with wooden tables and chairs (one table has high-backed white leather dining chairs) and a woodburning stove. An upstairs dining room has a striking barrel-vaulted ceiling (it was originally a dormitory for masons working on the reconstruction of the church after a fire in 1348). Harveys Best and guests such as Jennings Sneck Lifter and Whitstable East India Pale Ale on handpump and 11 wines by the glass;

background music. The very prettily planted garden has rustic furniture under smart umbrellas and lovely views of rolling pasture dotted with sheep and lined with oak trees.

Free house ~ Licensees Mike and Sue Chappell ~ Real ale ~ Open 11.30-11; 12-10.30 Sun ~ Bar food 12-2.30, 6.30-9; 12-3, 6-8.30 Sun ~ Restaurant ~ Children welcome ~ Dogs welcome ~ Wi-fi

HENLEY   SU8925
Duke of Cumberland Arms

(01428) 652280 ~ www.dukeofcumberland.com
Off A286 S of Fernhurst; GU27 3HQ

Charming country pub with two character dining rooms, local beers and enjoyable food

It's hard to imagine that the lane on which this pretty little stone-built 16th-c cottage stands was once the main road from London to Chichester – coaches would stop here and change horses. Two small rooms have big scrubbed oak tables on brick or flagstoned floors, low ceilings, rustic decorations and an open fire. Harveys Best, Langham Best Bitter and Hip Hop and London Beer Factory Chelsea Blonde tapped from the cask and several wines by the glass; background music and board games. A dining extension has a light and more modern feel plus cosy sofas in front of a woodburning stove and fine views. From seats and picnic-sets on decking and in the charming big, tiered garden there are more beautiful Surrey Hills views; the many ponds contain trout.

Free house ~ Licensee Simon Goodman ~ Real ale ~ Open 11.45-11.30; 12-10.30 Sun ~ Bar food 12-2, 7-9; not Sun or Mon evenings ~ Restaurant ~ Well behaved children welcome ~ Dogs allowed in bar ~ Wi-fi

HIGH HURSTWOOD   TQ4925
Hurstwood

(01825) 732257 ~ www.thehurstwood.com
Hurstwood Road off A272; TN22 4AH

Friendly dining pub with chatty bar area, first class food and seats in the garden

The main emphasis here is on the excellent food – but regulars do drop in for a pint and a chat and they keep Harveys Best and IPA and Sharps Doom Bar on handpump, ten good wines by the glass and a fair choice of spirits and cocktails; staff are attentive. The U-shaped and beamed open-plan interior has high spindleback chairs against the counter, and an area beside the log fire in the tiled Victorian fireplace with a couple of leather sofas, armchairs and two tables. The dining areas have tables set with red gingham napkins, little plants and church candles in rustic ironwork candlesticks, chairs that range from farmhouse to captain's to cushioned dining ones on bare boards, hunting prints and other artwork on pale painted walls above a grey dado, various lamps and lanterns, and a piano (which does get played). French windows at one end open out to decking with seats and tables, which leads down to a grassed area where there are more seats.

Free house ~ Licensees Martin and Lenka Spanek ~ Real ale ~ Open 11.30-11; 12-5.30 Sun; closed Sun evening except bank holidays ~ Bar food 12-2.30, 6.30-9.30; 12-3 Sun ~ Children welcome ~ Dogs allowed in bar ~ Wi-fi

HORSHAM

Black Jug

(01403) 253526 – www.brunningandprice.co.uk/blackjug
North Street; RH12 1RJ

Busy town pub with wide choice of drinks, efficient staff and rewarding food

There's a good mixed crowd of office workers, theatre-goers and couples here and the atmosphere is always lively. The single, large, early 20th-c room has a long central bar, a nice collection of sizeable dark wood tables and comfortable chairs on a stripped-wood floor, bookcases and interesting old prints and photographs above a dark wood-panelled dado on cream walls; board games. A spacious, bright conservatory has similar furniture and lots of hanging baskets. Harveys Best and Marstons Pedigree New World with guests such as Courage Directors and Butcombe Haka on handpump, 16 wines by the glass, 150 malt whiskies, 30 rums and farm cider. The pretty, flower-filled back terrace has plenty of garden furniture; parking is in the council car park next door, as the small one by the pub is for staff and deliveries only.

Brunning & Price ~ Tenant Alastair Craig ~ Real ale ~ Open 11.30am-11pm; 12-10.30 Sun ~ Bar food 12-10 (9.30 Sun) ~ Children welcome till 5pm ~ Dogs allowed in bar ~ Wi-fi

HORSTED KEYNES

Crown

(01825) 791609 – www.thecrown-horstedkeynes.co.uk
The Green; RH17 7AW

Super food in beamed 16th-c inn, character bar with real ales, fine wines and seats outside; bedrooms

Of course, much emphasis is placed on the highly thought-of food here (cooked by the chef-patron), but there's also a proper bar with heavy beams, big flagstones, a huge inglenook fireplace, simple furniture and chairs against the counter where they keep Harveys Best, Long Man Copper Hop and St Austells Tribute on handpump and 20 wines by the glass; staff are helpful and convivial. There's also a two-way fireplace with a leather sofa on one side and spreading dining areas on the other, with all manner of high-backed wooden and leather dining chairs around rustic-style tables on red-patterned carpet, more beams and timbering and bare brick walls. Seats in the terraced back garden overlook the village green and cricket pitch and there are also picnic-sets at the front.

Free house ~ Licensee Mark Raffan ~ Real ale ~ Open 12-3, 6-11; 12-5 Sun; closed Mon ~ Bar food 12-2.30, 6-9; 12-4.30 Sun ~ Restaurant ~ Children welcome ~ Dogs allowed in bar ~ Wi-fi ~ Bedrooms: £90

LICKFOLD

Lickfold Inn

(01789) 532535 – www.thelickfoldinn.co.uk
NE of Midhurst, between A286 and A283; GU28 9EY

Tudor country pub with impressive food in bars and upstairs restaurant, friendly staff, a thoughtful choice of drinks and attractive garden

It's a surprise to find this little gem tucked away in the countryside with such inventive and delicious food on offer. But this is no straightforward restaurant – it's a proper pub with a working bar and a great deal of easy-going character. The two bar rooms have heavy Tudor beams, a fine herringbone brick floor, comfortable sofas to each side of a woodburning stove, chapel chairs, armchairs, Georgian settles and more sofas with scatter cushions and nice old tables (some with fine in-laid panels); it's fun to be able to watch the kitchen hard at work behind a big glass window. Bowman Lapwing and Swift One and Langham Best Bitter on handpump, a dozen wines by the glass and several gins. Upstairs, the restaurant has more heavy beams, pale grey upholstered dining chairs around dark polished wood tables on bare boards, a few standing timbers and another woodburning stove. Outside, a terrace has plenty of seats and tables and there's also a garden across the drive on several levels with more seats, and a big enclosure of chickens.

Free house ~ Licensee Tom Sellers ~ Real ale ~ Open 11.30-10; 11.30-11.30 Sat; 11.30-8.30 Sun; closed Mon, winter Tues, first two weeks Jan ~ Bar food 12-2, 7-9 ~ Restaurant ~ Children welcome ~ Dogs allowed in bar ~ Wi-fi

LURGASHALL   SU9327

Noahs Ark

(01428) 707346 – www.noahsarkinn.co.uk
Off A283 N of Petworth; GU28 9ET

Busy old pub in nice spot with neatly kept rooms, real ales and pleasing food using local produce

An inn since 1537, this old place is in a lovely spot overlooking the village green and cricket pitch. Inside, the simple, traditional bar, popular with locals, has a bustling atmosphere and bar stools by the counter where they serve Greene King IPA and Abbot and a guest such as Hogs Back TEA on handpump, 20 wines by the glass and a fine bloody mary. There are also beams, a mix of wooden chairs and tables, parquet flooring and an inglenook fireplace. Open to the top of the rafters, the dining room is spacious and airy with church candles and fresh flowers on light wood tables; a couple of comfortable sofas face each other in front of an open woodburning stove; background music and board games. The pub's border terrier is called Gillie and visiting dogs may get a dog biscuit. There are tables in a large side garden.

Greene King ~ Lease Henry Coghlan and Amy Whitmore ~ Real ale ~ Open 11-11; 11-midnight Sat; 12-10 (8 in winter) Sun ~ Bar food 12-2.30, 7-9.30; 12-3 Sun ~ Restaurant ~ Children welcome ~ Dogs allowed in bar ~ Wi-fi

MARK CROSS   TQ5831

Mark Cross Inn

(01892) 852423 – www.themarkcross.co.uk
A267 N of Mayfield; TN6 3NP

Sizeable pub with interconnected rooms, real ales and popular food (including brunch), and good views from seats in the garden

In warm weather, the benches and tables on the terrace and the picnic-sets on grass get snapped up quickly by customers keen to enjoy the far-reaching views; there's also a children's play fort. Inside, it's a big place on several linked levels but kept cosy with church candles and open fires, shelves lined with books and stone bottles, gilt-edged mirrors, big clocks, large house plants and fresh flowers.

There's all manner of seating from farmhouse, mate's and cushioned dining chairs to settles and stools grouped around dark shiny tables on rugs and bare boards, and the walls are lined almost frame to frame with photographs, prints, paintings and old newspaper cuttings. Helpful staff serve Caledonian Deuchars IPA, Fullers London Pride, Long Man Best and Shepherd Neame Spitfire on handpump and good wines by the glass; daily papers and background music.

Whiting & Hammond ~ Manager Amy Glenie ~ Real ale ~ Open 9am-11pm (midnight Fri, Sat); 9-10.30 Sun ~ Bar food 12-9.30 (9 Sun) ~ Restaurant ~ Children welcome ~ Dogs allowed in bar ~ Wi-fi

OVING   SU9005

Gribble Inn

(01243) 786893 – www.gribbleinn.co.uk
Between A27 and A259 E of Chichester; PO20 2BP

Own-brewed beers in bustling village pub with well liked bar food and pretty garden

For over 30 years, this 16th-c thatched pub has brewed its own ales. On handpump, these might include Fuzzy Duck, Gribble Ale, Pig's Ear, Plucking Pheasant, Quad Hopper, Reg's Tipple and three seasonal ales, such as Sussex Quad Hopper or strong Wobbler Ale; they also stock 30 gins, 30 vodkas and unusual rums. The chatty bar features a lot of heavy beams and timbering while the other various linked rooms have a cottagey feel and sofas around two roaring log fires; board games. The barn houses a venue for parties. There are seats outside in a covered area and more chairs and tables in the pretty garden with its apple and pear trees.

Badger ~ Licensees Simon Wood and Nicola Tester ~ Real ale ~ Open 11-11; 12-9 Sun ~ Bar food 12-9; 12-4 Sun ~ Restaurant ~ Children welcome away from bar ~ Dogs allowed in bar ~ Wi-fi

PETWORTH   SU9721

Angel

(01798) 342153 – www.angelinnpetworth.co.uk
Angel Street; GU28 0BG

Medieval building with 18th-c façade, chatty atmosphere in beamed bars, friendly service and good, interesting food; bedrooms

This is a smart town pub with the feel of a country inn. The interconnected rooms have kept many of their original features. The front bar has beams, a log fire in an inglenook fireplace and an appealing variety of old wooden and cushioned dining chairs and tables on wide floorboards. It leads through to the main room with high chairs by the counter where they keep a beer named for the pub (from Langham) plus a guest such as Dorking Smokestack Lightnin' and Firebird Pacific Gem on handpump, 22 wines by the glass from an extensive list and a good range of malt whiskies and gins; board games. Staff are courteous and helpful. There's also high-backed brown leather and antique chairs and tables on pale wooden flooring, the odd milk churn and french windows to a three-level terrace garden. The cosy and popular back bar is similarly furnished, with a second log fire.

Free house ~ Licensee Murray Inglis ~ Real ale ~ Open 10.30am-11pm; 11.30-10.30 Sun ~ Bar food 12-2.30, 6.30-9.30; 12-2.30, 6-9 Sun ~ Children welcome ~ Dogs welcome ~ Wi-fi ~ Live jazz summer Sun 4pm ~ Bedrooms: £140

RINGMER

TQ4313

Cock

(01273) 812040 – www.cockpub.co.uk
Uckfield Road – blocked-off section of road off A26 N of village turn-off; BN8 5RX

Country pub with a wide choice of popular bar food, real ales in character bar and plenty of seats in the garden

You can be sure of a warm welcome in this 16th-c former coaching inn from the friendly licensees and their helpful staff. The unspoilt bar has traditional pubby furniture on flagstones, heavy beams, a log fire in an inglenook fireplace, Harveys Best and a couple of guests such as Beachy Head Legless Rambler and Dark Star Hophead on handpump, 12 wines by the glass and a dozen malt whiskies. There are also three dining areas; background music. Outside, on the terrace and in the garden, are lots of picnic-sets with views across open fields to the South Downs. The owners' dogs are called Bailey and Tally, and visiting dogs are offered a bowl of water and a chew. This is sister pub to the Highlands at Uckfield.

Free house ~ Licensees Ian, Val, Nick and Matt Ridley ~ Real ale ~ Open 11-3, 6-11.30; 11-10.30 Sun ~ Bar food 12-2 (2.30 Sat), 6-9.30; 12-8.30 Sun ~ Restaurant ~ Well behaved children welcome but no toddlers ~ Dogs allowed in bar ~ Wi-fi

ROBERTSBRIDGE

TQ7323

George

(01580) 880315 – www.thegeorgerobertsbridge.co.uk
High Street; TN32 5AW

Former coaching inn with good food and ales and seats in courtyard garden; comfortable bedrooms

Quietly civilised and well run, this handsome old village inn is popular with both locals and visitors. There's a log fire in a brick inglenook fireplace with a leather sofa and a couple of armchairs in front – just the place for a quiet pint and a chat – plus high bar stools by the counter where they serve Harveys Best and Franklins English Garden on handpump, good wines by the glass and a farm cider. A dining area leads off here with elegant high-backed beige tartan or leather chairs around a mix of tables (each with fresh flowers and a tea-light) on stripped floorboards and more tea-lights in a small fireplace; background music. The back terrace has plenty of seats and tables.

Free house ~ Licensees John and Jane Turner ~ Real ale ~ Open 12-11; 12-9 Sun; closed Mon ~ Bar food 12-2.30, 6.30-9; 12-7 Sun ~ Children welcome but must be accompanied by an adult at all times ~ Dogs allowed in bar ~ Wi-fi

RYE

TQ9220

Ypres Castle

(01797) 223248 – www.yprescastleinn.co.uk
Gun Garden; steps up from A259, or down past Ypres Tower; TN31 7HH

Traditional pub with several real ales, quite a choice of bar food and seats in garden

Perched beside a stepped path just beneath the medieval Ypres Tower, this bustling pub has views down over the River Rother from its sheltered garden. Inside, it's unpretentious and traditional: the main bar has wall banquettes with pale blue cushions, an open fire in a stone fireplace with a mirror above and easy chairs in front, assorted chairs and tables (each set with a modern oil lamp) and local artwork. Stools line the blue-panelled counter where they keep Harveys Best and guests such as Adnams Broadside, Long Man Long Blonde, Old Dairy Copper Top and Timothy Taylors Landlord on handpump, eight wines by the glass and farm cider; background music and board games. The back dining room has paintings and pictures of Rye and similar furnishings to the bar; there's another dining room at the front.

Free house ~ Licensee Garry Dowling ~ Real ale ~ Open 12-11 (10.30 Sun) ~ Bar food 12-3, 6-9 (8 Fri); 12-3 Sun ~ Children welcome ~ Dogs welcome ~ Wi-fi ~ Live music Fri and Sun evenings

SALEHURST   TQ7424
Salehurst Halt
(01580) 880620 ~ www.salehursthalt.co.uk
Village signposted from Robertsbridge bypass on A21 Tunbridge Wells–Battle; Church Lane; TN32 5PH

Bustling country local in quiet hamlet with easy-going atmosphere, real ales, well liked bar food and seats in pretty back garden

There's always a cheerful crowd of chatty locals here – especially on Wednesday evenings when the bellringers from the church next door pile in. To the right of the door is a small stone-floored area with a couple of tables, a settle, a TV and an open fire. Furniture includes a nice long scrubbed pine table, a couple of sofas and a mix of more ordinary pubby tables and wheelback and mate's chairs on the wood-strip floor; occasional background music, board games and books on shelves. Dark Star American Pale Ale, Harveys Best and Isfield Flapjack on handpump, farm cider, several malt whiskies and eight wines by the glass. The cottagey and charming back garden has views over the Rother Valley and the summer barbecues and pizzas from the wood-fired oven are extremely popular; a terrace has metal chairs and tiled tables.

Free house ~ Licensee Andrew Augarde ~ Real ale ~ Open 12-11.30 (10.30 Sun); closed Mon ~ Bar food 12-2.30, 7-9.30; 12.30-3 Sun ~ Children welcome ~ Dogs allowed in bar ~ Wi-fi

UCKFIELD   TQ4720
Highlands
(01825) 762989 ~ www.highlandsinn.co.uk
Eastbourne Road/Lewes Road; TN22 5SP

Busy, well run pub with plenty of space, real ales and well thought-of food; seats outside

A favourite spot in this big, bustling place is the area around the bar counter where customers chat over a pint or a glass of wine or read the newspapers: high tartan benches, high leather chairs around equally high tables and armchairs here and there. Harveys Best and a couple of guests such as Black Cat Original and Dark Star Hophead on handpump, 15 wines by the glass and a dozen malt whiskies. Service from friendly, helpful young staff is good. The large, spreading restaurant on the right is split into two by a dividing wall with bookcase wallpaper, and has painted rafters in high ceilings, big glass lamps and walls decorated with local photographs and animal pictures. Also, all manner of cushioned dining and painted farmhouse chairs, long chesterfield sofas, upholstered banquettes and scatter cushions on settles around wooden tables on the part carpeted, part wooden and part ceramic flooring; background music. There's also an end bar with more long chesterfields, a pool area, TV, fruit machine and an open fire. Outside is a decked smoking shelter, a children's play area and picnic-sets on a terrace and on grass. This is sister pub to the Cock at Ringmer.

Ridley Inns ~ Managers Ian, Val, Nick and Matt Ridley ~ Real ale ~ Open 11-11 (midnight Sat); 11-10.30 Sun ~ Bar food 12-2.30, 6-9.30; 12-9.30 Sat; 12-6 Sun ~ Restaurant ~ Children welcome ~ Dogs allowed in bar ~ Wi-fi

WARNINGLID   TQ2425
Half Moon

(01444) 461227 – www.thehalfmoonwarninglid.co.uk
B2115 off A23 S of Handcross or off B2110 Handcross–Lower Beeding; RH17 5TR

Simply furnished pub with real ales, rewarding food, lots of wines by the glass and seats in sizeable garden; bedrooms

Although there's obviously a strong emphasis on the imaginative food here, the lively locals' bar has a proper pubby atmosphere, straightforward wooden furniture on bare boards and a small Victorian fireplace; a room just off here has oak beams and flagstones. A couple of steps lead down to the dining areas, which have a mix of wooden chairs, cushioned wall settles and nice old tables on floorboards, plank panelling and bare brick, and old village photographs; there's also another open fire and a glass-covered well. Adnams Broadside, Harveys Best and Hurst Founders Best Bitter on handpump, around 18 wines by the glass, several malt whiskies and a farm cider. The sheltered, sizeable garden has picnic-sets on a lawn and a spectacular avenue of trees with uplighters that glow at night-time.

Free house ~ Licensee James Amico ~ Real ale ~ Open 11.30-3, 5.30-11; 11.30-11 Sat; 12-9 Sun ~ Bar food 12-2, 6-9.30; 12-3 Sun ~ Restaurant ~ Children welcome ~ Dogs allowed in bar ~ Wi-fi ~ Bedrooms: $120

DOG FRIENDLY HOTELS, INNS AND B&Bs

ALFRISTON   TQ5203
George

(01323) 870319 – www.thegeorge-alfriston.com
High Street, Alfriston, Polegate, East Sussex BN26 5SY

$120; 5 beamed rooms. Venerable inn in lovely village with comfortable, heavily beamed bars, massive hop-hung beams, lots of copper and brass, open fires (one in a huge stone inglenook), several real ales, a comfortable lounge with standing timbers and sofas, good, interesting food in the candlelit restaurant, and a flint-walled garden with seats; the South Downs Way and Vanguard Way cross here and Cuckmere Haven is close by. Dogs allowed in all bedrooms and everywhere in pub.

BATTLE   TQ7414
Powder Mills Hotel

(01424) 775511 – www.powdermillshotel.com
Powdermill Lane, Battle, East Sussex TN33 0SP

$140; 49 individually decorated rooms, including 6 suites. Attractive 18th-c creeper-clad manor house in 150 acres of park and woodland with four lakes and outdoor swimming pool, and next to the 1066 battlefield; country-house atmosphere, log fires and antiques in elegant day rooms, attentive service and good modern cooking in Orangery restaurant; resident dogs. Dogs allowed in ground-floor bedrooms and other public areas, but not in restaurant; £10.

BEPTON
SU8618
Park House Hotel
(01730) 819020 – www.parkhousehotel.com
Bepton, Midhurst, West Sussex GU29 0JB

£135; 21 attractive rooms – 12 in main house, 9 in cottages. Quietly set, family-run country house in ten acres of grounds near Goodwood and Cowdray Park, with outdoor and indoor swimming pools, grass tennis courts, croquet, lawn bowls, six-hole golf course and putting green; a comfortable drawing room, an honesty bar and good seasonal english cooking in the formal dining room – particularly good breakfasts; spa, gym and fitness centre; lots of walks nearby. Dogs allowed in some bedrooms; £15.

BRIGHTON
TQ3004
Grand
(01273) 224300 – www.grandbrighton.co.uk
97–99 Kings Road, Brighton, East Sussex BN1 2FW

£200; 201 smart rooms and suites, many with sea views. Famous Victorian hotel with marble columns and floors and fine moulded plasterwork in the luxurious and elegant day rooms; courteous, helpful service, very good contemporary british cooking, fine wines, popular afternoon teas, extensive breakfasts, and a spa with steam room, treatments and gym; walks for dogs on the beach (not during the summer). Dogs allowed in all bedrooms, and away from food areas; £30.

BRIGHTON
TQ3004
Granville
(01273) 326302 – www.granvillehotel.co.uk
124 Kings Road, Brighton, East Sussex BN1 2FY

£100; 24 individually themed rooms, some with sea views. Seafront boutique hotel with contemporary furnishings, a US barbecue restaurant and sleek bar on the lower ground floor, attentive friendly service, traditional breakfasts and international dishes, and seats and tables on the summer terrace. Dogs allowed in some bedrooms and bar; £15.

BRIGHTON
TQ3004
Hotel du Vin
(01273) 718588 – www.hotelduvin.com
2–6 Ship Street, Brighton, East Sussex BN1 1AD

£180; 49 well equipped and comfortable rooms and suites. Close to the seafront in the popular Lanes area, this hotel is housed in an unusual collection of part gothic-styled buildings; lots of wood, brick, glass and a feeling of space, a bustling bar area and wine bar, good bistro food using fresh local ingredients in the clubby-style restaurant, a fine wine list and helpful young staff; attached pub too. Dogs allowed in all bedrooms; bed and bowl; £10.

BRIGHTON
TQ3303
Malmaison

(01273) 041482 – www.malmaison.com
Waterfront, Brighton Marina Village, Brighton, East Sussex BN2 5WA

From £100; 71 contemporary rooms. Seafront hotel opposite the marina, with bright, modern rooms – some with sea views, others facing inland – a spacious bar, brasserie and a terrace; chain restaurants and multiplex cinema next door and a short bus ride from central Brighton – undergoing complete refurbishment as we went to press. Dogs allowed in all bedrooms and bar; bed and bowl; £10.

CHICHESTER
SU8601
Spire Cottage

(01243) 778937 – www.spirecottage.co.uk
Church Lane, Hunston, Chichester, West Sussex PO20 1AJ

£90; 3 pretty rooms including 1 in annexe with private entrance and garden; also self-catering. Country cottage built from the old spire of Chichester Cathedral, with a relaxed and friendly atmosphere, and good breakfasts with home-made preserves and local bacon and eggs in the pretty dining room with its winter log fire. Dogs allowed in garden bedroom; £5.

CHILGROVE
SU8214
White Horse

(01243) 519444 – www.thewhitehorse.co.uk
High Street, Chilgrove, Chichester, West Sussex PO18 9HX

£110; 15 comfortable, contemporary rooms, each with a little private courtyard (two also have a hot tub). Handsome whitewashed coaching inn with plenty of room for a drink or a meal and a cheerful mix of customers; throughout there are beams and timbering, flagstones and coir carpet, leather wall seats, wooden dining chairs and all sorts of country knick-knacks – stuffed animals, china plates, riding boots, flower paintings, dog drawings, stone bottles and books on shelves; there's also a dining room with a huge painting of a galloping white horse, mirrors and big metal chandeliers, and lots of seats outside on a two-level terrace and grass; real ales, good wines by the glass, first class food and friendly staff; good surrounding walks. Dogs allowed in all bedrooms and bar; bed and bowl; £15.

CLIMPING
TQ0000
Bailiffscourt Hotel

(01903) 723511 – www.hshotels.co.uk
Climping Street, Climping, Littlehampton, West Sussex BN17 5RW

£300; 39 lovely rooms, many with four-poster beds, winter log fires and super views. Mock 13th-c manor and other buildings built only 90 years ago but with tremendous character – fine old iron-studded doors, huge fireplaces, heavy beams and so forth – in 30 acres of coastal pastures and walled gardens: open fires, antiques, tapestries and fresh flowers, elegant furnishings, enjoyable modern english food in the mullion-windowed restaurant and courteous, helpful staff; spa with indoor swimming pool, gym and treatment rooms, plus outdoor swimming pool, tennis and croquet. Dogs allowed in some bedrooms and lounges; mat, bowl and biscuits; £15.

TQ3024

Ockenden Manor Hotel

(01444) 416111 – www.hshotels.co.uk
Ockenden Lane, Cuckfield, Haywards Heath, West Sussex RH17 5LD

£339; 28 individually decorated, pretty rooms. Dating from 1520, this carefully extended manor house has antiques, fresh flowers and an open fire in the elegant sitting room, a well stocked, cosy bar, beautifully presented modern cooking in the panelled restaurant and super views of the South Downs from the nine-acre garden; spa with indoor and outdoor linked swimming pools, sauna, steam room, gym and treatment rooms. Dogs allowed in most bedrooms; bowl and bedding; £15.

DONNINGTON

SU8501

Blacksmiths

(01243) 785578 – www.the-blacksmiths.co.uk
Selsey Road, Donnington, Chichester, West Sussex PO20 7PR

£130; 3 airy, attractive rooms. This carefully refurbished white-painted pub, close to the Chichester Canal towpath, looks lovely. It has a bar with wooden wall seats with scatter cushions, wide floorboards and an open fire, a couple of dining rooms with grey leather or wooden chairs and watercolour pictures, and a terrace surrounded by glass panels with teak tables beneath parasols, a fire pit and far-reaching country views; real ales, good breakfasts and rewarding food using produce from their farm and kitchen garden and their own eggs. Dogs allowed in all bedrooms and everywhere except restaurant.

EAST HOATHLY

TQ5116

Old Whyly

(01825) 840216 – www.oldwhyly.co.uk
Halland Road, East Hoathly, Lewes, East Sussex BN8 6EL

£145; 4 quiet spacious rooms. Handsome Georgian manor house in a lovely garden with a lake, tennis court and swimming pool; fine antiques, paintings and an open fire in the restful drawing room, delicious food (dinner by arrangement) in the elegant dining room and super breakfasts with their own honey and duck and chicken eggs; plenty of walks nearby and very near to Glyndebourne (hampers can be provided). Dogs allowed in all bedrooms (not to be left unattended) and drawing room.

EASTBOURNE

TV6198

Grand Hotel

(01323) 412345 – www.grandeastbourne.co.uk
King Edwards Parade, Eastbourne, East Sussex BN21 4EQ

From £190; 152 individually designed rooms, many with sea views. Gracious and very well run Victorian hotel with views of the sea and the cliffs at Beachy

Head; a genuinely friendly atmosphere, spacious, comfortable lounges with lots of fine original features and lovely flower arrangements, imaginative food in two smart but unstuffy restaurants, popular afternoon teas and courteous, helpful service; spa with treatment, sauna and steam rooms, gym and indoor and outdoor swimming pools. Dogs allowed in some bedrooms but not public areas; bed, bowl and meal provided; £20.

EWHURST GREEN   TQ7924
White Dog
(01580) 830264 – www.thewhitedogewhurst.co.uk
Ewhurst Green, Robertsbridge, East Sussex TN32 5TD

£95; 3 airy rooms. Friendly, family-run village pub with magnificent views of Bodiam Castle (National Trust) from seats in garden; a bustling bar with hop-draped beams, wood panelling, farm implements and horsebrasses, a roaring log fire in an inglenook fireplace and real ales on handpump; also a flagstoned dining room and a games room; well liked lunchtime and evening food using local seasonal produce, and tasty breakfasts; walks in surrounding fields and footpaths. Dogs allowed in all bedrooms and bar; bowl and treats; £10.

LEWES   TQ4109
Shelleys
(01273) 472361 – www.the-shelleys.co.uk
High Street, Lewes, East Sussex BN7 1XS

£195; 19 homely rooms. Once owned by relatives of the poet, this stylish and spacious 17th-c townhouse hotel is warm and friendly, with good food, nice breakfasts and bar lunches in an elegant dining room, popular morning coffee and afternoon teas, and terrace with seats in the quiet back garden. Dogs allowed in all bedrooms; £10.

MIDHURST   SU8821
Spread Eagle Hotel
(01730) 816911 – www.hshotels.co.uk
South Street, Midhurst, West Sussex GU29 9NH

£159; 39 pretty, well equipped rooms. Historic 15th-c coaching inn with log fires in inglenook fireplaces, stained-glass windows, beams and sloping floors, lots of sofas and armchairs, and very good modern british food in the candlelit restaurant or summer conservatory; picturesque grounds with plenty of seats; spa with indoor swimming pool, gym and sauna, steam and treatment rooms. Dogs allowed in some bedrooms; bed and bowl; dog food can be provided; £15.

PETWORTH   SU9721
Angel
(01798) 342153 – www.angelinnpetworth.co.uk
Angel Street, Petworth, West Sussex GU28 0BG

£140; 6 newly refurbished, comfortable rooms. Medieval in origin, this place has been carefully renovated to create a smart town pub with the feel of a country inn, with several interconnected bars, all manner of nice old chairs and tables on slate and wooden floors, open fires, genuinely friendly service, well kept local beers, 22 wines by the glass from an extensive list and several malt whiskies and gins, very good breakfasts, lunches and evening meals, and seats in the pretty three-level garden. Dogs allowed in one bedroom and bar; £10.

RUSHLAKE GREEN

TQ6218

Stone House

(01435) 830553 – www.stonehousesussex.co.uk
Rushlake Green, Heathfield, East Sussex TN21 9QJ

£215; 7 traditional rooms with antiques and lovely fabrics, some with four-posters. In 1,000 acres of pretty countryside (with plenty of walks and country sports) and surrounded by an 18th-c walled garden, this lovely house was built at the end of the 15th c and extended in Georgian times; log fires, antiques and family heirlooms in the drawing room, a quiet library, interesting modern british evening meals in the panelled dining room and excellent breakfasts. Closed Christmas/New Year week, mid February to mid March. Dogs allowed in all bedrooms, but not in public rooms.

RYE

TQ9120

Jeakes House

(01797) 222828 – www.jeakeshouse.com
Mermaid Street, Rye, East Sussex TN31 7ET

£120; 11 pretty rooms overlooking the rooftops of this medieval town or across the marsh to the sea. Fine 16th-c building, well run and friendly, with good breakfasts in the galleried dining room, much character in the honesty bar and parlour with period furnishings and antiques, swagged curtains and a warm fire, and a peaceful atmosphere; nearby fields for walking. Dogs allowed in all bedrooms and elsewhere except dining room; £5.

RYE

TQ9220

Rye Lodge Hotel

(01797) 223838 – www.ryelodge.co.uk
Hilders Cliff, Rye, East Sussex TN31 7LD

£105; 18 comfortable rooms. Family-run hotel close to the town and with fine views across the estuary and Romney Marsh; caring, friendly service, an elegant and comfortable bar and lounge, a breakfast area (no lunch or dinner but plenty of places to eat in Rye) and an indoor swimming pool and sauna. Dogs allowed in most bedrooms, bar and lounge; £8.

RYE

TQ9120

Ship

(01797) 222233 – www.theshipinnrye.co.uk
The Strand, Rye, East Sussex TN31 7DB

£125; 10 cheerfully decorated rooms. Appealingly quirky 16th-c pub with an easy-going atmosphere in opened-up rooms, beams and timbers, comfortable armchairs and sofas and other traditional seats and tables on stripped boards, flagstones and some carpeting, a log fire in a stripped-brick fireplace, a stuffed boar's head, real ales and local cider and perry, and a short choice of interesting dishes; lots of footpaths and beach walks. Dogs allowed in all bedrooms and anywhere in the pub; breakfast sausage included; £10 per stay.

SOUTH HARTING   SU7819
White Hart
(01730) 825124 – www.the-whitehart.co.uk
The Street, South Harting, West Sussex GU31 5QB

£124; 6 comfortable, character rooms. A sympathetically renovated 16th-c village inn with plenty of charm; the bars and dining area have beams and standing timbers, a couple of woodburning stoves, an open fire, bare boards, flagstones and an attractive mix of furniture, as well as a mural of a white hart, country prints, antlers, candles and fresh flowers; good choice of drinks, enjoyable food (including breakfast for non-residents) and friendly staff; the terrace and garden have seats and picnic-sets under parasols, the surrounding countryside is lovely and Uppark (National Trust) is nearby. Dogs allowed in all bedrooms and bar.

TICEHURST   TQ6830
Bell
(01580) 200234 – www.thebellinticehurst.com
High Street, Ticehurst, Wadhurst, East Sussex TN5 7AS

£100; 7 quirky rooms each with a silver birch tree, plus 4 standalone lodges. Sensitively restored former coaching inn with heavy beams and timbering in two main rooms, a log fire in the inglenook, a happy jumble of wooden chairs around tables of various sizes, some unusual decorations, real ales and good wines by the glass; interesting food in the relaxed adjoining dining room, a comfortable sitting room with another open fire and, in what was the carriage room, benches on either side of a very long table; seats in the extended back terraced garden. Dogs allowed in all bedrooms, lodges and bar; £10.

TILLINGTON   SU9622
Horse Guards
(01798) 342332 – www.thehorseguardsinn.co.uk
Upperton Road, Tillington, Petworth, West Sussex GU28 9AF

£115; 3 light rooms. An 18th-c dining pub prettily set in a lovely village, with a neatly kept, beamed front bar, good country furniture on bare boards, a log fire and thoughtfully chosen drinks; other rambling rooms, similarly furnished, have more open fires and original panelling, fresh flowers and a gently civilised atmosphere; the delicious food from a short seasonal menu uses home-grown produce, and service is genuinely welcoming and helpful; resident cat and chickens; the 800-year-old church opposite is worth a visit; walks in Petworth Park (National Trust) and South Downs National Park. Dogs allowed in one bedroom and anywhere in the pub; bowl and bed; £10 per stay.

WEST HOATHLY
TQ3632

Cat

(01342) 810369 – www.catinn.co.uk
North Lane, West Hoathly, West Sussex RH19 4PP

£120; 4 comfortable rooms. An extremely popular 16th-c inn with a friendly, hands-on landlord who welcomes both drinkers and diners; the lovely old bar has beams, proper pubby tables and chairs on an old wooden floor, a fine log fire in an inglenook fireplace, real ales, local cider and locally made sparkling wines; there are also airy dining rooms, a contemporary-style garden room that opens on to a terrace and throughout you'll find hops, china platters, brass and copper ornaments and a gently upmarket atmosphere; the tempting food uses local suppliers and breakfasts are good; the cocker spaniel is called Harvey; steam train enthusiasts can visit the Bluebell Railway, and the Priest House in the village is fascinating. Dogs allowed in all bedrooms and bar; mat and bowl; £10.

WINCHELSEA
TQ9017

Strand House

(01797) 226276 – www.thestrandhouse.co.uk
Tanyards Lane, Winchelsea, East Sussex TN36 4JT

£175; 13 low-beamed, character rooms, including 3 in cottage. Warmly friendly little hotel in two ancient buildings with a log fire in the comfortable sitting room, a quiet reading room with books and games, delicious afternoon teas and nice breakfasts; towpath and beach walks. Closed first three weeks of January. Dogs allowed in three bedrooms, but not in public rooms; treats; £7.50.

WITHYHAM
TQ4935

Dorset Arms

(01892) 770278 – www.dorset-arms.co.uk
Buckhurst Park, Withyham, Hartfield, East Sussex TN7 4BD

£105; 6 attractive rooms in the Old School House. This bustling 18th-c village inn is part of the Buckhurst Estate and although there's a strong emphasis on the particularly good food, it's a proper pub with a friendly and informal beamed bar with real ales and good wines, an open fire, armchairs and a few simple seats and tables; also a cottagey dining room with pretty curtains, bookshelves to each side of a small fireplace, horse pictures and pieces of china, and another couple of rooms; staff are friendly and courteous and there's plenty of seating outside on the front terrace and in the lawned garden. Dogs allowed in all bedrooms and bar.

Warwickshire
with Birmingham and West Midlands

MAP 4

DOG FRIENDLY PUBS

ALDERMINSTER   SP2348
Bell
(01789) 450414 – www.thebellald.co.uk
A3400 Oxford–Stratford; CV37 8NY

Gently civilised 18th-c inn with sympathetically modernised character bars, a new two-storey restaurant, excellent modern cooking and thoughtful choice of drinks; bedrooms

Part of the Alscot Estate, this is a civilised Georgian coaching inn with a friendly, easy-going atmosphere. The open-plan rooms cleverly manage to create a contemporary feel that goes well with the many original features: beams, standing timbers, flagstoned or wooden floors and open fires. The bustling bar serves Alscot Ale and Monkey (named for the pub from North Cotswold), North Cotswold Shagweaver, Purity Pure UBU and a guest such as Stratford Upon Avon Stratford Gold on handpump, a dozen wines by the glass and proper cocktails (including a special bloody mary). The bar is comfortably furnished with a mix of traditional wooden chairs and tables, upholstered sofas, armchairs in front of open fires, high bar chairs by the blue-painted counter and daily papers; background music. The new two-storey restaurant is stylish and contemporary. The bottom floor, with stunning chandeliers, is decorated in soft pastels and silvers and has folding doors leading directly to the terrace, while the top floor has attractive chairs around polished copper tables on dark floorboards, seats on a balcony and panoramic views across the Stour Valley; there's also a private dining room with its own decked area and lawn. An appealing courtyard and gardens have seats and tables looking over water meadows and the lovely valley.

Free house ~ Licensee Emma Holman-West ~ Real ale ~ Open 9am-11pm ~ Bar food 12-2.30, 6.30-9 (9.30 Fri, Sat); 12-3, 6.30-8.30 Sun ~ Restaurant ~ Children welcome ~ Dogs allowed in bar ~ Wi-fi ~ Bedrooms: £95

BARSTON

SP1978

Malt Shovel

(01675) 443223 – www.themaltshovelatbarston.com

3 miles from M42 junction 5; A4141 towards Knowle, then first left into Jacobean Lane/ Barston Lane; B92 0JP

Well run country dining pub full of happy customers, with an attractive layout, good service and seats in sheltered garden

This bustling place feels just right whether you're popping in for a drink and a chat or enjoying a first class meal. The light and airy bar rambles extensively around the zinc-topped central counter with big terracotta floor tiles neatly offset by dark grouting, and cream, tan and blue paintwork. Sharps Doom Bar and Wells Bombardier Burning Gold on handpump and 18 wines by the glass served by efficient, neatly dressed staff. Furnishings are comfortable, with informal dining chairs and scatter-cushioned pews around stripped-top tables of varying types and sizes. There are cheerful fruit and vegetable paintings on the walls, and french café-style shutters. The sheltered back garden has a weeping willow and picnic-sets, and the terrace and verandah have cushioned teak seats and tables.

Free house ~ Licensee Helen Somerfield ~ Real ale ~ Open 12-12; 12-11 Sun ~ Bar food 12-2.30, 6-9.30; 12-4 Sun ~ Restaurant ~ Children welcome away from restaurant ~ Dogs allowed in bar

GAYDON

SP3654

Malt Shovel

(01926) 641221 – www.maltshovelgaydon.co.uk

Under a mile from M40 junction 12; B4451 into village, then over roundabout and across B4100; Church Road; CV35 0ET

Bustling pub in a quiet village with a nice mix of pubby bar and smarter restaurant

There's always a good mix of customers in this cheerful village pub, all keen to enjoy the tasty food cooked by the landlord. Mahogany-varnished boards through to bright carpeting link the entrance with the bar counter to the right and a woodburning stove on the left. The central area has a high-pitched ceiling, milk churns and earthenware containers in a loft above the bar and three steps that lead up to a space with comfortable sofas overlooked by a big stained-glass window; reproductions of classic posters line the walls. Sharps Doom Bar, Shepherd Neame Spitfire, St Austell Tribute and Timothy Taylors Golden Best on handpump, with 11 wines by the glass and two farm ciders. A busy eating area has fresh flowers on a mix of kitchen, pub and dining tables; background music, darts. The pub's jack russell is called Mollie.

Enterprise ~ Lease Richard and Debi Morisot ~ Real ale ~ Open 11-3, 5-11; 11-11 Fri, Sat; 12-10.30 Sun ~ Bar food 12-2, 6.30-9 ~ Restaurant ~ Children welcome ~ Dogs allowed in bar ~ Wi-fi

HUNNINGHAM   SP3768

Red Lion

(01926) 632715 – www.redlionhunningham.co.uk
Village signposted off B4453 Leamington–Rugby just E of Weston, and off B4455
Fosse Way 2.5 miles SW of A423 junction; CV33 9DY

Civilised and friendly place, a good range of drinks and well liked food

Friendly and easy-going, this riverside pub has a light open-plan interior that's been cleverly sectioned and appealingly furnished. There are pews with scatter cushions, an assortment of antique dining chairs and stools around nice polished tables on bare boards (a few big rugs here and there), contemporary paintwork and walls hung with film and rock star photographs; one long wall is a papered mural of bookshelves. A cosy room has tub armchairs around an open coal fire, and they keep a beer named for the pub (from Greene King), Greene King Abbot and a changing guest on handpump, ten wines by the glass and 40 malt whiskies; background music. The garden has picnic-sets that look across to the arched 14th-c bridge over the River Leam and there's a basket of rugs for customers to take outside; more picnic-sets are set out at the front of the building.

Greene King ~ Manager Richard Merand ~ Real ale ~ Open 11-11 (10.30 Sun) ~ Bar food 12-9 ~ Restaurant ~ Children welcome ~ Dogs allowed in bar ~ Wi-fi

ILMINGTON   SP2143

Howard Arms

(01608) 682226 – www.howardarms.com
Village signed with Wimpstone off A3400 S of Stratford; CV36 4LT

Lovely mellow-toned interior, lots to look at and enjoyable food and drink; bedrooms

With good nearby hill walks and a pretty setting beside the village green, this golden-stone inn is doing well under its newish licensees. Several beamed and flagstoned rooms (recently refurbished) have a nice mix of furniture ranging from pews and rustic stools to leather dining chairs around all sorts of tables, rugs on bare boards, shelves of books, candles and a log fire in a big inglenook. Hook Norton Hooky, St Austell Proper Job, Timothy Taylors Landlord and Wye Valley HPA on handpump, 20 wines by the glass and a thoughtful choice of whiskies and brandies; background music, TV. The big back garden has seats under parasols and a colourful herbaceous border.

Free house ~ Licensee Robert Jeal ~ Real ale ~ Open 9am-11pm; 11-10.30 Sun ~ Bar food 12-3, 6-9.30; 12-8 Sun ~ Restaurant ~ Children welcome ~ Dogs allowed in bar ~ Wi-fi ~ Bedrooms: £90

LEAMINGTON SPA   SP3166

Star & Garter

(01926) 359960 – www.starandgarterleamington.co.uk
Warwick Street; CV32 5LL

Bustling town-centre pub with open-plan rooms, good food and drink and friendly welcome

This fine old places is just a few minutes from the shopping heart of this bustling town and usefully open all day, so there are always customers popping in and out. It's been carefully renovated, with plenty of space for both drinking and dining, and although open-plan it has distinct cosy and quieter spots created by cleverly positioned furniture. At the front by big windows, the bar has cushioned wall seats upholstered in quirky eastern european fabric, as well as blue leather banquettes, red leather armchairs and small wooden stools around mixed tables on bare boards. High stools line the counter where they keep a beer named for the pub (from Greene King), Greene King Abbot, IPA and Morlands Old Golden Hen and St Austell Tribute on handpump, 14 wines by the glass plus champagne and prosecco, 13 gins and ten malt whiskies; background music. Leading back from here, a dining area has black, brown or red leather back-to-back banquettes down one side, elegant contemporary wooden dining chairs on more bare boards and an open kitchen. Up some steps is a second bar area with blue tubs seats, bright scatter cushions and some bold paintwork. The atmosphere is lively and friendly and staff are helpful and attentive.

Peach Pub Company ~ Lease Colin Barber ~ Real ale ~ Open 11-11; 9am-midnight Sat; 9am-10.30pm Sun ~ Bar food 12-10; 9am-10pm Sat; 9am-9pm Sun ~ Children welcome ~ Dogs allowed in bar ~ Wi-fi

PRESTON BAGOT   SP1765
Crabmill

(01926) 843342 – www.thecrabmill.co.uk
A4189 Henley-in-Arden to Warwick; B95 5EE

Comfortable décor, open fires and particularly good food and drink in converted mill

This rambling former cider mill is praised for its impressive food, served by helpful staff, and the range of drinks. There's a gently civilised atmosphere and it's attractively decorated throughout with contemporary furnishings and warm colour combinations. A smart two-level lounge has comfortable sofas and chairs, low tables, big table lamps and a couple of rugs on bare boards. The elegant, low-beamed dining area is roomy with caramel leather banquettes and chairs at pine tables, while the beamed and flagstoned bar area has stripped-pine country tables and chairs and snug corners; open fires. From the gleaming metal bar counter they serve Purity Pure Gold and UBU and Sharps Doom Bar on handpump and nine wines by the glass; background music. There are plenty of tables (some under cover) in the large, attractive, decked garden.

Free house ~ Licensee Sally Coll ~ Real ale ~ Open 11-11; 12-6 Sun ~ Bar food 12-2.30, 6-9.30; 12-4 Sun ~ Restaurant ~ Children welcome ~ Dogs allowed in bar ~ Wi-fi

SHIPSTON-ON-STOUR   SP2540
Black Horse

(01608) 238489 – www.blackhorseshipston.com
Station Road (off A3400); CV36 4BT

16th-c pub with simple country furnishings, well kept ales, an extensive choice of thai food and seats outside

The oldest and only thatched building in the village, this ancient stone tavern is chocolate-box pretty with its flowering baskets and tubs. Low-beamed, character bars lead off a central entrance passage with some fine old flagstones and floor tiles and two open fires (one an inglenook). There are also wheelbacks, stools, rustic seats and tables and built-in wall benches, half-panelled or exposed stone walls, and plenty of copper kettles, pans and bed warmers, horse tack and toby jugs. Friendly staff serve Prescott Hill Climb, Ringwood Old Thumper and Wye Valley The Hopfather on handpump, several wines by the glass, a dozen gins and ten malt whiskies; background music, TV, darts and board games. The little dining room has pale wooden tables and chairs on bare boards. There are a couple of benches on the front cobbles, contemporary seats and tables on a partly covered raised decked area at the back and picnic-sets on grass.

Free house ~ Licensee Gabe Saunders ~ Real ale ~ Open 12-3, 6-11; 6-11 Mon; 12-midnight Fri-Sun ~ Bar food 12-2.30, 6-10; not Mon ~ Restaurant ~ Children welcome ~ Dogs allowed in bar ~ Wi-fi

SHIPSTON-ON-STOUR   SP2540
Horseshoe
(01608) 662190 – www.horseshoeshipston.com
Church Street; CV36 4AP

Cheerful local with welcoming regulars, traditional furnishings, real ales and honest food and seats outside

There's a friendly and chatty, easy-going atmosphere in this pretty 17th-c timbered coaching inn. The two rooms that form the open, carpeted bar have straightforward red-upholstered cushioned wall seats and wheelback chairs around scrubbed wooden tables, country prints on lemon-yellow walls, copper pans hanging on the bressummer beam over the open fire (with books and stone jars on shelves to one side) and stools against the counter; juke box. There's Adnams Southwold, Sharps Doom Bar and Wadworths 6X on handpump and several wines by the glass, and service is cheerful and courteous. The end dining room is similarly furnished. The back terrace has contemporary seats and tables on decking; aunt sally.

Enterprise ~ Manager Baggy Saunders ~ Real ale ~ Open 10am-11pm ~ Bar food 12-2.30, 6-9; not Sun evening ~ Children welcome ~ Dogs welcome ~ Wi-fi

WARMINGTON   SP4147
Falcon
(01295) 692120 – www.brunningandprice.co.uk/falcon
B4100 towards Shotteswell; OX17 1JJ

Carefully extended and restored roadside pub with spreading bar and dining rooms, a fine choice of drinks and food, and seats outside

Reopened after a beautiful restoration by Brunning & Price, this 18th-c pub was originally built to take advantage of what was a busy turnpike road. It's a handsome golden-stone inn and the interconnected bar and dining areas have much character and plenty to look at. There are beams, mirrors over several open fires, rugs on pale floorboards, elegant metal chandeliers, prints and photos covering pale-painted walls, bookshelves, house plants and stone bottles. Cushioned Edwardian-style chairs and leather armchairs are grouped around a wide mix of tables and the main dining room has a central fire pit. Friendly young staff serve Phoenix Brunning & Price Original and White Monk and guests such as Cottage Goldrush, Gun Dog Ales Hotdog, Kendricks Webb Ellis and White Horse Black Horse Porter on handpump, 15 wines by the glass, 68 gins and numerous malt whiskies; background music. The garden has good quality seats and tables under a gazebo.

Brunning & Price ~ Manager Peter Palfi ~ Real ale ~ Open 11-11 (10.30 Sun) ~ Bar food 12-10 (9.30 Sun) ~ Restaurant ~ Children welcome ~ Dogs allowed in bar ~ Wi-fi

DOG FRIENDLY HOTELS, INNS AND B&Bs

ARMSCOTE   SP2444

Fuzzy Duck

(01608) 682635 – www.fuzzyduckarmscote.com
Armscote, Stratford-upon-Avon, Warwickshire CV37 8DD

£140; 4 comfortable, thoughtfully equipped bedrooms – each named after a species of duck. Set in a picturesque hamlet, this refurbished Georgian coaching inn is now part-pub and part-boutique inn; as well as the bar with an open fire there are three interconnected dining rooms with wooden tables on pale floorboards, a two-way woodburner in an open fireplace, cartoons and arty photos and fresh flowers; at the back is a decked terrace with seats under big parasols and a small lawn with fruit trees; friendly staff, real ales, a good wine list and inventive food with home-baked bread and their own ice-creams; plenty of walks in the surrounding rolling countryside and Stratford-upon-Avon is close by. Dogs allowed in all bedrooms and everywhere in pub.

BIRMINGHAM   SP0687

Hotel du Vin

(0121) 794 3005 – www.hotelduvin.com
25 Church Street, Birmingham, West Midlands B3 2NR

From £89; 66 stylish, contemporary rooms. A converted eye hospital, this grand red-brick Victorian building is in the old city centre, in the Jewellery Quarter; it has a friendly, informal atmosphere, bistro-style food in the club-like restaurant where wine bottles line the windowsills (the wine list is exceptional), real ales and pubby food in the basement 'pub', another bar with cocktails and afternoon tea, and helpful young staff; gym and beauty treatments. Dogs allowed in two bedrooms; bed, bowl and treats; £10.

HAMPTON-IN-ARDEN   SP2080

White Lion

(01675) 442833 – www.thewhitelioninn.com
10 High Street, Hampton-in-Arden, Solihull, West Midlands B92 0AA

£90; 9 nice rooms – 5 in pub, 4 in former bakery. Former farmhouse with a relaxed atmosphere, a mix of furniture trimly laid out in the carpeted bar, low-beamed ceilings and local memorabilia on cream walls, real ales on handpump, airy, modern dining areas with light wood and cane chairs on stripped floorboards, popular traditional food and tasty breakfasts; the church opposite is mentioned in the Domesday Book; nearby walks. Dogs allowed in bedrooms and anywhere in the pub.

LONG COMPTON   SP2832

Red Lion

(01608) 684221 – www.redlion-longcompton.co.uk
Main Street, Long Compton, Shipston-on-Stour, Warwickshire CV36 5JS

£100; 5 pretty rooms. Lovely old coaching inn with a warmly welcoming landlady and lots of original features to look out for – exposed stone, flagstones, beams and rambling corners with old-fashioned built-in settles, leather armchairs and a woodburning stove in the roomy lounge, a simpler public bar with real ales, and good popular food; resident chocolate labrador, Cocoa; tables out in the big back garden with play area, and walks in the surrounding countryside. Dogs allowed in bedrooms and anywhere in the pub.

LOWER BRAILES

SP3139

George

(01608) 685788 – www.georgeinnbrailes.com
High Street, Lower Brailes, Warwickshire OX15 5HN

£70; 6 rooms. This bustling stone inn was built in the 14th c to house the stonemasons constructing the interesting village church; there's a beamed and panelled back bar with a cheerful atmosphere and chatty locals, as well as a roomy front bar with flagstones and an inglenook fireplace, and a separate restaurant; real ales, farm cider and well liked, nicely priced food; aunt sally and picnic-sets (some blue-painted) in the sizeable and sheltered back garden and on the terrace; good nearby walks. Dogs allowed in two bedrooms and bar; £5.

STRATFORD-UPON-AVON

SP2054

Macdonald Swans Nest Hotel/Bear

(01789) 266804 – www.macdonaldhotels.co.uk
(01789) 265540 – www.thebearfreehouse.co.uk
Bridgefoot, Stratford-upon-Avon, Warwickshire CV37 7LT

£129–£245; 68 comfortable rooms. Large riverside hotel a short walk from the theatres; adjacent is a proper pub (the Bear) with eight real ales on handpump on the pewter bar, fine wines by the glass, armchairs, sofas and scatter-cushioned banquettes, and good value, popular bar food; thoroughly professional staff, seats on a waterside lawn; adjoining is a french brasserie with an outdoor terrace; guests can use the spa and swimming pool in the sister hotel opposite. Dogs allowed in some bedrooms and anywhere in the pub; £15.

STRATFORD-UPON-AVON

SP2054

Mercure Shakespeare

(02477) 092802 – www.mercure.com
Chapel Street, Stratford-upon-Avon, Warwickshire CV37 6ER

£165; 78 rooms. Smart chain hotel in a series of handsome, lavishly modernised Tudor merchants' houses, with a convivial bar, a bar-lounge (popular for morning coffee, light lunches and afternoon teas), an italian restaurant, quick friendly service, enjoyable breakfasts and seats in the terraced garden; very close to the theatres. Dogs allowed in 11 annexe bedrooms; £10.

Wiltshire

MAP 2

DOG FRIENDLY PUBS

ALDBOURNE   SU2675
Blue Boar

(01672) 540237 – www.theblueboarpub.co.uk
The Green (off B4192 in centre); SN8 2EN

Busy local with simple pubby furnishings in bar, cottagey restaurant serving traditional food and seats outside

Picnic-sets at the front make the most of the charming location by the pretty village green here and the window boxes are lovely in summer. The heavily beamed bar has built-in wooden window seats, tall farmhouse chairs and other red-cushioned pubby chairs on flagstones or bare boards, a woodburning stove in an inglenook fireplace with a stuffed boar's head and large clock above it, horsebrasses on the bressumer beam and a notice board with news of beer festivals and live music events. Wadworths IPA, 6X, Swordfish and a guest ale on handpump, eight wines by the glass, 17 malt whiskies and a farm cider. The back restaurant is beamed and cottagey with standing timbers, dark wooden chairs and tables on floorboards and rugs, and plates displayed on a dresser.

Wadworths ~ Tenants Michael and Joanne Hehir ~ Real ale ~ Open 11.30-3, 5.30-11.30; 11.30am-midnight Fri, Sat; 12-11 Sun ~ Bar food 12-2 (2.30 Fri, Sat), 6.30-9; 12-4 Sun ~ Restaurant ~ Children welcome ~ Dogs allowed in bar ~ Wi-fi ~ Live music regularly

BRADFORD-ON-AVON   ST8261
Castle

(01225) 865657 – www.flatcappers.co.uk
Mount Pleasant, by junction with A363, N edge of town; extremely limited pub parking but spaces in nearby streets; BA15 1SJ

Substantial stone inn with local ales, popular food including breakfasts, plenty of character and fine views; bedrooms

The unspoilt bar here has a lot of individual character, a wide range of seats (church chairs, leather armchairs, cushioned wall seating and brass-studded leather dining chairs) around chunky pine tables on dark flagstones, church candles, fringed lamps and a good log fire; daily papers, background music and board games. A bare-boards snug on the right is similar in style. Cheerful staff serve a beer named for the pub (from Three Castles Brewery), Dark Star Original, Plain Inntrigue and Sheep Dip, Quantock White Hind and Three Castles Barbury Castle on handpump and several wines by the glass; they hold a beer and music festival twice a year. The seats at the front of this handsome stone building offer sweeping town views, while in the back garden you look across lovely countryside. There is wheelchair access at the back of the pub.

Free house ~ Licensee Ben Paxton ~ Real ale ~ Open 9am-11pm ~ Bar food 8.30am-10pm (9.30pm Sun) ~ Children welcome but must be seated from 7.30pm ~ Dogs allowed in bar ~ Wi-fi ~ Bedrooms: £100

CORSHAM   ST8670

Methuen Arms

(01249) 717060 – www.themethuenarms.com
High Street; SN13 0HB

Charming hotel with character bars, friendly staff, imaginative food, good wines and ales, and seats outside; comfortable bedrooms

In a bustling market town, this handsome Georgian inn is run by professional licensees and their warmly friendly staff. It's civilised yet informal and there's always a good mix of both drinkers and diners. The proper little front bar has a log fire, a big old clock under a sizeable mirror, an assortment of antique dining chairs and tables, rugs on elm floorboards and evening candlelight. Drinks include Butcombe Bitter, Prescott Hill Climb and St Austell Tribute on handpump, 12 wines by the glass, ten malt whiskies and quite a few gins; background music. Across the green-painted bar counter is a second small bar, with similar furnishings, bare boards and rugs and a couple of armchairs. The dining room has settles (carved and plain), high-backed dining chairs with wooden arms around old sewing-machine tables, an open fire with tea-lights, black and white photographs of large local houses on sage green paintwork and swagged curtains. Another room leads off here, and there's also a restaurant at the back. The garden to the side of the building has seats and tables. Breakfast is available to non-residents.

Free house ~ Licensees Martin and Debbie Still ~ Real ale ~ Open 12-11 (10.30 Sun) ~ Bar food 12-3, 6-10 ~ Restaurant ~ Children welcome ~ Dogs allowed in bar ~ Wi-fi ~ Bedrooms: £120

CRUDWELL   ST9592

Potting Shed

(01666) 577833 – www.thepottingshedpub.com
A429 N of Malmesbury; The Street; SN16 9EW

Civilised but relaxed dining pub with low-beamed rooms, an interesting range of drinks and creative cooking; seats in the big garden

There's a good welcome under the newish owners for all customers here, and that includes dogs who might get a treat from the bar and a greeting from the pub dog, Milton. Low-beamed rooms rambling around the bar have bare stone walls, open fires and woodburning stoves (one in a big worn stone fireplace), mixed plain tables and chairs on pale flagstones, armchairs in one corner and daily papers. Four steps lead up into a high-raftered area with wood flooring, and there's another separate, smaller room that's ideal for a lunch or dinner party. Also, lots of country prints and more modern pictures, fresh flowers, candles and some quirky, rustic decorations such as a garden-fork door handle, garden-tool beer pumps and so forth. A fine range of drinks includes Bath Gem, Butcombe Bitter, Flying Monk Elmers and Timothy Taylors Landlord on handpump, as well as 21 wines and champagne by the glass, three farm ciders, home-made seasonal cocktails and local fruit liqueurs; background music and board games. There are sturdy teak seats around cask tables as well as picnic-sets out on the side grass among weeping willows. Good access for those in need of extra assistance. They also own the hotel across the road.

Enterprise ~ Lease Alex Payne ~ Real ale ~ Open 11-11 ~ Bar food 12-2.30, 6-9; 12-3,
6.30-8.30 Sun ~ Restaurant ~ Children welcome ~ Dogs welcome ~ Wi-fi

EAST KNOYLE
ST8731

Fox & Hounds

(01747) 830573 – www.foxandhounds-eastknoyle.co.uk
Village signposted off A350 S of A303; The Green (named on some road atlases),
a mile NW at OS Sheet 183 map reference 872313; or follow signpost off B3089,
about 0.5 miles E of A303 junction near Little Chef; SP3 6BN

Pretty thatched village pub with splendid views, welcoming service,
good beers and popular, enjoyable food

This 15th-c pub is in a charming spot by the village green and also overlooks
Blackmore Vale. Three linked areas – on different levels around the central
horseshoe-shaped servery – have big log fires, plentiful oak woodwork and
flagstones, comfortably padded dining chairs around big scrubbed tables, and a
couple of leather sofas; the furnishings are all very individual and uncluttered.
There's also a small light-painted conservatory restaurant. Hop Back Summer
Lightning, Otter Amber and Palmers Copper Ale on handpump, a dozen wines by
the glass and Thatcher's farm cider; background music and skittle alley. There
are marvellous views over into Somerset and Dorset from picnic-sets, the nearby
woods are good for a stroll and the Wiltshire Cycleway passes through the village.

Free house ~ Licensee Murray Seator ~ Real ale ~ Open 11.30-3, 5.30-11 (10 Sun) ~
Bar food 12-2.30, 6.30-9 ~ Children welcome ~ Dogs welcome ~ Wi-fi

EDINGTON
ST9353

Three Daggers

(01380) 830940 – www.threedaggers.co.uk
Westbury Road (B3098); BA13 4PG

Rejuvenated village pub with open fires, beams and candlelight, helpful
staff, enjoyable food (including breakfasts) and own-brew beers;
bedrooms

The thoughtful choice of drinks in this appealing brick pub includes their own
hand-pumped Three Daggers beers – Daggers Ale, Black, Blonde and Edge
(brewed in the farm shop building) – 14 wines by the glass, ten malt whiskies
and a couple of farm ciders. The interior is heavily beamed and open-plan with a
friendly, easy-going atmosphere: leather sofas and armchairs at one end in front
of a woodburning stove, kitchen and chapel chairs and built-in planked wall seats
with scatter cushions, leather-topped stools against the counter, and a cosy nook
with just one table. A two-way fireplace opens into the candlelit restaurant, which
has similar tables and chairs on a dark slate floor, and lots of photos of local
people and views. Stairs lead up to another dining room with beams in a high roof
and some unusual large wooden chandeliers; background music, darts and board
games. The airy conservatory has tea-lights or church candles on scrubbed kitchen
tables and wooden dining chairs. Just beyond this are picnic-sets on grass plus a
fenced-off, well equipped children's play area. Do visit their farm shop opposite.

Free house ~ Licensee Robin Brown ~ Real ale ~ Open 10am-11pm (10.30pm Sun) ~
Bar food 12-2.30, 6-9; 12-3, 6-9.30 Sat; 12-4, 6-8 Sun ~ Restaurant ~ Children welcome ~
Dogs allowed in bar ~ Wi-fi ~ Live music Fri/Sat evenings ~ Bedrooms: £95

FONTHILL GIFFORD

ST9231

Beckford Arms

(01747) 870385 – www.beckfordarms.com
Hindon Lane; from Fonthill Bishop, bear left after tea rooms through Estate gate;
from Hindon follow High Street signed for Tisbury; SP3 6PX

18th-c coaching inn with character bar and restaurant, unfailingly good food, thoughtful choice of drinks and an easy-going atmosphere; comfortable bedrooms

There's an almost country-house hotel feel to this golden-stone coaching inn with its civilised yet informal atmosphere – and a friendly welcome from courteous staff. The main bar has various old wooden dining chairs and tables on parquet flooring, a huge fireplace and bar stools beside the counter where they keep an interesting range of drinks: Keystone Phoenix (named for them), Yeovil Stout Hearted and a changing guest on handpump, 15 wines by the glass, 20 malt whiskies, farm cider and winter mulled wine and cider, and cocktails such as a bellini using locally produced peach liqueur and a bloody mary using home-grown horseradish. The cosy sitting room is stylish with comfortable sofas facing one another across a low table with newspapers, a nice built-in window seat among other chairs and tables, and an open fire in a stone fireplace with candles in brass candlesticks and fresh flowers on the mantelpiece. There's also a separate restaurant and private dining room. Much of the artwork on the walls is by local artists. They host film nights on occasional Sundays and will provide water and bones for dogs (the pub dog is called Elsa). The mature rambling garden has seats on a brick terrace, hammocks under trees, games for children, a dog bath and boules.

Free house ~ Licensees Dan Brod and Charlie Luxton ~ Real ale ~ Open 8am-11pm (10.30 Sun) ~ Bar food 12-3, 6-9.30 (9 Sun) ~ Children welcome ~ Dogs welcome ~ Wi-fi ~ Bedrooms: $95

GREAT BEDWYN

SU2764

Three Tuns

(01672) 870280 – www.threetunsbedwyn.co.uk
Village signposted off A338 S of Hungerford, or off A4 W of Hungerford via Little Bedwyn;
High Street; SN8 3NU

Carefully refurbished village pub with real ales and highly rated food

The chef-owner and his wife run this neatly kept 18th-c village inn with a great deal of care and enthusiasm. The beamed front bar is traditional and simply furnished with pubby stools and chairs on bare floorboards, and has an open fire, artwork by local artists on the walls and plenty of original features. They keep quickly changing ales from small local breweries including Three Tuns (brewed by Betteridge), a seasonal beer from Butcombe and West Berkshire Swift Pale Ale on handpump, 14 wines by the glass, several malt whiskies, gins and vodkas and Sheppy's farm cider. French doors in the back dining room lead into the garden where there are tables and chairs and an outdoor grill. Cooked by the landlord using seasonal ingredients from local producers and making everything in-house, the food is particularly good. The Kennet & Avon Canal runs through the village and the pub is on the edge of Savernake Forest, which has lovely walks and cycle routes.

Free house ~ Licensees James and Ashley Wilsey ~ Real ale ~ Open 10am-midnight; 12-6 Sun; closed Sun evening, Mon, first week Jan ~ Bar food 12.30-2.30, 6-9.30; 12.30-9.30 Fri, Sat; 12-3 Sun ~ Restaurant ~ Children welcome ~ Dogs welcome ~ Wi-fi

HOLT
ST8561

Toll Gate

(01225) 782326 – www.tollgateinn.co.uk
Ham Green; B3107 W of Melksham; BA14 6PX

16th-c stone pub with cheerful staff, woodburning stoves in bars, real ales and popular food; pretty bedrooms

This former weavers' shed is a friendly place with a good mix of both locals and visitors. The relaxed bar has real character with seats by a woodburner, a mix of tables and chairs on pale floorboards and plenty of paintings by local artists for sale. Box Steam Half Sovereign and Tunnel Vision (the brewery is in the village), Butcombe Bitter and Fullers London Pride with a guest such as Sharps Doom Bar on handpump, 16 wines by the glass, interesting gins and three farm ciders; background music, TV and board games. The dining room leads off the bar with high-backed leather and other cushioned chairs, a second woodburner, fresh flowers and cream window blinds. Up a few steps, the high-raftered restaurant is similarly furnished with white deer heads on a dark blue wall and church windows (this used to be a workers' chapel). The sun-shaded and paved back terrace has seats and tables, and there's a boules pitch. There is wheelchair access to the bar, but not to the loos.

Free house ~ Licensees Laura Boulton and Mark Hodges ~ Real ale ~ Open 10am-11pm (midnight Sat); 10-4 Sun ~ Bar food 12-2, 6.30-9; 12-9 Sat; 12-4 Sun ~ Restaurant ~ Children welcome ~ Wi-fi ~ Live music outside in summer ~ Bedrooms: £70

MANTON
SU1768

Outside Chance

(01672) 512352 – www.theoutsidechance.co.uk
Village (and pub) signposted off A4 just W of Marlborough; High Street; SN8 4HW

Popular dining pub, civilised and traditional, nicely reworked with sporting theme; interesting modern food

The 20-times champion jump jockey A P McCoy co-owns this charming country pub that's usefully open all day. The three small linked rooms have hops on beams, flagstones or bare boards, and mainly plain pub furnishings such as chapel chairs and a long-cushioned pew; one room has a more cosseted feel, with panelling and a comfortable banquette. The décor celebrates unlikely horse-racing winners Caughoo, Foinavon, Mr Spooner's Only Dreams (a 100–1 winner at Leicester in 2007) and the odd-gaited little Seabiscuit who cheered many thousands of Americans with his dogged pursuit of victory during the Depression. There's a splendid log fire in the big main fireplace and maybe fresh flowers and candlelight; background music and board games. Wadworths IPA, 6X and a guest from Wadworths on handpump and eight good wines by the glass served by neatly dressed young staff; background music, board games and TV. A suntrap side terrace has contemporary tables with metal frames and granite tops, while the good-sized garden has sturdy rustic tables and benches under ash trees; they have private access to the local playing fields and children's play area. There are plenty of walks and things to see and do nearby.

Wadworths ~ Tenant Howard Spooner ~ Real ale ~ Open 12-11 ~ Bar food 12-2, 6-9; 12-3, 6-8 Sun ~ Children welcome ~ Dogs welcome ~ Wi-fi

MARSTON MEYSEY

SU1297

Old Spotted Cow

(01285) 810264 – www.theoldspottedcow.co.uk
Off A419 Swindon–Cirencester; SN6 6LQ

An easy-going atmosphere in cottagey bar rooms, friendly young staff, lots to look at, well kept ales and enjoyable food; bedrooms

This is a smashing little pub with a very friendly landlady and staff. You'll see many cows of all sorts around the bars, and some of them are actually spotted: paintings, drawings, postcards, all manner and colour of china objects and embroidery and toy ones too. The main bar has high-backed cushioned dining chairs around chunky pine tables on wooden floorboards or parquet, a few rugs here and there, an open fire at each end of the room (with comfortable sofas in front of one), fresh flowers and brass candlesticks with candles, and beer mats and bank notes pinned to beams. Butcombe Gold, Otter Bitter and Timothy Taylors Landlord on handpump, ten wines by the glass, summer farm cider and quite a few gins and malt whiskies. Two cottagey dining rooms lead off here with similar tables and chairs, a couple of long pews and a big bookshelf. There are seats and picnic-sets on the front grass and a children's play area beyond a big willow tree. A classic car show is held here on the late May Bank Holiday.

Free house ~ Licensee Anna Langley-Poole ~ Real ale ~ Open 11-11; 11-6.30 Sun ~ Bar food 12-2, 7-9; 12-3 Sun ~ Restaurant ~ Children welcome but must be over 8 in bar ~ Dogs allowed in bar ~ Wi-fi ~ Bedrooms: £95

MONKTON FARLEIGH

ST8065

Muddy Duck

(01225) 858705 – www.themuddyduckbath.co.uk
Signed off A363 Bradford–Bath; BA15 2QH

Grand stone building with character bar and dining room, open fire, real ales, good food and seats at the front and back; bedrooms

In a pretty village not far from Bath, this is a convivial and imposing 17th-c stone inn. The bar and dining room are furnished in a similar manner, with wooden and upholstered chairs around tables of all shapes on bare boards or parquet flooring, armchairs in front of an open fire, cushioned pews, the odd duck ornament, beams, half-panelled walls and low-hanging lamps. High red leather chairs line the counter where friendly staff serve Butcombe Bitter, St Austell Proper Job and Timothy Taylors Landlord on handpump and good wines by the glass; background music and board games. In front of the building there's an impressive wisteria and picnic-sets under parasols; at the back, colourful tables and chairs sit in a fairy-lit, gravelled courtyard with views over open country.

Punch ~ Lease Tom Lakin ~ Real ale ~ Open 12-11; 12-9 Sun ~ Bar food 12-2.30, 6-9; 12-3, 6-9.30 Sat; 12-4 Sun ~ Restaurant ~ Children welcome ~ Dogs allowed in bar ~ Wi-fi

NEWTON TONY

SU2140

Malet Arms

(01980) 629279 – www.maletarms.com
Village signposted off A338 Swindon–Salisbury; SP4 0HF

Smashing village pub with no pretensions, a good choice of local beers and highly thought-of food

Those who like their pubs neat and tidy might find this place a little worn about the edges, but for most of us this just adds to the genuine, unspoilt character. The landlord and his staff are friendly and enthusiastic and sure to make you welcome. The low-beamed interconnecting rooms have a mix of tables of different sizes with high-winged wall settles, carved pews, chapel and carver chairs, and lots of pictures of local scenes and from imperial days. The main front windows are said to be made from the stern of a ship, and there's a log and coal fire in a huge fireplace. The snug is noteworthy for its fantastic collection of photographs and prints celebrating the local aviation history of Boscombe Down, alongside archive photographs of Stonehenge festivals of the 1970s and '80s. At the back is a homely, red-painted dining room. Four real ales on handpump come from breweries such as Butcombe, Flack Manor, Hop Back, Itchen Valley, Ramsbury, Stonehenge and Triple fff and they also keep 40 malt whiskies, eight wines by the glass and Weston's Old Rosie cider; board games. The country cooking uses seasonal game from local shoots (some bagged by the landlord), lamb raised in the surrounding fields and free-range local pork. There are seats on the small front terrace with more on grass and in the back garden. The road to the pub goes through a ford, and it may be best to use an alternative route in winter when the water can be quite deep.

Free house ~ Licensees Noel and Annie Cardew ~ Real ale ~ Open 11-3, 6-11; 12-4 Sun; closed Sun evening ~ Bar food 12-2.30, 6.30-9.30; 12-2.30 Sun ~ Restaurant ~ Children allowed only in restaurant or snug ~ Dogs allowed in bar

PITTON   SU2131
Silver Plough

(01722) 712266 ~ www.silverplough-pitton.co.uk
Village signed from A30 E of Salisbury (follow brown signs); SP5 1DU

Bustling country dining pub with popular, reasonably priced bar food, good drinks and nearby walks; bedrooms

With notably helpful and friendly staff, a warm atmosphere and a cheerful mix of both locals and visitors, this pub is a winner. The comfortable, nicely kept front bar has plenty to look at: black beams strung with hundreds of antique boot warmers and stretchers, pewter and china tankards, copper kettles, toby jugs, earthenware and glass rolling pins and so forth. Seats include half a dozen cushioned antique oak settles (one elaborately carved, next to a very fine reproduction of an Elizabethan oak table) around rustic pine tables. Badger First Call, K&B Sussex Bitter and Tanglefoot on handpump and 13 wines by the glass served from a bar made from a hand-carved Elizabethan overmantel. The back bar is simpler, but still has a big winged high-backed settle, cases of antique swords and some substantial pictures, and there are two woodburning stoves for winter warmth; background music. The skittle alley is for private use only. The quiet south-facing lawn has picnic-sets and other tables beneath parasols and there are more seats on the heated terrace; occasional barbecues. There are plenty of walks in the surrounding woodland and on downland paths.

Badger ~ Tenants Katie Hunter and Mike Reeves ~ Real ale ~ Open 12-3, 6-11; 12-8.30 Sun ~ Bar food 12-2, 6-9; 12-7.30 Sun ~ Restaurant ~ Children welcome ~ Dogs allowed in bar ~ Wi-fi ~ Bedrooms: £60

POULSHOT
ST9760

Raven

(01380) 828271 – www.ravenpoulshot.co.uk
Off A361; SN10 1RW

Pretty village pub with friendly licensees, enjoyable beer and food and seats in a walled back garden

The welcoming, professional licensees take great care of their pretty half-timbered pub – and of their customers too. The two cosy, black-beamed rooms are spotlessly kept with comfortable banquettes, pubby chairs and tables and an open fire. Wadworths IPA and 6X plus a changing guest tapped from the cask and 13 wines by the glass; background music is played in the dining room only. The jack russell is called Faith and the doberman Harvey. There are picnic-sets under parasols in the walled back garden and the pub is just across from the village green. There are plenty of good nearby walks.

Wadworths ~ Tenants Jeremy and Nathalie Edwards ~ Real ale ~ Open 11.30-3, 6.30-11; 12-3.30, 7-10.30 Sun; closed Sun evening Oct-Easter, Mon end Oct-early May ~ Bar food 12-2 (2.30 Sun), 6.30-9 ~ Restaurant ~ Children welcome ~ Dogs allowed in bar ~ Wi-fi

RAMSBURY
SU2771

Bell

(01672) 520230 – www.thebellramsbury.com
Off B4192 NW of Hungerford, or A4 W; SN8 2PE

Lovely old inn with a civilised feel, character bar and dining rooms, and a thoughtful choice of both drinks and food; spotless bedrooms

Not surprisingly, this handsome and civilised 300-year-old former coaching inn does get extremely busy at peak times, so it's best to arrive early or pre-book a table in the restaurant. Throughout, the original features and contemporary paintwork and furnishings blend well together; the two rooms of the bar have tartan-cushioned wall seats and pale wooden dining chairs around assorted tables, country and wildlife paintings, interesting stained-glass windows and a woodburning stove. Neat, efficient staff serve Ramsbury Bitter, Gold and a seasonal ale plus a guest such as Muirhouse Chocolate Mild on handpump, a dozen wines by the glass and 20 malt whiskies. A cosy room between the bar and restaurant has much-prized armchairs and sofas before an open fire, a table of magazines and papers, a couple of portraits, stuffed birds and a squirrel, books on shelves and patterned wallpaper. The restaurant, smart but relaxed, is similarly furnished to the bar with white-clothed tables on bare boards or rugs, oil paintings and winter-scene photographs on beige walls; fresh flowers decorate each table. A nice surprise is the charming back café with white-painted farmhouse, tub and wicker chairs on floorboards, where they offer toasties, buns, cakes and so forth – it's very popular for morning coffee and afternoon tea. The garden has picnic-sets on a lower terrace and raised lawn, with more on a little terrace towards the front.

Free house ~ Licensee Alistair Ewing ~ Real ale ~ Open 12-11 (10 Sun) ~ Bar food 12-2.30, 6-9; 12-3, 6-8 Sun ~ Restaurant ~ Children welcome ~ Dogs allowed in bar ~ Wi-fi ~ Bedrooms: £110

ROWDE

ST9762

George & Dragon

(01380) 723053 – www.thegeorgeanddragonrowde.co.uk
A342 Devizes–Chippenham; SN10 2PN

Gently upmarket inn with good food, west country ales and a relaxed atmosphere; bedrooms

Handy for walks along the nearby Kennet & Avon Canal, this is a 16th-c former coaching inn with plenty of character. The two low-ceilinged rooms have beams, large open fireplaces, wooden dining chairs (some straightforward and others rather elegant) and wall seats with scatter cushions around candlelit tables, antique rugs and walls hung with old pictures and portraits; the atmosphere is pleasantly chatty. From the rustic bar counter, friendly staff serve Butcombe Bitter and Prescott Track Record on handpump and several wines by the glass. The pretty back garden has tables and chairs.

Free house ~ Licensee Christopher Day ~ Real ale ~ Open 12-3 (4 Sat), 6.30-11; 12-4 Sun; closed Sun evening ~ Bar food 12-3 (4 weekends), 6.30-10 ~ Restaurant ~ Children welcome ~ Dogs allowed in bar ~ Bedrooms: £95

SHERSTON

ST8585

Rattlebone

(01666) 840871 – www.therattlebone.co.uk
Church Street; B4040 Malmesbury–Chipping Sodbury; SN16 0LR

17th-c village pub with rambling rooms, real ales and good bar food using local and free-range produce; friendly staff

There's a great deal of character here as well as a bustling atmosphere helped along by chatty customers. The rambling rooms are softly lit and in the public bar and long back dining room you'll find beams, standing timbers and flagstones, pews, settles and country kitchen chairs around an assortment of tables, and armchairs and sofas by roaring fires. Butcombe Bitter, Flying Monk Elmers and St Austell Tribute on handpump, 20 wines by the glass from a thoughtful list, local cider and home-made lemonade; background music, darts, board games, TV and games machine. Outside is a skittle alley and three boules pitches, often in use by one of the many pub teams; a boules festival is held in July, as well as mangold hurling (similar to boules, but using cattle-feed turnips) and other events. The two pretty gardens include an extended terrace where they hold barbecues and spit roasts. Wheelchair access.

Youngs ~ Tenant Jason Read ~ Real ale ~ Open 12-3, 5-11 (midnight Fri); 12-midnight Sat; 12-11 Sun ~ Bar food 12-2.30, 6-9.30; 12-5 Sun ~ Restaurant ~ Children welcome ~ Dogs allowed in bar ~ Wi-fi ~ Live music last weekend of month

SOUTH WRAXALL

ST8364

Longs Arms

(01225) 864450 – www.thelongsarms.com
Upper S Wraxall, off B3109 N of Bradford-on-Avon; BA15 2SB

Friendly licensees for well run and handsome old stone inn with plenty of character, real ales and first class food

The enthusiastic, convivial landlord here comes in for special praise for the thoughtfulness and care he shows all his customers. The bar has windsor and other pubby chairs around wooden tables on flagstones, a fireplace with a woodburning stove and high chairs by the counter where they keep Wadworths Horizon and 6X and a changing guest on handpump and ten wines and prosecco by the glass. Another room has cushioned and other dining chairs, a nice old settle and a wall banquette around a mix of tables on carpeting, fresh flowers and lots of prints and paintings; board games. There are tables and chairs in the pretty walled back garden, which also has raised beds and a greenhouse for salad leaves and herbs.

Wadworths ~ Tenants Rob and Liz Allcock ~ Real ale ~ Open 12-3.30, 5.30-11.30; 12-5 Sun; closed Sun evening, Mon, three weeks Jan ~ Bar food 12-2.30, 5.30-9.30; 12-3 Sun ~ Children welcome ~ Dogs welcome ~ Wi-fi

SWINDON   SU1384
Weighbridge Brewhouse
(01793) 881500 – www.weighbridgebrewhouse.co.uk
Penzance Drive; SN5 7JL

Stunning building with stylish modern décor, own microbrewery ales, a huge wine list, a big range of popular food and helpful staff

At any one time you'll find six of their own-brew ales here, such as Weighbridge Brinkworth Village, Pooleys Gold, Poppy Red, Renegade, Swindon Pale Ale and Weighbridge Best; also, 20 wines by the glass, 30 malt whiskies and a cocktail menu. The bar area has comfortable brown leather chesterfields and wood and leather armchairs around a few tables on dark flagstones, much-used blue bar chairs against the long dimpled and polished steel counter and a sizeable carved wooden eagle on a stand. The fantastic-looking, stylishly modern open-plan dining room has a steel-tensioned high-raftered roof (the big central skylight adds even more light), attractive high-backed striped chairs and long wall banquettes, bare brick walls, candles in red glass jars on windowsills and a glass cabinet at the end displaying about 1,000 bottled beers from around the world. Metal stairs lead up to an area overlooking the dining room below with big sofas and chairs beside a glass piano; another room on the same level is used for cosier dining occasions. There are seats on an outside terrace.

Free house ~ Licensees Anthony and Allyson Windle ~ Real ale ~ Open 11.30am-midnight; 12-10.30 Sun ~ Bar food 12-2, 6-9.30; 12-8 Sun ~ Restaurant ~ Children welcome before 8pm ~ Dogs allowed in bar ~ Live music Thurs-Sat evenings

TOLLARD ROYAL   ST9317
King John
(01725) 516207 – www.kingjohninn.co.uk
B3081 Shaftesbury–Sixpenny Handley; SP5 5PS

Pleasing contemporary furnishings in carefully opened-up pub, courteous, helpful service, good drinks and excellent food; pretty bedrooms

Opened in 1859, this was named after one of King John's hunting lodges and although regulars do drop in for a pint, most customers are here for the creative food. It's gently civilised and friendly and the open-plan L-shaped bar has a relaxed atmosphere, a log fire, nice little touches such as a rosemary plant and tiny metal buckets of salt and pepper on scrubbed kitchen tables, dog-motif cushions, a screen made up of the sides of wine boxes, and candles in big glass jars. An attractive mix of seats takes in spindlebacks, captain's and chapel chairs (some built into the bay windows) plus the odd cushioned settle, and there are big terracotta floor tiles, lantern-style wall lights, hound, hunting and other photographs, and prints of early 19th-c scientists. Ringwood Best, Sharps Doom Bar and Waylands Sixpenny 6d Gold on handpump and wines from a good list. A second log fire has fender seats on each side and leather chesterfields in front, and there's also a stuffed heron and grouse and daily papers. Outside at the front are seats and tables beneath parasols, with more up steps in the raised garden where there's also an outdoor kitchen pavilion.

Free house ~ Licensee Lee Hart ~ Real ale ~ Open 11-11 ~ Bar food 12-2.30, 7-9.30; 12-3, 7-9 Sun ~ Restaurant ~ Children welcome ~ Dogs welcome ~ Wi-fi ~ Bedrooms: £140

UPTON SCUDAMORE ST8647
Angel
(01985) 213225 – www.theangelinn.co.uk
Off A350 N of Warminster; BA12 0AG

Bustling bar and dining rooms where old and new features blend together, real ales, good wines, well thought-of food and seats in garden; attractive bedrooms

The bar in this 16th-c coaching inn has built-in tartan-cushioned wall seats, some farmhouse chairs and tables on stripped floorboards and stools against the counter where they serve Butcombe Bitter and Sharps Doom Bar on handpump and good wines by the glass; service is friendly and helpful. Steps lead up to an informal dining room with more farmhouse chairs around rustic tables on more bare boards, plus big hanging ceiling lights, paintings and fresh flowers; the upper restaurant is stylish with cushioned elegant chairs around polished tables on tartan carpet. The terraced back garden has modern chairs and tables under parasols, with sofas and more seats and tables among flower tubs and pots. Longleat House & Safari Park is nearby.

Free house ~ Licensee Sharon Cornelius ~ Real ale ~ Open 11.30-3, 5.30-11 (10 Sun); see website for opening times in winter ~ Bar food 12-2, 6.30-9 ~ Restaurant ~ Children welcome ~ Dogs allowed in bar ~ Wi-fi ~ Bedrooms: £100

DOG FRIENDLY HOTELS, INNS AND B&Bs

BRADFORD-ON-AVON ST8361
Woolley Grange
(01225) 864705 – www.woolleygrangehotel.co.uk
Woolley Green, Bradford-on-Avon, Wiltshire BA15 1TX

£120; 25 very individual, characterful rooms. Civilised Jacobean manor house with a relaxed, informal atmosphere, lovely flowers, log fires and antiques in comfortable, panelled sitting rooms, plenty of original features and genuinely friendly, helpful staff; interesting modern food using home-grown and other local produce in the restaurant, as well as marvellous breakfasts and light lunches in the Orangery; outdoor heated swimming pool, and a spa with treatment, steam and sauna rooms and indoor swimming pool; ornamental and kitchen gardens, and a field that dogs can use. Dogs allowed in bedrooms and anywhere except restaurant; bed, bowl and biscuits; £15.

CASTLE COMBE
ST8377

Manor House

(01249) 782206 – www.manorhouse.co.uk
Castle Combe, Chippenham, Wiltshire SN14 7HR

£240; 48 sumptuous rooms, some in mews cottages. 14th-c manor house in 360 acres of countryside with an italian garden and parkland, an 18-hole golf course (with its own club house and restaurant), croquet and fishing; wood panelling, antiques, log fires and fresh flowers and a warm, friendly atmosphere; extensive breakfasts, light lunches and afternoon teas in the convivial Clubhouse bar, exceptional food in the smart Bybrook restaurant, and courteous, helpful staff. Dogs allowed in two cottage bedrooms and grounds; bowl and bed; £25.

CHICKSGROVE
ST9730

Compasses

(01722) 714318 – www.thecompassesinn.com
Lower Chicksgrove, Tisbury, Salisbury, Wiltshire SP3 6NB

£95; 4 simply designed rooms; also self-catering cottage. Lovely 14th-c thatched inn with plenty of surrounding country walks and an unchanging bar of real character; old bottles and jugs hang from beams, there are farm tools and traps on the part-stripped stone walls, high-backed wooden settles forming snug booths around tables on the mainly flagstoned floor and a log fire; real ales and interesting food (including smashing breakfasts) served by helpful, friendly young staff; quiet garden with seating on terraces and in a flagstoned courtyard. Dogs allowed in all bedrooms (but not on beds) and anywhere in pub.

CRICKLADE
SU1093

Red Lion

(01793) 750776 – www.theredlioncricklade.co.uk
74 High Street, Cricklade, Swindon, Wiltshire SN6 6DD

£85; 5 attractive rooms. Well run 16th-c inn with walks nearby along the Thames Path; all sorts of bric-a-brac and old street signs on the stone walls of the bar, an open fire, traditional seats and tables on red carpet, ten real ales including some from their on-site Hop Kettle microbrewery, over 60 bottled beers, five farm ciders and several gins and malt whiskies; the more formal dining rooms, with pale wooden farmhouse tables and chairs and a woodburning stove, serve imaginative food (they make their own butter, bread, ice-creams, chutneys and jellies); large back garden with picnic-sets. Dogs allowed in two bedrooms and bar.

CRUDWELL
ST9592

Rectory Hotel

(01666) 577194 – www.therectoryhotel.com
Crudwell, Malmesbury, Wiltshire SN16 9EP

£165; 12 lovely airy rooms. Elegant, welcoming country house hotel, formerly the rectory to the Saxon church next door, in three acres of attractive landscaped Victorian gardens with an outdoor heated swimming pool; comfortable sitting room and bar, open fires and antiques, interesting, enjoyable food using seasonal local produce in the panelled restaurant, a relaxed atmosphere and unpretentious service; their sister establishment, the Potting Shed pub across the road, is excellent; lots of nearby footpaths and bridleways. New owners arrived at the hotel in 2016, so there may be changes. Dogs allowed in all bedrooms and everywhere except restaurant; welcome box (treats, blanket, bowl).

EAST CHISENBURY
SU1352

Red Lion

(01980) 671124 – www.redlionfreehouse.com
East Chisenbury, Pewsey, Wiltshire SN9 6AQ

£150; 5 well equipped, boutique-style bedrooms in a separate building with private decks beside the River Avon. Thatched village inn renowned for exceptional food from the hard-working chef-owners (using meat from home-reared pigs, their own eggs, home-grown produce and other local suppliers) but they also have a fine range of drinks including real ales and 30 wines by the glass; one long room is split into different areas, with a woodburner in a brick inglenook fireplace at one end, black leather sofa and armchairs, assorted tables and chairs, pretty flowers and church candles; there's another dining room and seats outside on terrace and grass; excellent breakfasts; own-made dog treats. Dogs allowed in one bedroom and bar; bowl and treats; £10.

HINDON
ST9132

Lamb

(01747) 820573 – www.lambhindon.co.uk
High Street, Hindon, Salisbury, Wiltshire SP3 6DP

£129; 18 contemporary rooms. Smart, attractive old pub-hotel (refurbished in 2015) with a roomy bar with log fire, two flagstoned lower sections with a very long polished table, pews and settles, pictures and prints, a comfortable sitting room, a good choice of drinks including plenty of malt whiskies, polite service from smartly dressed staff, enjoyable bar and restaurant food and good breakfasts; tables on the terrace and in the garden across the road; boules. Dogs allowed in ten bedrooms and bar; bed, bowl, toy and treats; £20.

LACOCK
ST9168

At the Sign of the Angel

(01249) 730230 – www.signoftheangel.co.uk
6 Church Street, Lacock, Chippenham, Wiltshire SN15 2LB

£129; 5 charmingly old bedrooms with antiques. Fine 15th-c wool merchant's house in a lovely National Trust village, lots of character, heavy oak furniture, beams and big fireplaces, a restful oak-panelled lounge, good english cooking in three candlelit restaurants using their own and other local produce, and generous breakfasts with home-made bread and their own eggs; streamside garden. Dogs allowed in bedrooms only; £15.

LOWER CHUTE
SU3153

Hatchet

(01264) 730229 – www.thehatchetinn.com
Lower Chute, Andover, Wiltshire SP11 9DX

£85; 7 cosy rooms. Neatly kept, 13th-c thatched pub tucked away down country lanes with a convivial landlord and a peaceful local feel; a very low-beamed bar with a splendid 16th-c fireback in the huge fireplace (and a roaring winter log fire), a mix of captain's chairs and cushioned wheelbacks around oak tables, real ales and several farm ciders; well liked traditional bar food and hearty breakfasts; resident patterdale/lakeland cross, Marmite; plenty of nearby footpaths. Dogs allowed in two bedrooms; £10.

MALMESBURY

ST9387

Old Bell

(01666) 822344 – www.oldbellhotel.com
Abbey Row, Malmesbury, Wiltshire SN16 0BW

£115; 33 attractive modern rooms, some in coach house. With some claim to being one of England's oldest hotels and standing in the shadow of the Norman abbey, this fine wisteria-clad building has traditionally furnished rooms with open fires (one in an early 13th-c hooded stone fireplace), plenty of comfortable sofas and armchairs, helpful service, good, attractively presented food, afternoon teas and nice breakfasts, and seats in the garden. Dogs allowed in some coach house bedrooms and public areas, but not restaurant; £10.

MARLBOROUGH

SU1969

Lamb

(01672) 512668 – www.thelambinnmarlborough.com
5 The Parade, Marlborough, Wiltshire SN8 1NE

£80; 7 light, cottagey rooms. Friendly, family-run former coaching inn, tucked away in a side street, with a good mix of customers in its bustling bar, lots of hop bines, straightforward pubby seats and tables, a two-way woodburning stove, Cecil Aldin prints on red walls, real ales tapped from the cask, and maybe the easy-going bulldog wandering about; large helpings of popular food cooked by the landlady and hearty breakfasts; River Kennet walks are nearby and it's a short drive to Savernake Forest. Dogs allowed in bedrooms and anywhere in the pub.

NETTLETON

ST8377

Fosse Farmhouse

(01249) 782286 – www.fossefarmhouse.com
Nettleton, Chippenham, Wiltshire SN14 7NJ

£125; 3 pretty rooms; also self-catering. Friendly, 18th-c Cotswold-stone house filled with decorative french antique furniture and english chintzes; a comfortable drawing room, a homely dining room and good food cooked by the owner; seats in the garden; nearby walks including the Macmillan Way. Dogs allowed in two bedrooms; bed, bowl and treats; £15.

PURTON

SU0987

Pear Tree

(01793) 772100 – www.peartreepurton.co.uk
Church End, Purton, Swindon, Wiltshire SN5 4ED

£119; 17 pretty rooms. Impeccably run former vicarage with elegant day rooms, fresh flowers, a conservatory restaurant with creative modern english cooking using home-grown herbs and wines from their own vineyard, and afternoon teas; helpful, caring staff; seven acres of grounds and walks nearby. Dogs allowed in all bedrooms (not to be left unattended) and public areas except restaurant; welcome pack including bowl, towel and chews.

TEFFONT EVIAS
ST9931

Howards House

(01722) 716392 – www.howardshousehotel.co.uk
Teffont Evias, Salisbury, Wiltshire SP3 5RJ

£190; 9 pretty rooms, some overlooking the grounds. Partly 17th-c stone house (recently redecorated) in two acres of attractive gardens with ancient box hedges, croquet and kitchen garden; fresh flowers, beams and an open fire in the restful sitting room; delicious modern cooking, fine breakfasts, afternoon teas and impeccable service; walks all round. Dogs allowed in bedrooms; £15.

UPTON LOVELL
ST9441

Prince Leopold

(01985) 850460 – www.princeleopoldinn.co.uk
Upton Lovell, Warminster, Wiltshire BA12 0JP

£75; 6 cottagey bedrooms. An enjoyable village pub with a friendly welcome from the licensees and pleasing décor; there's a simply furnished, panelled bar busy with chatty locals, a cosy little snug with an open fire and book-lined wall, two other linked rooms with scrubbed tables and wooden dining chairs, and a light and airy back restaurant overlooking the River Wylye; the riverside garden has its own charming bar and seats and tables; highly rated food, real ales and helpful staff. Dogs allowed in all bedrooms, bar and lounge; £10.

WARMINSTER
ST8944

Bishopstrow Hotel

(01985) 212312 – www.bishopstrow.co.uk
Bishopstrow, Warminster, Wiltshire BA12 9HH

£175; 32 stylish rooms. Charming ivy-clad Georgian house in 27 acres of grounds with an outdoor swimming pool, indoor and outdoor tennis courts and fishing on River Wylye; a very relaxed friendly atmosphere, two comfortable lounges (where afternoon tea is taken) with original features, chandeliers, log fires and paintings; delicious inventive food in the main restaurant and more informal meals in the conservatory; spa with sauna, steam and treatment rooms, gym and indoor swimming pool; walks in the grounds and nearby. Dogs allowed in all bedrooms and public areas away from restaurants; £10.

WHITLEY
ST8866

Pear Tree

(01225) 704966 – www.peartreewhitley.co.uk
Top Lane, Whitley, Melksham, Wiltshire SN12 8QX

£120; 8 lovely rooms – 4 in main inn, 4 in converted barn. Attractive honey-coloured stone dining pub (former 17th-c farmhouse) under new management; revamped beamed interior with plenty of contemporary/rustic charm – mismatched furniture, exposed beams and stonework, rugs on flagstone and timber floors – in front bar, restaurant and airy garden room; inventive food, real ales and friendly attentive service; terrace and pretty garden. Dogs allowed in three bedrooms, bar and garden room; treats; £10.

Worcestershire

MAP 4

DOG FRIENDLY PUBS

BRANSFORD   SO8052
Bear & Ragged Staff
(01886) 833399 – www.bearatbransford.co.uk
Off A4103 SW of Worcester; Station Road; WR6 5JH

**Well run dining pub with pleasant places to sit both inside and out
and well liked food and drink**

In a hamlet tucked away in the Teme Valley, this is a friendly, gently civilised
dining pub – but there's a relaxing bar as well: Hobsons Twisted Spire and
Sharps Doom Bar on handpump, ten wines by the glass, several malt whiskies and
quite a few brandies and liqueurs. The restaurant is more formal with upholstered
dining chairs, proper tablecloths and linen napkins. These interconnecting rooms
give fine views of attractive rolling country (as do the pretty garden and terrace).
In winter, there's a warming open fire; background music and darts. Good
disabled access and facilities.

Free house ~ Licensee Lynda Williams ~ Real ale ~ Open 12-2.30, 6-11; 12-4 Sun ~ Bar food
12-2, 6-9; 12-2.30 Sun ~ Restaurant ~ Children welcome ~ Dogs allowed in bar ~ Wi-fi

BRETFORTON   SP0943
Fleece
(01386) 831173 – www.thefleeceinn.co.uk
*B4035 E of Evesham: turn S off this road into village; pub is in central square by church;
there's a sizeable car park at one side of the church; WR11 7JE*

**Marvellously unspoilt medieval pub owned by the National Trust;
bedrooms**

Many of the furnishings here are original and heirlooms of the family that
owned this lovely former farm for around 500 years; it was bequeathed to
the National Trust in 1977. The fine country rooms include a great oak dresser
holding a priceless 48-piece set of Stuart pewter, two grandfather clocks,
ancient kitchen chairs, curved high-backed settles, a rocking chair and a rack
of heavy pointed iron shafts, probably for spit roasting in one of the huge
inglenook fireplaces; two other log fires. As well as massive beams and exposed
timbers, there are worn and crazed flagstones (scored with marks to keep out
demons) and plenty of oddities such as a great cheese-press and set of cheese
moulds and a rare dough-proving table; a leaflet details the more bizarre items.
Malvern Hills Black Pear, Purity Mad Goose, Uley Pigs Ear, Wye Valley Bitter

and a guest or two on handpump, six wines by the glass, a similar number of malt whiskies and four farm ciders; board games. They hold an asparagus auction at the end of May, as part of the Vale of Evesham Asparagus Festival, and also host the village fête on August Bank Holiday Monday. The calendar of events also includes morris dancing and the village silver band plays here regularly. The lawn, with fruit trees around a beautifully restored thatched and timbered barn, is a lovely place to sit, and there are more picnic-sets and a stone pump-trough in the front courtyard. If you're visiting to enjoy the famous historic interior, best to go midweek as it can get very busy at weekends.

Free house ~ Licensee Nigel Smith ~ Real ale ~ Open 10am-11pm; 10.30am-11pm Sun ~ Bar food 12-2.30, 6.30-9; 12-8 Sun ~ Children welcome ~ Dogs welcome ~ Wi-fi ~ Bedrooms: £97.50

BROADWAY SP0937

Crown & Trumpet

(01386) 853202 – www.crownandtrumpet.co.uk
Church Street; WR12 7AE

Honest local with good real ale and decent, good value food; bedrooms

Warmly welcoming and run by a charming landlord and his helpful staff, this is an old-fashioned, unpretentious place with a good mix of both regulars and visitors. The bustling beamed and timbered bar has a cheerful, easy-going feel, antique dark high-backed settles, large solid tables and a blazing log fire. You'll find a beer named for the pub (from Stanway) plus Prescott Chequered Flag, Stroud Tom Long and Timothy Taylors Landlord on handpump, alongside nine wines by the glass, ten malt whiskies, Black Rat perry and cider, Orchard Pig chilli and ginger or marmalade ciders, mulled wine and a good range of soft drinks. There's an assortment of pub games, including darts, cribbage, shut the box, dominoes, bar skittles and ring the bull, as well as a games machine, TV and background music. The hardwood tables and chairs outside, set among flowers on a slightly raised front terrace, are popular with walkers.

Laurel (Enterprise) ~ Lease Andrew Scott ~ Real ale ~ Open 11-11 (midnight Sat); 11-11 Sun ~ Bar food 12-2.30, 5.45-9.30; 12-9.30 Fri-Sun ~ Children welcome ~ Dogs allowed in bar ~ Wi-fi ~ Live jazz/blues Thurs evening, 1960s-80s music Sat evening ~ Bedrooms: £68

CHILDSWICKHAM SP0738

Childswickham Inn

(01386) 852461 – www.childswickhaminn.co.uk
Off A44 NW of Broadway; WR12 7HP

Bustling dining pub with highly regarded food, good drinks choice, attentive staff and seats in neat garden

The chatty bar in this bustling pub is full of friendly regulars (often with their dogs too) and there are leather sofas and armchairs and Lancaster Northern Hemisphere Hopped Ale and Sharps Atlantic on handpump, ten wines by the glass (Friday evening special deals on champagne and prosecco), malt whiskies and farm cider; background music. There are two dining areas, one with high-backed dark leather chairs on terracotta tiles, the other with country kitchen chairs on bare floorboards. Both have contemporary artwork on part-timbered walls painted cream or pale violet; an open fire and woodburning stove. Outside, the neat garden has rush-seated chairs and tables on decking and also separate areas under parasols. The surrounding countryside offers many lovely walks. Disabled facilities.

Punch ~ Tenant Carol Marshall ~ Real ale ~ Open 11.30-11; 12-11 Sun ~ Bar food 12-2, 6-9;
12-8 (6 in winter) Sun ~ Restaurant not Sun evening or Mon lunch ~ Children welcome ~
Dogs allowed in bar ~ Wi-fi

CUTNALL GREEN   SO8868

Chequers

(01299) 851292 – www.chequerscutnallgreen.co.uk
Kidderminster Road; WR9 0PJ

**Bustling roadside pub with plenty of drinking and dining space in
interesting rooms and rewarding food**

This interesting pub was built some 90 years ago on the site of an old coaching
inn, and is a clever mix of ancient and modern: red-painted walls between
beams and timbering, broad floorboards and weathered quarry tiles, and warm
winter fires. There are leather sofas and tub chairs, high-backed purple and red
or ladderback dining chairs around all sorts of tables, plenty of mirrors giving the
impression of even more space, brass plates and mugs, candles and fresh flowers.
Sharps Doom Bar, Wye Valley HPA and a guest from Marstons on handpump
and 14 wines by the glass. One elegant but cosy room, known as the Players
Lounge, has photographs of the landlord, Mr Narbett, who is a former chef for
the England football team. The pretty garden has three 'beach huts' to hire,
chairs with barrel tables and sofas, heaters and parasols. This is sister pub to
the Bell & Cross at Holy Cross (see below).

Free house ~ Licensees Roger and Jo Narbett ~ Real ale ~ Open 12-11 (10.30 Sun) ~ Bar
food 12-9 (9.15 Fri, 9.30 Sat, 8.30 Sun) ~ Restaurant ~ Children welcome ~ Dogs allowed in
bar ~ Wi-fi

HOLY CROSS   SO9278

Bell & Cross

(01562) 730319 – www.bellandcrossclent.co.uk
*2 miles from M5 junction 3: A491 towards Stourbridge, then follow Clent signpost off
on left; DY9 9QL*

**A delightful old interior, good food, staff with a can-do attitude
and a pretty garden**

The perfect place for a break from the M5, this well run pub has a cosy bar
where chatty locals are served by neatly dressed courteous staff. Enville
Ale, Otter Bitter, Timothy Taylors Landlord and Wye Valley HPA on handpump
and 12 wines by the glass. The four attractively decorated dining rooms (with
a choice of carpet, bare boards, lino or nice old quarry tiles) have a variety
of moods, from snug and chatty to bright and airy; background music. Décor
includes theatrical engravings on red walls, nice sporting prints on pale green
walls, and racing and gun dog pictures above a black panelled dado; most
rooms have coal fires. The lovely garden has a spacious lawn, and the terrace
offers pleasant views – both have seating. This is sister pub to the Chequers at
Cutnall Green (see above).

Enterprise ~ Lease Roger and Jo Narbett ~ Real ale ~ Open 12-3, 6-11; 12-9 Sun ~
Bar food 12-2, 6-9 (9.15 Fri, 9.30 Sat); 12-7 Sun ~ Restaurant ~ Children welcome ~
Dogs allowed in bar ~ Wi-fi

MALVERN   SO7845

Nags Head

(01684) 574373 – www.nagsheadmalvern.co.uk
Bottom end of Bank Street, steep turn down off A449; WR14 2JG

A delightfully eclectic layout and décor, remarkable choice of ales, tasty lunchtime bar food and warmly welcoming atmosphere

This cheerful pub is always packed with customers keen to enjoy the marvellous range of ales and easy-going atmosphere. A series of snug, individually decorated rooms, separated by a couple of steps and with two open fires, have leather armchairs, pews sometimes arranged as booths and a mix of tables (including sturdy ones stained different colours). There are bare boards here, flagstones there, carpet elsewhere, plenty of interesting pictures and homely touches such as house plants, shelves of well thumbed books and daily papers; board games. If you struggle to choose from the 15 or so beers on handpump, you'll be offered a taster by the professional, friendly staff: Banks's Bitter, Bathams Best Bitter, Brains Rev James, Burning Sky Plateau, Burton Bridge Sovereign Gold, Connoisseur Lucem, Jennings Cumberland, Marstons Pedigree New World, Otter Bitter, Purity Pure Ubu, Ringwood Fortyniner, St Georges Charger, Dragons Blood and Friar Tuck, and Woods Shropshire Lad. Also, two farm ciders, 30 malt whiskies, a dozen gins, ten bottled craft ales/lagers and ten wines by the glass. The front terrace and garden have picnicsets, benches and rustic tables as well as parasols and heaters.

Free house ~ Licensee Alex Whistance ~ Real ale ~ Open 11am-11.15pm (11.30pm Fri, Sat); 12-11 Sun ~ Bar food 12-2.30, 6.30-8.30; 12-2.30, 7-8.30 Sun ~ Restaurant ~ Children welcome ~ Dogs welcome ~ Wi-fi

NEWLAND   SO7948

Swan

(01886) 832224 – www.theswaninnmalvern.co.uk
Worcester Road (set well back from A449 just NW of Malvern); WR13 5AY

Popular, interesting pub with six real ales and seats in the big garden

This bustling, creeper-clad pub has six real ales and tasty food. The dimly lit dark-beamed bar is quite traditional, with a forest canopy of hops, whisky-water jugs, beakers and tankards. Several of the comfortable and clearly individually chosen seats are worth a close look for their carving, and the wall tapestries are interesting. The carved counter has their own St Georges Dragons Blood and Friar Tuck plus Purity Mad Goose, Ringwood Fortyniner, a guest from Marstons and another changing guest on handpump, as well as several wines, malt whiskies and four farm ciders. On the right is a broadly similar red-carpeted dining room and beyond it, in complete contrast, an ultra-modern glass garden room; background music and board games. The garden itself is as individual as the pub, with a cluster of huge wooden casks topped with flowers, even a piano doing flower-tub duty – and a set of stocks on the pretty front terrace.

Free house ~ Licensee James Crane ~ Real ale ~ Open 12-11.30 ~ Bar food 12-2.30, 6.30-9; 12-3, 7-9 Sun ~ Restaurant ~ Children welcome but not in bar after 8pm ~ Dogs welcome ~ Wi-fi

TENBURY WELLS
SO6468

Talbot

(01584) 781941 – www.talbotinnnewnhambridge.co.uk
Newnham Bridge; A456; WR15 8JF

Carefully refurbished coaching inn with character bar and dining rooms and highly rated food; bedrooms

This 19th-c coaching inn is in lovely Teme Valley countryside and has a friendly, gently civilised atmosphere. There are nice old red and black and original quarry tiles, bare floorboards, open fires, hops and candlelight, with the bar and dining rooms being quite different in style. There's an assortment of dark pubby, high-backed painted wooden and comfortably upholstered dining chairs around a variety of tables, leather tub chairs and sofas here and there, bookshelves, old photographs of the local area, table lights and standard lamps, and some elegant antiques dotted about. It gets pretty busy at the weekend when you'll need to book a table in advance. Hobsons Best Bitter and Wye Valley HPA on handpump, local cider and good wines by the glass.

Free house ~ Licensee Barnaby Williams ~ Real ale ~ Open 12-11; 12-9 Sun; closed first two weeks Jan ~ Bar food 12-2.30, 7-9.30; 12-7.30 Sun ~ Children welcome ~ Dogs allowed in bar ~ Wi-fi ~ Live music last Fri of month Sept-Feb ~ Bedrooms: £90

DOG FRIENDLY HOTELS, INNS AND B&Bs

AB LENCH
SP0151

Manor Farm House

(01386) 462226 – www.wolseylodges.com
Ab Lench, Evesham, Worcestershire WR11 4UP

£45; 2 rooms. Comfortable 250-year-old house in a rural spot with a lovely fenced half-acre garden; two reception rooms (one has beams and a huge inglenook fireplace), a study with TV, interesting objects collected from around the world by the friendly, dog-loving owner and nice breakfasts; one resident dog and a cat; plenty of surrounding fields for walks. Dogs allowed anywhere; treats and bowl.

BROADWAY
SP0937

Broadway Hotel

(01386) 852401 – www.cotswold-inns-hotels.co.uk/the-broadway-hotel
The Green, Broadway, Worcestershire WR12 7AA

£180; 19 beautifully and recently refurbished rooms; also a self-catering cottage in the village. Lovely 15th-c half-timbered building, once a monastic guesthouse, with a galleried and timbered bar of real character, a cosy sitting room with an inglenook fireplace (morning coffee and afternoon teas are served here), an elegant, light brasserie restaurant with contemporary furnishings and imaginative food; animal-themed artwork throughout; attentive staff and seats outside on the terrace; plenty of nearby walks. Dogs welcome in four bedrooms, bar and sitting room; must be kept under control; £10.

EVESHAM

SP0443

Evesham Hotel

(01386) 765566 – www.eveshamhotel.com
Coopers Lane, off Waterside, Evesham, Worcestershire WR11 1DA

£115; 37 individually furnished rooms – some are themed. Small, friendly hotel with eccentric touches, under new ownership since late 2015; two lounges, a well stocked bar, a dining room serving good breakfasts and enjoyable, interesting lunches and evening meals; indoor swimming pool and two and a half acres of grounds with croquet and putting; dogs can walk in the garden or along the nearby River Avon. Dogs allowed in bedrooms and one lounge; blanket, treats and water bowl; £10.

GREAT MALVERN

SO7647

Cowleigh Park Farm

(01684) 566750 – www.cowleighparkfarm.co.uk
Cowleigh Road, Malvern, Worcestershire WR13 5HJ

£85; 3 rooms; also 2 self-catering cottages. Charming black and white timbered 17th-c farmhouse on the edge of Malvern, with an acre of grounds and surrounded by lovely countryside – it's on the Worcestershire Way; carefully restored and furnished with beams and an inglenook fireplace in the sitting room, good breakfasts with home-made bread and preserves; resident collie. Dogs allowed in bedrooms; £5.

HIMBLETON

SO9459

Phepson Farm

(01905) 391205 – www.phepsonfarm.co.uk
Phepson, Droitwich, Worcestershire WR9 7JZ

£80; 6 attractive rooms – 4 in renovated farm buildings; also 3 self-catering cottages. Relaxed and friendly 17th-c farmhouse on a 50-acre sheep farm (in the same family for a century) with a sizeable fishing lake and walks both on the farm and along the nearby Wychavon Way; comfortable guests' lounge and very good breakfasts with local sausages and their own conserves in a separate dining room; resident dogs and cats. Closed two weeks over Christmas and New Year. Dogs allowed in four bedrooms.

KEMPSEY

SO8548

Walter de Cantelupe

(01905) 820572 – www.walterdecantelupe.co.uk
34 Main Road, Kempsey, Worcester, Worcestershire WR5 3NA

£80; 3 rooms. Traditional inn with a friendly landlord, a carpeted bar with beams and an inglenook fireplace, a pleasant mix of furniture, three real ales on handpump plus summer cider, enjoyable food and seats in the walled garden. Dogs allowed in bedrooms and bar; £5.

KNIGHTWICK

SO7355

Talbot

(01886) 821235 – www.the-talbot.co.uk
Bromyard Road, Knightwick, Worcester, Worcestershire WR6 5PH

£110; 11 good rooms. Rambling country hotel with a heavily beamed and extended traditional lounge bar with a mix of seats, a winter log fire and a vast stove in a central stone hearth; their own-brewed Teme Valley ales, farm cider and a sedate dining room serving inventive seasonal food (using own-grown vegetables, home-reared pigs and home-made bread, pickles and jam); there's also a back public bar, an airy garden room and tables and seats outside by the River Teme; lots of fantastic walks nearby. Dogs allowed in some bedrooms, bar and lounge; bedding, bowls and treats; £10.

MALVERN WELLS

SO7742

Cottage in the Wood

(01684) 588860 – www.cottageinthewood.co.uk
Holywell Road, Malvern Wells, Worcestershire WR14 4LG

£128–£198; 30 traditionally decorated rooms, some in separate nearby buildings. New owners for this Georgian dower house with quite splendid views across the Severn Valley and marvellous walks from the grounds; antiques, log fires and comfortable seats in the public rooms, modern british cooking and an extensive wine list in the attractive restaurant. Dogs allowed in ground-floor bedrooms, but not in public areas; bedding, bowl and biscuits; £10.

Yorkshire

DOG FRIENDLY PUBS

BECK HOLE   NZ8202
Birch Hall
(01947) 896245 – www.beckhole.info/bhi.htm
Off A169 SW of Whitby, from top of Sleights Moor; YO22 5LE

Extraordinary place in lovely valley with friendly landlady, real ales and simple snacks

Quite unique, this tiny pub-cum-village shop remains resolutely unchanged. It's in stunning surroundings in a beautiful steep valley village by a bridge over a river and close to Thomason Foss waterfall, so walkers with their dogs make up many of the customers. The two simple rooms have built-in cushioned wall seats, wooden tables (one embedded with 136 pennies), flagstones or composition flooring, unusual items such as a tube of toothpaste priced 1/-3d, and a model train running around a head-height shelf. Black Sheep, North Yorkshire Beckwater and a guest such as Hambleton Goldfield on handpump and several malt whiskies and wines by the glass. Food consists of bar snacks – local pork pie, butties, scones and their famous beer cake – and the shop sells postcards, sweets and ice-creams. There are benches outside in a streamside garden and one of the wonderful nearby walks is along a disused railway. They have a self-catering cottage to rent.

Free house ~ Licensee Glenys Crampton ~ Real ale ~ No credit cards ~ Open 11-11; 11-3, 7.30-11 Weds-Sun in winter; closed Mon evening in winter, all day Tues Nov-Apr ~ Bar food available during opening hours ~ Children in small family room ~ Dogs welcome

BLAKEY RIDGE   SE6799
Lion
(01751) 417320 – www.lionblakey.co.uk
From A171 Guisborough–Whitby follow Castleton, Hutton-le-Hole signposts; from A170 Kirkby Moorside–Pickering follow Keldholm, Hutton-le-Hole, Castleton signposts; OS Sheet 100 map reference 679996; YO62 7LQ

Extended pub in fine scenery and open all day; popular food; bedrooms

On cold, misty days, walkers find this isolated 16th-c inn quite a haven. The low-beamed rambling bars have open fires, a few big high-backed rustic settles around cast-iron-framed tables, lots of small dining chairs, a nice leather sofa and stone walls hung with old engravings and photographs of the pub under snow (it can easily get cut off in winter – 40 days is the record so far). The fine choice of beers on handpump might include Black Sheep Best, Copper Dragon Golden Pippin,

Theakstons Best, Old Peculier and Paradise Ale, Thwaites Wainwright and a changing guest; they have 13 wines by the glass and several malt whiskies; background music and games machine. The inn is situated at the highest point of the North York Moors National Park (1,325 feet above sea level) and the valley views are breathtaking.

Free house ~ Licensees Barry, Diana, Paul and David Crossland ~ Real ale ~ Open 10am–11pm (midnight Sat) ~ Bar food 12–10 ~ Restaurant ~ Children welcome ~ Dogs allowed in bar ~ Wi-fi ~ Bedrooms: £86

CRAY   SD9479
White Lion

(01756) 760262 – www.whitelioninncray.com
B6160 N of Kettlewell; BD23 5JB

Refurbished and reopened inn under newish owners, open fires in bar and dining room, a fair choice of food and seats outside; bedrooms

Some 1,100 feet up by Buckden Pike, this former drovers' hostelry is set in lovely countryside and is popular with walkers. Throughout, there are lovely big flagstones and beams and the bar has button-back leather chesterfield sofas and armchairs in front of a woodburning stove, a cushioned window seat, books on shelves and a brass chandelier; a simple little back room (good for wet dogs) has some tables and chairs. Black Sheep Best, Hop Studio Pale and Wharfedale Blonde on handpump and eight wines by the glass. The attractive dining room has antique-style dining chairs around chunky tables, an open fire, some exposed stone walling and bits and pieces of old farming equipment; background music. In warm weather you can sit at picnic-sets above the quiet steep lane or on flat limestone slabs in the middle of the shallow stream that tumbles down opposite.

Free house ~ Licensee Dennis Peacock ~ Real ale ~ Open 12–10.30 ~ Bar food 12–2.30, 6–8.30 ~ Restaurant ~ Children welcome ~ Dogs allowed in bar ~ Wi-fi ~ Bedrooms: £130

HALIFAX   SE1027
Shibden Mill

(01422) 365840 – www.shibdenmillinn.com
Off A58 into Kell Lane at Stump Cross Inn, near A6036 junction; keep on, pub signposted from Kell Lane on left; HX3 7UL

300-year-old interesting pub with a cosy rambling bar, four real ales and inventive, top class bar food; luxury bedrooms

Tucked away at the bottom of a peaceful wooded valley, this 17th-c restored mill is particularly well run. The rambling bar is full of nooks and crannies and the bustling atmosphere is helped along by a good mix of locals and visitors. Some cosy side areas have banquettes heaped with cushions and rugs, well spaced attractive old tables and chairs, and candles in elegant iron holders giving a feeling of real intimacy; also, old hunting prints, country landscapes and a couple of big log fires. A beer named for them (from Moorhouses) plus Black Sheep, Little Valley Withens IPA and Stod Fold Gold on handpump and 21 wines by the glass from a wide list. There's also an upstairs restaurant; background music. Outside on the pleasant heated terrace are plenty of seats and tables, and the building is prettily floodlit at night. There are lovely walks nearby.

Free house ~ Licensee Glen Pearson ~ Real ale ~ Open 12–11 (10.30 Sun) ~ Bar food 12–2, 5.30–9; 12–2.30, 5.30–9.30 Fri, Sat; 12–7.30 Sun ~ Restaurant ~ Children welcome ~ Dogs allowed in bar ~ Wi-fi ~ Bedrooms: £125

LEDSHAM

SE4529

Chequers

(01977) 683135 – www.thechequersinn.com

1.5 miles from A1(M) junction 42: follow Leeds signs, then Ledsham signposted; Claypit Lane; LS25 5LP

Friendly village pub with hands-on landlord, log fires in several beamed rooms, real ales and interesting food; pretty back terrace

---

A neatly kept and very well run village pub. The several small, individually decorated rooms have plenty of character, with low beams, log fires, lots of cosy alcoves, toby jugs and all sorts of knick-knacks on the walls and ceilings (cricket fans will be interested to see a large photo in one room of four yorkshire heroes). From the little old-fashioned, panelled-in central servery they offer Brown Cow Sessions Pale Ale, Leeds Best, Theakstons Best, Timothy Taylors Landlord and a guest beer on handpump and eight wines by the glass. The lovely sheltered two-level terrace at the back has lots of tables among roses, and the hanging baskets and flowers are very pretty. RSPB Fairburn Ings reserve is not far and the ancient village church is worth a visit.

Free house ~ Licensee Chris Wraith ~ Real ale ~ Open 11-11; 12-6 Sun ~ Bar food 12-9; 12-5 Sun ~ Restaurant ~ Children until 8pm ~ Dogs allowed in bar ~ Wi-fi

LEVISHAM

SE8390

Horseshoe

(01751) 460240 – www.horseshoelevisham.co.uk

Off A169 N of Pickering; YO18 7NL

Friendly village pub with super food, neat rooms, real ales and seats on the village green; bedrooms

---

A warmly friendly pub run by two brothers. The bustling bars have beams, blue banquettes, wheelback and captain's chairs around a variety of tables on polished wooden floors, vibrant landscapes by a local artist on the walls and a log fire in the stone fireplace; an adjoining snug has a woodburning stove, comfortable leather sofas and old photographs of the pub and the lovely village. Served by the courteous staff are Black Sheep and guests such as Cropton Yorkshire Moors and Timothy Taylors Golden Best on handpump, half a dozen wines by the glass and 15 malt whiskies; background music. There are seats on the attractive green, with more in the back garden. The North York Moors National Park is nearby and the historic church is worth a visit. This is sister pub to the Fox & Rabbit in Lockton.

Free house ~ Licensees Toby and Charles Wood ~ Real ale ~ Open 11-11 (10.30 Sun) ~ Bar food 12-2, 6-8.30 ~ Children welcome ~ Dogs allowed in bar ~ Wi-fi ~ Bedrooms: £80

LOCKTON

SE8488

Fox & Rabbit

(01751) 460213 – www.foxandrabbit.co.uk

A169 N of Pickering; YO18 7NQ

Neatly kept pub with fine views, a friendly atmosphere, real ales and highly regarded food

---

Set in a lovely spot, this is an attractive pub with a warm welcome for all. The interconnected rooms have beams, panelling and some exposed stonework, wall settles and banquettes, dark pubby chairs and tables on tartan carpet, a log fire and an inviting atmosphere; fresh flowers, brasses, china plates, prints and old local photographs too. The locals' bar is busy and cheerful and there are panoramic views from the comfortable restaurant – it's worth arriving early to bag a window seat. Black Sheep, Cropton Yorkshire Moors and Timothy Taylors Golden Best on handpump, seven wines by the glass, 12 malt whiskies and home-made elderflower cordial; background music, games machine, pool, juke box and board games. Outside are seats under parasols and some picnic sets. The inn is in the North York Moors National Park, so there are plenty of surrounding walks. They have a caravan site. This is sister pub to the Horseshoe in Levisham.

Free house ~ Licensees Toby and Charles Wood ~ Real ale ~ Open 11am-11.30pm ~ Bar food 12-2, 5-8.30 ~ Restaurant ~ Children welcome ~ Dogs allowed in bar ~ Wi-fi

LOW CATTON   SE7053
Gold Cup

(01759) 371354 – www.goldcuplowcatton.com
Village signposted with High Catton off A166 in Stamford Bridge or A1079 at Kexby Bridge; YO41 1EA

Friendly, pleasant pub with attractive bars, real ales, decent dependable food, seats in garden and ponies in paddock

For 27 years the hospitable licensees in this comfortable white-rendered house have been offering sustenance to their wide mix of customers. The neatly kept bar has a bustling atmosphere, plenty of smart tables and chairs on stripped wooden floors, quite a few pictures, an open fire at one end opposite a gas-effect stove and coach lights on the rustic-looking walls. The spacious restaurant, with solid wooden pews and tables (said to be made from a single oak tree), has pleasant views of the surrounding fields. Theakstons Best Bitter on handpump; background music and pool. There's a grassed area in the garden for children and the back paddock houses three ponies, Cinderella, Dobbin and Polly. The pub has fishing rights on the adjacent River Derwent.

Free house ~ Licensees Pat and Ray Hales ~ Real ale ~ Open 12-2.30, 6-11; 12-11 Sat; 12-10.30 Sun; closed Mon lunchtime ~ Bar food 12-2, 6-9; 12-9 Sat; 12-8 Sun ~ Restaurant ~ Children welcome ~ Dogs allowed in bar ~ Wi-fi

MARTON-CUM-GRAFTON   SE4263
Punch Bowl

(01423) 322519 – www.thepunchbowlmartoncumgrafton.com
Signed off A1 3 miles N of A59; YO51 9QY

Refurbished old inn in lovely village, with character bar and dining rooms, real ales, accomplished food and seats on terrace

This is a handsome and particularly well run old inn with many original features: the main bar is beamed and timbered with a built-in window seat at one end, lots of red leather-topped stools, and cushioned settles and church chairs around pubby tables on flagstones or bare floorboards. Black Sheep Best, Rudgate Jorvik Blonde and Timothy Taylors Boltmaker on handpump, 20 wines by the glass and a dozen malt whiskies. Open doorways lead to five separate dining areas, each with an open fire, heavy beams and an attractive mix of cushioned wall seats and wooden or high-backed red dining chairs around antique tables on oak floors; the red walls are covered with photographs of vintage car races and racing drivers, sporting-themed cartoons and old photographs of the pub and village. Up a swirling staircase is a coffee loft and a private dining room. There are seats and tables in the back courtyard where they hold summer barbecues.

Free house ~ Licensee Michael Ibbotson ~ Real ale ~ Open 12-3, 5-11; 12-11.30 Sat; 12-10.30 Sun ~ Bar food 12-2.30, 5.30-9.30; 12-8 Sun ~ Children welcome ~ Dogs allowed in bar ~ Wi-fi

MOULTON
NZ2303

Black Bull

(01325) 377556 – www.theblackbullmoulton.com

Just E of A1, a mile E of Scotch Corner; DL10 6QJ

Character pub with a traditional bar, a large open restaurant, good choice of drinks, high quality food and courteous efficient service

The friendly bar in this carefully refurbished pub has a convivial feel with high chairs against the counter where they serve Black Sheep Best, Theakstons Boltmaker and a guest beer on handpump, 18 wines by the glass and over 20 malt whiskies. There's some original panelling and leather wall seating topped with scatter cushions, and the dining area has cushioned wooden chairs around a mix of tables on pale flagstones, a couple of leather armchairs in front of a woodburner in a brick fireplace, some horse tack, and stone bottles, wooden pails and copper items on windowsills. The new dining extension with tall windows and a wooden floor has attractive brown-orange high-backed dining chairs or cushioned settles and a rather nice wire bull; background music. Doors from here lead out to a neat terrace with modern seats and tables among pots of rosemary or tall bay trees.

Free house ~ Licensee Michael Ibbotson ~ Real ale ~ Open 12-3, 5-11; 12-midnight Sat; 12-11 Sun ~ Bar food 12-2.30, 5.30-9.30; 12-3, 6-9.30 Sun ~ Restaurant evening ~ Children welcome ~ Dogs allowed in bar ~ Wi-fi

ROBIN HOOD'S BAY
NZ9505

Laurel

(01947) 880400

Bay Bank; village signed off A171 S of Whitby; YO22 4SE

Delightful little pub in unspoilt fishing village with neat friendly bar and real ales

Things here remain quite unchanged and the charming landlord welcomes all to his little local at the bottom of a row of fishermen's cottages. The neatly kept beamed main bar has an open fire and is decorated with old local photographs, Victorian prints and brasses and lager bottles from across the world. There's Adnams Southwold and Theakstons Best and Old Peculier on handpump; darts, board games and background music. In summer, the hanging baskets and window boxes are lovely. There's no food but you can bring in sandwiches from the tea shop next door. This is one of the prettiest and most unspoilt fishing villages to be found on the north-east coast.

Free house ~ Licensee Brian Catling ~ Real ale ~ No credit cards ~ Open 12-11 (10.30 Sun); 4-11 Mon-Thurs in winter ~ Children in snug bar only ~ Dogs welcome

SANDHUTTON
SE3882

Kings Arms

(01845) 587887 – www.thekingsarmssandhutton.co.uk

A167, 1 mile N of A61 Thirsk–Ripon; YO7 4RW

Cheerful pub with friendly service, interesting food and beer, and comfortable furnishings; bedrooms

On race days at nearby Thirsk racecourse, it's best to book way ahead if you want a table in this charming village inn. It's still run by the friendly father and son team and while there's quite a focus on food, there remains a traditional pubby atmosphere. The bar has an unusual circular woodburner in one corner, a high central table with four equally high stools, modern ladderback wooden dining chairs around light pine tables, a couple of cushioned wicker armchairs, some attractive modern bar stools and photographs of the pub in years gone by. Black Sheep, Rudgate Viking, Theakstons Best, Village Brewer White Boar Bitter and Walls Gun Dog Bitter on handpump, 11 wines by the glass and efficient, friendly service. The two connecting dining rooms have similar furnishings to the bar (plus some high-backed brown leather dining chairs), arty flower photographs on cream walls and a small woodburning stove; background music, darts, board games and TV. There's a small beer garden and they have secure bike storage with air and puncture repair kits and a heated towel rail for drying wet kit.

Free house ~ Licensees Raymond and Alexander Boynton ~ Real ale ~ Open 12-11 (midnight Sat); 12-10 Sun ~ Bar food 12-2.30, 5.30-9; 12-9 Sat; 12-5 Sun ~ Restaurant ~ Children welcome ~ Dogs allowed in bar ~ Wi-fi ~ Bedrooms: £70

SHEFFIELD   SK4086

Kelham Island Tavern

(0114) 272 2482 – www.kelhamtavern.co.uk
Kelham Island; S3 8RY

Busy little local with fantastic real ales, basic but decent lunchtime food, a friendly welcome and pretty back garden

The knowledgeable, well organised and friendly staff in this busy tavern keep the 13 interesting ales on handpump in tip top condition. There's always a mild and a stout or porter on offer and their regulars include Abbeydale Deception, Acorn Barnsley Bitter, Bradfield Farmers Blonde and Pictish Brewers Gold, with guests from breweries such as Arbor, Blue Bee, Brass Castle, Dark Star, Hop Studio, North Riding, Siren Craft, Tiny Rebel and Yorkshire Dales; also, a changing craft beer, a german wheat beer, a belgian fruit beer, an interesting range of bottled ales, two farm ciders and around 30 malt whiskies. It's a busy backstreet local with a wide array of cheerful customers and pubby furnishings; dominoes and board games. The unusual flower-filled back courtyard garden has plenty of seats and tables, and the front window boxes regularly win awards.

Free house ~ Licensee Trevor Wraith ~ Real ale ~ Open 12-midnight ~ Bar food 12-3 (not weekends) ~ Children allowed in back room ~ Dogs welcome ~ Live folk Sun evenings

WELBURN   SE7168

Crown & Cushion

(01653) 618777 – www.thecrownandcushionwelburn.com
Off A64; YO60 7DZ

Plenty of dining and drinking space in well run inn with real ales and particularly good food – and seats outside

This is a carefully refurbished and extended 18th-c inn. The little tap room has rustic tables and chairs on wide floorboards, high stools around an equally high central table, beams and timbering, with Black Sheep, Brass Castle Malton Amber, Rudgate Jorvik and York Guzzler on handpump and 19 wines by the glass served by friendly, helpful staff. The other attractively refurbished, interconnecting rooms are for dining and on different levels: smart high-backed chairs mix with wooden ones and an assortment of cushioned settles and wall seats around various tables on flagstones or red and black floor tiles. There are open fires and a woodburning stove, old prints of the pub and local scenes on painted or exposed stone walls and lots of horsebrasses, copper pans and kettles and old stone bottles; background music. Contemporary tables and chairs sit on a terrace with picnic-sets below and a long-reaching view across to the Howardian Hills. The pub is handy for Castle Howard.

Free house ~ Licensee Michael Ibbotson ~ Real ale ~ Open 12-3, 5.30-11; 12-11 Fri-Sun ~ Bar food 12-3, 5.30-9 (9.30 Fri, Sat); 12-8 Sun ~ Restaurant ~ Children welcome ~ Dogs allowed in bar ~ Wi-fi

WIDDOP   SD9531
Pack Horse

(01422) 842803 – www.thepackhorse.org

The Ridge; from A646 on W side of Hebden Bridge, turn off at Heptonstall signpost (as it's a sharp turn, coming out of Hebden Bridge the road signs direct you around a turning circle), then follow Slack and Widdop signposts; can also be reached from Nelson and Colne, on high, pretty road; OS Sheet 103 map reference 952317; HX7 7AT

Friendly pub up on the moors and liked by walkers for generous, tasty honest food, four real ales and lots of malt whiskies

Considering its isolation high up on the moors, this friendly, traditional walkers' pub is remarkably popular as a cosy haven. The bar has welcoming winter fires, window seats cut into the partly panelled stripped-stone walls (from where you can take in the beautiful views), sturdy furnishings and horsey mementoes. Black Sheep and Thwaites Wainwright plus guests such as Cottage Conquest and Greyhawk Blonde Obsession on handpump, over 100 single malt whiskies and some irish ones, and 11 wines by the glass. The friendly golden retrievers are called Padge and Purdey. There are seats outside in the cobblestoned beer garden and pretty summer hanging baskets. They have a smart self-catering apartment for rent.

Free house ~ Licensee Andrew Hollinrake ~ Real ale ~ Open 12-3, 5.30-11; 12-11 Sat, Sun; closed Mon except bank holidays; no weekday lunchtime opening in winter ~ Bar food 12-2, 5.30-9; 12-7 Sun ~ Children welcome ~ Dogs welcome

DOG FRIENDLY HOTELS, INNS AND B&Bs

AUSTWICK   SD7668
Traddock

(01524) 251224 – www.thetraddock.co.uk

Austwick, Settle, Yorkshire LA2 8BY

£125; 12 individually decorated rooms, many with views. Surrounded by the Yorkshire Dales National Park and fantastic walks, this is a warmly friendly and homely country house; two warm and comfortable lounges with sofas, open fires, antiques and brocade curtains, a little bar, smashing breakfasts, light lunches, afternoon teas and interesting evening meals in the traditionally furnished restaurant, helpful, courteous service and seats outside on the terrace and in the garden. Dogs allowed in all bedrooms and (on a lead) anywhere in the hotel except the dining rooms; £5.

BAINBRIDGE

SD9390

Rose & Crown

(01969) 650225 – www.theprideofwensleydale.co.uk
Bainbridge, Leyburn, North Yorkshire DL8 3EE

£80; 9 pretty rooms, including some with four-posters. 15th-c coaching inn overlooking the lovely village green, with antique settles and other old furniture in the beamed and panelled bars, open log fires, a cosy residents' lounge and enjoyable pubby food in both the bars and restaurant; walks nearby. Dogs allowed in some bedrooms and bar.

BOLTON ABBEY

SE0753

Devonshire Arms Hotel

(01756) 710441 – www.thedevonshirearms.co.uk
Bolton Abbey, Skipton, North Yorkshire BD23 6AJ

£185; 40 individually furnished rooms with thoughtful extras; also 2 self-catering cottages. Close to the priory itself and on the Duke of Devonshire's 30,000-acre estate, this civilised former coaching inn is carefully furnished with fine antiques and paintings from Chatsworth; three comfortable lounges serving all-day light snacks and afternoon teas, beautifully presented, excellent food (using food from kitchen garden) in two smart, formal restaurants, super breakfasts and faultless service; tennis, mountain bike hire and spa with indoor swimming pool, treatment, sauna and steam rooms and gym. Dogs allowed in all bedrooms and public areas (on a lead) but not restaurants; welcome pack, bedding and treats; £10.

BOROUGHBRIDGE

SE3966

Black Bull

(01432) 322413 – www.blackbullboroughbridge.co.uk
6 St James Square, Boroughbridge, York, North Yorkshire YO51 9AR

£75; 6 rooms. A handy stop-off point from the A1, this is an attractive town pub with lots of separate drinking and eating areas and plenty of cheerful locals; the main bar area has a big stone fireplace and comfortable seats, there's a cosy snug with traditional wall settles, a tap room, a lounge bar and a restaurant; a good choice of drinks and pubby food that includes hot and cold sandwiches and a pie of the day; the borzoi is called Spot and the two cats Kia and Mershka; nearby walks. Dogs allowed in bedrooms and bar; bowl and treats.

BRADFIELD

SK2290

Strines Inn

(0114) 285 1247 – www.thestrinesinn.webs.com
Strines, Bradfield, Sheffield, South Yorkshire S6 6JE

£85; 3 rooms with four-posters. A pub since the 18th c but actually five centuries older, this friendly place is surrounded by superb Peak District scenery and many customers are walkers with their dogs; the main bar has black beams liberally decked with copper kettles and so forth, quite a menagerie of stuffed animals, homely red plush-cushioned traditional wooden wall benches and small chairs, and a coal fire in the rather grand stone fireplace; two other rooms to the right and left are similarly furnished and serve real ales and reasonably priced food; picnic-sets outside, as well as swings, a play area, peacocks and geese. Dogs allowed in all bedrooms and anywhere in the pub; £5.

CONSTABLE BURTON SE1690

Wyvill Arms

(01677) 450581 – www.thewyvillarmsbedandbreakfast.co.uk
Constable Burton, Leyburn, North Yorkshire DL8 5LH

£90; 7 rooms. Well run, 18th-c former farmhouse with a small bar area, a winter fire in an elaborate stone fireplace, a mix of seating and a finely worked plaster ceiling with the Wyvill family's coat of arms; a second bar has various alcoves, leather seating around old oak tables, a model train on a railway track running around the room and there's a reception area with a huge leather sofa, another open fire and an old leaded stained-glass church window partition; imaginative food using home-grown produce and game from the estate across the road, and enjoyable breakfasts; Constable Burton Hall and Gardens are opposite. Dogs allowed in some bedrooms and bar and front eating area; £10 per stay.

COXWOLD SE5377

Fauconberg Arms

(01347) 868214 – www.fauconbergarms.com
Coxwold, York, North Yorkshire YO61 4AD

£95; 8 comfortable rooms. Friendly, family-run 17th-c inn with a heavily beamed and flagstoned bar, log fires, attractive oak chairs plus more usual furnishings, nicely chosen local photographs and other pictures on contemporary paintwork, plenty of malt whiskies, real ales and a thoughtful choice of wines; the candlelit dining room is quietly elegant and the popular food includes smashing breakfasts; Byland Abbey (English Heritage) and lots of walks nearby. Dogs allowed in all bedrooms and bar, but not dining room; bone; £10.

CRAYKE SE5670

Durham Ox

(01347) 821506 – www.thedurhamox.com
West Way, Crayke, York, North Yorkshire YO61 4TE

£120; 6 comfortable rooms, in main building or renovated farm cottages; self-catering cottage too. Friendly, well run inn on the hill up which the Grand Old Duke of York marched his men; the old-fashioned, relaxed lounge bar has a huge inglenook fireplace, interesting satirical carvings in the panelling, polished copper and brass and venerable furniture on flagstones and the bottom bar has a large framed print of the original famous Durham Ox, and the Burns Bar has a woodburning stove, exposed brickwork and large french windows; real ales, 20 wines by the glass and a dozen malt whiskies; helpful staff serve the imaginative food (they bake their own bread and use local produce); the courtyard has plenty of seats and tables and fantastic views over the Vale of York. Dogs allowed in most bedrooms and bar.

CROPTON
SE7588

New Inn

(01751) 417330 – www.newinncropton.co.uk
Cropton, Pickering, North Yorkshire YO18 8HH

£105; 9 rooms; also self-catering cottage. Modernised village pub with famous own-brewed beers (six at any one time) and a genuinely warm welcome; the bar has traditional seats and tables, wood panelling and a small fire, there's a downstairs conservatory with historical posters, and a modern restaurant with straightforward pubby food; the brewery shop and tours are popular. Dogs allowed in two outside bedrooms and bar; £10.

DOWNHOLME
SE1197

Bolton Arms

(01748) 823716 – www.boltonarmsdownholme.com
Downholme, Richmond, North Yorkshire DL11 6AE

£70; 2 rooms. This friendly little stone-built village inn has a bar with beams, carpeting, a log fire, comfortable plush wall banquettes, lots of gleaming brass and drinks advertisements on the walls, fairly priced drinks and efficient service; there's also a dining room and a conservatory and the tasty pubby dishes are cooked by the landlord; marvellous views from seats in the neat garden and a lower terrace. Dogs allowed in both bedrooms.

EAST WITTON
SE1486

Blue Lion

(01969) 624273 – www.thebluelion.co.uk
East Witton, Leyburn, North Yorkshire DL8 4SN

£109; 15 individually decorated rooms, in the main house and converted stables. Warmly civilised 18th-c coaching inn with an informal little bar, a good mix of drinkers and their dogs mingling happily with those waiting to eat, high-backed antique settles and windsor chairs on rugs and flagstones, a log fire, daily papers, sporting caricatures and other pictures, real ales and excellent wines (including champagne) by the glass; the elegant candlelit restaurant offers delicious, inventive food served by courteous, charming and attentive staff; large back garden and nearby walks. Dogs allowed in some bedrooms and bar; towel; £10 per stay.

ELSLACK
SD9249

Tempest Arms

(01282) 842450 – www.tempestarms.co.uk
Elslack, Skipton, North Yorkshire BD23 3AY

£100; 21 comfortably modern rooms, some with hot tubs. Stylish and understated 18th-c stone pub with three log fires and a wide mix of customers (plenty of dog-walkers); cushioned armchairs, built-in wall seats with comfortable cushions and all sorts of tables, amusing prints on cream walls, half a dozen real ales, wines by the glass and highly enjoyable and generously served food; resident dogs Milly and Lottie; lots of lovely surrounding walks. Dogs allowed in two bedrooms and bar; £10.

FELIXKIRK   SE4684

Carpenters Arms

(01845) 537369 – www.thecarpentersarmsfelixkirk.com
Felixkirk, Thirsk, North Yorkshire YO7 2DP

£165; 10 modern lodge-style rooms, most built around the garden. In a picturesque small village on the edge of the moors, this friendly pub was once a carpenter's workshop; the opened-up bars have dark beams and joists, candlelight and fresh flowers, a relaxed atmosphere, real ales and a good choice of wines by the glass; a snug seating area has tartan armchairs in front of a double-sided woodburner, and the red-walled dining area has traditional prints and antique and country kitchen chairs around scrubbed tables on flagstones; seating outside on a raised decked terrace overlooks the landscaped garden; food is inventive and well presented; plenty of short and long walks nearby. Dogs allowed in three bedrooms and bar; blanket, bedding and bowl; £8.

GRINTON   SE0498

Bridge Inn

(01748) 884224 – www.bridgeinn-grinton.co.uk
Grinton, Richmond, North Yorkshire DL11 6HH

£82; 5 neat rooms. Former coaching inn with lovely surrounding walks in a pretty Swaledale village; traditional, comfortable bars, leather armchairs and sofas in front of two log fires, a relaxed atmosphere, several real ales and malt whiskies and an extensive two-part dining room with cream and brown décor and a modicum of fishing memorabilia; bar food is tasty and the breakfasts are good; the church opposite is known as the Cathedral of the Dales; resident labrador, Teale, and new kitten, Bobbie. Dogs allowed in all bedrooms and elsewhere except the restaurant; £7 per stay.

HALIFAX   SE0829

Holdsworth House

(01422) 240024 – www.holdsworthhouse.co.uk
Holmfield, Halifax, West Yorkshire HX2 9TG

£139; 38 individually decorated, quiet rooms. Lovely, immaculately kept 17th-c stone house a few miles outside Halifax in its own neatly maintained grounds; antiques, fresh flowers and fires in comfortable lounges, lots of sitting areas in the two bar rooms, friendly, particularly helpful staff and three carefully furnished dining rooms serving enjoyable, inventive food, brasserie-style lunches, very popular afternoon teas and delicious breakfasts. Dogs allowed in ten bedrooms and public areas except dining areas; bedding, bowl and treats; £10.

HAROME   SE6481

Pheasant

(01439) 771241 – www.thepheasanthotel.com
Mill Street, Harome, Helmsley, North Yorkshire YO62 5JG

£200; 16 lovely, well equipped rooms (including a separate cottage). Carefully converted from a 17th-c village smithy and barns and overlooking the village duck pond, the beamed bar has stuffed pheasants and an inglenook fireplace, the cosy sitting room opens on to a pretty terrace, and the elegant restaurant serves beautifully presented and inventive food using the best local produce; also, light lunches, quite a choice of afternoon teas and excellent breakfasts; indoor heated swimming pool and nearby walks. Dogs allowed in two courtyard rooms and terrace; bed; £26 per stay.

HARROGATE
SE2956
Alexa House

(01423) 501988 – www.alexa-house.co.uk
26 Ripon Road, Harrogate, North Yorkshire HG1 2JJ

£100 without breakfast; 13 rooms, some in former stable block. Attractive Victorian house with friendly staff, a comfortable lounge with an honesty bar, marvellous breakfasts (extra £10 per person) in the bright dining room and lots of pubs and restaurants nearby for evening meals. Dogs allowed in stable bedrooms only, not in main building; walk map.

HARROGATE
SE3055
Hotel du Vin

(01423) 608121 – www.hotelduvin.com
Prospect Place, Harrogate, North Yorkshire HG1 1LB

£189; 48 stylish rooms including 4 airy loft suites. Made up of eight Georgian-styled houses and close to the town centre, this relaxed and informal hotel has a bustling atmosphere, a cellar snug, a sleek, comfortable brasserie serving imaginative bistro-style food and superb wines, and well informed, helpful staff; spa with treatment rooms, and courtyard garden with seating. Dogs allowed in all bedrooms and public areas except brasserie; blanket and bowl; £10.

HAWNBY
SE5690
Laskill Grange

(01439) 798268 – www.laskillgrange.co.uk
Easterside, Hawnby, Helmsley, North Yorkshire YO62 5NB

£95; 6 rooms, some in beamed converted outbuilding; also 7 self-catering cottages. Attractive and welcoming creeper-covered stone house on a large sheep and cattle farm near Rievaulx Abbey and with lots of nearby walks; an open fire, antiques and books in the comfortable lounge, a conservatory overlooking the garden and super breakfasts using home-grown produce (evening meals on request); free trout fishing on their lake; resident labrador Tosh, swans and ducks. Dogs allowed in all bedrooms, not dining room.

HELMSLEY
SE6183
Black Swan

(01439) 770466 – www.blackswan-helmsley.co.uk
Market Place, Helmsley, North Yorkshire YO62 5BJ

£155–£205; 45 attractive, contemporary rooms. Striking Georgian house and adjoining Tudor rectory given a careful modern makeover though keeping many original features like beams, panelling and big open fireplaces; a convivial bar for pubby lunches, a tea room where their renowned afternoon teas are served, and a more formal restaurant with enjoyable modern food in the evening including six-course tasting menus, and Sunday lunches; seats in the charming sheltered garden. Dogs allowed in most bedrooms, bar and lounge; bowl; £10 per stay.

HELPERBY
SE4370
Oak Tree
(01423) 789189 – www.theoaktreehelperby.com
Raskelf Road, Helperby, York, North Yorkshire YO61 2PH

£120; 6 well equipped rooms. Pretty brick pub with slate, oak and weathered brick retaining some original character in the informal bar; church chairs and elegant wooden dining chairs, open fires, bold red walls, real ales and a friendly atmosphere; also a main dining room with a large woodburner in a huge brick fireplace, ornate mirrors and striking artwork and french windows leading to a terrace with seating; first class food served by helpful staff; breakfasts (available to non-residents too on weekend); walks by river and in woodland nearby. Dogs allowed in one bedroom and in bar.

KILBURN
SE5179
Forresters Arms
(01347) 868386 – www.forrestersarms.com
Kilburn, York, North Yorkshire YO61 4AH

£90; 10 neat rooms. Friendly old coaching inn opposite the pretty village garden, with traditional pubby furnishings in the carpeted lounge, a big log fire in the cosy lower bar, a second bar in what was the stable with the manger and stalls still visible (look for the carvings by Robert 'Mouseman' Thompson), real ales, wines by the glass and enjoyable food in the separate restaurant. Dogs allowed in all bedrooms and away from dining room; £10.

KNARESBOROUGH
SE3457
Best Western Dower House
(01423) 863302 – www.dowerhouse-hotel.co.uk
Bond End, Knaresborough, North Yorkshire HG5 9AL

£123; 29 well equipped rooms. Creeper-clad 15th-c former dower house with a contemporary bar and reception lounge where you can take morning coffee, afternoon teas and light lunches, a second lounge with an open fire, an informal restaurant with enjoyable food served by helpful staff, and plenty of seats and tables outside in the garden; spa with treatment rooms, indoor swimming pool and gym, and walks along the River Nidd. Dogs allowed in some bedrooms, lounge and bar; £10.

KNARESBOROUGH
SE3556
Newton House Hotel
(01423) 863539 – www.newtonhouseyorkshire.com
5-7 York Place, Knaresborough, North Yorkshire HG5 0AD

£115; 12 very well equipped rooms. Elegant family-run 18th-c house close to the river and market square, with a warm welcome for guests of all ages, a comfortable sitting room with books and daily papers, a licensed honesty bar and good generous english breakfasts in the dining room; no evening meals but plenty of places close by; they provide a list of local walks. Dogs allowed in two bedrooms, not dining room; bed, bowl, towel and home-made biscuits; £10.

LASTINGHAM   SE7390
Lastingham Grange

(01751) 417345 – www.lastinghamgrange.com
High Street, Lastingham, York, North Yorkshire YO62 6TH

£210; 11 rooms; also self-catering cottage. Attractive, family-run stone-walled country house in 12 acres of neatly kept gardens and fields – with the moors beyond (marvellous walks); a relaxed homely atmosphere in the traditionally furnished lounge where complimentary afternoon tea is served, open fires, well liked food generously served in the airy dining room, good breakfasts and extremely helpful service. Closed December-February. Dogs allowed in all bedrooms and elsewhere except dining room.

LEEDS   SE3033
42 The Calls

(0113) 244 0099 – www.42thecalls.co.uk
41 The Calls, Leeds, West Yorkshire LS2 7EW

£124.50; 41 attractive, contemporary rooms and suites incorporating interesting original features. Stylish modern hotel in a converted riverside grain mill in a surprisingly peaceful spot overlooking the River Aire; genuinely friendly staff, super breakfasts with a dozen varieties of sausage and home-made conserves, room service for light snacks but can eat next door in Brasserie Forty 4 restaurant (a separate business). Dogs allowed in all bedrooms; bowl; £10.

LEEDS   SE3033
Malmaison

(0113) 398 1000 – www.malmaison.com
1 Swinegate, Leeds, West Yorkshire LS1 4AG

£85–£225; 100 well equipped, slinky rooms. This is a stylish, modern hotel in what was once a bus company office, with bold, modern furnishings, comfortable contemporary bar, busy brasserie with leather booths and good international dishes given an up-to-date twist, decent breakfasts, popular Sunday brunches and helpful, friendly service. Dogs allowed in some bedrooms and lobby only; mat and bowl; £10.

LEYBURN   SE1190
Sandpiper

(01969) 622206 – www.sandpiperinn.co.uk
Market Place, Leyburn, North Yorkshire DL8 5AT

£90; 2 charming rooms. 17th-c inn in lovely spot with a warmly friendly landlord, a cosy beamed bar with chatty locals, a log fire, cushioned wall seats around a few tables, local ales and 75 malt whiskies; also, a back snug, an attractive restaurant with fresh flowers and excellent food cooked by the landlord, who also makes his own bread and ice-creams; pretty summer hanging baskets and flowering climbers on the front terrace; walks nearby. Closed two weeks early January. Dogs allowed in both bedrooms, bar and snug, but not restaurant; £10.

LINTON IN CRAVEN
SD9962
Fountaine

(01756) 752210 – www.fountaineinnatlinton.co.uk
Linton, Skipton, North Yorkshire BD23 5HJ

£99; 5 rooms in converted barn. Neatly kept pub in a charming village with civilised bar rooms, attractive cushioned wall benches and stools around copper-topped tables, lots of wall prints, log fires (one in a beautifully carved heavy wooden fireplace), five real ales and popular food usefully served all day, terrace with seating and attractive hanging baskets; super surrounding walks in the Yorkshire Dales National Park. Dogs allowed in three bedrooms and bar; bed and bowl.

MALHAM
SD9062
Lister Arms

(01729) 830330 – www.listerarms.co.uk
Malham, North Yorkshire BD23 4DB

£101; 15 attractive bedrooms with views over the village green or the Yorkshire Dales National Park, plus 8 new rooms in converted barn (available from end of 2016). Handsome, creeper-covered inn with a cosy bar with cushioned dining chairs and leather or upholstered armchairs around antique wooden tables on slate flooring, with a big deer's head above the inglenook fireplace; there's also another bar with rustic slab tables and comfortable wall seats, a dining room with a woodburning stove, and a flagstoned and gravelled courtyard with tables and benches; fine walks all around. Dogs allowed in all bedrooms and bars; £15 per stay.

MASHAM
SE2179
Swinton Park

(01765) 680900 – www.swintonpark.com
Masham, Ripon, North Yorkshire HG4 4JH

From £195; 31 huge, well equipped rooms with estate views. Grand luxury castle hotel dating in part from 17th c and still an ancestral home; quite a choice of sumptuously decorated day rooms (though the atmosphere is relaxed and friendly) plus a bar in the former family museum/chapel, a private cinema and a snooker and Victorian games room; imaginative food in elegant restaurant using seasonal produce from the extensive walled garden and 20,000-acre estate; 200 acres of parkland and gardens, falconry, fishing, new spa with pool, gym, treatment rooms, sauna and brasserie, and popular cookery school. Dogs allowed in five bedrooms only, not in public rooms; £25.

MONK FRYSTON   SE5029

Monk Fryston Hall Hotel

(01977) 682369 – www.monkfrystonhallhotel.co.uk
Main Street, Monk Fryston, Leeds, West Yorkshire LS25 5DU

£99; 29 comfortable rooms, some recently refurbished. Handsome Benedictine
manor house in 30 acres of secluded gardens with a lake and mature woodland;
many original features such as inglenook fireplaces, oak panelling and stone
mullioned windows, a lounge and bar with antiques, paintings, fresh flowers and
log fires, interesting modern cooking in the elegant restaurant, lighter pubby-style
lunches, hearty breakfasts and friendly, helpful staff. Well behaved dogs allowed
in all bedrooms and public areas, not in restaurant; £5.

OTLEY   SE2143

Chevin Country Park Hotel

(01943) 467818 – www.crerarhotels.com/chevin-country-park-hotel-spa
Yorkgate, Otley, West Yorkshire LS21 3NU

£89; 49 rooms, some in log cabins deep in the woods; also self-catering. Built of
swedish logs and offering walks through 44 acres of woodland (lots of wildlife),
this comfortable hotel has a lounge with leather sofas, an informal cosy bar,
a conservatory bar and lakeside restaurant, a wide choice of food from good
breakfasts through light lunches and afternoon teas to smart, contemporary
evening meals, and friendly, helpful staff; spa with treatment rooms, hot tub,
sauna, steam room, indoor swimming pool, gym and tennis court. Dogs allowed
in some bedrooms and snug; £10.

PICKERING   SE7984

White Swan

(01751) 472288 – www.white-swan.co.uk
Market Place, Pickering, North Yorkshire YO18 7AA

£169; 21 luxurious rooms. Smart, civilised 16th-c coaching inn on the edge
of the North York Moors National Park, run by the same family for over
30 years; the little bar is relaxed and has a log fire, comfortable sofas, some wood
panelling, an extensive (and very good) wine list and local beers, smart lounges
have more open fires, attractive prints and all sorts of seats and tables on bare
boards or carpet, the attractive restaurant has yet another fire and ancient
flagstones, and the residents' lounge is in a converted beamed barn; excellent
food and delicious breakfasts served by courteous, efficient staff. Dogs allowed
in six bedrooms (not to be left unattended), bar and lounge; £12.50.

PICKHILL   SE3483

Nags Head

(01845) 567391 – www.nagsheadpickhill.co.uk
Pickhill, Thirsk, North Yorkshire YO7 4JG

£87; 7 comfortable rooms. Neatly kept dining pub, handy for the A1, with
an enthusiastic long-serving landlord and a bustling tap room decorated with
jugs, coach horns and ale-yards hanging from beams and masses of ties; also,
a smarter lounge with plush seating and an open fire, a library-themed restaurant,

local beers, a thoughtful choice of wines, whiskies and vintage Armagnacs, and consistently good food using local game (some shot by the landlord); boules, quoits and a nine-hole putting green. Dogs allowed in two bedrooms (not to be left unattended), not in public areas; towel.

RICHMOND
NZ1700
Millgate House
(01748) 823571 – www.millgatehouse.com
Millgate, Richmond, North Yorkshire DL10 4JN

£125–£165; 6 rooms, some overlooking the garden; also self-catering. Georgian townhouse with lots of interesting antiques and lovely plants, a peaceful drawing room, warm, friendly owners offering meticulous attention to detail, and good breakfasts in charming dining room that overlooks the award-winning and really special garden (no dogs here but riverside walks nearby); two resident whippets. Dogs allowed in all bedrooms (not to be left unattended).

RIPLEY
SE2860
Boars Head
(01423) 771888 – www.boarsheadripley.co.uk
Ripley, Harrogate, North Yorkshire HG3 3AY

£125; 25 individually decorated rooms – 9 in main house, 10 in courtyard, 6 in separate house. Smart coaching inn with a friendly bar-bistro and an informal, relaxed atmosphere; walls are hung with golf clubs, cricket bats and jolly little drawings of cricketers or huntsmen and a boar's head (part of the family coat of arms), and some furniture came from the attic of next-door Ripley Castle; real ales, malt whiskies and 20 wines by the glass, and good, popular food using produce from their kitchen garden. Dogs allowed in some bedrooms, bar-bistro and lounge, not in dining areas; bed, bowl and treats; £10.

RIPON
SE3171
Old Deanery
(01765) 600003 – www.theolddeanery.co.uk
Minster Road, Ripon, North Yorkshire HG4 1QS

£125; 11 comfortable rooms. Carefully modernised 17th-c hotel built on the site of a former monastery, next to Ripon Cathedral, with a fine old oak staircase, comfortable leather sofas and log fire in the lounge, a convivial bar, imaginative modern food in the attractive, candlelit dining room, bistro-style lunches and popular afternoon teas, good breakfasts, attentive service and a one-acre garden; canal and River Ure walks nearby. Dogs allowed in most bedrooms, bar and reception area; £5.

ROECLIFFE
SE3765
Crown
(01423) 322300 – www.crowninnroecliffe.com
Roecliffe, North Yorkshire YO51 9LY

£100; 4 charming, country-style bedrooms. The hard-working Mainey family continue to welcome cheerful crowds of both locals and visitors to their lovely inn; the bar has a contemporary colour scheme of dark reds and off-whites, with a mix of tables on flagstones and plaid carpet, a log fire, pleasant prints and local real ales; first class food using their own smokehouse and home-baked bread is served in a small olive-green, candlelit bistro and a more formal restaurant, the garden has rattan sofas and tables on decking, and the village green is opposite. Dogs allowed in all bedrooms and bar.

SEDBUSK SD8790
Stone House Hotel
(01969) 667571 – www.stonehousehotel.com
Sedbusk, Hawes, North Yorkshire DL8 3PT

£140; 24 rooms. Small, warmly friendly Edwardian hotel in a stunning setting with magnificent views and marvellous walks; a country-house atmosphere, log fires and appropriate furnishings, an attractive oak-panelled drawing room, a library/billiard room, and a pleasant extended dining room with good, honest food served by helpful staff; P G Wodehouse stayed here as a guest of the original owner who employed a butler called Jeeves – it was on him that Wodehouse based his famous character. Dogs allowed in some bedrooms and on lead in public areas except dining room; blanket.

SKIPSEA TA1655
Village Farm
(01262) 468479 – www.villagefarmskipsea.co.uk
Back Street, Skipsea, East Yorkshire YO25 8SW

£80; 3 quiet, attractive rooms. Carefully renovated traditional farmhouse and outbuildings set around a central courtyard with nearby walks along 40 miles of beach; dining room serving good evening meals and hearty breakfasts; resident cat, Tosca. Dogs allowed in all bedrooms; £5.

STUDLEY ROGER SE2970
Lawrence House
(01765) 600947 – www.lawrence-house.co.uk
Studley Roger, Ripon, North Yorkshire HG4 3AY

£120; 3 spacious, lovely rooms with peaceful views. Attractive Georgian house in two acres of lovely gardens on the edge of Studley Royal and Fountains Abbey where there are 100 acres to walk in; fine antiques and paintings, a roaring log fire in the drawing room, enjoyable breakfasts and a cosseting atmosphere; resident border/lakeland terriers, Mole and Rattie. Dogs allowed in bedrooms, not in public rooms.

THORNTON WATLASS SE2385
Buck
(01677) 422461 – www.buckwatlass.co.uk
Thornton Watlass, Ripon, North Yorkshire HG4 4AH

£90; 5 recently refurbished rooms. Honest village pub and very much the heart of the community with a friendly welcome for all from the licensees; a pleasantly traditional bar has upholstered wall settles, a fine mahogany bar counter, local artwork on the walls and a brick fireplace, and the lounge (overlooking the cricket green) has large prints of the pub's cricket teams, signed bats and so forth, well kept beers and a dozen malt whiskies; popular Sunday jazz, generously served honest food and particularly good breakfasts; quoits; walks nearby. Dogs allowed in all bedrooms, residents' lounge and bars; £10.

WEST WITTON   SE0688
Wensleydale Heifer
(01969) 622322 – www.wensleydaleheifer.co.uk
West Witton, Leyburn, North Yorkshire DL8 4LS

£160; 13 smart rooms. Stylish restaurant-with-rooms with log fires, oak beams and comfortable leather sofas, a cosy, informal food bar and extensive main, formal restaurant, excellent, interesting food with emphasis on fish/seafood and grills, big breakfasts and attentive, helpful service. Dogs allowed in all bedrooms; bed and treats; £10.

WILLERBY   TA0230
Best Western Willerby Manor Hotel
(01482) 652616 – www.willerbymanor.co.uk
Well Lane, Willerby, Hull, East Yorkshire HU10 6ER

£138; 51 individually decorated rooms. Originally the home of an Edwardian shipping merchant, this carefully extended hotel is surrounded by three acres of gardens; a friendly modern bar, enjoyable breakfasts, lunches, afternoon teas and evening meals in the attractive Figs brasserie, helpful service, lots of seats and tables on the terrace, and health club with swimming pool. Dogs allowed in ground-floor bedrooms; mat; £10.

YORK   SE5952
Grange Hotel
(01904) 644744 – www.grangehotel.co.uk
1 Clifton, York, North Yorkshire YO30 6AA

£146; 41 individually decorated rooms. Close to the Minster, this handsome Regency mansion has elegant and deeply comfortable lounges with open fires, oil paintings, gilt-edged mirrors and fresh flowers, a stylish modern brasserie in the original brick-vaulted cellars, interesting, contemporary cooking, afternoon teas and good breakfasts, and warmly friendly staff; nearby riverside walks and gardens. Dogs allowed in all bedrooms and one dining area; £20 per stay.

YORK   SE5951
Hotel du Vin
(01904) 557350 – www.hotelduvin.com
89 The Mount, York, North Yorkshire YO24 1AX

From £120; 44 stylish rooms and suites. Fine early 19th-c building, once an orphanage, close to the historic city centre; stylish brasserie and attractive, informal area with wicker armchairs and navy sofas, chatty bar, modern, bistro-style food including a popular Sunday brunch, a good choice of wines by the glass, friendly, helpful young staff and seats and tables in the courtyard and terrace. Dogs allowed in all bedrooms; bowl and basket; £10.

YORK   SE5948

Middlethorpe Hall

(01904) 641241 – www.middlethorpe.com
Bishopthorpe Road, Middlethorpe, York, North Yorkshire YO23 2GB

£230; 29 elegant rooms with pretty fabrics, most in the adjoining courtyard. Lovely, immaculately restored William III country house in 20 acres of neat gardens and parkland; antiques, paintings and fresh flowers in comfortable, quiet day rooms (plenty of fine original features), excellent, imaginative food in the panelled dining rooms, afternoon tea, very good breakfasts and courteous, helpful service; spa with indoor swimming pool, treatment rooms, sauna and gym. Dogs allowed in some bedrooms only.

London

MAP 3

DOG FRIENDLY PUBS

CENTRAL LONDON

Admiral Codrington

(020) 7581 0005 – www.theadmiralcodrington.co.uk
Mossop Street, SW3 2LY; South Kensington tube

Long-standing Chelsea landmark with easy-going bar and pretty restaurant, popular food and seats outside

Bustling and with a gently civilised atmosphere, this tucked-away pub has a good mix of customers dropping in and out all day. A central dark-panelled bar has high red chairs beside the counter with more around equally high tables on either side of the log-effect gas fire, button-back wall banquettes with cream and red patterned seats, little stools and plain wooden chairs around a medley of tables on black-painted boards, patterned wallpaper above a dado and a shelf with daily papers. There are ornate flower arrangements, a big portrait above the fire, several naval prints and quiet background music. The friendly, helpful staff serve London Beer Factory Chelsea Blonde, Upham Tipster and a guest beer on handpump, good wines by the glass and, of course, their famous bloody mary. The light and airy restaurant area is a total contrast: high-backed pretty wall seats and plush dining chairs around light tables, an open kitchen, fish prints on pale blue paintwork, a second fireplace and an impressive retractable skylight. The back garden has chunky benches and tables under a summer awning.

Free house ~ Licensee Ben Newton ~ Real ale ~ Open 11.30-11 (midnight Weds, Thurs, 1am Fri, Sat); 12-10.30 Sun; closed 24-26 Dec ~ Bar food 12-3, 6-10 (11 Thurs, Fri); 12-4, 7-11 Sat; 12-9 Sun ~ Restaurant ~ Children welcome but not in bar after 7pm ~ Dogs allowed in bar ~ Wi-fi

CENTRAL LONDON

Alfred Tennyson

(020) 7730 6074 – www.thealfredtennyson.co.uk
Motcomb Street, SW1X 8LA; Knightsbridge tube

Bustling and civilised with good drinks choice, rewarding food and friendly, helpful service

The interesting food and drinks and relaxed, civilised atmosphere draw plenty of customers to this pub in a quiet residential area. Apart from one table surrounded by stools beside the bar counter, there are high-backed upholstered dining chairs around wooden tables on parquet flooring, comfortable leather wall seats and eclectic décor that encompasses 19th-c postcards to nobility, envelopes displayed address-side out, Edward Lear illustrations and World War II prints – plus antique books on windowsills. Friendly, helpful staff serve Canopy Journeyman and Cubitt 1788 (named for the pub from Canopy) on handpump, cocktails and 23 wines by the glass. The upstairs restaurant has leather chairs and wooden tables on more parquet and a huge mirror above an open fire. Above that is a room for private hire, while up again is a cosy loft used for monthly events such as cheese tastings. The front pavement has tables and chairs beneath a striped awning.

Cubitt House ~ Lease Adam Quigley ~ Real ale ~ Open & bar food 8am-11pm; 9am-11pm Sat; 9am-10pm Sun ~ Children welcome ~ Dogs allowed in bar ~ Wi-fi

CENTRAL LONDON
Grazing Goat

(020) 7724 7243 – www.thegrazinggoat.co.uk
New Quebec Street, W1H 7RQ; Marble Arch tube

A good mixed crowd of customers, restful décor, a thoughtful choice of drinks and good interesting food; bedrooms

Tucked away behind busy Oxford Street and Selfridges department store, this is a stylish pub with a rustic feel. It has a big gilt-edged mirror above an open fire and plenty of spreading dining space with white cushioned and beige dining chairs around pale tables on bare boards, sage green or light oak-panelled walls, hanging lamps and lanterns and some goat memorabilia dotted about. Efficient, friendly staff serve Canopy Journeyman and Cubitt 1788 (named for the pub from Canopy), 23 wines by the glass and Weston's cider. The upstairs restaurant is more formal. Glass doors open on to the street where there are a few wooden-slatted chairs and tables.

Cubitt House ~ Licensee Adam Quigley ~ Real ale ~ Open & bar food 7.30am-11pm (10.30pm Sun) ~ Restaurant ~ Children welcome ~ Dogs allowed in bar ~ Wi-fi ~ Bedrooms: £250

CENTRAL LONDON
Lamb & Flag

(020) 7497 9504 – www.lambandflagcoventgarden.co.uk
Rose Street, off Garrick Street, WC2E 9EB; Covent Garden, Leicester Square tube

Historic yet unpretentious, full of character and atmosphere, with six real ales and pubby food

This is the most characterful pub in Covent Garden, so you'll never have it to yourself – but customers spill out on to the pavement, even in winter. It's an unspoilt and, in places, rather basic old tavern: the more spartan front room leads into a cosy, atmospheric, low-ceilinged back bar with high-backed black settles and an open fire. Fullers ESB, London Pride, Olivers Island, Seafarers, Summer Ale and a seasonal beer plus a couple of guests from breweries such as Adnams and Butcombe on handpump, as well as 12 wines by the glass and 25 malt whiskies. The upstairs Dryden Room is often less crowded and has more seats (though fewer beers). There's a lively and well documented history: Dryden was nearly beaten to death by hired thugs outside, and Charles Dickens made fun of the Middle Temple lawyers who frequented it when he was working in nearby Catherine Street.

Fullers ~ Manager Tim Adams ~ Real ale ~ Open 11-11; 12-10.30 Sun ~ Bar food 12-9 ~ Restaurant ~ Children in upstairs dining room only ~ Dogs allowed in bar ~ Wi-fi ~ Live jazz first Sun evening of month

CENTRAL LONDON
Orange

(020) 7881 9844 – www.theorange.co.uk
Pimlico Road, SW1W 8NE; Sloane Square tube

Carefully restored pub with simply decorated rooms, thoughtful choice of drinks and good modern cooking; bedrooms

At the heart of Pimlico, this restored Georgian inn has an easy-going, gently civilised feel and courteous, friendly staff. The two floors of the pub itself have huge sash windows on all sides making the interconnected rooms light and airy; throughout, the décor is shabby-chic and simple and the atmosphere easy-going and chatty. The high-ceilinged downstairs bar has wooden dining chairs around pale tables on bare boards, an open fire at one end and a big carved counter where they keep Canopy Journeyman and Cubitt 1788 (named for the pub from Canopy), 23 wines by the glass, Weston's cider and a lengthy cocktail list. The dining room to the right, usually packed with cheerful customers, is decorated with prints, glass bottles and soda siphons, big house plants and a few rustic knick-knacks. Upstairs, the linked restaurant rooms are similarly furnished with old french travel posters and circus prints on cream walls, more open fireplaces, big glass ceiling lights and chandeliers and quiet background jazz.

Cubitt House ~ Licensee Adam Quigley ~ Real ale ~ Open & bar food 8am-11.30pm (midnight Fri, Sat); 8am-10.30pm Sun ~ Restaurant ~ Children welcome ~ Dogs allowed in bar ~ Wi-fi ~ Bedrooms: £240

CENTRAL LONDON
Punchbowl

(020) 7493 6841 – www.punchbowllondon.com
Farm Street, W1J 5RP; Green Park tube

Bustling, rather civilised pub with good wines and ales, enjoyable food and helpful service

This tucked-away Mayfair pub has real character – the nicest part is at the back where several panelled booths have suede bench seating, animal scatter cushions, some etched glasswork and church candles on tables. Elegant spoked chairs are grouped around dark tables on worn floorboards, a couple of long elbow shelves are lined with high chairs and one fireplace has a coal fire while the other is piled with logs. At the front it's simpler, with cushioned bench seating and pubby tables and chairs on floor tiles. All sorts of artwork from cartoons to oil paintings line the walls and the ceiling has interesting old hand-drawn street maps; background music. Adnams Broadside, Caledonian Deuchars IPA and a beer named for the pub on handpump, good wines by the glass and professional, friendly service. The smart dining room on the first floor has plush furnishings, large artworks and a huge gilt mirror above an open fire; there are private dining facilities too.

Free house ~ Licensee Ben Newton ~ Real ale ~ Open 12-11 (9 Sun) ~ Bar food 12-3.30, 5.30-10; 12-10 Sat; 12-8 Sun ~ Restaurant ~ Children welcome if seated and dining ~ Dogs allowed in bar ~ Wi-fi

CENTRAL LONDON

Star

(020) 7235 3019 – www.star-tavern-belgravia.co.uk
*Belgrave Mews West, behind the German Embassy, off Belgrave Square, SW1X 8HT;
Knightsbridge, Hyde Park Corner tube*

**Bustling local with restful bar, upstairs dining room, Fullers ales,
well liked bar food and colourful hanging baskets**

Outside peak times, there's a restful, local feel to this tucked-away pub in its
cobbled mews. The small bar is pleasant, with sash windows, a wooden
floor, stools by the counter, an open winter fire and Fullers ESB, London Pride
and Olivers Island plus a guest beer on handpump, nine wines by the glass and
a few malt whiskies. An arch leads to the main seating area where there are
well polished tables and chairs and good lighting; there's also an upstairs dining
room. In summer, the front of the building is covered with an astonishing array
of hanging baskets and flowering tubs. It's said that this is where the Great Train
Robbery was planned.

Fullers ~ Manager Marta Lemieszewska ~ Real ale ~ Open 11-11; 12-11 Sat; 12-10.30 Sun
~ Bar food 12-3, 5-9; 12-4, 5-9 Sun ~ Restaurant ~ Children welcome ~ Dogs welcome ~
Wi-fi

CENTRAL LONDON

Thomas Cubitt

(020) 7730 6060 – www.thethomascubitt.co.uk
Elizabeth Street, SW1W 9PA; Sloane Square tube, Victoria tube/rail

**Belgravia pub with a civilised but friendly atmosphere and enterprising
food and drink**

Named after the legendary builder and located in well heeled Elizabeth Street,
this bustling place has a bar with miscellaneous Edwardian-style dining chairs
around wooden tables on stripped parquet flooring, and architectural prints and
antlers on panelled or painted walls; open fires and lovely flower arrangements.
Attentive staff serve Canopy Journeyman and Cubitt 1788 (named for the pub
from Canopy), 23 wines by the glass, Weston's cider and cocktails. The more
formal dining room upstairs has smart upholstered wooden chairs around white-
clothed tables, candles in wall holders, a few prints, house plants and window
blinds; background music. In warm weather, the floor-to-ceiling glass doors are
pulled back to the street where there are cordoned-off tables and chairs.

Cubitt House ~ Licensee Adam Quigley ~ Real ale ~ Open 12-11 (10 Sun) ~ Bar food – 12-10
(9 Sun) ~ Restaurant ~ Children welcome ~ Dogs allowed in bar ~ Wi-fi

NORTH LONDON

Hare

(020) 8954 4949 – www.hareoldredding.com
Brookshill/Old Redding, HA3 6SD; Hatch End rail

**Carefully modernised old pub with plenty of drinking and dining space,
friendly staff and enjoyable food**

This extended early 19th-c pub is attractively contemporary inside with
interconnected bar and dining rooms. The bar has tartan cushions on a long
leather wall seat, upholstered and leather dining chairs around a medley of tables

and a long counter lined with bar stools. Fullers London Pride and a changing
guest beer on handpump and several wines by the glass. The stylish brasserie has
a woodburning stove, a long beige button-back leather wall seat, leather-seated
chairs around simple tables, rugs on bare boards and candles in lanterns, and
there's also a similarly furnished dining area with more rugs on black slates.
A little room with burgundy-painted wall planking is just right for a small group.
Throughout, there are church candles on substantial holders, dried lavender in
rustic jugs and modern artwork. The back garden has seats and tables under a
gazebo, deck chairs on the lawn and piles of blankets for cooler weather; there
are also some picnic-sets out in front.

White Brasserie Company ~ Manager Amanda Radcliffe ~ Real ale ~ Open 11-11 (10 Sun) ~
Bar food 12-10 (10.30 Fri, Sat); 12-9 Sun ~ Restaurant ~ Children welcome ~ Dogs allowed
in bar ~ Wi-fi

NORTH LONDON
Holly Bush

(020) 7435 2892 – www.hollybushhampstead.co.uk
Holly Mount, NW3 6SG; Hampstead tube

**Unique village local, with good food and drinks, and lovely
unspoilt feel**

This bustling old place was originally a stable block and is tucked away
among some of Hampstead's most villagey streets. The old-fashioned front
bar has a dark sagging ceiling, brown and cream panelled walls (decorated
with vintage advertisements and a few hanging plates), open fires, bare
boards and secretive bays formed by partly glazed partitions. The slightly
more intimate back room, named after the painter George Romney, has an
embossed red ceiling, panelled and etched glass alcoves, and ochre-painted
brick walls covered with small prints; lots of board and card games. Fullers
ESB, IPA, London Pride and Olivers Island plus a guest such as Adnams Ghost
Ship on handpump, as well as 15 malt whiskies and 14 wines by the glass from
a good wine list. The upstairs dining room has table service at the weekend, as
does the rest of the pub on Sundays. There are benches on the pavement.

Fullers ~ Manager Ben Ralph ~ Real ale ~ Open 12-11 (10.30 Sun) ~ Bar food 12-10; 12-8
Sun ~ Restaurant ~ Children welcome ~ Dogs welcome ~ Wi-fi

NORTH LONDON
Princess of Wales

(020) 7722 0354 – www.lovetheprincess.com
Fitzroy Road/Chalcot Road, NW1 8LL; Chalk Farm tube

**Friendly place with three different seating areas, enjoyable food,
wide choice of drinks and funky garden**

Spread over three floors, this bustling pub usefully offers some kind of food all
day at weekends. The main bar, at ground level, is open-plan and light with big
windows looking out to the street, wooden tables and chairs on bare boards and
plenty of high chairs against the counter: Sambrooks Wandle and a beer named
for the pub (also from Sambrooks) plus a changing guest ale on handpump,
16 wines by the glass, 11 malt whiskies and good cocktails. Upstairs, the smarter
dining room has beige- and white-painted chairs, leather sofas and stools around
wooden tables on more bare boards, big gilt-edged mirrors and chandeliers; two
TVs. Orange and green plush banquettes create a diner-like feel in the colourful

Garden Room downstairs, and doors lead out to the suntrap garden with its
Bansky-style mural, framed wall mirrors and picnic-sets (some painted pink
and purple) under parasols.

Free house ~ Licensee Lawrence Santi ~ Real ale ~ Open 11am-midnight; 10am-midnight
Sat; 10am-11.30pm Sun ~ Bar food 12-2.30, 6-10.30; 12-10.30 weekends ~ Restaurant ~
Children welcome ~ Dogs allowed in bar ~ Wi-fi

SOUTH LONDON
Earl Spencer

(020) 8870 9244 – www.theearlspencer.co.uk
Merton Road, SW18 5JL; Southfields tube

Good, interesting food and six real ales in busy but friendly pub

This sizeable Edwardian pub has a cheerful, chatty atmosphere and is
particularly well run. There are cushioned wooden, farmhouse and leather
dining tables around all sorts of tables on bare boards, standard lamps, modern
art on the walls and an open fire. The back bar has long tables, pews and benches,
and stools line the U-shaped counter where efficient, friendly staff serve six ales
on handpump. These include Belleville Calif-Oregon Amber, By the Horns The
Mayor of Garratt, East London Foundation Bitter, Sambrooks Wandle, Wimbledon
Tower SPA and a weekly changing guest beer. Also, 20 wines by the glass,
50 british gins, 12 british vodkas and 20 malt whiskies; they also sell 23 kinds
of cigar. There are picnic-sets out on the front terrace.

Enterprise ~ Lease Michael Mann ~ Real ale ~ Open 4-11 Mon-Thurs; 11am-midnight Fri,
Sat; 12-10.30 Sun ~ Bar food 7-10 Mon-Thurs; 12.30-3.30, 7-10 Fri, Sat; 12.30-4, 7-9.30
Sun ~ Children welcome ~ Dogs allowed in bar ~ Wi-fi

SOUTH LONDON
Jolly Gardeners

(020) 8870 8417 – www.thejollygardeners.co.uk
Garrett Lane, SW18 4EA; Earlsfield rail

**High quality food in bustling corner street pub, local ales, a relaxed
atmosphere and courtyard garden**

With the 2010 *MasterChef* winner at the helm, this Victorian corner pub gets
packed in the evenings with customers keen to enjoy the notably good food.
The L-shaped front bar has high stools around equally high tables, high-backed
black leather dining chairs around straightforward tables, pale floorboards and
more stools at the counter where friendly, chatty staff serve Belleville Northcote
Blonde and Sambrooks Wandle on handpump and a dozen wines by the glass.
Similar furnishings lead back to more of a dining area where there's an open fire.
Paintwork is dark grey (as is the dado), décor is minimal and the atmosphere is
easy-going; background music and TV. The airy conservatory is simply furnished
with cushioned wooden chairs around wood-topped tables on floorboards and
doors lead out to the decked courtyard garden. Here there are heaters, big
parasols, a much-used barbecue, wall seating with scatter cushions, picnic-sets
and contemporary tables and chairs.

The Lads Pub Co ~ Tenant Stephen Robb ~ Real ale ~ Open 12-11 (midnight Fri, Sat);
12-8 (7 in winter) Sun ~ Bar food 12-3, 6-10; 12-5 Sun ~ Restaurant ~ Children welcome ~
Dogs allowed in bar ~ Wi-fi

SOUTH LONDON

Latchmere

(020) 7223 3549 – www.thelatchmere.co.uk

Battersea Park Road, SW11 3BW; Clapham Junction rail

Busy, well run pub with open-plan drinking and dining areas, enjoyable food and drink, and seats in garden; upstairs theatre

Recently refurbished, this Battersea landmark remains a cheerful, bustling place with a good mix of customers. The open-plan areas include a log fire with leather sofas to either side, a group of tub chairs in one corner, and cushioned Edwardian-style dining chairs, two-sided banquettes and red leather wall seating around wooden tables on bare floorboards. There are some model yachts, big mirrors, animal prints, photographs and posters, and evening candles. Stools line the counter where efficient, friendly staff serve Sharps Doom Bar, St Austell Liquid Sunshine and Timothy Taylors Landlord on handpump, 19 wines by the glass, and cocktails. Outside, the heated terraced garden has several small booths down one side, a larger one for a private party and plenty of tables and chairs. The award-winning theatre is on the first floor.

Three Cheers Pub Co ~ Manager Tom Peake ~ Real ale ~ Open 11-11; 11am-midnight Fri, Sat; 11-10.30 Sun ~ Bar food 12-2.30, 6-10.30; 12-4, 5-10.30 Sat; 12-9 Sun ~ Restaurant ~ Children welcome until 7pm ~ Dogs welcome ~ Wi-fi

SOUTH LONDON

Rose & Crown

(01689) 869029 – www.the-roseandcrown.co.uk

Farnborough Way (A21), BR6 6BT; Chelsfield rail

Sizeable pub on the edge of London with surprisingly large back garden, character bars, a wide choice of food and drink and cheerful service

You might be forgiven for thinking that a pub on a large roundabout on the outskirts of London might not be your first port of call for a drink or meal – but you'd be mistaken in this case. It's been completely renovated and refurbished to create open-plan interconnected rooms with alcoves and smaller, cosier areas too. Every shape and size of Edwardian-style dining chairs, leather tub seats, upholstered stools and coloured button-back banquettes are grouped around all manner of polished tables on rugs, bare boards or black and white tiles. Walls are hung with frame-to-frame prints and pictures, there are house plants, church candles, lots of mirrors and hundreds of books on shelves, and three log fires (one's a woodburner). The place hums with cheerful customers, all ably looked after by chatty, efficient and friendly staff. A beer named for the pub (from Youngs), Youngs Bitter, Blonde, Bombardier and Special and a guest from Larkins on handpump, and 16 wines by the glass. The biggest surprise is the big back garden which has colourful beach huts and cabanas, chairs and tables on a terrace, picnic-sets on grass and a sizeable children's play area.

Whiting & Hammond ~ Manager Lee Scott ~ Real ale ~ Open 11-11; 12-10.30 Sun ~ Bar food 12-9.30 (9 Sun) ~ Restaurant ~ Children welcome ~ Dogs allowed in bar ~ Wi-fi

SOUTH LONDON
Royal Oak

(020) 7357 7173 – www.harveys.org.uk
Tabard Street/Nebraska Street, SE1 4JU; Borough tube, London Bridge tube/rail

Old-fashioned corner house with particularly well kept beers and honest food

This bustling pub has the look and feel of a traditional London alehouse – you'd never imagine it had been painstakingly transformed by Sussex brewery Harveys just a few years ago. The place is always packed with customers of varying ages, all keen to enjoy the full range of Harveys ales plus a guest from Fullers on handpump and Thatcher's cider. The two little L-shaped rooms (the front bar is larger and brighter, the back room cosier with dimmer lighting) meander around the central wooden servery, which has a fine old clock in the middle. The rooms are done out with patterned rugs on wooden floors, plates running along a delft shelf, black and white scenes or period sheet music on red-painted walls, and an assortment of wooden tables and chairs. There's disabled access at the Nebraska Street entrance.

Harveys ~ Tenants John Porteous, Frank Taylor ~ Real ale ~ Open 11-11; 12-9 Sun ~ Bar food 12-2.45, 5-9.15; 12-8 Sun ~ Children welcome until 9pm ~ Dogs welcome

SOUTH LONDON
Victoria

(020) 8876 4238 – www.thevictoria.net
West Temple Sheen, SW14 7RT; Mortlake rail

Excellent food in attractive inn, airy conservatory and cosy bar and seats in pretty garden; bedrooms

After a walk in nearby Richmond Park, this well run, friendly inn is just the place for lunch. The bar has leather sofas facing each other beside a fireplace, and wooden seats and tables in a bow window with more on bare boards around the counter. Sambrooks Wandle, Timothy Taylors Landlord and a guest such as Twickenham Naked Ladies on handpump, 25 wines by the glass from a good list and home-made elderflower cordial; background music. A light and airy back conservatory restaurant has dark chunky furniture and doors that open out into a pretty garden. Here, there are plenty of seats and tables under a huge parasol and an outside bar.

Enterprise ~ Lease Greg Bellamy ~ Real ale ~ Open 11-11 (10.30 Sun) ~ Bar food 12-10 ~ Restaurant ~ Children welcome ~ Dogs allowed in bar ~ Wi-fi ~ Bedrooms: £135

WEST LONDON
Bell

(020) 8941 9799 – www.thebellinnhampton.co.uk
Thames Street, Hampton, TW12 2EA; Hampton rail

Bustling pub by the Thames with seats outside, real ales, a good choice of food and friendly service

There's a good bustling atmosphere and a wide mix of customers in this friendly riverside pub. The interconnected rooms have wooden dining and tub chairs around copper-topped or chunky wooden tables, comfortably upholstered wall seats with scatter cushions, mirrors, old photographs and lots of church candles. From the long panelled bar counter here, helpful staff serve Caledonian Deuchars

IPA and guests such as Adnams Jack Brand Mosaic Pale Ale, Sambrooks Wandle and Sharps Doom Bar on handpump, 20 wines by the glass and speciality teas and coffees. There are plenty of contemporary seats and tables in the garden, which has heaters, lighting and booth seating; summer barbecues.

Authentic Inns ~ Lease Simon Bailey ~ Real ale ~ Open 11-11 (midnight Fri, Sat) ~ Bar food 12-3, 6-10; 12-10 Sat; 12-9 Sun ~ Restaurant ~ Children welcome ~ Dogs allowed in bar ~ Wi-fi ~ Live music Sat evening

WEST LONDON

Dove

(020) 8748 9474 – www.dovehammersmith.co.uk
Upper Mall, W6 9TA; Ravenscourt Park tube

Character pub with a lovely riverside terrace, cosily traditional front bar and an interesting history

One of London's best-known pubs, this old-fashioned riverside place is in the Guinness World Records for having the smallest bar room – the front snug, a mere 4'2" by 7'10". The bar is cosy, traditional and unchanging, with black panelling and red leatherette cushioned built-in wall settles and stools around assorted tables. It leads to a bigger, similarly furnished back room that's more geared to eating, which in turn leads to a conservatory. Fullers ESB, London Pride, Olivers Island, a changing seasonal ale plus a guest or two on handpump and 19 wines by the glass including champagne and sparkling wine. Head down steps at the back to reach the verandah with its highly prized tables looking over a low river wall to the Thames Reach just above Hammersmith Bridge; a tiny exclusive area, reached up a spiral staircase, is a prime spot for watching rowers on the water. The pub has played host to many writers, actors and artists over the years (there's a fascinating framed list on a wall); it's said to be where 'Rule Britannia' was composed and was a favourite with Turner, who painted the view of the Thames from the delightful back terrace, and with Graham Greene. The street itself is associated with the foundation of the arts and crafts movement – William Morris's old residence Kelmscott House (open certain afternoons) is nearby.

Fullers ~ Manager Sonia Labatut ~ Real ale ~ Open 11-11; 12-10.30 Sun ~ Bar food 12-10; 12-8 ~ Children welcome ~ Dogs welcome ~ Wi-fi

WEST LONDON

Duke of Sussex

(020) 8742 8801 – www.thedukeofsussex.co.uk
South Parade, W4 5LF; Chiswick Park tube, South Acton rail

Attractively restored Victorian local with interesting bar food, a good choice of drinks and a lovely big garden

On a warm day, the unexpectedly big garden behind this well run pub is a real treat – there are seats and tables under parasols, nicely laid out plants, carefully positioned lighting and (if it gets cooler in the evening) heaters. The classy, simply furnished bar has some original etched glass, chapel and farmhouse chairs around scrubbed pine and dark wood tables, and huge windows overlooking Acton Green. The big horseshoe-shaped counter, lined with high bar stools, is where they serve a beer named for the pub (from Greene King), Portobello VPA, Sharps Own and Triple fff Citra Sonic on handpump, 30 wines by the glass and 15 malt whiskies. Off here is a dining room, again with simple wooden furnishings on parquet, but also six-seater booths, chandeliers, antique lamps, a splendid skylight framed by colourfully painted cherubs and a couple of big mirrors, one above a small tiled fireplace.

Greene King ~ Manager Matt Mullett ~ Real ale ~ Open 12-11 (11.30 Fri, Sat); 12-10.30 Sun ~ Bar food 12-10 (10.30 Fri, Sat); 12-9 Sun ~ Restaurant ~ Children welcome ~ Dogs allowed in bar ~ Wi-fi

WEST LONDON
Malt House

(020) 7084 6888 – www.malthousefulham.co.uk
Vanston Place, SW6 1AY; Fulham Broadway tube

Creative food and good drinks choice in refurbished Georgian pub, stylish bar and dining areas and hidden-away garden; bedrooms

Dating from 1729, this large refurbished corner pub has a good, bustling atmosphere in its U-shaped bar. There are big windows, high ceilings, wooden or tiled floors, green leather button-back wall seating and dark wooden dining chairs around pale-topped tables and groups of sofas and armchairs dotted here and there. Planked walls are hung with watercolours, there's a lot of cream paintwork and some bookshelf wallpaper. Contemporary high chairs line the counter where helpful staff serve Brakspears Bitter, Marstons Pedigree New World Pale Ale and a guest beer on handpump, eight good wines by the glass, 11 malt whiskies and a farm cider. The small paved back garden has pretty hanging baskets, fairy lights, candles in lanterns and candy-striped benches around wooden tables.

Brakspears ~ Lease Jessica Chanter ~ Real ale ~ Open 10am-11pm; 11-11 Sun ~ Bar food 8am-2.30, 6-10; 12-9 Sun ~ Restaurant ~ Children welcome ~ Dogs welcome ~ Wi-fi ~ Bedrooms: £145

WEST LONDON
Mute Swan

(020) 8941 5959 – www.brunningandprice.co.uk/muteswan
Palace Gate, Hampton Court Road, KT8 9BN; Hampton Court rail

Handsome pub close to the Thames with sunny seats outside, relaxed bar, upstairs dining room and imaginative food and drinks choice

Just yards from the River Thames (though there's no view), this remains a friendly, busy and well run pub. The light and airy bar has four big leather armchairs grouped around a low table in the centre, while the rest of the room has brown leather wall seats, high-backed Edwardian-style cushioned dining chairs around dark tables and rugs on bare boards. The walls are covered in interesting photographs, maps, prints and posters and there are sizeable house plants, glass and stone bottles on the windowsills and a woodburning stove; the atmosphere is informal and relaxed. Brunning & Price Phoenix Original, Hogs Back TEA, Sharps Coaster and Tillingbourne Falls Gold on handpump, a carefully chosen wine list with 19 by the glass, farm cider and 75 malt whiskies; staff are efficient and helpful. A metal spiral staircase – presided over by an elegant metal chandelier – leads up to the dining area where there are brass-studded caramel leather chairs around well spaced tables on bare boards or carpeting, and numerous photographs and prints. The tables and chairs on the front terrace get snapped up quickly and the pub is opposite the gates to Hampton Court Palace. There are a few parking spaces in front, but you'll probably have to park elsewhere.

Brunning & Price ~ Manager Alisha Craigwell ~ Real ale ~ Open 11-11 (midnight Fri, Sat); 11-10.30 Sun ~ Bar food 12-10 (9.30 Sun) ~ Restaurant ~ Children welcome in upstairs restaurant only ~ Dogs allowed in bar ~ Wi-fi

WEST LONDON
Old Orchard

(01895) 822631 – www.brunningandprice.co.uk/oldorchard
Off Park Lane, Harefield, UB9 6HJ; Denham rail (some distance away)

Wonderful views from the front garden, a good choice of drinks and interesting brasserie-style food

The position here is pretty special: from tables on the front terrace and in the garden you look down to the narrowboats on the canal and across to the lakes that are part of the conservation area known as the Colne Valley Regional Park – it's a haven for wildlife. Inside, the open-plan rooms have an attractive mix of cushioned dining chairs around all sizes and shapes of dark wooden tables, lots of prints, maps and pictures covering the walls, books on shelves, old glass bottles on windowsills and rugs on wood or parquet flooring. One room is hung with a sizeable rug and some tapestry. There are daily papers to read, three cosy coal fires, big pot plants and fresh flowers. Half a dozen real ales on handpump served by friendly, efficient staff include Phoenix Brunning & Price Original, Mighty Oak Oscar Wilde and Tring Side Pocket for a Toad alongside guests such as Leighton Buzzard Black Buzzard, Mole Rucking Mole, Thornbridge Jaipur and Tiny Rebel One Inch Punch; also, 24 wines by the glass, 140 malt whiskies and six farm ciders. The atmosphere throughout is civilised and easy-going.

Brunning & Price ~ Manager Dan Redfern ~ Real ale ~ Open 11.30-11; 12-10.30 Sun ~ Bar food 12-10 (9.30 Sun) ~ Children welcome ~ Dogs welcome ~ Wi-fi

WEST LONDON
White Horse

(020) 7736 2115 – www.whitehorsesw6.com
Parsons Green, SW6 4UL; Parsons Green tube

Cheerfully relaxed local with big terrace, excellent range of carefully sourced drinks and imaginative food

On summer evenings and weekends, the front terrace – overlooking Parsons Green itself – has something of a continental feel with its many seats and tables; there are barbecues most sunny evenings. Inside, the stylishly modernised U-shaped bar has a gently upmarket and chatty atmosphere, plenty of leather chesterfield sofas and wooden tables, huge windows with slatted wooden blinds, flagstone and wood floors, and winter coal and log fires (one in an elegant marble fireplace). There's also an upstairs dining room with its own bar. The impressive range of drinks takes in real ales such as Harveys Best, Oakham JHB and guest beers such as Flack Manor Double Drop, Mallinsons Summit, Moor Confidence, Siren Undercurrent, Thornbridge Windle and Twickenham Sundancer on handpump, eight craft ales, six of the seven Trappist beers, around 135 other foreign bottled beers, several malt whiskies and 20 good wines by the glass. They hold three beer festivals a year (one celebrating American beer and two spotlighting regional breweries).

Mitchells & Butlers ~ Manager Danny Daws ~ Real ale ~ Open 9.30am-11.30pm (midnight Thurs-Sat) ~ Bar food 9.30am-10.30pm ~ Restaurant ~ Children welcome ~ Dogs welcome ~ Wi-fi

WEST LONDON

Windsor Castle

(020) 7243 8797 – www.thewindsorcastlekensington.co.uk
Campden Hill Road, W8 7AR; Notting Hill Gate tube

Genuinely unspoilt, with lots of atmosphere in tiny, dark rooms and lovely summer garden

Unchanging and full of character, there's a lot of old-fashioned charm here, with a wealth of dark oak furnishings, sturdy high-backed built-in elm benches, time-smoked ceilings, soft lighting and a coal-effect fire. Three of the tiny unspoilt rooms have their own entrance from the street, but it's much more fun trying to navigate through the minuscule doors between them inside. Usually fairly quiet at lunchtime, it tends to be packed most evenings. The panelled and wood-floored dining room at the back overlooks the garden. Black Sheep, Fullers London Pride, Hop Back Summer Lightning, Harviestoun Summer Legend, Portobello Bronze Star, Sharps Doom Bar, Salopian Hop Twister and Wells Bombardier on handpump, decent house wines, farm ciders, malt whiskies and jugs of Pimms. The garden, on several levels, has tables and chairs on flagstones and feels secluded thanks to the high ivy-covered walls; heaters for cooler evenings.

Mitchells & Butlers ~ Manager Andrew Davidson ~ Real ale ~ Open 12-11 (10.30 Sun) ~ Bar food 12-10 (9 Sun) ~ Restaurant ~ Children in eating area of bar ~ Dogs welcome ~ Wi-fi

DOG FRIENDLY HOTELS, INNS AND B&Bs

CENTRAL LONDON

Chesterfield Mayfair

(020) 7491 2622 – www.chesterfieldmayfair.com
35 Charles Street, W1J 5EB; Green Park tube

£320; 107 well equipped, pretty rooms and suites. Charming hotel with particularly courteous and helpful staff, a relaxed club-style bar with a resident pianist, a light and airy conservatory for lunches and afternoon teas, and a smart, attractive restaurant for fine dining; Hyde Park is close by for walks. Dogs allowed in all bedrooms and public areas; bed, bowls and treats; dog-sitting and dog-walking available.

CENTRAL LONDON

Draycott Hotel

(020) 7730 6466 – www.draycotthotel.com
26 Cadogan Gardens, SW3 2RP; Sloane Square tube

From £318; 35 traditionally designed rooms and suites. Made up of three Edwardian townhouses with fine staircases, this is an informal and enjoyable small hotel with a library, a drawing room for afternoon tea, a breakfast room (the breakfasts are of real quality), genuinely helpful staff and a one-acre garden; no restaurant. Dogs allowed in three bedrooms and public areas if well behaved (not in garden).

CENTRAL LONDON
Levin

(020) 7589 6286 – www.thelevinhotel.co.uk
28 Basil Street, SW3 1AS; Knightsbridge tube

£345; 12 comfortable, carefully furnished rooms. Family-run small hotel in the heart of Knightsbridge, with a comfortably modern entrance hall and reception/lounge, an honesty bar, a bustling basement brasserie for continental breakfasts and simple all-day food, and helpful, friendly staff. Dogs allowed in all bedrooms and public areas except brasserie.

CENTRAL LONDON
Malmaison

(020) 7012 3700 – www.malmaison.com
18-21 Charterhouse Square, EC1M 6AH; Barbican tube

£253; 97 stylish, modern, very well equipped rooms and suites. Large, elegant red-brick Victorian hotel converted from a nurses' residence for St Bartholomew's hospital and set in the cobbled courtyard of leafy Charterhouse Square near Smithfield Market; imaginative modern cooking in the brasserie, a chic bar off the spacious lobby with comfortable sofas, and helpful, attentive service; the Thames Path for scenic riverside walks is just under a mile away. Dogs allowed in some bedrooms and lobby; bed; £10.

CENTRAL LONDON
Rubens

(020) 7834 6600 – www.rubenshotel.com
39 Buckingham Palace Road, SW1W 0PS; Victoria tube/rail

£245; 161 luxurious rooms and suites and 2 apartments. Opposite Buckingham Palace and near Victoria station, this attractive hotel has comfortable lounges, a couple of bars, various restaurants including one with a popular and extensive buffet-style carvery and the Library restaurant with à la carte classics, and views of the Royal Mews; nearby parks for walks. Dogs allowed in some bedrooms and public areas; bed, bowl and treats; other services available on request.

CENTRAL LONDON
South Place Hotel

(020) 3503 0000 – www.southplacehotel.com
3 South Place, EC2M 2AF; Liverpool Street tube/rail

£390; 80 well equipped, contemporary bedrooms. Smart but relaxed hotel behind Liverpool Street station – very handy for the City and Shoreditch, with a casual chop house downstairs and a more formal rooftop restaurant specialising in seafood (the hotel is run by the D&D London restaurant chain); various bars include a rooftop terrace and a cosy library bar; sauna, steam room and

24-hour gym. Small to medium-sized dogs allowed in some bedrooms and ground-floor bar and restaurant; bed, bowl and toy; £50 per stay.

SOUTH LONDON

Bermondsey Square Hotel

(020) 7378 2450 – www.bermondseysquarehotel.co.uk
Bermondsey Square, Tower Bridge Road, SE1 3UN; London Bridge tube/rail

From £159; 90 modern rooms including 4 suites. Modern medium-rise hotel south of the river near Tower Bridge and London Bridge, with a glass-fronted lounge/restaurant with leather sofas and armchairs and serving bistro-style food all day. Dogs allowed in some bedrooms and lounge; bed, blanket and bowl; £20.

WEST LONDON

Portobello Hotel

(020) 7727 2777 – www.portobellohotel.com
22 Stanley Gardens, W11 2NG; Notting Hill Gate tube

£345; 21 rooms decorated in colourful and very individual styles. Relaxed and informal hotel (liked by music and show business celebrities) on a quiet residential street, with plenty of eccentric character, big plants and flower arrangements, and a sitting room (also where the enjoyable breakfasts are served) with comfortable sofas and armchairs and an honesty bar. Small dogs allowed in two bedrooms only; bed, bowl and treats; £25 per stay.

Scotland

DOG FRIENDLY PUBS

ANCRUM
NT6224

Cross Keys

(01835) 830242 – www.ancrumcrosskeys.com
Off A68 Jedburgh–Edinburgh; TD8 6XH

Simply decorated village pub with a high reputation for local ales and particularly good food

Perched above Ale Water for 200 years and overlooking the village green, this cheerful pub is the hub of local life. But there are usually just as many visitors too, as the reputation of the innovative food has spread far and wide. The easy-going, simply furnished bar has dogs and regulars vying for the fire, wall seats, minimal décor and stools against the counter where they serve Born in the Borders Foxy Blonde and a guest ale from a local brewery such as Born in the Borders on handpump, a good choice of wines and a healthy number of malt whiskies; a newish side bar is for both drinking and eating. The blue-walled dining room has chunky tables and chairs on bare boards, an open kitchen and, again, minimal décor. The food, creatively presented and with some unusual touches, uses local and foraged ingredients. Service is helpful and friendly. There's a back garden with picnic-sets and a gate that leads down to the water. A few tables and chairs are set out in front of the stone building.

Free house ~ Licensee John Henderson ~ Real ale ~ Open 5pm-midnight (1am Fri, Sat); 12-12 Sun; closed weekday lunchtimes ~ Bar food 5.30-9 Weds-Sun; 12-2, 5.30-9 Sat; 12-2, 5.30-8 Sun ~ Restaurant ~ Children welcome ~ Dogs allowed in bar ~ Wi-fi

APPLECROSS
NG7144

Applecross Inn

(01520) 744262 – www.applecross.uk.com/inn/
Off A896 S of Shieldaig; IV54 8LR

Wonderfully remote pub on famously scenic route on west coast; particularly friendly welcome, real ales and good seafood; bedrooms

If you wish to stay here, you'll have to book months ahead as customers from all over the world will also be wanting a place. But it will be worth it for the extraordinary drive through miles of spectacularly wild, unpopulated scenery to get there and for the inn's breathtaking backdrop towards Raasay and Skye. The alternative route, along the single-track lane winding around the coast from just south of Shieldaig, has equally glorious sea loch (and then sea) views nearly all the way. The no-nonsense, welcoming bar has a woodburning stove, exposed stone walls, upholstered pine furnishings and a stone floor; An Teallach Crofters Pale Ale and Isle of Skye Red on handpump, over 50 malt whiskies and a good, varied wine list; board games. The tables in the shoreside garden enjoy magnificent views. There's a new outdoor eating area for summer use. Some disabled facilities.

Free house ~ Licensee Judith Fish ~ Real ale ~ Open 11am-11.30pm (midnight Sat); 12.30-11.30 Sun ~ Bar food 12-9 ~ Children welcome till 8.30pm ~ Dogs welcome ~ Wi-fi ~ Live music first Sun of month 3-6pm ~ Bedrooms: £130

EDINBURGH   NT2573
Bow Bar
(0131) 226 7667
West Bow; EH1 2HH

Cosy, enjoyably unpretentious pub with an excellent choice of well kept beers

This is a cheerfully traditional alehouse and a haven of old-fashioned drinking with a splendid range of real ales. The rectangular bar has an impressive carved mahogany gantry, and from the tall 1920s founts on the bar counter, knowledgeable staff dispense eight well kept real ales: regulars such as Alechemy Bowhemia Pale, Cromarty Happy Chappy and Stewart 80/- and five quickly changing guests; regular beer festivals. Also on offer are some 320 malts, including five 'malts of the moment', a good choice of rums, 60 international bottled beers and 20 gins. The walls are covered with a fine collection of enamel advertising signs and handsome antique brewery mirrors, and there are sturdy leatherette wall seats and café-style bar seats around heavy narrow tables on the wooden floor. Food – lunchtime-only – consists of pies. No children allowed.

Free house ~ Licensee Mike Smith ~ Real ale ~ Open 12-midnight; 12.30-11.30 Sun ~ Bar food 12-3 ~ Dogs welcome ~ Wi-fi

RATHO   NT1470
Bridge
(0131) 333 1320 – www.bridgeinn.com
Baird Road; EH28 8RA

Canalside inn with cosy bar and airy restaurant, a thoughtful choice of drinks and enjoyable food; attractive bedrooms

This is a charming inn next to the Union Canal. The cosy bar has an open fire with leather armchairs to either side and a larger area with a two-way fireplace and upholstered tub and cushioned wooden chairs on pale boards around a mix of tables; a contemporary and elegant dining room leads off. Belhaven St Andrews Ale, Bridge Friendly Fire ISA and a changing guest from Inveralmond on handpump, 36 wines by the glass and 50 malt whiskies. The main restaurant is light and airy with up-to-date pale oak settles, antique-style chairs and big windows overlooking the water. Seats on the terrace share the same view. A unique part of the friendly licensees' business here is their summer restaurant barge, which travels from the inn down the canal to the Almondell Aqueduct over the River Almond; there's a full kitchen team on board and you can have lunch, afternoon tea or supper. The particularly good food uses their own pork and lamb and produce grown in their walled garden.

Free house ~ Licensees Graham and Rachel Bucknall ~ Real ale ~ Open 9am-11pm; 11am-midnight Fri, Sat; 11-11 Sun ~ Bar food 12-3, 5-9; 12-9 Sat; 12-8 Sun ~ Restaurant ~ Children welcome but not in bar after 8pm ~ Dogs allowed in bar ~ Wi-fi ~ Live music monthly ~ Bedrooms: £90

THORNHILL   NS6600

Lion & Unicorn

(01786) 850204 – www.lion-unicorn.co.uk
Main Street (A873); FK8 3PJ

Busy, interesting pub with emphasis on its home-made food; friendly staff and bedrooms

Parts of this neatly kept inn date from 1635 and there's an original fireplace with a log fire in a high brazier almost big enough to drive a car into. The back bar has pubby character, some exposed stone walls, wooden flooring and stools lined along the counter where they keep An Teallach Ale and Caledonian Deuchars IPA on handpump and several wines by the glass; log fires. This opens to a games room with a pool table, juke box, fruit machine, darts, TV and board games. The more restauranty-feeling beamed and carpeted front room is traditionally furnished and set for dining; background music. Outside there are benches in a gravelled garden and a lawn with a play area.

Free house ~ Licensee Fiona Stevenson ~ Real ale ~ Open 12-midnight (1am Fri, Sat) ~ Bar food 12-9 ~ Restaurant ~ Children welcome ~ Dogs allowed in bar ~ Wi-fi ~ Bedrooms: £75

DOG FRIENDLY HOTELS, INNS AND B&Bs

ACHILTIBUIE   NC0208

Summer Isles Hotel

(01854) 622282 – www.summerisleshotel.co.uk
Achiltibuie, Ullapool, Ross-shire IV26 2YQ

£140–£250; 11 comfortable rooms; also self-catering cottage. Beautifully placed above the sea towards the end of a very long and lonely road and with plenty of surrounding walks; warm, friendly, well furnished hotel with delicious set menus using fresh local ingredients, lovely puddings and excellent selection of scottish cheeses; also a locals' bar well stocked with malt whiskies. Closed November-March. Dogs allowed in most bedrooms only (not to be left unattended); £20 per stay.

ALYTH   NO2448

Tigh Na Leigh

(01828) 632372 – www.tighnaleigh.com
22-24 Airlie Street, Alyth, Perthshire PH11 8AJ

£110; 5 comfortably furnished, well equipped rooms (all with spa baths). Former Victorian doctor's house with friendly, helpful owners, an informal and relaxing atmosphere and interesting contemporary decor; three different lounges – one with a log fire, one with a TV and another with books, daily papers and a computer; super breakfasts with home-made preserves, and good meals using local, seasonal produce (some home-grown) in conservatory dining room; resident cats Tom and Bunny; landscaped gardens and dog walks in nearby park. Closed December, January. Dogs allowed in all bedrooms and public areas, but not in dining room; towel; £7.50.

ARDEONAIG

NN6635

Ardeonaig Hotel

(01567) 820351 – www.ardeonaighotel.co.uk
Ardeonaig, Killin, Perthshire FK21 8SY

£120; 17 rooms including 2 cottage suites and 5 shielings (thatched huts). Extended 17th-c farmhouse on south shore of Loch Tay, with log fire in snug and lounge, library with fine views, lunchtime bar food and more formal evening dining using fresh local produce; salmon fishing rights on the loch – trout fishing too – a drying and rod room, shooting/stalking can also be arranged, lots of surrounding walks. Dogs allowed in all bedrooms (not to be left unattended) and public areas except restaurant; £15 per stay.

ARDUAINE

NM7910

Loch Melfort Hotel

(01852) 200233 – www.lochmelfort.co.uk
Arduaine, Oban, Argyll PA34 4XG

£158; 25 well equipped rooms with stunning sea views over Asknish Bay – 5 in main house, rest in cedar wing. Comfortable modern hotel popular in summer with passing yachtsmen (own moorings), nautical charts and marine glasses in airy bar, good food in bistro and restaurant including excellent local seafood; pleasant foreshore walks, 17 acres of grounds including outstanding springtime woodland gardens (National Trust); two resident dogs. Closed December-January except Christmas and New Year. Dogs allowed in six ground-floor rooms only; £9.

AUCHENCAIRN

NX8249

Balcary Bay Hotel

(01556) 640217 – www.balcary-bay-hotel.co.uk
Auchencairn, Castle Douglas, Dumfriesshire DG7 1QZ

£160; 20 rooms with fine views. Once a smugglers' haunt, this charming hotel has wonderful views over the bay, neat grounds running down to the water, comfortable public rooms (one with a log fire), a relaxed atmosphere and good food; lots of walks. Closed December-February. Dogs allowed in bedrooms only.

BALQUHIDDER

NN4719

Monachyle Mhor Hotel

(01877) 384622 – www.mhor.net
Balquhidder, Lochearnhead, Perthshire FK19 8PQ

Hotel £195; 16 prettily furnished rooms with fine views, some overlooking Voil and Doine lochs. Remote 18th-c farmhouse hotel four miles west of Balquhidder on 2,000-acre estate with good food using own game, cured meats and herbs; private fishing and stalking for guests; resident black lab, Black Betty, and jack russell, Tinker. Closed two weeks January. They also run the cheaper Mhor 84 motel at the head of the glen, with seven bedrooms, a games room and all-day food. Dogs allowed in four bedrooms, bar and lounge; £10.

BRIDGE OF CALLY   NO1451

Bridge of Cally Hotel

(01250) 886231 – www.bridgeofcallyhotel.com
Bridge of Cally, Blairgowrie, Perthshire PH10 7JJ

£100; 18 rooms. Adjoining 1,500 acres of private moorland, this former drovers' inn is a friendly, family-run place with good value home-made food including seasonal game in the popular restaurant and a comfortable chatty bar; salmon fishing, stalking, shooting, golf and skiing are all locally available. Closed December except Christmas and New Year. Well behaved dogs allowed in four bedrooms and bar; £10.

CALLANDER   NN6207

Highland Guesthouse

(01877) 330269 – www.thehighlandguesthouse.co.uk
8 South Church Street, Callander, Perthshire FK17 8BN

£75; 10 rooms. Georgian house just off the main street with friendly owners, homely residents' lounge and cosy bar, good scottish breakfasts; pleasant back garden (no dogs), plenty of surrounding walks and outdoor activities. Small, well behaved dogs allowed in bedrooms, but not in public rooms; £5 per stay.

CALLANDER   NN6208

Poppies

(01877) 330329 – www.poppieshotel.com
Leny Road, Callander, Perthshire FK17 8AL

£95; 9 comfortable rooms. Small private hotel with excellent food in popular and attractive candlelit dining room including a very good value early evening menu, comfortable lounge, cosy bar with over 120 malt whiskies and good wine list, helpful friendly owners, seats in the front garden. Closed most of January. Dogs allowed in two bedrooms only.

EAST HAUGH   NN9556

East Haugh House

(01796) 473121 – www.easthaugh.co.uk
East Haugh, Pitlochry, Perthshire PH16 5TE

£130–£150; 13 rooms – 5 in converted bothy and 1 with open fire; also 2-bedroom lodge (can also be self-catering). Family-run turreted stone house with lots of character, delightful fishing-themed bar, house party atmosphere and particularly good food including local seafood, game in season and home-grown vegetables cooked by chef-proprietor; excellent shooting, stalking and salmon and trout fishing on surrounding local estates; plenty of good walks nearby. Closed Christmas. Dogs allowed in three ground-floor bedrooms and lodge, bar and snug; £10.

EDINBURGH

NT2776

Malmaison

(0131) 468 5000 – www.malmaison.com
1 Tower Place, Leith, Edinburgh EH6 7DB

£120; 100 stylish, well equipped rooms and suites, some with harbour views. Converted baronial-style seamen's mission – thoroughly refurbished in 2016 – in the fashionable docks area of Leith, with very good food in the brasserie with terrace and a smart cocktail bar; friendly service, 24-hour gym, free parking, dog walks in nearby Leith Links. Dogs allowed in all bedrooms and lobby; bed and bowl; £10.

ERISKA

NM9043

Isle of Eriska Hotel

(01631) 720371 – www.eriska-hotel.co.uk
Ledaig, Oban, Argyll PA37 1SD

£350; 26 comfortable rooms; also self-catering. In a wonderful position on a small island linked by bridge to the mainland, this impressive baronial hotel has a very relaxed country house atmosphere, log fires, pretty drawing room, Michelin-starred restaurant, comprehensive wine list and exemplary service; leisure complex with indoor swimming pool, sauna and gym, nine-hole golf course, clay-pigeon shooting and lovely surrounding walks, plenty of wildlife including tame badgers who come nightly to the library door for bread and milk; one resident labrador. Closed January. Dogs allowed in most bedrooms (not to be left unattended), not in public rooms; towel and treats.

FORTROSE

NH7256

Anderson

(01381) 620236 – www.theanderson.co.uk
Union Street, Fortrose, Inverness, Inverness-shire IV10 8TD

£99; 9 rooms. Seaside hotel with friendly, enthusiastic owners, two homely bars with a vast collection of international bottled beers and 250 malt whiskies, a light, airy dining room with an open fire and good international food using the best local ingredients (smashing fish and shellfish); walks on the nearby beach. Closed mid November to mid December. Dogs allowed in some bedrooms and bar.

GAIRLOCH

NB8175

Old Inn

(01445) 712006 – www.theoldinn.net
Flowerdale Glen, Gairloch, Ross-shire IV21 2BD

£120; 17 rooms. Quietly positioned old inn in charming waterside setting with a chatty and relaxed public bar serving their own-brewed beers and over 20 malt whiskies; paintings and murals on exposed stone walls, traditional tables and chairs, a warming woodburning stove and another woodburner in the residents' lounge; well liked food using local fish and game, and they also smoke their own meat, fish and cheese; you can sit by trees beside the stream and there are good walks from the door. Closed early November to early March. Dogs allowed in some bedrooms and bar, but not residents' lounge; bed and bowl; £10.

GATEHOUSE OF FLEET
NX6054
Cally Palace
(01557) 814341 – www.callypalace.co.uk
Gatehouse of Fleet, Castle Douglas, Dumfriesshire DG7 2DL

£150; 56 rooms – 31 in main house, 25 in newer forest wing. 18th-c country mansion, a hotel since 1934, with marble fireplaces and ornate ceilings in the public rooms, relaxed cocktail bar and sunny conservatory, enjoyable food in elegant dining room (smart dress required), evening pianist and helpful, friendly staff; 18-hole golf course, croquet and tennis, indoor leisure complex with heated swimming pool; plenty of walks. Closed January and weekdays first half of February. Dogs allowed in all bedrooms and foyer; £5.

GIFFORD
NT5367
Tweeddale Arms Hotel
(01620) 810240 – www.tweeddalearmshotel.com
High Street, Gifford, Haddington, East Lothian EH41 4QU

£90; 14 rooms. Civilised late 17th-c inn in quiet village; comfortable sofas and chairs in tranquil lounge, dining room with wide choice of good daily changing food and charming service; nice walks nearby. Dogs allowed in some bedrooms and bar, not in lounge or restaurant; £10.

GLASGOW
NS5567
Hotel du Vin
(0141) 339 2001 – www.hotelduvin.com
1 Devonshire Gardens, Glasgow G12 0UX

£140; 49 opulent rooms. Elegant, cosseting hotel a little way out from the city centre; luxurious Victorian furnishings, fresh flowers, exemplary staff and fine modern cooking in the stylish restaurant (afternoon tea too), plus a bar, cigar shack and whisky room; parks nearby for dogs to exercise. Dogs allowed in all bedrooms and bar; bedding and bowl; £10.

GLASGOW
NS5865
Malmaison
(0141) 572 1000 – www.malmaison.com
278 West George Street, Glasgow G2 4LL

£120; 72 well equipped, individually decorated rooms, some with french windows. Stylishly converted former greek orthodox 19th-c church, striking central wrought-iron staircase, a well stocked bar in vaulted crypt and enjoyable modern food in attractive brasserie, relaxed contemporary atmosphere and friendly staff; nearby park for exercising dogs. Dogs allowed in all bedrooms and in public rooms not serving food; mat and bowls; £10.

GLENFINNAN

NM9080

Glenfinnan House Hotel

(01397) 722235 – www.glenfinnanhouse.com
Glenfinnan, Fort William, Inverness-shire PH37 4LT

£155; 14 homely rooms. In lovely grounds beside Loch Shiel (plenty of surrounding walks), this Victorian hotel has a comfortable drawing room, a bustling bar with traditional furnishings and local music, log fires, particularly good breakfasts, light bar lunches and french/scottish-influenced evening meals using the best local produce, and genuinely friendly, helpful service. Closed November to mid March. Dogs allowed in all bedrooms and public areas, but not restaurant; £8.

GLENROTHES

NO2902

Balbirnie House

(01592) 610066 – www.balbirnie.co.uk
Markinch, Glenrothes, Fife KY7 6NE

£190; 31 traditionally furnished rooms, plus 1 triplex. Handsome Georgian country house hotel in 400-acre park landscaped in Capability Brown style; fresh flowers, open fires and antiques in gracious public rooms, good bistro food or more creative cooking in evening Orangery restaurant, comprehensive wine list. Dogs allowed in all bedrooms, but not public areas; £20.

INNERLEITHEN

NT3236

Traquair Arms

(01896) 830229 – www.traquairarmshotel.co.uk
Innerleithen, Peebles, Peeblesshire EH44 6PD

£90; 15 comfortable rooms; also self-catering cottages in converted stables. Friendly modernised inn with traditional scottish food in bars and attractive dining room, two bars serving over 30 malt whiskies and good Traquair ale brewed nearby; pretty and recently refubished garden and lots of walks in the surrounding area. Closed two weeks January. Dogs allowed in two bedrooms and bar, but not restaurant; £10.

INVERNESS

NH6342

Loch Ness Country House Hotel

(01463) 230512 – www.lochnesscountryhousehotel.co.uk
Loch Ness Road, Inverness, Inverness-shire IV3 8JN

£195; 11 rooms including 6 suites with own lounge and 2 garden cottages. This is an 18th-c italianate mansion in six acres of well tended gardens and woodland, a short walk from the River Ness and Caledonian Canal; comfortably elegant with log fires and fresh flowers, enterprising food using local ingredients (some home-grown), generous breakfasts, around 200 malt whiskies; lots of walks and golf courses nearby. Closed first two weeks January. Dogs allowed in garden cottages only; £10.

ISLE OF GIGHA

NR6448

Gigha Hotel

(01583) 505254 – www.gigha.org.uk
Isle of Gigha, Argyll PA41 7AA

£90; 12 rooms; also self-catering cottages. Traditional hotel overlooking Ardminish Bay towards Kintyre, small and attractive with bustling bar (popular with yachtsmen and locals), neatly kept, comfortable residents' lounge and restaurant serving local seafood; fields for dogs to exercise in. Dogs allowed in some bedrooms and bar; £7 (maximum £21).

ISLE OF IONA

SM2824

Argyll Hotel

(01681) 700334 – www.argyllhoteliona.co.uk
Iona, Argyll PA76 6SJ

£167; 17 simply furnished rooms, some with water views. Locally run former croft house looking over the Sound of Iona (beach and hill walks just a few minutes away), with three traditionally furnished lounges, a TV room, log fires and lots of books, good wholesome food in the dining room using seasonal organic produce from their kitchen garden and local crofts, and a friendly, relaxed atmosphere. Closed end October to end March. Dogs allowed in all bedrooms, not in dining areas; beanbag bed and bowl; £15 per stay.

ISLE OF ISLAY

NR2558

Port Charlotte Hotel

(01496) 850360 – www.portcharlottehotel.co.uk
Port Charlotte, Isle of Islay, Argyll PA48 7TU

£210; 10 rooms, 9 with sea views. Made up of former cottages by the water in a lovely Georgian village with sweeping views over Loch Indaal, this bustling hotel has a civilised bare-boards pubby bar with padded wall seats and modern art, a comfortable back bar, a separate restaurant and roomy conservatory, an exceptional collection of about 250 Islay malt whiskies, enjoyable food using local seafood and good breakfasts; walks nearby and on the beach. Well behaved dogs allowed in all bedrooms only.

ISLE OF WHITHORN

NX4736

Steam Packet Inn

(01988) 500334 – www.thesteampacketinn.biz
Harbour Row, Isle of Whithorn, Newton Stewart, Dumfriesshire DG8 8LL

£80; 7 rooms, most with harbour views. Friendly family-run inn with big picture windows overlooking the picturesque working harbour; inside, you'll find a comfortable low-ceilinged bar with plush banquettes, stripped-stone walls and a woodburner; a lower beamed dining room with another woodburner, rugs on wooden flooring and quite a choice of bar food, plus a small eating area off the lounge bar and an airy conservatory leading into the garden; you can walk from here to the remains of St Ninian's kirk. Dogs allowed in all bedrooms, bars and conservatory.

ISLE ORNSAY   NG7012

Eilean Iarmain

(01471) 833332 – www.eileaniarmain.co.uk
Isle Ornsay, Isle of Skye, Inverness-shire IV43 8QR

£195; 16 individual rooms including 4 suites (those in main hotel are the best), all with fine views; also self-catering cottages. Sparkling white hotel on sheltered bay overlooking the Sound of Sleat, some Gaelic-speaking staff and locals, cheerful bar with open fire, dining conservatory and restaurant with lovely sea views, and very good food including local fish and seafood, real ales from Skye plus own range of whiskies. Well behaved dogs allowed in three bedrooms, bar and lounge; £10.

ISLE ORNSAY   NG7015

Kinloch Lodge

(01471) 833333 – www.kinloch-lodge.co.uk
Isle Ornsay, Isle of Skye, Inverness-shire IV43 8QY

£340; 19 comfortable rooms. Surrounded by rugged mountain scenery at the head of Loch Na Dal, this charming white-painted stone hotel has a relaxed atmosphere in its traditionally furnished and attractive drawing rooms, antiques, portraits, flowers, log fires, a whisky bar and first class imaginative food; cookery courses; plenty of surrounding walks; children by arrangement. Closed two weeks January. Dogs welcome in all bedrooms only; £20 (£10 winter).

KELSO   NT7233

Ednam House Hotel

(01573) 224168 – www.ednamhouse.com
Bridge Street, Kelso, Roxburghshire TD5 7HT

£150; 32 rooms including 2 suites. Large Georgian manor house by the River Tweed with three acres of gardens; three distinctive lounges with antiques and plenty of comfortable seating, good choice of whiskies in log-fire bar, excellent food in large candlelit dining room overlooking the river, a lovely informal atmosphere and particularly good, friendly service; shooting and fishing by arrangement. Dogs allowed in all bedrooms and everywhere except restaurant; blanket and treats.

KILBERRY   NR7164

Kilberry Inn

(01880) 770223 – www.kilberryinn.com
Kilberry, Tarbert, Argyll PA29 6YD

£215 including dinner; 5 ground-floor rooms. Homely and warmly welcoming inn on west coast of the Knapdale peninsula with fine sea views, old-fashioned character, very good traditional home cooking relying on fresh local ingredients; resident jack russell. Closed January to mid March, weekdays November, December. Dogs allowed in one bedroom only; bedding and biscuits.

KILCHRENAN

NN0824

Ardanaiseig

(01866) 833333 – www.ardanaiseig.com
Kilchrenan, Taynuilt, Argyll PA35 1HE

£218; 16 lovely, big, themed rooms with views of the loch or gardens, plus self-catering boat shed and cottage. Handsome Scottish baronial mansion quietly set in its own natural gardens and woodland right on Loch Awe; antiques-filled reception areas, comfortable squashy sofas, bold colour scheme and décor, marvellous modern cooking, super afternoon tea and very friendly young staff; fishing, archery, photography and other activities can be arranged. Sometimes closed January-March; check website. Dogs allowed in all bedrooms and everywhere except dining room; £20.

KILCHRENAN

NN0421

Taychreggan Hotel

(01866) 833211 – www.taychregganhotel.co.uk
Kilchrenan, Taynuilt, Argyll PA35 1HQ

£149; 18 rooms. Civilised hotel (originally a drovers' inn) on the shores of Loch Awe with fine garden and 40 acres of grounds where dogs can walk; comfortable airy bar serving light lunchtime and early evening food, polite, efficient staff, good dinners in restaurant, a carefully chosen wine list and dozens of malt whiskies; activities such as clay-pigeon shooting, fishing and falconry can be arranged. Closed January. Dogs allowed in all bedrooms and some public areas; £10.

KILNINVER

NM8523

Knipoch Hotel

(01852) 316251 – www.knipochhotel.co.uk
Knipoch, Oban, Argyll PA34 4QT

£165; 19 rooms. Well kept Georgian hotel in lovely countryside overlooking Loch Feochan; fine family portraits, log fires, fresh flowers and polished furniture in comfortable lounges, dining rooms and bar, carefully chosen wines and fine selection of whiskies (some pre-war), excellent seasonal food including their own smoked salmon; lovely walks from the door. Closed December, January. Dogs allowed in some bedrooms and reception, but not other public areas; £10 per stay.

KINCLAVEN BY STANLEY

NO1436

Ballathie House Hotel

(01250) 883268 – www.ballathiehousehotel.com
Stanley, Perth, Perthshire PH1 4QN

£120; 53 traditional rooms, some luxurious and some in newer riverside building and separate (cheaper) sportsman's lodge. Turreted Victorian mansion on vast estate with fine salmon fishing on the River Tay (lodge accommodation and facilities for fishermen) and plenty of sporting opportunities; comfortable and relaxed drawing room, separate lounge, dining room and bar, good modern scottish cooking, croquet, putting and lots of space for dogs to walk. Dogs allowed in most bedrooms and some public areas; £20 per stay.

KIRK YETHOLM

NT8228

Border Hotel

(01573) 420237 – www.borderhotelyetholm.co.uk
The Green, Kirk Yetholm, Kelso, Roxburghshire TD5 8PQ

£95; 5 rooms. Welcoming and comfortable village-green hotel at one end of the Pennine Way and start of Scottish National Trail; cheerfully unpretentious bar with beams, flagstones, a log fire, Borders scenery etchings and murals; snug side rooms and a comfortable lounge with another fire, neat conservatory and spacious dining room with fishing-themed décor and enjoyable food; walks from the front door. Dogs allowed in all bedrooms and bar; £5.

KIRKTON OF GLENISLA

NO2160

Glenisla Hotel

(01575) 582223 – www.glenisla-hotel.com
Glenisla, Blairgowrie, Perthshire PH11 8PH

£80; 6 recently refurbished cosy rooms. Old coaching inn in lovely quiet position with lots of country pursuits all around; convivial, traditionally furnished beamed bar with open fire, drawing room with comfortable sofas, flowers and books, games room, enjoyable seasonal food and hearty scottish breakfasts in elegant dining room, well kept real ales. Dogs allowed in all bedrooms and bar (except at mealtimes); £5.

MEIKLEOUR

NO1539

Meikleour Arms

(01250) 883206 – www.meikleourarms.co.uk
Meikleour, Perthshire PH2 6EB

£110; 9 bedrooms including 4 in new annexe; also self-catering cottages. Enjoyable country inn, part of the Meikleour Estate, with a historic and spectacular beech hedge nearby – it's the tallest in the world; there's a main bar with comfortable seating, fishing/shooting pictures, open wood fires, scottish beers, 50 malt whiskies and attentive, friendly staff; also a more formal, tartan-carpeted dining room and seating outside in the garden with distant Highland views; interesting food using produce from their own walled garden and the Estate, and good breakfasts; plenty to see and do nearby – including one of the best salmon beats in Scotland. Dogs allowed in all bedrooms and bar.

MELROSE

NT5433

Burts Hotel

(01896) 822285 – www.burtshotel.co.uk
Market Square, Melrose, Roxburghshire TD6 9PN

£140; 20 smart little rooms. Welcoming 18th-c family-run hotel close to abbey ruins in beautifully unspoilt small town; warming fire, classic pubby furniture on carpet, scottish prints on pale green walls and real ales, farm cider and some 80 malt whiskies served by notably helpful staff; the restaurant is elegant and the food most enjoyable (good breakfasts too). Closed one week January. Dogs allowed in some bedrooms and bar-bistro; blanket and walks map.

NEWTON STEWART

NX4165

Creebridge House

(01671) 402121 – www.creebridge.co.uk
Creebridge, Newton Stewart, Dumfriesshire DG8 6NP

£116; 18 rooms. Attractive country house hotel in three acres of gardens; relaxed friendly atmosphere, open fire in comfortable drawing room, cheerful bar with woodburner and wide choice of good food including fine local fish and seafood in garden restaurant; forest walks nearby. Usually closed three weeks January. Dogs allowed in some bedrooms and bar.

NEWTON STEWART

NX4266

Kirroughtree House Hotel

(01671) 402141 – www.kirroughtreehousehotel.co.uk
Newton Stewart, Dumfriesshire DG8 6AN

£120; 16 comfortable rooms with fine views, some with own sitting room. Early 18th-c mansion with lavish Victorian/Edwardian extension, in six acres of grounds close to Galloway Forest Park; oak-panelled lounge with open fire, oil paintings, antiques and french windows leading out to the garden, elegant dining rooms and excellent food, and particularly helpful, personal service; pitch and putt, croquet and plenty to do nearby. Dogs allowed in lower ground-floor bedrooms, but not in public areas; £10 per stay.

NEWTONMORE

NN6892

Crubenbeg House

(01540) 673300 – www.crubenbeghouse.com
Falls of Truim, Newtonmore, Inverness-shire PH20 1BE

£85; 4 well equipped rooms. Carefully run guesthouse with wonderful views from all rooms, charming, friendly owners, lots of teddy bears (Mrs England collects them), open fire in comfortable, homely guest lounge and good breakfasts in light and airy dining room; can arrange packed lunches and light suppers (not Mon or Tues evenings, or July, August); lots of surrounding walks and activities. Dogs allowed in all bedrooms (not to be left unattended) and other areas, but not in restaurant.

PITLOCHRY

NN9162

Killiecrankie Hotel

(01796) 473220 – www.killiecrankiehotel.co.uk
Killiecrankie, Pitlochry, Perthshire PH16 5LG

From £280 with dinner; 10 spotless rooms. Comfortable country hotel in four acres of grounds with splendid mountain views; traditional, green-panelled bar, cosy sitting room with books and games, a relaxed atmosphere and friendly owners; excellent, well presented, locally sourced food and good wine list in elegant restaurant and less formal bistro; two resident cocker spaniels; fine nearby walks. Closed January to mid March. Dogs allowed in some bedrooms (must not be left unattended) and bar; £10.

PORT APPIN
NM9045
Airds Hotel
(01631) 730236 – www.airds-hotel.com
Port Appin, Appin, Argyll PA38 4DF

£340 including dinner; 11 lovely rooms including 3 suites; also 2 self-catering cottages. Instantly relaxing 18th-c inn with fine views of Loch Linnhe and the island of Lismore, blissfully comfortable day rooms, professional, courteous staff and charming owners; the food is exceptional (as is the wine list), there are lots of surrounding walks, with more on Lismore (small boat every hour), clay-pigeon shooting and riding. Usually closed first two weeks December. Dogs allowed in all bedrooms (must not be left unattended), not in public areas; £10.

PORTPATRICK
NX0252
Knockinaam Lodge
(01776) 810471 – www.knockinaamlodge.com
Portpatrick, Stranraer, Dumfriesshire DG9 9AD

£190; 10 individual rooms. Neatly kept little country house hotel with comfortable, pretty rooms, open fires, wonderful food and friendly, caring service, panelled whisky bar with over 120 malts; 30 acres of grounds stretching down to secluded beach, dramatic surroundings and fine cliff walks. Dogs allowed in three bedrooms, but not public areas; £20 per stay.

SCARISTA
NG0092
Scarista House
(01859) 550238 – www.scaristahouse.com
Scarista, Harris, Isle of Harris, Inverness-shire HS3 3HX

£235; 3 rooms in main house, 3 suites in annexe, all with sea views; self-catering cottage. Wonderful wild countryside and empty beaches surround this small isolated hotel (a former manse), which has antiques-furnished rooms, open fires, plenty of books and CDs (no TV) and a warm friendly atmosphere; impressive wine list and good food in candlelit dining room using organic home-grown vegetables and herbs, hand-made cheeses, their own eggs, home-made bread, cakes, yoghurt and marmalade, and lots of fish and shellfish; excellent for wildlife, walks and fishing; resident pug, Maud, spaniel, Tess, and Misty the cat. Closed three weeks October-November, also mid December-March. Dogs allowed in all bedrooms and one sitting room.

SCONE
NO1526
Murrayshall House
(01738) 551171 – www.murrayshall.co.uk
Scone, Perth, Perthshire PH2 7PH

£150; 41 rooms including 16 suites, plus lodge sleeping 6. Handsome mansion set in 350 acres of park and woodland where dogs may walk, very popular with golfers (it has two courses); comfortable elegant public rooms including two bars and restaurant with imaginative food and good wines; a friendly, relaxed atmosphere and helpful staff. Usually closed first two weeks January. Dogs allowed in some bedrooms.

SCOURIE

NC1544

Scourie Hotel

(01971) 502396 – www.scourie-hotel.co.uk
Scourie, Lairg, Sutherland IV27 4SX

£125; 23 rooms, some with views to Scourie Bay. A haven for anglers, with 46 exclusive beats on 25,000-acre estate; snug bar and cocktail bar, two comfortable lounges and good food using plenty of local game and fish in smart dining room; fine walks on the doorstep. Closed October-April. Dogs allowed in all bedrooms, lounge and part of bar (on lead); £10 (maximum £40).

SHIEL BRIDGE

NG9319

Kintail Lodge Hotel

(01599) 511275 – www.kintaillodgehotel.co.uk
Glenshiel, Kyle, Ross-shire IV40 8HL

£150; 12 big rooms. Pleasantly informal and fairly simple former shooting lodge on Loch Duich, with magnificent views, two acres of gardens, residents' lounge bar and comfortable sitting room, good well prepared food including local seafood in conservatory restaurant and fine collection of malt whiskies; there's also a separate locals' bar, bunkhouse and trekkers' lodge; good variety of local walks. Closed ten days before Christmas. Dogs allowed in all bedrooms and public areas except breakfast room and restaurant.

SHIELDAIG

NG8153

Tigh an Eilean

(01520) 755251 – www.tighaneilean.co.uk
Shieldaig, Strathcarron, Ross-shire IV54 8XN

£140; 11 tranquil rooms. Attractive hotel in outstanding position with lovely view of pine-covered Shieldaig Island and the sea, and within easy reach of NTS Torridon Estate, Beinn Eighe nature reserve and the Applecross peninsula; the two-storey bar (separate from the hotel) is gently contemporary and relaxed with lots of timbering, scottish ales and a dozen wines by the glass; delicious food, including local fish and seafood, is served in the first-floor dining room or on the decked balcony with its magnificent loch and village view; they also have several sitting rooms with guidebooks, a restaurant and seats in a sheltered little courtyard. Closed January. Dogs allowed in all bedrooms, one sitting room and bar.

SLIGACHAN

NG4829

Sligachan Hotel

(01478) 650204 – www.sligachan.co.uk
Sligachan, Isle of Skye, Inverness-shire IV47 8SW

£140; 21 bright, comfortable bedrooms; also self-catering cottages, bunkhouse and camping. Stunningly set hotel in the heart of the Cuillin mountains with fantastic walks from the doorstep; there's a spacious, pine-clad main bar with tartan carpeting, hearty food, own-brewed ales and over 400 malt whiskies; also a more sedate lounge bar with leather armchairs and a coal fire, and a separate restaurant for evening meals (open to non-residents too);

an interesting little museum charts the history of the hotel and its famous climbers. Closed mid November to February. Dogs allowed in three bedrooms and bars; bed, bowl and bone; £5.

SPEAN BRIDGE   NN2490
Letterfinlay Lodge Hotel
(01397) 712622 – www.letterfinlaylodgehotel.co.uk
Letterfinlay, Spean Bridge, Inverness-shire PH34 4DZ

£109; 18 rooms including 3 suites. Secluded and genteel country house on the edge of Loch Lochy, with picture window in extensive modern bar overlooking the water, comfortable reading room, good popular food in sun lounge and conservatory, friendly attentive service; grounds run down through rhododendrons to the jetty and the loch (dogs may walk here), fishing can be arranged. Dogs allowed in one bedroom only; £20 per stay.

SPITTAL OF GLENSHEE   NO0971
Dalmunzie Castle Hotel
(01250) 885224 – www.dalmunzie.com
Glenshee, Blairgowrie, Perthshire PH10 7QG

£205; 17 individual rooms with fine views and named after local families. Old-fashioned turreted Victorian shooting lodge peacefully set in huge estate among spectacular mountains, plenty of walks nearby, golf course, tennis and fishing; comfortable drawing room, open fires in two other lounges, cosy, informal bar and antiques-filled library, good inventive country house cooking in candlelit restaurant using local produce, and hearty breakfasts. Dogs allowed in all bedrooms (must be well behaved) and some public areas; £10.

STEIN   NG2656
Stein Inn
(01470) 592362 – www.steininn.com
Stein, Waternish, Isle of Skye IV55 8GA

£77; 5 rooms, all with sea views; self-catering apartment too. Skye's oldest inn standing just above a sheltered inlet with views out to the Hebrides and quite glorious sunsets; the unpretentious bar has much character, sturdy country furnishings, flagstones, partly panelled stripped-stone walls, a double-sided stove, scottish ales and over 135 malt whiskies; smartly uniformed staff serve a short menu of good, simple food using local fish and highland meat – breakfasts are tasty too. Dogs allowed in all bedrooms and bar (not 6–9.30pm); £5 per stay.

STRONTIAN   NM8161
Kilcamb Lodge Hotel
(01967) 402257 – www.kilcamblodge.co.uk
Strontian, Acharacle, Argyll PH36 4HY

£185; 11 country house-style rooms. Warm, friendly little hotel in 22 acres by Loch Sunart, with log fires in two comfortable lounges, carefully cooked food using fresh ingredients, good choice of malt whiskies in small bar and a relaxed atmosphere; dogs welcome in grounds and on hotel's secluded beach, resident terrier, Spike; no young children. Closed January. Dogs allowed in five bedrooms only; bed, towel and treats; dog-sitting available; £10.

SWINTON
Wheatsheaf
NT8347

(01890) 860257 – www.wheatsheaf-swinton.co.uk
The Green, Swinton, Berkwickshire TD11 3JJ

£119; 11 comfortable bedrooms and cottage. A restaurant-with-rooms in a pretty Borders village surrounded by rolling countryside and only a few miles from the River Tweed; there's a small bar with armchairs, oak settles and an open fire, a relaxed lounge bar and a conservatory as well as the more formal restaurant with excellent cooking; attentive, friendly staff and seating outside. Dogs allowed in some bedrooms, cottage and bar; £5.

TARBERT
Stonefield Castle Hotel
NR8671

(01880) 820836 – www.bespokehotels.com/stonefieldcastle

£155; 32 traditional rooms. With wonderful Loch Fyne views and 60 acres of surrounding wooded grounds where dogs can walk, this 1837 baronial mansion has a panelled lounge bar and other comfortable sitting areas, good food and super views in the restaurant, and a separate snooker room; fishing and horse-riding can be arranged. Dogs allowed in all bedrooms and public areas, but not restaurant; bedding, bowl and treats; £10 per stay.

THORNHILL
Trigony House
NX8893

(01848) 218127 – www.trigonyhotel.co.uk
Closeburn, Thornhill, Dumfriesshire DG3 5EZ

£120; 9 rooms. In four acres of garden and woodland, this friendly Edwardian shooting lodge is now a country house hotel with wonderful walks a short drive away; a cosy lounge and bar with open fires, traditional furniture and games, light bar lunches (by reservation) and delicious, interesting food using home-grown produce in the pretty dining room with french windows on to the garden, and hearty breakfasts; resident miniature daschund, Kit, golden retriever, Roxy, and yorkie/pug cross, Lola; new spa (autumn 2016) with treatment room and outdoor hot tub, and they can arrange riding, falconry, shooting, fishing and cycling. Dogs allowed in all bedrooms and throughout hotel except dining room; welcome pack including treat, toy and walks map; dog-sitting available; £9.50.

TIRORAN
Tiroran House Hotel
NM4727

(01681) 705232 – www.tiroran.com
Tiroran, Isle of Mull, Argyll PA69 6ES

£185–£235; 11 comfortable rooms, some in annexe; also 2 self-catering cottages. Friendly hunting lodge in 56 acres of lovely grounds on the shores of Loch Scridain (lots of walks); two cosy sitting rooms, a log fire, helpful guidebooks, a candlelit dining room and vine-covered conservatory, tea and home-made cakes or champagne on arrival, excellent, beautifully presented evening meals and hearty scottish breakfasts; resident border terrier, Penny, chocolate lab, Captain Hastings, golden lab, Colonel Mustard, and two cats, Pixie and Paddy. Closed mid November to mid March. Dogs allowed in four bedrooms; not in public rooms.

TOBERMORY   NM5055
Highland Cottage
(01688) 302030 – www.highlandcottage.co.uk
24 Breadalbane Street, Tobermory, Isle of Mull, Argyll PA75 6PD

£160; 6 cosy rooms; self-catering house too. Spotlessly kept small hotel rebuilt from an old cottage, run by friendly, helpful, hands-on owners (Mrs Currie also cooks the highly enjoyable food); a sitting room with views over Tobermory Bay, an honesty bar, an attractive dining room and hearty breakfasts. Closed mid October to late March. Dogs allowed in all bedrooms, but not in public rooms.

TORRIDON   NG8854
Torridon
(01445) 791242 – www.thetorridon.com
Torridon, Achnasheen, Ross-shire IV22 2EY

£370; 18 comfortable rooms including separate cottage. Built in 1887 as a shooting lodge, this turreted stone house is spectacularly placed in 58 acres at the foot of Ben Damph by Upper Loch Torridon; unusual ornate ceilings, panelling and log fires; innovative cooking and a whisky bar with 365 malts; they also run the dog-friendly Torridon Inn nearby as a cheaper alternative. Closed January. Dogs allowed in cottage but not in main hotel.

ULLAPOOL   NH1293
Ceilidh Place
(01854) 612103 – www.theceilidhplace.com
14 West Argyle Street, Ullapool, Ross-shire IV26 2TY

£150; 13 simply furnished rooms, most with own bathroom, plus 11 rooms in bunkhouse across road. White-painted hotel in quiet street, attractive conservatory dining room and café-bar with modern prints, plants and central woodburner, also a comfortable living room with honesty bar and balcony to sit out on; good locally sourced food all day and nice choice of wines and whiskies; relaxed, friendly atmosphere; books and radios in bedrooms rather than a TV; art exhibitions, live music and theatre, bookshop; resident border collie, Rieff; river walk from the door. Dogs allowed in all bedrooms and everywhere; £12 per stay.

WALKERBURN   NT3637
Windlestraw Lodge
(01896) 870636 – www.windlestraw.co.uk
Galashiels Road, Tweed Valley, Walkerburn, Peeblesshire EH43 6AA

£175; 6 lovely rooms. Handsome little Edwardian hotel looking over the River Tweed and surrounding forests, with two-acre garden and marvellous nearby walks; several lounges and a bar with plenty of original features, open fires, comfortable seating and family photographs, an elegant restaurant offering beautifully presented, inventive food using the best local produce and extensive breakfasts; two resident cocker spaniels. Closed mid December to mid February. Dogs allowed in some bedrooms (not to be left unattended) and in sun room after dinner; £10 per stay.

WEEM

NN8449

Ailean Chraggan

(01887) 820346 – www.aileanchraggan.co.uk
Weem, Aberfeldy, Perthshire PH15 2LD

£110; 4 rooms. Family-owned inn in two acres with fine views of the mountains; homely, simple bar with a chatty feel and a wide mix of customers, scottish ales, over 100 malt whiskies and good wines, a comfortably carpeted modern lounge and adjoining neatly old-fashioned dining room, inventive food and good breakfasts; nice walks from the door. Dogs allowed in one bedroom and bar.

Wales

DOG FRIENDLY PUBS

COLWYN BAY   SH8478

Pen-y-Bryn

(01492) 533360 – www.brunningandprice.co.uk/penybryn
B5113 Llanwrst Road, on southern outskirts; when you see the pub, turn off into
Wentworth Avenue for the car park; LL29 6DD

**Spacious open-plan modern bungalow overlooking the bay, with reliable
brasserie-style food all day, good range of drinks and obliging staff**

Don't be put off by the rather unprepossessing exterior of this pub because,
once inside, it's charming. Extending around the three long sides of the bar
counter, you'll find welcoming coal fires, oriental rugs on pale stripped boards,
a mix of seating and well spaced tables, shelves of books, a profusion of pictures,
big pot plants, careful lighting and dark green old-fashioned school radiators.
A fine choice of drinks served by knowledgeable, perky young staff includes
Phoenix Brunning & Price Original plus Adnams Ghost Ship, Heavy Industry
Collaborator, Purple Moose Snowdonia Ale and Tomos Watkin Blodwens Beer
on handpump, well chosen good value wines including 19 by the glass and
65 malt whiskies; board games and background music. The big windows at the
back look over seats and tables on the terraces and in the sizeable garden and
then out to the sea and the Great Orme. In summer, the award-winning flowering
tubs and hanging baskets are lovely.

Brunning & Price ~ Manager Andrew Grant ~ Real ale ~ Open 11.30-11; 11-11 Sat; 11-10.30
Sun ~ Bar food 12-9.30 (9 Sun) ~ Children welcome ~ Dogs allowed in bar ~ Wi-fi

EAST ABERTHAW   ST0366

Blue Anchor

(01446) 750329 – www.blueanchoraberthaw.com
Village signed off B4265; CF62 3DD

**Thatched character pub with cosy range of low-beamed little rooms,
making a memorable spot for a drink**

The snug low-beamed little rooms of this atmospheric place date back nearly
650 years, making it one of the oldest pubs in Wales. There's a central
servery and the character rooms leading off have tiny doorways, open fires
(including one in an inglenook with antique oak seats built into the stripped
stonework) and other seats and tables worked into a series of chatty little
alcoves. The more open front bar still has an ancient lime-ash floor and keeps

Brains Bitter, Theakstons Old Peculier, Wadworths 6X, Wye Valley HPA and a guest from Tomos Watkin on handpump, as well as farm cider and eight wines by the glass. Rustic seats shelter peacefully among tubs and troughs of flowers outside, with stone tables on a newer terrace. The pub can get very full in the evenings and on summer weekends; tasty, traditional food. A path from here leads to the shingle flats of the estuary.

Free house ~ Licensee Jeremy Coleman ~ Real ale ~ Open 11-11; 12-10.30 Sun ~ Bar food 12-2, 6-9; 12-3 Sun ~ Restaurant ~ Children welcome ~ Dogs allowed in bar ~ Wi-fi

GRESFORD
SJ3453

Pant-yr-Ochain

(01978) 853525 – www.brunningandprice.co.uk/pantyrochain
Off A483 on N edge of Wrexham: at roundabout take A5156 (A534) towards Nantwich, then first left towards the Flash; LL12 8TY

Particularly well run dining pub with good food all day, a very wide range of drinks and pretty lakeside garden

Surrounded by herbaceous borders, the tables and chairs on the terrace in front of this elaborately gabled 16th-c place look over a lake with waterfowl; there are more seats spread around the attractive grounds. The light and airy rooms inside are stylishly decorated with a wide range of interesting prints and bric-a-brac, and a good mix of individually chosen country furnishings, including comfortable seats for relaxing as well as more upright ones for eating. One area is set out as a library, with floor-to-ceiling bookshelves, there's a good open fire, and a popular dining conservatory overlooking the garden; board games. The impressive line-up of drinks served by well trained staff includes Phoenix Brunning & Price Original and guests such as Big Hand Havok, Hawkshead Brodies Prime Export, Purple Moose Snowdonia Ale and Stonehouse Off the Rails on handpump, 17 wines by the glass, around 80 malt whiskies and a good choice of gins and vodkas. Good disabled access.

Brunning & Price ~ Licensee James Meakin ~ Real ale ~ Open 11-11; 12-10.30 Sun ~ Bar food 12-9.30 (9 Sun) ~ Children welcome ~ Dogs allowed in bar ~ Wi-fi

LLANFIHANGEL-Y-CREUDDYN
SN6676

Y Ffarmers

(01974) 261275 – www.yffarmers.co.uk
Village signed off A4120 W of Pisgah; SY23 4LA

Welsh- and English-speaking pub with traditional furnishings in bar and dining areas, local ales and especially good food

The chef-landlord and his wife work hard to attract both drinkers and diners to their bilingual pub, which is very much the hub of the community. It's been carefully and simply refurbished, with high chairs and stools against the green-painted counter where they keep local ales on handpump such as Evan Evans Cwrw, Mantle Moho and maybe a guest from Montys, farm ciders and six wines by the glass; background music, TV and darts. There's a woodburning stove in a little fireplace, cushioned armed wheelback chairs, mate's chairs and a box settle around dark tables (each set with fresh flowers), wooden floors and walls painted white or red. As well as a sunken terrace with seats, there's a lawn with picnic-sets under parasols. The 13th-c village church is opposite.

Free house ~ Licensees Esther Prytherch and Rhodri Edwards ~ Real ale ~ Open 12-2, 6-11 (midnight Sat); 12-2, 7-11 Sun; closed Mon, winter Sun evening, first week Jan ~ Bar food 12-2, 6-9; not Sun evening, Mon, Tues lunchtime ~ Restaurant ~ Children welcome ~ Dogs allowed in bar ~ Wi-fi

LLANGOLLEN   SJ2142

Corn Mill

(01978) 869555 ~ www.brunningandprice.co.uk/cornmill
Dee Lane, very narrow lane off Castle Street (A539) just S of bridge; nearby parking can be tricky, may be best to use public park on Parade Street/East Street and walk; LL20 8PN

Fascinating riverside building with fine views, personable young staff, super food all day and good beers

The interior of this cleverly restored watermill has been interestingly refitted with pale pine flooring on stout beams, a striking open stairway with gleaming timber and tensioned steel rails, and mainly stripped-stone walls. Quite a lot of the old machinery is still in place, including the huge waterwheel (often turning) and there are good-sized dining tables, big rugs, thoughtfully chosen pictures (many to do with water) and several pot plants. One of the two serving bars, away from the water, has a much more local feel with regulars sitting on bar stools, pews on dark slate flagstones and daily papers. Helpful young staff serve Phoenix Brunning & Price Original and Facers DHB on handpump with a couple of guests such as Otter Summer Light and Phoenix Arizona; also, farm cider, around 50 sensibly priced malt whiskies and a decent wine choice with around a dozen by the glass. There are seats on a raised deck at the front that overlook the rushing millrace and rapids below; you can also watch steam trains arriving and leaving the station on the opposite riverbank.

Brunning & Price ~ Manager Andrew Barker ~ Real ale ~ Open 11-11 (10.30 Sun) ~ Bar food 12-9.30 (9 Sun) ~ Restaurant ~ Children welcome ~ Dogs allowed in bar ~ Wi-fi

LLANMADOC   SS4493

Britannia

(01792) 386624 ~ www.britanniainngower.co.uk
The Gower, near Whiteford Burrows (NT); SA3 1DB

Fine views from seats behind this popular pub with more in the big garden, well liked food and ales and friendly staff

As this 18th-c dining pub is on the north coast of the Gower peninsula, there are lovely nearby walks. You can warm yourself afterwards by the newly installed woodburning stove in the refurbished beamed bar and enjoy a pint of Marstons Pedigree and Sharps Doom Bar on handpump and several wines by the glass; darts and TV. The beamed restaurant has attractive modern wooden tables and chairs on a striped carpet and paintings on bare stone walls. The picnic-sets on the raised decked area at the back of the building have marvellous views over the Loughor estuary and get snapped up quickly in warm weather; there are also tables out in front and in the big garden. They have a rabbit hutch and an aviary with budgies, cockatiels, quails and a parrot.

Enterprise ~ Tenants Martin and Lindsey Davies ~ Real ale ~ Open 12-11 ~ Bar food 12-2.30, 6.30-8.30; all day weekends ~ Restaurant ~ Children welcome ~ Dogs allowed in bar ~ Wi-fi

MOLD SJ2465
Glasfryn
(01352) 750500 – www.brunningandprice.co.uk/glasfryn
N of the centre on Raikes Lane (parallel to the A5119), just past the well signposted Theatr Clwyd; CH7 6LR

Lively open-plan bistro-style pub with inventive all-day food, nice décor and wide choice of drinks

There's a lively, cheerful atmosphere and wide mix of customers in this neat and rather unassuming-looking pub. The open-plan interior is cleverly laid out to create plenty of nice quiet corners with a mix of informal, attractive country furnishings, turkey-style rugs on bare boards, deep red ceilings (some high), a warming fire and plenty of close-hung homely pictures; background music. Phoenix Brunning & Price Original plus guests such as Crouch Vale Brewers Gold, Hobsons Best, Roosters Yankee, Salopian Darwins Origin, Tatton Best and Timothy Taylors Boltmaker on handpump, 22 wines by the glass, 30 gins, 25 rums, 60 malt whiskies and farm cider. On warm days, the wooden tables on the large front terrace are a restful place to sit, providing sweeping views of the Clwydian Hills. Theatr Clwyd is just over the road.

Brunning & Price ~ Manager Graham Arathoon ~ Real ale ~ Open 10.30am-11pm (10.30pm Sun) ~ Bar food 12-9.30 (9 Sun) ~ Children welcome ~ Dogs allowed in bar ~ Wi-fi

MONKNASH SS9170
Plough & Harrow
(01656) 890209 – www.ploughandharrow.org
Signposted 'Marcross, Broughton' off B4265 St Brides Major–Llantwit Major – turn left at end of Water Street; OS Sheet 170 map reference 920706; CF71 7QQ

Old building full of history and character, with a huge log fire and a good choice of real ales

They keep a fine range of eight real ales on handpump or tapped from the cask in this historic pub, such as Bass, Cwrw Ial Haf Gwyn, Purple Moose Glaslyn Ale, Sharps Atlantic, Valley Forge Vanilla Porter, Wye Valley HPA and a guest from Mumbles or Tomos Watkin; they usually hold beer festivals in June and September. Also, a good range of local farm cider and welsh and scottish malt whiskies. The unspoilt main bar with its massively thick stone walls used to be the scriptures room and mortuary (some of the building once formed part of a monastic grange); it has ancient ham hooks in the heavily beamed ceiling, an intriguing arched doorway at the back, broad flagstones and a comfortably informal mix of furnishings that includes three fine stripped-pine settles. There's a log fire in a huge fireplace with a side bread oven large enough to feed a village; background music in the left-hand room. The front garden has picnic-sets. A path from the pub leads through the wooded valley of Cwm Nash to the coast, revealing a spectacular stretch of cliffs around Nash Point. Dogs are welcome in the bar, but not while food is served.

Free house ~ Licensee Paula Jones ~ Real ale ~ Open 12-11 (10.30 Sun) ~ Bar food 12-2.30 (5 weekends), 6-9; not Sun evening ~ Restaurant ~ Children welcome ~ Dogs allowed in bar ~ Live music Sat evening

OVERTON BRIDGE

SJ3542

Cross Foxes

(01978) 780380 – www.brunningandprice.co.uk/crossfoxes
A539 W of Overton, near Erbistock; LL13 0DR

**Terrific river views, contemporary food and an extensive range
of drinks in bustling, well run pub**

A fine range of drinks in this 18th-c coaching inn includes 40 malt whiskies,
30 Armagnacs, 28 gins and lots of wines by the glass – plus Phoenix Brunning &
Price Original, Brakspears Bitter, Jennings Queen Bee, Marstons EPA, Wychwood
Jester Jack and a couple of guests on handpump and a farm cider; service is friendly
and efficient. The ancient low-beamed bar, with its red tiled floor, dark timbers, warm
fire in the big inglenook and built-in old pews, is more traditional than most pubs in
the Brunning & Price group, though the characteristic turkey rugs, large pot plants
and frame-to-frame pictures are present, as they are in the dining areas; board games
and newspapers. Big windows all round the airy dining conservatory look over the
River Dee, as do seats and tables on the raised terrace and picnic-sets on grass.

Brunning & Price ~ Manager Ian Pritchard-Jones ~ Real ale ~ Open 11-11 (10.30 Sun) ~
Bar food 12-9.30 (9 Sun) ~ Children welcome ~ Dogs allowed in bar ~ Wi-fi

PANTYGELLI

SO3017

Crown

(01873) 853314 – www.thecrownatpantygelli.com
*Old Hereford Road N of Abergavenny; off A40 by war memorial via Pen Y Pound,
passing leisure centre; Pantygelli also signposted from A465; NP7 7HR*

**Country pub in fine scenery, attractive inside and out, with good food
and drinks**

On the edge of the Brecon Beacons National Park, this highly thought-of pub
is run by warmly friendly licensees. Wrought-iron and wicker chairs on the
flower-filled front terrace look up from the lush valley to the hills and there's
also a smaller back terrace surrounded by lavender. Inside, the dark flagstoned
bar, with sturdy timber props and beams, has a log fire in a stone fireplace, a
piano at the back with darts opposite, Bass, Montys Pale Ale, Rhymney Best and
Tomos Watkin Cwrw Haf on handpump from the slate-roofed counter, Gwatkin's
farm cider, seven good wines by the glass, local organic apple juice and good
coffees. On the left are four smallish, linked, carpeted dining rooms, the front
pair separated by a massive stone chimneybreast; thoughtfully chosen individual
furnishings and lots of attractive prints by local artists make it all thoroughly
civilised. Also, background music, darts and board games.

Free house ~ Licensees Steve and Cherrie Chadwick ~ Real ale ~ Open 12-2.30 (3 Sat),
6-11; 12-3, 6-10.30 Sun; closed Mon lunchtime ~ Bar food 12-2, 7-9; not Sun evening or Mon
~ Restaurant ~ Children welcome ~ Dogs allowed in bar ~ Wi-fi

PENNAL

SH6900

Riverside

(01654) 791285 – www.riversidehotel-pennal.co.uk
A493; opposite church; SY20 9DW

**Carefully refurbished pub with tasty food and local beers, and efficient
young staff; bedrooms**

This bustling pub is just inside the southern boundary of Snowdonia National Park, with plenty of fine surrounding walks. Most people are here to enjoy the wide choice of good quality food but there's quite a range of thoughtful drinks too. The neatly furnished rooms have green and white walls, slate tiles on the floor, a woodburning stove, modern light wood dining furniture and some funky fabrics. High-backed stools are lined up along the stone-fronted counter where they serve Purple Moose Glaslyn, Salopian Golden Thread and Tiny Rebel Cwtch with a guest from Vale of Glamorgan on handpump, 30 malt whiskies, 30 gins, 12 wines by the glass and farm cider; background music and dominoes. There are seats and tables in the garden, and they also run a Georgian guesthouse in the pretty village.

Free house ~ Licensees Glyn and Corina Davies ~ Real ale ~ Open 12-3, 6-11; 12-midnight Sat; 12-11 Sun; closed Mon; two weeks Jan ~ Bar food 12-2 (2.30 Sun), 6-9 ~ Restaurant ~ Children welcome ~ Dogs allowed in bar ~ Wi-fi ~ Bedrooms: £75

PENTYRCH   ST1081

Kings Arms

(029) 2089 0202 ~ www.kingsarmspentyrch.co.uk
Church Road; CF15 9QF

Village pub very much part of the community with a perky bar, civilised lounge and top class food

Although many customers are here to enjoy the fantastic food cooked by the chef-patron, this 16th-c longhouse is not a straightforward dining place. It's very much a proper pub with plenty of regulars, and the cosy bar has a cheerful atmosphere, an open log fire in a sizeable brick fireplace and a mix of seats on flagstones. There's Brains Bitter and SA and guests from Grey Trees and Tiny Rebel on handpump, 14 wines by the glass and up to ten malt whiskies, all served by helpful, friendly staff. There's also a comfortable lounge and a cosy restaurant. Plenty of seats on a terrace and picnic-sets under parasols in the garden.

Free house ~ Licensee Andrew Aston ~ Real ale ~ Open 12-11; 12-midnight Sat; 12-8 Sun ~ Bar food 12-3, 5.30-9.30; 12-9.30 Sat; 12-4 Sun ~ Restaurant ~ Children welcome ~ Dogs allowed in bar ~ Wi-fi

PONTYPRIDD   ST0790

Bunch of Grapes

(01443) 402934 ~ www.bunchofgrapes.org.uk
Off A4054; Ynysangharad Road; CF37 4DA

Bustling pub with a fine choice of drinks in friendly, relaxed bar, delicious inventive food and a warm welcome for all

As well as exceptional food, this fine 18th-c pub offers a fantastic range of drinks too. Served by knowledgeable, friendly and efficient staff, these might include their own Otley O2 Croeso and three Otley guests plus other quickly changing guests such as Crouch Vale Amarillo, Dark Star Hophead and Salopian Hop Twister on handpump. They hold around six beer and music festivals each year, and also keep continental and american ales on draught or in bottles, a couple of local ciders or perrys, eight wines by the glass and good coffee. The cosy bar has an informal, relaxed atmosphere, comfortable leather sofas, wooden chairs and tables, a roaring log fire, newspapers to read and background music and board games. There's also a restaurant with elegant high-backed wooden dining chairs around a mix of tables and black and white local photo-prints taken by the landlord (an ex-professional photographer). A deli offers home-baked bread and chutneys, home-cooked ham, local eggs and quite a choice of welsh cheeses and so forth, and they hold regular themed cookery evenings. There are seats outside on decking.

Free house ~ Licensee Nick Otley ~ Real ale ~ Open 11am-11.30pm; 12-11 Sun ~ Bar food 12-8.30 (7 Fri); 12-6.30 Sat ~ Restaurant ~ Children welcome ~ Dogs allowed in bar ~ Wi-fi

ST GEORGE   SH9775
Kinmel Arms
(01745) 832207 ~ www.thekinmelarms.co.uk
Off A547 or B5381 SE of Abergele; LL22 9BP

Stylish food in bustling inn, a wide choice of drinks, courteous staff and lovely position; bedrooms

The countryside surrounding this 17th-c sandstone inn is stunning and there are good walks from the front door. It has mullioned windows and handsome carriage-lamps at the front, and also a bar with sofas on either side of a woodburning stove, an attractive mix of nice old wooden chairs and tables on the wooden floor and seats against the counter (with stained glass above) where they keep Great Orme Welsh Gold and Spitting Feathers Thirst Quencher on handpump, 21 wines by the glass and farm cider; service is helpful and friendly. The restaurant, with rattan chairs around marble-topped tables, has big house plants, contemporary art painted by Tim Watson (one of the owners) and evening candles and twinkling lights. To one side is a tea room with silver teapots and pretty bone china cups and saucers – it's here that you can buy their hampers, chutneys, port and cheese boxes and so forth. There are picnic-sets out in front.

Free house ~ Licensees Lynn Cunnah-Watson and Tim Watson ~ Real ale ~ Open 11-11 (11.30 Fri, Sat); closed Sun, Mon ~ Bar food 12-2, 6-9 (9.30 Fri, Sat); light meals all day; afternoon tea 2-4.30pm ~ Restaurant ~ Children welcome but not in bedrooms ~ Dogs allowed in bar ~ Wi-fi ~ Bedrooms: £135

STACKPOLE   SR9896
Stackpole Inn
(01646) 672324 ~ www.stackpoleinn.co.uk
Village signed off B4319 S of Pembroke; SA71 5DF

Busy pub, a good base for the area, with enjoyable food and friendly service; comfortable bedrooms

It's not surprising this pub is so popular with walkers since it's very near the Pembrokeshire Coast Path and the Bosherston Lily Ponds; they even have a walkers' lunch menu. There's an area around the bar with pine tables and chairs, but most of the pub, L-shaped on four different levels, is given over to diners, with neat light oak furnishings, ash beams and low ceilings to match; background music and board games. Brains Rev James, Felinfoel Best Bitter and Double Dragon and a changing guest ale on handpump, 14 wines by the glass, 15 malt whiskies and two farm ciders. Attractive gardens feature colourful flower beds and mature trees and there are plenty of picnic-sets at the front.

Free house ~ Licensees Gary and Becky Evans ~ Real ale ~ Open 12-3, 6-11; 12-11 Sat, Sun ~ Bar food 12-2.15, 6.30-9 ~ Restaurant ~ Children welcome ~ Dogs allowed in bar ~ Wi-fi ~ Bedrooms: £90

TINTERN
SO5300

Anchor

(01291) 689582 – www.theanchortintern.co.uk
Off A466 at brown Abbey sign; NP16 6TE

Wonderful setting for ancient inn next to Tintern Abbey ruins and river, historic features, plenty of space and good ales and food

Tintern Abbey's magnificent ruins (floodlit at night) are right next to this medieval building and can be enjoyed from picnic-sets on the terrace and in the front garden and from the Garden Room. The bar was originally a cider mill attached to the abbey's orchard and the horse-drawn cider press is the central feature; also, little plush stools around circular tables, heavy beams, flagstones, four real ales such as Otter Bitter, Wye Valley Butty Bach and a couple of guests on handpump and local ciders served by friendly, hard-working staff. The restaurant was once the ferryman's cottage and boat house and is connected to the abbey's north wall: bare stone walls, high-backed leather dining chairs around all sorts of tables and more flagstones. There's also an airy café (open 9am-5pm) with colourfully painted chairs and a 100-year-old olive tree. The River Wye is just behind and lots of walks surround the inn.

Free house ~ Licensee Robert Parkin ~ Real ale ~ Open 11-11 (10.30 Sun) ~ Bar food 12-2.45, 6-9; 12-3.45, 5.30-7.30 Sun ~ Restaurant ~ Children welcome ~ Dogs allowed in bar ~ Wi-fi

USK
SO3700

Nags Head

(01291) 672820
The Square; NP15 1BH

Spotlessly kept and traditional in style with a hearty welcome and good food and drinks

Standards here remain consistently high and customers are full of praise for the way the long-serving and friendly Key family run this handsome coaching inn. The traditional main bar is cheerily chatty and cosy, with lots of well polished tables and chairs packed under its beams (some with farming tools, lanterns or horsebrasses and harness attached), as well as leatherette wall benches and various sets of sporting prints and local pictures – look out for the original deeds to the pub. Tucked away at the front is an intimate little corner with some african masks, while on the other side of the room a passageway leads to a dining area; background music. There may be prints for sale, and perhaps a group of sociable locals. They offer nine wines by the glass, along with Brains Rev James and SA and a guest such as Sharps Doom Bar on handpump. The church is well worth a look. The pub has no parking and nearby street parking can be limited.

Free house ~ Licensee Key family ~ Real ale ~ Open 10.30-3, 5-11 ~ Bar food 12-2, 5.30-9 ~ Restaurant ~ Children welcome ~ Dogs welcome ~ Wi-fi

DOG FRIENDLY HOTELS, INNS AND B&Bs

ABERDOVEY   SN6196

Penhelig Arms Hotel

(01654) 767215 – www.penheligarms.com
27-29 Terrace Road, Aberdovey, Gwynedd LL35 0LT

£99; 15 comfortable, modern rooms – 4 in impressively furnished annexe, with
lovely views. In a fine spot overlooking the Dovey estuary, this 18th-c hotel has a
fishermens' bar with a log fire, panelling and traditional furnishings, real ales, 20
wines by the glass and a dozen malt whiskies served by efficient, friendly staff,
well thought-of food using local fresh fish in the bar or more formal restaurant,
good breakfasts and sunny terrace; walks on five miles of beach. Dogs allowed in
all but one bedroom and bar, but not in restaurant; blanket, bedding and bowl; £10.

ABERGAVENNY   SO2914

Angel Hotel

(01873) 857121 – www.angelabergavenny.com
15 Cross Street, Abergavenny, Gwent NP7 5EN

£99; 34 well equipped, contemporary rooms, some in mews and cottages. A
former coaching inn with a Georgian façade, this family-run hotel is on the edge
of the Brecon Beacons (marvellous walks); it has a bustling bar (liked by locals
too), a comfortable lounge where their award-winning afternoon teas are served,
a smart restaurant with excellent modern european dishes and particularly good
breakfasts; walks nearby along River Usk. Dogs allowed in some bedrooms and
bar, but not in restaurant; bedding and bowl; £25.

ABERSOCH   SH3126

Porth Tocyn Hotel

(01758) 713303 – www.porthtocynhotel.co.uk
Bwlch Tocyn, Pwllheli, Gwynedd LL53 7BU

£150; 17 individually designed rooms, most with sea views; also self-catering
cottage. On a headland overlooking Cardigan Bay, this comfortable and homely
place – converted from a row of lead miners' cottages – has been run by the same
hard-working family for nearly 70 years; several cosy interconnecting sitting rooms
with antiques, books and fresh flowers, a sunny conservatory, most enjoyable
cooking from light lunches through an imaginative dinner menu to a huge Sunday
buffet lunch; helpful young staff, lots of space in the pretty garden, heated swimming
pool in summer and hard tennis court; good walks and plenty of outdoor activities.
Closed November to mid March. Dogs allowed in all bedrooms, not in public rooms.

BEAUMARIS   SH6076

Bull

(01248) 810329 – www.bullsheadinn.co.uk
Castle Street, Beaumaris, Anglesey LL58 8AP

£110; 26 well equipped bedrooms, some traditional, some contemporary in
design – in main building or adjacent Townhouse. Historic inn in an attractive

seaside town, with a delightful beamed and rambling bar with a log fire, real ales and several gins, copper and china jugs and interesting reminders of the town's past (a rare 17th-c brass water clock, cutlasses and even an oak ducking stool), a busy, stylishly modern brasserie and a very good, more formal restaurant upstairs with a wine list that runs to 120 bottles; also a pretty courtyard with a vast door. Dogs allowed in two bedrooms in main building and bar; bed and bowl; £15.

BRECHFA

SN5230

Ty Mawr

(01267) 202332 – www.wales-country-hotel.co.uk
Brechfa, Carmarthen, Dyfed SA32 7RA

£115; 6 simple rooms. A former farmhouse and school, this tranquil hotel is on the edge of the Brechfa forest (lots of walks) and has rambling rooms with beams, exposed stone walls and open fires, friendly, helpful owners and staff and good, honest food including generous breakfasts, suppers and packed lunches (on request). Dogs allowed in all bedrooms, but not in restaurant or breakfast room.

BROAD HAVEN

SM8616

Druidstone Hotel

(01437) 781221 – www.druidstone.co.uk
Broad Haven, Haverfordwest, Dyfed SA62 3NE

£80–£180; 11 rooms, some with sea views, some with shared bathrooms; self-catering cottages also. Alone on the coast above a fine beach with exhilarating cliff walks, this roomy and informally friendly hotel (run by the same family since the 1940s) has something of a folk-club and Outward Bound feel at times; it's extremely winning and relaxing if you take to its unique combination of good wholesome and often memorably inventive food (including themed nights), slightly fend-for-yourself approach amid elderly furniture and glorious seaside surroundings; resident parsons terrier, Dash, and six cats. Dogs allowed in all bedrooms and public areas except restaurant.

CAERNARFON

SH4759

Plas Dinas

(01286) 830214 – www.plasdinas.co.uk
Bontnewydd, Caernarfon, Gwynedd LL54 7YF

£129; 10 individually furnished, well equipped rooms overlooking the garden; also self-catering lodge. A lovely former gentleman's residence between the mountains and the sea in 15 acres of grounds; friendly, helpful owners (one also cooks the top class food), a comfortable big drawing room with an open fire, afternoon tea with home-made chocolate brownies, a gun room with interesting royal memorabilia and a smart restaurant; resident dogs Malta and Blue; fantastic walks. Small dogs allowed in some bedrooms and drawing room; towel and treats; £10.

CONWY   SH7577

Sychnant Pass House

(01492) 596868 – www.sychnant-pass-house.co.uk
Sychnant Pass Road, Conwy, Gwynedd LL32 8BJ

£155; 12 rooms including 2 suites (named after Welsh hymn tunes). Victorian
house in two acres among the foothills of Snowdonia National Park; big
comfortable sitting rooms, log fires, a relaxing, friendly atmosphere and enjoyable
food (the restaurant is open to non-residents too); heated swimming pool, spa
and outdoor hot tub. Closed two weeks January. Dogs allowed in all bedrooms
and lounge; £20 per stay.

CRICKHOWELL   SO2118

Bear

(01873) 810408 – www.bearhotel.co.uk
High Street, Crickhowell, Powys NP8 1BW

£129; 35 appealing rooms, some with hot tubs and four-posters. Interesting inn
run by the same convivial family for many years, with a splendid old-fashioned
bar area, real ales, 30-plus malt whiskies and vintage and late-bottled ports,
heavily beamed lounge with roaring log fire, plenty of fine antiques, fresh flowers;
comfortable reception rooms, too; imaginative food and enjoyable breakfasts
served by genuinely helpful staff; river and canal walks within ten minutes.
Dogs allowed in courtyard bedrooms and bar.

EGLWYSFACH   SN6895

Ynyshir Hall

(01654) 781209 – www.ynyshirhall.co.uk
Eglwysfach, Machynlleth, Dyfed SY20 8TA

£200; 10 individually decorated rooms. Carefully run Georgian manor house
in 14 acres of landscaped gardens adjoining the Ynyshir coastal bird reserve;
particularly good service, antiques, log fires and paintings in the light and airy
public rooms, fantastic food in Michelin-starred restaurant with tasting menus at
lunch and dinner, and delicious breakfasts; resident great dane and kelpie; lots to
do nearby. Closed two weeks January. Dogs allowed in two bedrooms; £20 per stay.

FELINFACH   SO0933

Griffin

(01874) 620111 – www.eatdrinksleep.ltd.uk
Felinfach, Brecon, Powys LD3 0UB

£135; 7 tastefully decorated rooms. Classy, relaxed dining pub with a proper
back bar with scrubbed kitchen tables on bare boards, leather sofas by a log
fire and a bright blue and ochre colour scheme; interesting drinks including real
ales, local cider, welsh spirits and fine wines by the glass; two smallish, attractive
dining rooms with terracotta or white-painted stone walls, excellent, imaginative
food using local produce (some from own kitchen garden), breakfasts are hearty
and nicely informal; resident dogs Max and Lottie. Dogs allowed in all bedrooms,
bar and at some tables in dining rooms; towels, mat, bowl and treats.

GELLILYDAN

SH6939

Tyddyn-du Farm

(01766) 590281 – www.snowdoniafarm.com
Gellilydan, Blaenau Ffestiniog, Gwynedd LL41 4RB

£110; 4 self-contained ground-floor suites in former stables or barn. 400-year-old farmhouse on organic working sheep farm in the heart of Snowdonia, with beams and exposed stonework, and big inglenook fireplaces in lounge; suites are very well equipped with whirlpool bath, fridge, microwave and private patio/garden; children can help bottle-feed the lambs and look at goats, sheep, alpacas and shetland ponies; one sheepdog, Pero; lovely country and mountain views and fine walks, including short one to their own Roman site. Dogs allowed in all suites and public areas except dining room; £4.

GLYNARTHEN

SN3149

Penbontbren Farm

(01239) 810248 – www.penbontbren.com
Glynarthen, Llandysul, Dyfed SA44 6PE

£125; 5 lovely suites with own sitting room and terrace; also self-catering cottage. Former farmhouse, now a luxury B&B, in 32 acres of grounds with nearby beaches for walks; charming, helpful owners, exceptional breakfasts in the carefully converted barn with crisply clothed tables and pretty flowers – plenty of places close by for evening meals; resident king charles spaniels. Dogs allowed in all suites and elsewhere except breakfast room; £10 (free if you mention this guide!).

LLANARMON DYFFRYN CEIRIOG

SJ1532

Hand

(01691) 600666 – www.thehandhotel.co.uk
Llanarmon Dyffryn Ceiriog, Llangollen, Clwyd LL20 7LD

£115; 13 rooms, some in converted stables. Comfortable rural hotel (a former drovers' inn) in remote valley looking out to the Berwyn Mountains; black-beamed carpeted bar with good inglenook log fire, mix of chairs and settles and old prints on cream walls, local beers, fair-priced wines by the glass and several malt whiskies; the largely stripped-stone dining room has a woodburner and tasty food served by friendly staff (splendid breakfasts too); there's also an attractive residents' lounge; three resident whippets; walks from the door among sheep. Dogs allowed in three bedrooms and bar, but not dining room; £8.

LLANARMON DYFFRYN CEIRIOG

SJ1532

West Arms

(01691) 600665 – www.thewestarms.com
Llanarmon Dyffryn Ceiriog, Llangollen, Clwyd LL20 7LD

£115; 16 comfortable character rooms, including 2 suites. Charming 16th-c beamed and timbered inn in lovely surroundings, cosy atmosphere in picturesque upmarket lounge bar full of antique settles, sofas, even an elaborately carved confessional stall, good original bar food strong on local produce, friendly staff, nice range of wines, malt whiskies and three well kept local ales, more sofas in old-fashioned entrance hall, comfortable back bar too, roaring log fires, good restaurant; pretty lawn running down to River Ceiriog, good walks. Dogs allowed in all bedrooms and public areas except restaurant; £10.

LLANBERIS

SH6655

Pen-y-Gwryd

(01286) 870211 – www.pyg.co.uk
Nant Gwynant, Caernarfon, Gwynedd LL55 4NT

£90–£110; 18 rooms – most with shared bathroom. Unchanging 19th-c mountain inn set beneath Snowdon and the Glyders and run by the same family since 1947, with lots of climbers' mementoes; homely slate-floored log cabin bar has built-in wall benches and sturdy country chairs looking out at surrounding mountain landscapes, a smaller room has a collection of illustrious boots from famous climbs and there's a cosy panelled room too; welsh ales, simple, good value meals, hearty traditional breakfasts and packed lunches; they even have their own chapel, sauna and outdoor natural pool; endless walks in surrounding Snowdonia National Park. Closed January-February. Dogs allowed in 16 bedrooms and bar, not in dining room; £5.

LLANDRILLO

SJ0337

Tyddyn Llan

(01490) 440264 – www.tyddynllan.co.uk
Llandrillo, Corwen, Clwyd LL21 0ST

£190; 12 pretty rooms and 1 garden suite. Restaurant-with-rooms set in an elegant and relaxed Georgian house with three acres of lovely gardens surrounded by the Berwyn mountains; fresh flowers in comfortable public rooms, enterprising food including gourmet and tasting menus using the best ingredients and an impressive wine list; fine forest walks and watersports nearby; two resident cats. Closed two weeks January. Dogs allowed in most bedrooms only; £10.

LLANDUDNO

SH7882

St Tudno

(01492) 874411 – www.st-tudno.co.uk
15 North Parade, Llandudno, Gwynedd LL30 2LP

£80; 18 individually decorated rooms, some with sea views. Opposite the pier, this smart, well run seaside hotel has genuinely helpful and friendly staff; Victorian-style décor in restful sitting room, a convivial bar lounge, relaxed coffee lounge for good light lunches and dinner, and an attractive italian-style restaurant. Dogs allowed in all bedrooms, bar, coffee lounge and residents' lounge; £7.50.

LLANFAIR DYFFRYN CLWYD

SJ1355

Eyarth Station Guest House

(01824) 703643 – www.eyarthstation.com
Llanfair Dyffryn Clwyd, Ruthin, Clwyd LL15 2EE

£85; 5 pretty rooms. Carefully converted old railway station with quiet gardens and wonderful views; friendly relaxed atmosphere, log fire in airy and comfortable beamed lounge, good breakfasts and evening meals in dining room (more lovely views); sun terrace and lots of walks; under new ownership so some changes are likely. Dogs allowed in all bedrooms and public areas, but not in dining room; £6.

LLANFERRES
SJ1860

Druid

(01352) 810225 – www.thedruidinn.com
Ruthin Road, Llanferres, Mold, Clwyd CH7 5SN

£82; 5 rooms. Friendly extended 17th-c whitewashed inn in choice walking country; fine views from civilised, smallish plush lounge and bigger beamed back bar with its two handsome antique oak settles, pleasant mix of more modern furnishings, quarry-tiled area by the log fire; real ales, 30 malt whiskies and reasonably priced, generously served food. Dogs allowed in all bedrooms and anywhere except dining room.

LLANGAMMARCH WELLS
SN9447

Lake Country House

(01591) 620202 – www.lakecountryhouse.co.uk
Llangammarch Wells, Powys LD4 4BS

£195; 32 charming, pretty rooms. Particularly well run 1860s half-timbered hotel in 50 acres of grounds, with plenty of wildlife, well stocked trout lake, tennis, riding and walking; deeply comfortable tranquil drawing room with antiques, paintings and log fire, wonderful afternoon teas (in summer under the chestnut tree overlooking the river), courteous service, fine wines and good modern british cooking in elegant candlelit dining room, breakfast served in the orangery; spa with swimming pool, outdoor hot tub and treatment rooms; resident brown labrador called Molly. Dogs allowed in 20 bedrooms, reception and oak room; £15.

LLANWDDYN
SJ0219

Lake Vyrnwy Hotel

(01691) 870692 – www.lakevyrnwy.com
Llanwddyn, Oswestry, Powys SY10 0LY

£174; 52 individually furnished rooms – some overlooking the huge lake. Large, impressive Tudor-style mansion in a 26,000-acre estate – 16,000 acres are dedicated to the RSPB; conservatory looking over the water, log fires and sporting prints in the comfortable and elegant public rooms, convivial bar, a relaxed atmosphere and good food using their own lamb and game from the estate and home-made preserves, chutneys, mustards and vinegars, enjoyable teas too; spa with treatments. Dogs allowed in some bedrooms, bar and on lead in grounds; £10; they also have free heated kennels.

LLANWRTYD WELLS
SN8746

Carlton Riverside

(01591) 610248 – www.carltonriverside.com
Irfon Crescent, Llanwrtyd Wells, Powys LD5 4ST

£90; 4 well equipped rooms. Warmly friendly owners run this restaurant-with-rooms; two lounges with large squishy sofas and modern glass coffee tables, a well stocked bar, contemporary restaurant overlooking the River Irfon and old stone bridge, exceptionally good modern british cooking using top quality local produce and a thoughtful wine list, super breakfasts with home-made bread and marmalade; good walks straight from the door. Dogs allowed in all bedrooms but not in public rooms.

MONTGOMERY

SO2296

Dragon

(01686) 668359 – www.dragonhotel.com
Market Square, Montgomery, Powys SY15 6PA

£79; 20 rooms. 17th-c black and white timbered, family-run hotel with a pleasant grey-stone tiled hall, comfortable residents' lounge, beamed bar and popular Bistro 7 restaurant serving real ales, craft beers, local wines and spirits; indoor swimming pool, bike hire and countryside walks. Dogs allowed in ten bedrooms and some public areas; £10-£15.

NEWPORT

SN0539

Golden Lion

(01239) 820321 – www.goldenlionpembrokeshire.co.uk
East Street, Newport, Pembrokeshire, Dyfed SA42 0SY

£100; 13 well appointed rooms. Welcoming village inn with a nice balance of comfortable dining and pubby character – a smashing all-rounder; cosy beamed rooms with distinctive old settles, changing beers, local cider, wines by the glass, malt whiskies and pleasant staff; the dining room has elegant blond wood oak furniture, whitewashed walls and potted plants and serves enjoyable, carefully presented food; walks from the door to the sea. Dogs allowed in one bedroom and bar, not in dining room; £15.

NEWPORT

SN0539

Llys Meddyg

(01239) 820008 – www.llysmeddyg.com
East Street, Newport, Pembrokeshire, Dyfed SA42 0SY

£120; 8 large, bright rooms. Once a Georgian coaching inn, this is now a restaurant-with-rooms in the Pembrokeshire Coast National Park, with extensive walks from the front door; you can expect warmly welcoming owners and staff, a comfortable sitting room, a cosy and informal flagstoned cellar bar, good artwork and open fires, a wooden-shuttered restaurant with fresh flowers and candlelight, first class imaginative food using local seasonal ingredients (home-smoked, foraged or shot) and excellent breakfasts. Closed first week January. Dogs allowed in three bedrooms and bar.

OLD RADNOR

SO2559

Harp

(01544) 350655 – www.harpinnradnor.co.uk
Old Radnor, Presteigne, Powys LD8 2RH

£105; 5 pretty rooms. Welcoming 15th-c inn in superb hilltop position with lovely views and good walks nearby; traditional bars with log fires, some slate flooring and antique settles, real ales, local cider and quite a few malt whiskies, lots of local books, maps and guides for residents; character dining rooms, appealing food using local produce. Dogs allowed in all bedrooms and bar.

OXWICH   SS5086

Oxwich Bay Hotel

(01792) 390329 – www.oxwichbayhotel.co.uk
Oxwich, Gower Peninsula, West Glamorgan SA3 1LS

£110; 26 rooms – 12 in main house and 14 in various cottages. Comfortable hotel on edge of beach in a lovely area, with a restaurant/lounge bar with panoramic views and a summer outdoor dining area; food served all day, friendly staff and a welcome for families; eight acres of grounds in which dogs can walk. Dogs allowed in cottage bedrooms and part of restaurant/bar; £10.

PRESTEIGNE   SO3164

Radnorshire Arms

(01544) 267406 – www.radnorshirearmshotel.com
High Street, Presteigne, Powys LD8 2BE

£85; 19 rooms – 11 in main building, 8 garden rooms. Rambling, handsomely timbered hotel dating from the 16th c with many later additions, elegantly moulded beams and fine dark panelling in the lounge bar, latticed windows, enjoyable food (including morning coffee and afternoon tea), separate recently refurbished restaurant, well kept real ales and politely attentive service; walks nearby or in the garden. Dogs allowed in garden rooms, and public areas outside of food times; £15.

PUMSAINT   SN6540

Dolaucothi Arms

(01558) 650237 – www.thedolaucothiarms.co.uk
Pumsaint, Camarthen, Dyfed SA19 8UW

£80; 3 simply furnished bedrooms – each with a decanter of port and fresh biscuits. A genuinely welcoming National Trust-owned pub (part of the Dolaucothi Estate); there's a chatty bar with a woodburning stove, red and black floor tiles, welsh ales (they have an August Bank Holiday beer festival) and farm cider; also a terracotta-painted dining room with another woodburner, heavy welsh dressers and big flagstones and walls hung with local art, maps and old local photos; the neat garden overlooks the Cothi River where the pub has four miles of fishing rights; pub cat, Lily, and chickens; pleasing food using produce from their kitchen garden includes popular pies and curries. Closed two weeks January. Dogs allowed in one bedroom and bar; £10.

RAGLAN   SO3608

Clytha Arms

(01873) 840206 – www.clytha-arms.com
Clytha, Abergavenny, Gwent NP7 9BW

£90; 3 comfortable rooms. Rural inn in its own extensive, well cared-for grounds on the edge of Clytha Park and a short stroll from the riverside path by the Usk; comfortable, light and airy bar and lounge with scrubbed wood floors, pine settles and a good mix of old country furniture, a couple of warming fires and an impressive array of drinks (they hold a cider and beer festival); hearty modern food is available in the bar, lounge and contemporary linen-set restaurant, part-welsh and part-spanish tapas menu plus other enjoyable dishes and good breakfasts; five resident dogs. Dogs allowed in all bedrooms and bar; bed and bowl.

REYNOLDSTON   SS4691
Fairyhill
(01792) 390139 – www.fairyhill.net
Reynoldston, Swansea, West Glamorgan SA3 1BS

£200; 8 comfortable rooms. 18th-c hotel in 24 wooded acres with croquet, a trout stream and a lake with wild ducks; log fire in comfortable drawing room, cosy bar, lovely food and excellent wine list in attractive dining room using local produce (some from own walled garden), hearty breakfasts, a leafy terrace and personal friendly service. Closed 1-25 January. Dogs allowed in some bedrooms; £10.

RHAYADER   SN9869
Beili Neuadd
(01597) 810211 – www.beilineuadd.co.uk
Rhayader, Powys LD6 5NS

£80; 6 rooms – 3 in farmhouse, 3 bunkhouse rooms (sleeping 16) in converted stone barn; also self-catering chalet. Charming, partly 16th-c stone-built farmhouse with panoramic views set in quiet countryside; beams, polished oak floorboards, log fires and nice breakfasts in garden room; own dogs, cats, pigs, sheep and chickens; walks in paddocks, garden and surrounding area. Dogs allowed in all rooms and some public rooms.

SKENFRITH   SO4520
Bell
(01600) 750235 – www.skenfrith.co.uk
Skenfrith, Abergavenny, Gwent NP7 8UH

£150; 11 rooms, some with four-posters. Elegant but relaxed inn by a bridge over the River Monnow and close to the impressive medieval ruin of Skenfrith Castle; there are two bars with flagstones, a big inglenook fireplace, comfortable sofas, a couple of pews and lots of tables and chairs; good wines by the glass, local ales and cider, malt whiskies and interesting food using the best local produce (including their own vegetables and pigs) and generous breakfasts; new residents' sitting room with plenty of books, magazines and board games, and a terrace with seating under parasols; good nearby walks. Dogs allowed in most bedrooms and most public areas except restaurant; £20.

ST DAVIDS   SM7524
Warpool Court Hotel
(01437) 720300 – www.warpoolcourthotel.com
St Davids, Haverfordwest, Dyfed SA62 6BN

£195; 22 attractive rooms, some with sea views; also self-catering cottage. Originally built as St Davids cathedral school in 1870 and bordering National Trust land, this popular hotel has lovely views over St Bride's Bay; Ada Williams' collection of lovely hand-painted tiles can be seen in the public rooms and some bedrooms, the food in the elegant restaurant is imaginative (good for vegetarians too) and staff are helpful; attractive quiet gardens (walks here and in surrounding fields), heated summer swimming pool, tennis and croquet, games room with table tennis and pool. Closed November-March. Dogs allowed in most bedrooms but not public area; £10.

TINTERN PARVA
SO5300

Parva Farmhouse

(01291) 689411 – www.parvafarmhouse.co.uk
Tintern, Chepstow, Gwent NP16 6SQ

£86; 8 comfortable rooms, most with river view. Friendly 17th-c stone farmhouse with a large beamed lounge with leather chesterfields, woodburner, honesty bar and books (no TV downstairs); very good food and wine (some from local vineyard) in cosy inglenook restaurant; 50 metres from the River Wye, Tintern Abbey nearby and lots of walks in lovely surrounding countryside; resident border terrier cross. Dogs allowed in two bedrooms and residents' lounge; £5.

TY'N-Y-GROES
SH7774

Groes

(01492) 650545 – www.groesinn.com
Ty'n-y-groes, Conwy, Gwynedd LL32 8TN

£125; 14 well equipped rooms, some with terraces or balconies; also self-catering cottage and log cabin. Delightful 15th-c former drovers' inn of much character; rambling, low-beamed and thick-walled rooms with antique settles, old clocks, portraits, hats and tins hanging from walls, cheerful log fires, own-brewed beers, wines by the glass and maybe a harpist playing; several options for enjoying the good food (using local lamb, salmon and game) include an airy conservatory and a smart white-linen restaurant; seats in idyllic back garden and on terracing. Dogs allowed in all bedrooms and bar; bowl and treats; £10–£20.

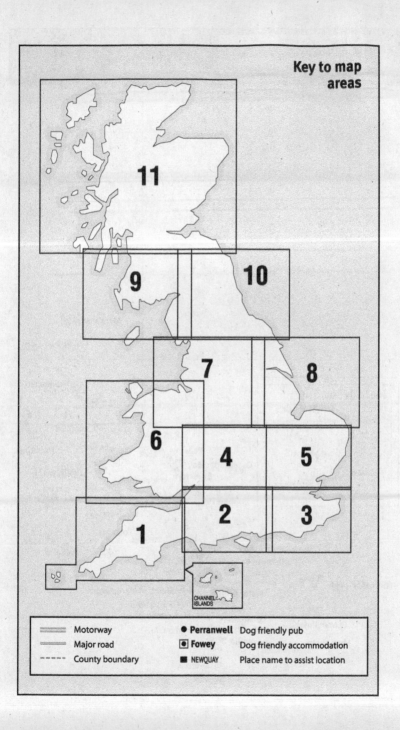

Key to map areas

Motorway	**Perranwell** Dog friendly pub
Major road	⊙ Fowey Dog friendly accommodation
County boundary	■ NEWQUAY Place name to assist location

CHANNEL ISLANDS

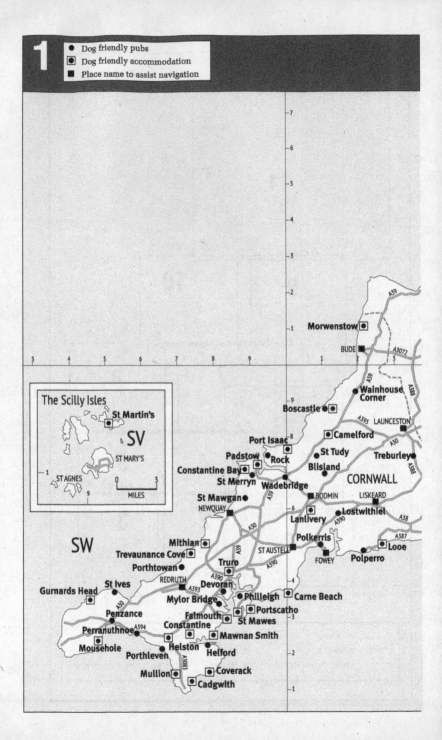

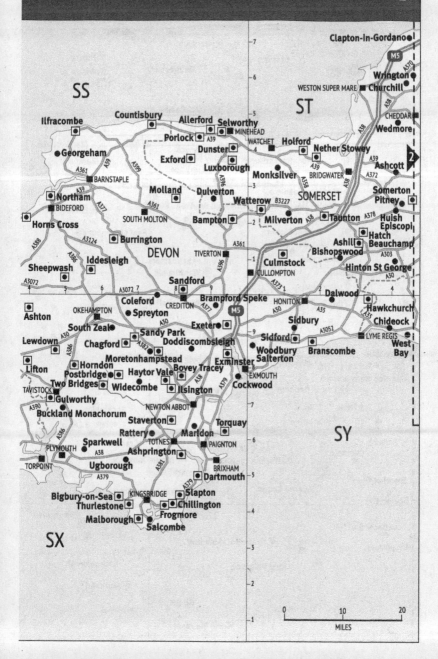

2

- Dog friendly pubs
- Dog friendly accommodation
- Place name to assist navigation

Oldbury-on-Severn · Tetbury

Thornbury · Westonbirt · Crudwell

GLOUCESTERSHIRE · Purton

Didmarton · Malmesbury · Swindon

M4 · M5 · Sherston · A3102 · M4

Castle Combe

Bristol · Nettleton · CHIPPENHAM · Marlborough

Wraxall · Corsham · CALNE · Manton

Monkton Farleigh · Whitley · Lacock · Great Bedwyn

Bath · MELKSHAM · Rowde

Stanton Wick · South Wroxall · Broughton Gifford · DEVIZES

Monkton Combe · Holt · WILTSHIRE

Combe Hay · Midford · Bradford-on-Avon · Poulshot

MIDSOMER NORTON · TROWBRIDGE

Ston Easton · Babington · Edington · East Chisenbury

Priddy · Mells

CHEDDAR · Holcombe · Upton Scudamore

WELLS · Croscombe · Frome · Warminster

SHEPTON MALLET · Newton Tony

GLASTONBURY · SOMERSET · Upton Lovell · AMESBURY

ST · WYLYE

Hindon · Cricklade · Pitton

Kingsdon · Bourton · Fonthill Gifford · Teffont Evias · SALISBURY

Babcary · WINCANTON · East Knoyle · Chicksgrove

Charlton Horethorne · West Stour

Corton Denham · SHAFTESBURY · Tollard Royal

Odcombe · Trent · Rockbourne · Stuckton

YEOVIL · Sherborne · Farnham · FORDINGBRIDGE · Fritham

Barwick · Sturminster Newton

Chetnole · DORSET · Cranborne

Hazelbury Bryan · Tarrant Monkton

Evershot · Middlemarsh · Plush · BLANDFORD FORUM · RINGWOOD

Beaminster · Cerne Abbas · Wimborne Minster

Bransgore

Nettlecombe · CHRISTCHURCH

Bridport · DORCHESTER · Lower Bockhampton · POOLE

East Knighton · Bournemouth

WAREHAM · Studland

WEYMOUTH · Kingston · SWANAGE

Worth Matravers

SY

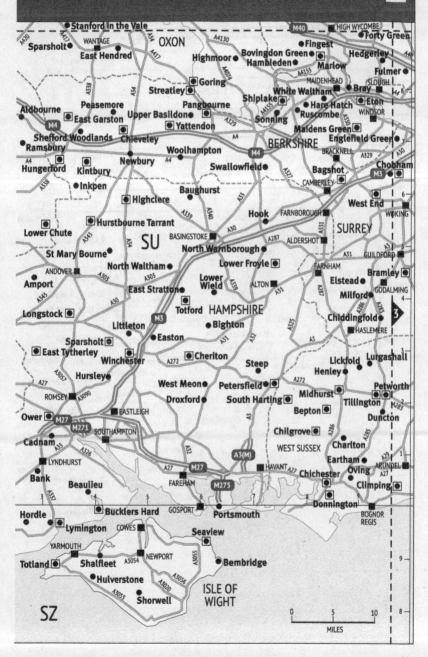

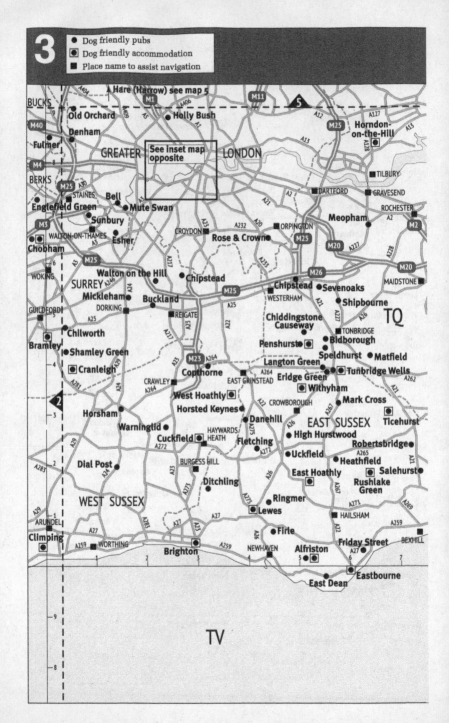

3
- ● Dog friendly pubs
- ◉ Dog friendly accommodation
- ■ Place name to assist navigation

▲ Hare (Harrow) see map 5

BUCKS

Old Orchard ● Holly Bush

Denham

Fulmer

GREATER   See Inset map opposite   LONDON

BERKS

STAINES   Bell ● Mute Swan

Eng3field Green ● Sunbury

Chobham   WALTON-ON-THAMES   Esher

WOKING   Walton on the Hill   Chipstead

SURREY   Mickleham   Buckland

Chilworth   DORKING   REIGATE

Bramley ● Shamley Green

● Cranleigh   Copthorne

Horsham   CRAWLEY   West Hoathly ◉

Warninglid   Horsted Keynes ●

Cuckfield ◉   HAYWARDS HEATH   Fletching

Dial Post   BURGESS HILL

Ditchling

WEST SUSSEX   Ringmer

Lewes

ARUNDEL   Firle

Climping ◉   WORTHING   Brighton   NEWHAVEN   Alfriston

East Dean   Eastbourne

TILBURY

GRAVESEND

DARTFORD   ROCHESTER

ORPINGTON   Meopham   M2

CROYDON   Rose & Crown ●

Chipstead ● Sevenoaks

WESTERHAM   Shipbourne

Chiddingstone Causeway   TONBRIDGE

Penshurst ◉ ● Bidborough

Langton Green   Speldhurst ● Matfield

EAST GRINSTEAD   Eridge Green ● ■ Tunbridge Wells

● Withyham

CROWBOROUGH   Mark Cross

Danehill   EAST SUSSEX   Ticehurst

High Hurstwood

Robertsbridge ●

Uckfield   Heathfield

East Hoathly ◉   Salehurst ◉

Rushlake Green

HAILSHAM

Friday Street   BEXHILL

Horndon-on-the-Hill

MAIDSTONE

TQ

TV

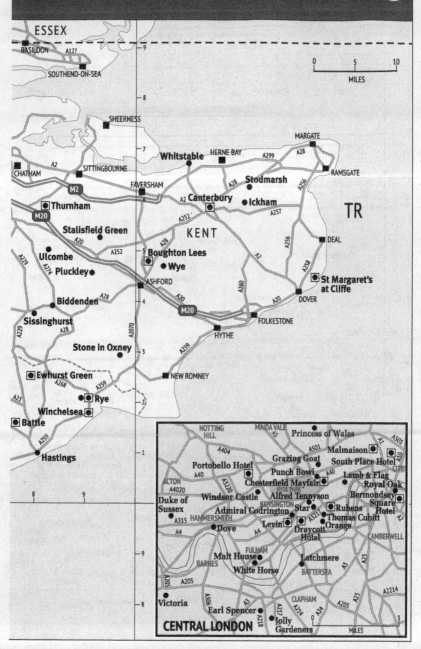

ESSEX

BASILDON A127

SOUTHEND-ON-SEA

0   5   10
MILES

SHEERNESS

MARGATE

WHITSTABLE HERNE BAY A299 A28 RAMSGATE

CHATHAM A2 SITTINGBOURNE

M2 FAVERSHAM

Thurnham A2 Canterbury Stodmarsh

M20 Ickham A257

Stalisfield Green KENT A256 DEAL

A20 A28

Ulcombe A252 Boughton Lees A2

Pluckley Wye St Margaret's
at Cliffe

ASHFORD A260 A258

Biddenden A28 A20 DOVER

M20 FOLKESTONE

Sissinghurst A28 A2070

A29 HYTHE

Stone in Oxney A259

Ewhurst Green A268 A259 NEW ROMNEY

A21 Rye

Winchelsea

Battle

A259

Hastings

8 9

TR

NOTTING
HILL MAIDA VALE Princess of Wales A501

Malmaison A10

A404 A5 Grazing Goat South Place Hotel CITY

Portobello Hotel Punch Bowl Lamb & Flag

ACTON A40 A3220 Chesterfield Mayfair A40 Royal Oak

A4020 Alfred Tennyson Bermondsey
Square
Hotel

Duke of
Sussex Windsor Castle KENSINGTON Star Rubens

Admiral Codrington A321 Thomas Cubitt

HAMMERSMITH A315 Levin Orange

A4 Dove A4 Draycott
Hotel CAMBERWELL

FULHAM

Malt House Latchmere A3

BARNES White Horse BATTERSEA

A205 A306 A205

Victoria CLAPHAM A2214

Earl Spencer A3 A217 A205

A306 A24

Jolly
Gardeners 0 3

CENTRAL LONDON MILES

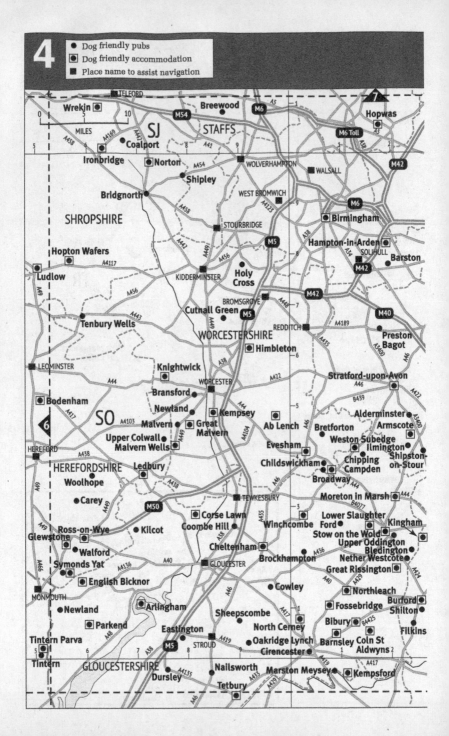

4
- Dog friendly pubs
- Dog friendly accommodation
- Place name to assist navigation

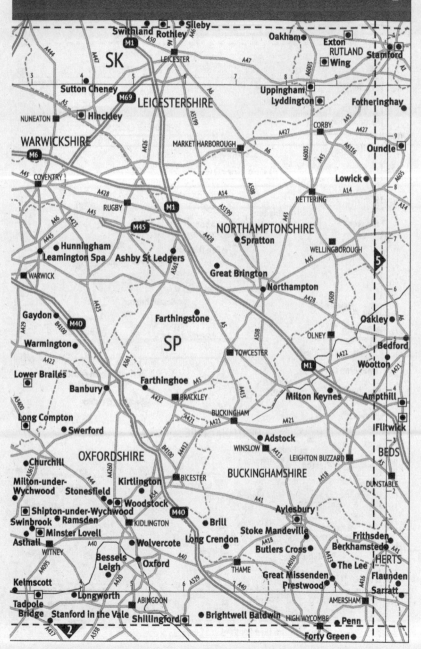

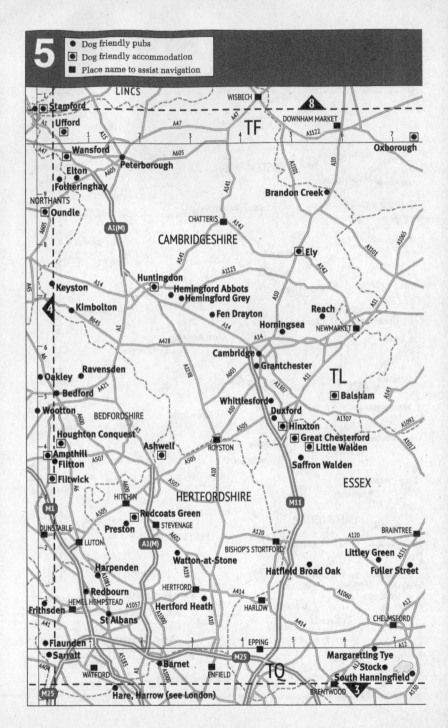

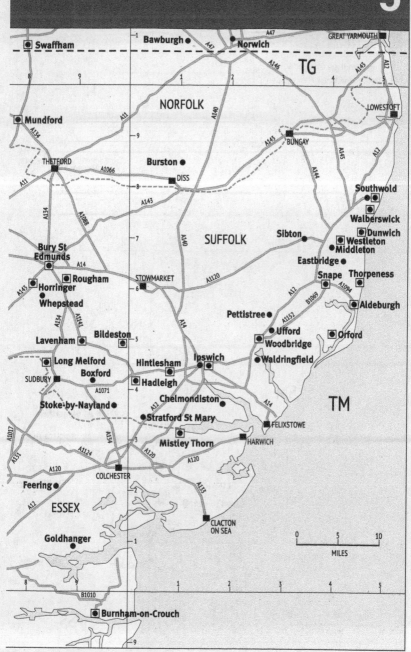

5

Swaffham

Bawburgh Norwich GREAT YARMOUTH

A47 A146 TG A143 A12

NORFOLK

A11 LOWESTOFT

Mundford

A134 A145 BUNGAY

THETFORD Burston A144 Southwold

A1066 DISS A145 Walberswick

A11 A143 A32 Dunwich

A134 A1088 SUFFOLK Sibton Westleton

A140 Middleton

Bury St Eastbridge

Edmunds A14 A1120 Snape Thorpeness

A145 Rougham STOWMARKET A12 Aldeburgh

Horringer A1094

Whepstead B1069

A134 A1141 Pettistree Orford

Lavenham Bildeston A1152

Ufford

Long Melford Hintlesham Ipswich Woodbridge

SUDBURY Boxford Waldringfield

A1071 Hadleigh

Stoke-by-Nayland Chelmondiston

A12 Stratford St Mary A14 TM

A1017 Mistley Thorn FELIXSTOWE

A351 A1124 A134 HARWICH

A120 A120 A120

COLCHESTER

Feering A133

A12 ESSEX

Goldhanger CLACTON
ON SEA

0   5   10

MILES

B1010

Burnham-on-Crouch

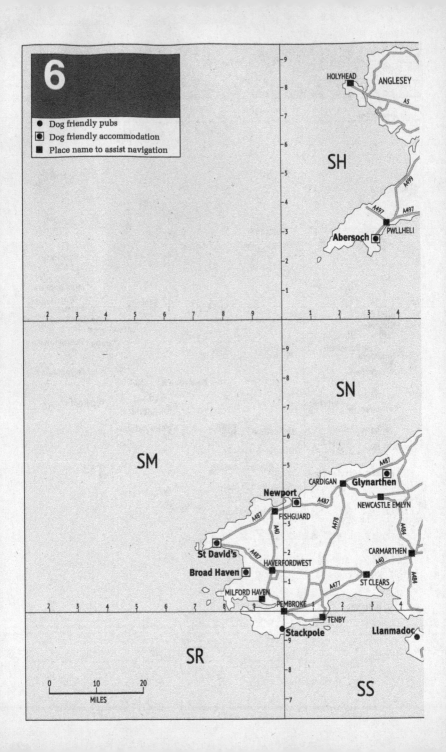

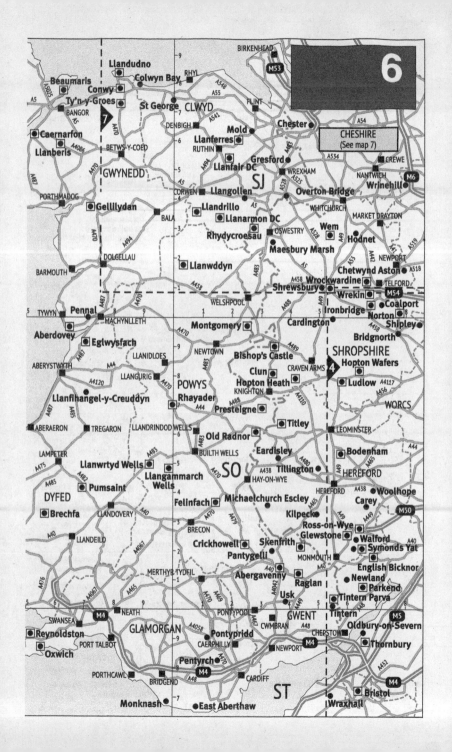

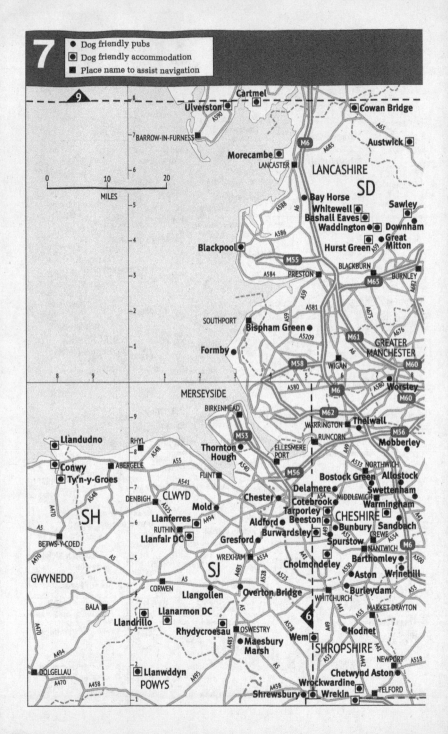

7

- ● Dog friendly pubs
- ◉ Dog friendly accommodation
- ■ Place name to assist navigation

9

—8 **Cartmel** ■
Ulverston ◉
—7 **BARROW-IN-FURNESS** ■

A590
Cowan Bridge ◉
A65

M6
A585
Austwick ◉

—6 **Morecambe** ◉
LANCASTER ■

LANCASHIRE

SD

0   10   20
MILES

—5 ● **Bay Horse**
A588
Whitewell ◉
Bashall Eaves ◉
Waddington ● ◉ **Downham**
A6
A586
Sawley ●

—4
Great Mitton
Hurst Green ● ◉
A59

Blackpool ◉
M55
BLACKBURN ■

—3
A584
PRESTON ■
A59
M65
BURNLEY ■
A682
A675

—2
A581

SOUTHPORT ■
—1 **Bispham Green** ●
A5209
M61
GREATER MANCHESTER
M60

Formby ●
A6
M58
WIGAN ■

MERSEYSIDE
A580
M6
A580
Worsley ■
M60

—9
BIRKENHEAD ■
M62
WARRINGTON ■
Thelwall ●
RUNCORN ■
M56

Llandudno ◉
RHYL ■
—8
A548
A55
Thornton Hough ●
A540
ELLESMERE PORT ■
M56
Mobberley ●

Conwy ◉
ABERGELE ■
A55
FLINT ■
A49
NORTHWICH ■
A533
Allostock ■

Ty'n-y-Groes ◉
A541
Bostock Green ●
Swettenham ●

—7
DENBIGH ■
CLWYD
Chester ●
Delamere ●
MIDDLEWICH ■
Warmingham ●

A548
A525
Mold ●
Cotebrook ●
Tarporley ●
CHESHIRE
Sandbach ■

—6
Llanferres ●
A494
Aldford ●
Beeston ●
Bunbury ◉
A41
SH
RUTHIN ■
Burwardsley ●
Spurstow ◉
CREWE ■
M6

A5
BETWS-Y-COED ■
Llanfair DC ●
Gresford ●
NANTWICH ■

A5
—5
WREXHAM ■
A534
Barthomley ●
A500
A470
SJ
A483
A528
A525
Cholmondeley ●
A530
Aston ● **Wrinehill** ●

GWYNEDD
CORWEN ■
A5
Overton Bridge ●
A41
Burleydam ●
A53

A470
BALA ■
Llangollen ●
WHITCHURCH ■
MARKET DRAYTON ■

—3
Llandrillo ◉
Llanarmon DC ◉
A5
6
A49
Hodnet ●

A494
Rhydycroesau ◉
OSWESTRY ■
A528
Wem ◉
SHROPSHIRE

Maesbury Marsh ●
A483
NEWPORT ■
A518

—2
A458
A5
Chetwynd Aston ●
■ DOLGELLAU
A470
Llanwddyn ◉
A495
Wrockwardine ■
A442
TELFORD ■

A458
POWYS
A458
Shrewsbury ◉ ● **Wrekin** ■

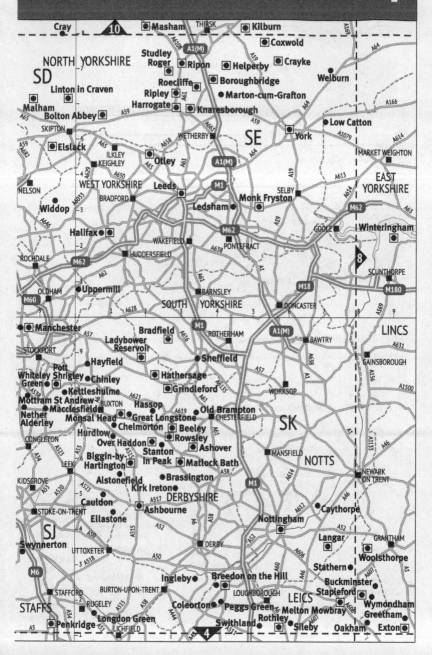

Cray · Masham · THIRSK · Kilburn
10
· Coxwold
NORTH YORKSHIRE · Studley Roger · Ripon · Helperby · Crayke
SD A1(M)
· Linton in Craven · Roecliffe · Boroughbridge · Welburn
· Ripley · Marton-cum-Grafton
· Malham · Harrogate · Knaresborough
· Bolton Abbey
SKIPTON · Low Catton
· Elslack **SE** · York
ILKLEY MARKET WEIGHTON
KEIGHLEY · Otley
NELSON · Leeds EAST
WEST YORKSHIRE YORKSHIRE
BRADFORD SELBY
· Widdop · Ledsham · Monk Fryston
· Halifax WAKEFIELD GOOLE · Winteringham
ROCHDALE HUDDERSFIELD PONTEFRACT
M62 **8**
· Uppermill BARNSLEY SCUNTHORPE
OLDHAM **M18** **M180**
M60 SOUTH YORKSHIRE DONCASTER
LINCS
· Manchester · Bradfield ROTHERHAM A1(M)
STOCKPORT · Ladybower BAWTRY
Reservoir · Sheffield GAINSBOROUGH
Pott · Hayfield
Whiteley Shrigley · Chinley · Hathersage WORKSOP
Green
· Kettleshulme · Grindleford
Mottram St Andrew BUXTON · Hassop SK
Nether · Macclesfield · Great Longstone · Old Brampton
Alderley · Monsal Head CHESTERFIELD
· Chelmorton · Beeley NOTTS
Hurdlow · Rowsley
· Over Haddon · Ashover
Biggin-by- · Stanton MANSFIELD
Hartington in Peak · Matlock Bath NEWARK
LEEK · Alstonefield · Brassington ON TRENT
KIDSGROVE Kirk Ireton **M1**
· Cauldon DERBYSHIRE
STOKE-ON-TRENT · Ashbourne · Caythorpe
· Ellastone
SJ · Nottingham GRANTHAM
Swynnerton · Langar · Woolsthorpe
UTTOXETER
DERBY
M6 · Stathern
· Ingleby · Breedon on the Hill · Buckminster
STAFFORD BURTON-UPON-TRENT LOUGHBOROUGH · Stapleford
· Wymondham
STAFFS RUGELEY · Coleorton · Peggs Green **LEICS** · Greetham
· Melton Mowbray
· Penkridge · Longdon Green · Swithland Rothley · Exton
LICHFIELD · Sileby · Oakham
4

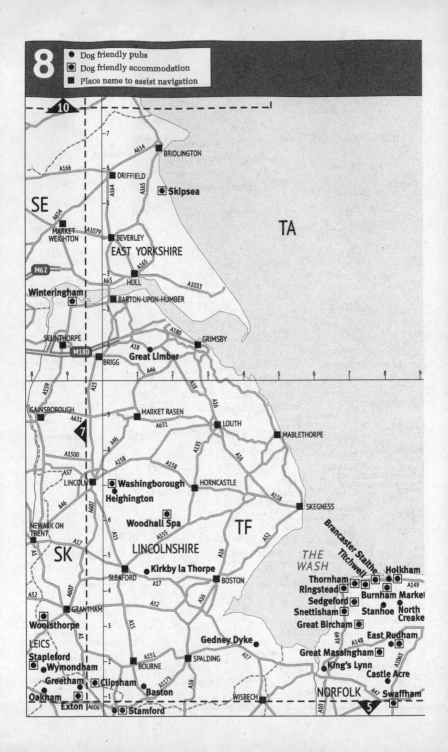

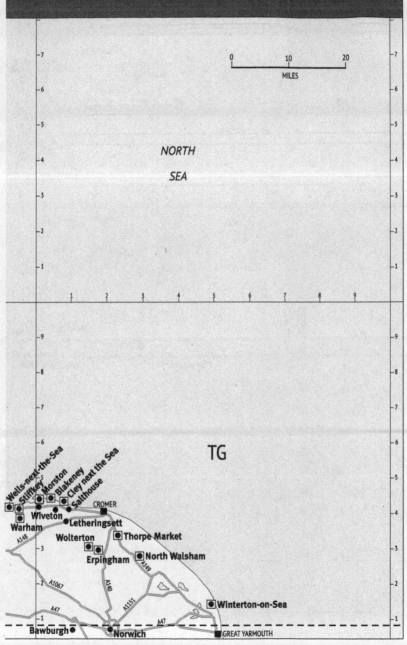

8

0   10   20
MILES

-7

-6

-5

-4   NORTH

-3   SEA

-2

-1

1 2 3 4 5 6 7 8 9

-9

-8

-7

-6   TG

-5

Wells-next-the-Sea
Stiffkey   Morston
Blakeney   Cley next the Sea
Salthouse

Wiveton   CROMER
Warham   Letheringsett
A148
Wolterton   Thorpe Market
-3
Erpingham   North Walsham
A149

-2   A1067
A140   A1151

-1   A47   A47
Bawburgh   Norwich   GREAT YARMOUTH

Winterton-on-Sea

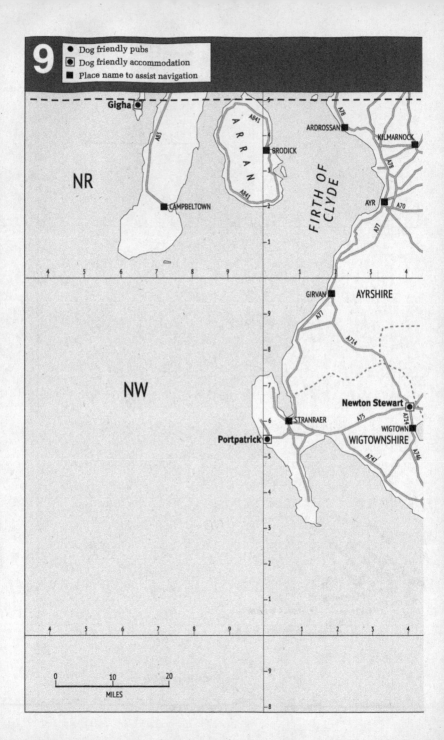

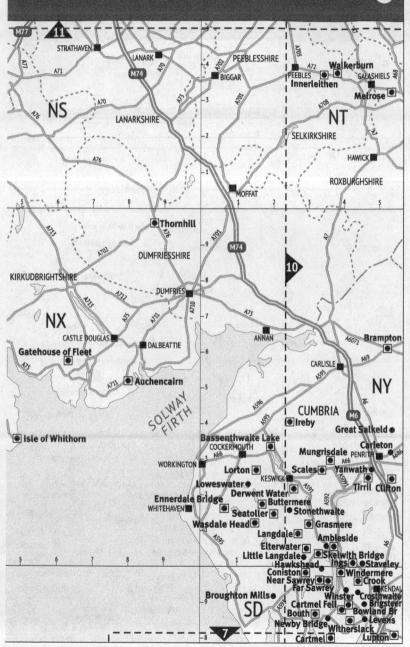

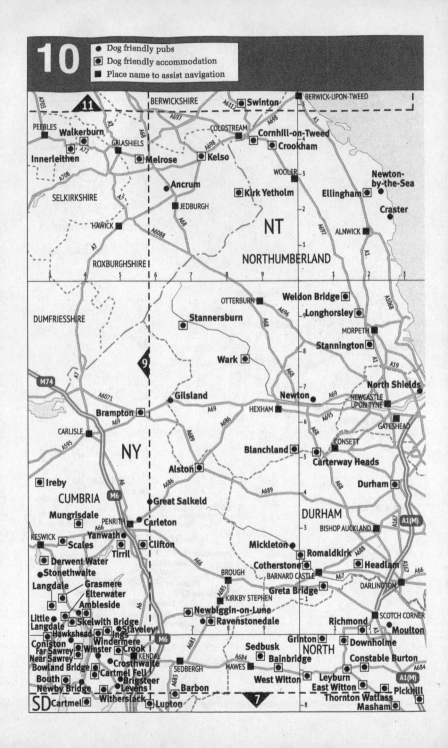

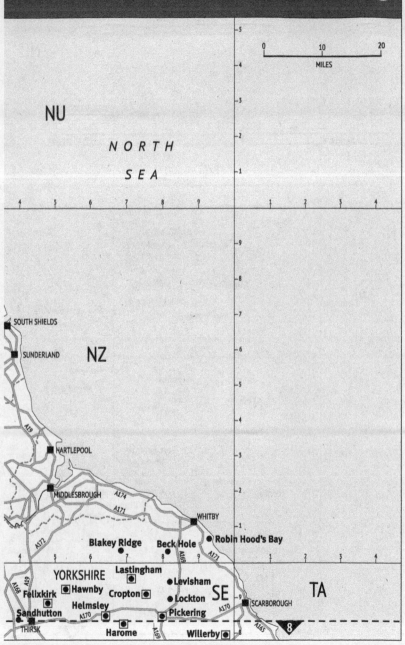

0   10   20
MILES

NU

NORTH

SEA

SOUTH SHIELDS

SUNDERLAND

NZ

HARTLEPOOL

MIDDLESBROUGH   A174

A171

WHITBY

Robin Hood's Bay

Blakey Ridge   Beck Hole

YORKSHIRE   Lastingham

Felixkirk   Hawnby   Cropton   Levisham

Sandhutton   Helmsley   Lockton   SE   TA

THIRSK   A170   Pickering   SCARBOROUGH

Harome   Willerby

A19

A168

A172

A169

A165

8

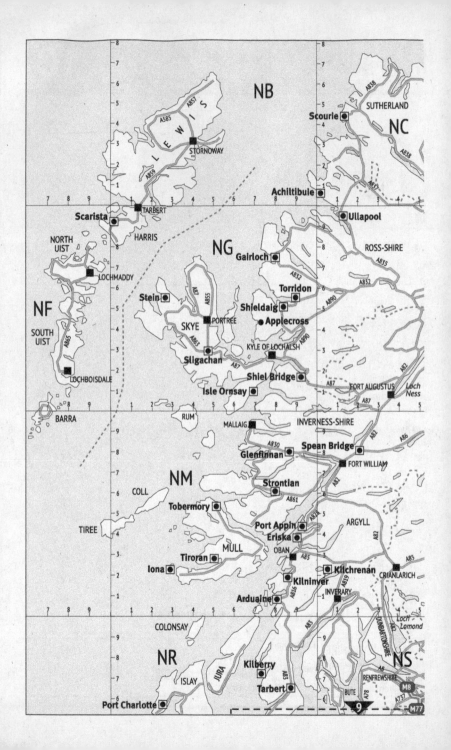

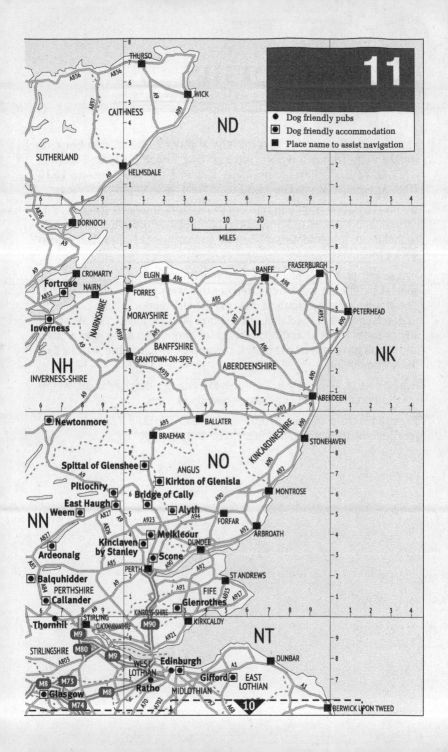

Report forms

Please report to us: you can use the tear-out forms in this book or simply write to our freepost address: Dog Friendly Guide, Freepost RTJR-ZCYZ-RJZT, Perrymans Lane, Etchingham, East Sussex TN19 7DN. Alternatively, you can email us at **feedback@goodguides.com**.

We need to know what you think of the establishments featured in this edition, and we need to know about other places you think are worthy of inclusion. It would also be helpful to know about ones that should *not* be included.

Please tell us how welcome you felt with your dog, and about any special facilities or welcoming touches that were provided for your dog. The atmosphere and character are particularly important, so please try to describe what is special about a venue. And we need to know about any changes in décor and furnishings too. Food and drink also matter, and if you have stayed overnight, please tell us about the standard of the accommodation.

It helps enormously if you can provide contact details for anywhere new, although a website address is usually enough.

Though we try to answer all letters, please understand if there's a delay (particularly in summer, our busiest period).

I have been to the following places in the *Good Guide to Dog Friendly Pubs, Hotels and B&Bs 2017* in the last few months, found them as described, and confirm that they deserve continued inclusion:

continued overleaf

PLEASE GIVE YOUR NAME AND ADDRESS ON THE BACK OF THIS FORM

Report continued...

Your own name and address (block capitals please)

....

....

....

Postcode...

Please return to

Dog Friendly Guide
Freepost RTJR-ZCYZ-RJZT
Perrymans Lane
Etchingham
East Sussex
TN19 7DN

IF YOU PREFER, YOU CAN SEND
US REPORTS BY EMAIL:

feedback@goodguides.com